REAL WORLD FREEHAND 5.0|5.5

Elizabeth —
I can not give you the world,
but I can give you some tools
so that we can hold the world
together — in the palm of our hands.
With love and admiration!
— S

Real World FreeHand 5.0|5.5

by
Olav Martin Kvern

AN OPEN HOUSE BOOK

PEACHPIT PRESS

for Neil Selmer Kvern, Craig Stanley Kvern,
& Laurie Ann McNutt,
my siblings

REAL WORLD FREEHAND 5.0|5.5
Olav Martin Kvern

Copyright © 1996 by Olav Martin Kvern

PEACHPIT PRESS
2414 Sixth St.
Berkeley, California 94710
(510) 548-4393
(510) 548-5991(fax)

Find us on the World Wide Web at: http://www.peachpit.com
Peachpit Press is a division of Addison-Wesley Publishing Company

Editor: Stephen F. Roth
Copy editor: Jeff Carlson
Indexer: Jan C. Wright
Cover design: Ted Mader & Associates (TMA)
Cover illustration: Robert Dietz
Interior design, illustration, and production: Olav Martin Kvern

NOTICE OF RIGHTS
All rights reserved. No part of this book may be reproduced or transmitted in any form by any means, electronic, mechanical, photocopying, recording, or otherwise, without the prior written permission of the publisher. For information on getting permission for reprints and excerpts, contact Trish Booth at Peachpit Press.

DISCLAIMER
The information in this book is distributed on an "As Is" basis, without warranty. While every precaution has been taken in the preparation of the book, neither the author nor Peachpit Press, shall have any liability to any person or entity with respect to any loss or damage caused or alleged to be caused directly or indirectly by the instructions contained in this book or by the computer software and hardware products described in it.

ISBN 0-201-88360-0

9 8 7 6 5 4 3 2 1

Printed and bound in the United States of America

FOREWORD ❧ *by* JAMES VON EHR

If I weren't one of the authors of FreeHand, I'd want this book to teach me how to use it. Actually, I'd want Ole to teach me, but he lives two thousand miles away. And he probably would get pretty tired of showing me the tricky parts over and over and over again. With *Real World FreeHand*, I have his advice and insight any time I need them.

When we started working on FreeHand, we had a vision of an easy-to-use, yet extraordinarily powerful graphics program. We wanted it to be usable by both novices and professional designers, and give results limited only by a person's artistic ability. It should be as intuitive as a pencil, but as powerful as a mind link to a hallucination machine. We've come a long way in those years. Of course, we aren't quite up to the level of our vision yet. But it wouldn't have been much of a vision if we could achieve it in just a few years of programming.

We had another vision too—one of talented artists working with computers, multiplying their abilities a hundredfold, and avoiding the dull, routine work of aligning things that simply refused to align; of specifying type, then setting the job aside while waiting for the galleys to come back from the typesetting house; of doing what our first ad agency did—cutting that type apart letter by letter and hand setting it with just the right spacing; of hearing the client ask to change a word in the middle of one of those blocks when the final deadline is tomorrow morning. With FreeHand, everything is malleable until the moment when a scanning laser beam starts to reveal the billions of pixels that make up your page on the drum of a laser printer or to the film of an imagesetter.

We also thought everybody ought to have a chance to undo their mistakes. Any mistakes. A bunch of mistakes. Imagine how much bolder you could be in real life if you had a chance to undo some of your blunders. Call your broker and tell him to undo that stock you sold last week. Go back two years and change your mind about marrying that bum who just passed out on the couch. You can't do that in real life, but you sure can with FreeHand. It is an underappreciated fact that FreeHand lets you undo more than just the easy things. FreeHand is the only program I have ever seen that lets you undo *every* editing operation, as many as 99 operations back.

I am really happy with what we finally achieved in FreeHand 5 and 5.5 (née Spork). Our Spork development team worked for months fixing bugs that companies who don't care as much about perfection as Macromedia would have shipped with. They kept improving it even after it was good enough, kept working on it until they were sick of it, in fact. I think there are three factors in our success: we really care about doing the best job we know how, we have several very smart software engineers working on it, and we have some awesomely talented users who continue to tell us how to make it even better.

Reading the drafts of this book is a lot like reading a biography of your own daughter. The writer talks about her accomplishments. Her beauty. Her charm. Her high-pitched whiny voice. Well, no writer is perfect. Fortunately, Ole laughs with us on those few occasions where the reality differs from the vision. And he goes on to explain those hard parts step by step in a way that almost anybody can understand.

I've reconsidered my first sentence. I do want this book, even though I did write a lot of FreeHand. *Real World FreeHand* is a great study guide: we'll continue to improve the parts of FreeHand Ole finds great, and we'll rework the parts Ole finds need lots of explaining. Reader, you've made two good choices. Crank up FreeHand and get started with *Real World FreeHand*. I think you'll have fun with both.

Jim Von Ehr
Vice President and General Manager,
Digital Arts Group
Macromedia, Inc.

Introduction xix

What's New in FreeHand? xxvii

CHAPTER 1 ## FreeHand Basics 1
The Publication Window 4
    Info Bar 5
    Scroll Bars 5
    Page Icons 5
    View Mode Popup Menu 5
    Magnification Popup Menu 6
    Multiple Windows 7
    Multiple Publications 7
    Page and Pasteboard 8
    Bleed Area, Page Size, and Paper Size 8
    Rulers 9
    Zero Point 10
    Guides 11
    Snap to Guides 17
FreeHand's Palettes 18
Changing Document Defaults 23
Setting Up Pages 24
    Using the Document Inspector 24
    Using the Setup Inspector 29
    What About the Page Setup Dialog Box? 32
Moving Around in Your Publication 33
    Zooming 33

      Scrolling 36
          Moving from Page to Page 38
  Using FreeHand's Toolbox 38
          Pointer Tool 40
          Text Tool 40
          Rectangle Tool 40
          Polygon Tool 42
          Ellipse Tool 43
          Line Tool 43
          Freehand Tool 43
          Pen Tool 46
          Knife Tool 46
          Point Tool 47
          Rotation Tool 47
          Reflection Tool 48
          Scaling Tool 48
          Skewing Tool 48
          Tracing Tool 48
          Magnifying Glass 49
  Constraining Tools 49
  What's on My Page? 51
          Points and Paths 51
          Basic Shapes 54
          Text Blocks 54
          Imported Graphics 54
  Thinking Objectively 56
  Selecting and Deselecting Elements 57
  Moving Elements 60
  Working with Layers 62
          Default Layers 62
          Using the Layers Palette 63
  FreeHand and the Edit Menu 70
          Clone 70
          Duplicate 70
  Preferences 71
          Colors 72
          Document 76
          General Editing 78
          Object Editing 80
          Text Editing 82

Importing and Exporting	85
Palettes	86
Redraw	88
Sounds	93
Spelling	94
Expert Document	95
Expert Editing	97
Expert Import/Output	99
The Tao of FreeHand	101

CHAPTER 2 **Drawing** 103

Basic Shapes	106
Drawing Lines	108
Resizing Rectangles and Ellipses	109
Proportionally Resizing Rectangles and Ellipses	109
Changing a Rectangle's Corner Radius	110
Converting Rectangles and Ellipses into Paths	110
Points and Paths	112
Thinking Like a Line	113
Winding	113
Control Handles	114
Flatness	115
Path-Drawing Tools	116
Freehand Tool	116
Pen Tool	120
Using the Point Tool	122
Xtra Drawing Tools	126
Arc Tool	126
Spiral Tool	127
Fractalize Xtra	130
Manipulating Control Handles	130
Automatic Curvature	132
Issuing a Retraction	132
Drawing Techniques	133
Ways to Draw Paths	133
Drawing with the Knife Tool	136
Keeping Paths Simple	137
Selecting and Moving Points	138
Flipping and Flopping	139

Open and Closed Paths 139
Splitting and Joining Paths 142
    Splitting Paths 142
    Joining Paths 144
Composite Paths 145
    Editing Composite Paths 147
Path Operations 148
    Correcting Path Direction 149
    Reversing Path Direction 149
    Removing Overlap 150
    Simplifying Paths 150
    Blending 151
    Intersect 164
    Punch 166
    Union 166
    Crop 167
    Expand Stroke 167
    Inset Path 168
    Path Operations and Preferences 169
    Running Path Operations from the Operations Palette .. 170
Tracing 170
    Manual Tracing 170
    Autotracing 172
Strokes 173
    Basic Strokes 173
    Custom Strokes 177
    PostScript Strokes 180
    Editing Strokes 181
    Removing Strokes 182
Fills 182
    Editing Fills 193
    Removing Fills 194
Working with Graphic Styles 194
    Thinking About Styles 195
    Creating Styles by Example 196
    Creating Styles by Specifying Attributes 198
    Applying Styles 199
    Redefining Styles 200
    Basing One Style on Another 200
    Duplicating Styles 202

Styles and Local Formatting 204
Moving Styles from One Publication to Another 205
Merging Styles 206
Adding Styles to Your Defaults File 206
Charting and Graphing................................ 206
Bar and Column Charts.......................... 208
Stacked Bar and Stacked Column Charts 210
Line and Area Charts 211
Pie Charts 213
Perspective Projection................................ 216
Single-View Perspective.......................... 218
Blending and Single-View Perspective 219
Multiview Perspective 219
Oblique Projection 220
Creating Grids for Oblique Projection................ 221
Axonometric Projection 223
Drawing Conclusions 224

CHAPTER 3 **Text and Type** 225
Entering and Editing Text 228
Auto-expanding Text Blocks...................... 232
Entering and Editing Text with the Text Editor 236
Moving the Cursor............................. 237
Selecting Text 238
Entering Special Characters 238
Checking Spelling 240
Finding and Changing Text 243
Setting the Range 243
Finding Text 243
Changing Text 245
Working with Text Blocks 248
Copying and Pasting Text 248
Linking Text Blocks 254
Multicolumn and Multirow Text Blocks 255
Borders and Fills for Text Blocks 258
Adding Borders to Rows, Columns, or Cells 259
Character Formatting 262
Font 264
Type Style 269
Size.. 269

Leading	270
Baseline Shift	272
First line leading	273
Applying Colors to Text	275
Stretching Characters Horizontally	280
Text Effects	280
Kerning	286
Paragraph Formatting	288
Alignment	289
Spacing	291
Hyphenation	294
Paragraph Indents	295
Hanging Punctuation	296
Tabs	297
Setting Tabs with the Edit Tab Dialog Box	302
Spacing Before and After Paragraphs	304
Controlling Widows	305
Paragraph Rules	307
Working with Text Styles	309
Global versus Local Formatting	310
Styles Are More Than Formatting	311
Creating a Text Style	311
Applying a Text Style	314
Editing Styles	316
Automatic Copyfitting	321
Joining Text to a Path	324
Flowing Text Inside Paths	329
Wrapping Text around Objects	330
Converting Characters into Paths	332
Inline Graphics	337
Creating an Inline Graphic	337
Working with Inline Graphics	338
After Words	340

CHAPTER 4 **Importing and Exporting** ... 341

Importing Anything	344
About Graphic File Formats	346
PNTG and TIFF	346
PICT and EPS	346
Importing Object PICTs	349

- Importing Charts from Microsoft Excel
  and Adobe Persuasion 350
- Importing PICTs from CAD Programs 352
- Working with TIFFs 353
  - Halftones 353
  - TIFFs, Screen Frequency, and Resolution 354
  - TIFF Controls 356
  - Working with the Image Dialog Box 357
  - Resizing Images to Your Printer's Resolution 360
  - Cropping TIFF Images 362
  - Creating an Outline Mask for a TIFF Image 364
  - Creating a Vignette Mask for a TIFF Image 365
  - Preseparating Color TIFFs 367
  - Running Photoshop Plug-Ins 368
- Importing EPS Graphics 372
  - If You See an "X" Instead of a Graphic 373
  - Importing FreeHand EPS 373
  - Importing Illustrator EPS 374
  - Creating Your Own EPS Graphics 375
  - Creating Invisible EPS Graphics 376
  - Creating Visible, Nonprinting Graphics 377
- Linking and Embedding 378
- Extracting Embedded Graphics 380
- Importing Text 382
  - Importing Text-Only Files 382
  - Importing RTF 384
  - Importing Text Tagged with XPress Tags 388
- Exporting 391
  - Creating EPS Graphics 394
  - FreeHand, TIFFs, and PageMaker 6 397
  - Exporting Publications in Adobe Illustrator Format 399
  - Copying: Another Way to Export 400
  - Placing FreeHand Graphics in Page-Layout Programs .. 401
  - Converting FreeHand 3 EPS Files
    to Illustrator 1.1 EPS Format 404
- Rasterizing FreeHand Objects 412
  - Using the Create PICT Image Xtra 412
  - From FreeHand to Photoshop 414
- Publishing and Subscribing 415
- Managing Linked Files 419

Working with PDF 420
The Best of All Possible Worlds 421

CHAPTER 5 **Transforming** 329
    Grouping and Transformation 426
    Transformation Shortcuts 426
Moving 429
    Moving Path Contents and Fills 430
    Moving by Dragging 432
    Moving "By the Numbers" 433
    Moving Objects with the Inspector 434
    Moving by Pressing Arrow Keys 435
Scaling. 435
    Scaling Contents, Fills, and Lines 435
    Using the Scaling Tool 435
    Using the Scale Palette 437
    Scaling with the Pointer Tool 439
    Scaling with the Object Inspector 440
Rotating 440
    Using the Rotation Tool 440
    Using the Rotate Palette 441
    Rotating Multiple Selected Objects 443
    Rotating Contents and Fills. 444
    Rotating Selected Points 444
    Rotation and Path Direction. 444
    Rotation and Perspective Drawing. 445
Reflecting 447
    Using the Reflection Tool 447
    Using the Reflect Palette 448
    Reflection and Path Direction. 449
    Reflecting Contents and Fills 449
Skewing 450
    Using the Skewing Tool. 450
    Using the Skew Palette. 452
    Skewing Contents and Fills 453
    Skewing and Perspective Drawing 453
Creating Clipping Paths 454
    Using Paste Inside to Crop Imported Images 456
    Creating a Color Change Where an
        Object Crosses a Color Boundary 457

Creating the Illusion of Transparency
  Using Clipping Paths 458
  Creating Transparent Text 459
Locking Objects 461
Aligning and Distributing................................ 461
  Aligning Objects 462
  Distributing Objects............................... 462
Transformation Xtras 464
  Fisheye Lens Tool 464
  3D Rotation Tool 465
My Life Was Transformed 466

CHAPTER 6   **Color** 467
Color Printing 470
  The Printing Process 471
  Spot and Process Inks 472
  New Screening Technologies 472
Color in FreeHand 474
  Spot Color or Process Color or Both? 474
  Is What You See Anything Like What You'll Get? 475
  Controlling Your Color-Viewing Environment 476
  Color Models 477
  FreeHand's Color Libraries 478
FreeHand's Color Controls 479
  Drag and Drop Color............................. 479
  Color List 479
  The Color Mixer.............................. 481
Creating and Adding Colors........................... 482
  Adding Colors from a Color Library 483
  Creating a Color 485
  Creating Color Libraries 486
  Importing Colors from PageMaker 490
  Adding Colors from Illustrator..................... 492
  Importing Colors from Other Applications 492
Editing Colors 493
  Converting Spot Colors to Process Colors 493
Applying Colors................................ 496
  Applying Colors to Text 497
  Applying Colors to Groups 497
  Applying Colors to Imported Graphics 498

    Creating Duotones 498
    Removing Colors 500
    Copying Colors 500
Color Xtras. 501
    Color Control 501
    Darken Colors 502
    Desaturate Colors. 503
    Lighten Colors 503
    Name All Colors 504
    Randomize Named Colors 504
    Saturate Colors 505
    Sort Color List by Name 505
    Delete Unused Named Colors 505
    Eyedropper Tool 505
Creating Spot-Color Tint Builds 507
    Using Blending to Create Process-Color Tint Builds 508
    Substituting Process Colors for Spot Colors 509
Trapping. 510
    Object-Level Overprinting 512
    Ink-Level Overprinting 513
    Manual Trapping 513
    Spot-Color Trapping 514
    Trapping Lines 518
    Trapping Text. 519
    Advanced Spot-Color Trapping 520
    Trapping Spot-Color Graduated Fills 520
    Trapping Spot-Color Radial Fills 522
    Process-Color Trapping 523
    Simple Process-Color Trapping 523
    Complex Process-Color Trapping 525
    Trapping Process-Color Graduated and Radial Fills 525
    Trapping Imported Images 526
    Using the Trapping Xtra 526
Separating Color Images. 528
    Preseparating Color Images 529
    FreeHand and OPI 529
    Do-It-Yourself "Stochastic" Screening. 530
    Stochastic Screening Without an Imagesetter 533
Color Me Gone 536

INTRODUCTION   XVII

CHAPTER 7 **Printing** 537
    The FreeHand Print Dialog Box 540
        Copies 540
        Pages 541
        Paper Source 541
        Destination 541
        Tile... 542
        Scale.. 544
        Print Options 544
    Printing and Page Setup 545
        Page Size and Paper Size 545
        Page Orientation and Paper Orientation 545
        Printing Signatures............................... 547
    FreeHand Printing Options 549
        Printer Type 549
        Paper Size 549
        Halftone Screen 551
        Transfer Function 551
        Printer Marks 552
        Page Labels 552
        Imaging Options 553
        Separations 553
    Output Options 555
        Printing Invisible Layers 555
        Split Complex Paths............................. 555
        Image Data 556
        Flatness 557
    FreeHand and PPDs 557
        PPDs—Who's on First? 558
    Rewriting PPDs 559
        What's in a PPD? 559
        Adding Custom Paper Sizes to PPDs 559
    Preparing a FreeHand File for Imagesetting 568
        Printing PostScript to Disk 568
        Taking a FreeHand Publication to a Service Bureau 571
    The Golden Rules 572
    Printing Troubleshooting............................. 574
    Fortune Cookie 576

CHAPTER 8 **PostScript** 577
What Is PostScript? 579
What's PostScript Got to Do with FreeHand? 580
Writing Your Own EPS Files 581
Looking at FreeHand's PostScript 583
Looking at FreeHand's PostScript Resources 585
    Variables in FreeHand's PostScript 589
Changing FreeHand's PostScript 590
    Making Textured Fills Transparent 590
    Overprinting TIFFs 592
Creating Your Own PostScript Effects 594
    Typing PostScript in the Fill and Stroke Inspectors 595
    Creating and Using a UserPrep File 598
    Creating External Resource Files 601
    Creating Custom PostScript Strokes 608
    Creating Custom Fill Effects 618
PostScript Postscript 628

APPENDIX A **System** 629

APPENDIX B **Your FreeHand Installation** 653

APPENDIX C **Resources** 665

Index 669

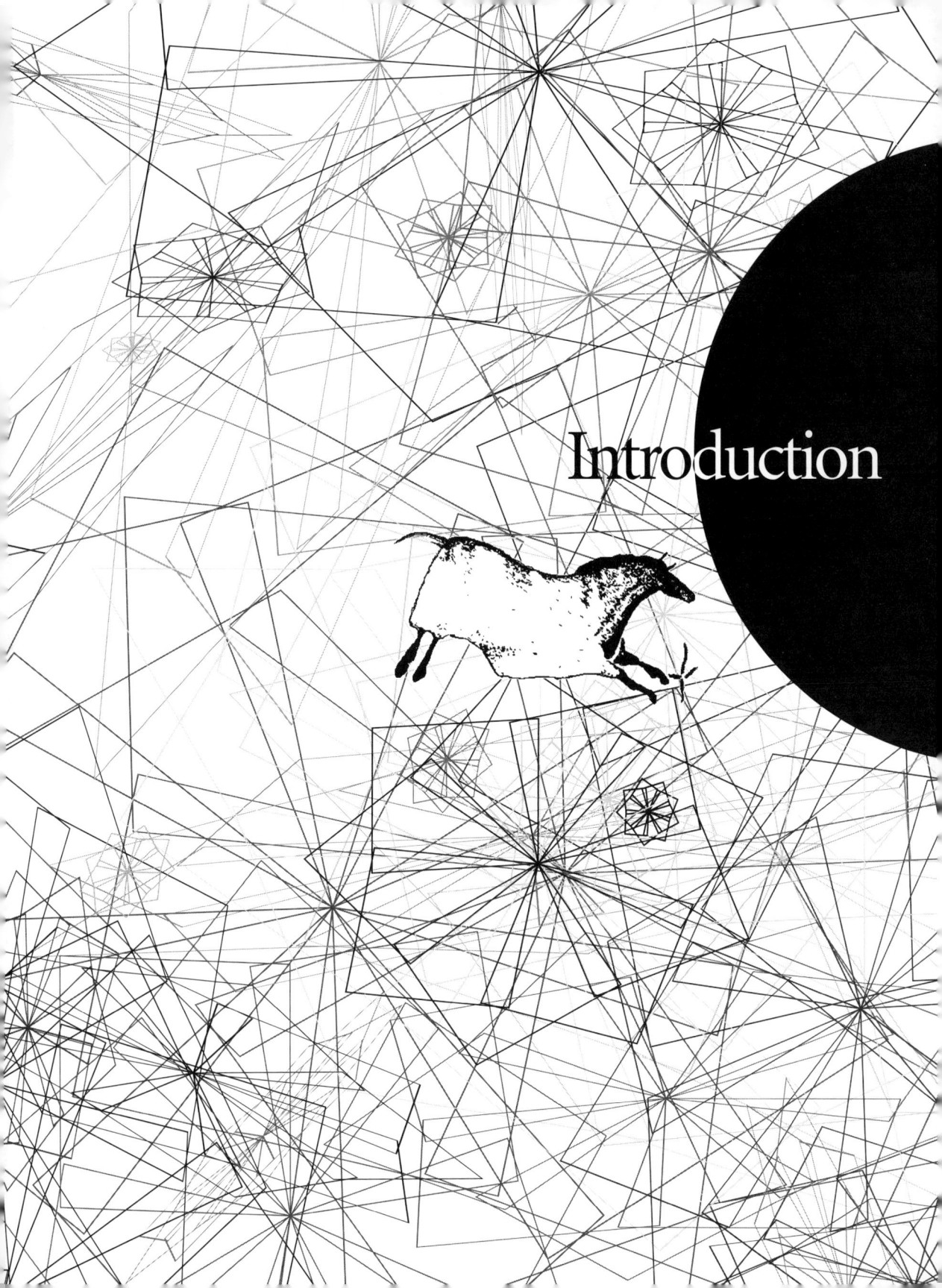

Introduction

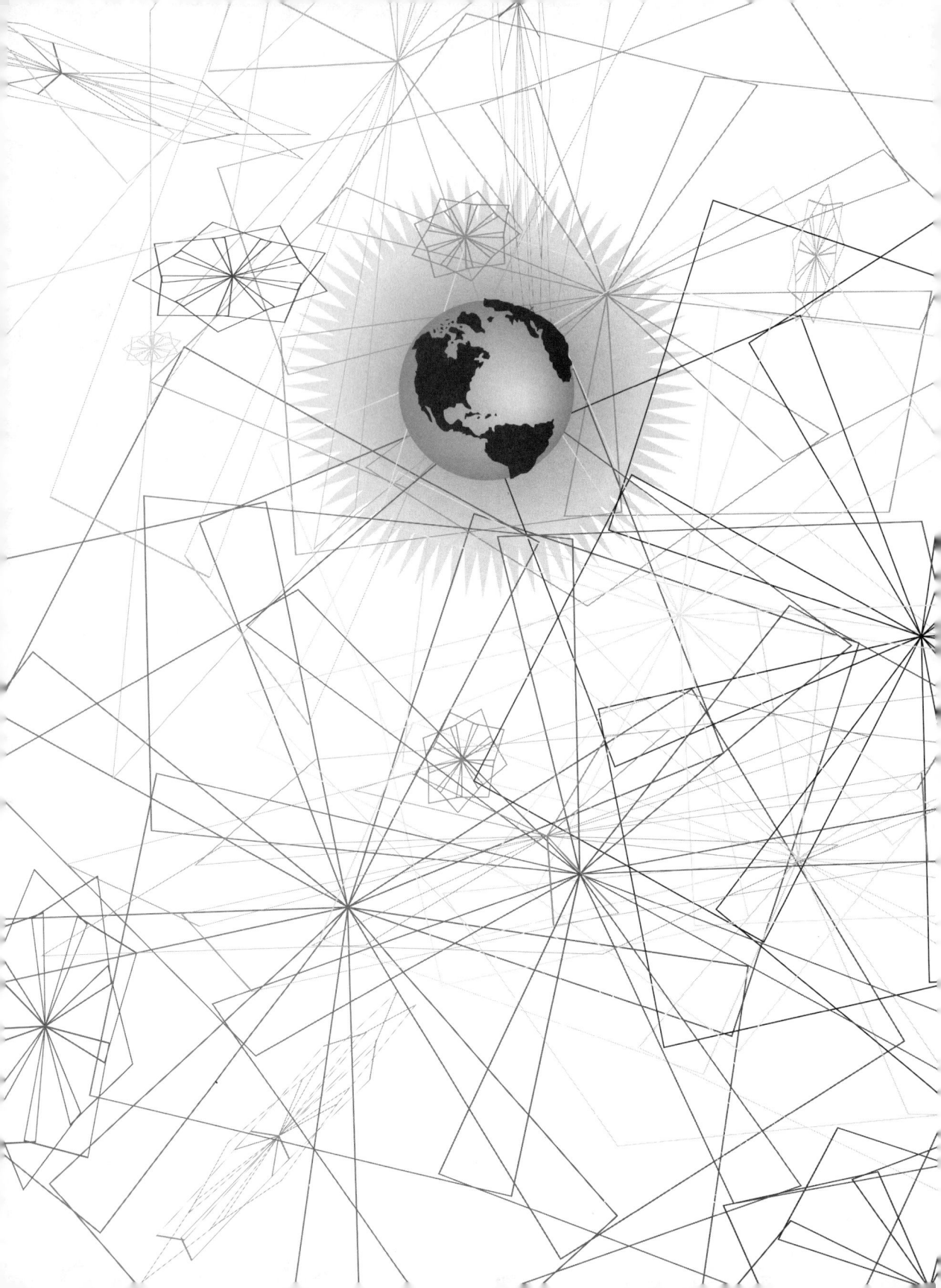

INTRODUCTION

I don't read Finnish. But there it was, in the mail: a review of my book in a Finnish magazine. Did they like it? Hate it? I couldn't tell.

I wasn't thinking about it, much, right at that moment—I was busy throwing things into a bag to take to the hospital. Leslie, my wife, was in labor, and it was time to go.

The next night, as I was rocking my newborn son to sleep, our anesthetist, a friendly, interesting woman (who had, only a few hours before, been poking a big needle into Leslie's back), stopped by to see how we were doing. Business was slow at Ballard Hospital's birthing center—we were the only "customers," and it was the middle of the night. I rocked, we talked.

In the course of our conversation, she mentioned that she'd emigrated to the United States from Finland.

What could I do? I pulled the crumpled review out of my coat pocket and asked if she'd glance at it and tell me whether the reviewer liked the book or not. She insisted on doing a full translation of the text—in trade for a copy of the book for her son, a FreeHand user.

And the review? It was a rave.*

So here we are again. If you're a new reader, welcome. If you read the previous edition of this book, welcome back!

---

*"Vaikka FreeHandin tuntisi miten hyvin tahansa, löytyy tästä kirjasta silti uutta tietoa," which we quoted on the back of the book, means, more or less (according to my translator), "Even if you think you know everything about FreeHand, you'll learn something from this book."

The Wild Ride

"Adobe's just acquired Aldus."

The news made my head spin. First, it was good news for a product I love. PageMaker, as an entity, would probably benefit. Second, it was very bad news for another product I love. FreeHand. There was no way that FreeHand would benefit from having its marketer (Aldus) acquired from the maker of its chief competitor (Adobe, and Adobe Illustrator, respectively). I thought, and it seemed likely, that Adobe would do everything they could to hang on to the marketing rights to FreeHand, while, simultaneously, doing very little to sell it. FreeHand would wither and die.

I wasn't the only person thinking this way—Altsys, the software development company that's always written FreeHand, sued immediately to get FreeHand back. And then—to make a long and involved legal story short—something unexpected happened.

They won.

FreeHand went back to Altsys, and Altsys merged with Macromedia, becoming Macromedia's Graphics Products Division. I was hoping that Altsys would try marketing FreeHand on their own, but, so far, it looks like they've made a good deal—Macromedia seems inclined to leave them alone. Which means they can go on doing what they do best: making FreeHand the best illustration tool on the market; pushing it farther into new fields, like page layout.

I think we're in for a wonderful ride.

Where I'm Coming From

Why should you listen to what I have to say about working with FreeHand? I've worked as a technical, medical, archaeological, and veterinary illustrator, as well as a general-purpose book and magazine illustrator. I've also worked as a designer, typesetter, paste-up slave, and art director.

More importantly, I bring my experience as a FreeHand user. I really have been through the long shifts (some of them longer than 40 hours) trying to get FreeHand files to print. On most of those late nights and early mornings, I could have been home in bed if

I'd known just one key piece of information. But I didn't. There was no one to tell me.

I'm here to tell you.

If some piece of information in this book saves you one late night, one early morning, or gets your file to print on the first pass through the imagesetter instead of the second or third, I will have succeeded in my purpose.

Once, a janitor found me pounding on a Linotronic film processor (an ML-314, for you hardware tweaks) with a wastebasket. At 4:00 AM. I'd been up for more than 36 hours, and it'd just eaten a job that'd taken six hours to run on an imagesetter. I wrote this book in the hope that I could save others from repeating this scene.

Organization

This book's pretty simple: first, I'll show you how to get things into FreeHand; next, I'll talk about how to work with elements in FreeHand; and, finally, I'll tell you how to get your work out of FreeHand. Then, in Chapter 8, "PostScript," I'll show you how to extend FreeHand and make it do more than it could when it came out of the box.

What's New in FreeHand 5.5. This is for people who've been using FreeHand 3, 4, or 5 and want to know what's changed since then. The section works like an expanded table of contents: there's an overview of each new feature, followed by a page number where you can find further information.

Chapter 1: FreeHand Basics. This chapter is your orientation to the world of FreeHand. In it, I describe the publication window, selecting objects, moving objects, working with FreeHand's toolbox, and an overview of the way that you create and import elements into FreeHand (including basic path drawing).

Chapter 2: Drawing. This is all about using FreeHand's drawing tools—from creating and joining paths to applying lines and fills, creating styles, working with blends, creating charts and graphs, and drawing using perspective.

Chapter 3: Text and Type. This chapter deals with working with text in FreeHand—how to enter, edit, and format text. It covers wrapping text around graphics, specifying type, FreeHand's type effects, joining text to a path, and converting text into paths.

Chapter 4: Importing and Exporting. FreeHand doesn't exist in a vacuum. You need to be able to import images from scanners and color image-editing programs, or to be able to import EPS graphics from other PostScript drawing programs. You need to be able to import text from your word processor. This chapter shows you how, and where, FreeHand fits in with your other applications. Topics include working with TIFFs, importing PICTs, importing formatted and unformatted text, opening and importing EPS files created in other programs, and converting old FreeHand 3 EPS files to Illustrator 1.1 EPS format so that you can open them.

Chapter 5: Transforming. This chapter shows you how to manipulate FreeHand elements you've drawn, typed, or imported, and describes how to use the transformation (skewing, scaling, rotation, and reflection) tools.

Chapter 6: Color. In this chapter, I cover creating and applying colors in FreeHand. I also discuss color models, the history of color printing, creating duotones, and controlling the conditions under which you view and create color publications.

Chapter 7: Printing. It don't mean a thing if you can't get it on paper or film. Here's how to do that, plus a bunch of tips that'll save you money at your imagesetting service bureau and your commercial printer. In this chapter, I also talk about the various options contained in FreeHand's Print and Print Options dialog boxes and how they affect your publications.

Chapter 8: PostScript. How to use PostScript when working with FreeHand, and how to add features to FreeHand. I wrote this chapter because I want to demythologize the process of adding PostScript strokes and fills to FreeHand. You don't have to have an engineering degree, or be a rocket scientist, to add unique touches to FreeHand that'll make it truly your own program.

Disclaimer

Some of the techniques in this book involve modifying either FreeHand's subsidiary files (like PPDs) or modifying FreeHand itself. While I've tried to make the procedures (in these cases, anyway) as complete and accurate as possible, you need to be aware that you're proceeding entirely at your own risk. Given that, there are a few things you can do to make everything less risky.

Work on copies of files. If you don't keep your original files in their original state, how can you ever go back to where you started? Always back up your files before you try altering them.

Remember that not everyone will have your system. You can't expect your friends and your imagesetting service bureau to be absolutely up-to-date with your current modifications if you don't give them to them. Therefore, if your publication requires a custom page size you've written into a PPD, make sure that your imagesetting service bureau has the PPD.

Clean up after yourself. If you change any of FreeHand's PostScript printing routines in a printer's RAM, make sure that you change them back to their original state before anyone else sends a job to that printer or imagesetter. Nothing is more embarrassing for you or as much of a bother to everyone else as having your name and "DRAFT" print across all of the jobs printed on a particular printer because you forgot to change *showpage* back to its original definition. This, in fact, is a great way to provoke the villagers to come after you with torches and pitchforks.

Don't call Macromedia technical support if something you read in this book doesn't work. They didn't write this book and shouldn't be expected to support it. This book is not a Macromedia product, and they have no control over its content. I'm not kidding. Write to me, instead. My mail addresses are listed in Appendix C, "Resources."

Acknowledgments

Thanks to the FreeHand engineering team (and related folks, in no particular order): Samantha Seals-Mason and Pete Mason (did anyone here mention red wine?), Steven Johnson (without his clues, I wouldn't have been able to start—let alone finish—Chapter 8, "PostScript"), Katharine Green, the incomparable Brian Schmidt, John Ahlquist, Mark Zartler, Kevin Bottner, Doug Benson, Anna Sturdivant, Robert Hurst, Delores Highsmith, Cassandra Rose, Lorin Rivers, Kevin Crowder, Rusty Williams, and, especially, to Jim Von Ehr for his inspiring foreword.

Thanks to Tamis Nordling and Nick Allison at *Adobe Magazine* (and Harry Edwards of *Aldus Magazine*) for making me a better writer (and for being great to work with).

Thanks to the Seattle Gilbert and Sullivan Society, and their photographer, Ray O. Welch, for giving me permission to use some of their archival photographs as example images. Special thanks to the amazing Ed Poole for the free use and abuse of his moustache.

Thanks to Ted Nace for being a great publisher (and the only publisher I've ever had to loan money to so he could take me out to dinner), and to my editor and good buddy, Steve Roth, for his help whipping the manuscript into shape (no one does it better). Jeff Carlson and Cindy Bell did a fantastic job proofreading and copy editing, and carl juarez helped with last-minute production and illustration work. Jan C. Wright, the Queen of Indexing, pulled together a great index in record time (with help from Keri Bero). Thanks to the other denizens of the Seattle Desktop Publishing Commune/Ghetto/Grotto—David "did you borrow my hard drive?" Blatner, Don "Zap!" Sellers, Marci "Queen of Room Service" Eversole, Steve "thumper" Broback, Krista "no nickname yet" Carreiro, and the always elegant Michele Dionne.

Finally, thanks to my wonderful wife, Leslie Renée Simons, and to my son, Max Olav Kvern, for their encouragement, understanding, and support.

Olav Martin Kvern
Republic of Fremont
Seattle, 1995

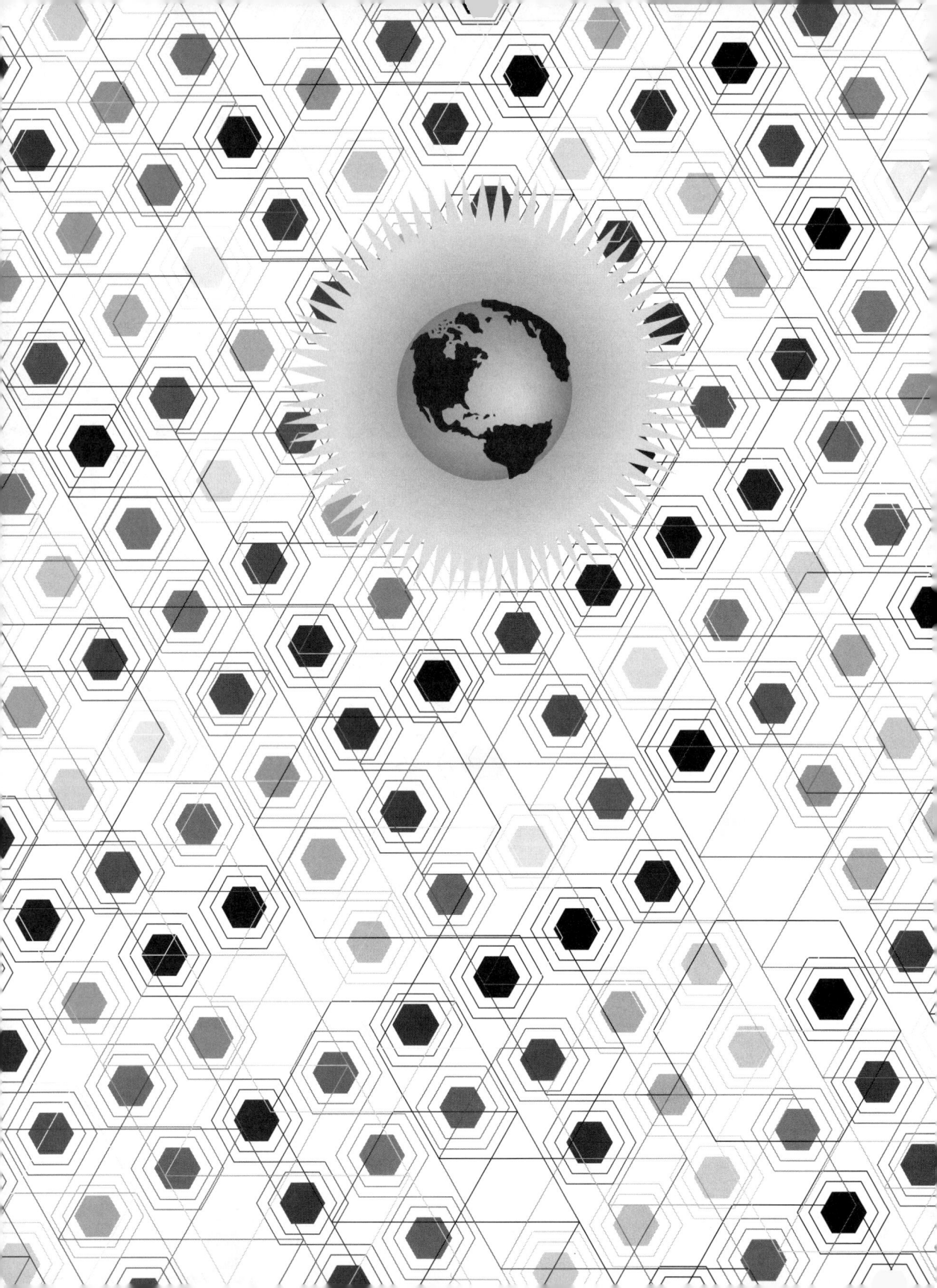

WHAT'S NEW IN FREEHAND

Do you wish that software companies would just stop updating their products for a bit? Not long—just long enough for us to figure out how to use the current version. Wouldn't that be great?

I'm not holding my breath.

FreeHand 5 wasn't as different from FreeHand 4 as FreeHand 4 was from FreeHand 3, but the stretch of time between the two versions was very short: *Aldus* FreeHand 4 had just appeared, it seemed, when *Macromedia* started shipping FreeHand 5 (for more on the corporate hurly-burly surrounding FreeHand, see "The Wild Ride" in the Introduction).

Because of this rapid change, lots of you have gone from FreeHand 3 straight to FreeHand 5.5, skipping FreeHand 4 and 5 altogether. And lots of you didn't have time to get used to FreeHand 4 before FreeHand 5 arrived. So, in this section, I'll include new things in FreeHand 4, as well as the things that changed between FreeHand 4, FreeHand 5, and FreeHand 5.5.

What's New Since FreeHand 5?

FreeHand 5.5 adds the following features.

Photoshop Plug-Ins. You can run Photoshop plug-ins in FreeHand 5.5. Most of the time, this means you can apply special effects to

XXIX

images in FreeHand, but some Photoshop file format and image acquisition plug-ins work, as well. See page 368.

Rasterizing FreeHand Objects. Using the Create PICT Image Xtra, FreeHand can convert objects in a FreeHand publication into bitmap images. Once you've saved the images, you can take them into Photoshop, or another image editing program, and manipulate them as you would any other image. See page 412.

Inline Graphics. FreeHand 5.5 can embed graphics in text blocks. This can come in very handy when you need to attach a graphic to a piece of text. See page 337.

PDF Import. Adobe Acrobat's PDF files are becoming a standard method of interchanging documents between different publishing programs. FreeHand 5.5 can read PDFs, converting the objects in the PDF into editable FreeHand objects. If you want to bring a publication you've produced in QuarkXPress or Adobe PageMaker into FreeHand, PDF is your ticket. See page 420.

Auto-Expanding Text Blocks. FreeHand 5 introduced the concept of text blocks that grow as you add text to them—but imposed some limitations (mainly that the text in an auto-expanding text block was always formatted as left aligned). FreeHand 5.5 takes auto-expanding text blocks a step further, making them handle paragraphs of any alignment. See page 232.

Cropping. FreeHand 5.5's new path operation, "Crop," gives you yet another way to work with the area of overlap between two paths. See page 167.

Extract. Because a variety of FreeHand's operations embed images in your publication, you'e got to have some way to get them out again. That's where "Extract" comes in. Use this feature to save embedded TIFFs and EPS files as to disk. See page 380.

Photoshop EPS Export. I often want to take my FreeHand artwork into Photoshop. Photoshop can't open FreeHand files or EPSes, and saving files in Illustrator fomat loses too much information (placed images and styles, for example, disappear). When you want to rasterize FreeHand paths in Photoshop, you can save the file in the new Photoshop EPS format—Photoshop will be able to open and process the EPS. See page 414.

What's New Since FreeHand 4?

Altsys had 120 days from the date they knew they'd be getting the product back to the first day that they could ship it (see "The Wild Ride" in the Introduction). Many companies would have done nothing more than change the product's packaging, but those crazy Texans decided to update the entire product.

Interface First, FreeHand 4 users will note the nifty gray 3D interface (which you can change back to the FreeHand 4 "look," if you want; see page 87). In addition, many of the user interface ideas used in FreeHand 4 have been improved and polished.

Expanded Preferences. FreeHand 4 kept lots of its preferences hidden in a text file. FreeHand 5 took those preferences, added a few more, and put them in a beautiful and intimidating series of dialog boxes. See page 71.

Increased Magnification. It's true—you can edit bacteria at actual size in FreeHand's 256,000% magnification. See page 34.

FreeHand Xtras. To software developers, FreeHand's support for add-on products (called "Xtras") make it the most advanced piece of software in shrink-wrap. FreeHand comes with a variety of Xtras (including some useful ones), and more are available from third-party developers. See page 126.

Illustrator Plug-Ins. FreeHand can run most of the plug-ins that work with Adobe Illustrator—including most of the plug-ins that come in the Illustrator package. Some of them are useful. See page 657.

Hiding All Palettes. The palettes are handy, but they can get in the way. You can quickly hide them all by pressing Command-Shift-H. See page 22.

Drag-and-Drop Styles. In FreeHand 4, you could apply colors by dragging color swatches out of color wells and dropping them on objects. In FreeHand 5, you can do the same thing with paragraph styles (another new feature of FreeHand 5). See page 315.

More Export Formats. FreeHand 5 supports more import and export formats than previous versions—mostly Illustrator formats corresponding to releases of that product. See page 398.

Page Layout

FreeHand continues to expand into territory usually claimed by PageMaker and XPress.

Larger Page and Pasteboard Size. FreeHand's maximum page size is now 222 by 222 inches—up from FreeHand 3's 40-by-40-inch limit, and up from FreeHand 4's 54-by-54 inch limit. This also means that the pasteboard's larger (the maximum page size in FreeHand is the size of the pasteboard). See page 27.

Zooming in the Document Inspector. It was frustrating. In FreeHand 4, you'd often have a very hard time moving pages in the Document Inspector—the thumbnail views of the pages were frequently too small to work with. In FreeHand 5, three buttons at the top of the Document Inspector's view of the pasteboard give you a way to zoom in and out on your publication. See page 24.

Text and Type

The biggest changes between FreeHand 4 and FreeHand 5 came in the areas of text and type.

Auto-expanding text blocks. FreeHand 5 introduced the idea of the automatically-expanding text block—a text block that gets bigger as you enter more text into it. FreeHand 5.5 improves on this feature. See page 232.

The Return of the Text Editor. In FreeHand 3, all text had to be entered through the Text dialog box—you couldn't edit text on the page. FreeHand users complained. In FreeHand 4, you could edit text on the page, but the Text dialog box disappeared. FreeHand users complained. In FreeHand 5, you can do both—edit text on the page, or use the Text Editor dialog box. See page 236.

Displaying/Hiding Text Rulers. Tired of looking at the Text (or Tab) ruler as you edit text? Put it away by pressing Command-\. See page 230.

Paragraph Styles. You might not know it, but you're always categorizing the different pieces of text you see. You know which paragraphs are headings, which are subheads, and which paragraphs are body text. Styles work the same way. When you use paragraph styles in FreeHand, you're helping FreeHand think about the text the way you already do. See page 309.

Spelling. FreeHand's spelling dialog box gives you the ability to check and change the spelling of the text in your publications. See page 240.

Search and Replace. With FreeHand's Find Text dialog box, you can search for words or phrases in your FreeHand publications. In addition, you can change the text you find to something else. See page 243.

Tab Leaders. Want to fill a tab with a leader character? Or change a tab's alignment? See page 305.

Vertical Line Tracks Tabs. When you drag a tab on the Text Ruler, you can have FreeHand display a vertical line running through the tab. It's another of FreeHand's myriad preferences. See page 82.

Improved text color controls. In FreeHand 4, it was sometimes difficult to apply a color to text. FreeHand 5 makes it easier. See page 275.

Color

Some parts of FreeHand's user interface for working with color moved around a bit in FreeHand 5, and various Xtras made working with color more convenient.

Tints Moved to the Color Mixer. FreeHand 4 had a separate Tint palette—FreeHand 5 moved the tint controls into a panel in the Color Mixer. Press Command-Shift-Z to display the Tint panel (same keyboard shortcut, different palette). See page 481.

Split Color well in the Color Mixer. Want to see a "before and after" view of your color as you edit it? You can split the large color well at the bottom of the Color Mixer to do just that. See page 74.

Automatic Color Naming. When you drag a color swatch into the Color List, FreeHand 5 assigns a new color name to the color. The color name is based on the color specification of the color swatch you're dragging. See page 73.

Color Xtras. Color Xtras can remove any unused colors you might have in your Color List, or increase or decrease brightness of a series of colors. You can even randomize the colors in the publication. See page 501.

Trap Xtra. FreeHand 5's Trap Xtra does a good job of trapping FreeHand publications that are too complicated to trap manually, but not so complicated that you want to use TrapWise. See page 526.

What's New Since FreeHand 3?

What changed between FreeHand 3 and FreeHand 5? What didn't? When I started writing *Real World FreeHand 4*, I thought I'd be able to revise *Real World FreeHand 3* (and thereby achieve an hourly pay rate approaching the minimum wage). Instead, I found I'd have to rewrite the book to keep up with all the changes in FreeHand. It was fun, though—I found I was frequently changing text from "you can't do that in FreeHand" to "you can do that in FreeHand."

Interface in Your Face

If you've been using FreeHand 3, it's obvious from the time you start FreeHand 5.5 that FreeHand has a new user interface. The new look is built around eleven palettes (seven of them are new), which replace about 70 separate dialog boxes in FreeHand 3. See page 12.

Inspector Palette. The Inspector is the most important palette in FreeHand. You use the it to set paragraph formatting options, to specify fills and strokes, to create new pages, and to arrange pages on FreeHand's pasteboard. FreeHand's Inspector palette replaces more than 30 of FreeHand 3's modal dialog boxes. See page 13.

Color List. FreeHand's Color List replaces FreeHand 3's Colors palette. What the Color List does is pretty similar to the old palette, but how it does it is very different. See page 384.

Color Mixer. This is the place where you create and edit colors. It's a palette, so you don't have to take your eyes off your publication while you work with color, as you did in FreeHand 3's Colors dialog box. See page 481.

Type Specifications Palette. You use the Type Specifications palette to set the font, type style, and size of your text. See page 263. I sure wish leading were in this palette, but it's in the Character Inspector—see page 262 for more on the Character Inspector.

Align Palette. FreeHand's Align palette takes the functions of FreeHand 3's Align dialog box and puts them in a palette. See page 462.

Transform Palette. The Transform Palette puts FreeHand's transformations (move, scale, rotate, and skew) on your screen—making them easier to reach than they were in FreeHand 3. See page 426.

Halftone Palette. You use the Halftone palette to quickly set halftone type, screen angle, and screen frequency for a selected object. See page 18.

Styles Palette. The new Styles palette works differently—and, in my opinion, better—than FreeHand 3's version. You now define and edit styles by example—the quickest and easiest way to work with styles. See page 18.

Layers Palette. FreeHand's new Layers palette is easier to use, though, in some ways, a little less capable than FreeHand 3's Layers palette (there's no longer a Multilayer shortcut for making the current layer the only active layer—you've got to turn layers on and off to accomplish the same thing). See page 63.

Minimizing and Maximizing Palettes. You can display palettes in a "minimized" form, where only the palette's title bar is visible, by clicking the zoom box in the palette's title bar. When you want to display the entire palette again, click the zoom box and the palette expands to its full size. See page 22.

Page Layout   In the first edition of this book, in a description of the Pages control in the Print dialog box, I said, "Whenever I see this, my heart leaps up. Can you imagine a multipage FreeHand? Wouldn't that be great? Are you ready to start calling Aldus and Altsys?"

I guess enough of us called.

Multiple Pages, Multiple Sizes, Multiple Page Orientations. You can create as many pages, in as many different page sizes and orientations as you can fit on FreeHand's pasteboard. You can view and work on any single page, or any number of pages, at any time—making FreeHand an ideal choice when you have to work with multipage spreads, such as brochures. See page 24.

Print Spreads Using Manual Tiling. Being able to position multiple pages on the pasteboard is great—but you really need a way to print more than one of those pages on a single sheet of paper or imagesetter film. Luckily, FreeHand includes this capability (though I can't tell if it does so by intention or accident). See page 542.

Drawing   All of FreeHand 3's drawing features are still with us—and some of the tools (like the Knife tool) have even gotten better. In addition, FreeHand adds some new drawing tools.

Point Tool. FreeHand's toolbox looks about the same as the toolbox in FreeHand 3, with a few important differences. The biggest change is that the individual point-drawing tools from FreeHand 3 have been combined into the Point tool. When you're using this tool, a click produces a corner point. Hold down Option key as you click, and you place a curve point. Hold down Control as you click, and FreeHand places a connector point. See page 122.

Calligraphic Pen Tool. FreeHand 3's Variable Stroke tool gave FreeHand users a way to create paths shaped like brush strokes. FreeHand 4 built on this feature, adding the Calligraphic Pen tool. Use this tool to create thick and thin paths that look like they were drawn with a calligraphic nib. See page 120.

Polygon tool. FreeHand's Polygon tool makes it easy to draw any equilateral polygon, such as pentagons, octagons, and hexagons. You can also use it to draw stars with any number of points. See page 42.

Improved Knife Tool. FreeHand 3's Knife tool could only cut paths one path at a time. In FreeHand 5, the Knife tool works like—well, like a knife would (or, really, more like a chain saw!). It cuts every selected path you drag it across. See page 46.

Editable Arrowheads. When you don't see the arrowhead you want on the Arrowhead menus in FreeHand's Stroke Inspector, you can create your own. See page 176.

Path Operations

Path operations make it easy to create shapes that would be difficult or impossible to draw by hand—you can draw basic shapes (rectangles, polygons, and ellipses) and use the path operations to turn these basic shapes into more complex paths. See page 105.

Punch. Select two closed, overlapping paths and choose Punch from the Path Operations submenu of the Arrange menu when you want to cut the shape of the frontmost path out of the path behind it. Punch uses the frontmost object as a "cookie cutter." See page 166.

Union. Choose Union when you want to join overlapping (closed) paths together while deleting the area(s) where the paths overlap. See page 166.

Intersect. When you select two closed, overlapping paths and choose Intersect from the Path Operations submenu of the Arrange menu, FreeHand deletes the original paths, leaving only the area defined by their intersection. See page 164.

Simplify. Simplify analyzes a path and removes extraneous points on the path. Autotracing, for example, sometimes generates more points than are strictly necessary to describe a path. See page 150.

Correct Direction. Choose Correct Direction when you want to set a selected path's direction of the current path to clockwise. This path operation, and its counterpart, Reverse Direction, are particularly handy when you want to change the way text joins to a path. See page 149.

Reverse Direction. Reverse Direction does just what it says—it changes the direction of a path from whatever it currently is to its opposite (from clockwise to counterclockwise, for example). See page 149.

Remove Overlap. Choose Remove Overlap to remove any areas of a single path where the path crosses over itself. This path operation comes in handy when you're cleaning up complex paths you've generated by autotracing. See page 150.

Expand Stroke. Expand Stroke converts a closed path into a composite path, or converts an open path into a closed path that follows the open path's shape. You can specify the width of the new path as you use Expand Stroke. See page 167.

Inset Path. Inset Path creates another version of the selected shape, a precise distance inside (or outside) the current shape. See page 168.

Text and Text Blocks

You can edit your text just as you see it in your layout—no more trips to the dreaded Text dialog box (unless you want to go there—see page 236).

You can even edit text that's been joined to a path this way—just select the Text tool and click it in some text that's joined to a path. The insertion point follows the baseline of the type as it shifts and slants around the path.

Creating and Editing Text Onscreen. To create a text block, select the Text tool and drag it on the page (you can also simply click the Text tool on the page, but drag-creating a text block gives you control over the width and height of the text block). To add text to your new text block, start typing. See page 228.

Sizing Text Blocks To Fit Text. After you've finished typing text in a text block, you might want to resize the text block to fit the text. If so, select the text box with the pointer tool, and double-click the link box (the box that appears outside the lower-right corner of the text block). FreeHand sizes the text block so that it's no larger than the text it contains. See page 232.

Specifying a Text Block's Inset. If you want, you can specify an inset for your text block—essentially, the inset is a margin inside the text block. See page 259.

Multicolumn and Multirow Text Blocks. A FreeHand text block can contain up to 100 rows and 100 columns—which, when combined with FreeHand's new tabs and paragraph formatting, makes FreeHand a great choice for creating tables. See page 255.

Creating Borders on Text Blocks. FreeHand's text blocks—and the rows and columns they contain—can be stroked and filled. The same fill and stroke apply to all of the cells and cell borders inside the text block. See page 258.

Linking Text Blocks. FreeHand's text blocks, (like those found in QuarkXPress or Adobe PageMaker), can be linked together so that text can flow from one text block to another. By linking text blocks, you can create articles that flow over several magazine pages, for example. See page 254.

Typography

FreeHand is now equipped with a fairly complete set of paragraph formatting controls, including indents and tabs, space above and below, and controls for hyphenation and justification. In addition, FreeHand now features range kerning and hanging punctuation.

Formatting Paragraphs. You use the Paragraph Inspector, Alignment Inspector, and Spacing Inspector to format paragraphs in your FreeHand text blocks. See page 288.

Paragraph Rules. You can attach up to two rules to paragraphs in FreeHand—one rule above the paragraph; one rule below the paragraph. These rules are vertically centered in the space above and below the paragraph, and flow with the text as you edit or reformat the text. See page 307.

Setting Tabs. FreeHand's text blocks can contain left, right, center, and decimal alignment, and wrapping tabs. Wrapping tabs create a column inside a column of your text block, and are unique to FreeHand—no other page-layout or illustration program that I know of has anything like them. They're great for creating columns within columns, or for creating columns of unequal widths inside a text block (columns set with the Column Inspector always divide a text block evenly). See page 297.

Hanging Indents. As in both Microsoft Word and PageMaker, you can create a hanging indent by dragging the left margin icon to the right of the first-line indent icon, and then setting a left tab at the same position as the left margin icon. See page 300.

Range Kerning. When you want to tighten or loosen the spaces between all of the characters in a selection, use FreeHand's Range Kern field—which you can see in the Character palette. Enter a kerning value here, and FreeHand tightens (or loosens) the spaces between the selected characters. See page 286.

Automatic Hanging Punctuation. Because we don't "see" punctuation when we're reading, a line beginning (or, in some cases ending) with punctuation (especially quotation marks) doesn't look like it aligns with other lines in the surrounding text. It's a kind of typographic optical illusion. To compensate, try FreeHand's hanging punctuation—which moves the punctuation slightly beyond the edge of the text column. See page 296.

Automatic Copyfitting. When you've got too much text (or too little text) to fill a column, you can direct FreeHand to squash (or expand) the leading and/or the type size to get the text to fit in the text blocks you've allocated for the story. See page 321.

Wrap Text Around Objects. When you want text to avoid a path on your page, use FreeHand's new Text Wrap feature. See page 330.

Flow Text Inside Objects You can flow text inside any closed path—it's like the opposite of a text wrap. Use this effect when you want to create angled columns, or when you need nonrectangular text blocks. Text inside a path is always a single column and a single row, but you can still use tabs to create multiple columns if you need to. See page 329.

Importing and Exporting

FreeHand's always been strong in the area of import and export, and it's gotten even stronger. See Chapter 4, "Importing and Exporting," on page 343.

Editable FreeHand EPS. When you export a FreeHand publication as an EPS, you can choose to embed the original FreeHand file in the EPS—which means that you can open and edit the EPS just as you would any FreeHand publication file. No more having to keep two versions of the file around (one in EPS format, one in FreeHand 3's native file format). Layers, styles, colors, and other FreeHand features are all preserved when you create an editable EPS. See page 394.

Text File Import and Export. FreeHand can import text files you've saved as text-only (ASCII) or Rich Text Format (RTF). RTF is an ASCII coding system that's supposed to be able to describe anything you can have in a Microsoft Word file. PageMaker, Microsoft Word, and other page-layout and word-processing programs can save text files as RTF. See page 382.

The nice thing about RTF is that local formatting—typestyles, type sizes, and font changes—is retained when you place the document in FreeHand. Because FreeHand doesn't import RTF paragraph styles, that information in the RTF file is ignored and discarded. The text formatting remains the same, but it's local formatting.

FreeHand can also save text files as RTF or ASCII. When you export, FreeHand exports all of the text in your document, not just the text you've selected. See page 391.

Color

FreeHand 5 builds on FreeHand 3's legacy of strong color production tools, and adds a new ease of use and immediacy to working with color.

Color Wells and Color Swatches. As you look at FreeHand's palettes, you'll see lots of little squares of color. These are color wells, and they're the key to using color in FreeHand. See page 479.

When you position your cursor over a color well (in the Color List, the Color Mixer, the Inspector, or the Tints palette) and drag, a small square of color emerges from the color well and follows the cursor. We call the moving square of color a "color swatch." See page 479.

Drag-and-Drop Color. You can drag color swatches from any color well to any other color well, but you can also drop the color swatches directly on objects in your publication to apply the color to the object (or, in the case of a path, to the path's fill or stroke). See page 479.

Drag-and-Drop Graduated Fills. To create a graduated fill using drag-and-drop, hold down Option as you drop a color swatch onto a path. See page 186.

Drag-and-Drop Radial Fills. To create a radial fill using drag-and-drop, hold down Control as you drop a color swatch onto the path. See page 188.

Automatic Tint Generation. To quickly create tints based on the current color, drag a color swatch from the Color List (or any other color well) and drop it into the base color well in the Tints section of the Color Mixer. FreeHand creates tints in 10 percent increments. You can also create custom tint percentages. See page 481.

CHAPTER

FreeHand Basics

1

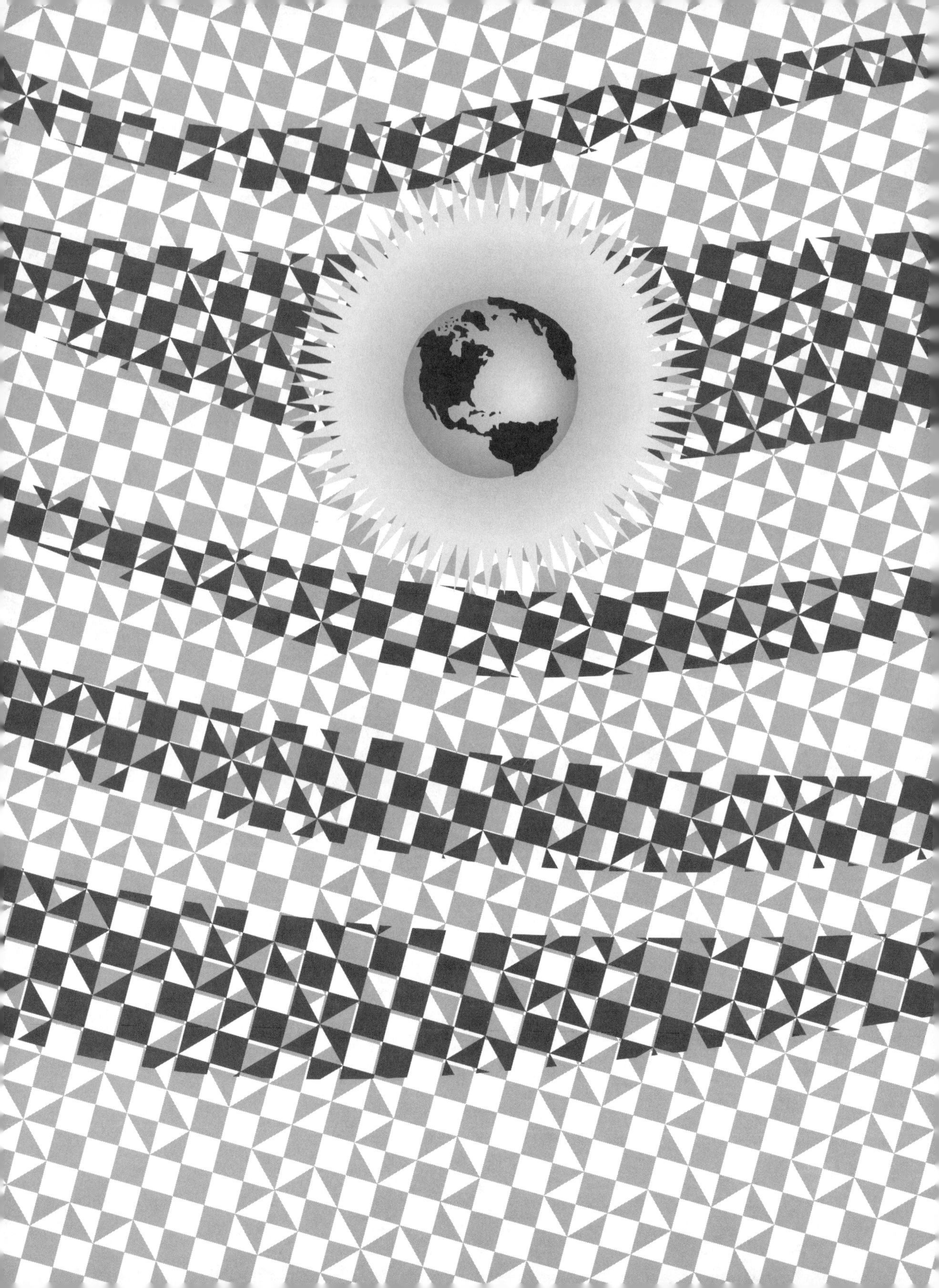

CHAPTER ONE ❦ FREEHAND BASICS

Start FreeHand, and you enter another world—a software model of a graphic artist's studio. Most programs are based on some real-world model: PageMaker works like a layout board, Excel works like an accountant's worksheet, and Word works like a reasonably smart electric typewriter. Metaphors like these make computer software "user-friendly"—partly because they give us something we're familiar with, and partly because they give the program a logic of its own.

In this chapter, I'll show you around the virtual reality that is FreeHand. There'll be lots of definitions of terms (how can you know what I'm talking about unless we're using the same vocabulary?) and "maps" of FreeHand's screen (how can you tell where you're going unless you know the lay of the land?). Almost all of the concepts and practices covered here are covered in greater depth in other chapters. In those cases, I'll provide a cross reference to the more detailed explanation.

I'll also be going through some techniques for changing the way FreeHand looks and behaves, because I believe that the tools you use should fit your working habits. Someday, all of our software will be completely modular and completely customizable, but until that day arrives, there's always ResEdit.

At the end of the chapter, I'll run through my list of rules for using FreeHand. You can take them or leave them; there are many different ways to approach FreeHand, and my methods are not necessarily the ones that'll work best for you. Some of my habits are rooted in the dim and primordial past (giant ground sloths, woolly mammoths, and Linotronic L100s roamed the earth), and some, while true today, may not apply when this book reaches your hands. That's the thing about computer software—as soon as you really know something, it's obsolete.

The Publication Window

When you open or create a FreeHand publication, you view and work on the publication in the publication window (see figure 1-1). FreeHand's publication window gives you a view on FreeHand's pasteboard—the place everything happens in FreeHand.

In addition to the standard Macintosh title bar, close box, and zoom box (click it to make your publication window the size of the screen; click it again to return the publication window to its previous size), FreeHand's publication window holds several other controls and features.

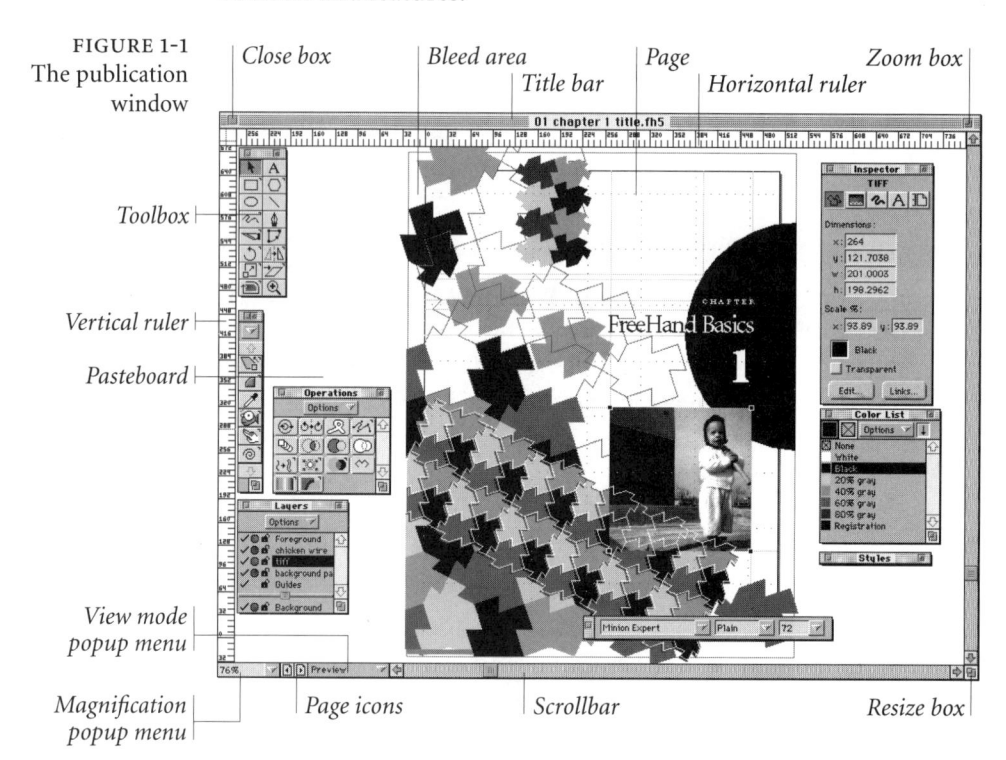

FIGURE 1-1
The publication window

Close box   *Bleed area*   *Page*   *Zoom box*
Title bar   *Horizontal ruler*

Toolbox

Vertical ruler

Pasteboard

View mode popup menu

Magnification popup menu   *Page icons*   *Scrollbar*   *Resize box*

FREEHAND BASICS 5

Info Bar Immediately below the title bar, FreeHand's Info Bar displays information about the current state of the selected object and the position of the cursor or selected object (see figure 1-2). You can display and hide the Info Bar by pressing Command-Shift-R, but you can't move it, as you could in FreeHand 3.

FIGURE 1-2
FreeHand's Info Bar

```
h:0        v:0
```

Info Bar showing that you've got nothing selected, and that your cursor is off the page. "h" shows the horizontal position of the cursor; "v" shows the vertical position of the cursor. FreeHand measures these coordinates from the publication's current zero point.

```
ch:473.4735   cv:528.6805   angle:135
```

When you rotate an object, the Info Bar looks like this. "ch" shows the horizontal center of the object; "cv" shows the vertical center; "angle" shows you the angle of rotation.

Scroll Bars The most obvious, least convenient, and slowest way to change your view of your publication is to use a scroll bar (that is, to click in a scroll bar, drag a scroll handle, or click one of the arrows at either end of a scroll bar). For more on better ways to get around, see "Moving Around in Your Publication," later in this chapter.

Page Icons Now that FreeHand publications can contain multiple pages, you need a way to move from one page to another. One way is to click the left page icon to move to the previous page in your publication, and click the right page icon to move to the next page. There's a better way to get from page to page, however: double-click the pages in the thumbnail view of FreeHand's pasteboard in the Document Inspector (for more on how to do this, see "Moving Around in Your Publication," later in this chapter).

View Mode Popup Menu Choose Preview or Keyline from this popup menu to switch between FreeHand's two view modes. You can also press Command-K to switch viewing modes.

In Preview mode, FreeHand renders the objects you've drawn as they'll be printed. In Keyline mode, FreeHand shows you only the outlines of the objects on the page (see figure 1-3).

FIGURE 1-3
Preview and
Keyline viewing
modes

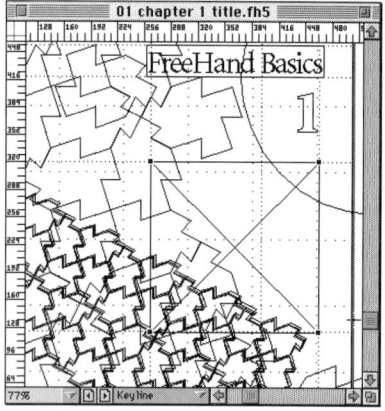

Preview mode

Keyline mode (note that the TIFF becomes a box)

Each viewing mode has advantages and disadvantages. In Preview mode, you'll see something resembling your printed publication, but you'll also wait longer for it to display; Keyline mode redraws quickly but doesn't usually resemble the printed publication. It's easier to select points in Keyline mode, and it's easier to select objects in Preview mode. You'll find yourself switching between Preview and Keyline often.

Note that you can also set specific layers to display in either Keyline or Preview mode using the Layers palette. For more on how to do this, see "Working with Layers," later in this chapter.

Magnification Popup Menu

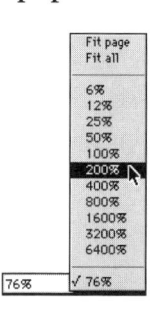

Choose the magnification at which you want to view your publication from this popup menu, and FreeHand magnifies (or reduces) the view of the publication you see in the publication window. Again, there are several better ways to do this, as shown in "Moving Around in Your Publication," later in this chapter.

Note that these views aren't the only magnifications available—using the magnifying glass, you can achieve any magnification you want. For more on using the magnifying glass, see "Magnifying Glass," later in this chapter.

Note, too, that the maximum magnfication cited in the Magnification popup menu isn't the ultimate magnification FreeHand's capable of. I don't actually know what the limit is—but I do know that you can zoom in far enough to draw bacteria at actual size (see Appendix B, "Your FreeHand Installation").

FREEHAND BASICS 7

Multiple Windows If you want to open more than one window on your publication, choose "New Window" from the Window menu (or press Command-Option N). The new window obscures the original window, so you'll have to drag and resize windows to see both views at once (see figure 1-4). Alternatively, you can use the Window menu to move from one window to another—each window appears in the list of open publications at the bottom of the menu.

Sometimes, when you're working with a multi-page document, it's easier to display pages in multiple windows than it is to scroll or zoom from page to page. This is especially true if you're copying objects from one page to another.

Multiple Publications You can have as many different publications open as FreeHand can fit into your machine's RAM. You move between open publications by choosing their file names from the Window menu, or by clicking on their windows, just as you'd switch between applications (see figure 1-4).

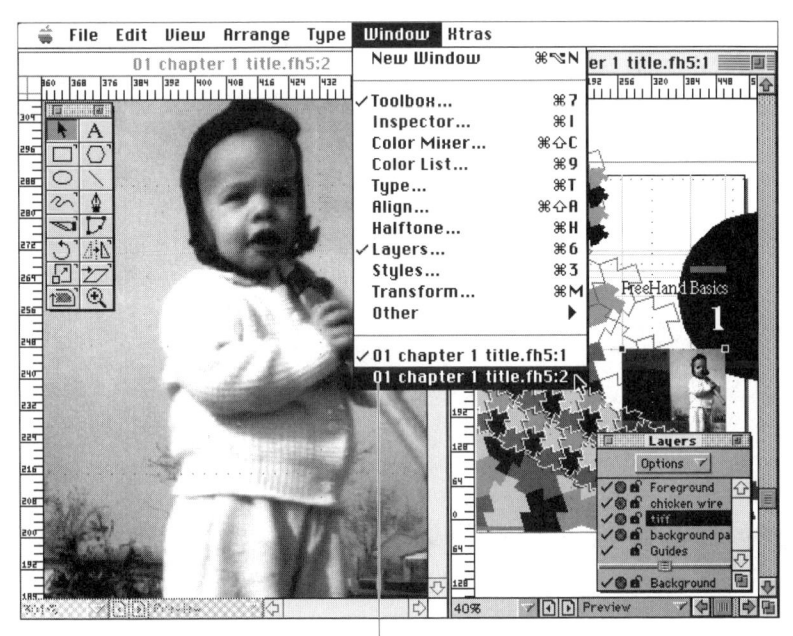

FIGURE 1-4
Window menu

List of open publications or windows. FreeHand displays a check beside the title of the active window.

Page and Pasteboard

Like most other page layout programs, FreeHand is built around the concept of pages—areas on which you place graphic elements. Pages float on the pasteboard—a 222-inch square area. In FreeHand 5, you can create as many pages as you want, provided they all fit on the pasteboard. You can use areas of the pasteboard that don't contain pages for temporary storage of the elements you're working with—just drag the elements off the page, and they'll stay on the pasteboard until you need them.

Bleed Area, Page Size, and Paper Size

Objects can extend past the edge of the page, into an area of the pasteboard that's defined as the bleed. What's the point of having a "bleed?" Sometimes, you want to print objects that extend beyond the edge of your page (they'll be clipped off at the edge of the page when your commercial printer cuts your pages, but, sometimes, that's just the design effect you want).

Each page's bleed is shown in the publication window by line (a gray line on color and grayscale monitors, or a dotted line if you're working in black and white) surrounding the page. Different pages can have bleed areas of different sizes.

The size of the bleed, the page size, and the size of the paper (that is, the paper size you want to use when you print your *final* copy) all affect each other. In FreeHand, the page size you define in the Document Inspector should be the same as the final size of the document's page after it's been printed by a commercial printer. You define the paper size—the physical size of the paper in your printer—in the Print Options dialog box. When you're printing to an imagesetter, the paper size is a defined area on the imagesetter's film roll (or sheet, for drum imagesetters).

If your publication's page size (without the bleed) is the same as the paper size you've chosen in the Print Options dialog box, you can expect FreeHand to neatly clip off the bleed area you've specified. Choose a larger paper size in the Print Options dialog box than your publication's page size when you want to print bleeds (choose Letter.Extra when you're printing a letter-size publication with a bleed, for example). If want to learn how to create new paper sizes for imagesetters (I don't know of any laser printer that can handle custom paper sizes), see "Rewriting PPDs" in Chapter 7, "Printing."

FREEHAND BASICS

Rulers Command-R displays or hides FreeHand's rulers—handy measuring tools that appear along the top and left sides of your publication window (see figure 1-5). They're marked off in the units of measurement specified in the Setup Inspector. The actual increments shown on the rulers vary somewhat with the current page view; in general, you'll see finer increments and more ruler tick marks at 800% size than you'll see at 12% size.

As you move the cursor, lines in the rulers (called shadow cursors) display the cursor's position relative to the rulers (see figure 1-6). When you select an object, FreeHand highlights areas on the rulers that correspond to the size and position of the object (I call this the "shadow selection").

FIGURE 1-5
FreeHand's rulers

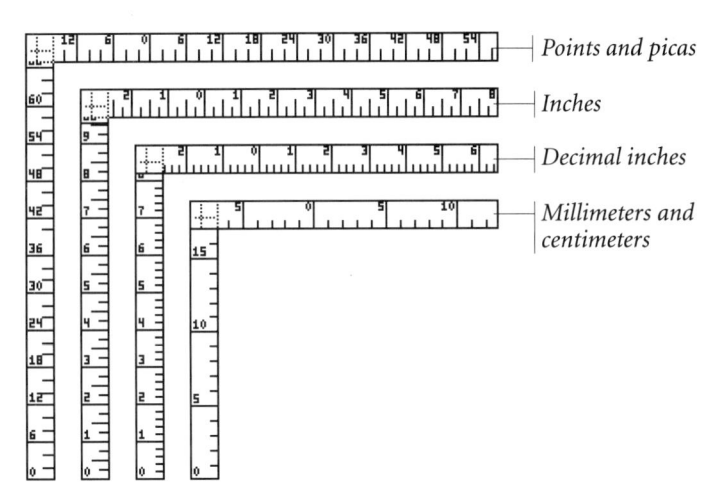

Points and picas

Inches

Decimal inches

Millimeters and centimeters

FIGURE 1-6
Shadow cursors and shadow selection

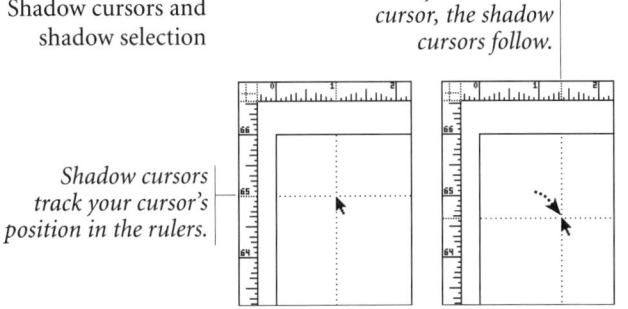

As you move the cursor, the shadow cursors follow.

As you move an object, the shadow selection shows the width and height of the object on the rulers.

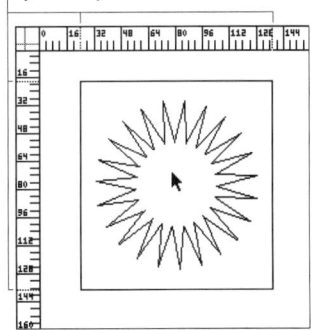

Shadow cursors track your cursor's position in the rulers.

Zero Point

The intersection of the zero measurement on both rulers is called the zero point. In FreeHand, the default location of the zero point is at the lower-left corner of the current page. To control the location of the zero point you use the zero-point marker (see figure 1-7), which you see at the upper-left corner of your screen (when you have the rulers displayed). You can think of it as the point where the two rulers intersect on the page, even though you can't see the point itself.

To move the zero point, drag the zero-point marker to a new position (see figure 1-8). As you drag, intersecting dotted lines show you the position of the zero point. When you've moved the zero point to the location you want, release the mouse button. The rulers now mark off their increments based on this new zero point.

If you need to reposition only the horizontal or vertical ruler's zero point, drag the zero-point marker along the other ruler—the one you don't want to change—until the zero point is where you want it (see figure 1-9).

Tip:
Resetting the Zero Point

To reset the zero point to the lower-left corner of the page, double-click the zero-point marker.

FIGURE 1-7
Zero-point marker

Zero-point marker

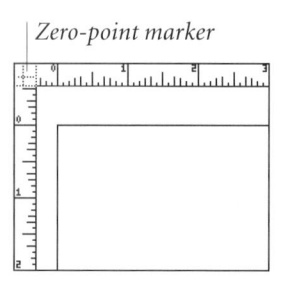

FIGURE 1-8
Repositioning the zero point

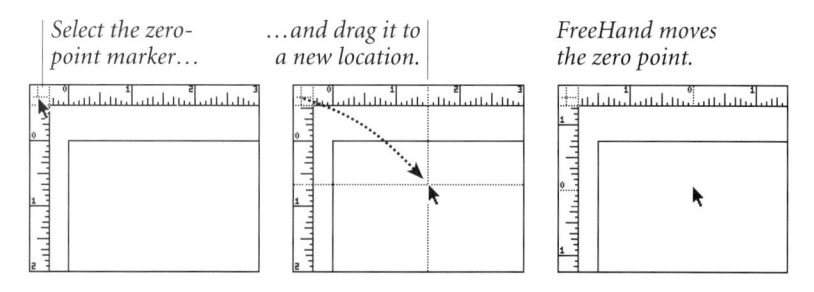

Select the zero-point marker...

...and drag it to a new location.

FreeHand moves the zero point.

FIGURE 1-9
Repositioning only one
of the zero points

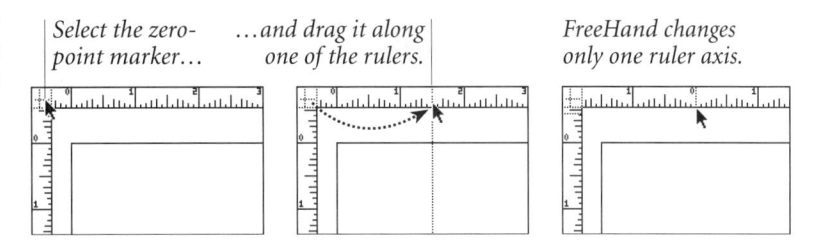

Select the zero-point marker... *...and drag it along one of the rulers.* *FreeHand changes only one ruler axis.*

Guides

Guides are nonprinting guidelines you use when you're aligning items on a page. In FreeHand 5, you'll find two kinds of guides.

- Ruler guides are the guides you might remember from FreeHand 4—or, for that matter, from other programs, such as PageMaker or Quark XPress—they're straight lines that run all of the way across the page. Ruler guides are always either vertical or horizontal (just like the rulers).

- Custom guides are paths you've drawn in FreeHand and converted to guides. Custom guides can be any shape, any length, at any angle relative to the page, and can be turned back into paths at any time.

As far as I can tell, there's no limit to the number of guides you can use in a publication.

Adding ruler guides. To add a ruler guide, position the cursor over a ruler and drag the cursor onto the page or pasteboard. As you drag the cursor off the ruler, a line follows the cursor, showing you where your new ruler guide will fall. When you've got the line where you want it, release the mouse button. FreeHand positions a new ruler guide at this location (see figure 1-10).

FIGURE 1-10
Positioning
a ruler guide

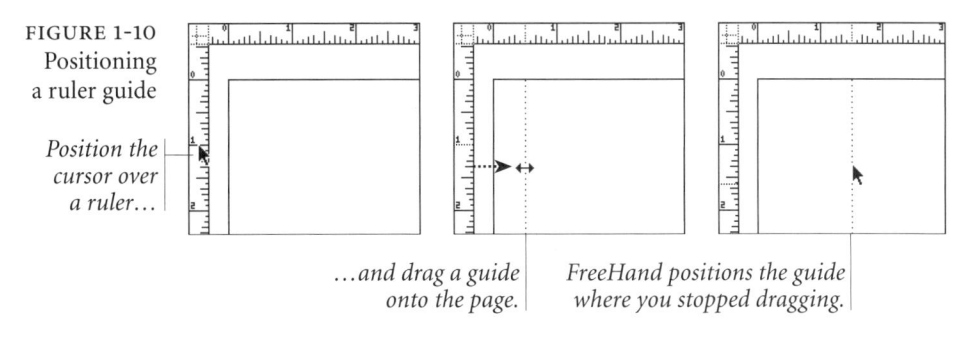

Position the cursor over a ruler...

...and drag a guide onto the page. *FreeHand positions the guide where you stopped dragging.*

Adding custom guides. To add a custom guide, select a path you want to use as a guide and click on the default Guides layer in the Layers palette (see figure 1-11). FreeHand converts the selected path into a guide. You'll be able to tell immediately that the path is a guide, because FreeHand changes its color to the Guides color, and because FreeHand removes any formatting that's been applied to the stroke of the path, rendering custom guides as one-pixel wide lines at any screen magnification (the formatting's only gone until you release the guide).

FIGURE 1-11
Creating a custom guide

Select the path or paths you want to convert to a guide…

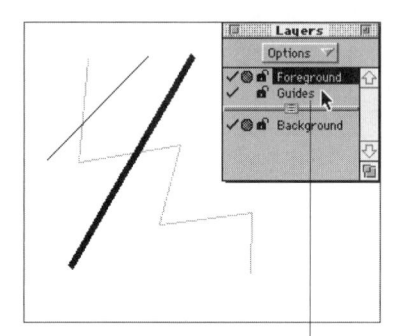

…and click the Guides layer. FreeHand converts the paths to custom guides.

Tip:
When You Want a Wide Guide

What can you do when you'd like your custom guide to be the same width as the formatted path you've used to create it? Before you convert the path to a guide, select the path and choose "Expand stroke" from the Path Operations submenu of the Arrange menu. FreeHand displays the Expand Stroke dialog box. Enter a value in the Width field that's equal to the stroke weight of the path, and FreeHand creates a composite path that's the width of the formatted path (see figure 1-12). Once you've done that, you can convert the path to a guide and you'll have the wide guide you were looking for. Though I haven't ever had a need for this, I'm betting some of you will.

Adding guides numerically. When you know precisely where you want a ruler guide to appear, use the Guides dialog box to add the guide (see figure 1-13).

FREEHAND BASICS 13

FIGURE 1-12
Creating a guide that's the width of a path

Select the path you want to turn into a guide.

Choose "Expand Stroke" from the Path Operations submenu of the Arrange menu.

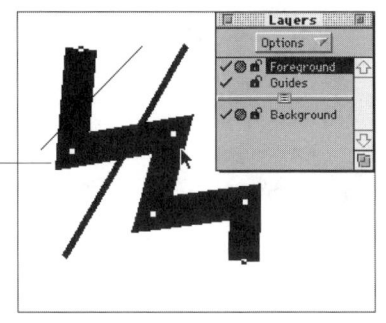

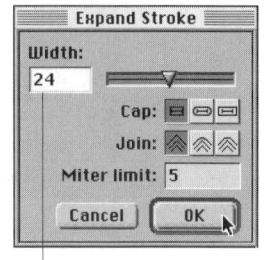

Enter the width of the stroke in the Expand Stroke dialog box.

FreeHand expands the path.

Click the Guides layer.

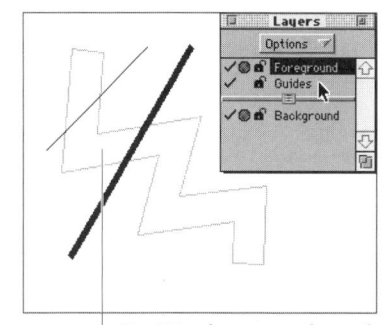

FreeHand converts the path to a guide that follows the outline of the original path.

1. Choose "Edit Guides" from the View menu. FreeHand displays the Guides dialog box.

2. Click the Add button. FreeHand displays the Add Guides dialog box.

3. Enter the type of ruler guide you want to add (vertical or horizontal), the number of guides you want, and the range you want those guides to fill. Use the Count option to enter a specific number of guides, or turn on the By Increment option to enter the distance you want between guides (in this case, the actual number of guides entered depends on the values in the first and Last fields—you'll get as many guides as will fit in the defined range). Set the range of pages you want to apply these guide settings to using the Page Range fields.

4. Press Return to close the Add Guides dialog box. FreeHand adds the guides to the list in the Guides dialog box.

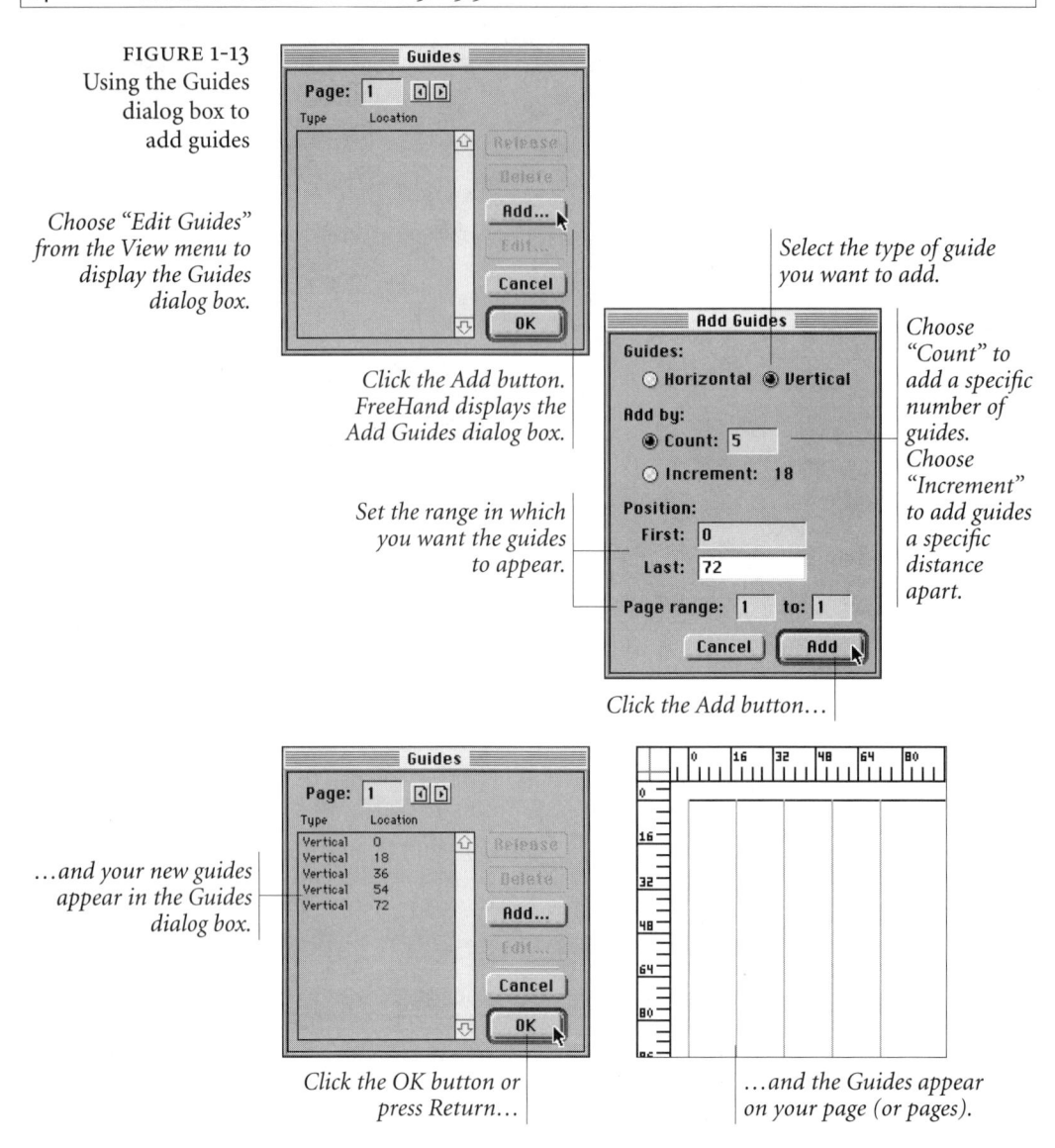

FIGURE 1-13
Using the Guides dialog box to add guides

Choose "Edit Guides" from the View menu to display the Guides dialog box.

Click the Add button. FreeHand displays the Add Guides dialog box.

Select the type of guide you want to add.

Choose "Count" to add a specific number of guides. Choose "Increment" to add guides a specific distance apart.

Set the range in which you want the guides to appear.

Click the Add button...

...and your new guides appear in the Guides dialog box.

Click the OK button or press Return...

...and the Guides appear on your page (or pages).

5. Press Return (or click the OK button). FreeHand adds the guides to your page (or pages, if you specified a range).

Removing Guides. When you want to remove a ruler guide, position the Pointer tool above the ruler guide and drag the ruler guide back onto the ruler (see figure 1-14). If you can't select the ruler guide, you've probably got Lock Guides turned on. Turn it off by choosing "Lock Guides" from the View menu.

FIGURE 1-14
Removing a
ruler guide

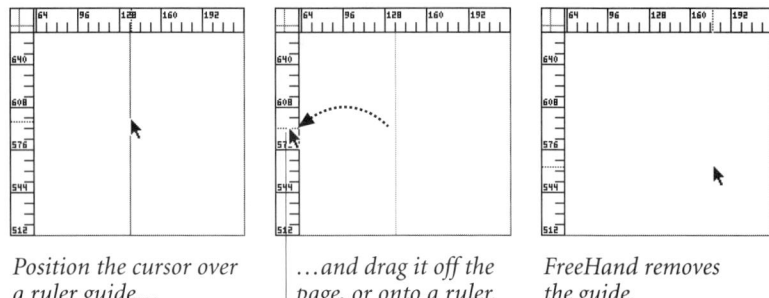

Position the cursor over a ruler guide... | *...and drag it off the page, or onto a ruler.* | *FreeHand removes the guide.*

In FreeHand 4, you had to drag the ruler guide all the way off the page to remove it. What did this mean if you couldn't see an edge of the current page? It meant you had to zoom out, then drag the guide off of the page. Or it meant that FreeHand would scroll your view of the page as you dragged a guide. Most FreeHand users didn't want to do either (and I agreed with them), and felt that you shouldn't have to change your view of the page to remove a guide. If, on the other hand, you *liked* the way it worked in FreeHand 4, you can make FreeHand 5 work that way, too—just check Dragging a Guide Scrolls the Window in the General Editing Preferences dialog box, and you can have it your way.

To delete a guide, double-click the guide. FreeHand displays the Edit Guides dialog box, which shows a list of the guides on the current page. The guide you clicked is highlighted in the list. Click the Delete button, and FreeHand removes the guide from the page (see figure 1-15).

You could, of course, bring up the Edit Guides dialog box by choosing "Edit guides" from the View menu, then locate and select

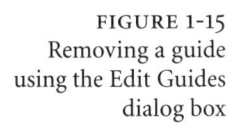

FIGURE 1-15
Removing a guide
using the Edit Guides
dialog box

Double-click the guide you want to remove.

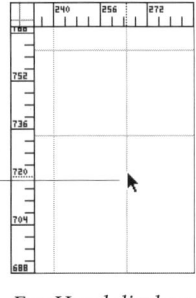

FreeHand displays the Guides dialog box.

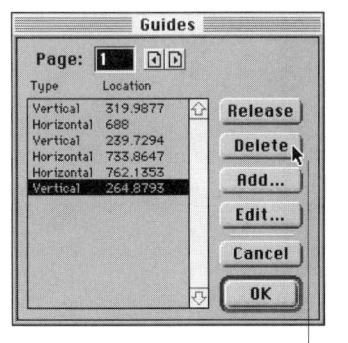

Click the Delete button.

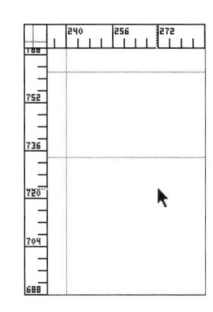

FreeHand deletes the guide.

the guide you want to remove in the list of guides. I prefer the double-click technique, because it brings up the Edit Guides dialog box with the guide you clicked selected. If you don't do this, it's hard to tell which guide is which by looking at the guide positions in the dialog box.

Removing multiple guides. To remove more than one guide at a time, hold down Shift and select more of the guides in the list, then click the Delete button. Want to get rid of all the guides on the current page? Hold down Shift and drag through the list. Once you've selected all of the guides, click the Delete button.

Converting custom guides to paths. To convert a custom guide back into a normal path, double-click the guide. FreeHand displays the Edit Guides dialog box, and selects the guide you clicked in the list of guides. Click the Release button. FreeHand converts the guide back to a path (see figure 1-16). Any formatting applied to the path before you turned it into a guide reappears.

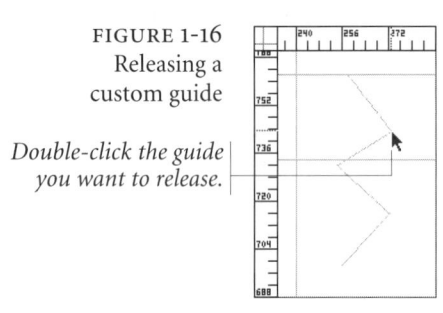

FIGURE 1-16
Releasing a custom guide

Double-click the guide you want to release.

FreeHand displays the Guides dialog box.

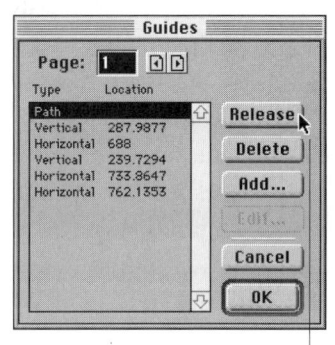

Click the Release button.

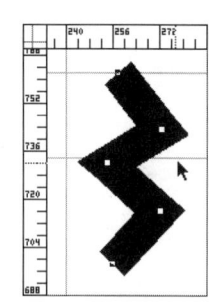

FreeHand converts the guide into a path, complete with its original formatting.

Editing guides. Want to change the location of a guide? Drag the guide to a new position. If you want to move the guide to a specific vertical or horizontal coordinate, use the Guides dialog box (see figure 1-17).

1. Choose "Edit Guides" from the View menu. FreeHand displays the Guides dialog box.

FIGURE 1-17
Editing guide positions

Double-click the guide you want to edit.

FreeHand displays the Guides dialog box.

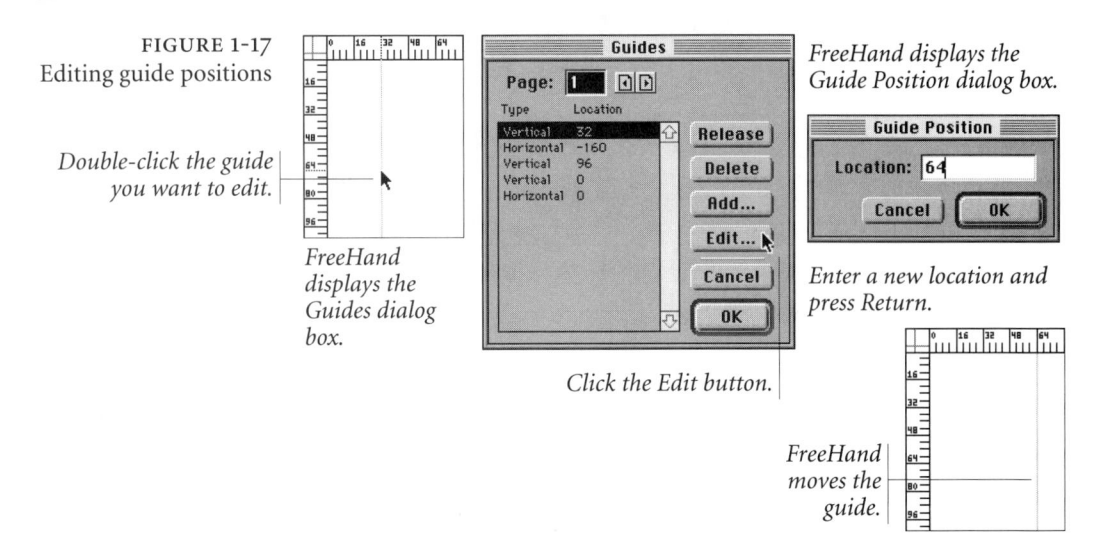

Click the Edit button.

FreeHand displays the Guide Position dialog box.

Enter a new location and press Return.

FreeHand moves the guide.

2. Select the guide you want to change from the list of guides.

3. Click the Edit button. FreeHand displays the Edit Guide dialog box.

4. Enter the position you want to move the guide to.

5. Press Return to close the Edit Guides dialog box. FreeHand changes the position of the guide in the list of guides in the Guides dialog box.

6. Press Return (or click the OK button). FreeHand moves the guide.

Snap to Guides Ruler guides are especially useful in conjunction with the Snap to Guides option (toggle this option on and off by pressing Command-;). When you've turned on Snap to Guides, objects within the distance you've set (in the Snap Distance field of the Editing Preferences dialog box) automatically snap into alignment with the ruler guide (see figure 1-18). For more on snapping in general, see "Snap Distance," later in this chapter.

To see how this works, turn on Snap to Guides, draw a box, position a ruler guide, and drag the box toward the guide. When the box gets within your specified distance of the guide, it snaps right to it. You can almost feel the magnetic pull of the guide in the

FIGURE 1-18
Snap to Guides

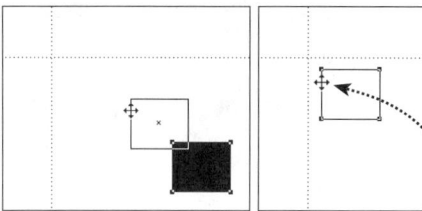

When you're dragging an object with Snap to Guides turned on, nothing happens...

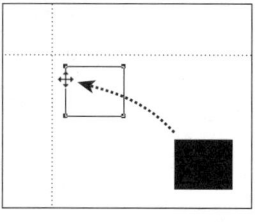

...until you drag the object within a certain distance of a ruler guide. At this point, the guides seem to pull the object toward them...

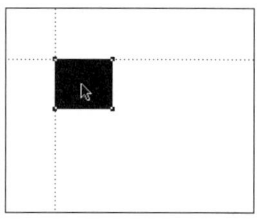

...until the object snaps to the guide (or guides).

mouse as you move the box closer to the guide. There's nothing actually affecting the movement of your mouse, of course, but it's a useful illusion.

FreeHand's Palettes

FreeHand's palettes work two ways—they display information on the publication (or about the object you've got selected), and they provide controls for changing the publication and the objects in it. The palettes are an integral part of FreeHand's user interface, and are the key to doing almost everything you can do in FreeHand (see figure 1-19).

- Toolbox
- Layers palette
- Styles palette
- Halftone palette
- Type Specifications palette
- Color List
- Color Mixer
- Tints palette
- Transform palette
- Align palette
- Inspector
- Xtra Tools palette
- Operations palette

FREEHAND BASICS 19

FIGURE 1-19
FreeHand's palettes

Toolbox

Xtra tools palette

Display the Inspector's different panels by clicking these buttons.

The Inspector displays different controls and information depending on what you've selected.

Click these buttons to display the different panels of the Transform palette.

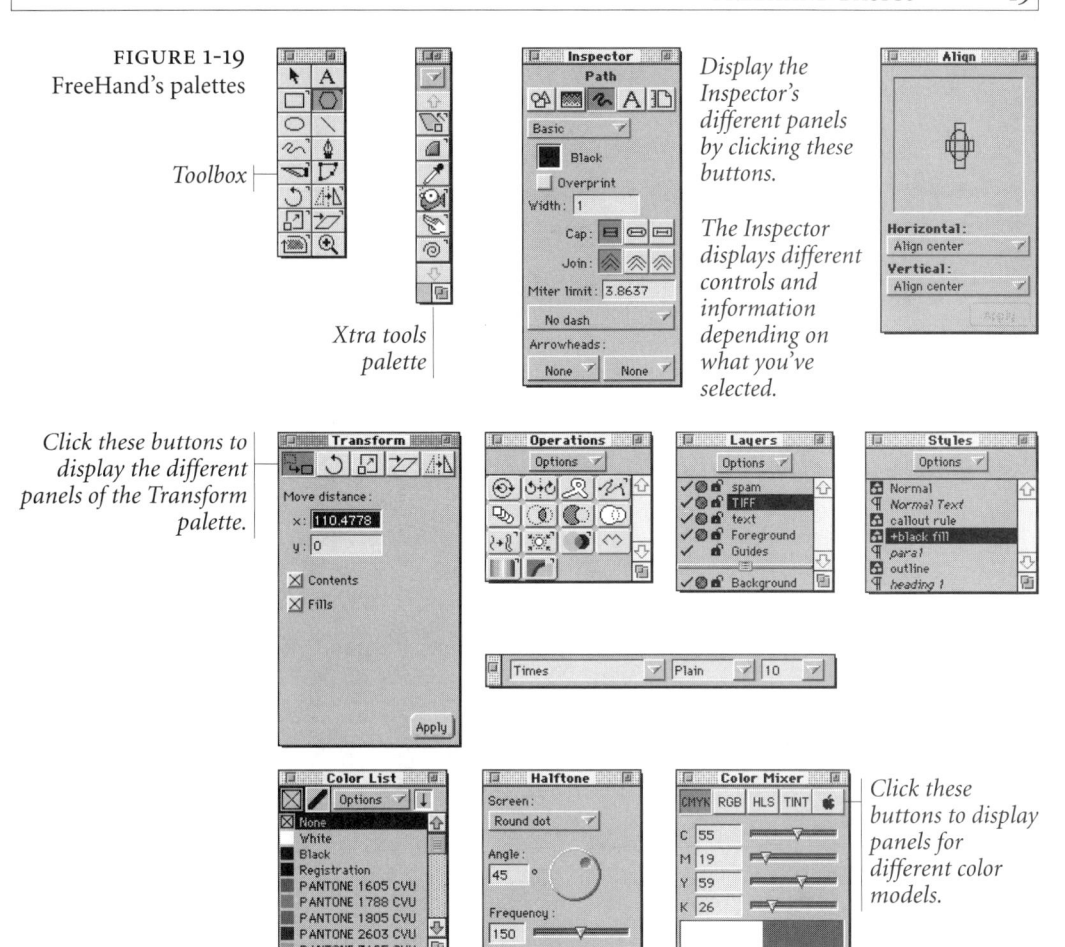

Click these buttons to display panels for different color models.

You don't have to use the menus to display or hide the palettes—an action called "toggling." You can use keyboard shortcuts to save yourself lots of mouse movement (see Table 1-1).

The Inspector is the palette you'll use most when you work with FreeHand. I refer to each of the subpanels of the Inspector as an Inspector, such as the Paragraph Inspector, the fill Inspector, and the Stroke Inspector (see figure 1-20). This saves me from having to say things like "the Character subpanel of the Type section of the Inspector."

Do you really have to click the different icon buttons in the Inspector to display the different sections of the Inspector? No—you can use keyboard shortcuts for almost all of the Inspectors. Take a look at Table 1-2 on page 22.

TABLE 1-1
Palette keyboard shortcuts

Palette:	To display or hide the palette, press:
Align palette	Command-Shift-A
Color List	Command-9
Color Mixer	Command-Shift-C
Halftone palette	Command-H
Inspector	Command-I
Layers palette	Command-6
Styles palette	Command-3
Toolbox	Command-7
Transform palette	Command-M
Type Specifications palette	Command-T

Note that there is no keyboard shortcut for the Setup Inspector, where you set up the publication's grid and measurement system. This seems like an oversight to me.

Tip:
Applying Palette Changes

When you make a change in a palette using a button or a popup menu, that change takes effect immediately. When you make a change by entering a value in a field, however, you have to press Return to let FreeHand know you're done entering text. In the Transform palette or the Align palette, you can click the Apply button or press Return to apply your changes. When you're finished making changes in the Inspector, press Return to apply your changes (there's no Apply button).

Tip:
Moving Through fields

To move from one field to the next in a palette, press Tab. To move from one field to the previous, press Shift-Tab.

Tip:
Cycling Through Palettes

To cycle through all of the visible palettes containing fields, press Command-` (accent grave; it's just below the ~, or tilde, symbol). Each press of Command-` takes you to the next available palette. Why only palettes containing text fields? Because there's not much

FREEHAND BASICS 21

FIGURE 1-20
The many faces of the Inspector

The Object Inspector displays different options depending on the element you've selected.

When you select a text block, the Object Inspector displays three panels full of options.

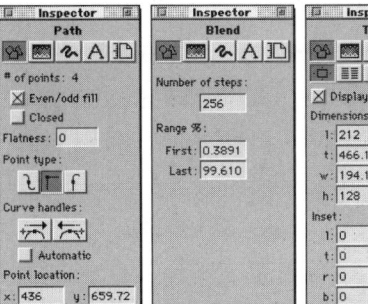

Object Inspector (point selected)

Object Inspector (blend selected)

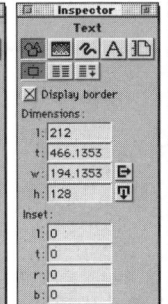

Object Inspector (text selected)

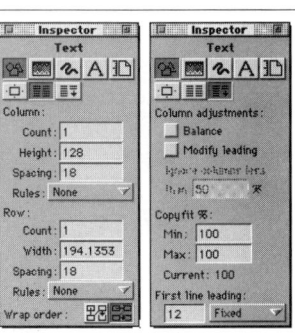

Column Inspector

Copyfit Inspector

You use the Fill and Stroke Inspectors to set the formatting of FreeHand paths (and the fill and stroke of type).

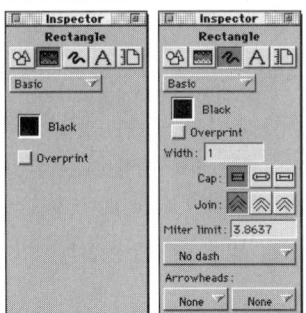

The Document Inspector is where you create, duplicate, arrange, and delete pages. In the Setup Inspector, you control the units of measurement, grid, and constraint angle.

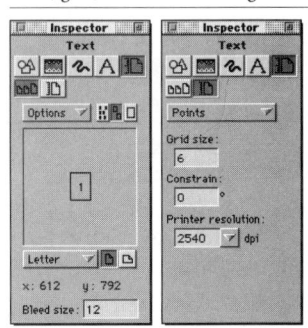

Fill Inspector (Basic fill)

Stroke Inspector (Basic stroke)

Document Inspector

Setup Inspector

You'll find most of FreeHand's type formatting features in the four panels of the Text Inspector.

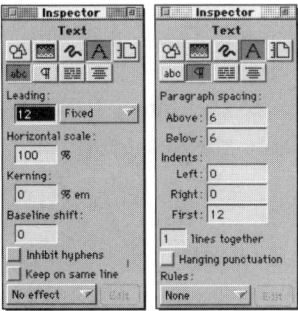

Character Inspector

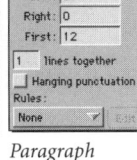

Paragraph Inspector

Spacing Inspector

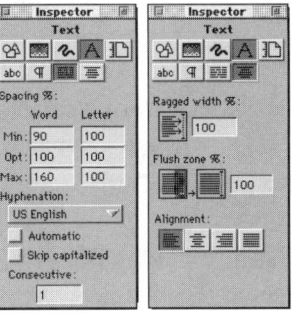

Alignment Inspector

TABLE 1-2
Inspector keyboard shortcuts

To display the:	Press:
Document Inspector	Command-Option-D
Fill Inspector	Command-Option-F
Column Inspector*	Command-Option-R
Copyfit Inspector*	Command-Option-C
Object Inspector	Command-Option-I
Stroke Inspector	Command-Option-L
Alignment Inspector	Command-Option-A
Character Inspector	Command-Option-T
Paragraph Inspector	Command-Option-P
Spacing Inspector	Command-Option-K

* Only appears when a text block is selected

point using a keyboard shortcut to move to a palette in which you have to use the mouse anyway. It's great, on the other hand, to be able to jump from the Size field in the Type Specifications palette to the Leading field in the Paragraph Inspector without moving the mouse.

Tip: Zipping and Unzipping Palettes

With all these floating palettes, it's easy to run out of room on your screen to see anything but the palettes. While there are keyboard shortcuts to display or hide all of the palettes, you might like this better: you can shrink a palette down to just its title bar by clicking the zoom box at the right end of the title bar. This is called "zipping" a palette (and, at this point, the palette is "zipped"). The title bar stays on the screen (see figure 1-21). When you want to display the entire palette, click the box again, and the palette expands to its full size.

Tip: Now You See 'Em…

In FreeHand 4, you couldn't display or hide *all* of the palettes with a single keystroke. In FreeHand 5, press Command-Shift-H (for "hide"), and all of the palettes currently displayed disappear; press it again, and they reappear.

If you want to hide the Toolbox when you hide the palettes, check the Hiding Palettes Hides the Toolbox option in the Palettes Preferences dialog box.

FIGURE 1-21
Zipping and unzipping palettes

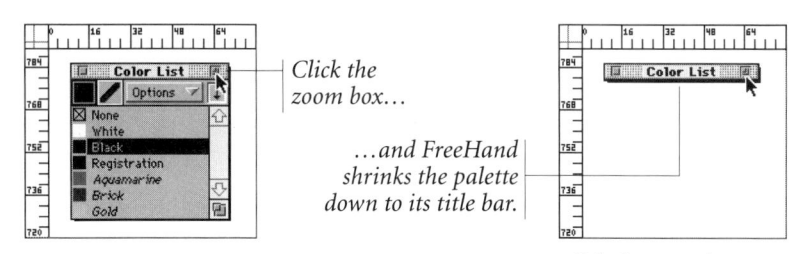

Click the zoom box...

...and FreeHand shrinks the palette down to its title bar.

Click the zoom box again to see all of the palette.

Changing Document Defaults

"Defaults" are the settings you start out with when you start Free-Hand. FreeHand has two kinds of defaults—application defaults (which, for the most part, correspond to the settings in the Preferences dialog boxes—see "Preferences," later in this chapter), and document defaults. FreeHand's defaults control page size, fill type and color, available styles, type specifications, and other details.

When you create a new FreeHand document, do you immediately add a set of colors to the Colors List, change the default line weight, display the rulers, or add styles to the Style palette? If you do, you probably get tired of making those changes over and over again. Wouldn't it be great if you could tell FreeHand to create new documents using those settings?

You can. Open the file named FreeHand Defaults that's in the same folder as FreeHand, make the changes you want using Free-Hand's dialog boxes and palettes, and save the file (using the same file name) as a template. Make sure that the new file replaces the original file.

The next time you create a new FreeHand document (changing the " FreeHand Defaults" file has no effect on existing documents); it'll appear with the same defaults as you specified in the defaults file (for more on working with defaults files—even working with multiple defaults files, see "Preferences," later in this chapter).

This technique goes for objects, as well. If you find you're always copying a corporate logo into your publications, add it to your FreeHand Defaults template, and it'll appear in every new document you create.

Tip: Reverting to FreeHand's Original Defaults

If you've gotten hopelessly away from FreeHand's original defaults and want to go back to them, move the FreeHand Defaults file out of the folder containing your FreeHand application and put it somewhere else. Or rename the file. When FreeHand can't find the defaults file, it creates new documents using the original default settings (which are stored inside FreeHand).

Setting Up Pages

The first thing you do when creating a publication is to set up your publication's pages using the Document Inspector and the Setup Inspector. You can always make changes in these palettes, if you need to; changing the values here only changes the underlying pages and their associated settings, and won't change anything you've drawn or imported (objects might end up sitting on the pasteboard, but they won't disappear or change shape).

Using the Document Inspector

To display the Document Inspector, click the Document button in the Inspector palette, then click the Pages button (or, better, press Command-Option-D). The Document Inspector displays a window in the middle of the Inspector, showing you a miniaturized view of FreeHand's pasteboard (see figure 1-22).

Zooming in the Document Inspector. In FreeHand 4, small document pages (say, for example, business cards) could end up being *very* small in the Document Inspector's thumbnail view of the pasteboard. These tiny pages (some not more than one pixel on a side) were very hard to arrange on the pasteboard—there were, after all, only so many pixels to work with in the Inspector's view of the world. Worse yet, in FreeHand 4 you couldn't zoom in to get a better grip on your pages using the Document Inspector.

FIGURE 1-22
Document Inspector

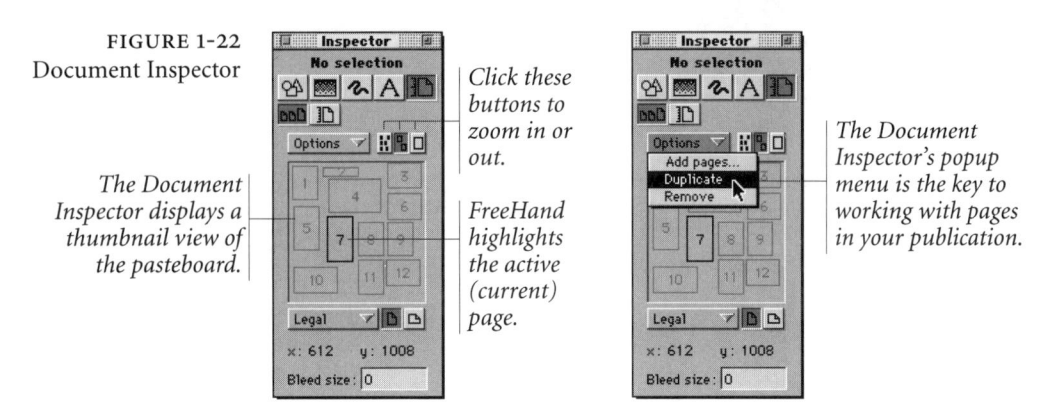

The Document Inspector displays a thumbnail view of the pasteboard.

Click these buttons to zoom in or out.

FreeHand highlights the active (current) page.

The Document Inspector's popup menu is the key to working with pages in your publication.

In FreeHand 5, you can change the view that the Document Inspector uses to display your publication's pages. The buttons above the Inspector's thumbnail view of the pasteboard control the view of the Pasteboard (see figure 1-23).

Scrolling in the Document Inspector. To change your view of the Pasteboard, position the cursor inside the thumbnail view in the Document Inspector, and drag. The cursor turns into the grabber hand, and FreeHand scrolls your view of the pasteboard as you drag (see figure 1-24).

Adding pages. To add a new page, choose Add Pages from the pop-up menu at the top of the palette (see figure 1-25). FreeHand displays the Add Pages dialog box. Choose a page size (the current page size is the default) and press Return. FreeHand adds a new page (or pages) to your file, and positions them on the pasteboard.

FIGURE 1-23
Zooming in the Document Inspector

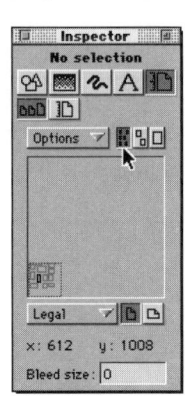

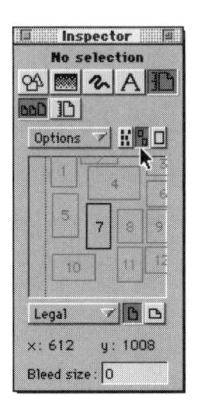

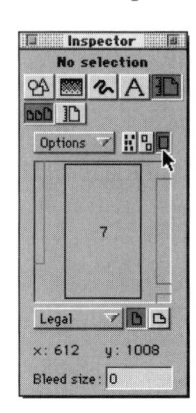

FIGURE 1-24
Scrolling your view
of the Pasteboard

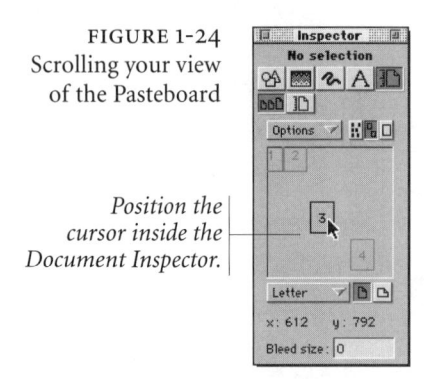

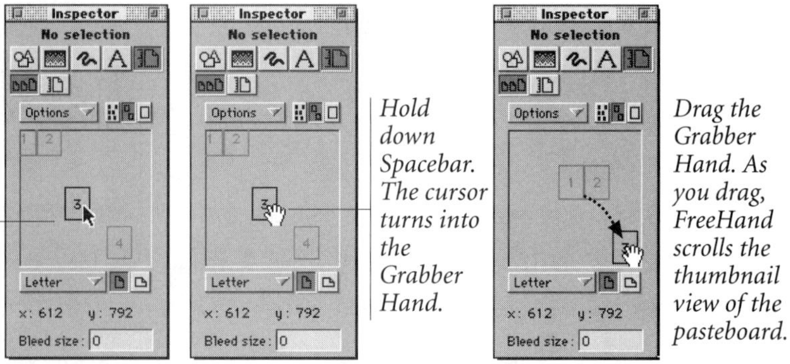

Position the
cursor inside the
Document Inspector.

Hold down Spacebar. The cursor turns into the Grabber Hand.

Drag the Grabber Hand. As you drag, FreeHand scrolls the thumbnail view of the pasteboard.

FIGURE 1-25
Adding pages

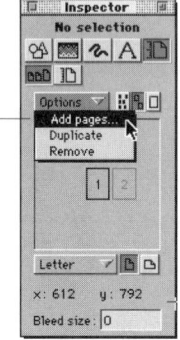

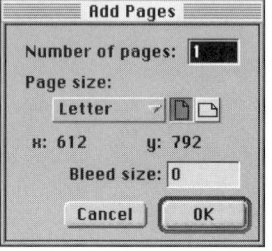

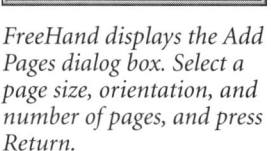

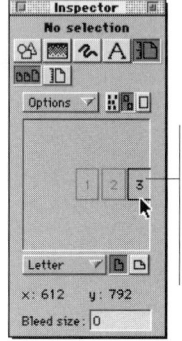

Choose "Add pages"
from the popup menu.

FreeHand displays the Add Pages dialog box. Select a page size, orientation, and number of pages, and press Return.

A new page (or pages) appears in the Document Inspector.

You can change your page setup at any time by clicking the page in the Document Inspector—its outline changes to black when it's the current selection—and choosing a new page size from the popup menu below the window.

Rearranging pages. To rearrange your pages on the pasteboard, drag the page icons around in the Document Inspector. FreeHand won't let you position one page on top of another, so it's easy to get pages to abut perfectly. Bleed areas, on the other hand, do overlap other pages, as they should (see figure 1-26).

As you move the pages around in the Document Inspector, note that their page numbers change. FreeHand numbers pages according to their position on the pasteboard—the page closest to the upper-left corner of the pasteboard is always the first page, the next closest is the second page, and so on.

FIGURE 1-26
Rearranging pages

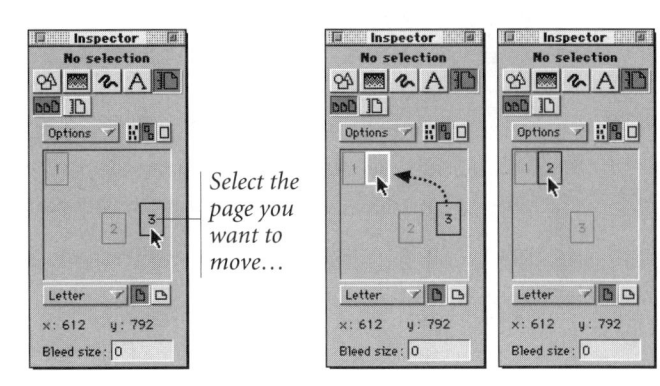

Select the page you want to move...

...and drag the page to a new location on the pasteboard.

Duplicating pages. To create a duplicate page of an existing page, click the page in the Document Inspector and choose Duplicate from the popup menu. FreeHand adds the duplicated page to your pasteboard, if there's room to add it.

Removing pages. To remove a page, click the page in the Document Inspector and choose Remove from the popup menu.

Page size. Generally, you'll want to enter the page size you want for your printed publication. I see far too many people (especially those who should know better) laying out single business cards in the middle of a 51-by-66-pica (that's 8.5-by-11-inch) page. Try not to do this; it wastes film and time when you go to your imagesetting service bureau (if you operate the imagesetter yourself, it's even more important). If your design features elements that extend beyond the edge of the page, use the Bleed option, described later in this section.

You can specify any page size from six by six picas (one inch square) to 1,332 by 1,332 picas (222 inches square) However, as you specify your page size, remember the paper sizes available for the printer you'll be using for your final printing. Linotronic L300s, for example, print on a roll of film that, while very long, is just 11.7 inches (70 picas) wide. When you need the larger page sizes, you can always look for an imagesetter that uses wider film, or you can print tiles (selected parts) of your publication and paste them together (see Chapter 7, "Printing," for more on tiling).

Tiling is ugly, and I try to avoid it. There are often better ways to create large layouts (I tend to create them small, print them at high resolution, then enlarge them using a commercial printer's copy camera).

You can print multiple pages on a single sheet of paper or film using manual tiling to print "reader spreads" or "page spreads." For more on printing reader spreads and page spreads (imposition), see Chapter 7, "Printing."

Tip: Getting That Big Page to fit

FreeHand sometimes refuses to create a page or change a page size—you'll enter a custom page size, and get the message "Could not complete the 'Set page info' command because an object would be placed off the pasteboard," or "Could not complete the 'Set page info' command because the page would overlap another page." You get these messages even when you know that there's plenty of room on the pasteboard (or between pages) to add the new page or change the page size. What gives?

Here's the deal: FreeHand calculates the space available for the new (or changed) page from that page's lower-left corner. If the page would extend within six picas (one inch) of the edge of the pasteboard, or over another page, in either dimension, measured from the current location of the lower-left corner of the page, Free-Hand refuses to create (or change) your page.

The solution? Move the page farther left and/or down on the pasteboard, or move other pages to make room for the new page or new page size.

Page orientation. If you're using one of the preset page sizes, you can choose a Tall or Wide orientation. If you're creating a custom page size, the measurements you enter in the X and Y fields determine the page's height and width, respectively. If you want a Wide orientation page, enter a larger value in the X field than you've entered in the Y field. It's that simple.

Once again, try to keep the printer you'll be using for your final printing in mind. In some cases, you might find yourself laying things out sideways to get them onto a film roll's limited width (though you can flip the printing orientation of your publication by rewriting the PPD you're using—see "Rewriting PPDs" in Chapter 7, "Printing").

Bleed. Enter the amount of space you want to print that extends beyond the edge of the page. The value you enter here is added to all four sides of the page. Again, keep the page sizes of your final output device in mind as you enter the bleed area. If your publication's page size is 10 by 12 picas and your imagesetter's page size is 11 by 13 picas, the largest bleed area you'd be able to use is 6 points (though you could always rewrite the PPD file you're using to accommodate a larger bleed, provided the imagesetter you're printing to can handle it).

Using the Setup Inspector

Click the Document Setup button in the Document Inspector palette to display the Setup Inspector (see figure 1-27).

Unit of measure. Choose your favorite unit of measure from the popup menu in the Setup Inspector. I prefer points and/or picas, because they're the measurement system of type, and type is the backbone of all of my designs, but I'll try not to be a fascist about it. You can always override the current unit of measure for setting your type in dialog boxes, as shown in Table 1-3.

Grid Size. The value you enter in this field controls the distance between intersections of a nonprinting grid on each page in your publication (see figure 1-28). The grid starts at the zero point on the rulers and moves when you move the zero point.

When you choose Grid from the View menu, FreeHand displays the grid on your screen. The appearance of the grid varies, depending on the size of the grid, the current units of measurement, and the current magnification—at higher magnifications,

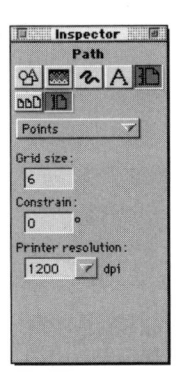

FIGURE 1-27
Setup Inspector

FIGURE 1-28
The grid

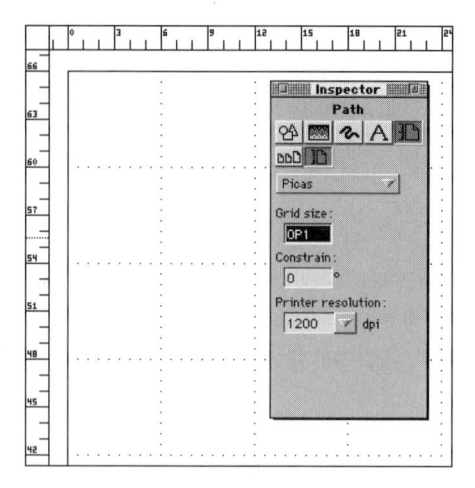

TABLE 1-3
Overriding units of measurement

If you want this value:	Type this in the dialog box:
7 inches	7i
22 points	p22
11 picas	11p*
6 picas, 6 points	6p6*
23.4 millimeters	23.4m*

* There are approximately 236,220.4 picas in a kilometer.

you'll see a point at each grid intersection. The grid is the same for every page in a publication—you can't use different grids on different pages. When you choose Snap to Grid, objects you're creating, moving, or resizing snap to the grid. Snap to Grid works whether the grid's visible or not.

You can't enter a value smaller than one point or larger than 720 points in the Grid Size field.

Tip:
Avoiding Accuracy

Most of the time, when I'm working with a FreeHand publication, I don't want or need to know the location of an object (or my cursor, or a guide) with anything like the kind of accuracy that FreeHand displays in the info bar by default. In fact, the extra decimal places become distracting. Here's an example: you want to position a rule 24 points from the bottom of the page, and no matter how hard you try to match the tick mark on the ruler, the info bar displays the rule's position as 24.21806. Why can't I get the object into the right position? What's happening?

There are only so many pixels on your screen. At certain views, it might not be possible to "hit" specific coordinates without some help, because that location is "between" two rows of pixels. Clearly, zooming in to a higher magnification will help, but the best thing to do is to set Grid to a small value, such as one point, and turn on Snap to Grid. Now, when you drag the rule, it snaps to each point location, and the info bar will read in whole points—no more distracting decimals.

Constrain. The value you enter in the Constrain field controls the angle FreeHand uses when you constrain tools (see "Constraining Tools," later in this chapter).

The angle you enter here also affects how FreeHand draws rectangles and ellipses (see figure 1-29). If you've entered "30" in the Constrain field, rectangles and ellipses you create are constrained to 30 and 120 degrees (rather than the default 90 and 180 degrees).

FIGURE 1-29
Setting a constraint angle

Enter an angle here to set the angle of constraint.

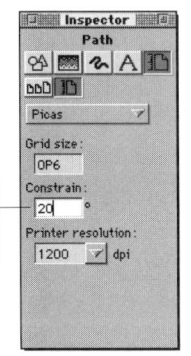

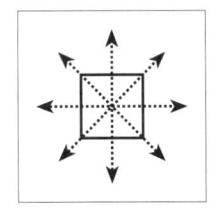

When the constraint angle is "0" (the default), holding down Shift as you drag an object constrains its movement to 45-degree angles.

If you change the angle, the constraint axes are based on the angle you entered.

The Constrain field also affects the way FreeHand draws basic shapes.

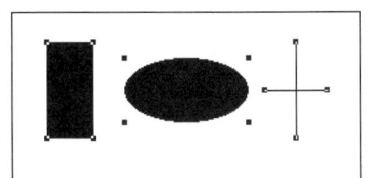

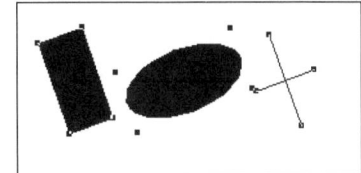

Constraint angle: 0

Constraint angle: 20

Printer Resolution. Type a value in the Printer Resolution field that corresponds to the resolution of the printer you intend to use for final output of your publication, or choose a value from the defaults listed in the popup menu. FreeHand uses this value to calculate the optimum number of steps to use in a graduated fill, a radial fill, or a blend (see Chapter 2, "Drawing"). FreeHand also uses this value for sizing bilevel bitmaps to the resolution of the output device ("magic stretching," to you PageMaker fans out there). For more on why you might need to stretch bilevel bitmaps to your printer's resolution, see "Resizing Images to Your Printer's Resolution" in Chapter 4, "Importing and Exporting."

What About the Page Setup Dialog Box?

Choosing Page Setup from the file menu brings up the LaserWriter driver's dialog boxes and printing options. Almost every setting found in these dialog boxes is overridden by settings in FreeHand's Document Inspector and Print and Print Options dialog boxes.

There's still one important setting in these dialog boxes, however. If you're having trouble printing a document containing multiple downloadable fonts, choose Page Setup from the file menu to bring up the LaserWriter Page Setup dialog box. Click the Options button. The LaserWriter Options dialog box appears (see figure 1-30). Turn on Unlimited Downloadable Fonts in a Document (if it's already on, leave it on), and then press Return twice to close the dialog boxes.

Many jobs that FreeHand would otherwise print have been canceled because this simple option was off. If your job isn't printing, try checking this option. Most of the time, however, you want to leave this option turned off—it slows printing (it downloads

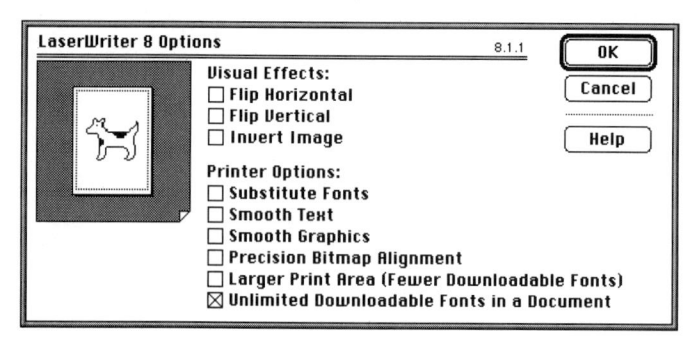

FIGURE 1-30
LaserWriter Options dialog box

fonts and flushes them from memory every time they're used—this makes more RAM available, but means you have to download fonts far more often).

Moving Around in Your Publication

FreeHand offers three ways to change your view of the publication: zooming, scrolling, and moving from page to page. Zooming changes the magnification of the pages inside the publication window. Scrolling changes the view of the publication in the publication window without changing the magnification. Moving from page to page can be thought of as either automated scrolling or zooming, but I'm not sure which.

Zooming

Most of the time, I use zooming (that is, changing magnifications of the view of the publication) rather than scrolling (that is, changing the view of the publication without changing magnification) to move from one area of the page or pasteboard to another.

Zooming with the View menu. The View menu offers FreeHand's "standard" magnifications, or views, and provides keyboard shortcuts for most of them (see Table 1-4).

TABLE 1-4
Magnification keyboard shortcuts

To reach this magnification:	Press:
Fit Page	Command-W
Fit All	None
12%	None
25%	None
50%	Command-5
75%	Command-7
100%	Command-1
200%	Command-2
400%	Command-4
800%	Command-8

All of these commands except fit Page center the object you've selected in the publication window. If there's no object selected, these shortcuts zoom in or out based on the center of the current view. fit Page centers the publication in the publication window. This makes fit Page the perfect "zoom-out" shortcut.

Zooming with the Magnifying Glass. Another zooming method: choose the Magnifying Glass, point at an area in your publication, and click. FreeHand zooms to the next larger view size (based on your current view—from 100% to 200%, for example), centering the area you clicked on in the publication window. Hold down Option and the Magnifying Glass tool changes to the Reducing Glass tool. Click the Reducing Glass tool and you'll zoom out.

Tip:
Switching to the Magnifying Glass

Hold down Command-spacebar to temporarily change any tool into the Magnifying Glass to zoom in; or hold down Option-Command-spacebar to change any tool into the Reducing Glass to zoom out (see figure 1-31).

Tip:
The Best Way to Zoom In

To zoom in, press Command and hold down the spacebar to turn the current tool (whatever it is) into the Magnifying Glass tool, then drag the Magnifying Glass in the publication window. As you drag, a rectangle (like a selection rectangle) appears. Drag the rectangle around the area you want to zoom in on, and release the mouse button. FreeHand zooms in on the area, magnifying the area to the largest size that fits in the publication window (see figure 1-32).

To zoom out, use one of the keyboard shortcuts—Command-W, for fit Page, is especially handy.

Tip:
What's the Most Accurate View in FreeHand?

Lots of FreeHand users have noticed that elements seem to shift slightly as they zoom in and out, and have wondered which magnification is most accurate. It's simple: it's the 256,000% view. Interestingly, the fit Page view is pretty good, too.

If something's a point off in the 256,000% view, it sometimes looks like it's about a mile away in the fit Page view. Which is good. You want to know when lines aren't where you want them, so a little exaggeration is a good thing.

FREEHAND BASICS 35

FIGURE 1-31
Magnifying Glass

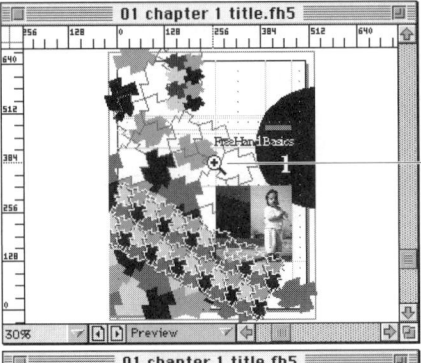

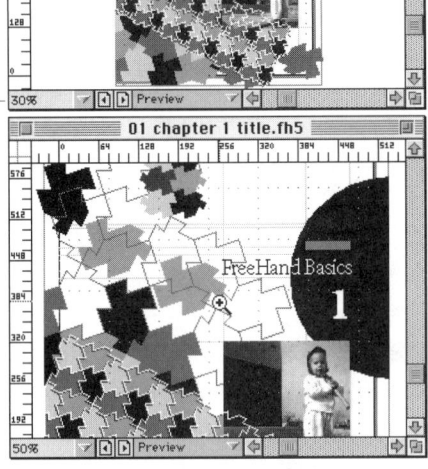

Press Command-spacebar and the cursor turns into the Magnifying Glass.

As you zoom, FreeHand displays the magnification percentage.

Click the Magnifying Glass, and FreeHand zooms in to the next "standard" magnification level (that is, those seen on the Magnification submenu of the View menu).

To zoom out, hold down Command-Option-spacebar to turn any tool into the Reducing Glass, and click again.

FIGURE 1-32
Drag magnification

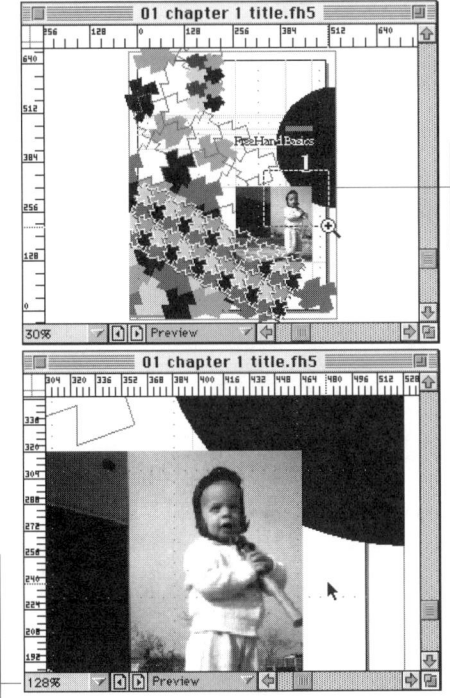

Drag the Magnifying Glass around the area you want to zoom in on and release the mouse button.

FreeHand zooms in on the area you selected.

You can hold down Option as you drag the Reducing Glass to zoom out. I've never found a use for this technique, myself.

When you use drag magnification, you can use percentages other than those seen on the Magnification submenu.

The final arbiters of accuracy are the numbers in the Object Inspector. If points don't seem to line up, select them by turn and look at their coordinates in the Object Inspector. By comparing their numeric positions, you'll know exactly where they are, and whether they're where you want them.

Entering a zoom percentage. If you want to zoom to a specific magnification percentage, enter the percentage you want in the Magnification field and press Return. FreeHand zooms to the percentage you specified.

Tip:
Maximum zoom

Want to zoom in as far as you can go? Hold down Command-Control-Spacebar. The cursor turns into the Magnifying Glass. Click, and you'll zoom in to 256,000% (or whatever you've set as your maximum zoom percentage—see Appendix B, "Your FreeHand Installation" for more on setting FreeHand's maxmimum magnification percentage).

Tip:
Minimum zoom

To zoom out to FreeHand's minimum zoom percentage (6%) hold down Command-Control-Option-Spacebar and click. FreeHand zooms out to the 6% view.

Scrolling

As I said earlier in this chapter, I rarely use the scroll bars to scroll. So how do I change my view of my publication? I use the Grabber Hand, or I let FreeHand do the scrolling for me as I move objects.

Scrolling with the Grabber Hand. You can also change your view of the publication using the Grabber Hand. Provided you're not editing text, holding down the spacebar turns the cursor into the Grabber Hand (if you *are* editing text, you'll enter spaces, which probably isn't what you want to do). As long as you keep pressing the mouse button, you can slide the publication around in the publication window (see figure 1-33).

Scrolling as you drag objects. Don't forget that you can change your view by dragging objects off the screen (see figure 1-34). If you know an object should be moved to some point below your current view, select the object and drag the cursor off the bottom

FREEHAND BASICS 37

FIGURE 1-33
Grabber Hand

Hold down the spacebar with any tool selected to turn the cursor into the Grabber Hand.

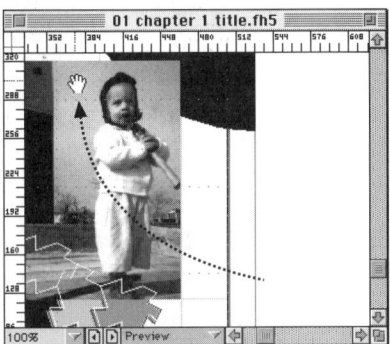

Use the Grabber Hand to drag your publication around in the window.

FIGURE 1-34
Scrolling by dragging

As you drag an object, FreeHand scrolls the current window to keep up with your dragging.

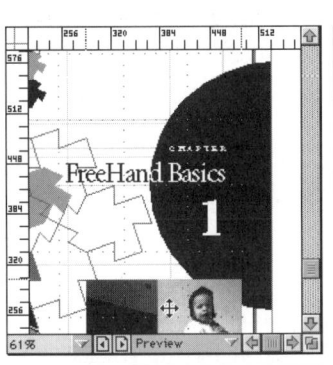

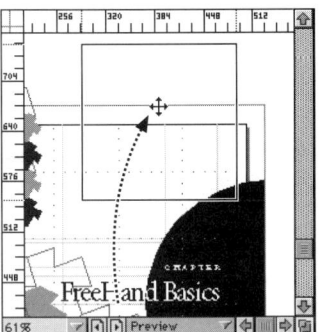

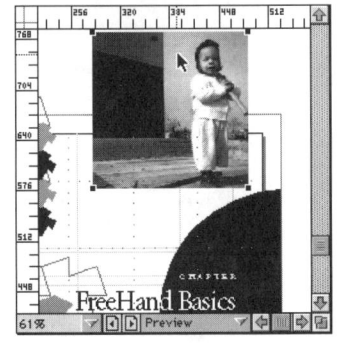

of the publication window. The window scrolls as long as the cursor is off the bottom of the screen and the mouse button is down. Sometimes it's the best way to get something into position.

Moving from Page to Page

You move between pages in your FreeHand publication by scrolling (the slow way), or by clicking on the next page and previous page icons (the ones at the bottom of the publication window), but the best method is to display the Document Inspector (press Command-Option-D) and double-click the thumbnail of the page you want to move to. FreeHand moves to the page and displays it in fit Page view.

Using FreeHand's Toolbox

If FreeHand is your workshop, and the menus and palettes are where you collect the wood, nails, and paint you use, the toolbox is where you keep your saws, hammers, and brushes.

Some of the following descriptions of the tool functions aren't going to make any sense unless you understand how FreeHand's points and paths work, and that discussion falls in "Points and Paths," later in this chapter. You can flip ahead and read that section, or you can plow through this section, get momentarily confused (remember that confusion is a great state for learning), and then become enlightened when you reach the descriptions of points and paths.

Or, you can flip ahead to Chapter 2, "Drawing" for even more on points and paths. It's your choice, and either method works. This is precisely the sort of nonlinear information gathering that hypertext gurus say can't be done in books.

You can break FreeHand's toolbox into four main conceptual sections (as shown in figure 1-35).

- Tools for drawing basic shapes (the Rectangle, Polygon, Ellipse, and Line tools)

- Path-drawing tools (the Point, Freehand, and Pen tools, also known as the freeform drawing tools)

FIGURE 1-35
Tools in the toolbox

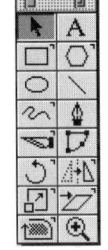

Toolbox

When you see this symbol on a tool, it means that you can view and set options for the tool by double-clicking on the tool in the Toolbox.

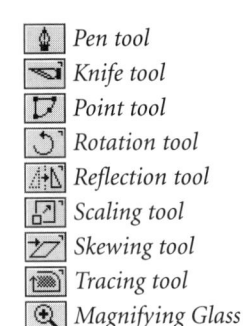

Pointer tool	Pen tool
Text tool	Knife tool
Rectangle tool	Point tool
Polygon tool	Rotation tool
Ellipse tool	Reflection tool
Line tool	Scaling tool
Freehand tool*	Skewing tool
Variable Stroke tool*	Tracing tool
Calligraphic Pen tool*	Magnifying Glass

*Can't see more than one of these tools? That's because they share the same slot in the Toolbox. Only one of them can be visible at a time—double-click the tool in the Toolbox to display the FreeHand Tool dialog box, where you can choose which tool you want to work with.

- Transformation tools (the Rotation, Reflection, Skewing, and Scaling tools)
- The Text tool

The basic shape tools draw complete paths containing specific numbers of points in specific positions on the path, while the path-drawing tools draw paths point by point. The transformation tools act on objects you've drawn, typed, or imported, and the Text tool is for entering text.

The remaining tools don't really fit into a single category—the Pointer tool is for selecting objects, the Knife tool is for splitting points and paths, and the Magnifying Glass tool is for changing your view of your publication.

The tool descriptions in the following section are brief and are only intended to give you a feeling for what the different tools are and what they do. For more on drawing objects with the drawing tools, see Chapter 2, "Drawing." To learn more about entering text with the Text tool, see Chapter 3, "Text and Type." For more on working with the Transformation tools, see Chapter 5, "Importing and Exporting."

Note: Talking about FreeHand's tools and their use can get a little confusing. When you select a tool in the toolbox (or press the keyboard shortcut to select a tool), what does the cursor become? In the previous edition of this book, I used the same wording as in FreeHand's documentation: "When you select a tool, the cursor turns into a crosshair." I didn't like that, because I think the cursor remains the cursor (and because we couldn't decide between "cross hair" or "crosshair"—either one sounds uncomfortable). Therefore, in this book, I'll use phrases like "select a tool and drag" or "select a tool and drag the tool."

Toolbox Keyboard Shortcuts. You can choose most of the tools in FreeHand's toolbox through keyboard shortcuts. This is usually faster than going back to the toolbox and clicking on the tool (see Table 1-5).

Pointer Tool

You use the Pointer tool to select and transform objects. You can press 0 (zero) or Shift-F10 to select the Pointer tool. You can temporarily switch to the Pointer tool by holding down Command when any other tool is selected.

Text Tool

You enter and edit text using the Text tool. To create a text block, select the Text tool and click on a point in the publication window; a text block appears with a flashing text-insertion point (or cursor) in the first line of the text block. To edit text, select the Text tool and click in a text block. If you want to edit text using the Text Editor, select the text block (using either the text tool or the Pointer tool) and press Command-Option-E. FreeHand opens the story you selected in the Text Editor. For more on entering, editing, and formatting text, see Chapter 3, "Text and Type." To select the Text tool, press A or F9.

Rectangle Tool

Use the Rectangle tool to draw rectangles. If you hold down Shift as you draw a rectangle, you draw squares.

Note that you can always draw rectangles and squares using the other drawing tools, but that the rectangles drawn using the Rectangle tool have some special capabilities (see Table 1-6 on page 50). Press 1 (on either the keyboard or on the numeric keypad) or F1 to select the Rectangle tool.

TABLE 1-5
Toolbox keyboard shortcuts

Tool:	Key:
Pointer tool	0*, or Shift-F10
Pointer tool (temporary)	Hold down Command and the current tool turns into the Pointer tool. Release Command and the cursor changes back into the selected tool.
Text tool	A, or Shift-F9
Rectangle tool	1* or Shift-F1
Polygon tool	2* or Shift-F2
Ellipse tool	3* or Shift-F3
Line tool	4* or Shift-F4
Freehand tool	5* or Shift-F5
Pen tool	6* or Shift-F6
Knife tool	7* or Shift-F7
Point tool	8* or Shift-F8
Magnifying Glass	Hold down Command-spacebar and the current tool turns into the Magnifying Glass. Release Command-spacebar and the Magnifying Glass turns back into the selected tool. If your cursor is inside a text block, make sure you press Command slightly before you press spacebar, or you'll get a bunch of spaces in the text block.
Reducing Glass	Hold down Command-Option-spacebar and the current tool turns into the Reducing Glass. Release Command-Option-spacebar and the Reducing Glass turns back into the selected tool.

* The number keys on the numeric keypad work, too.

If you want to draw rectangles with rounded corners, double-click the Rectangle tool. FreeHand displays the Rectangle Tool dialog box. Drag the slider or enter a number to set the corner radius you want to use for your rounded corners (see figure 1-36).

If you draw a rectangle with square corners and then decide that you'd rather its corners were rounded, you can always change them using the Corner Radius field in the Object Inspector. Until, that is, you ungroup the rectangle—once you do that, the rectangle becomes a normal path (and you'll have to make the corners rounded using path-drawing techniques).

FIGURE 1-36
Specifying rounded corners

Double-click the Rectangle tool to display the Rectangle Tool dialog box. Enter a corner radius and press Return.

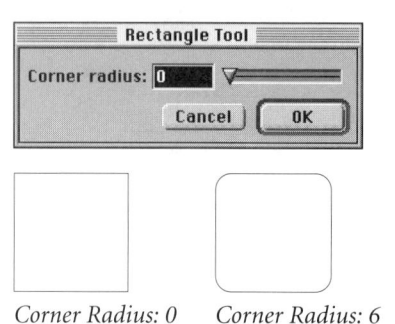

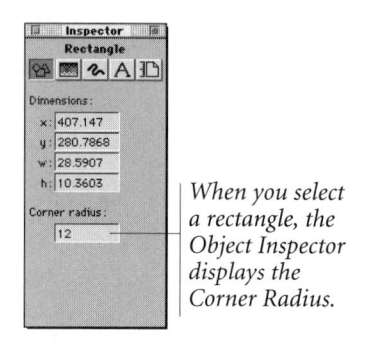

Corner Radius: 0   Corner Radius: 6

When you select a rectangle, the Object Inspector displays the Corner Radius.

Polygon Tool

The Polygon tool makes it easy to draw equilateral polygons, such as pentagons, hexagons, and dodecagons. (Polygons are closed geometric objects that have at least three sides; they're equilateral if each side is the same length.) You can also use the Polygon tool to draw stars.

To change which polygon the Polygon tool draws, double-click the tool in the toolbox. FreeHand displays the Polygon Tool dialog box (see figure 1-37), where you can specify the number of sides you want your star or polygon to have, and how acute (or obtuse) you want the star's interior angles to be. You can drag a slider for polygons or stars from three to 20 sides or points, or enter a larger number.

Clicking the slider after entering a larger number resets the number to 20. The preview is dynamically updated as you drag the slider or enter a number. For stars, there's another slider for changing the interior angles of the star from acute to obtuse.

Press 2 (on either the keyboard or on the numeric keypad) or F2 to select the polygon tool.

FIGURE 1-38
Polygon tool controls

Double-click the Polygon tool to define what kind of polygons the Polygon tool draws.

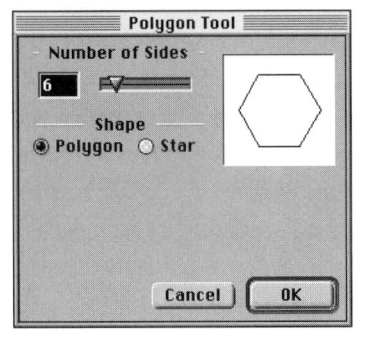

Drag the slider to set the number of sides in the polygon, or enter a number.

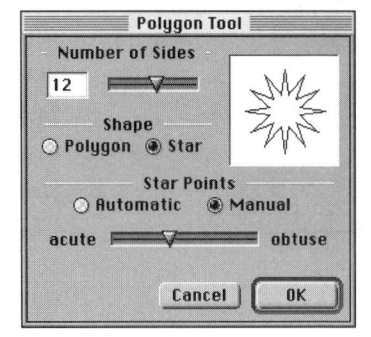

Click Star, and options appear for drawing star-shaped polygons. Enter a number to specify the number of points you want for the star, then drag the Star Points slider to set the sharpness of the star's points.

Ellipse Tool

Use the Ellipse tool to draw ellipses. If you hold down Shift as you draw an ellipse, you draw circles. Note that you can always draw ellipses and circles using other drawing tools, but that the ellipses drawn using the Ellipse tool offer some special capabilities (see Table 1-6, later in this chapter). If you ungroup these ellipses, you lose those capabilities.

Press 3 (on either the keyboard or on the numeric keypad) or F3 to select the Ellipse tool.

Line Tool

Use the Line tool to draw straight lines. If you hold down Shift as you drag the Line tool, the lines you draw will be constrained to 0-, 90-, and 45-degree angles (relative to the current default axis—see "Constrain" on page 31).

Press 4 (on either the keyboard or on the numeric keypad) or F4 to select the Line tool.

Freehand Tool

Select the Freehand tool (it's not the FreeHand tool), hold down the mouse button, and scribble. The Freehand tool creates a path that follows your mouse movements, adding points according to its settings.

If you double-click the Freehand tool, the Freehand Tool dialog box appears. This dialog box lets you customize the way the Freehand tool works. The Freehand tool is really three tools—the Freehand, Variable Stroke, and Calligraphic Pen tools. To change from one tool to another, choose the appropriate option at the top of the Freehand Tool dialog box. The options you see in the dialog box depend on which tool you've selected. Note that the paths you draw using the Freehand tool are open paths (unless you intentionally close them), while the paths drawn using the variable stroke and calligraphic pen tools are closed paths.

Press 5 (on either the keyboard or on the numeric keypad) or F5 to select the Freehand tool.

Freehand tool. The Tight fit option draws more points along the path as you draw, and the Draw Dotted Line option controls the way your path appears as you draw it. With Draw Dotted Line on, the Freehand tool simply places a series of dots as you draw and waits until you stop drawing to connect the dots and display the path you've drawn (see figure 1-38).

FIGURE 1-38
Freehand tool options

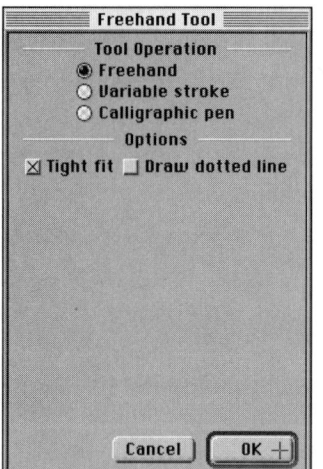

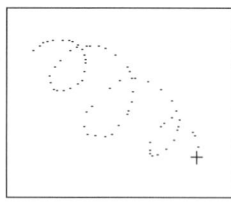

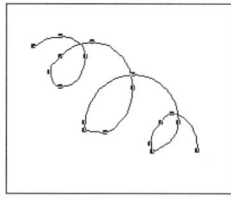

Draw Dotted Line displays the path as a dotted line as you draw.

With Draw Dotted Line off, FreeHand displays the path as you draw.

Variable Stroke tool. The Variable Stroke tool (also known as the "variable blob tool") is good for creating paths that look like brush strokes (see figure 1-39). Tight fit and Draw Dotted Line are the same as those for the Freehand tool. In the Minimum and Maximum fields, enter the minimum and maximum widths you want for paths you create using the Variable Stroke tool.

If you have a pressure-sensitive drawing tablet (such as those made by Wacom and Kurta), you can use pressure to control the width of paths you draw using the Variable Stroke tool. If you

FIGURE 1-39
Variable Stroke
tool options

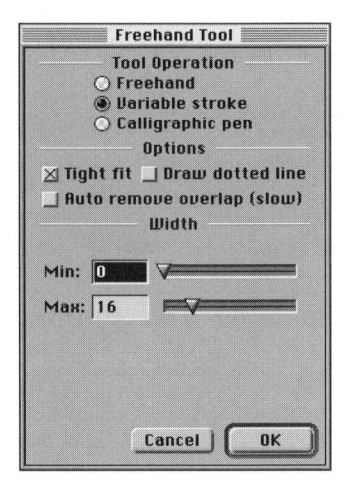

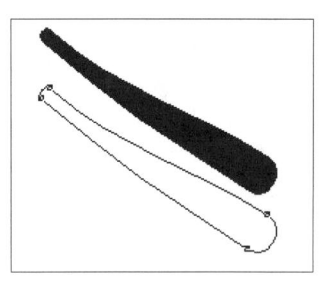

Use the Variable Stroke tool, to create paths that look like brushstrokes.

don't have a pressure-sensitive tablet, however, you can get similar effects. As you drag the Variable Stroke tool on your page, press 2 (or the Right Arrow key) to make your path get wider, or press 1 (or the Left Arrow key) to make your path narrower.

Calligraphic Pen tool. The Calligraphic Pen tool draws paths that look like they were drawn with a lettering pen (see figure 1-40). Tight fit and Draw Dotted Line are the same as those for the Freehand tool. When you choose fixed in the Width section of the dialog box, the paths you draw are a single, fixed width. When you choose Variable, the Calligraphic Pen tool simulates a pen with a flexible nib.

FIGURE 1-40
Calligraphic Pen
tool options

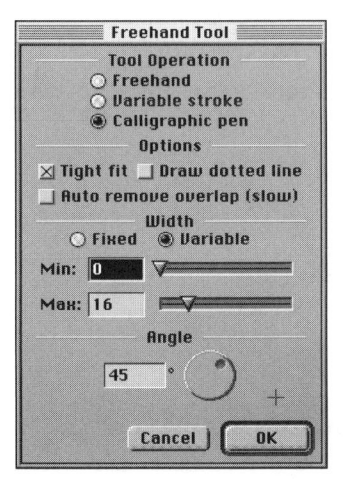

Drag the Calligraphic Pen tool to create paths that look like hand lettering.

Like the Variable Stroke tool, the Calligraphic Pen tool is pressure-sensitive and uses the same keyboard shortcuts.

Pen Tool

You use the Pen tool to draw paths containing both straight and curved line segments (that is, paths containing both curve and corner points). Illustrator users will recognize the Pen tool immediately, because it works the same as Illustrator's Pen tool. Click the Pen tool to create a corner point; drag to create a curve point.

Knife Tool

The Knife tool splits paths or points. Just select a path or point, choose the Knife tool, point at a path or point, and click, and FreeHand splits the path or point into separate paths where you clicked. Drag the Knife tool, and you'll see a line extending from the point at which you started dragging. You're not actually drawing anything—you're just defining a path that cuts through any other selected path it encounters. Knife tool? They should have named it the "chainsaw" tool!

Press 7 (on the keyboard or on the numeric keypad) or F7 to select the Knife tool. For more on splitting paths, see "Splitting Paths" in Chapter 2, "Drawing."

Double-click the Knife tool, and FreeHand displays the Knife Tool dialog box (see figure 1-41).

Straight or Freehand. When you choose the Straight option, dragging the Knife tool produces a straight "cutting" path. Click the Freehand option, and the Knife tool picks up the current settings of the Freehand tool. That's right—you can cut things with a pressure-sensitive calligraphic knife, if you want. See "Drawing with the Knife tool," in Chapter 2, "Drawing."

Width. The value you enter in the Width field sets the width of the swath you're cutting through things with your Chainsaw—I mean Knife—tool. As you'd expect, entering larger values gives your Knife a thicker blade.

Close Cut Paths. Choose the Close Cut Paths option if you want FreeHand to close the paths you've cut using the Knife tool (if

FIGURE 1-41
Knife tool options

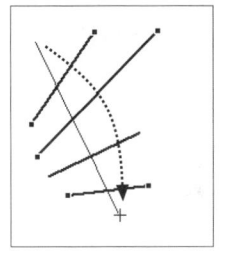

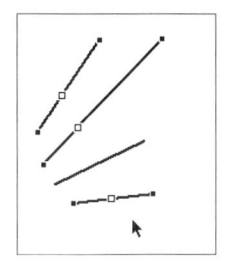

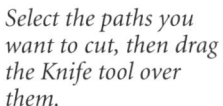

Select the paths you want to cut, then drag the Knife tool over them.

FreeHand cuts the selected paths; other paths are not affected.

you're cutting closed paths, you'll usually want this turned on; for open paths, you'll probably want it turned off (see "Drawing with the Knife Tool," in Chapter 2, "Drawing").

Tight fit. When you turn on the Tight fit option, you're directing FreeHand to more closely monitor the motion of the Knife tool as you drag it on the page. This means that it produces more irregular cuts in paths when you're using the "Freehand" form of the Knife tool.

Point Tool

Use the Point tool to place points on your page (the FreeHand manuals call this tool the "Bezigon" tool, but I find I can't—I just can't—type the word). You can create curve points, corner points, or connector points. To add a corner point, all you need to do is click. To create a curve point, hold down Option and click. Add a connector point by holding down Control and clicking. As you position points, bear in mind that you can always change any kind of point into any other kind of point, and that you can always change the curve of line segments attached to points.

For more on corner points, curve points, and connector points, see "Points and Paths," later in this chapter.

Rotation Tool

To rotate an object, select the Rotation tool from the toolbox, select the object, and drag the Rotation tool on your page. The point at which you start dragging specifies the center of rotation. If you want to rotate an object around its center, hold down Control as you drag.

Reflection Tool The Reflection tool creates a mirror image of an object around the object's vertical or horizontal axis (or both), around an angled axis, or around a fixed location on your page or pasteboard. To reflect an object, select the object, select the Reflection tool, then drag the Reflection tool on the page to flip the object. The point at which you start dragging determines the axis about which you're reflecting the object. Hold down Control as you drag if you want to reflect the object around its center point.

Scaling Tool To scale (or resize) an object, select the object, select the Scaling tool, and drag the Scaling tool to size the selected object. The point at which you start dragging determines the center point around which you're sizing the object. Hold down Shift as you drag to retain the object's proportions as you scale it. If you want to scale the object around its center point, hold down Control as you drag.

If you want to do your scaling numerically, double-click the Scaling tool—FreeHand will display the Scale section of the Transform palette.

For more about sizing or scaling objects, see "Scaling" in Chapter 5, "Transforming."

Skewing Tool Skewing alters the vertical or horizontal axes (or both) of objects, which makes them appear as though they're on a plane that's been slanted relative to the plane of the publication. To skew a selected object, select the Skewing tool from the toolbox and drag it on your page. As you drag, FreeHand skews the object. The point at which you start dragging sets the point around which the object skews (this means that the object will move, unless you've started dragging in precisely the center of the object). To skew the object around its center point, hold down Control as you drag.

To use the Skewing section of the Transform palette, double-click the Skewing tool—FreeHand displays the Skewing section of the Transform palette.

For more on skewing objects, see "Skewing" in Chapter 5, "Transforming."

Tracing Tool To automatically trace objects in your publication, select the Tracing tool and drag a selection rectangle around the objects you want to trace. Many people have the idea that the Tracing tool is only for tracing bitmaps, which isn't true—it'll trace anything you can have on a FreeHand page.

If you double-click the Tracing tool, the Tracing Tool dialog box appears (see figure 1-42). The Tight option adds more points to the paths generated by the tracing process. Trace Background and Trace Foreground are pretty straightforward. Choose Trace Background if you want to trace anything on a background layer; choose Trace Foreground if you want to trace things in the foreground layer(s).

FIGURE 1-42
Tracing tool settings

Magnifying Glass

Use the Magnifying Glass to change your view of the publication. Holding down Option changes the Magnifying Glass tool (which zooms in) into the Reducing Glass (which zooms out). To temporarily switch to the Magnifying Glass, hold down Command-spacebar, and then click the area you want to magnify, or drag a selection rectangle around it. To temporarily switch to the Reducing Glass, hold down Command-Option-spacebar, and then click or drag to zoom out.

For more on using the Magnifying Glass, see "Zooming," earlier in this chapter.

Constraining Tools

Most Macintosh drawing applications (beginning with MacPaint) have the concept of constraint: that holding down some key (usually Shift) makes tools behave differently. Usually, constraint limits movement to vertical and horizontal axes, relative to the sides of your Macintosh screen (though some applications limit movement to 45-degree tangents of the current location). Table 1-6 shows how constraint works in FreeHand.

TABLE 1-6
Effect of constraint on tools

Tool:	Constraint:
Pointer tool	If you're moving an object, holding down Shift limits the movement of the object to 45-degree tangents from the point at which you started dragging. You can hold down Shift at any time as you drag the object to get this effect. If you're selecting objects, holding down Shift extends the selection to include the next object or set of objects you click.
Polygon tool	Hold down Shift to constrain the rotation of the polygon's axis to 15-degree increments as you draw it.
Rectangle tool	Hold down Shift to draw squares.
Ellipse tool	Hold down Shift to draw circles.
Line tool	Hold down Shift to constrain the Line tool to draw lines in 45-degree increments (that is, 0, 45, and 90 degrees, where 0 degrees is horizontal and 90 degrees is vertical, relative to your publication).
Freehand tool	Hold down Option to constrain line segments to straight lines (from the point you held down the key); hold down Option-Shift to constrain line segments to 45-degree angles.
Pen tool	Shift constrains the next point placed to a 45-degree tangent from the previous point on the path.
Knife tool	Same as Line tool.
Point tool	Same as Pen tool.
Magnifying Glass	None
Reducing Glass	None

Additionally, you should note that constraint (holding down Shift) is affected by the angle you entered in the Constrain field of the Setup Inspector. All constraint, including drawing, is based on the angle you enter (see "Constrain," earlier in this chapter).

What's on My Page?

A FreeHand page can contain four kinds of objects: paths, basic shapes, text blocks, and imported graphics.

Points and Paths

Because so much of working with FreeHand depends on understanding the concept of points and paths, I've written about it in several places in this book. The following section is an overview of the topic. For more (much more) on points and paths, see "Points and Paths" in Chapter 2, "Drawing."

In FreeHand, continuous lines are called paths. Paths are made up of several points and the line segments drawn between those points. A point can have curve control handles attached to it which control the curve of the line segments associated with the point (see figure 1-43).

Many people call these handles "Bezier control points" (which is the technical, mathematical term for them), or "Bezier control handles." I find it confusing talking about two different kinds of "points," so I call them "control handles" or "curve handles," and use "point" to refer to the point on the path. It's simple: there are points, and those points might, or might not, have control handles attached to them.

FIGURE 1-43
Paths, points, and control handles

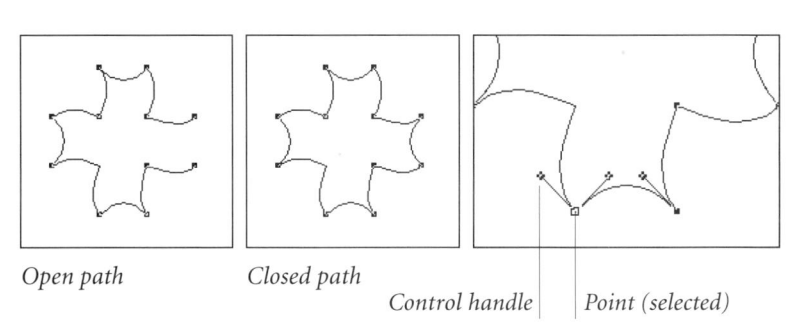

Open path   *Closed path*

Control handle   *Point (selected)*

Points come in three different flavors—curve points, corner points, and connector points. Each type of point has its own special properties.

- A curve point adds a curved line segment between the preceding and following points along the path. Curve points are shown onscreen as small circles and have curve control handles placed along a straight line from the curve point itself (see figure 1-44).

    The curve handle following the point controls the curve of the line segment following the curve point on the path; the curve handle preceding the point controls the curve of the line segment preceding the curve point on the path. Curve points are typically used for adding smooth curves to a path (see figure 1-45).

- A corner point adds a straight line segment between the current point and the preceding point on the path (see figure 1-46). Corner points are typically used to create paths containing straight line segments.

- A connector point adds a curved line segment following the point on the path. A connector point is something like a curve or corner point with one curve control handle extended and connects corner points and curve points (see figure 1-47). I've been using FreeHand for years, and I have yet to use a connector point.

You can always drag curve control handles out of corner and connector points. Select the point, hold down Option, and drag a curve control point out of the point. The first curve handle controls the curve of the line segment following the point along the path; the second curve handle controls the curve of the line segment preceding the point along the path.

What points should you use? Any type of point can be turned into any other type of point, and anything you can do with one kind of point can be done with any other kind of point. Given these two points (so to speak), you can use the kinds of points and drawing tools you're happiest with and achieve exactly the results you want. There is no "best way" to draw with FreeHand's freeform

FIGURE 1-44
Curve points

Control handle...
...controlling the curve of this line segment
Curve point
Control handle...

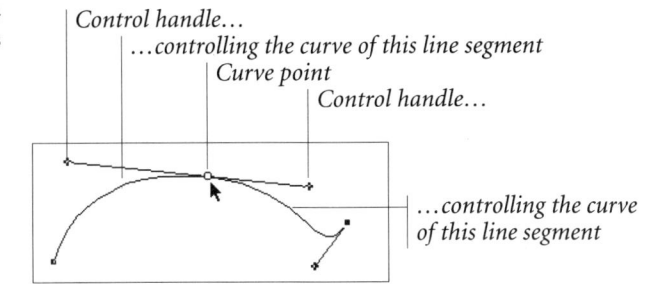

...controlling the curve of this line segment

FIGURE 1-45
Adjusting handles on curve points

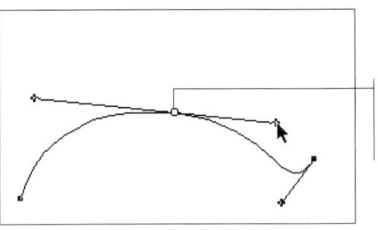

Select one of the curve points, then position the cursor over one of the control handles...

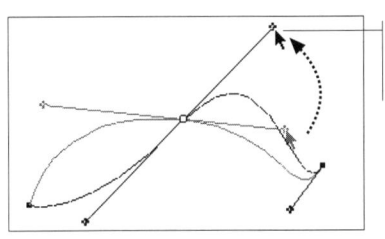

...and drag it to a new position. When you drag one handle of a curve point, the other handle moves, too.

FIGURE 1-46
Corner points

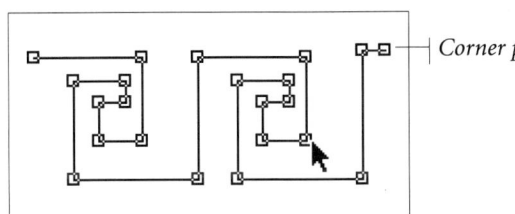

Corner point

FIGURE 1-47
Connector points

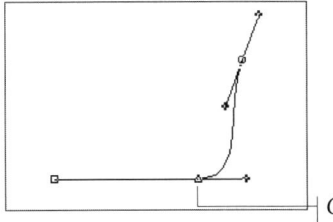

Connector point

drawing tools, but it helps to understand how the particular method you choose works.

I always use the Point tool, and place corner points to draw straight line segments. I add curves later, once I've placed points where I want them along the path. This seems easiest to me; what you like may be different. Experiment until you find what method of drawing suits you best. For more on working with points and paths, see Chapter 2, "Drawing."

Basic Shapes The Rectangle, Polygon, Ellipse, and Line tools draw basic shapes (that's what I call them, anyway). The Line tool draws a straight line segment between two points, which then behaves exactly as if you'd drawn it by placing two corner points. The other three tools draw paths with specific properties and points in specific places. It's as you'd expect: the Rectangle tool draws rectangles, the Ellipse tool draws ellipses, and the Polygon tool draws polygons. Objects drawn with the basic shapes tools act like grouped paths, but have certain special properties, as shown in Table 1-7.

Text Blocks FreeHand's text blocks can contain any number of typefaces, paragraph formats, colors, and sizes of type. Text blocks can also be linked to each other (so text flows between them as you edit the copy, reshape text blocks, or change formatting), and can be linked across pages. Text can flow along a path (that is, have its baseline follow a path), and can be flowed inside a path (see figure 1-48).

For more on FreeHand's text-handling capabilities, see Chapter 3, "Text and Type."

Imported Graphics FreeHand can import graphics saved in the PICT, EPS (including DCS), paint-type (MacPaint), and TIFF (including CMYK TIFF) formats. PICT object graphics are disassembled into their component objects on import and are converted into FreeHand elements you can edit just as if you'd drawn them in FreeHand. EPS graphics you've opened (as opposed to placed) are also converted into FreeHand elements. TIFF, paint, and EPS files you've placed are handled very much like a FreeHand group, except that they cannot be ungrouped. You can use all of FreeHand's transformation tools (for scaling, rotation, reflection, and skewing) to manipulate imported graphics (see figure 1-49).

For more on working with imported graphics, see Chapter 4, "Importing and Exporting."

TABLE 1-7
Special properties of basic shapes

Shape:	Special properties:
Rectangle	The Object Inspector for rectangles contains fields specifying the object's X and Y (horizontal and vertical) coordinates, W and H (width and height), as well as a field for specifying the rectangle's corner radius. (If you ungroup the rectangle, you won't be able to change its corner radius using the Object Inspector.) If you hold down Option as you draw a rectangle, FreeHand positions the center of the rectangle at the point where you started dragging, drawing the rectangle out from that point.
Ellipse	The Object Inspector for ellipses contains fields specifying the object's X and Y (horizontal and vertical) coordinates, W and H (width and height). If you hold down Option as you draw an ellipse, FreeHand positions the center of the ellipse at the point where you started dragging, drawing the ellipse out from that point.
Polygon	When you select a polygon, the Object Inspector displays the same information as it would if you selected a freeform path. If you hold down Option as you draw a polygon, FreeHand positions the center of the polygon at the point where you started dragging.

FIGURE 1-48
Text blocks

FIGURE 1-49
Imported graphics

Thinking Objectively

FreeHand's world is made up of objects (also called elements)—points, line segments, paths, basic shapes, text blocks, groups, and imported graphics. Each class of object has certain attributes that you can view and edit by selecting the object and looking at the Object Inspector.

The Object Inspector provides an extremely powerful way of looking at objects in your publication—by the numbers. If you want a rectangle to occupy exactly a certain space in your publication, you can always type the numbers right into the palette. Can I prove it to you? To position a six-by-six-pica rectangle three picas from the top and three picas from the left edge of your publication, follow these steps.

1. Reset the zero point to the upper-left corner of the publication (see "Rulers," earlier in this chapter).

2. Draw a rectangle with the Rectangle tool. Anywhere. Any size. I don't care.

3. Without deselecting the rectangle or selecting anything else, press Command-Option-R, then press Command-` to select the text in the X field in the Inspector.

4. In the X field, type "3p" (that's three picas from the left edge of the page). Press Tab to move to the Y field. Type "-3p" (that's three picas down from the top of the page) in the Y field, and press Tab to move to the W(idth) field. Enter "6p" and press Tab to move to the H(eight) field. In the H field, enter "6p".

5. Press Return.

The rectangle snaps into the position specified in the Object Inspector. You could have drawn it using the shadow cursors, Snap to Guides, or ruler guides—it's true. But, in this case, all you had to do was some typing, and the rectangle is positioned perfectly, exactly where you want it. If you know where something has to go, try using the Object Inspector to get it there. It can beat dragging, measuring, and waiting for the screen to redraw.

Selecting and Deselecting Elements

Before you can act on an object, you have to select it. You select objects with the Pointer tool by clicking them, dragging a selection rectangle over them, or by Shift-selecting (select one object, hold down Shift, and select another object). You can also choose Select All from the Edit menu.

When you select an object, FreeHand displays the object's selection handles. FreeHand displays selected objects a little bit differently depending on the method you've used to select them and the type of object you've selected. figure 1-50 shows you the differences.

To deselect objects, click an uninhabited area of the page or pasteboard, or press Command-Tab.

FIGURE 1-50
Selecting objects

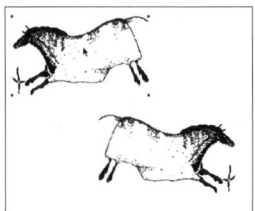

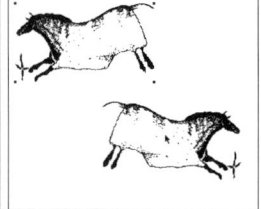

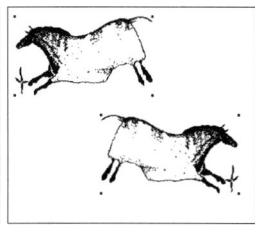

Shift-selecting

Click on one object to select it.

Hold down Shift, and click on another object.

You've selected both objects.

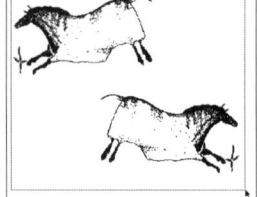

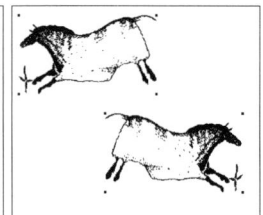

Drag-selecting

Position the cursor outside the group of objects you want to select…

…and drag a selection rectangle over the objects.

You've selected all of the objects inside the rectangle.

Tip: Deselect All

Pressing Command-Tab deselects all selected objects. This is particularly handy when you're having trouble deselecting an object at a high magnification—you can't see the currently selected object's selection handles because the object is larger than your page view. Pressing Command-Tab is easy, fast, and guaranteed to deselect all objects. Actually, if you're not entering text in a text block, you can just press Tab to deselect all objects. If your cursor is inside a text block, of course, you'll enter a tab character in the text block.

Tip: Selecting Parts of Paths

Sometimes, you only want to work on specific points in a path, rather than working on the path as a whole. To do this, drag a selection rectangle over only the points you want to select. If you want to select several points but can't reach them all with one selection rectangle, select some of the points by dragging a selection rectangle, then hold down Shift and drag more selection rectangles until you've selected all of the points you want.

Tip: Selecting Paths Instead of Points

If you've selected a path by dragging a selection rectangle over part of it, you've probably got some points specifically selected. While you sometimes want to do this, it can cause problems—when you drag the path, it's likely that the unselected points on the path stay put while the selected points move. To select the path as a whole when you've got some specific points selected, press ` (accent grave), located on the upper left of your keyboard underneath the ~ or tilde—see figure 1-51).

FIGURE 1-51
Selecting paths only

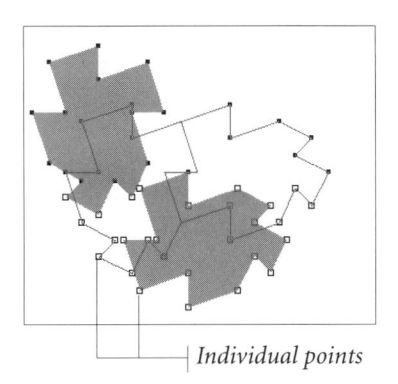

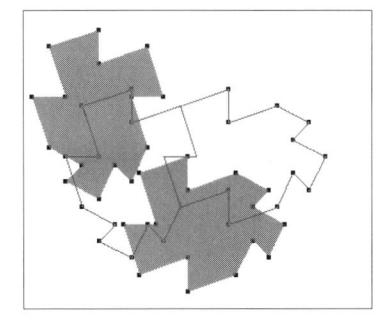

Individual points

Press ` (accent grave) and FreeHand selects the paths as paths, rather than as individual points.

Tip:
Select Through Objects

To select an object that's behind another object (or objects), hold down the Control key and click through the stack of objects until the selection handles of the individual object you want to select appear (see figure 1-52).

FIGURE 1-52
Selecting through stacks of objects

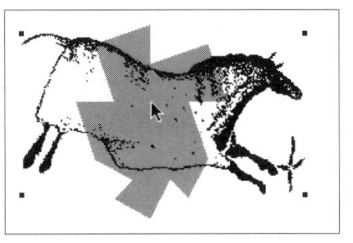

Control-click once to select the object on top of the stack.

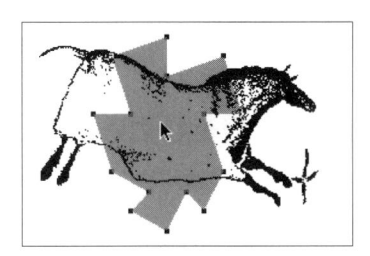

Control-click again to select the next object in the stack.

Tip:
Subselecting Items in a Group

You don't have to ungroup a group of objects to edit the objects in the group—you can select them and work with them just as if they were outside the group. Hold down Option and click on the element that you want to edit inside a group. While it's selected, you can change its attributes, text, shape, or position. When you deselect the subselected item, it goes back to being part of the group (see figure 1-53).

FIGURE 1-53
Subselecting items inside groups

Point at an object inside a group.

Hold down Option and click to select the object.

You can move or edit the object, but it remains inside the group (in this example, I've changed an object's color and position).

If you're trying to select an object in a group that's behind other objects, hold down Option and Control as you click through the stack of elements. You can also select multiple buried objects this way by holding down Control-Option-Shift as you click through the stack of objects.

This set of features is flexible enough that you can select any number of groups or individual objects through a stack of items containing groups or individual elements.

When you have an object inside a group selected, and you want to select and act on the group, press ` (accent grave). FreeHand selects the group. When you're working with groups nested inside other groups, each press of ` selects the next encompassing group.

Moving Elements

You can move individual points, sets of points, paths, groups or imported graphics—or sets of selected points, paths, or objects. Moving any single object is simple: just position the Pointer tool over the object (but not over a point in the path), hold down the mouse button, and drag the object to wherever you want it (see figure 1-54).

FIGURE 1-54
Moving by dragging

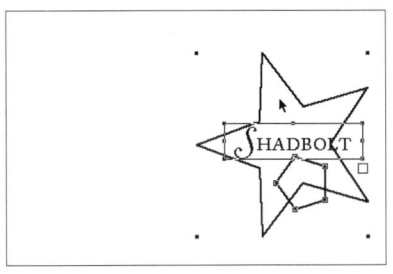

Select the objects you want to move...

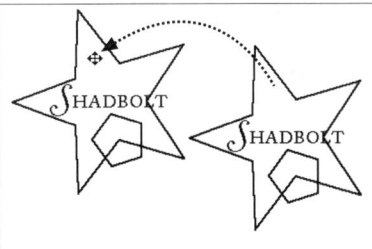

...and drag them to a new position.

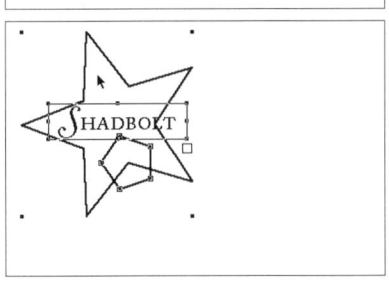

When the objects are where you want them, drop them (that is, stop dragging and release the mouse button).

Okay, I admit that this is pretty basic, but I do get asked, honest.

To move more than one object at once, hold down Shift and click on the objects you want to move. When you reach the last object you want to select, position the Pointer tool over the object, and, while still holding down Shift, press the mouse button. If you want to constrain the object's movement, continue holding down Shift (if not, release the Shift key), and drag the selected objects to where you want them.

Alternatively, you can move objects using the Move palette. Select an object (or group of objects) and press Command-M to display the Transform palette (then click the Move icon at the top of the palette if the Move palette's not visible). Type the horizontal and vertical distance you want the selection to move in the fields, and press Return. FreeHand moves the object the distance you specified (see figure 1-55). For more on moving, see "Moving," in Chapter 5, "Transforming."

FIGURE 1-55
Moving objects using the Move palette

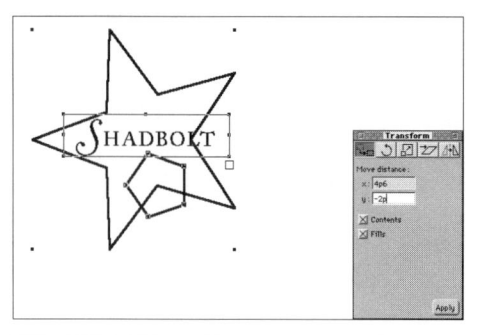

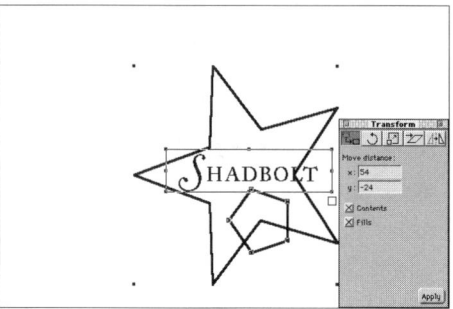

Select the objects you want to move and press Command-M to display the Transform palette (if it's not already visible). Click the Move icon to display the Move palette, type the distance you want to move the objects in the X and Y fields, and press Return (or click the Apply button).

FreeHand moves the objects as you specified.

Working with Layers

Many authors would save the intricacies of working with the Layers palette for later in the book. Sorry. The Layers palette is one of the most important tools at your disposal for speeding up the process of creating publications with FreeHand.

Like many CAD programs, FreeHand uses the concept of layers—transparent planes on which you create and place elements. Once you've gone beyond creating very simple publications, you'll find layers indispensable because they help you organize and control the elements in your publication.

Layers give you control over which parts of your publication redraw while you're working on the file. If, for example, you're correcting text in a publication containing large TIFF images, put the TIFFs on their own layer and make it invisible while you work on the text. Don't spend time displaying things you're not working on and don't need to see.

Default Layers

FreeHand has three default layers: Foreground, Guides, and Background. These layers are representative of the three major types of layers available in FreeHand (see figure 1-56). You can create or delete any number of background and foreground layers, but you can't create a new, or delete the existing, Guides layer.

- Foreground layers are where you do your drawing. In general, they're what you want to print, when you print.

- The Guides layer contains FreeHand's guides. Move the layer, and the guides move with it.

- Background layers are where you put objects you want to trace. Background layers don't print.

The line in the Layers palette defines the boundary between background and foreground layers. Layers above the line in the palette are foreground layers; layers below are background layers. Objects on the background layers are screened to 50 percent of their original color (this makes it easier to trace objects on the background layer).

FIGURE 1-56
Default layers

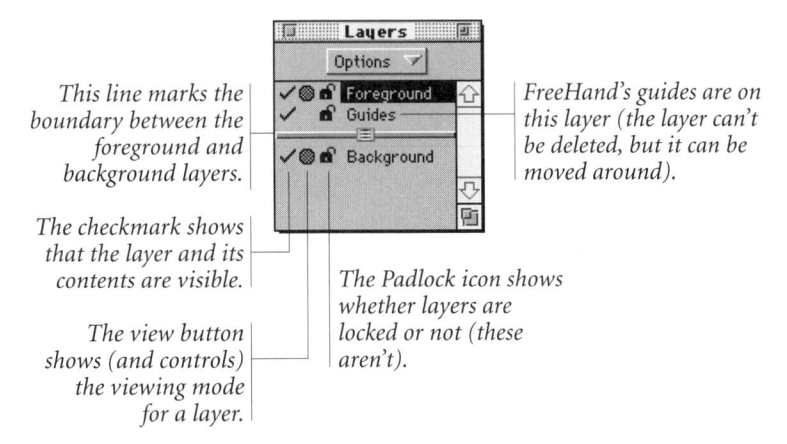

This line marks the boundary between the foreground and background layers.

The checkmark shows that the layer and its contents are visible.

The view button shows (and controls) the viewing mode for a layer.

FreeHand's guides are on this layer (the layer can't be deleted, but it can be moved around).

The Padlock icon shows whether layers are locked or not (these aren't).

Using the Layers Palette

Here are some of the things you can do using the Layers palette.

- Make the Layers palette visible or invisible
- Move objects from one layer to another
- Create new layers
- Remove layers (and their contents)

- Make layers visible or invisible
- Display layers in Preview or Keyline view
- Change the stacking order of layers
- Make layers foreground or background
- Make layers printing or nonprinting
- Copy the contents of entire layers to other layers
- Lock layers (objects on locked layers cannot be selected)
- Rename layers

Toggling the Layers palette. You can display and hide the Layers palette by pressing Command-6. If it's currently displayed, Command-6 hides it, and vice-versa.

Moving objects from one layer to another. To send an object or objects to a specific layer, select the objects and click the name of the layer in the Layers palette. FreeHand moves the selected objects to that layer (see figure 1-57).

Creating new layers. To create a new layer choose New from the popup menu at the top of the Layers palette. FreeHand adds a new layer to the Layers palette. If you want to change the default name FreeHand's assigned to the new layer, double-click on the layer's name in the Layers palette, type a new name for the layer, and press Return (see figure 1-58).

FIGURE 1-57
Moving objects from one layer to another

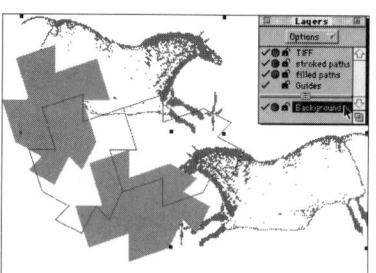

Select the objects you want to move (in this example, the objects are on the background layer).

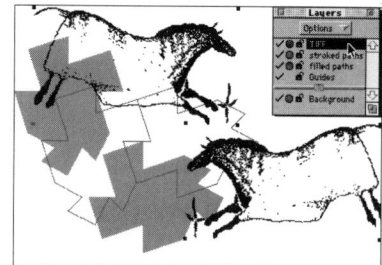

Click on the layer name in the Layers palette. FreeHand moves the objects to the layer.

FREEHAND BASICS 65

FIGURE 1-58
Creating and
naming a new layer

Select "New" from the
Layers palette popup
menu.

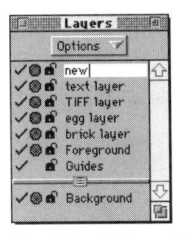

Double-click on the
new layer's name and
type the name you want
for the layer.

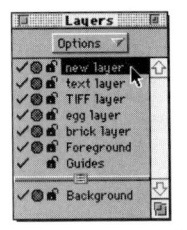

Press Return, and
FreeHand adds the new
layer's name to the
Layers palette.

Removing layers. To remove a layer, select the layer name in the Layers palette and choose Remove from the popup menu at the top of the palette. If there are objects on that layer, FreeHand asks if you want to remove those objects (see figure 1-59). If that's what you want to do, click OK and all of the objects on that layer will be deleted along with the layer. If you don't want the objects removed, click Cancel, and move the objects to other layers. Then try removing the layer again.

FIGURE 1-59
Removing layers

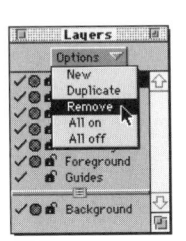

Select the layer you want
to remove and choose
Remove from the Layers
palette popup menu.

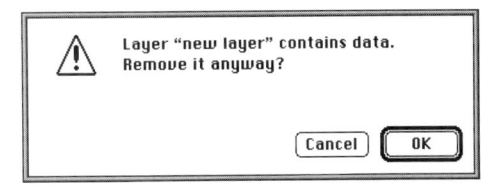

If there's anything on the layer, FreeHand
displays this message. Click OK (or press
Return) if you want to remove the objects on the
layer. Otherwise, click Cancel and move the
objects to other layers.

Tip:
Removing
Multiple Layers

Want to remove more than one layer at once? To select a contiguous range of layers (layers adjacent to each other in the Layers palette), hold down Shift and click on the layer names in the Layers palette. To select a series of layers that aren't in a range, hold down Command and click on the layers you want to select. Once you've selected the layers you want to remove, choose Remove from the Layers palette's popup menu (see figure 1-60).

FIGURE 1-60
Selecting and removing multiple layers

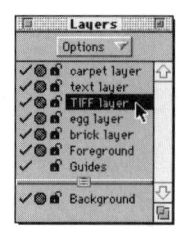

Select the start of the range...

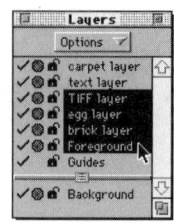

...then hold down Shift and click the end of the range. Shift-click inside the range to deselect layers you've selected.

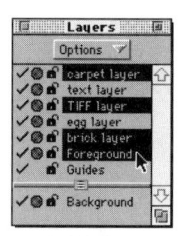

Or hold down Command and click on the layers you want to select (they don't have to be next to each other in the palette). To deselect a layer name, Command-click the layer again.

Once you've chosen the layers you want to delete, choose Remove from the Layers palette's Options menu.

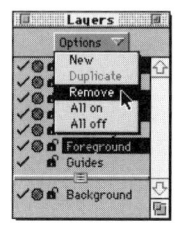

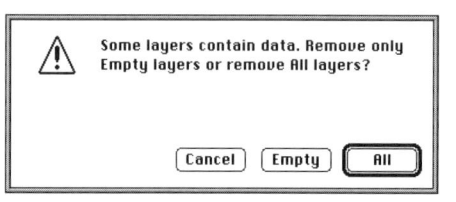

FreeHand displays this alert. Delete all of the selected layers by clicking the All button, or remove only the empty layers in the selection by clicking the Empty button.

Making layers visible or invisible. If you want to make all of the objects on a layer invisible, click the checkmark to the left of the layer's name in the Layers palette. Everything that's on that layer disappears (see figure 1-61). Don't worry. It's not gone; it's just not visible and can't be selected. To make the layer visible again, click the space to the left of the layer's name. The checkmark reappears, and the objects on the layer become visible.

You can make all layers visible by choosing All On from the popup menu at the top of the Layers palette, or make all layers invisible by choosing All Off. When you want to work on just one layer, choose All Off and then make that one layer visible.

Tip:
All On/All Off Shortcuts

To quickly hide all layers, hold down Option and click a checkmark to the left of a layer's name in the Layers palette. FreeHand hides all layers. To show all layers, Option-click to the left of a layer you've turned off. FreeHand displays all layers.

Changing your view of layers. You can set the viewing mode (Preview or Keyline) of a layer by clicking the view button to the left of

FREEHAND BASICS 67

FIGURE 1-61
Making layers visible
or invisible

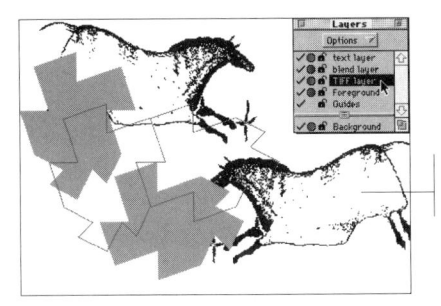

This figure is on the layer "TIFF layer".

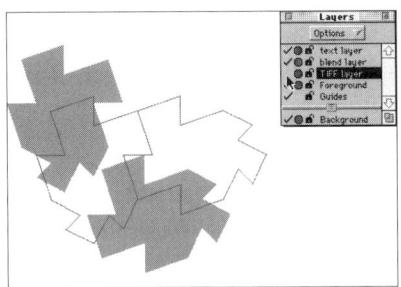

Click the checkmark to the left of the layer's name to make the layer invisible.

the layer's name in the Layers palette (see figure 1-62). When you do this, everything on the layer is displayed in the view you've chosen.

Tip:
Keyline/Preview
Shortcut

To switch all layers in keyline view, hold down Option and click the View button next to a layer that's already in keyline view. To switch all of the layers in a publication to preview mode, Option-click the View button to the left of a layer that's currently in preview mode.

Changing the stacking order of layers. The stacking order of the layers you use is determined by the order in which they appear in the Layers palette. Layers closer to the top of the Layers palette are

FIGURE 1-62
Changing the viewing
mode for a layer

TIFF layer, displayed in preview

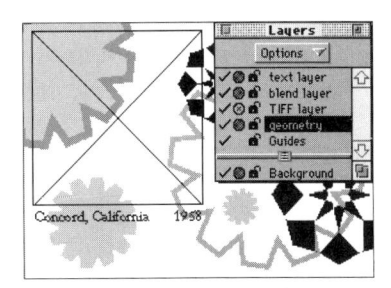

TIFF layers, in keyline mode.

farther to the front in your publication. If you want to move the contents of a specific layer closer to the front, drag the layer name closer to the top of the Layers palette (see figure 1-63).

Tip:
Moving the Guides Layer

To send the guides all the way to the back, drag the Guides layer below the line on the Layers palette. The Guides layer is now behind every foreground layer. If you want to move the Guides layer behind every background layer, drag the Guides layer to the bottom of the list in the Layers palette.

You can also move the Guides layer so that it falls behind one or more foreground layers.

FIGURE 1-63
Changing the stacking order of layers

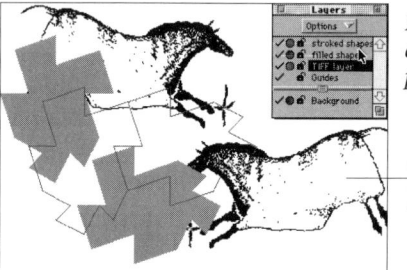

Drag the layer name up or down in the Layers palette.

This image is on the layer named "TIFF layer".

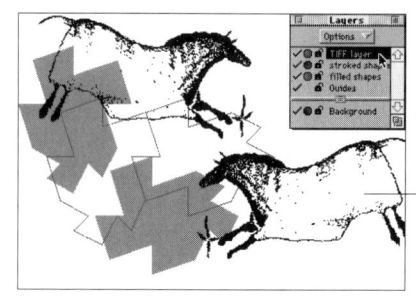

Drop the layer when it's where you want it.

The image comes to the front, along with any other objects on the same layer.

Making layers foreground or background. To make a layer a background layer, drag it below the line in the Layers palette. To make a background layer into a foreground layer, drag it above the line in the Layers palette. You can also drag the line up and down in the palette, making whole ranges of layers foreground or background.

Making layers printing or nonprinting. If you want to print only the visible foreground layers (the layers above the line in the palette with a checkmark to the left of their names), click All Visible

FREEHAND BASICS 69

Foreground Layers in the Print Options dialog box. If you want to print all foreground layers, whether they're visible or not, click All Foreground Layers.

Alternatively, you can make foreground layers into background layers to make them nonprinting, and vice versa.

The default Guides layer cannot be printed.

Copying layers. To copy all of the objects on a particular layer to a new layer, select the layer and choose Duplicate from the Layers palette's popup menu. FreeHand creates a new layer containing copies of all of the objects on the original layer. Your page won't look any different, of course, because the copied objects are exactly on top of the original objects.

Locking and unlocking layers. When you're working on a complex publication, it's too easy to select something you'd rather leave alone—or, worse, delete it. Instead of losing time "undoing" your mistakes, why not put the things you're done with (or, at least, not currently working on) on a layer of their own, and then keep them safe by locking the layer?

To lock a layer, click the Padlock icon to the left of the layer's name in the Layers palette (see figure 1-64). The objects on the layer remain visible, but you can't select them. You can still change the layer's position in the stacking order when it's locked.

To unlock a layer, click the Padlock icon to the left of the layer's

FIGURE 1-64
Locking and unlocking layers

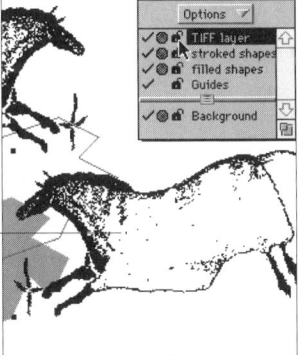

This image is on the layer you want to lock.

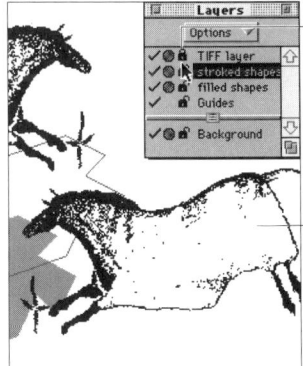

Click the Padlock to lock the layer.

Any objects you had selected on the locked layer become deselected. You won't be able to select this object again until you unlock the layer.

name. When the padlock's open, the layer is unlocked.

Renaming layers. You can rename a layer at any time. Double-click on the layer name in the Layers palette, type a new name for the layer and press Return.

Renaming layers makes not a bit of difference to FreeHand, but it might help you remember which layer contains which objects.

FreeHand and the Edit Menu

FreeHand works a little bit differently than other Macintosh applications, particularly in that you don't have to go through the Clipboard to copy items in your publication. Instead, you'll typically use Clone and Duplicate (which you'll find on FreeHand's Edit menu) inside a publication (you'll still need to use Cut and Copy to move items from publication to publication). Not only are Clone and Duplicate faster, they use less memory and have some useful features of their own.

Clone

The Clone command, Command-= (that's the equals sign), creates a copy of the selected object exactly on top of the original (see figure 1-65). This can be a little confusing at first, because the cloned object's selection handles look just the same as the selection handles of the original object. New FreeHand users sometimes end up with stacks of identical objects in their publications.

Placing the object in the same position, however, offers distinct advantages. If, for example, you know that you want a copy of a specific object two picas to the right and two picas down from the location of the original object, just clone the object, then display the Move palette, and move the object numerically. If you hadn't started in exactly the same position as the original object, you'd have to do a bunch of measuring to figure out where the copied object was supposed to go.

Duplicate

The Duplicate command (Command-D) creates a copy of the object at a slight offset from the selected object (see figure 1-66),

FIGURE 1-65
Cloning

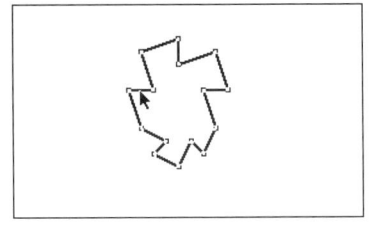

Select an object and press Command-= to clone it.

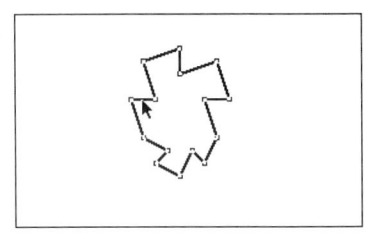

FreeHand places an exact copy of the object on top of the object. It doesn't look like a new object, but it's there.

FIGURE 1-66
Duplicating

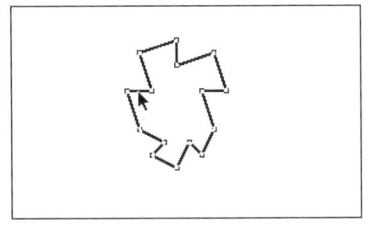

Select an object and press Command-D to duplicate it.

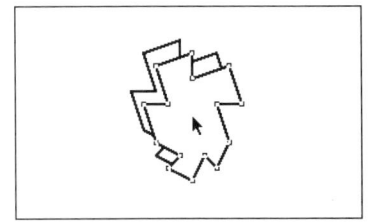

FreeHand places an exact copy of the object on the page.

or copies the object and repeats the last series of transformations (uses of the Move, Scaling, Rotation, Skewing, or Reflection tools). I'll cover more of the complex uses of the Duplicate command in Chapter 5, "Transforming."

Preferences

FreeHand 4 had lots of different preference settings that people never understood or used, and FreeHand 5 has even more. It's worth learning what the different choices are, however, because the Preferences dialog boxes are one place inside FreeHand where you can truly fine-tune FreeHand's performance and behavior. Preference settings are so useful, in fact, that I'm hoping that FreeHand 6 will have a Yet More Preferences dialog box, or a Son of More Preferences dialog box. The possibilities are endless.

When you choose Preferences from the file menu, FreeHand displays the Display panel of the Preferences dialog box. Click on the items in the list at the left side of the dialog box to display the different panels of the Preferences dialog box. From now on, I'll refer to each section of this dialog box as if it were a separate dialog box (as, in fact, each is).

Colors   The options in the Colors Preferences dialog box (see figure 1-67) affect FreeHand's user interface for working with colors—none of these settings actually change the way your colors are defined.

FIGURE 1-67
Colors preferences

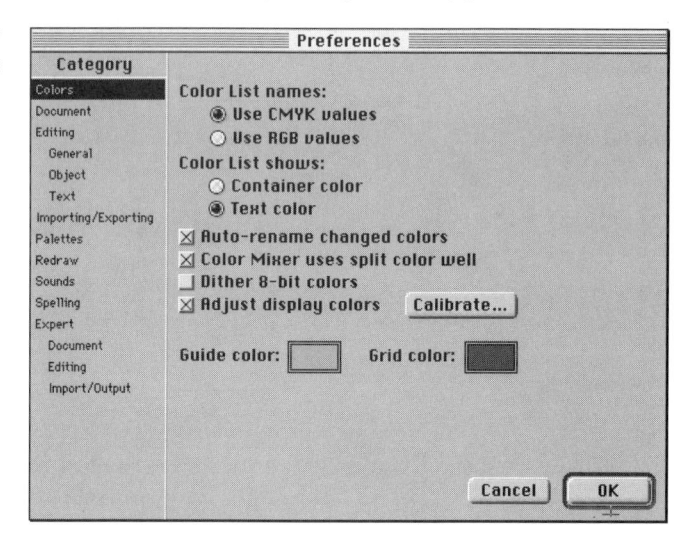

Color List Names. You've probably noticed that when you drag a color swatch into the Color List, FreeHand assigns a name to the color based on that color's components. By default, FreeHand names the color based on its CMYK values—which is what you get when you choose the Use CMYK Values option. If you'd rather see your colors named for their RGB values (what you see on your screen, more or less), turn on the Use RGB Values option. If you're working with process colors, do yourself a favor and stick with the default (see Chapter 6, "Color," for more on the ins and outs of color definitions).

Color List Shows. One of FreeHand's great features—the ability to apply a stroke and fill to the background of a text block—ends up causing a problem. What's the problem? When you select a text block, should the fill and Stroke buttons at the top of the Color List show the colors applied to the text block, or should they show the fill and stroke you've applied to the text itself? In FreeHand 4, the Color List settled on the former (the container) rather than the latter (the text). In FreeHand 5, you can choose for yourself. Choose the Container Color option to have the Color List show the colors of the fill and stroke applied to the text block; choose Text Color to work with the fill and stroke applied to the text itself (see figure 1-68).

FIGURE 1-68
Container color versus text color

When you select the Container Color option, the Color List displays the color of the text block when you select the text block with the Pointer tool...

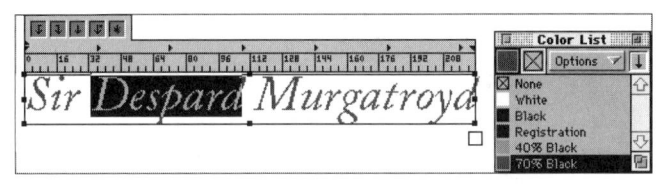

...and displays the color of the text when you select the text with the Text tool.

When you choose the Text Color option, FreeHand displays the color of the text in the Color List, regardless of the tool you use to select the text. While this is usually what you want, it makes it impossible to apply a color to the text block's background.

Auto-Rename Changed Colors. If this option were called "Auto-Rename Auto Named Changed Colors," it'd make (a little) more sense. It'd also be harder to say. If you check this option, FreeHand renames any automatically-named (that is, colors you've created but haven't typed a name for) colors as they're edited. If you add 10% cyan to a color FreeHand named "20C 50M 0Y 10K," FreeHand will change the color's name to "30C 50M 0Y 10K." If you don't want FreeHand to do this, turn this option off—but bear in mind that you'll have to keep closer track of your color definitions, as the name will no longer reflect the color values.

Color Mixer Uses Split Color Well. If, as you're editing a color, you like seeing a swatch of the original color next to a swatch of the edited color, turn this option on. It splits the color well at the bottom of the Color Mixer into two sections—one showing the original color, one showing the edited color (see figure 1-69).

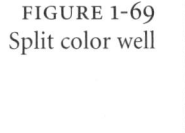

FIGURE 1-69
Split color well

Original color — Edited color

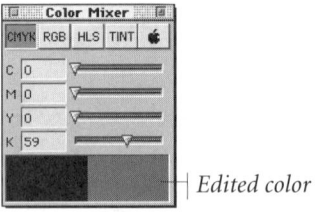

When you turn on the Split Color Well option, the Color Mixer looks like this when you're editing a color.

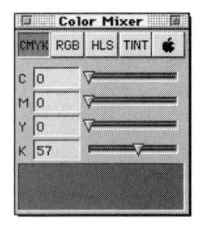

When you turn off the Split Color Well option, the Color Mixer shows only the edited (or current) color.

Dither 8-Bit Colors. If you're working with an eight-bit video system, you can check this box to make FreeHand dither colors (that is, use patterns of different-colored pixels) to represent the colors you're using in your publication. These dither patterns do not affect printing. Why does FreeHand need to use dithering? Because an eight-bit video system has only 256 colors available—which means it's easy to pick a color your system can't display.

Leave this box unchecked, and FreeHand will use the eight-bit color that's closest to the color you're working with.

This one's up to you—dithered colors more accurately represent the colors you've chosen, but you might not like the pixel patterns it creates. In any case, FreeHand always uses dithering to represent colors in graduated and radial fills.

Adjust Display Colors. When you click the Calibrate button in the Preferences dialog box, the Display Color Setup dialog box appears (see figure 1-70).

Click the Cyan, Magenta, and Yellow color wells to select the colors you want from the Apple Color Picker dialog box. Which colors are correct? I use the settings shown in Table 1-8; you can type the numbers right into the fields in the Color Picker. You might want to use different settings, however, depending on your monitor and viewing environment.

FIGURE 1-70
Adjusting your
color display

Click one of the color wells in
the Display Color Setup
dialog box...

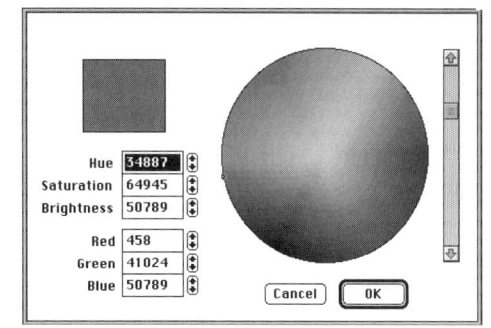

...And FreeHand displays the Apple Color
Picker, where you can choose a color that
matches (or comes close to matching) a
printed sample of the color you want to use.

TABLE 1-8
HSB and RGB color
settings for process
colors

Color	H	S	B	R	G	B
Cyan	32768	65535	65535	0	65535	65535
Magenta	54614	65535	65535	65535	0	65535
Yellow	10922	65535	65535	65535	65535	0
Black	65535	65535	65535	65535	65535	65535

You can also adjust the colors by holding a printed color sample next to your screen and modifying your display colors until they match the sample. Ideally, you'd only use printed process-color samples from the commercial printer and press you intend to use to produce the publication, printed on the paper stock you've chosen for the job (though I confess I've never done this myself).

You don't need to adjust all of the colors—once you've changed Cyan, Yellow, and Magenta, FreeHand adjusts the other colors accordingly (though you won't see a difference in the dialog box display until you close and reopen the dialog box).

These adjustments are for screen display only and have nothing to do with the percentages of process colors FreeHand will print. Don't trust your monitor. The colors you see on your screen are only there to remind you of which color you've applied to different objects. Specify your colors by referring to printed samples of the spot or process colors you want to use. For more on specifying colors, or on calibrating your monitor to display colors more accurately, refer to Chapter 6, "Color."

Guide Color. To change the color of FreeHand's ruler guides, click the color swatch. The Guide Color dialog box appears (I call this dialog box the Apple Color Picker). Click on the color in the color wheel you want to use for the nonprinting guides in your publication and press Return to close the dialog box. FreeHand uses the new color for displaying the ruler guides.

Grid Color. To change the color of FreeHand's grid, click on the color swatch to display the Grid Color dialog box, then choose a color in the Apple Color Picker's color wheel. After you press Return to close the dialog box, FreeHand displays the grid in the new color.

Document

The options in the Document Preferences dialog box (see figure 1-71) change the way FreeHand opens and exports publications.

Restore Last View When Opening Document. When this option is off, FreeHand displays page one of your publication at fit in Window view when you open it; when it's on, FreeHand displays the publication using the same view (or views) as you were using when you last saved it (that is, it returns you to the same page and the same zoom level).

Remember Window Size and Location. This option is a lot like the previous one. Do you want FreeHand to open your documents to a default window size and window position, or do you want your documents opened with windows the same as they were the last time you saved the publication? I like to come back to my work the way I left it, so I turn this option on.

FreeHand 4 Compatible Page Placement. FreeHand 5 features a larger pasteboard than FreeHand 4. This is great, until you open a

FIGURE 1-71
Document preferences

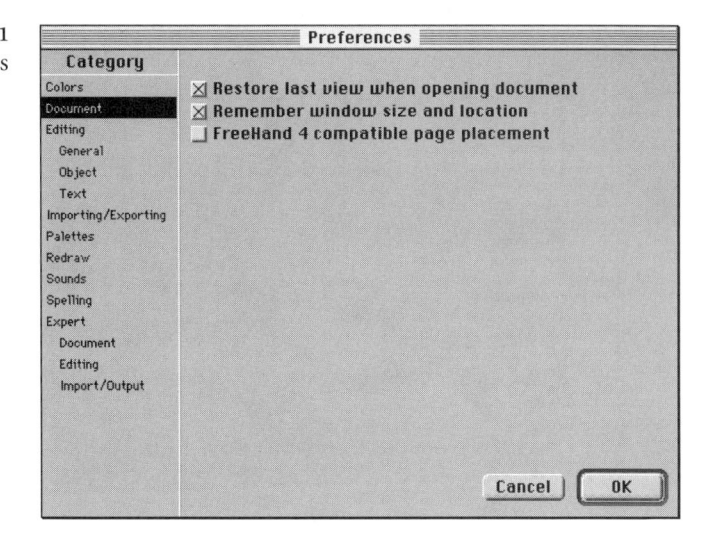

FreeHand 5 publication using FreeHand 4. What happens to all of the extra space on the pasteboard? It goes away, taking with it any pages that won't fit on FreeHand 4's pasteboard. If you plan to export documents in the FreeHand 4 file wformat, turn this option on—you'll then see an area marked off in the lower-left of the pasteboard (in the Document Inspector's thumbnail view of the pasteboard). This area is the same size as FreeHand 4's pasteboard, and any pages you drag inside this area will appear in any FreeHand 4 document you export (see figure 1-72).

FIGURE 1-72
FreeHand 4 compatible page placement

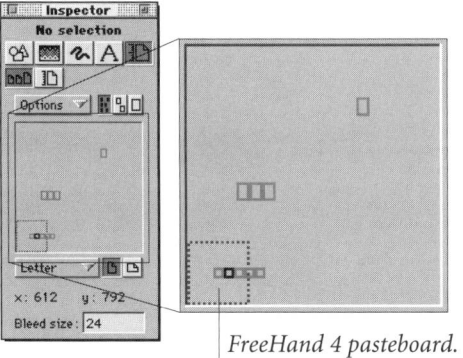

Document Inspector with the FreeHand 4 Compatible Page Placement option turned on.

FreeHand 4 pasteboard. Anything outside this area won't be exported when you export a FreeHand 4 publication.

Document Inspector with the FreeHand 4 Compatible Page Placement option turned off.

General Editing When you click the General option in the Editing section of the Preferences list, FreeHand displays what I call the General Editing Preferences dialog box (see figure 1-73). Some of the most important of FreeHand's preferences live here.

FIGURE 1-73
General Editing
Preferences dialog box

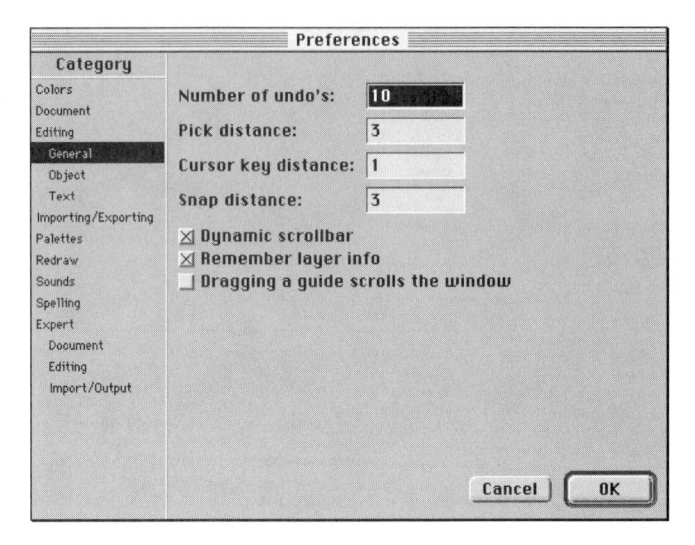

Number of Undo's. This option sets the number of actions held in FreeHand's Undo queue. Enter smaller numbers here if you find you don't use that many levels of Undo or want to save memory. Enter larger numbers here if you change your mind a lot and don't like the idea of using Save As and Revert when you're experimenting with possibilities. Remember, however, that each level of Undo adds to the amount of RAM that FreeHand uses (the amount of RAM consumed depends on the action). You can enter any number from one to 100 in this field.

Pick Distance. How close to the edge of an object do you have to click to select the object? How does FreeHand "know" you want to select the object? The value you enter in the Pick Distance field determines how close, in pixels, you can click before FreeHand decides you're trying to select the object. You can enter a value from zero to five pixels in this field—the lower the value, the more accurate your clicks have to be.

The Pick Distance field also controls how close you have to get to an object to apply a color to it using drag-and-drop color. If you're having trouble dropping color swatches on paths, you might want to increase the value you've entered in the Pick Distance field (for more information, see "Drag-and-Drop Color" in Chapter 6, "Color").

Cursor Key Distance. Enter a number in the Cursor Key Distance field to set the distance a selected object moves when you press the arrow keys to "nudge" an object.

Snap Distance. FreeHand has lots of different "snaps" under the View menu. There's Snap to Guides, Snap to Point, and Snap to Grid. Snap to Point makes FreeHand points snap together when you drag them to within a specified distance of each other. Snap to Guides snaps objects to ruler guides when you drag objects within a specified distance of them. Snap to Grid makes objects snap to an underlying grid, which you define in the Setup Inspector.

The number you enter in the Snap Distance field in the Editing Preferences dialog box sets the distance (in screen pixels) that all of the Snap commands rely on. Set the Snap Distance option to five pixels, and the next time you drag an object within five pixels of an active snap point (point, ruler guide, or grid intersection), FreeHand snaps the object to that point.

If you just can't seem to get one point to land on top of another so that you can close a path or connect the end of one path to the end of another (see "Open and Closed Paths" in Chapter 2, "Drawing," for more on closing paths), try increasing the number in the Snap Distance field. If, on the other hand, you're having a hard time keeping points from snapping together, enter a smaller number in the Snap Distance field.

Dynamic Scrollbar. When this option is off, FreeHand doesn't redraw the screen as you drag the slider in the scroll bars—it redraws when you stop dragging. If you want to see your publication as you scroll using the slider, check this box. Bear in mind, however, that turning this option on makes scrolling slower. Turn this option off if you're running low on RAM.

Note that both the Dynamic Scrollbar and the Redraw While Scrolling preferences sound like they address the same issue—they don't. The Redraw While Scrolling preference affects all scrolling methods; the Dynamic Scrollbar option applies only to scrolling by dragging the slider in the scroll bar.

Remember Layer Info. In FreeHand 3, you'd lose layer information when you cut, copied, or pasted objects, or when you grouped and ungrouped objects. The Remember Layer Info feature, which first appeared in FreeHand 3.1, gives you the option of keeping that layer information. With Remember Layer Info on, you can cut and paste, group and ungroup, as much as you like, and the objects you're working with always appear on their original layers.

If you're copying objects into a publication that doesn't contain the layers, FreeHand adds those layers to the publication. If you've deleted layers, and ungroup a group containing objects originally assigned to those layers, FreeHand adds the layers to the Layers palette.

If, on the other hand, you want to paste objects from other layers into the current layer, turn off Remember Layer Info.

Dragging a Guide Scrolls the Window. If you like to scroll your current view of the publication by dragging ruler guides, turn this option on. Once you do this, you can't remove ruler guides by dragging them to the rulers—you have to drag them all the way off the page (or use the Guides dialog box). This was the way ruler guides worked in FreeHand 4.

Object Editing

Click "Object" under "Editing" in the Preferences List, and Free-Hand displays the Object Editing Preferences dialog box (see figure 1-74). The options in this dialog box control various aspects of working with objects in your FreeHand publications.

Changing Object Changes Defaults. If you check the Changing Object Changes Defaults box, any changes you make to a selected object's attributes (colors, type specifications, fills, and strokes) are carried over to the next object you create. For example, if you've created a stroke and set its width to six points and its color to 20-percent gray, the next path you create has the same stroke width and color.

FIGURE 1-74
Object Editing
Preferences dialog box

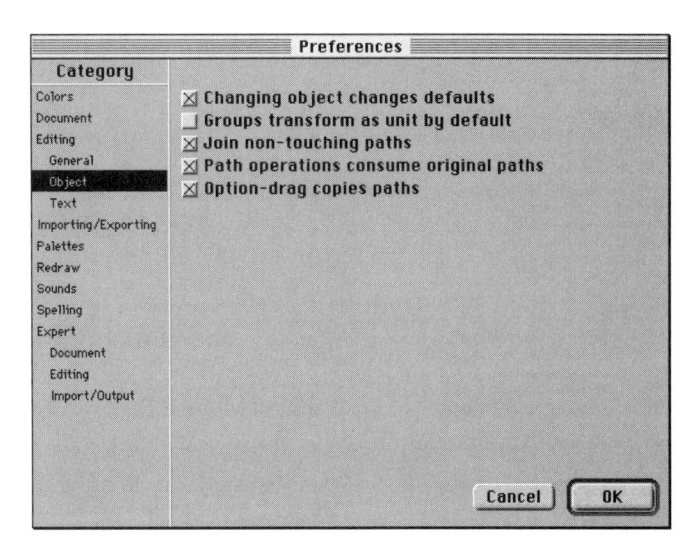

[Preferences dialog box showing Category list with Object selected, and options: Changing object changes defaults (checked), Groups transform as unit by default (unchecked), Join non-touching paths (checked), Path operations consume original paths (checked), Option-drag copies paths (checked)]

When this option's unchecked, you set defaults for the entire document by making changes to object attributes (colors, fills, lines, type specifications, and so on) without having any object selected. In this case, each new object you create picks up the publication's default attributes regardless of what changes have been made to selected objects created or modified previously.

Groups Transform As Unit by Default. When you're transforming (moving, scaling, skewing, or rotating) objects, you can choose to have the transformation affect the line weights and fills of objects in the group. If you don't want this to happen, uncheck this box. For more on Groups Transform as a Unit by Default, see Chapter 5, "Transforming."

Join Non-Touching Paths. When Join Non-Touching Paths is on, FreeHand joins the endpoints of open paths when you select the points and press Command-J (or choose Join Elements from the Arrange menu). With Join Non-Touching Paths turned off, FreeHand only joins the endpoints of paths that you draw or drag to within the distance in pixels you entered in the Pick Distance field.

Path Operations Consume Original Paths. In FreeHand 4, most of the path operations (on the submenu of the same name on the Arrange menu—and, for some reason, on *another* submenu of the same name on the Extras menu) would delete the original paths as they produced new paths from the selected objects. To retain the original paths, you had to clone the paths before running the path operation. In FreeHand 5, you can turn this option off and save your original paths—or you can turn it on and clone any paths you want to keep around before you run any path operations.

Option-Drag Copies Paths. Many Macintosh graphics applications (beginning with MacPaint and continuing through Illustrator and Photoshop) clone selected objects when you drag them while holding the Option key down. Turn this option on to have FreeHand join the club, or, if you feel the Option key is getting overloaded as it is, turn it off. Why might you think that? Because Option is used for "Bend-o-matic" path drawing (see "Bend-o-matic" in Chapter 2, "Drawing"), and for forcing a preview drag (see "Preview Drag," earlier in this chapter), and for dragging control handles out of points on a path (see "Manipulating Control Handles," in Chapter 2, "Drawing"). Still, I keep this one turned on.

Text Editing

The controls in the Text Editing Preferences dialog box, as you'd expect, affect the way that you work with text in your FreeHand publications (see figure 1-75).

Always Use Text Editor Dialog. If you always want to use the Text Editor to edit and enter text, turn this option on. Yes, I have met people who want to do this, and no, I don't think they're crazy—though they're mostly cartographers, and that's pretty close. If you prefer editing text on the page, leave this option turned off—you can always switch to the Text Editor dialog box by selecting a text block and pressing Command-Shift-E.

Track Tab Movement with Vertical Line. Here's one of my favorites: turn this on, and a vertical line appears when you drag a tab marker on the tab ruler (see figure 1-76). The line runs through the tab marker, through the text, and, in fact, all the way to the vertical ruler at the top of the page (provided, of couse, that you've got FreeHand's rulers turned on). This makes it very easy to see

FIGURE 1-75
Text Editing
Preferences
dialog box

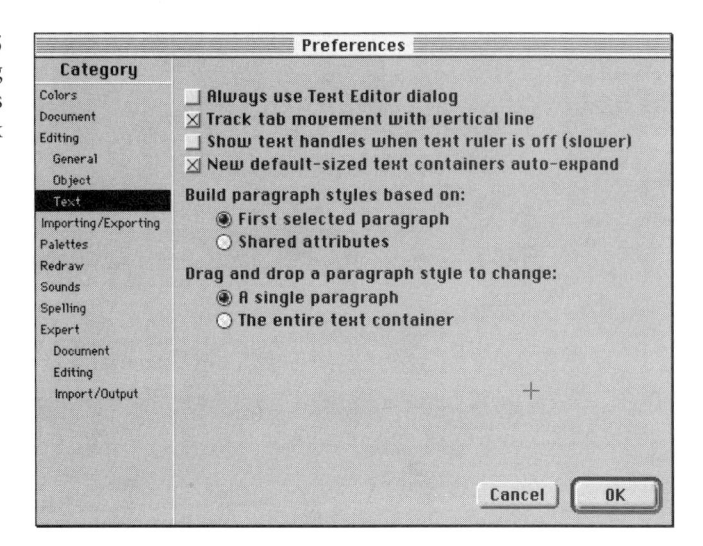

FIGURE 1-76
Tracking
tab movement

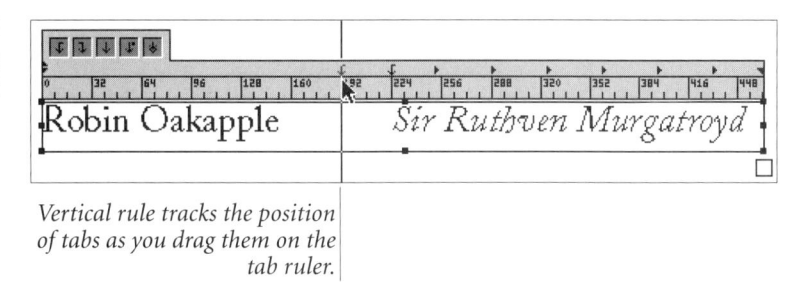

Vertical rule tracks the position of tabs as you drag them on the tab ruler.

where the tab's going, and even provides this book with another sleazy tip—see "Indent to Here," in Chapter 3, "Text and Type."

Show Text Handles When Text Ruler Is Off. If you've turned the Text Ruler off (by pressing Command-/), turning this option on displays the selection handles of a text block as you edit the text in that text block (FreeHand always displays text block handles when you select the text block with the Pointer tool). When this option is turned off, and you've turned off the Text Ruler, FreeHand won't display a text block's selection handles while you're editing text (see figure 1-77).

If you find you're doing lots of text block resizing as you edit, and you prefer to work without displaying the Text Ruler, you might want to turn this option on (see Chapter 3, "Text and Type," for more on working with the Text Ruler).

FIGURE 1-77
Displaying or hiding
text block handles

*Editing text with the
Show Text Handles When
Text Ruler Is Off option
turned off.*

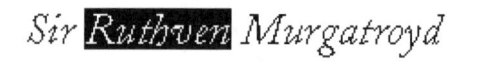

*Editing text with the
Show Text Handles When
Text Ruler Is Off option
turned on.*

New Default-Sized Text Containers Auto-Expand. What's a default-sized text container? It's what you get when you *click*—as opposed to *drag*—the text tool (see "Creating Text Blocks," in Chapter 3, "Text and Type"). If you're typing captions, or other one-line blocks of text, and want the text blocks to be the size of the text, turn this option on, then create your text blocks by clicking the text tool and typing. When you leave this option turned off, clicking the text tool will produce text blocks 18 picas wide by about 12 picas tall. In either case, dragging the text tool gives you the ability to create text blocks of any width and height.

Build Paragraph Styles Based On. When you're creating styles, and have multiple paragraphs selected, FreeHand needs to know whether you want to create a style based on all the paragraphs in the selection (turn on the Shared Attributes option), or on only the first paragraph in the selection (use the FreeHand first Selected Paragraph option).

If you choose the Shared Attributes option, you run the risk (or accrue the advantage, depending on your point of view) of creating paragraph styles that lack some attributes—if, for example, the paragraphs in your selection have more than one leading, your style won't include a leading value—which means that applying the style won't affect the leading of the paragraphs you're applying it to. While this has some uses, it might not be what you want (see "Defining Styles" in Chapter 3, "Text and Type").

Drag and Drop a Paragraph Style to Change. If you apply styles by dragging and dropping (see "Applying Styles" in Chapter 3, "Text and Type"), you can choose whether the style you're applying affects only the paragraph you dropped it on (turn on the A Single

Paragraph option), or affects all of the paragraphs in the text block (turn on The Entire Text Container option).

Importing and Exporting
Click "Importing/Exporting" in the Preferences List, and FreeHand displays the Import/Export Preferences dialog box (see figure 1-78).

Convert Editable EPS When Placed. FreeHand can open a wide variety of EPS formats and convert their contents to FreeHand objects. In general, these converted files print faster than placed EPS files—and they're editable, to boot (see "Importing EPS Graphics," in Chapter 4, "Importing and Exporting"). When you turn on the Convert Editable EPS When Placed option, FreeHand converts EPS files you bring into FreeHand using the Place command, just as it would if you opened the files using the Open command.

What's the difference? You save a step. If you use "Open," you'll have to copy the converted objects from a new, untitled publication into your current publication—but, if you use "Place," the converted objects appear as a group in your current publication.

Convert PICT Patterns to Grays. When you import object PICT files, such as those created by MacDraw or Canvas, FreeHand needs to know what to do with any PICT patterns used to represent shades of gray (like those you see when you choose Pattern

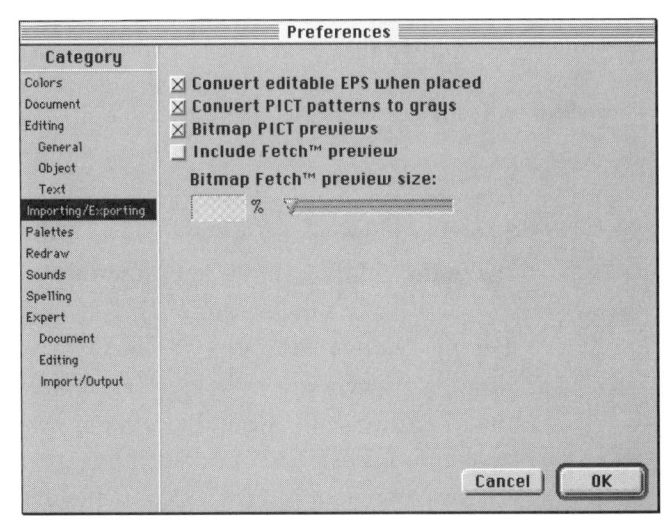

FIGURE 1-78
Importing/Exporting Preferences dialog box

from the popup menu in the fill Inspector). In my opinion, you should turn this preference on—and leave it that way.

PICT patterns are no substitute for real gray shades, and they don't print reliably on imagesetters. If you've just got to have those PICT patterns, go ahead and leave this option unchecked, but don't say I didn't warn you (for more on patterned fills, see "Patterned fills" in Chapter 2, "Drawing").

Note that this option has nothing to do with bitmap PICT files—bitmap PICT files are always converted to TIFF when you place or open them (for more on this conversion, see Chapter 4, "Importing and Exporting").

Bitmap PICT Previews. When this option is off, Macintosh EPS files you export from FreeHand contain object (or vector) PICT previews—almost like using a MacDraw file for a screen preview. Object PICT previews provide more accurate screen previews than bitmaps—but they also take substantially longer to draw on your screen, and can be larger than a TIFF preview of the same graphic.

Include Fetch Preview. If you plan to add exported FreeHand files to an Aldus Fetch image database, check this option. If you don't, leave it unchecked—the previews make your exported files larger.

When you check this option, you can choose how large you want to make the preview—using the Bitmap Fetch Preview Size option. As you'd expect, larger previews are more accurate representations of your file, and they also take up more space on disk. As you do this, remember that most people look at previews in Fetch in Thumbnail view, so you can probably get by with a small (say, 25 percent) preview.

Palettes

The settings in the Palettes Preferences dialog box tell FreeHand how you'd like to deal with a few small-but-important issues having to do with FreeHand's user interface (see figure 1-79).

Hiding Palettes Hides the Toolbox. Do you want the Toolbox to disappear when you hide FreeHand's palettes (by pressing Command-Shift-H)? Or would you like it to stay around? Check this option to make it disappear with the others, or leave it unchecked to leave it on your screen. It's your choice.

FIGURE 1-79
Palettes Preferences
dialog box

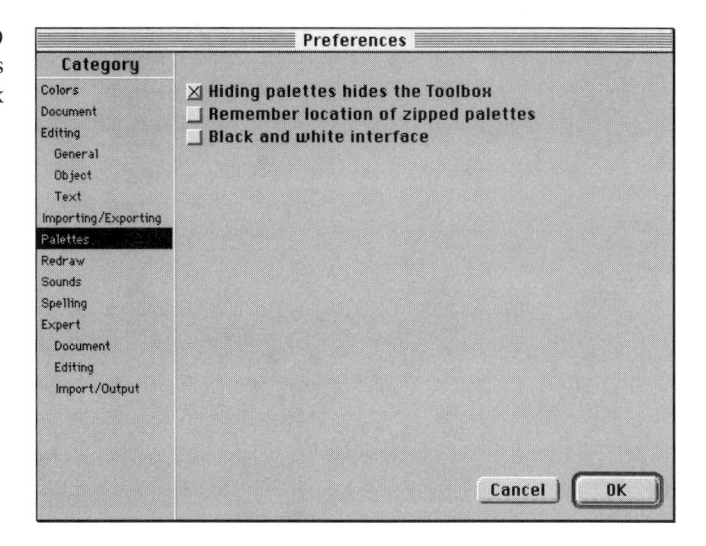

Remember the Location of Zipped Palettes. When you turn this option on, FreeHand keeps track of the location of a palette's title bar when you zip the palette. Unzip the palette, drag it to some new location, and then click the zip box to zip the palette back up again, and the zipped title bar of the palette reappears in the position it was in before you unzipped and moved the palette.

This is useful, because it means you can assign a "storage" area for your palettes, where you keep a stack of zipped title bars, and then set each palette to open to some more useful location on your screen. Park the palettes in some part of the screen that you rarely use, then set the unzipped palettes to appear in the areas you like to work in.

This wouldn't do us much good, of course, if we had to drag our cursor across the screen to unzip the palettes—but you don't have to use the zip box to unzip the palettes. Just press the keyboard shortcut for a particular palette that's zipped, and FreeHand will unzip the palette and move it to the pre-set location.

Use this technique consistently, and you'll always *know* where a particular palette is going to show up when you call for it.

Black and White Interface. As I mentioned earlier, FreeHand 5's controls—the dialog boxes, palettes, and buttons you work with on your screen—have a beautiful 3-D look. If you liked the way the controls looked in FreeHand 4—they're simpler, and they're drawn in black-and-white, not shades of gray—you can return to that look by checking this option (see figure 1-80). If you're working on a monochrome monitor, choosing the black-and-white version of the interface won't make your copy of FreeHand run faster, and it won't make it look any different.

FIGURE 1-80
Interface options

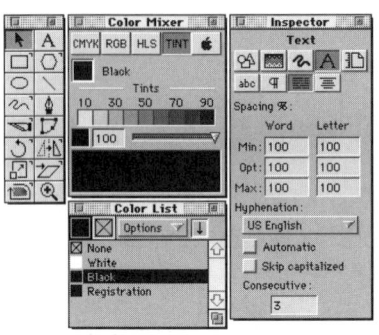

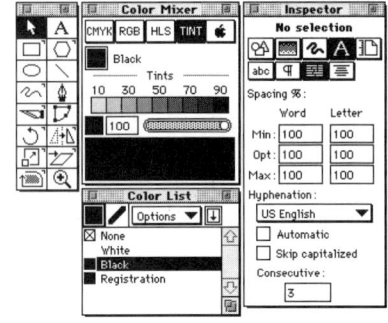

FreeHand palettes with the Black and White Interface option turned off.

FreeHand palettes with the Black and White Interface option turned on.

Redraw

The options in the Redraw Preferences dialog box control the way that FreeHand draws objects on your screen (see figure 1-81). Many of these preferences can speed up—or slow down—the time it takes FreeHand to draw the screen.

FIGURE 1-81
Redraw Preferences
dialog box

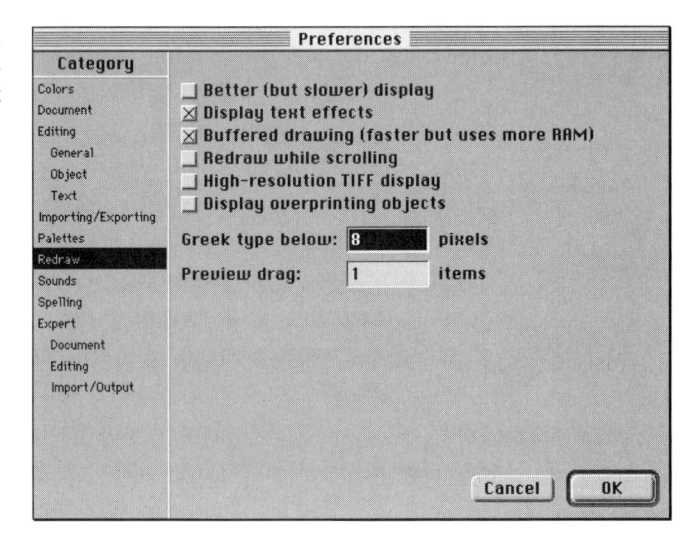

Better (but Slower) Display. When the Better (but Slower) Display option is turned off, FreeHand draws graduated and radial fills on screen more rapidly, using fewer gray steps to render them. Turn it on to see a better representation of your fills on screen. This option has no effect on the printing of the fills.

Display Text Effects. The Display Text Effects option displays any of FreeHand's text effects you've applied to text blocks in your publication. If you don't turn this option on, you'll see the text displayed at the correct size and leading, but without the effects. If the text effects extend beyond the text block (Zoom Text often does, for example), the selection rectangle shows the extent of the text and the effects when you move the text block. Turning this option on shows you your text effects, but slows down your screen display (see figure 1-82).

Buffered Drawing. From your Macintosh's point of view, you're very slow. And you don't do very much work, either. FreeHand makes use of the spare time between your mouse clicks and keystrokes drawing all of the objects in your publication—off screen,

FIGURE 1-82
Display Text
Effects option

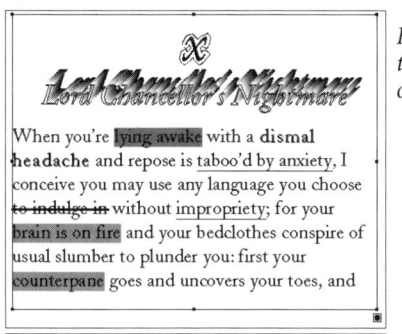

FreeHand's text effects with the Display Text Effects option turned on.

FreeHand's text effects with the Display Text Effects option turned off.

where you can't see them. Then, when you do something that requires FreeHand to redraw the screen, it blasts them onto the screen at once. This results in faster screen display.

The only drawback to the off-screen drawing technique is that it consumes more memory than drawing each object individually when redrawing the screen. Therefore, any time RAM is limited, FreeHand draws object by object.

Redraw While Scrolling. If you want FreeHand to redraw while you're scrolling, check this option. If you'd rather FreeHand waited to redraw the screen until you've finished scrolling, leave it unchecked. This option affects both scrolling using the scroll bars and scrolling using the Grabber Hand (for more on using the Grabber Hand to scroll, see "Moving Around in Your Publication," later in this chapter). FreeHand always redraws the screen when you scroll while you're dragging an object. Turning this option on makes scrolling slower.

High-Resolution TIFF Display. If you check this option, FreeHand gets its information about how to render a TIFF from the original TIFF file that's linked to your FreeHand publication, which means that FreeHand renders the best possible display of the TIFF image for your current magnification level. With this option off, FreeHand constructs a low-resolution screen version of the image and uses it for display at all magnification levels (see figure 1-83).

The tradeoff is the speed of screen redraw. High-resolution TIFF images can take forever to draw on your screen. Given this, it's a good idea to leave this option unchecked until those times when you absolutely must see all of the detail in the TIFF.

FIGURE 1-83
High- and low-resolution TIFF display options

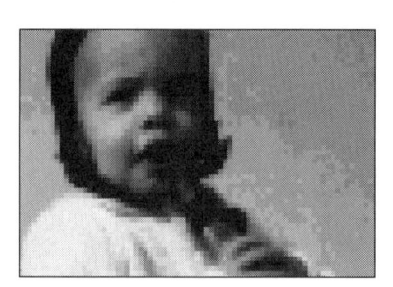

Low-resolution TIFF display

High-resolution TIFF display

Display Overprinting Objects. When you check this checkbox, FreeHand displays a pattern—a repeated "O"—inside any fill or stroke that's set to overprint. With this option on, you can quickly see what's set to overprint and what's not (see figure 1-84).

I don't leave this option on—I find the pattern distracting, and it looks too much like the pattern of repeating Cs FreeHand uses to denote a Custom fill (see "Custom fills," in Chapter 2, "Drawing"). But it's a great option to turn on just before you send your file out for imagesetting.

FIGURE 1-84
Displaying overprinting

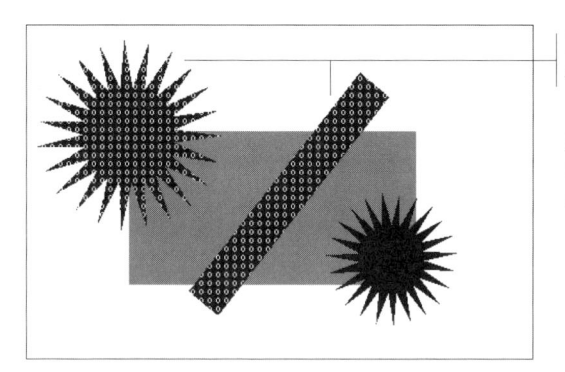

These two objects are set to overprint.

Display Overprinting Objects option turned on.

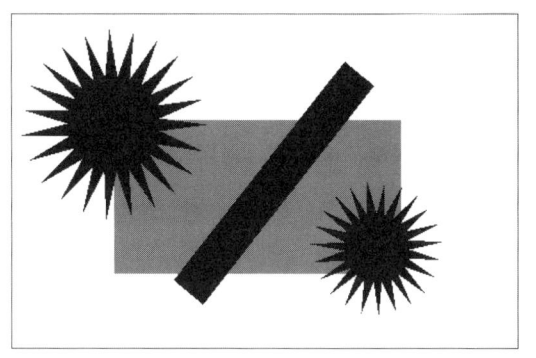

Display Overprinting Objects option turned off.

Greek Type Below N Pixels. This option displays type as a gray bar if it's shorter, in pixels, than the value you enter. As you zoom close to the text, you'll see the characters in the text block again (see figure 1-85). This happens because the type's taller, in pixels, at larger magnifications.

The advantage of using this option is that greeked type redraws much faster than the actual characters, speeding up your screen display. This option applies to both Preview and Keyline views.

FIGURE 1-85
Greeked type

24-point type at 100% view; Greek Type Below set to six points.

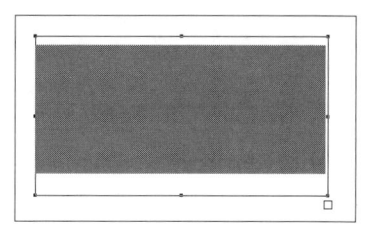

24-point type at 100% view; Greek Type Below set to 100 points.

Tip:
Greek All (or Almost All)

You can always choose to greek all (almost, anyway) of the text in your document at most views by entering "200"—the largest value you can enter—in the Greek Type Below field. This will greek all type below 200 points at 100% view, and all type below 400 points at most fit Page views (the exact magnification of the fit Page view depends on the size of your page).

Preview Drag. When you drag an object quickly, FreeHand displays only a box showing the general dimensions of the object. If you pause slightly before you drag the object, however, FreeHand displays the object itself as you drag (see figure 1-86). When the value in the Preview Drag field is one (FreeHand's default), FreeHand always displays a box (that is, not the objects themselves) when you're dragging more than one object. Increase this value, and you'll be able to see more objects as you drag them, but the amount of time you'll have to wait before FreeHand redraws the objects increases commensurately. You can enter values from zero to 32,000 (don't even think about it!) in this field.

FIGURE 1-86
Preview Drag

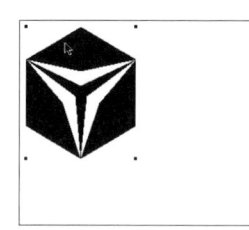

Select the object you want to move.

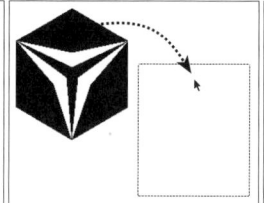

Drag quickly, and FreeHand displays only the object's bounding box as you drag.

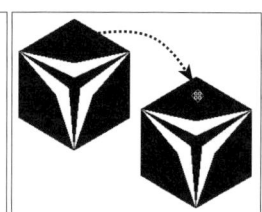

Wait a second (or tap Option) and FreeHand displays the object as you move it.

Tip:
Viewing Objects as You Drag Them

Tap the Option key as you start to drag an object or objects, and FreeHand displays the objects as you drag them (don't hold down Option, as this creates a copy of the objects you're dragging). It's a temporary way of turning on Preview Drag. So instead of increasing the value in the Preview Drag field, leave it at one—or even set it to zero—and tap Option when you want to see objects as you drag them.

Sounds

Choose Sounds from the Preferences list, and FreeHand displays the Sounds Preferences dialog box (see figure 1-87). When you check Snap Sounds Enabled, FreeHand plays a sound when a snap happens. When you're dragging an object toward a ruler guide, for example, you might want to hear it snap into position.

Snap to Grid, Snap to Point, Snap to H(orizontal)-Guide, Snap to V(ertical)-Guide. If you want to hear different sounds for different snaps, you can choose the sounds you want here—all of the sounds currently in your system appear in the popup menus. If you want to audition a particular sound before committing yourself to hearing it thousands of times, select the sound from the popup menu and press the appropriate Play button.

Snap Sounds Enabled. Turn on this checkbox to enable the snap sounds you've selected above.

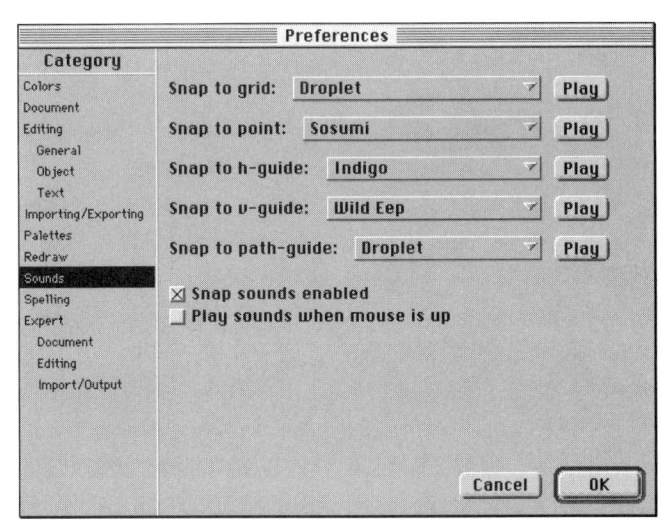

FIGURE 1-87
Sounds Preferences dialog box

Play Sounds When Mouse Is Up. Turn on this option if you want to hear the snap sounds whenever your cursor crosses a snap point, regardless of whether you're moving or sizing an object. This is actually useful when you're trying to draw something on a grid—you'll hear a sound if you're in the right place to start drawing. Most of the time, however, this makes FreeHand sound like an out-of-control video game.

Spelling

One of the great innovations of the word processing age is the spelling checker—something which, until now, we FreeHand users have been without. Now, however, we've got one, and we've got preference settings to go with it (see figure 1-88).

find Duplicate Words. Do you want FreeHand's spelling checker to let you know when it finds duplicate words in your text? ("He said he had had it up to here," for example, would produce an alert.) If so, turn this option on.

find Capitalization Errors. You can also ask FreeHand's spelling checker to look for possible errors in the capitalization of characters in your text. When this option is on, FreeHand will warn you if it encounters a lowercase letter at the start of a sentence.

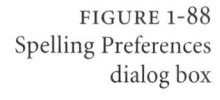

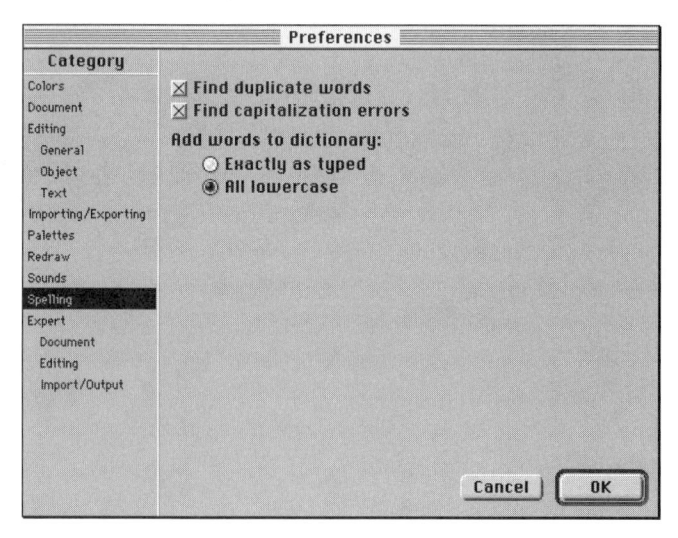

FIGURE 1-88
Spelling Preferences dialog box

Add Words to Dictionary. You know lots of words that aren't in FreeHand's spelling dictionary. Like your name. Or, almost certainly, *my* name. If you're tired of having FreeHand's spelling checker object to a word you frequently use in your publications, then the thing to do is enter that word in your user dictionary (see "Adding Words to FreeHand's User Dictionary" in Chapter 3, "Text and Type").

But wait—do you want Freehand to consider the case of the word you're entering? That is, do you want FreeHand to alert you to words that have the same spelling, but aren't capitalized in the same way as you entered them? That's where the Exactly as Typed and All Lowercase options come in. If you want FreeHand to check both the spelling and the capitalization of the word you're entering, turn on the Exactly As Typed option (then enter the word as you want it capitalized). If you want FreeHand to ignore the capitalization of the word as it checks the word's spelling, use the All Lowercase button.

I know—"all lowercase" sounds like FreeHand's spelling checker will flag a word as misspelled if its first character is capitalized (because it's in a title or at the start of a sentence, for example). That isn't how it works. Try to think of the buttons as "Case sensitive" and "Case insensitive." That makes a little more sense (not that this wording is FreeHand's fault alone—Word, PageMaker, and XPress all say the same thing).

Expert Document

While these preferences are named "Expert," don't be shy—there are things here just about everyone can use (see figure 1-89).

Default Template for New Documents. What's the name of the template file FreeHand bases new publications on? Whatever you enter here. By default, FreeHand's template file is named "FreeHand Defaults," but you can change that name to anything you want. The name you enter here must match the name of an existing file, and that file must have been saved as a template. If the names don't match, or if FreeHand can't find the file, or if the file wasn't saved as a template, FreeHand will create new publicatons based on the original, default settings (which also happen to be duplicated inside FreeHand for just such an occurrence).

FIGURE 1-89
Expert Document
Preferences dialog box

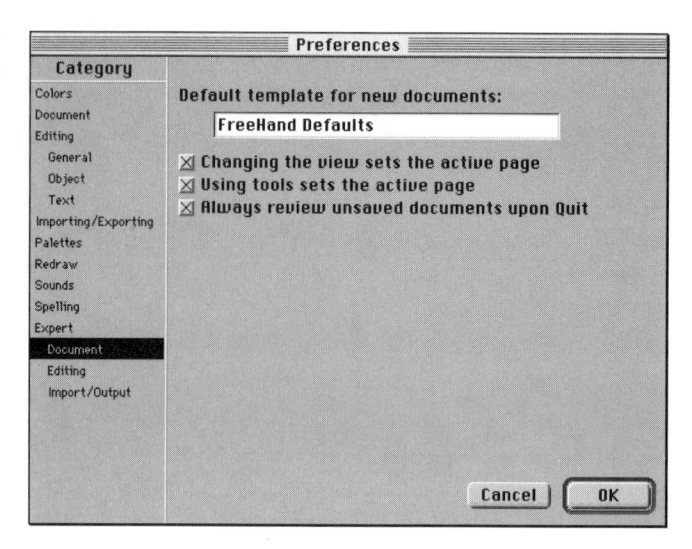

Tip:
Oops!

It's driving you crazy. You keep changing the default template (usually the "Freehand Defaults" file in your Freehand folder), but your new documents don't seem to be picking up the changes! What's going on?

It's likely that the template file's been renamed or deleted—go check the Default Template for New Documents field. Is there a filename in it? If not, enter one. If so, does that filename exactly match what you've been calling your template file? If not, change the name so that it matches, and create a new publication. The new publicaton appears with your new default settings in effect.

Tip:
Working with
Multiple Defaults
files

Suppose you do lots of work for two different clients. Each client has their own set of logos, their own favorite typeface and type size, and their own corporate colors. While you could load your defaults file with everything you needed to work on publications for either client, you'll have to make some compromises (do new files start off with the font favored by Client A or Client B?), and it can get confusing (is that a color I use for Client A, or is it Client B's?). Wouldn't it be great if you could have two default files—one for Client A and one for Client B?

You can—just create two template files, each containing the different settings. When you want to change defaults files, enter the new defaults file name in the Default Template for New Documents field of the Expert Document Preferences dialog box. From that point on, each new publication will be based on the template file you specify. Want to change it? Go enter another template name in the field.

Changing the View Sets the Active Page. In FreeHand, the "active page" is the page selected in the thumbnail view of the pasteboard in the Document Inspector (see figure 1-90). When this option is turned on, FreeHand sets the active page to the page taking up the largest percentage of your publication window—which might, or might not be the page you're working on. Since the active page determines the effect of the choices on the Magnification submenu of the View menu (or their keyboard equivalents), you can end up jumping to some other page—and away from your work—when you have this option turned on.

When this option is turned off, you set the active page by clicking the thumbnail of the page in the Document Inspector.

FIGURE 1-90
Active page

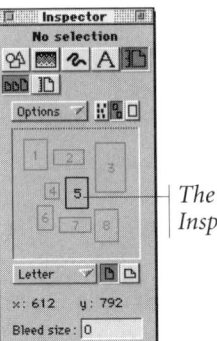

The page highlighted in FreeHand's Document Inspector is the active page.

Always Review Unsaved Documents Upon Quit. Are you sick of having FreeHand ask if you want to review unsaved publications when you quit? If so, turn this option off. I'm senile enough, at this point, that I like the reminder, so I leave it on.

Expert Editing

When you click "Editing" in the "Expert" section of the Preferences list, FreeHand displays the Expert Editing Preferences dialog box (see figure 1-91).

Default Line Weights. Do you find yourself wishing for different choices on the Stroke Weights submenu of the Arrange menu?

FIGURE 1-91
Expert Editing
Preferences dialog box

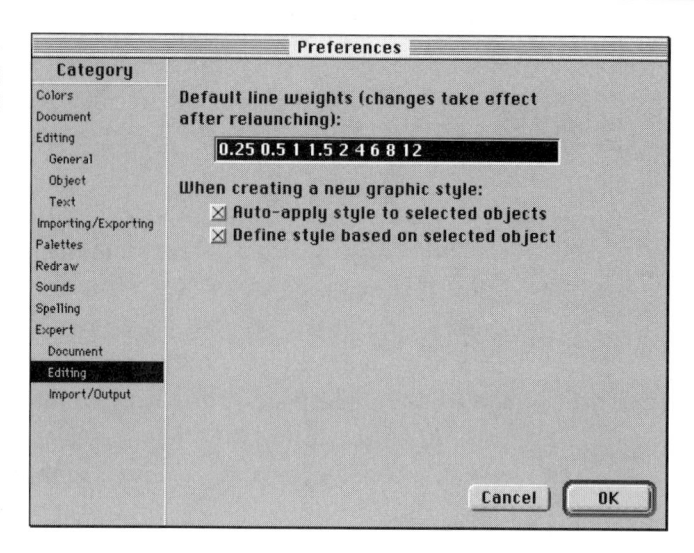

Suppose, for example, you're always working with a 3.5-point line. You can add (or subtract) line weights by entering (or deleting) them in the Default Line Weights field. If you want to add a stroke weight, type it here (separating it from other weights with a space). Restart FreeHand, and you'll see the weight you entered on the Stroke Weights submenu.

When Creating a New Graphic Style. Look. I try not to insist that the way I like to work is the best way to work (sometimes, I'm *sure* it's not). In this section, I'm trying to present FreeHand's features in a neutral, objective, and fair way, and leave the conclusions up to you. But, in this case, I've got to say that if you want to make your life easier, you'll just leave these two options checked (see "Creating Styles by Example," in Chapter 2, "Drawing" and in Chapter 3, "Text and Type").

When the Auto Apply Style to Selected Objects option is on, FreeHand applies a style you've created to the object that's selected when you create it. Ordinarily, you create a style based on an example object, so you definitely *want* the style applied to that object. Or maybe you don't—in which case you can turn this option off. But don't say I didn't warn you.

If you prefer defining styles using the Edit Style dialog box, and *never* want to define styles by example, you might think about turning the Define Style Based on Selected Object option off. If you're like me, and think that defining styles by example is the easiest and quickest way to define styles, you should leave this option turned on.

Expert Import/Output

The Expert Import/Output Preferences dialog box (click "Import/Export" under "Expert" in the Preferences list) contains interesting and useful settings that were hidden away in the FreeHand Preferences file in FreeHand 4. Now they're here—out in the open, where everyone can see and use them (see figure 1-92).

Name of UserPrep file. FreeHand's UserPrep files give you the ability to customize your PostScript printing. It's pretty simple—if FreeHand finds the file named in the Name of UserPrep file field inside the FreeHand folder, it sends the contents of the file to your printer prior to sending your print job. Technically speaking, the contents of the UserPrep file are merged into the PostScript output stream immediately after FreeHand downloads FreeHand's user dictionaries, but before FreeHand sends any of the document you're printing. You can control which, if any, UserPrep file gets sent by entering the file's name here. (See Chapter 8, "PostScript," for more on what you can do with a UserPrep file).

FIGURE 1-92
Expert Import/Export Preferences dialog box

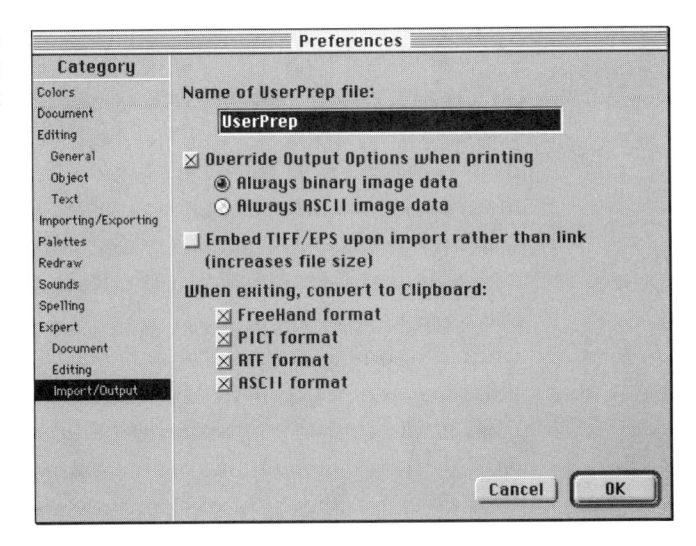

Override Output Options when Printing. Why would you ever want to override the Image Data options that you've set in the Output Options dialog box? I don't think you would, mostly—but you might if you're printing to a proof printer but exporting EPS files for use on an OPI-compliant prepress system. In this case, you'd probably be using the None (OPI Comments Only) option in the Output Options dialog box. By turning on the Always Binary Image Data option here, you'd be able to print images on your proof printer without changing the settings in the Output Options dialog box. (For more on the Output Options dialog box, see Chapter 9, "Printing.")

Embed TIFF/EPS Upon Import Rather than Link. By default, FreeHand doesn't store imported TIFF images or EPS graphics in your publications when you place them. Instead, FreeHand establishes a link to the file on disk. When the time comes to print or export the file, FreeHand goes out to the linked file and gets the information it needs. If you'd rather store—or "embed"—the file in your FreeHand publication, turn this option on. Your publication will increase in size by the size of the files—in effect, you end up storing the files twice. Still, it means you have only one file to worry about.

When Exiting, Convert to Clipboard. When you switch to another application, or when you quit FreeHand, you've probably seen the message "Converting Clipboard" go by on your screen. What's going on? FreeHand is rendering the contents of its internal Clipboard to the Macintosh Clipboard. This means that FreeHand has to convert FreeHand's native (AGX1) format into formats other applications can use, such as PICT, RTF, and ASCII (text-only)—just in case you want to paste objects you've copied from FreeHand into some other application.

If you think this process takes too long, you can turn off some or all of the conversions by checking the corresponding options. Don't turn off the FreeHand Format option if you're copying FreeHand objects to the Scrapbook for future use, however.

The Tao of FreeHand

Here are those rules I promised at the beginning of the chapter.

Keep it simple. I don't mean that you shouldn't create complex publications. I mean create publications with an understanding of what's difficult for PostScript printers (especially imagesetters) to do, and do those things sparingly. You can probably just fill a complex path with a tiled fill, for example, rather than drawing a rectangle, filling it with the tiled fill, and pasting it inside the path. If you've got to use Paste Inside, avoid having more than around 50 (and certainly fewer than 100 in all cases!) points on the containing path. If you don't, you'll get PostScript errors when you print. Understand, too, that adding RGB TIFFs or "colorizing" grayscale TIFFs dramatically increases printing time and makes it more likely you'll get a "VMerror" instead of a set of separations.

Again, I'm not saying that you shouldn't use these features or work with these file types—I'm saying that you should be conscious, as you use them, that they present a certain set of risks.

Use styles. I haven't really mentioned styles yet, but I will in Chapter 2, "Drawing," and again in Chapter 3, "Text and Type." Unless you work for people who never change their minds, and you never change your mind yourself, you need the ability to change things quickly and systematically—and that's where styles really shine. If you work for people who never change their minds, and you never change your mind yourself, please give me a call—I've never met anyone like you.

Use layers. And use them systematically. Not only will you find your publications easier to work with if you've spread the publication elements over several logical layers, but you'll be able to speed up your screen display, as well. Layers can speed printing, too.

Use trapping. I can't think of the number of color jobs I've ruined because of failing to think of trapping elements—especially type. See "Trapping" in Chapter 6, "Color."

Use color proofs. If you're working with process colors, it's an absolute necessity to make Cromalins (or Match Prints, or the equivalent) from the same negatives you intend to use to print the publication. They're expensive, but they're cheaper than thousands of publications printed the wrong way because the film was wrong. Believe me.

Talk to your commercial printer. This can often save you lots of time and money. The thing to remember when you're talking with your printer is that they're the experts. Don't be a jerk. Don't assume you know their job better than they do (you might, but don't assume you do). If possible, work out a printing contract for your job that spells out in exact terms what you expect of them and what they expect of you.

Talk to your imagesetting service bureau. first, ask them how to make PostScript files from FreeHand. If they don't know, start looking for another service bureau. Once you've found a service bureau that can answer that question, approach them very much the way you'd approach your commercial printer. A good working relationship with an imagesetting service bureau or inhouse imagesetter operator is essential.

CHAPTER

Drawing

2

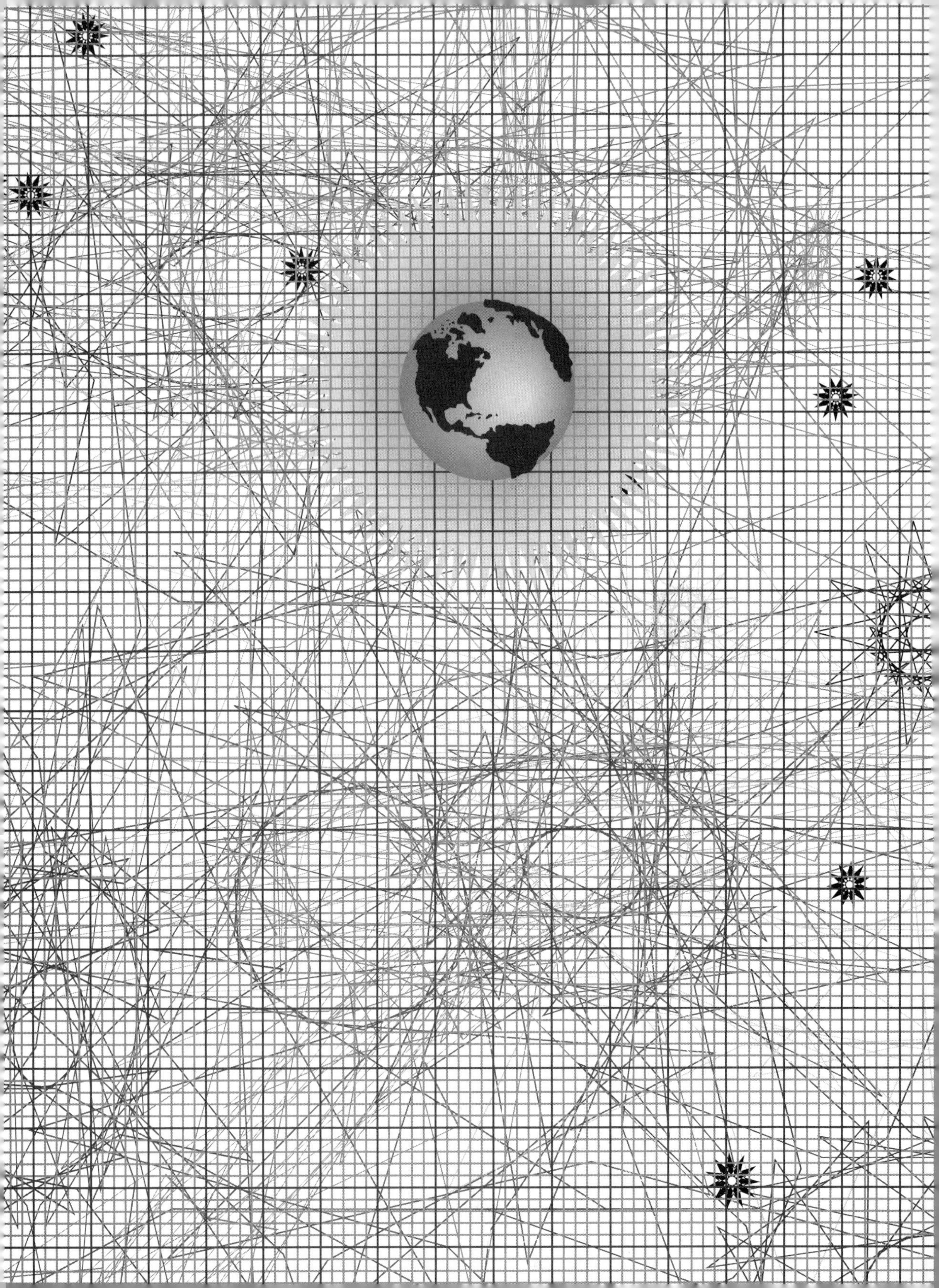

CHAPTER TWO   §   DRAWING

Human beings draw pictures.

The walls of caves inhabited since prehistoric times, the interiors of the tombs of the Pharaohs, and the development of desktop publishing all show that we're a kind of animal that likes to make marks on things. Drawing is at the center of us; it's one of the unique attributes that make us human.

Drawing is also at the heart of FreeHand. Seven of the 16 tools in the FreeHand toolbox are drawing tools. Using these tools, you can draw almost anything—from straight lines and boxes to incredibly complex freeform paths.

As I explained in Chapter 1, "FreeHand Basics," the lines you draw in FreeHand are made up of points, and the points are connected by line segments. A FreeHand line is just like a connect-the-dots puzzle. Connect all the dots in the right order, and you've made a picture, or part of a picture. Because points along a line have an order, or winding, we call the lines "paths," and you can think of each point as a milepost along the path. Or as a sign saying, "Now go this way."

The drawing tools can be divided into two types: the Rectangle, Polygon, Ellipse, and Line tools are for drawing basic shapes; the Freehand, Pen, and Point tools draw more complex, or "freeform," paths (see Figure 2-1).

Which tools should you use? Don't worry too much about the distinction. The basic shapes drawn with the basic shapes tools can be converted into freeform paths, and the freeform drawing tools

FIGURE 2-1
Drawing tools

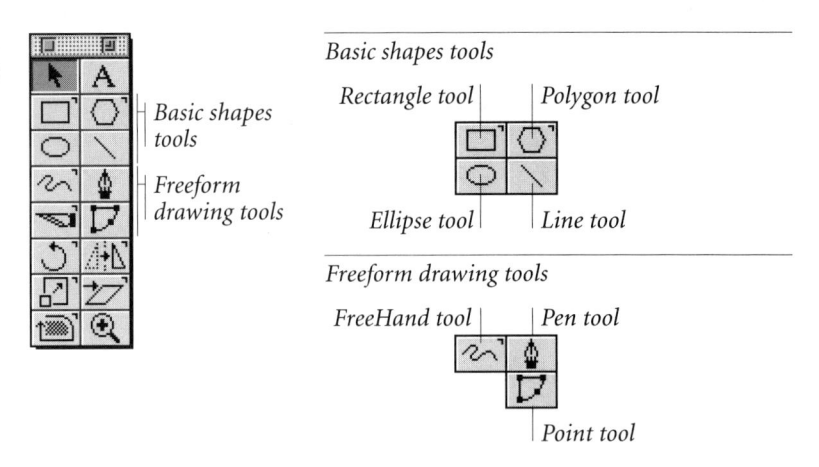

Basic shapes tools

Rectangle tool | Polygon tool

Ellipse tool | Line tool

Freeform drawing tools

FreeHand tool | Pen tool

Point tool

can be used to draw the same basic shapes. You can draw any path with any of the drawing tools (I was once stranded on a desert island with nothing but the Polygon tool, and survived), but some tools are better at some tasks, as I'll show you in the following sections.

Basic Shapes

The basic shape tools (the Rectangle, Polygon, Ellipse, and Line tools) don't draw anything you couldn't draw using the freeform drawing tools (discussed later in this chapter); they just make drawing certain types of paths easier. They're shortcuts.

The operation of the basic shapes tools is straightforward, but there are a few details you need to know. If you're a FreeHand aces, you might want to skip the next few paragraphs. It isn't that I'm getting paid by the word to write this (I'm not), but that I'm trying to cover all the bases. It's amazing, too, what people can miss when they're learning a software product; I've seen FreeHand gurus who could write their own PostScript fills and strokes but weren't aware that you could turn a rectangle drawn with the rectangle tool into a rounded-corner rectangle.

You can think of the paths drawn by the Rectangle and Ellipse tools as grouped paths. These paths have a few other special properties, as well, that you can't get by grouping a path drawn with the freeform drawing tools.

- You can edit the corner radius of rectangles drawn using the Rectangle tool.

- Basic shapes have a special constraint key you can use when you resize them, as described in the section, "Resizing Rectangles and Ellipses," below.

These magical properties disappear when you convert rectangles and ellipses into freeform paths (see "Converting Rectangles and Ellipses into Paths," below), and there's no way to convert the converted path back to its original state (apart from using Undo).

To draw a rectangle, ellipse, or polygon, follow the steps below (see Figure 2-2).

1. Select the appropriate tool from the toolbox (press 1 for the Rectangle tool, 2 for the Polygon tool, or 3 for the Ellipse tool).

    If you want to draw a rectangle with round (rather than square) corners, double-click the Rectangle tool and set the corner radius you want in the Rectangle dialog box before you start drawing.

    To specify what type of polygon you'll be drawing, double-click the Polygon tool and specify the polygon you want in the Polygon dialog box before you start drawing.

2. Position the cursor where you want one corner of the shape. Or position the cursor where you want the center of the shape, and hold down Option. When you use the first method, you draw from one corner of the shape. When you use the second method, you draw out from the center of the shape.

3. Press down the mouse button and drag the mouse. FreeHand draws a path, starting where you clicked the mouse button.

    If you hold down Shift as you draw with the Rectangle tool, you draw squares. Hold down Shift as you drag the Ellipse tool, and you draw circles. Holding down Shift as you drag the Polygon tool constrains the rotation of the

FIGURE 2-2
Drawing basic shapes

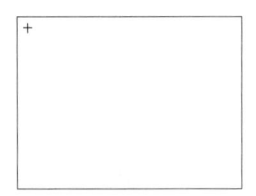

Select the basic shape tool (Rectangle, Polygon, or Ellipse)...

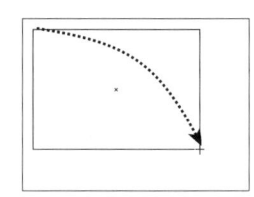

...and drag the tool in the publication window. When the basic shape looks the way you want it to...

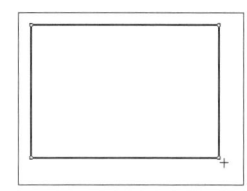

...stop dragging and release the mouse button.

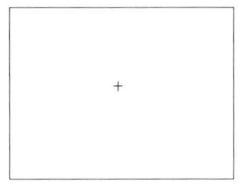

If you want to draw from the center of the basic shape (rather than from the corner)...

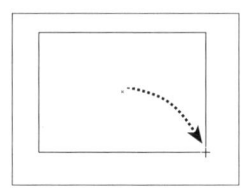

...hold down Option as you drag the tool. Polygons are always drawn from their center point.

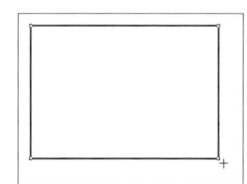

Stop dragging when the basic shape looks the way you want it to.

polygon (you can rotate the polygon as you draw) to 15-degree increments.

4. When the rectangle is the size and shape you want it to be, stop dragging and release the mouse button.

Drawing Lines

To draw a path as a single line segment between two corner points, follow these steps (see Figure 2-3).

1. Select the Line tool from the toolbox (or press 2).

2. Position the cursor where you want one end of the line to fall.

3. Press down the mouse button and drag the mouse. Free-Hand draws a line, starting where you clicked the mouse button. If you want to constrain your line to 45-degree increments (based on the angle you entered in the Constrain field of the Setup Inspector), hold down Shift as you draw the line.

DRAWING 109

FIGURE 2-3
Using the Line tool

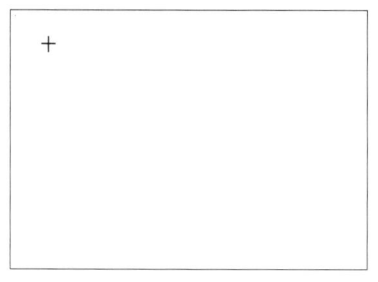

Position the line tool where you want one end of the line to start.

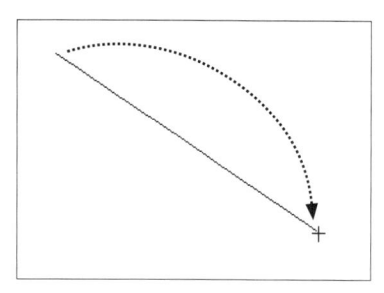

Drag the line tool across the page. Hold down Shift as you drag to constrain the line to 45-degree angles.

4. When the line is the length you want, stop dragging the mouse, and release the mouse button.

Resizing Rectangles and Ellipses

To resize any of the basic shapes, use the Pointer tool to select the rectangle or ellipse you want to resize and then drag any corner handle.

If you hold down Option as you drag a corner handle, FreeHand uses a special type of constraint that only works with groups (FreeHand thinks of rectangles and ellipses as groups), and resizes the object around its center point (see Figure 2-4). This is a very handy feature when you need to enlarge an object while leaving its center in the same place.

FIGURE 2-4
Special constraint for basic shapes

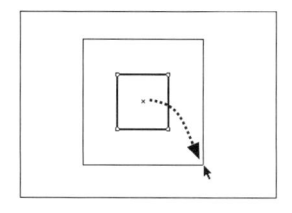

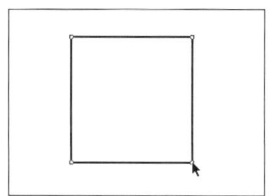

When you hold down Option as you resize a basic shape, FreeHand resizes the basic shape from its center.

Proportionally Resizing Rectangles and Ellipses

If you want to resize a rectangle or ellipse proportionally, you'd expect that you could just hold down Shift and drag a corner handle, but you can't—unless you're resizing a circle or a square—because holding down Shift and dragging a corner handle turns the object into a circle or square.

To resize a rectangle or ellipse proportionally, select the shape using the pointer tool, and then press Command-G to group the shape. Position the Pointer tool over any corner handle. Hold down Shift and drag the corner handle to resize the shape (see Figure 2-5). Ungroup the shape after you finish resizing it.

FIGURE 2-5
Proportionally resizing rectangles and ellipses

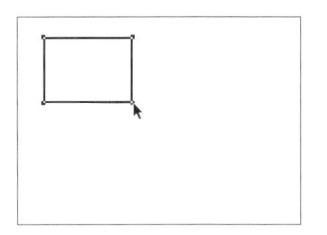

Select a basic shape, press Command-G, hold down Shift...

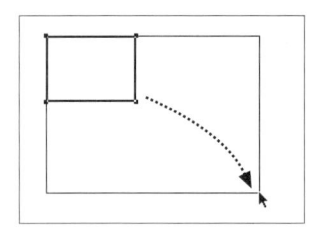

...and then drag the corner handle to proportionally resize the basic shape.

Changing a Rectangle's Corner Radius

To change a rectangle with square corners into a rectangle with rounded corners, select the rectangle with the Pointer tool and Press Command-Option-I to display the Object Inspector (if it's not already visible). Press Command-` to move your cursor to the Inspector, then tab to the Corner Radius field. After you enter the corner radius you want, press Return to apply your change. FreeHand converts the rectangle into a rectangle with rounded corners (see Figure 2-6).

To change a rectangle with rounded corners into one with square corners, enter 0 (zero) in the Corner Radius field.

FIGURE 2-6
Rounding corners

Select a rectangle and press Command-Option-B to display the Object Inspector.

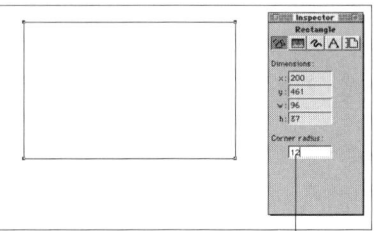

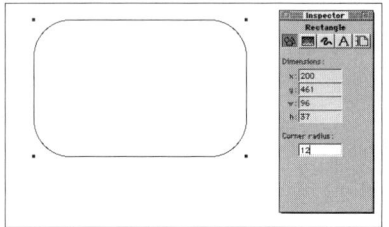

Type the corner radius you want in the Corner radius field.

Press Return, and FreeHand rounds the corners of the rectangle, using the corner radius you specified.

Converting Rectangles and Ellipses into Paths

Why would you want to convert a rectangle or an ellipse into a freeform path? Sometimes you want only part of a basic shape to connect to a path (see "Adding Round Corners to a Path," later in this chapter, for an example).

To turn a rectangle or an ellipse into a normal path, select the shape, and then press Command-U to ungroup it. The rectangle or ellipse becomes a freeform path, and can be manipulated as you'd manipulate any other freeform path (see Figure 2-7).

FIGURE 2-7
Converting basic shapes into paths

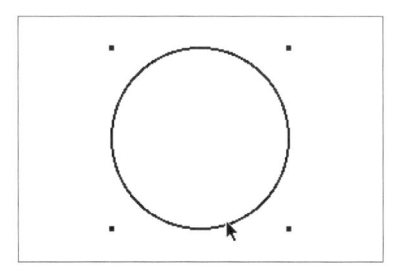

Select a rectangle or an ellipse and press Command-U.

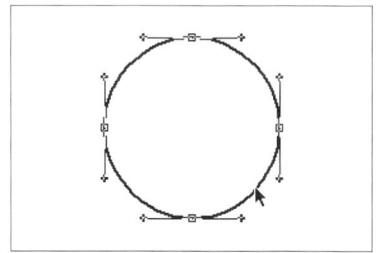

FreeHand converts the shape into a freeform path, which you can edit as you would any freeform path.

Tip:
Adding Round Corners to a Path

When you're drawing paths with the freeform path-drawing tools, it can be difficult to draw an arc with a specific corner radius (yes, even when you're drawing using the Arc tool). To do that, follow these steps (see Figure 2-8).

1. Double-click the Rectangle tool and set the corner radius you want in the Rectangle dialog box.

2. Draw a rectangle.

3. Without deselecting the rectangle, press Command-U to convert it to a path.

4. Select the points on the path on either side of the corner you want to add to your path and choose Split Element from the Arrange menu.

5. Select the corner you want and move it into position (you can delete the rest of the rectangle).

6. Join the round corner to the path (for more on joining paths, see "Joining Paths," later in this chapter).

Why don't we draw, ungroup, and split a circle to accomplish this same task? Because there's no way to specify the radius of the

FIGURE 2-8
Adding a round corner to a path

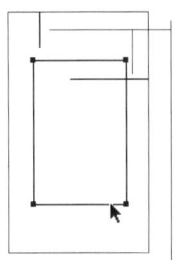

To add an arc with a corner radius of 24 points between these two lines, draw a rectangle and press Command-Option-B to display the Object Inspector. (If the Inspector's not already visible, press Command-I, first.)

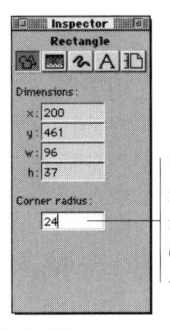

Type 24 in the Corner radius field and press Return.

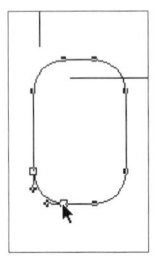

Select the points on either side of the arc you want.

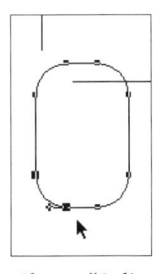

Choose "Split element" from the Element menu.

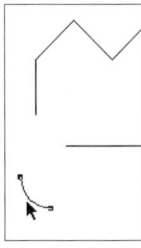

Drag the arc into position.

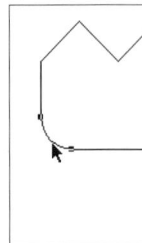

Join the arc to the path.

circle, short of drawing the circle to an exact size. It's far easier to enter a value for the corner radius in the Object Inspector.

Points and Paths

I briefly covered points and paths in Chapter 1, "FreeHand Basics," but there's still more to explain. Why is it that the most important things are often the ones that are the most difficult to learn?

When I first approached FreeHand and Illustrator, drawing by constructing paths, placing points, and manipulating control handles struck me as alien, as nothing like drawing at all. Then I started to catch on.

In many ways, when I used pens and rulers to draw, I was drawing lines from the point of view of everything *but* the line; in Free-Hand, I draw lines from the point of view of the line itself. This is neither better nor worse; it's just different and takes time to get used to. If you've just glanced at the toolbox and are feeling confused, I urge you to stick with it. Start thinking like a line.

DRAWING

Thinking Like a Line

Imagine that, through some mysterious potion or errant cosmic ray, you've been reduced in size so that you're a little smaller than one of the dots in a connect-the-dots puzzle. For detail and color, imagine the puzzles in a *Highlights* magazine in a dentist's office.

The only way out is to complete the puzzle. As you walk, a line extends behind you. As you reach each dot in the puzzle, a sign tells you where you are in the puzzle and how to get to the next dot in the path.

Get the idea? The dots in the puzzle are points. The route you walk from one dot to another, as instructed by the signs at each point, is a line segment. Each series of connected dots is a path. As you walk from one dot to another, you're thinking like a line.

Each point—from the first point in the path to the last—carries with it some information about the line segments that attach it to the previous and next points along the path.

Paths are made up of two or more points, connected by line segments, as shown in Figure 2-9. Even if the line attribute applied to the path is None, (and the line doesn't print or show up in Preview mode) there's still a line segment there.

FIGURE 2-9
A path

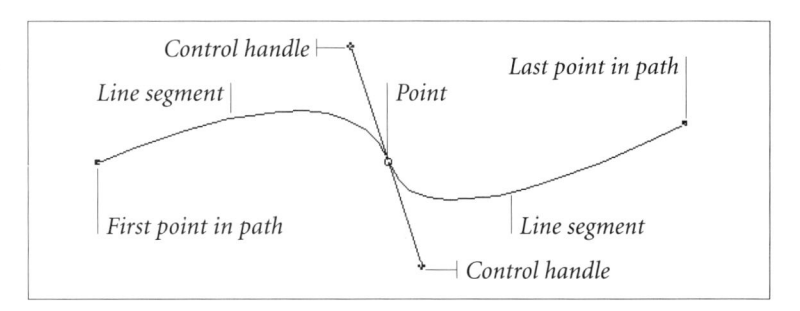

Winding

PostScript paths have a direction, also known as "winding" (as in "winding a clock"—nothing to do with the weather) that generally corresponds to the order and direction in which you place their points (see Figure 2-10). In our connect-the-dots puzzle, winding tells us the order in which we connect the dots.

When you create objects using the basic shapes drawing tools, FreeHand assumes a particular winding (see Figure 2-11). This is a useful thing to know, particularly when you're joining text to a path and want to control where that text begins (or ends) on the

FIGURE 2-10
The direction of a path

The numbers show the order in which you placed the points on the path.

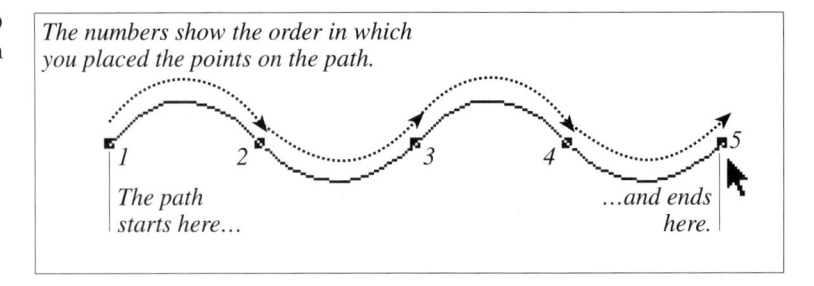

1 2 3 4 5

The path starts here...   *...and ends here.*

FIGURE 2-11
Winding for basic shapes

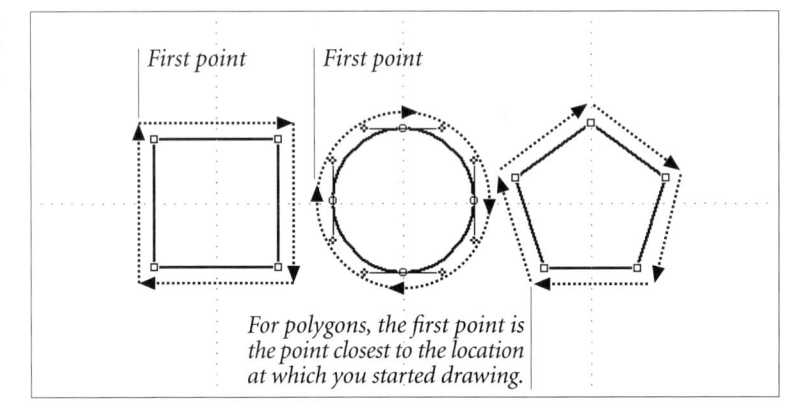

First point   First point

For polygons, the first point is the point closest to the location at which you started drawing.

path (FreeHand always positions the first character of text in a text block at the path's starting point, unless you're joining text to an object you've drawn with the basic shape tools, in which case it behaves differently; see "Joining Text to a Path," in Chapter 3, "Text and Type").

You can use FreeHand's new path operation Reverse Direction to reverse the winding of a path. To do this, select the path and choose Reverse Direction from the Path Operations submenu of the Arrange menu. FreeHand reverses the direction of the path.

Reflecting paths can also change their direction. You can use Reverse Direction to restore the original winding of the path.

Control Handles

You control the curvature of the line segments before and after each point with control handles. Points can have up to two control handles attached to them. Typically, corner points have none, connector points have one, and curve points have two (for more on the different types of points, see "Types of Points" in Chapter 1, "FreeHand Basics").

The first control handle you pull out of a point sets the curvature of the *next* line segment in the path along the direction (or winding) of the path. The second control handle sets the curvature of the line segment *before* the point (see Figure 2-12).

FIGURE 2-12
Control handles

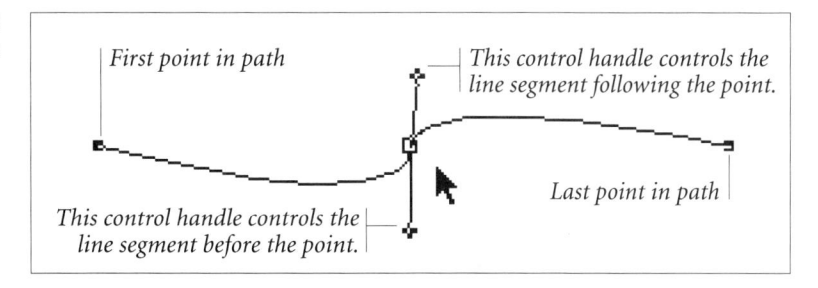

First point in path

This control handle controls the line segment following the point.

Last point in path

This control handle controls the line segment before the point.

Flatness

Besides winding, paths also have another property, flatness. Flatness is a PostScript property which controls how accurately curves are rendered on a PostScript printer. What? Can't the printer just print a curve? No. Laser printers, even PostScript laser printers, print by filling in pixels in a grid—just like MacPaint. Practically, this means that they only print straight lines. If you make the straight lines small enough, or short enough, however, they look like smooth curves. Flatness is PostScript's way of asking "How close is close enough?"

You can think of flatness this way: a flatness setting of one on a 300-dpi printer is equal to an inaccuracy in drawing curves of $\frac{1}{300}$ of an inch, or $\frac{1}{2540}$ of an inch on a Linotronic 300 at high resolution. The first is acceptable accuracy for proofing; the second is acceptable resolution for most publications. In fact, I've even gone to flatness settings of 3 without any problems when I knew I was going to be printing color separations at 2540 dpi. You can enter flatness values from 0 to 1000. Figure 2-13 shows the effect of increased flatness setting at 1270 dpi.

FIGURE 2-13
Flatness

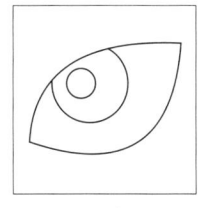

Flatness of 0

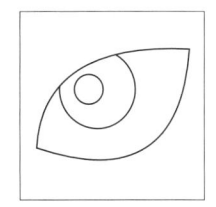

Flatness of 3

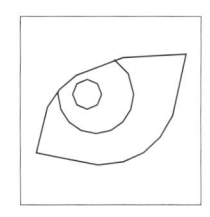

Flatness of 50

If you increase the Flatness setting to a high value—100, for example—you can see that smooth curves start to look like a series of line segments. A flatness setting of 0 ensures that the path prints at the highest level of accuracy possible, given the printer's resolution. This doesn't mean, however, that it's always the best choice.

Lower flatness settings take longer to print and use more of your printer's RAM (which is precious, unless you like PostScript error messages), because the printer has to draw more tiny line segments to render the path's curves. In fact, increasing the flatness sometimes eliminates PostScript errors that make a job unprintable, especially if there are a lot of points in the illustration you're trying to print.

To see a path's flatness, select the path and press Command-Option-I to bring up the Object Inspector.

Path-Drawing Tools

You use the freeform drawing tools—the Freehand tool, the Pen tool, and the Point tool—to create paths. The following sections discuss each freeform drawing tool. These tools have already been discussed, briefly, in Chapter 1, "FreeHand Basics," but this section gives you more detailed descriptions of their uses.

Freehand Tool The Freehand tool in the toolbox is actually three different tools: the Freehand tool, the Variable Stroke tool, and the Calligraphic Pen tool. You can switch between these tools by double-clicking the tool in the toolbox.

- The Freehand tool draws a single, open path that follows your cursor.
- The Variable Stroke tool draws closed paths that look like brushstrokes.
- The Calligraphic Pen tools draw closed paths that look like they were drawn with a flat-nib lettering pen.

Freehand tool. The simplest, quickest way to create a path on a FreeHand publication page is to use the Freehand tool. Just select the tool and scribble. As you drag the tool across the page, a path is created that follows your mouse motion (see Figure 2-14).

As you drag, FreeHand places corner and curve points along the path. You have some control over the placement of these points—double-click the Freehand tool to bring up the Freehand dialog box (see Figure 2-15).

The Tight Fit option controls the number of points FreeHand creates to construct the path. Turn off Tight Fit to create a simpler path, but bear in mind that the simplified path follows your mouse movements less accurately.

Draw Dotted Line displays the path you're drawing as a dotted line as you drag the Freehand tool. Turn Draw Dotted Line off to show the path as you draw it. Why would you want to do this? Drawing's a little faster with Draw Dotted Line turned on. I always leave it off. Note that when you've got Draw Dotted Line turned on, the path is drawn about the same way as it's always drawn in Illustrator.

FIGURE 2-14
Using the Freehand tool

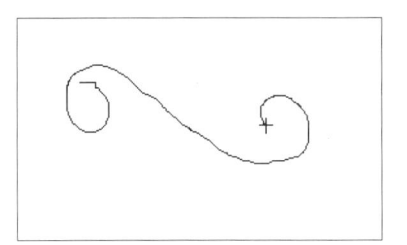

Select the Freehand tool and drag it across the page.

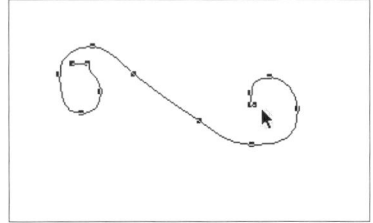

FreeHand creates a path that follows your mouse movements.

FIGURE 2-15
Freehand Tool dialog box

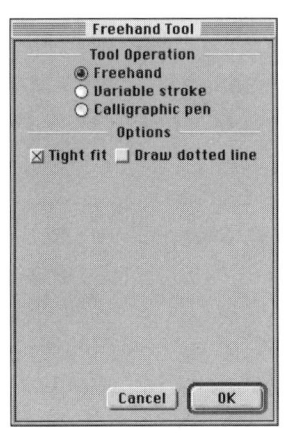

To set options for the Freehand tool's beshavior, double-click the Freehand tool.

If you need to back up along the path while you're drawing with the Freehand tool, hold down Command, and drag back along the path. To continue drawing the path, let go of Command and continue dragging the tool (see Figure 2-16).

If you need to create a straight line segment while you're drawing a path using the Freehand tool, hold down Option as you're dragging: each line segment you add forms a straight line from the last point on the path. If you want to constrain the angle of the straight line segment to 45-degree tangents (of the angle set in the Constrain field in the Document Setup Inspector), hold down Option-Shift as you drag the Freehand tool (see Figure 2-17).

FIGURE 2-16
Erasing part of a freeform path

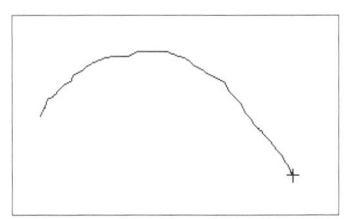

If you don't like what you've drawn with the Freehand tool...

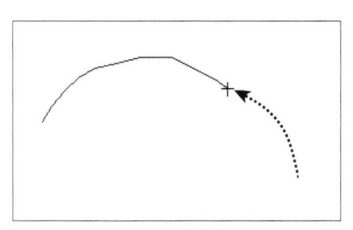

...hold down Command and drag back along the path.

FIGURE 2-17
Constraint and the Freehand tool

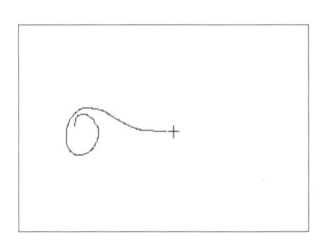

Hold down Option-Shift as you drag the Freehand tool...

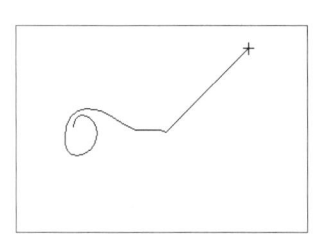

...and you constrain the lines you draw to 45-degree angles.

Though the Freehand tool is the easiest way to create paths in FreeHand, I've always found it to be one of the least useful. Why? Mice are wonderful things, and they're probably the best way we currently have of getting positioning information into computers (I've tried trackballs and pens, too), but they're far better for placing points and manipulating control handles than they are for drawing smooth lines.

Variable Stroke tool. The introduction of the wacky "variable blob tool" (known to serious persons as the Variable Stroke tool) in

FreeHand 3.1 gave FreeHand users a way to create paths shaped like brush strokes. To see the Variable Stroke tool's controls, double-click the Freehand tool in the toolbox, then click the Variable Stroke option at the top of the Freehand tool dialog box (see Figure 2-18).

If you have a pressure-sensitive tablet (such at those manufactured by Wacom, Calcomp, and Kurta), you can use the pressure of your stylus to change the widths of the path you draw with the Variable Stroke tool.

FIGURE 2-18
Variable Stroke tool

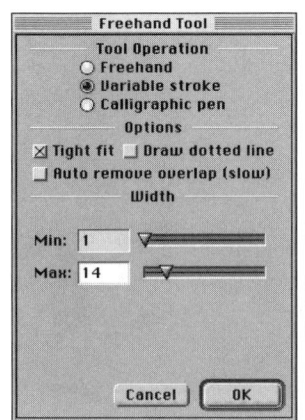

To set options for the Variable Stroke tool's behavior, double-click the Freehand tool and click the Variable Stroke option.

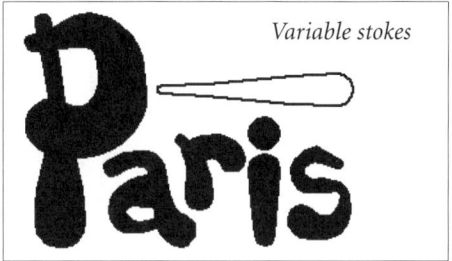

Variable stokes

Tip:
If You Don't Have a Tablet

What if you don't have a pressure-sensitive tablet? You can still use the tool's pressure-sensitivity. As you draw a path, press 2 (or right arrow) to increase the width of the path, or press 1 (or left arrow) to decrease its width. This technique takes a little practice, but you'll soon be drawing variable blobs as well as your friends with their fancypants tablets (see Figure 2-19).

FIGURE 2-19
Pressure without the pen

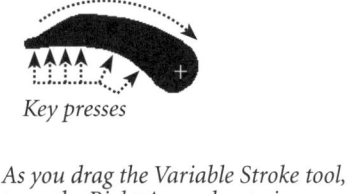

Key presses

As you drag the Variable Stroke tool, press the Right Arrow key to increase the width of the stroke; press the Left Arrow key to decrease the width.

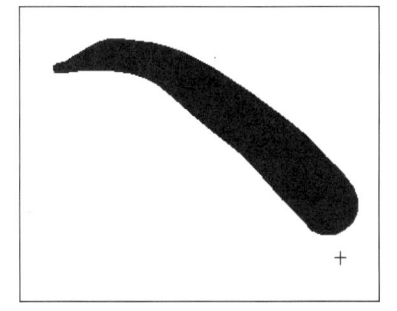

Calligraphic Pen tool. Choose the Calligraphic Pen tool when you want to create paths that resemble lines drawn with a pen. To use the Calligraphic Pen tool, double-click the Freehand tool in the toolbox, then click the Calligraphic Pen option. This is also where you set up the Calligraphic Pen's options (see Figure 2-20).

As with the Variable Stroke tool, you can use the Calligraphic Pen tool's pressure-sensitivity even if you don't have a pressure-sensitive tablet—as you draw a path, press 2 (or right arrow) to increase the width of the calligraphic stroke, or press 1 (or left arrow) to decrease its width.

FIGURE 2-20
Calligraphic Pen tool

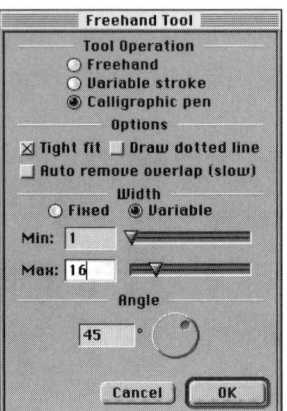

To set options for the Calligraphic Pen tool's behavior, double-click the Freehand tool and click "Calligraphic Pen."

Calligraphic pen strokes

Pen Tool

When you click with the Pen tool in the publication window, Free-Hand places corner points. If you drag the Pen tool, FreeHand places a curve point where you first started dragging—you determine the length of the control handles (and, therefore, the shape of the curve) by the distance you drag (see Figure 2-21). If you're an Illustrator user, you'll feel right at home—the Pen tool works just like the Pen tool in Illustrator.

FIGURE 2-21
The Pen tool

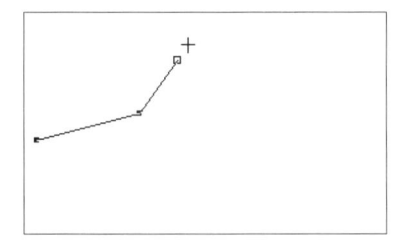

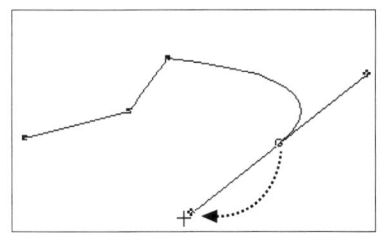

Click to create a corner point.   *Drag to create a curve point.*

To curve the line segment following a corner point, hold down Option as you place a corner point and drag. The control handle doesn't appear until you place the next point. Once you place the next point, the control handle appears and can be adjusted as you like (see Figure 2-22).

FIGURE 2-22
Dragging a control handle out of a corner point

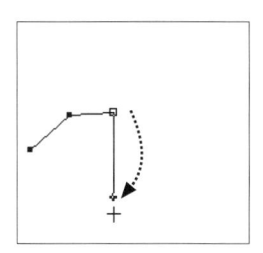

Hold down Option as you drag…

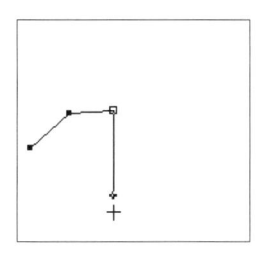

…and FreeHand creates a corner point with a single control handle.

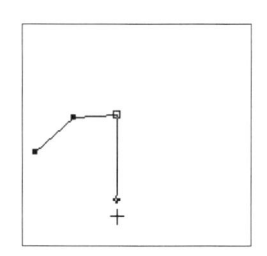

This control handle applies to the line segment following the corner point.

The trickiest thing about using the Pen tool this way is that you often don't see the effect of the curve manipulation until you've placed the next point. This makes sense in that you don't need a control handle for a line segment that doesn't yet exist, but it can be quite a brain-twister.

To convert a curve point you've just placed to a corner point, hold down Option after you've finished dragging out the curve point's control handles (see Figure 2-23). This creates a corner point with two control handles extended.

FIGURE 2-23
Converting a curve point to a corner point (with two control handles)

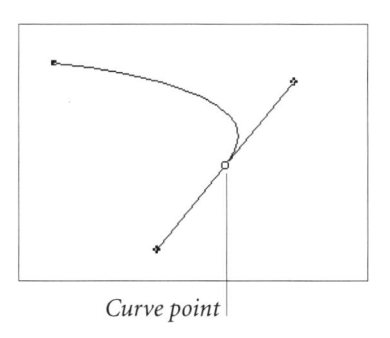

Curve point

Corner point

Drag out the curve point's handles as you normally would…

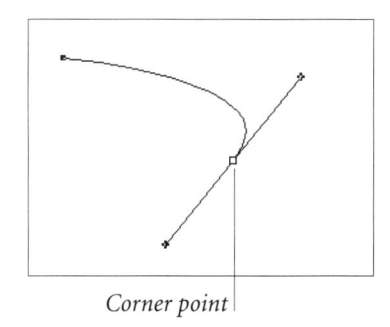

…then hold down Option and stop dragging. FreeHand converts the curve point to a corner point.

To convert a curve point you've just placed to a corner point with one control handle extended, hold down Option and click on the point. Just to make life interesting, this control handle applies to the line segment *before* the corner point along the path. Ordinarily, the first control handle dragged out of a corner point applies to the line segment *after* the point (see Figure 2-24).

You can change the position of points, as you'd expect, by holding down Command (which, as you'll recall, chooses the Pointer tool without deselecting the current tool), selecting the point, and dragging the point to a new location.

FIGURE 2-24
Converting a curve point to a corner point (with one control handle)

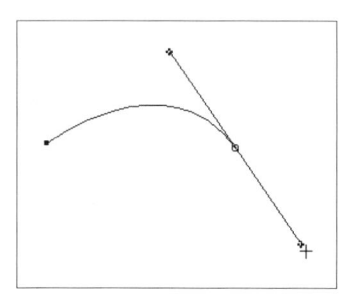

Position a curve point, hold down Option...

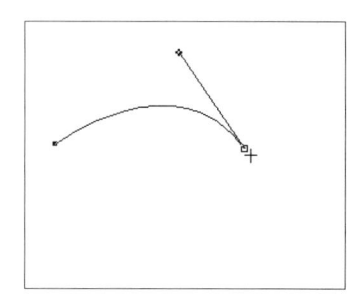

...and then click on the point to convert it into a corner point.

Using the Point Tool

Use the Point tool when you want to create paths point-by-point. Dragging the Point tool as you place a point moves the point—unlike the Pen tool, where dragging adjusts the curve of the line segments attached to the point you're placing. In general, you place points with the Point tool, then adjust the points' control handles to get the curves you want. Which tool is better—the Point tool or the Pen tool? Your answer depends on who you are and how you like to work. I'm a Point tool kind of guy, myself.

Placing corner points. When you click the Point tool on the page, you're placing corner points—points which have no control handles attached to them. Corner points look like small squares. Because corner points have no curve control handles attached to them (initially), the line segments between corner points are straight (see Figure 2-25).

You can drag curve levers out of corner points: place the corner point as you normally would, then hold down Command (to turn the cursor into the Pointer tool) and Option, and drag a control handle out of the corner point (see Figure 2-26).

Note that you can also drag a control handle out of a corner point any time by selecting the point with the pointer tool, then holding down Option, and dragging a control handle out of it.

The most significant difference between corner points and curve points is that the angle of control handles pulled out of corner points can be adjusted independently, while changing the angle of one control handle of a curve point changes the angle of the other control handle. This difference, in my opinion, makes corner points much more useful than curve points—especially given that you can do anything with a corner point you could do with a curve point or a connector point.

FIGURE 2-25
Corner points

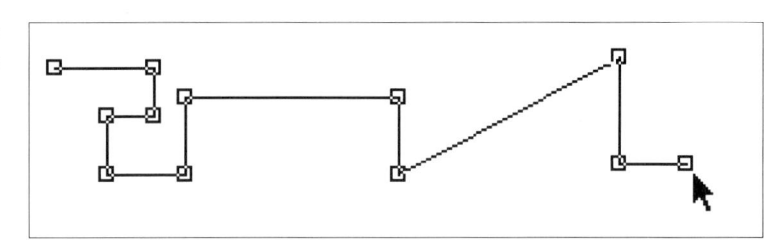

FIGURE 2-26
Dragging control handles out of corner points

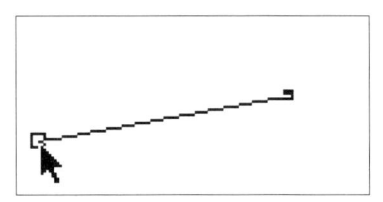

Select a corner point, hold down Option...

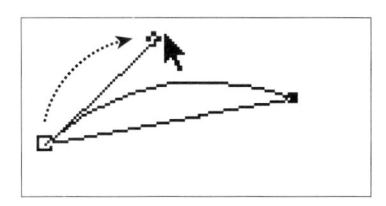

...and drag a control handle out of the point.

Corner points are more flexible than curve points, because you can adjust their control handles independently.

Adjusting control handles on corner points

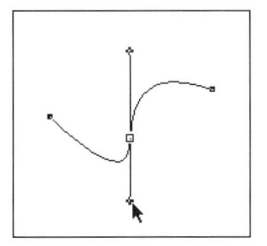

Point at a control handle...

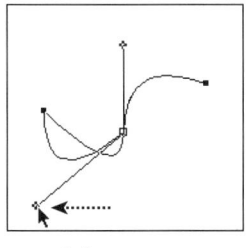

...and drag.

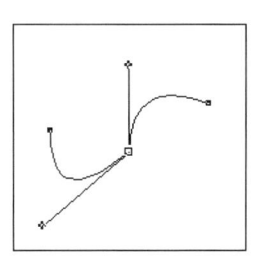

The handle moves independently of the other handle.

You can turn corner points into curve points by selecting the corner point, pressing Command-Option-I to display the Object Inspector, clicking the curve point button in the Inspector, and pressing Return to apply your change. The selected corner point becomes a curve point.

Placing curve points. Hold down Option as you click the Point tool, and you're placing curve points—points with two control handles pulled out of them. Curve points look like small circles. When you click to place a curve point, two control handles are extended from the point. How far the control handles are extended depends on the curve point's place in the path (see Figure 2-27).

You can increase or decrease the distance from one control handle to its curve point without moving the other curve point, but both handles move if you change the angle one of them presents to the curve point—they always move along the same axis. This makes them somewhat less flexible than corner points (see Figure 2-28).

FIGURE 2-27
Curve points

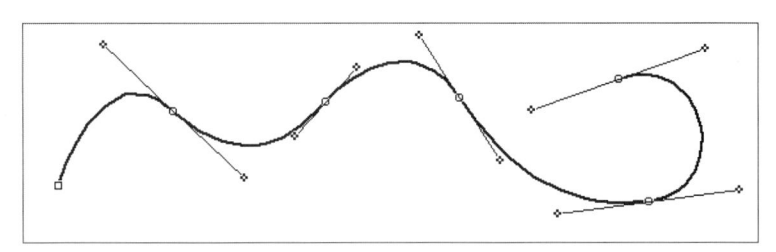

FIGURE 2-28
Manipulating control handles on curve points

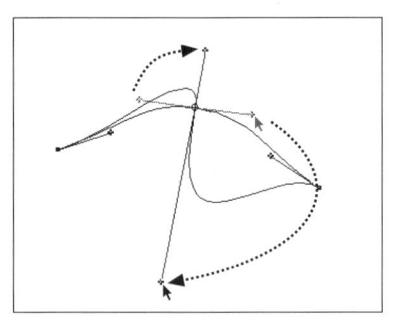

As you drag a control handle attached to a curve point, note that both control handles move as you drag.

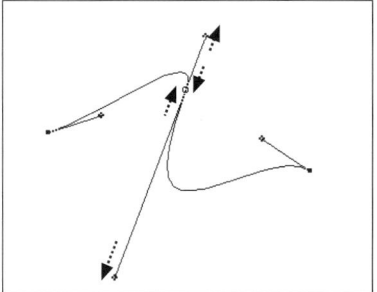

Control handles attached to curve points always move along the same axis.

You can turn curve points into corner points by selecting the curve point, pressing Command-Option-I (to display the Object Inspector), clicking the corner point button in the Inspector, and pressing Return to apply your change.

Placing connector points. If you hold down Option-Command and click the Point tool, you create connector points—points which may or may not have control handles pulled out of them depending on where they're placed in the path (and, I suspect, depending on their own whim). I never really have figured out connector points. Anyway, they look like little triangles.

If you place a curve point immediately after a connector point, the control handle for the line segment from the connector point to the curve point is extended from the connector point. This control handle is positioned along the axis formed by the connector point and the point preceding the connector point on the path, and is placed at the same distance from the connector point as the preceding point along this axis. When you drag the control handle, it moves along this axis (see Figure 2-29). If you want to change the curve, you'll have to convert the connector point into another type of point.

What's the use of connector points? They create smooth transitions between straight and curved line segments. I think of them as a sort of "half" curve point. They never seem to give me the curve I'm looking for, but you should experiment with them. In spite of my bias, they might be just what you're after.

FIGURE 2-29
Connector points

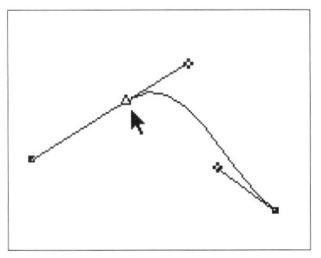

Connector points look like little triangles.

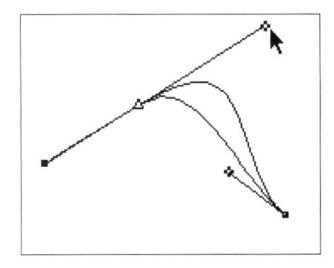

The control handle on a connector point can only move along its original axis.

Xtra Drawing Tools

FreeHand 5 arrives on your hard drive with several tools that don't appear in your Toolbox—they're FreeHand extensions, or "Xtras," and you can see them in the Xtra Tools palette (which you can display by pressing Command-Shift-K—see Figure 2-30). Two of the tools in this palette, the Arc tool and the Spiral tool, draw paths. In some ways, they're similar to the basic shapes tools: they draw a path with a specific shape and behavior.

While these tools aren't part of FreeHand's "core" code, they're every bit as fast and responsive as any tool you could choose in FreeHand's toolbox.

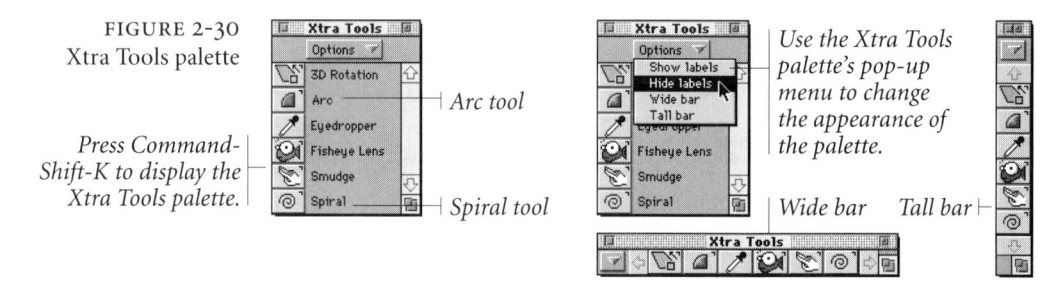

FIGURE 2-30
Xtra Tools palette

Press Command-Shift-K to display the Xtra Tools palette.

Arc tool

Spiral tool

Use the Xtra Tools palette's pop-up menu to change the appearance of the palette.

Wide bar   Tall bar

Arc Tool

The Arc tool draws—are you ready for this?—arcs (quarters of an ellipse). To draw an arc, select the Arc tool and drag it on the page—FreeHand creates an arc that follows the path you dragged (see Figure 2-31).

To set options for the Arc tool, double-click the tool in the Xtras palette. FreeHand displays the Arc dialog box (see Figure 2-32).

Create Open Arc. Turning on the Create Open Arc option makes the Arc tool draw a single curved line segment between two points. Turn "Create Open Arc" off, and you're drawing pie wedges.

FIGURE 2-31
Drawing arcs

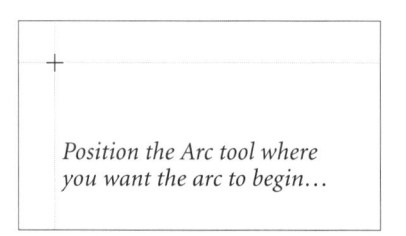

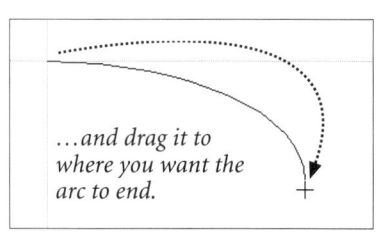

Position the Arc tool where you want the arc to begin...

...and drag it to where you want the arc to end.

DRAWING 127

FIGURE 2-32
Arc tool options

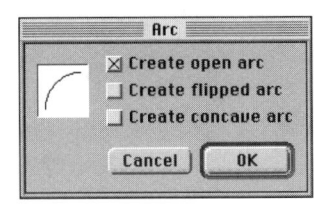

Double-click the Arc tool in the Xtra Tools palette to display the Arc dialog box.

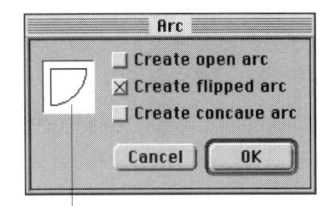

The preview window shows you the effect of the options you've chosen.

Create Flipped Arc. By default, the Arc tool draws the two top quarters of an ellipse—turn on the Create Flipped Arc option when you want to draw either of the bottom two quarters.

Create Concave Arc. Turn on the Create Concave Arc option when you want to create an arc that's the *inside* of a rectangle (the opposite of a pie wedge).

Like every other FreeHand tool, the Arc tool comes with several keyboard options.

- To toggle the Create Open Arc option on and off, hold down Command as you drag the Arc tool.

- To constrain the arcs you're drawing to circular arcs, hold down Shift as you drag the Arc tool.

- To toggle the settings of the Create Convex Arc option in the Arc dialog box, hold down Option as you drag the Arc tool.

- To toggle the Create Flipped Arc option in the Arc dialog box, hold down Control as you drag the Arc tool.

If, at some point, you decide you don't like or aren't using the Arc tool, you can remove it by deleting it or moving it out of the Xtras folder. When you restart FreeHand, the Arc tool will be gone.

Spiral Tool

Maybe it's just my clients, but it seems like everyone, all of a sudden, has a use for spirals. I don't know if they're out to hypnotize the world or if it's just some cosmic coincidence, but spirals—especially spirals with text joined to them—seem to be all the rage.

Whatever the case, FreeHand's Xtra Tools palette proudly displays a tool for drawing spirals. Select the Spiral tool from the Xtra Tools palette, then drag the tool on the page, and FreeHand draws a spiral, centered around the point at which you started dragging (see Figure 2-33).

FIGURE 2-33
Drawing spirals

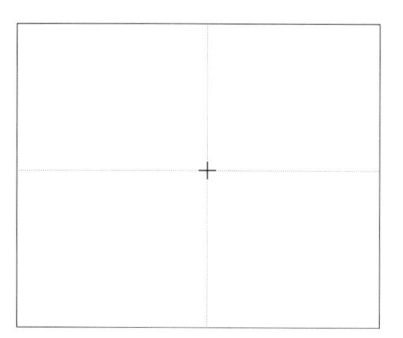

Position the Spiral tool where you want to locate the center of the spiral...

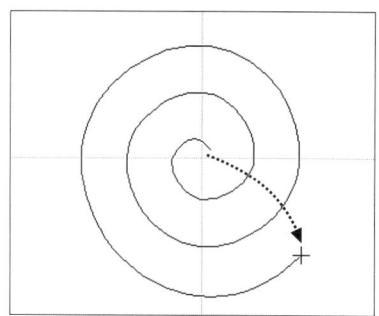

...and drag. As you drag, FreeHand creates a spiral. Stop dragging when the spiral looks the way you want it to.

Double-click the Spiral tool in the Xtra Tools palette, and FreeHand displays the Spiral dialog box (see Figure 2-34). I confess, this is one of those points in the book where I'd like to gloss over the controls in this dialog box. Just play with them and see what happens, I'd like to say. But, in the interest of being complete and authoritative, I'll grit my teeth and wade through the options.

Spiral Type. When you click the button on the right (in this section), the Spiral tool draws concentric spirals—spirals in which each successive line of the spiral is a set distance from the previous spiral. Clicking the button on the left directs FreeHand to draw "nautilus" spirals, in which each line is an increasing distance from the previous one (see Figure 2-35).

If you choose the nautilus spiral type, a new control appears in the Spiral dialog box: the Expansion slider/field. Enter a percentage in the field or drag the slider to set the rate of expansion.

Draw By. Choose "Rotation" from the Draw By popup menu to specify how many rotations you'd like to have in your spiral (which means that the size of the spiral determines the distance between

FIGURE 2-34
Spiral tool options

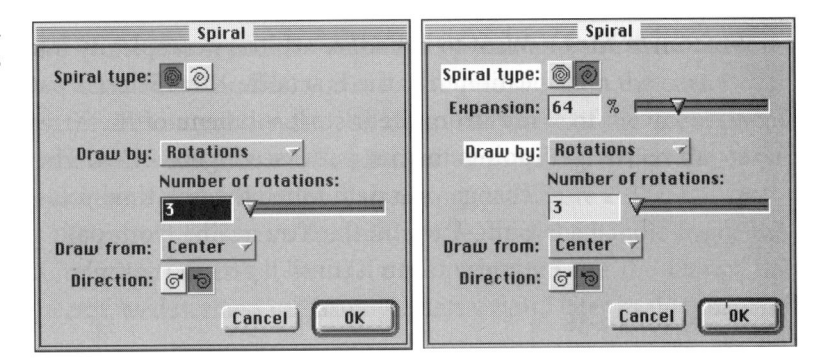

FIGURE 2-35
Nautilus and concentric spirals

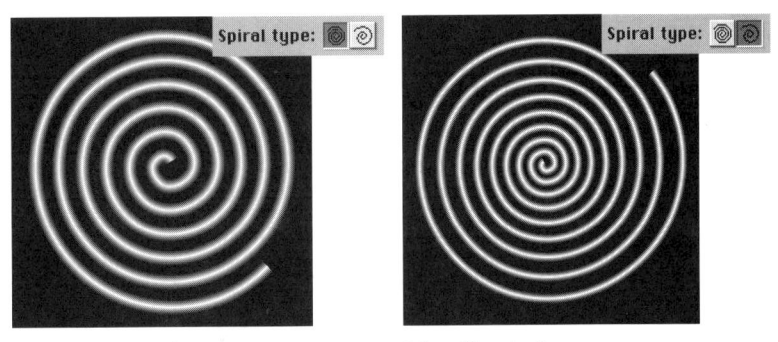

Concentric spiral   *Nautilis spiral*

the rotations of the spiral), or choose "Increments" to control the distance between rotations of the spiral. If you've chosen the nautilus spiral type, you'll see "Rotation" and "Starting Radius" on the popup menu; in this case, choosing "Starting Radius" gives you a way to set the initial radius of the spiral.

Draw From. If you want to draw your spirals from somewhere other than their center, choose "Corner" or "Edge" from the Draw From popup menu.

Direction. Use these buttons to determine the direction of rotation of the spirals.

If you don't use the Spiral tool, you can keep it from loading by moving or deleting the file "Spiral" from the Xtras folder in your FreeHand folder.

Tip:
Selecting
Multiple Points

You can select several points at once by dragging a selection rectangle over them. Once you have selected the points, their control handles appear. You can adjust any of the control handles without deselecting the other control handles, which means you can adjust control handles on a path while looking at the position of the path's other control handles (see Figure 2-39).

FIGURE 2-39
Selecting multiple points and adjusting curve control handles

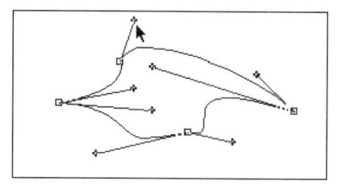

Drag a selection rectangle over a path to select all of the points on the path.

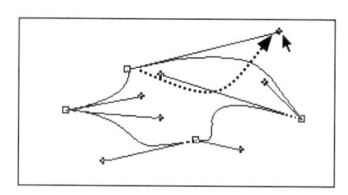

Now you can adjust control handles while looking at the positions of all of the control handles on the path.

Automatic Curvature

As you place curve or connector points along a path, FreeHand adds and adjusts curve control points where it thinks you'd like them. It's actually quite good at guessing. This is FreeHand's automatic curvature feature, which you can turn on or off for any point in your publication.

To turn automatic curvature on, select a point and press Command-Option-I to display the Object Inspector for that point. Check the Automatic checkbox, and FreeHand automatically decides how to extend control handles from the point, based on the point's position in the path.

When you adjust a control handle, it turns automatic curvature off for that point. If you decide you've made an error, and would like to return to FreeHand's automatic curvature, you can display the Object Inspector and turn on the Automatic curvature option (see Figure 2-40).

Issuing a Retraction

Click one of the Retract buttons in the Object Inspector and the associated control handle is pulled back into the point. No more not quite being sure if you'd dragged the handle inside the point! Anything you'd ordinarily do by dragging a curve control handle inside a point, you can do using the Retract buttons in the Object Inspector (see Figure 2-41).

FIGURE 2-40
Automatic curvature

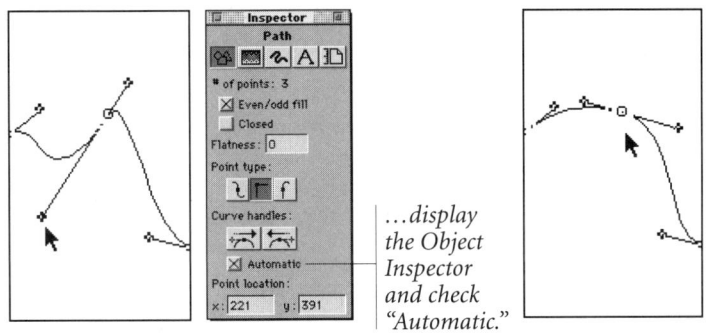

...display the Object Inspector and check "Automatic."

If you change your mind about an adjustment you've made to a control handle...

FreeHand returns the point's control handles to their default position.

FIGURE 2-41
Retracting control handles

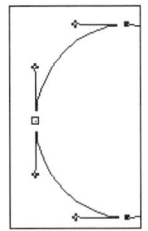

Select a point.

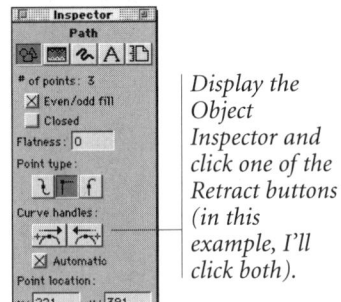

Display the Object Inspector and click one of the Retract buttons (in this example, I'll click both).

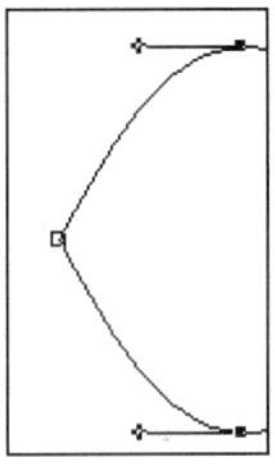

FreeHand retracts the point's control handles.

This Retract button affects curve of the line segment following the point.

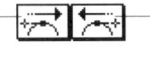

This Retract button affects curve of the line segment preceding the point.

Drawing Techniques

Now that you know all about the elements that make up paths, let's talk about how you actually use them.

Ways to Draw Paths

When you're drawing paths, don't forget that you can change the path after you've drawn it. I've often seen people delete entire paths and start over because they misplaced the last point on the path. Go ahead and place points in the wrong places; you can always change the position of any point on the path. Also, keep these facts in mind:

◆ You can always split the path.

- You can always add points to or subtract points from the path.

- You can always change tools while drawing a path.

It's also best to create paths using as few points as you can—but it's not required (after all, you can always use the Simplify Path operation). Create paths in whatever way you find works best for you—there's no "right" way to do it. I've talked with dozens of FreeHand users, and each one uses a slightly different method for putting points on a page.

The classical method. Use the Point tool to place curve, corner, and connector points, and place points one at a time. I call this the "classical" method, because it's how people were taught to place points in FreeHand 1.0. To construct a path using this method, you use the Point tool, holding down Option as you click to produce a curve point, or Option-Shift to produce a connector point (see Figure 2-42).

People who use this method of constructing paths keep one hand on the mouse and one hand hovering around the keyboard, because they'll change point type by pressing keys (as described in "Using the Point tool," earlier in this chapter).

FIGURE 2-42
The classical method

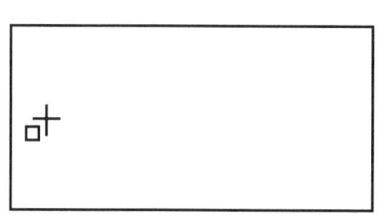

Choose the point tool and click to place a corner point.

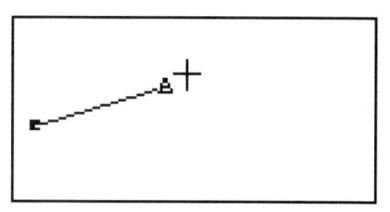

Hold down Control and click to place a connector point.

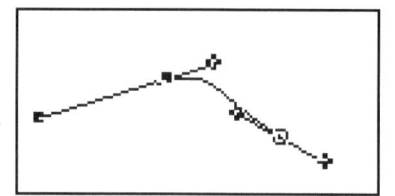

Hold down Option and click to place a curve point.

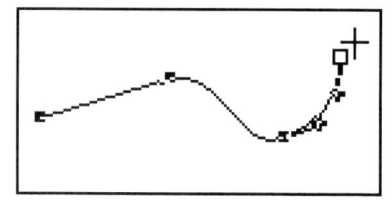

Continue placing points until you've drawn the path you want.

The "Illustrator" Method. Use the Pen tool only. I call this method the "Illustrator" method, because I've found that this set of users generally learned to use Illustrator before they started using Free-Hand. In this method, you click and drag the Pen tool to create paths containing only curve and corner points (see Figure 2-43).

FIGURE 2-43
The "Illustrator" method

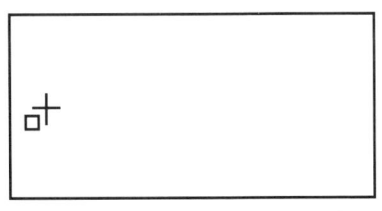

Choose the pen tool and click to place a corner point.

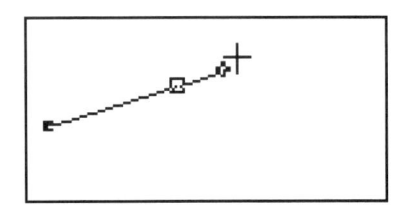

Option-drag a control handle out of the next corner point.

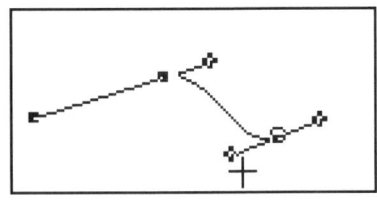

Drag out a curve point.

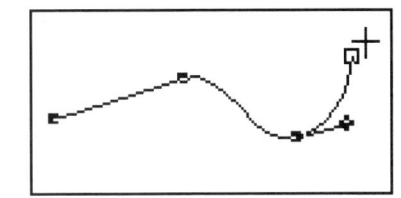

Click to place a corner point.

Drawing paths my way. Place corner points only, then pull control handles out of the points using the Option-Drag technique (see "The Quick Way to Make a Curve," earlier in this chapter). I call this method "my way," because it's how I do it. In this method, you use the Point tool to place corner points defining the path you want to create, then hold down Option and drag line segments to create the curves you want (see Figure 2-44).

I like this method because I can place points quickly where I know I want them to go, then work on the fine details of the curves when I can actually see the path changing as I drag—unlike using the Pen tool, where you're dragging control handles controlling a line segment you haven't yet placed. The disadvantage of this method is that you need to know where you're going to place points ahead of time, a skill you acquire by using the program a lot (see also "Keeping Paths Simple," below).

All three methods work well, and there's no reason not to mix and match methods in different situations. There's also no reason

FIGURE 2-44
My way

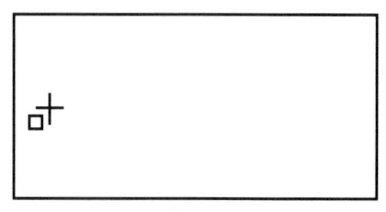

Choose the corner tool
and place a point.

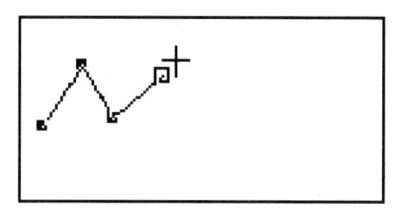

Click to place three
more corner points.

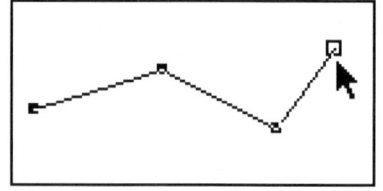

Drag the points into position.

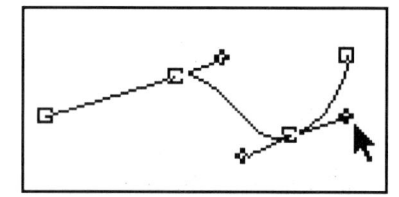

Drag out and adjust control handles,
or hold down Option and bend line
segments (see "The Quick Way to
Make a Curve," earlier in this
chapter).

not to mix these methods with the use of the Freehand tool, the basic shapes tools, autotracing, or blending.

Drawing with the Knife Tool

I've always liked working with scratchboard (or "scraperboard"), and woodcuts—I like the process of taking an area and cutting a drawing out of it. You can do the same with FreeHand 5's Knife tool. If the Knife tool could only draw straight lines, this technique wouldn't be so much fun—but the Knife tool can also act like the Freehand tool.

To try this neat technique, follow these steps (see Figure 2-45).

1. Draw a closed path and fill it with a basic fill.

2. Double-click the Knife tool. FreeHand displays the Knife tool dialog box.

3. Turn on the FreeHand option and the Cut Closed Paths option.

4. Hold down Command (to turn the Knife tool into the Pointer tool) and select the path you drew earlier.

FIGURE 2-45
Drawing with the
Knife tool

Double-click the Knife tool in the Toolbox to display the Knife Tool dialog box.

Select a filled path, then drag the Knife tool inside the path.

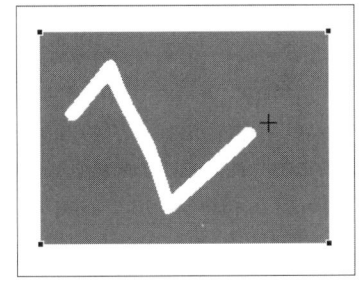

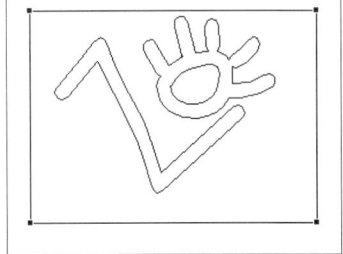

As you drag, the Knife tool cuts a hole in the path.

Drawing with the Knife tool creates composite paths, as you can see from this Keyline view.

5. Drag the Knife tool through the filled path. As you drag, FreeHand cuts a path out of the filled path.

Bear in mind, as you draw with the Knife tool, that you're creating compound paths. It's pretty easy to create a path that's too complex to print, so don't get carried away—especially if you plan to paste a TIFF inside the path.

Keeping Paths Simple

People who've just started working with FreeHand tend to use more points than they need to describe paths. Over time, they learn one of FreeHand's basic rules: Any curve can be described by two points and their associated control handles. No more, no less (see Figure 2-46). FreeHand's new "Simplify paths" path operator makes a great path-drawing instructor—draw a path and then run Simplify Paths on it (select the path, then select Simplify Paths from the Path operations submenu of the Arrange menu). Notice where FreeHand deletes and removes points on the path you've drawn, and you'll get a good lesson in path drawing. Note, however, that Simplify Paths is not perfect, and may sometimes change the shape of your path (you can always undo the action).

FIGURE 2-46
Any curve can be described by two points

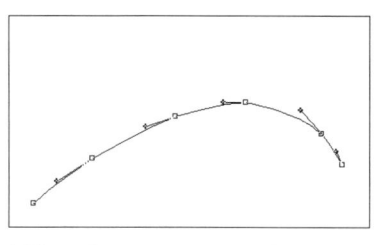

This path uses too many points.

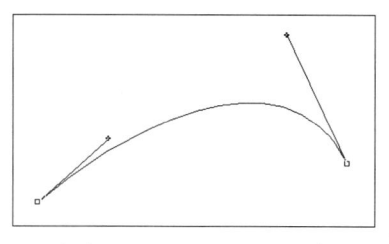

Here's the same curve, using only two points.

Selecting and Moving Points

If you've gotten this far, you probably know how to select points, but here are a few rules to keep in mind.

- You select a point by clicking on the point with the Pointer tool.

- You can select more than one point at a time by holding down Shift as you click on each point with the Pointer tool, or you can drag a marquee around a number of points to select them all.

- When you move a point, the control handles associated with that point also move, maintaining their same position relative to the point. Note that this means that the curves of the line segments attached to the point change, unless you're also moving the points on the other end of the incoming and outgoing line segments (see Figure 2-47).

FIGURE 2-47
Effect of moving a point on its attached line segments

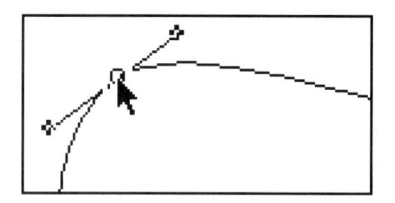

When you select and move a point…

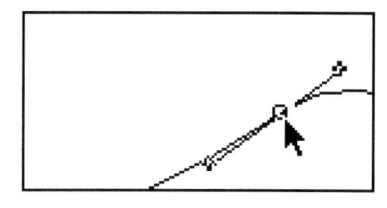

…the point's attached control handles move with the point.

Flipping and Flopping

I hate drawing objects from scratch when I don't have to, so I use flipping and flopping to create most of the objects I use in a FreeHand publication. What's flipping and flopping? It's the process of cloning an object and then selecting and moving some—not all—of the points on the cloned object. Look at Figure 2-48. Flipping and flopping depends on FreeHand's ability to select several points on a path without selecting the entire path.

Flipping and flopping come in especially handy when you need to create two paths—even paths of different shapes—which share a common boundary. Redrawing the boundary between two paths is not just boring, but can be quite difficult if the boundary is complex enough. I'm not averse to tackling difficult tasks; I just hate to make something more difficult than it has to be, so I use flipping and flopping even when the shapes sharing a boundary are very different.

FIGURE 2-48
Flipping and flopping

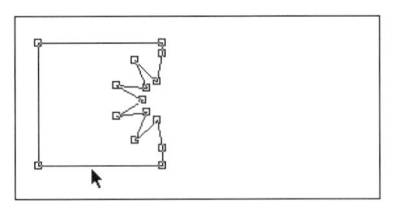

Clone the original object.

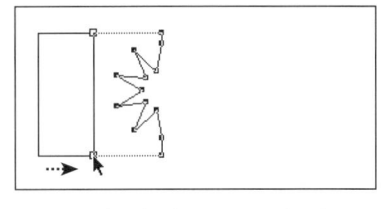

Select individual points on the clone and drag them...

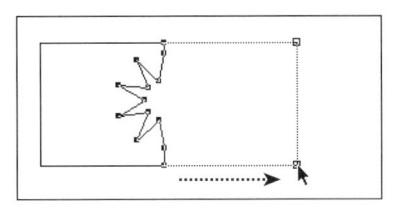

...until they're where you want them.

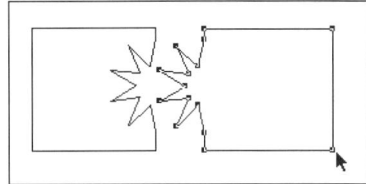

You now have two objects with an identical border.

Open and Closed Paths

You can think of an open path as a line and a closed path as a shape. Open paths can't be filled, have objects pasted inside them, or be manipulated using some path operations (Union, Punch, and Intersect). You can however, always join the endpoints of an open path to create a closed path, or split a closed path to create an open path (using either the Split Object command or the Knife tool).

To use FreeHand's Object Inspector to close a path, select the path, press Command-Option-I to display the Object Inspector (if it's not already visible), and then check the Closed checkbox in the Inspector. Press Return to apply your changes. FreeHand creates a straight line segment which joins the first point in the path to the last point in the path (see Figure 2-49).

FIGURE 2-49
Changing an open path into a closed path

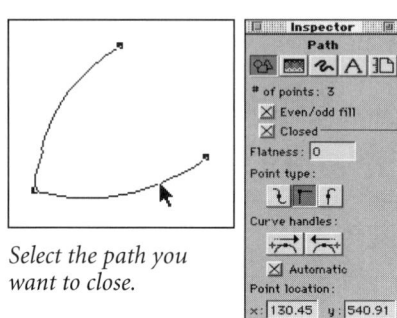

Select the path you want to close.

Display the Object Inspector and click the Closed checkbox.

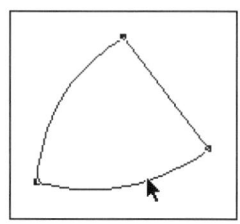

FreeHand closes the path with a straight line segment.

Similarly, you can use the Object Inspector to change a closed path into an open path by following the above procedure but unchecking the Closed option. When you do this, FreeHand removes the line segment which joins the first point in the path to the last point in the path. When you convert a closed path into an open path, any clipped (pasted-inside) objects or fills disappear. They haven't really vanished; if you then convert the open path into a closed path, the clipped objects and/or fills reappear.

Closing a path using the Object Inspector is great, but what if you've got a curved path you want to close but don't want to close with a straight line segment (see Figure 2-50)?

1. Select the path.

2. Press Command-= to clone the path. A copy of the path appears on top of the path.

3. Drag a marquee over two of the endpoints (they'll be right on top of each other, so it won't look like anything's selected).

FIGURE 2-50
Closing an irregular path

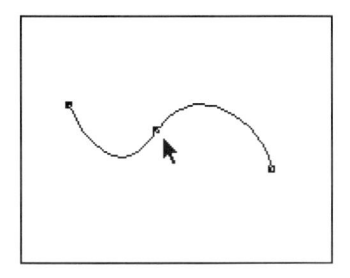

Select the path you want to make a closed path and clone it.

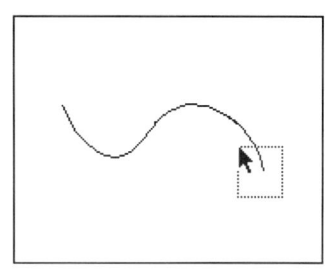

Drag a selection rectangle over the endpoints and press Command-J.

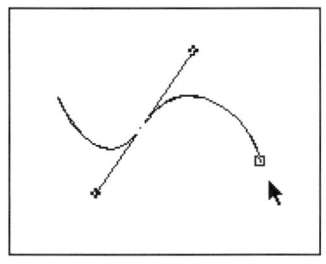

Display the Object Inspector and click "Closed." FreeHand closes the path.

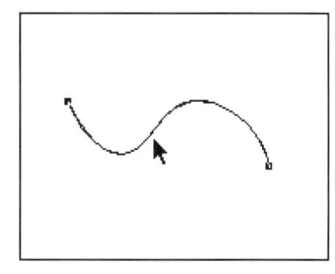

Now you can work with the path as you would with any closed path.

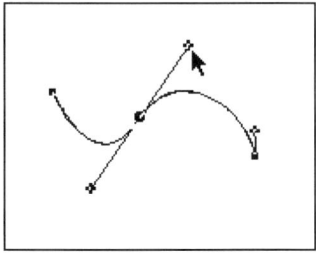

When you adjust the control handles on a closed path created with the above technique...

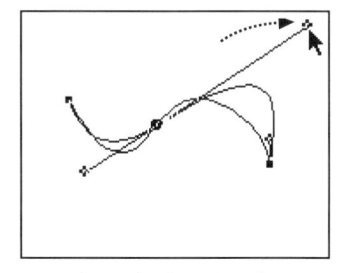

...you're only changing the curve of the lines on top. This may or may not be what you want.

4. Press Command-J to join the endpoints. FreeHand joins the two points into one point.

5. Press Command-Option-I to display the Object Inspector.

6. Check Closed and press Return. FreeHand closes the path.

At this point, you've got a closed path that's the same shape as the original, open path. Now you can join it to other closed paths to create compound paths.

Splitting and Joining Paths

You can always add points to or subtract points from a path in FreeHand. You can split an open or closed path into separate paths, or join paths to each other, or make a single path a closed path.

Splitting Paths   You can split a path in one of three ways.

- Select a point (or points) on the path with the Pointer tool, and then choose "Split object" (Command-Shift-J) from the Arrange menu.

- Select the path, then click the Knife tool on the path (or on a selected point on the path).

- Select the path, then drag the Knife tool over the path.

When you split a path by splitting a point, FreeHand creates a new point on top of the point you selected. This new point is connected to the line segment going to the next point along the path's winding (see Figure 2-51).

When you split a path using the Knife tool, two new points are created (see Figure 2-52).

To select one or the other of the two paths you've created by splitting the path, press Tab (to deselect everything), then click the path you want to select, or press ` (to select both paths), then hold down Shift and click the path you don't want selected.

When you split a path and create two new points, it can be very difficult figuring out which endpoint belongs to which path. It's simple, actually. The point closest to the start of the path (following the path's winding) becomes the point farthest to the back, and

FIGURE 2-51
Splitting a path by splitting points

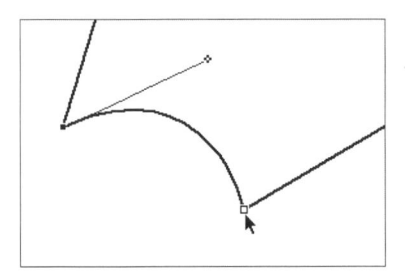

Select a point and choose "Split object" from the Element menu.

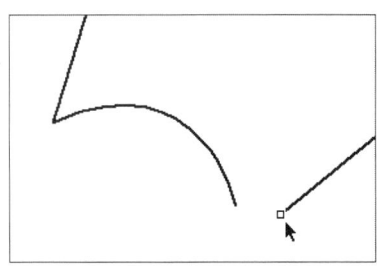

FreeHand splits the path at the point you selected.

FIGURE 2-52
Splitting a path by splitting a line segment

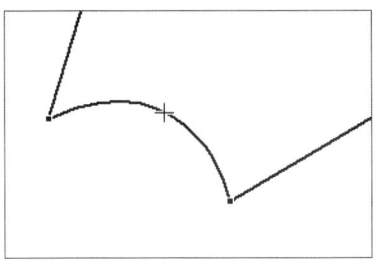

Select a path, select the knife tool, and then click on the path (or drag the knife tool across the path).

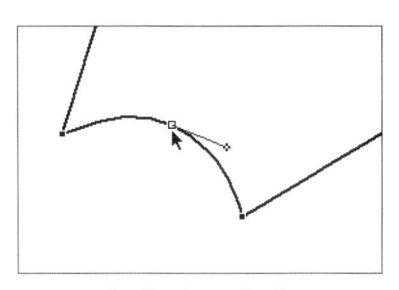

FreeHand splits the path where you clicked.

the point farthest from the start of the path is on top of it (see Figure 2-53). You can always use Bring To Front and Send To Back to change which point's on top.

You can use the Split element command to split any number of points. Drag a marquee over all the points you want to split, choose Split Object from the Arrange menu, and FreeHand splits all the points (see Figure 2-54).

FIGURE 2-53
Which point is on top?

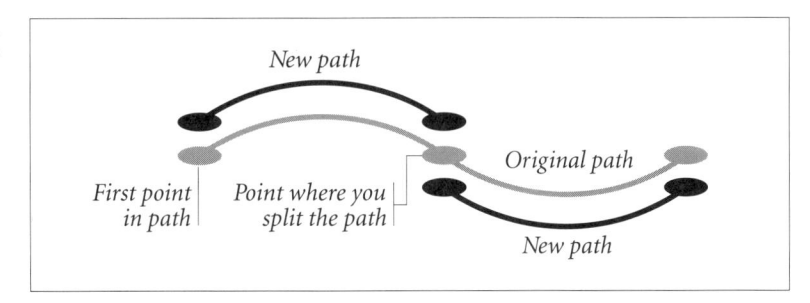

FIGURE 2-54
Splitting several points at once

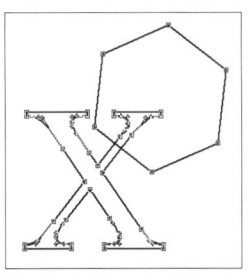

Drag a selection rectangle over the points you want to split.

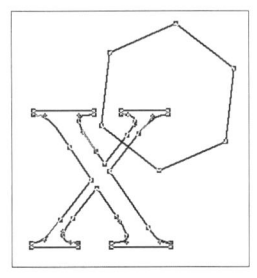

Choose Split Object from the Element menu. FreeHand splits all of the selected points.

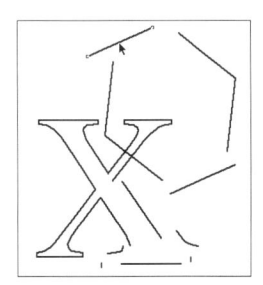

Now you can take the objects apart.

Joining Paths   You can join two open paths to create a single path, or you can join two closed paths to create a composite path. In this section, I'll talk about joining open paths. For more on joining closed paths to create composite paths, see the section "Composite Paths," later in this chapter.

To join points on two open paths and create a single path, drag the endpoints of the two open paths over each other. It's easier to do this when Snap To Point (on the View menu) is active. Usually, FreeHand joins the two points. If FreeHand—for whatever reason—won't join the points, drag a marquee over the two points and choose Join Objects from the Arrange menu (see Figure 2-55).

FIGURE 2-55
Joining two open paths

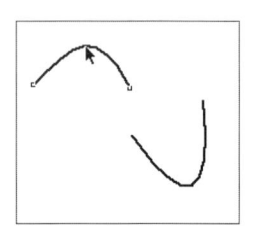

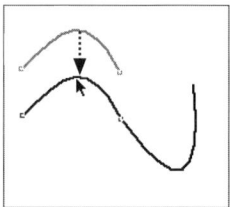

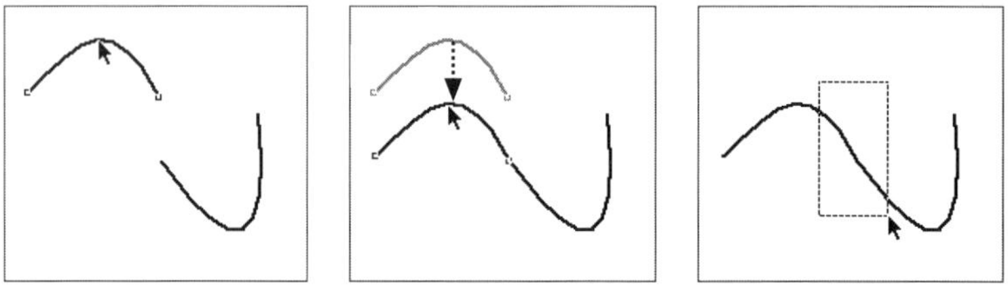

Move the paths so that their endpoints meet.

Drag a selection rectangle around the overlapping endpoints.

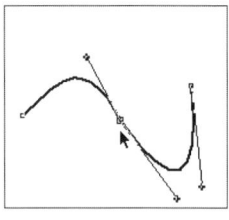

Press Command-Shift-J to join the points. The two paths become a single path.

Tip:
If "Join Objects" Is Grayed Out

If the Join Objects menu item is grayed out, one or both of the paths containing the points you've selected is probably a closed path, or both paths are open paths and you haven't selected a pair of points. If you're not sure if a path is closed or open, select the path and look at the Closed checkbox in the Object Inspector—if it's checked, the path is closed.

Tip:
If "Join Objects" Doesn't Do Anything

You can't join open paths without having two overlapping (or nearly overlapping) points selected. Move the paths or points so that two endpoints overlap, then drag a marquee over the two points, and choose Join Objects (or press Command-J) from the Arrange menu to join the paths.

Composite Paths

In the old days, not only did I have to walk miles to school in freezing weather, but I also had to perform impossibly difficult procedures just to create holes inside closed paths. While these rituals were kind of fascinating, they did nothing to help me hit my deadlines.

These days, creating holes in paths is easier—just make them into composite paths. Composite paths are made of two or more paths (which must be unlocked, ungrouped, and closed) which have been joined with Join Objects. Areas between the two paths, or areas where the paths overlap, are transparent (see Figure 2-56).

1. Select the ellipse tool from the toolbox.

2. Draw two ellipses, one on top of the other.

3. Fill the ellipses with some basic fill.

4. Select both ellipses.

FIGURE 2-56
Creating composite paths

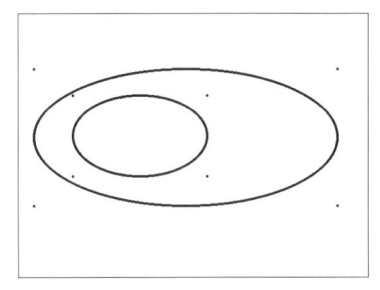

Create two ellipses using the ellipse tool.

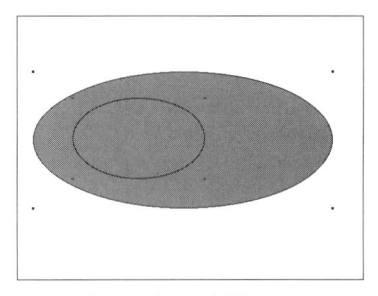

Apply the stroke and fill you want to the ellipses.

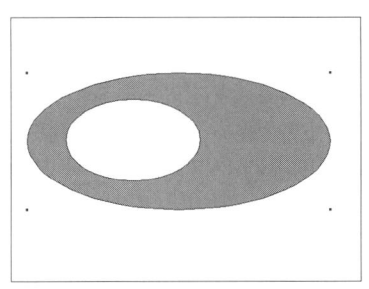

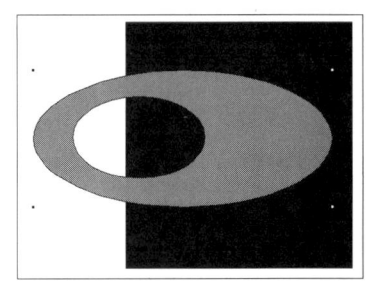

Press Command-J to join the ellipses.

You've just created a composite path. The inside of the shape is transparent.

5. Press Command-J to join the two ellipses.

What if you don't want transparent areas where the paths overlap? Select the composite path. Press Command-I to display the Inspector (if it's not already visible), and press Command-Option-I to display the Object Inspector. Uncheck the Even/Odd Fill option. This fills all the objects in the composite path with the same fill (see Figure 2-57).

FIGURE 2-57
Even/Odd fill and composite paths

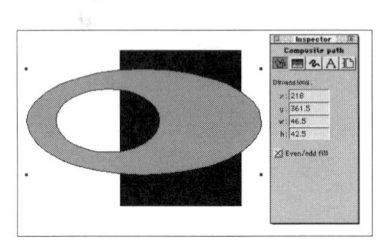

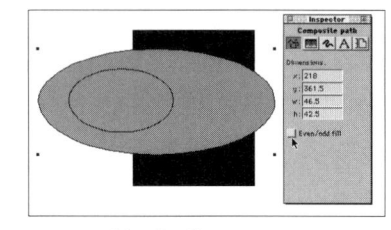

Even/Odd Fill on

Even/Odd Fill off

If you decide you don't want the paths to be composite paths, you can change them back into individual paths by selecting the composite path and then choosing Split Object from the Arrange menu.

Composite paths can be transformed just as you'd transform any other path.

When you convert characters to paths, FreeHand automatically converts the characters as composite paths (see Figure 2-58). This is great, because you can paste things inside composite paths.

FIGURE 2-58
Characters converted to paths are composite paths

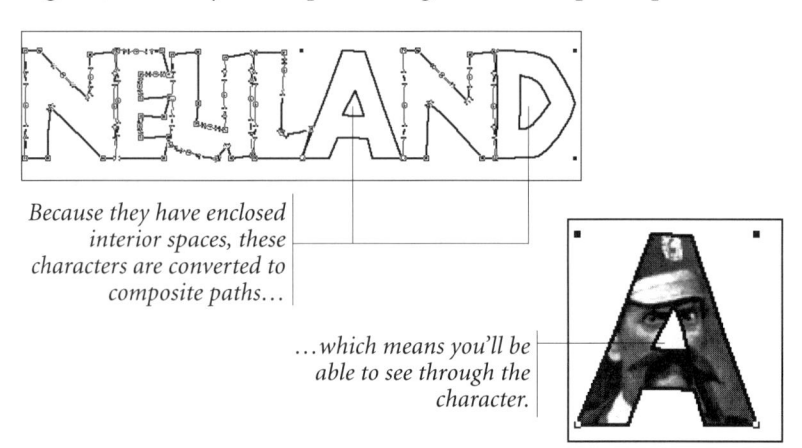

Because they have enclosed interior spaces, these characters are converted to composite paths…

…which means you'll be able to see through the character.

Composite paths work much like groups of objects, in that you can continue joining paths to the composite paths, just as you can group objects together with groups.

When you join new paths to a composite path, each new path is added to the path in order. When you split the composite path, the first time you choose Split Object removes the most recently appended subpath; the next Split Object removes the next most recently appended subpath; and so on.

Editing Composite Paths

You can subselect the individual subpaths that make up a composite path in the same way that you subselect objects inside a group—hold down Option and click on the object. Once an object is selected, you can alter the position of the path's points, move or otherwise transform the path, delete points, delete the entire path, or clone the path (see Figure 2-59).

FIGURE 2-59
Subselecting individual paths inside composite paths

For clarity, these two illustrations are shown in Keyline view.

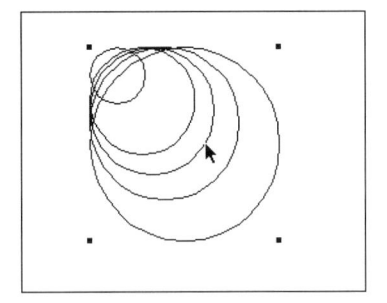

Select a composite path.

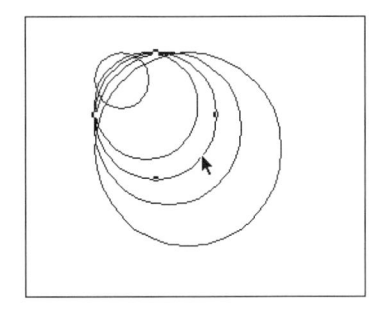

Hold down Option and click to select a subpath.

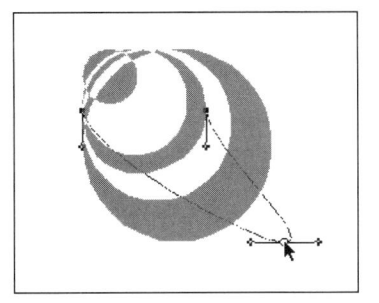

Modify the subpath.

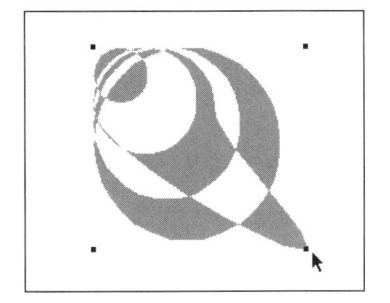

The subpath remains part of the composite path.

You can subselect multiple subpaths inside a composite path by holding down Shift as you select the subpaths. You can also select through any overlapping subpaths or objects by holding down Control and Option as you click on the subpaths, just as you can Control-click your way through stacks of objects. You can apply any of FreeHand's transformations to the subselected subpath.

When you join paths with different lines and fills, the composite path takes on the stroke and fill attributes of the path that's the farthest to the back.

Path Operations

FreeHand's path operations (the commands on the Path Operations submenu of the Arrange menu) fall into three conceptual groups, which don't necessarily match their grouping on the submenu. The path operations automate path-drawing tasks that would be difficult—if not impossible—to do manually.

- The path utilities (Correct Direction, Reverse Direction, Remove Overlap, and Simplify) are handy commands for cleaning up paths.

- The path-generating commands (Blend, Expand Stroke, and Inset Path) create new paths based on existing, selected paths, according to specific rules that differ from command to command.

- Intersection operations (Intersect, Punch, and Union) give you ways of manipulating the areas of intersection between two (or more) overlapping closed paths. You can remove the overlapping area from one of the paths using Punch, or join the two paths together while deleting the overlapping area using Union, or you can delete both of the original paths, leaving only the area defined by their intersection using Intersect.

In my opinion, the path operations are some of FreeHand's most important features. Why? First, the path operators make it easy for new users to create shapes they could never draw by hand: they can draw basic shapes (rectangles, polygons, and ellipses) and use the path operations to turn these basic shapes into the shapes they want. Second, illustrators and graphic artists benefit, because they can draw more accurately. I can't count the number of times I've seen FreeHand illustrations ruined because of paths that didn't quite meet, or paths that were too complex to print.

These features can also save you time, regardless of whether you're an amateur or a pro.

Correcting Path Direction

Most of the time, you could call Correct Path Direction, "make clockwise"—because that's what it does. You've probably noticed that you don't always get what you'd expect when you join paths to create a composite path. Sometimes, you'll see gaps in interior areas you'd expect would be filled. You can fix this problem by selecting the composite path and choosing Correct Direction (see Figure 2-60). Using Correct Direction has no effect on the shape of your path.

FIGURE 2-60
Correcting path direction

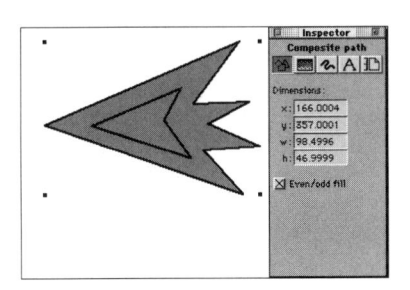

Before choosing Correct Direction—path doesn't fill properly.

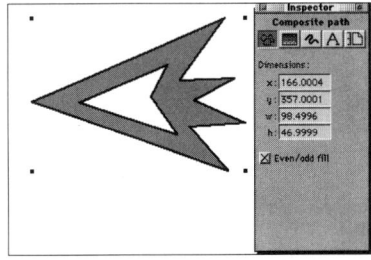

After "Correct Direction"

Reversing Path Direction

When you want to change a path's direction (for example, when you want an arrowhead to appear on the other end of an open path), choose Reverse Direction from the Path Operations submenu. FreeHand reverses the direction of the path (see Figure 2-61). Reverse Direction has no effect on the shape of your path.

FIGURE 2-61
Reversing path direction

Before "Reverse Direction"

After "Reverse Direction"

Removing Overlap

When a single FreeHand path crosses over itself, it becomes more difficult to print (and, to a certain extent, more difficult to edit). It's easy to create self-crossing paths when you're working with the Freehand tool, the Calligraphic Pen tool, or the Variable Stroke tool. It's also easy (it's practically unavoidable) to create composite paths which cross over themselves. Remove Overlap simplifies your paths by turning them into composite paths containing separate, closed paths (see Figure 2-62). It's kind of like a combination of Punch and Union, but works on a single path.

FIGURE 2-62
Removing overlap

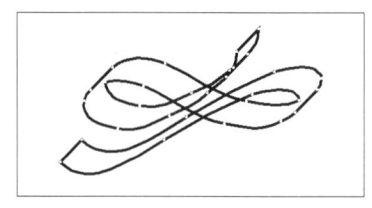

Before "Remove overlap"

After "Remove overlap"

Simplifying Paths

Okay, confess—here's something we've all done (at least once): we place a bilevel TIFF in FreeHand and trace it with the tracing tool, thereby generating a single path containing billions and billions of points—and then express surprise when the publication won't print. These days, we don't have to give up our sloppy habits (not that it'd be a bad idea…), provided we remember to select the path and run Simplify on it before we try to print (see Figure 2-63).

Simplify is also a great tool for new users who haven't quite gotten the hang of FreeHand's drawing tools—they can draw a path (new users typically use too many points when drawing), and then see how FreeHand thinks the path should be drawn.

FIGURE 2-63
Simplifying a path

Before "Simplify"

After "Simplify"

This path went from 177 to 127 points after simplification.

Remember: fewer points = easier printing.

Blending

Blending is a way of creating a number of paths, automatically, between two existing paths. Blending is one of FreeHand's most useful tools, especially for creating shaded objects. When Illustrator first introduced the world to blending, all of the marketing materials stressed this great new feature's ability to turn an "S" into a swan, or a "V" into a violin. That's pretty cool, *but how often do you actually need to do that?* Blending's actually a much less glamorous, much more useful tool (see Figure 2-64).

FIGURE 2-64
Blending

Select two points on two paths and choose Blend from the Path Operations submenu of the Arrange menu.

FreeHand fills in the intermediate blend objects.

Shading with blends   Keyline view of shading

FreeHand doesn't impose too many limitations on what, when, and how you can blend FreeHand objects. But there are a few things you've got to keep in mind.

You can blend any two ungrouped paths having like attributes. What do I mean by "like attributes?" I mean that you can blend a path containing a radial fill into a path containing another radial fill, but you can't blend a path containing a radial fill into a path containing a graduated fill.

When you try to blend paths having different stroke patterns, or patterned fills, the shapes of the objects blend, but the strokes or fills will flip from one to the other at the halfway point of the blend (see Figure 2-65).

Blending relies on reference points. When you're blending open paths, you have the option of selecting a "reference point." What's a "reference point?" It's a way of telling FreeHand, "Blend these

FIGURE 2-65
Blending paths with differing dashed strokes

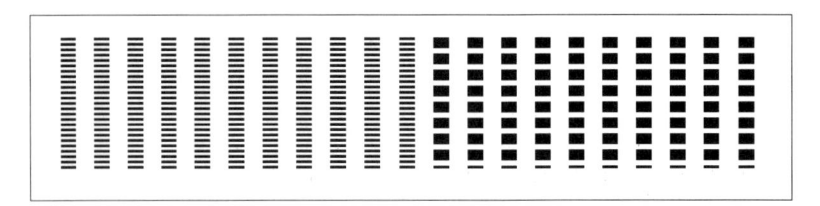

two objects from this point to that point" (see Figure 2-66). When you're blending closed paths, you *must* select a reference point on the paths before you can blend them.

FIGURE 2-66
Reference points

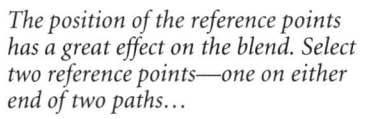

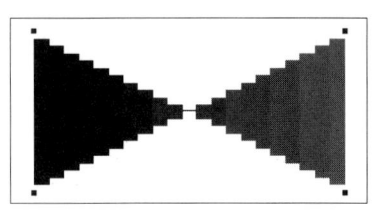

The position of the reference points has a great effect on the blend. Select two reference points—one on either end of two paths...

...and blend. In this example, the reference points make the blend flip over at its midpoint.

How many steps do you need? After picking reference points, the next most important part of creating a blend is the number you enter in the Number of Steps field in the Object Inspector (see Figure 2-67).

◆ The number you enter in the Number of Steps field is the number of steps you want in your blend, not including the original, selected objects.

FIGURE 2-67
Blend controls in the Object Inspector

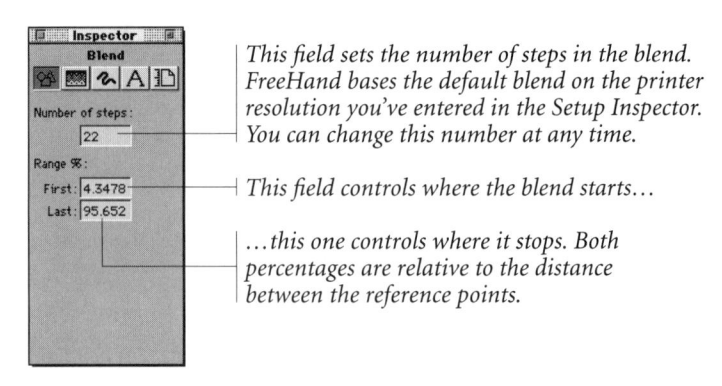

This field sets the number of steps in the blend. FreeHand bases the default blend on the printer resolution you've entered in the Setup Inspector. You can change this number at any time.

This field controls where the blend starts...

...this one controls where it stops. Both percentages are relative to the distance between the reference points.

- The number you enter in the First Blend field is the percentage of the distance between the original paths where you want to place the first blended path.

- The number you enter in the Last Blend field is the percentage of the distance between the original paths where you want to place the last blended path.

- Most of the time, you'll just type a number in the Number of Steps field and press Return. You can enter numbers in the other fields to create special blend effects (Figure 2-68).

FIGURE 2-68
Special blend effects

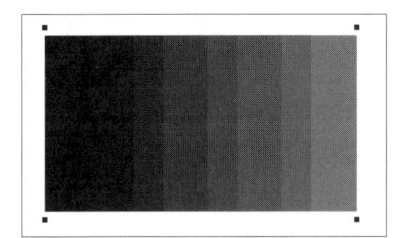

Normal blend: 19 blend steps; first blend step 5%; last blend step 95%.

Special blend: 19 blend steps; first blend step 20%; last blend step 80%.

When you're working with blends, you can determine the best number of blend steps to use, based on the length of the blend and the properties of your printer, by solving the following equation.

number of steps = (dpi ÷ lpi)^2 × % change in color

In this equation, *dpi* is the resolution of your final output device in dots per inch; *lpi* is the screen frequency you'll be using, in lines per inch. The value *% change in color* is just that, and it's easy to figure out if you're using spot colors.

If you're using process colors, figure out which component process color goes through the largest percentage change from one end of the blend to the other, and use that value for the % change in color part of the equation.

The purpose of this equation is to tell you the minimum number of steps you should use. Below this number of steps, you'll start losing gray levels, and bands of gray (or color) will appear in your blend. You can always use more blend steps than this, but you won't gain anything, and each additional blend step increases the complexity of your publication, therefore increasing the time your publication takes to print.

Also be aware that you never need more than 256 steps in a blend (unless you have to fill gaps between blend objects inside the blend), because that's the maximum number of gray levels a PostScript interpreter can render.

What if using the optimum number of blend steps means that gaps appear in your blend? This happens when your original blend objects aren't big enough to cover the distance from one blend step to the next. When this happens, you can either increase the number of blend steps you're using, or you can figure out how much larger you'll have to make your blend objects using the following equation.

distance blend has to cover ÷ number of steps = size of original object

Okay smart guy, you're saying, these equations work great for blending simple rectangles which happen to be running vertically or horizontally, but what about a diagonal blend between two like paths shaped like a camel's back (see Figure 2-69)? Huh? Huh?

It's easy—select the Line tool and draw a line from one point to another, then read the distance from the info bar.

You can also blend between intermediate objects to obtain an even higher degree of control over your graduated or radial fills.

FIGURE 2-69
Camel's hump blend

As you drag the Line tool, you'll see the distance between the two points in the Info Bar.

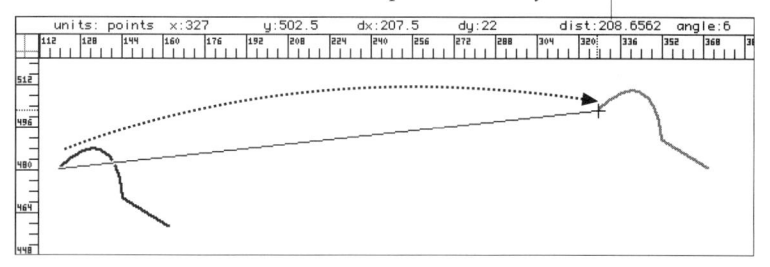

Blends and spot colors. Unlike FreeHand 3, FreeHand 5 lets you blend two spot-colored objects. Unfortunately, when you do this, FreeHand colors all the intermediate objects in the blend using process colors—which is almost certainly not what you want. Does this mean you're out of luck if you want to create tint builds by blending two spot colors? You're not—you can stack up two blends and set each spot color to overprint (see "Creating Tint Builds" in Chapter 6, "Color").

Alternatively, you can use one of the process colors (cyan, magenta, yellow, or black) as a substitute for each spot color in your publication, and blend away. For more on how to do this, see "Substituting Process Colors for Spot Colors" in Chapter 6, "Color."

Creating a blend. Now that you know the rules, let's create a blend (see Figure 2-70).

1. Select two ungrouped paths (with matching or compatible attributes).

FIGURE 2-70
Creating a blend

Select two reference points and choose Blend from the Path Operations submenu of the Arrange menu.

FreeHand creates your blend.

Enter the number of blend steps you want in the Object Inspector and press Return.

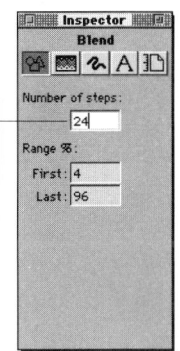

The blended objects are grouped.

Okay, this example's no more typical of the uses of blending than the swan or violin I mentioned earlier.

But it sure is fun!

2. Choose Blend from the Path operations submenu of the Arrange menu (or press Command-Shift-B).

Is Blend grayed out? If it is, your paths might not be of the same type (that is, you might have one open path and one closed path). If both of the paths are closed, you have to select a "reference point." If one of the paths is closed, you have to make it an open path, or make the other path closed.

FreeHand blends the paths you've selected. The original objects and the newly created paths are grouped together. I refer to the resulting group as a "blend."

If the attributes of the paths you're trying to blend are incompatible, FreeHand displays an alert (shown in Figure 2-71). Sorry, no blend. You'll have to track down what's different between the two paths, make changes, and try again.

FIGURE 2-71
What happens when you try blending incompatible objects

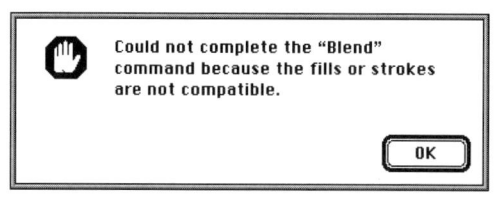

You can enter negative numbers (to -100%) in the First blend and Last blend fields. You can use this to extend the blend past the original objects by up to the distance between them. Of what possible use is this? I haven't found one yet.

Editing blends. If you want to change the number of steps in your blend, select the blended objects and press Command-Option-I to display the Object Inspector. Change the blend by entering new values in the Number of Steps, First blend, or Last blend fields, and press Return. FreeHand creates a new blend from the original objects (see Figure 2-72).

Changing the shape of the entire blend. You can change the shape and attributes of blended objects to a certain extent by changing the shape and attributes of the original shapes in the blend. Subselect the original path (or both original paths) by holding down

FIGURE 2-72
Editing blends

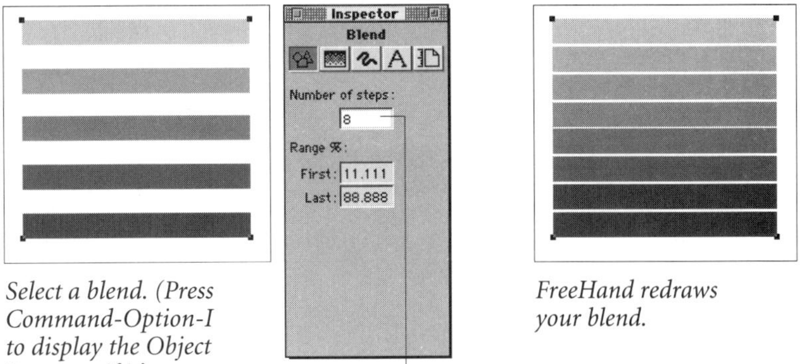

Select a blend. (Press Command-Option-I to display the Object Inspector if it's not already visible).

Enter a number in the Number of Steps field and Press Return.

FreeHand redraws your blend.

Option as you click on the path (you are subselecting an element in a group). Next, change the path's attributes and/or shape. As you change the path's shape and attributes, FreeHand recreates the blend on the fly based on the current shape and/or attributes (see Figure 2-73).

FIGURE 2-73
Changing the shape and attributes of blended objects

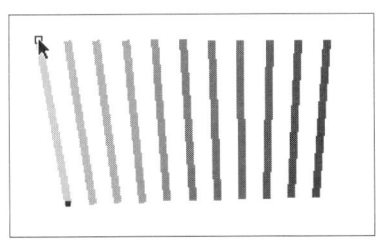

Hold down Option and click on the first or last object in the blend to subselect it.

Reshape the object. FreeHand alters the blend based on the new shape.

Editing an intermediate path in a blend. To edit one or more of the intermediate paths in the blend, ungroup the blend, select the path, and edit away. There's no way to get the changes you make to this intermediate point to ripple through the blend, however. If you want to do that, consider reblending between intermediate objects (see Figure 2-74).

Creating colors based on blend steps. When you create a blend, the colors applied to the intermediate paths in the blend are not automatically added to FreeHand's Color List. If you want to add

FIGURE 2-74
Editing intermediate
paths in a blend

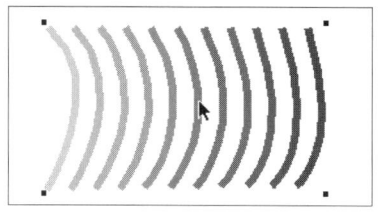

Select the blend you want to edit...

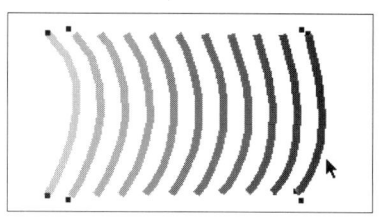

...and press Command-U to ungroup it.

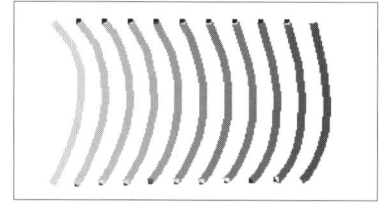

Press Command-U to ungroup the intermediate blend objects.

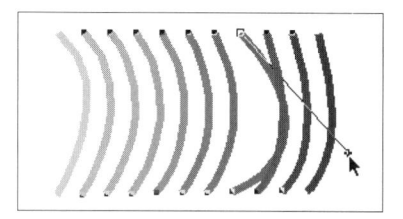

Now you can edit the intermediate blend objects.

one or more of the colors created by the blend to your Color List, this is the procedure (see Figure 2-75).

1. Select the blend.

2. Press Command-U twice to completely ungroup the blend (when you first press Command-U, FreeHand ungroups the original objects, but leaves the objects generated by the blend grouped; pressing Command-U again ungroups all the objects in the blend).

3. Select one of the objects you created by blending.

4. In the Color List, choose New from the popup menu. FreeHand adds a new color to the Color List. The new color is based on the color of the object you selected.

Tip:
Adding all of the colors in a blend

When you want to add *all* of the colors in a blend to your publication's Color List, ungroup the blend (twice), then choose Name All Colors from the Colors submenu of the Xtras menu. FreeHand adds all of the colors to your Color List, automatically assigning a name to each color as it does so. Bear in mind that this will add as many colors to your Colors List as there are steps in the blend.

FIGURE 2-75
Adding colors based on blended elements

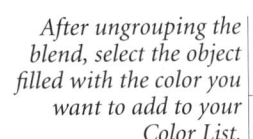

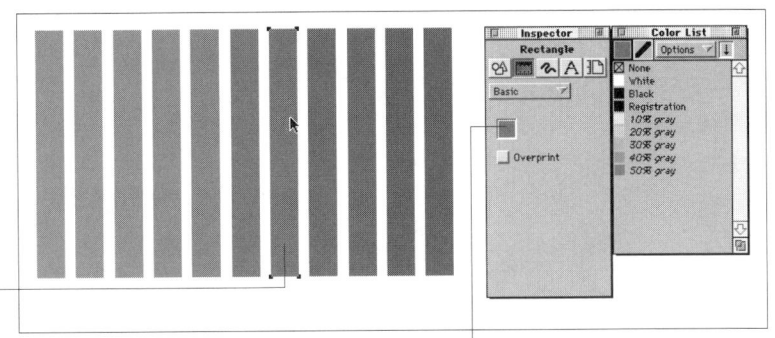

After ungrouping the blend, select the object filled with the color you want to add to your Color List.

When you select the object, its fill color appears in the color well in the Fill Inspector.

Drag a color swatch from the color well in the Fill Inspector to a blank area in the Color List (or drop it on the Add Arrow at the top of the Color List).

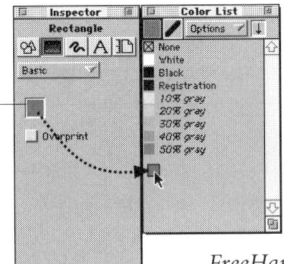

FreeHand adds the color to the Color List and automatically assigns a color name to the new color.

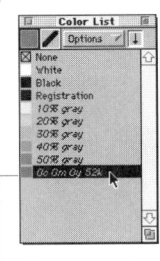

To change the color's name, double-click the color name in the Color List…

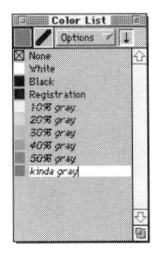

…and type a name for the color. When you're done typing, press Return.

Using blend to create graduated and radial fills. If you want total control over the creation of graduated or radial fills in FreeHand, use Blend, rather than the Graduated or Radial fill types. If you use Blend, you accrue several significant advantages.

- ◆ Control over the graduation. FreeHand's Graduated fill type offers you the choice between Linear and Logarithmic fill progressions, but blending can give you more control. By blending objects, you can make the blend go as rapidly or slowly from color to color as you choose.

- ◆ Control over trapping. See Chapter 7, "Printing," for more information on trapping graduated and radial fills.

- ◆ Optimization of your fill for printing on your final output device (printer or imagesetter).

- Superior screen display of fills.

The only disadvantage I can think of is that you've got many more objects on a page to worry about. Unless you ungroup them, however, they'll be treated as a single group.

Blends also produce very different-looking results. I find that I mix blends and graduated fills inside a publication to get the effects I want. If I want a graduated fill that doesn't follow the shape of an object, I'll often use a graduated fill. But if I want a graduated fill that does follow the shape of an object, I'll use a blend. Figure 2-76 shows the difference.

To create a graduated fill using Blend, follow these steps.

1. Create a path that has the fill attributes you want for one end of the graduation.

2. Create a path that has the fill attributes you want for the other end of the graduation.

3. Select one point from the first path, and then select a point from the second path.

4. Choose Blend from the Path Operations submenu of the Arrange menu.

5. Display the Object Inspector, if it's not already visible, by pressing Command-Option-I. Type a number in the Number of steps field and press Return.

FIGURE 2-76
Blends and graduated fills

Graduated fills don't follow the shape of the object.

Blends follow the shape of the object.

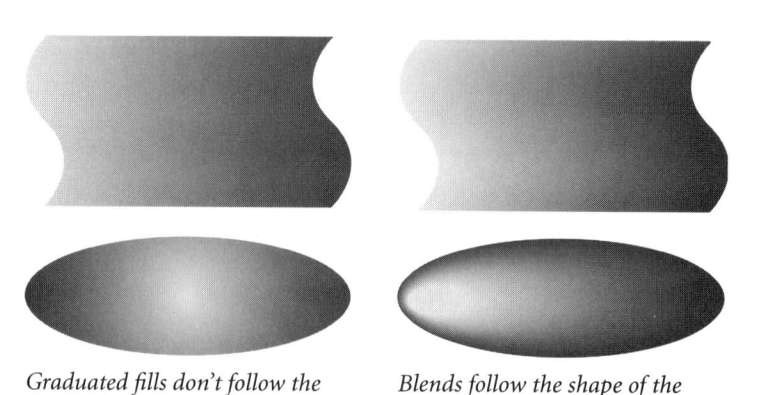

Blending with the Smudge Tool. If you've installed the Smudge tool (that is, if the file "Smudge" is in your Xtras folder), you can create a blend by dragging—it's almost like painting with a blend (see Figure 2-77). What do you have to do?

1. Display the Xtra Tools palette (press Command-Shift-K, if it's not already visible), then select the Smudge tool.

2. Hold down Command (to turn the cursor into the Pointer tool) and select the path you want to "smudge," then release Command and drag the Smudge tool. As you drag, Free-Hand extends a line from the original path, showing you the distance and direction of the blend you're creating.

3. Stop dragging, and FreeHand creates the blend.

Once you've created a blend using the Smudge tool, you can edit it as you would any other blend. For more on editing blends, see "Editing Blends," earlier in this chapter.

FIGURE 2-77
Creating a blend with the Smudge tool

You'll find the Smudge tool in the Xtra Tools palette (if the palette's not already visible, you can display it by pressing Command-Shift-K).

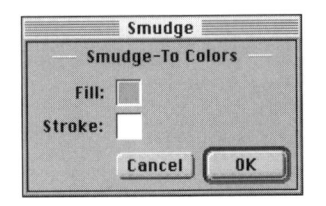

Double-click the Smudge tool in the Xtra Tools palette to display the Smudge dialog box.

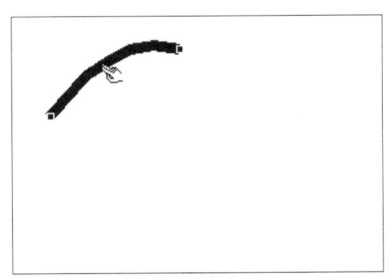

Position the Smudge tool over a path...

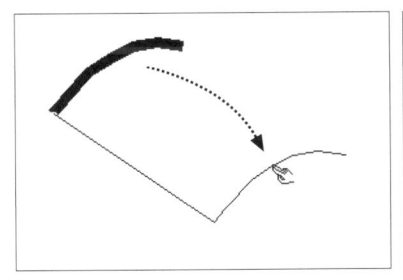

...and drag.

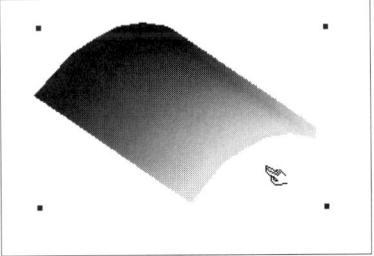

Stop dragging, and FreeHand creates a blend. Blends you create using the Smudge tool behave like any other FreeHand blend.

You can set options for the Smudge tool by double-clicking the tool in the Xtras palette. When you do this, FreeHand displays the Smudge dialog box. You can set the Fill and Stroke colors as you would any other FreeHand colors—drag a color swatch into the color well. Unlike most other color wells, double-clicking these won't bring up the Color Mixer and the Color List.

Blending with Multi-Color Fill Extra. What's the easiest way to create a rainbow? If you've installed the Multi-Color Fill Xtra (the file "Multi-Color Fills" is inside your Xtras folder), you can easily create graduated and radial fills that use more than two colors.

At this point, I've got to straighten a few things out—when you use this Xtra, you're not creating a *fill* (at least not in the way that you typically think of fills), you're creating a *blend*. The Multi-Color Fill Xtra gives you an easy way to automate the process of creating a series of blends. The individual blends inside the group that this Xtra creates behave just like other blends in FreeHand—as you'll see if you select the object you've "filled." Press Command-Shift-X (for "Cut Contents"), and then press Command-U (to ungroup the blend).

To use this Xtra, choose "Multi-Color Fill" from the Colors submenu of the Xtras menu. FreeHand displays the Multi-Color Fill dialog box (see Figure 2-78).

To change the location of a color in the blend, drag the appropriate color swatch back and forth above the preview bar (see Figure 2-79). Drop the swatch, and FreeHand changes the position of the color in the blend.

To add a color to your Multi-Color Fill, drag a color swatch into the Multi-Color Fill dialog box and drop it above the preview. FreeHand adds a new color to the blend and updates the preview (see Figure 2-80).

To remove a color from a multi-color fill, drag the swatch for the color you want to remove out of the dialog box and drop it. FreeHand removes the color from the blend and updates the blend and the dialog box (see Figure 2-81).

Unlike most other color swatches in FreeHand, double-clicking the color swatches in the Multi-Color Fill dialog box doesn't display or hide the Color Mixer or the Color List.

DRAWING 163

FIGURE 2-78
Using the Multi-Color Fill Xtra

Graduated Fill

Fill preview | *Color swatches*

Choose which fill type (Graduated or Radial) you want from this pop-up menu.

Set an angle for the graduated fill using either this field...

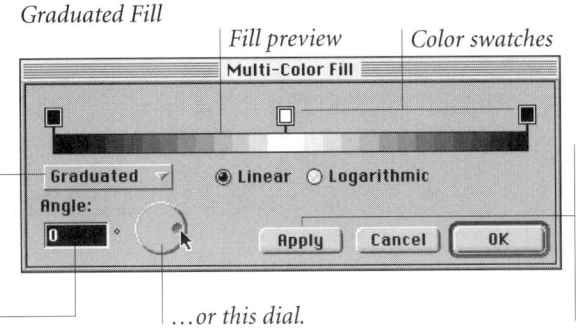

...or this dial.

Click the Apply button to see the multi-color fill applied to the selected path without closing the dialog box.

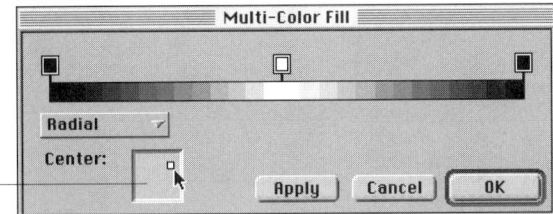

Radial Fill

Drag the square to set the center point of the radial fill.

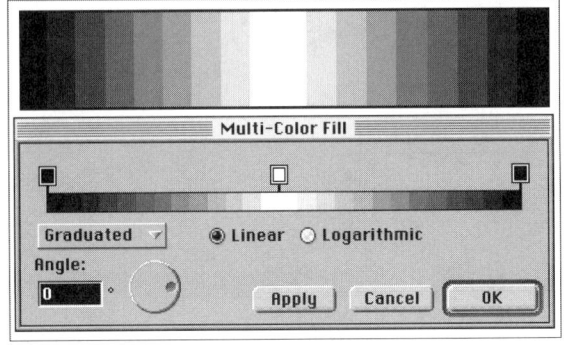

You don't have to close the Multi-Color Fill dialog box to see the effect of the settings on the blend—all you need to do is drag it out of the way and click the Apply button.

FIGURE 2-79
Changing the position of colors in the blend

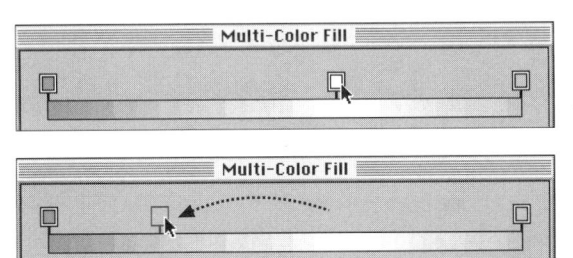

Drag the color swatches back and forth above the preview bar to change the appearance of the blend.

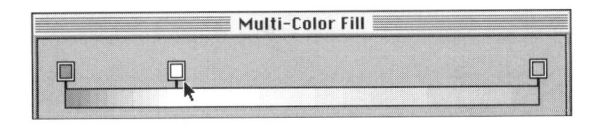

FIGURE 2-80
Adding colors
to the blend

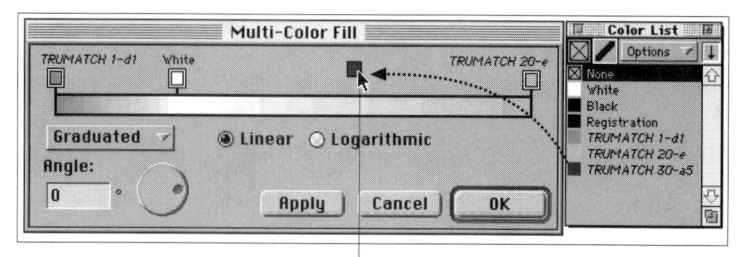

Drag a color swatch from the Color List and drop it above the preview bar...

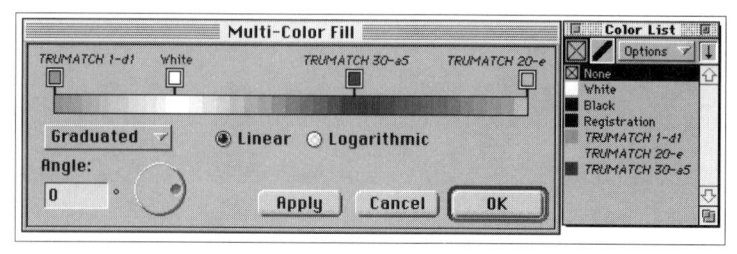

...and FreeHand adds that color to the blend.

FIGURE 2-81
Removing colors
from the blend

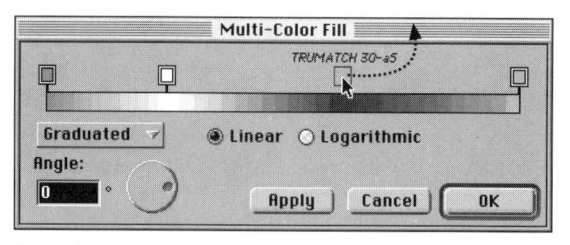

Drag the swatch away from the title bar.

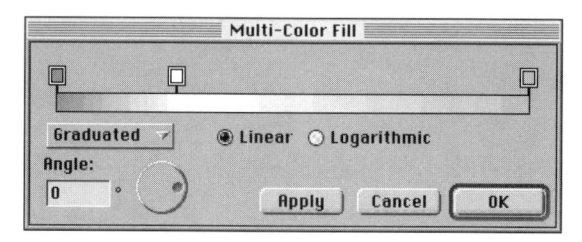

FreeHand removes the color from the blend.

Intersect   What do you do when you want to create a path that's defined by the intersection of two (or more) overlapping paths? Select the overlapping objects and choose Intersect from the Path operations submenu, and FreeHand creates the path for you. It's that simple (see Figure 2-82).

DRAWING 165

FIGURE 2-82
Using Intersect

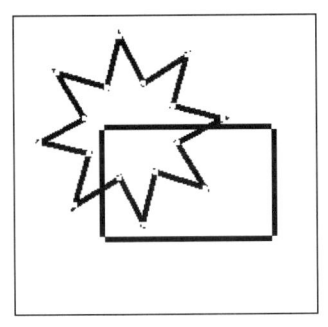

FreeHand deletes the areas shown in gray.

New path created by "Intersect"

Select two or more closed paths (in this example, the star shape is on top).

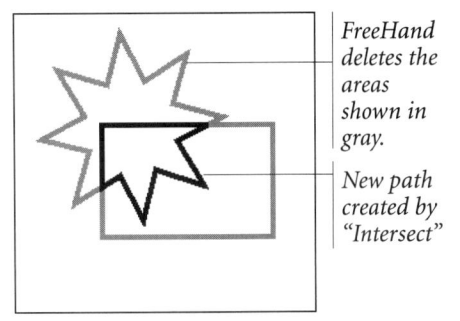

Choose Intersect from the Path Operations submenu of the Arrange menu. FreeHand creates a new path based on the intersection of the shapes, and deletes the original paths.

The following are a few things to keep in mind when you use Intersect.

- The path FreeHand generates when you choose Intersect takes on the formatting of the original path that's farthest to the back.

- If you run Intersect on a set of paths that don't intersect, FreeHand deletes all the paths.

- If you've turned on the Path Operations Consume Original Paths option in the Object Editing Preferences dialog box, FreeHand deletes the original paths as it creates the new path. If you want to keep the original paths, clone them before using Intersect, or turn off the Path Operations Consume Original Paths option.

Tip: Simulating the Effect of Transparency with Intersect

Hold down Option as you choose Intersect from the Path Operations submenu, or choose "Transparency" from the Path Operations submenu of the Xtras menu (or, for that matter, when you click the Intersect button in the Operations palette), and FreeHand displays the Transparency dialog box. Choose a percentage (0 percent equals complete transparency, 100 percent equals complete opacity—the same color as the topmost path) and press Return, and FreeHand colors the new path with a process color based on the colors of the intersecting objects (see Figure 2-83).

FIGURE 2-83
Transparency
dialog box

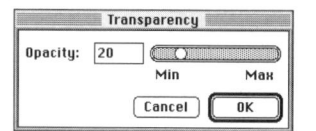

Hold down Option as you choose Intersect, and FreeHand displays the Transparency dialog box.

Transparency creates a new shape and colors it with a new color based on the colors of the original shapes.

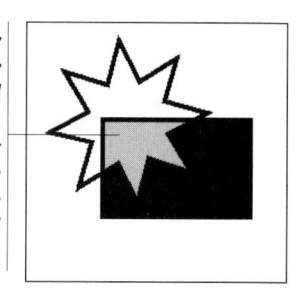

Punch

When you want to use one closed path to cut a hole in another closed path, use Punch. Position the path you want to use as the "cookie cutter" above the path you want to use as "cookie dough," and choose Punch from the Path Operations submenu. FreeHand deletes the area where the two paths overlap from the path that's farthest to the back (see Figure 2-84). When the topmost path is entirely within the path behind it, FreeHand turns the paths into a single composite path.

FIGURE 2-84
Punch effect

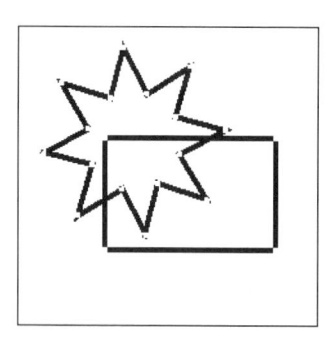

FreeHand deletes the areas shown in gray.

New path created by "Punch"

Select two or more closed paths (in this example, the star shape is on top).

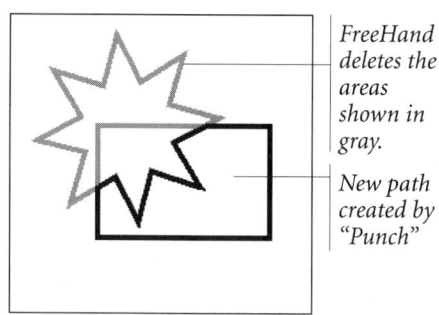

Choose Punch from the Path Operations submenu of the Arrange menu. FreeHand creates a new path by cutting the topmost path out of the paths behind it.

Union

Often, I want to create a single path from two or more overlapping closed paths, but I don't want the path to have holes in it, as it would if I made it a composite path using Join Elements. Union does just what I want—it combines two paths while removing any areas where they overlap from the new path (see Figure 2-85). If the paths I've selected don't overlap, FreeHand creates a composite path.

Union is great for creating complex paths from simple paths, such as rectangles and ellipses.

FIGURE 2-85
Using Union

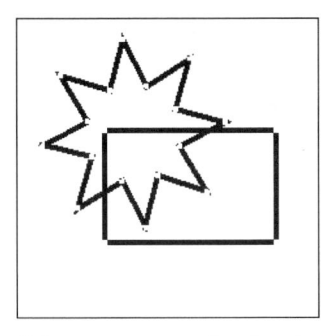

FreeHand deletes the areas shown in gray.

New path created by "Union"

Select two or more closed paths (in this example, the star shape is on top).

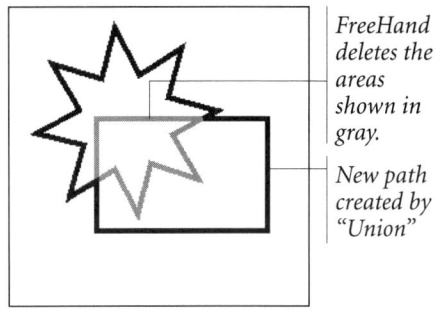

Choose Union from the Path Operations submenu of the Arrange menu. FreeHand creates a new path by merging the original paths and removing their areas of intersection.

Crop The Crop path operation is new in FreeHand 5.5. It's something like the opposite of Punch. Where Punch removes paths or parts of paths *inside* the area of the topmost path (the "cookie cutter"), Crop removes all paths *outside* that area. To use the Crop path operation, follow these steps (see Figure 2-86).

1. Position a path above some other paths.

2. Select the paths.

3. Choose Crop from the Path Operations submenu of the Arrange menu (or choose Crop from the Path Operations submenu of the Xtras menu). FreeHand crops the background paths into the area taken up by the cropping path.

The Crop path operation is nothing like the cropping tool found in other applications. Crop won't crop images unless those images have already been pasted inside a path. If that's the effect you're after, you can paste the image inside the path.

Expand Stroke Because I create lots of illustrations featuring geometric grids and lattices, I've often wanted a command that would take an open path I'd drawn and convert it into a closed path that I could fill or use as a clipping path. Expand Stroke creates two new paths, where each new path is a specific distance from the center of the original

FIGURE 2-86
Using Crop

This polygon is on top of the other selected objects.

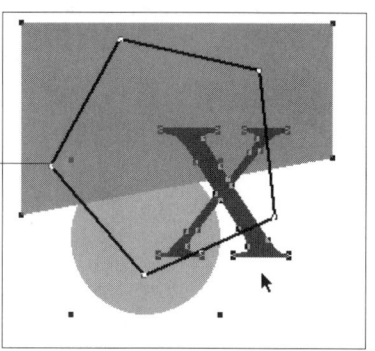

Select some objects and choose Crop from the Path Operations submenu of the Arrange menu.

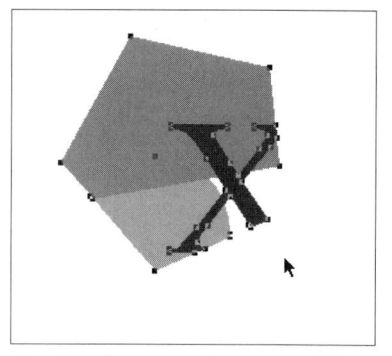

FreeHand removes that parts of the paths that aren't covered by the polygon.

path. One of the generated paths is a specific distance *outside* the original path; the other is the same distance *inside* the original path. Once FreeHand's created the paths, it joins them into a single, compound path (see Figure 2-87).

FIGURE 2-87
Using Expand Stroke

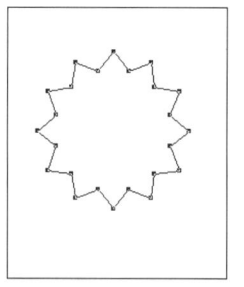

Select a path and choose Expand Stroke from the Path Operations submenu of the Arrange menu.

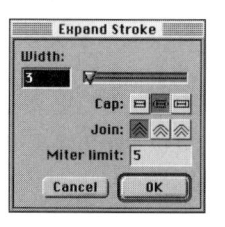

FreeHand displays the Expand Stroke dialog box. Enter the distance you want between the selected path and the new path in the Width field, and press Return.

FreeHand creates a new path, placing each new point a precise distance from each original point.

Inset Path

Inset Path works like Expand Stroke—but Inset Path only creates one new path, a specific distance inside or outside the original path (Figure 2-88). Note that scaling a path and using Inset Path produce (in most cases) very different results.

When you enter negative numbers in the Inset Path dialog box, FreeHand creates a new path *a* specific distance *outside* the original path ("inset path" becomes "outset path").

DRAWING 169

FIGURE 2-88
Using Inset Path

Select a path and
choose Inset Path
from the Path
Operations submenu
of the Arrange menu.

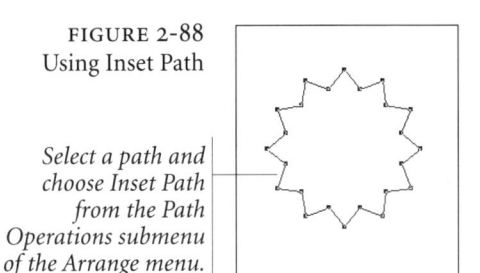

Clone the path first, if
you want to keep it in
its original shape—
"Inset path" operates on
the current path.

FreeHand displays the
Inset Path dialog box.
Enter the distance you
want between the
selected path and the
new path in the Width
field, and press Return.
Enter a negative
distance to make the
generated path larger
than the original path.

FreeHand creates a
new path, placing each
new point a precise
distance from each
original point.

Path Operations and Preferences

If you're getting tired of cloning paths before you run path operations on them, there's a preference you should know about. It's the Path Operations Consume Original Paths option in the Object Editing Preferences dialog box (see "Preferences," in Chapter 1, "FreeHand Basics"). When this option is off, FreeHand clones paths as you run path operations—and leaves your original paths alone. Turn this option on to have FreeHand delete the original paths while performing path operations (see Figure 2-89).

FIGURE 2-89
The Path Operations
Consume Original
Paths option

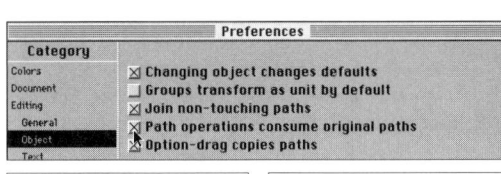

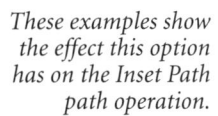

*Object Editing
Preferences dialog box.*

These examples show
the effect this option
has on the Inset Path
path operation.

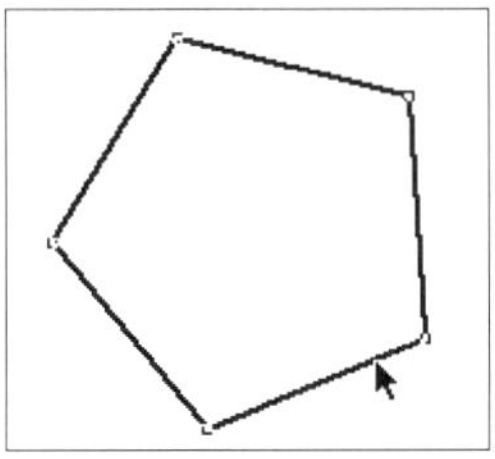

Original path.

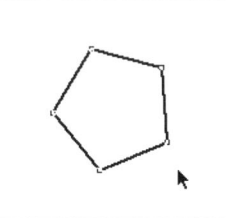

When the Path Operations Consume Original Paths option is on, FreeHand deletes the original path.

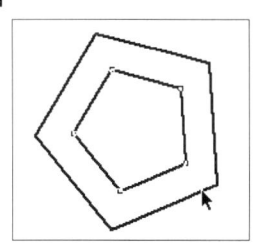

When the Path Operations Consume Original Paths option is off, FreeHand retains the original path.

Running Path Operations from the Operations Palette

Another way you can run FreeHand's path operations is to use the Operations palette (see Figure 2-90). To display the Operations palette, press Command-Shift-I. The path operations (and various other FreeHand operations) are represented by buttons in the palette (you can display the palette without labels once you get used to the appearance of the buttons).

FIGURE 2-90
Path operations on the Operations palette

The Operations palette takes up less room with "Show labels" turned off—but you've got to know your icons.

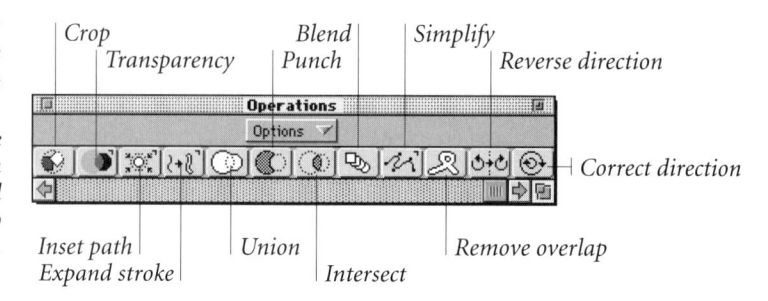

Tracing

When Illustrator 1.0 first appeared, tracing scanned artwork or MacPaint images was seen as the major use for the product. People just couldn't imagine creating entire pieces of artwork using a point-and-path drawing program. While times have changed—I think more people now use FreeHand and Illustrator to create illustrations without tracing—tracing is still a powerful option you can use in creating your FreeHand publication.

You can trace any object in FreeHand, and you can trace the object manually or use the Tracing tool.

Manual Tracing

To manually trace an image, follow these steps (see Figure 2-91).

1. Import an image. Make sure you've got High-Resolution TIFF Display turned on in the Preferences dialog box; this way, you'll see the high-resolution display of your imported image rather than a 72-dpi rendition.

2. Without deselecting the TIFF, click the Background layer in the Layers palette to send the image to the background. This grays the image and makes it easier to trace. You can also color the image some color (I like coloring it cyan, because

FIGURE 2-91
Manually tracing an imported image

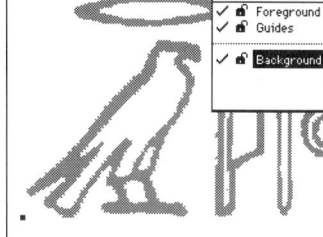

Import the image you want to trace.   *Send the image to a background layer.*

Place points and paths until…   *…you've traced the image.*

I'm used to tracing things drawn in nonreproducing blue pen) and send it to some other layer—just make sure you're doing the tracing on a layer that's in front of the layer you send the image to.

3. Lock the background layer by clicking on the padlock icon next to the layer's name in the Layers palette.

4. Zoom in on some portion of the image and start placing points.

5. When you're through tracing the image, delete the image from your illustration, or send it to some nonprinting layer.

Why not use the Tracing tool? The Tracing tool is great, but you're smarter than it is. Often, you can trace an image more quickly than you can autotrace it, given the amount of time it can take to clean up an autotraced image.

When you're tracing—particularly when you're tracing objects other than bitmaps—the larger the object is, the more accurate your tracing will be. I often copy objects I want to trace to a new document or a new page, trace them there, and then bring the resulting paths back into my publication.

Autotracing

First, I have to clear something up. In spite of what you might have heard elsewhere, you can autotrace *anything* on a FreeHand page. I have to mention this, because many people have the impression that you can only autotrace bitmapped images. In fact, you can autotrace text, paths, imported images—and even imported EPS graphics. Autotracing is a fast and fun way to create new paths from other FreeHand objects.

To autotrace an object, follow these steps (see Figure 2-92).

1. Select the Tracing tool from the toolbox. If you want to change the Tracing tool's settings, double-click the Tracing tool and make the changes you want in the Tracing tool dialog box.

2. Drag the cursor around the area you want to trace. Keep this area as small as you can—autotracing can take a long time and can generate paths containing lots of points. It's sometimes a little easier to autotrace a complex or large object in several passes, and then join the resultant paths. If you run out of memory while you're autotracing, select a smaller area to trace or quit FreeHand, increase FreeHand's RAM allocation in the Finder, and then try tracing again.

After you release the mouse button, FreeHand autotraces the object or objects you dragged a rectangle around. It's a good idea

FIGURE 2-92
Autotracing

Drag the tracing tool around the object you want to trace.

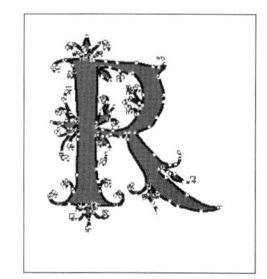

FreeHand traces the object.

to move the paths you've created to a new layer. Without deselecting the paths, choose New from the popup menu in the Layers palette. FreeHand creates a new layer and adds it to the top of the Layers palette. Click on the layer's name in the Layers palette to move the selected objects to that layer.

The current magnification has no effect on autotracing.

Strokes

Once you've created a path, you'll probably want to give the path some specific line weight, color, or other property. The process of applying formatting to a path is often called "stroking a path," and we refer to a path's appearance as its "stroke." Strokes specify what the outside of the paths looks like.

To apply a stroke to a path, you can choose one of FreeHand's default stroke widths from the Attributes menu, or you can specify a stroke using either the Stroke Inspector or the Styles palette.

Note that you can choose a number of predefined line weights from the Stroke Widths submenu of the Arrange menu. If you like, you can add new stroke weights to this submenu using the Expert Editing Preferences dialog box (see "Expert Editing Preferences," in Chapter 1, "FreeHand Basics"). These are great, as far as they go, but you'll be doing most of your serious work using the Stroke Inspector. To display the Stroke Inspector, press Command-Option-L (you can think of "L" as Line).

Use the Stroke Type popup menu (the popup menu directly below the Inspector buttons) in the Stroke Inspector to choose the type of stroke you want to use.

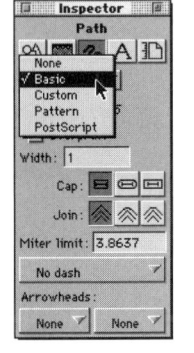

Basic Strokes

When you select Basic from the Stroke Type popup menu, the Stroke Inspector shows you the basic stroke attributes. Most of the time, you'll be working with basic strokes. Though they're not flashy, there are a few interesting tricks to using them, and a couple of things to look out for.

Color. Drag a color swatch from a color well in the Color List (or the Color Mixer, or from any other color well) into the color well in the Stroke Inspector to apply a color to your path. If you're working with a named color, the color's name appears next to the color well in the Stroke Inspector.

Overprint. Checking this option makes the stroke overprint, rather than knock out of, whatever's behind it. This setting overrides any ink-level overprinting settings in the Print options dialog box (see Figure 2-93). This might not seem like much, but if you're creating color publications, you'll find it's one of the most important features in FreeHand (see Chapter 6, "Color," for more about trapping).

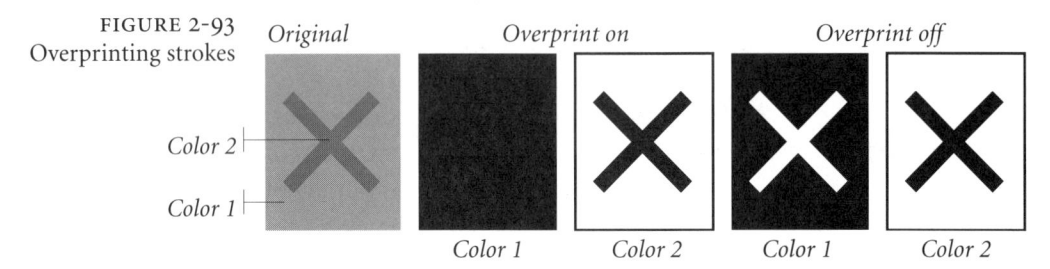

FIGURE 2-93
Overprinting strokes

Original   *Overprint on*   *Overprint off*

Color 2

Color 1

Color 1   Color 2   Color 1   Color 2

You won't see the effect of overprinting until you print separations of your publication. When you do that, you'll see something like these thumbnails.

Width. Enter a number to specify the width of your stroke. Don't type zero, even if it works to produce the finest stroke available on your 300-dpi printer, because a stroke weight of zero on an imagesetter produces an almost invisible line. If you want a hairline, use a .25-point stroke.

Cap. Select one of the Cap options to determine the shape of the end of the stroke (see Figure 2-94). The Cap option you choose has no visible effect on a closed path.

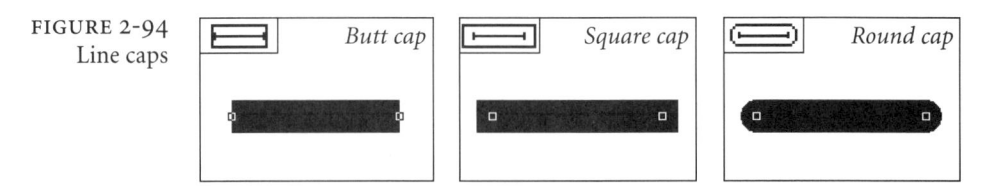

FIGURE 2-94
Line caps

Butt cap   *Square cap*   *Round cap*

Join. The Join option determines the way FreeHand renders corners—the place where two line segments meet in a point (see Figure 2-95).

FIGURE 2-95
Line joins

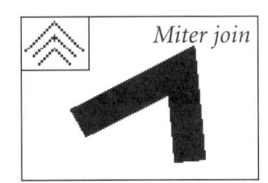

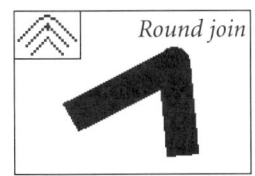

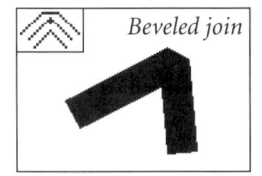

Miter join *Round join* *Beveled join*

Miter Limit. The number you enter in the Miter Limit field (from 2 to 180 degrees) sets the smallest angle for which FreeHand will use a mitered join. If the angle of the line join is less than the number you enter in the Miter limit field, FreeHand renders the corner as a beveled line join (see Figure 2-96).

FIGURE 2-96
Miter limit

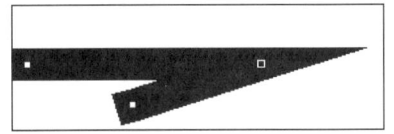

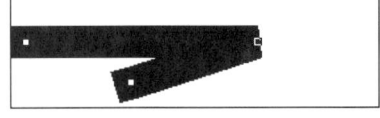

Miter limit of 2 *Miter limit of 30*

Dash. If you want a dashed line, choose one of the dash patterns from the Dash popup menu—that's the popup menu directly below the Miter Limit field (see Figure 2-97).

FIGURE 2-97
Dash patterns

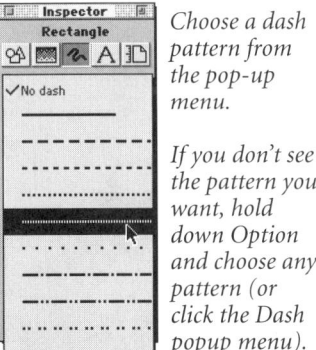

Choose a dash pattern from the pop-up menu.

If you don't see the pattern you want, hold down Option and choose any pattern (or click the Dash popup menu).

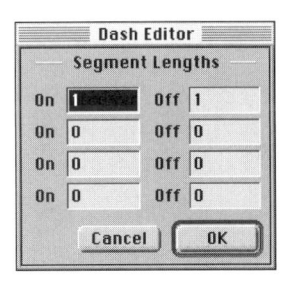

FreeHand displays the Dash Editor dialog box, where you can create your own dash pattern.

Tip:
Creating Your Own Dash Patterns

If you've looked at the Dash popup menu for a while and still don't see the dash pattern you're looking for, hold down Option and click the popup menu. The Dash Editor appears. In the Dash Editor, you can create a wide variety of dashed line patterns by entering different values in the Segment Lengths fields.

If you still can't find the dashed line style you want, you can create one using PostScript. See Chapter 8, "PostScript" for more on creating custom dashed lines.

Tip:
Editing Your Custom Dash Patterns

Once you've created a custom dash pattern, you can edit it. Hold down Option and choose the dash pattern from the Dash popup menu in the Stroke Inspector. FreeHand displays the Dash Editor, where you can edit the pattern.

Arrowheads. You can add arrowheads or (I guess) tailfeathers to any line you want by choosing an arrowhead style from the popup menus at the bottom of the Stroke Inspector. The leftmost popup menu applies to the first point in the path (according to the direction of the path); the rightmost popup menu applies to the last point in the path. You don't have to make choices from both of the popup menus (see Figure 2-98).

What if you can't find the arrowhead you need? You can make your own.

FIGURE 2-98
Arrowheads

Choose an arrowhead from either of the pop-up menus.

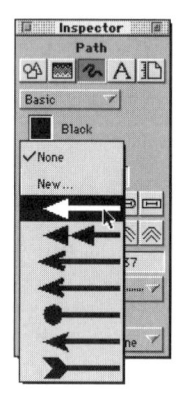

If you want to create your own arrowhead, choose New from the popup menu.

FreeHand displays the Arrowhead Editor dialog box.

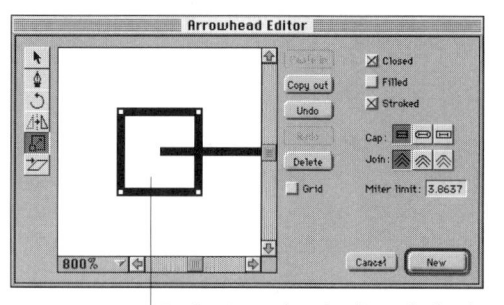

In the Arrowhead Editor dialog box, you can draw your new arrowhead, or you can paste in an arrowhead that you drew in the Publication window.

1. Draw the shape you want for your custom arrowhead using any of FreeHand's drawing tools. The shape can be anything you want, but it must be a single path.

2. Select the path you've drawn and press Command-C to copy it to the Clipboard.

3. If the Stroke Inspector isn't already visible, display it by pressing Command-L.

4. Choose New from one of the Arrowhead popup menus at the bottom of the Stroke Inspector. FreeHand displays the Arrowhead Editor.

5. Click the Paste In button. The path you copied to the Clipboard appears in the Arrowhead Editor. Scale it, change its shape, if you want. When the arrowhead looks the way you want it to, click the New button to create a new arrowhead style. FreeHand adds your arrowhead to the popup menus at the bottom of the Stroke Inspector, and you can apply it to any open path in your publication.

You can also draw the arrowhead in the Arrowhead Editor, but I find it easier to draw it on a FreeHand page (where more drawing tools are available).

Tip: Editing Arrowheads

You can edit any of the arrowheads shown in the Arrowhead popup menus—just hold down Option and choose the arrowhead you want to edit from the menu. FreeHand displays the Arrowhead Editor dialog box. When you're done editing the arrowhead, FreeHand changes the arrowhead's appearance in the popup menu to reflect your editing.

Custom Strokes

FreeHand's Custom stroke styles are something like the "graphic tapes" from Chartpak and Letraset (for those of you who remember what graphic production was like before computers). Like the graphic tapes, they come in handy when you need to do a custom border for a coupon or flyer.

When you choose a custom stroke from FreeHand's Effect popup menu, you'll see a preview of the stroke at the bottom of the

Stroke Inspector. The color and width settings for custom strokes all work exactly as described in "Basic Strokes," above.

Enter different values in the Length and Spacing text edit fields, and you can vary the custom stroke's appearance (see Figure 2-99, on the next page). The appearance of the Stroke Inspector for the Neon custom stroke is a little different—it doesn't have fields for Length and Spacing (they're irrelevant to the effect).

These stroke effects are PostScript, so they won't print on a non-PostScript printer.

Patterned Strokes. When you select Patterned, from the Stroke Type popup menu, the Stroke Inspector fills in with a variety of patterns you can apply to your path (see Figure 2-100). The color and width settings for patterned strokes work exactly as described in "Basic Strokes," above.

You choose a pattern by clicking on the swatch of the pattern you want in the bottom of the Stroke Inspector (to display other patterns, drag the slider at the bottom of the Inspector). If you want to edit the pattern you've chosen, click inside the cell containing the enlarged view of the pattern. It's like a miniature paint program—click on a black pixel and it turns white; click on a white pixel and it turns black. If you want to create a pattern entirely from scratch, click the Clear button to set all the pixels in the cell to white. Click on the Invert button to invert the pattern shown in the cell. As you make changes, the preview of the pattern changes to show you what you've done.

Patterned strokes have several significant limitations.

- The pattern in a patterned stroke is always the same size—72 dots per inch—regardless of the weight of the stroke.

- Patterned strokes won't separate into process colors unless you're printing to a PostScript Level 2 printer.

- Patterned strokes can take a long time to print.

- Patterned strokes have an opaque background, so the pattern won't knock out of whatever's behind them. The entire path will, instead.

FIGURE 2-99
Custom strokes

Here's an example of FreeHand's stock custom strokes. I printed each path using a pattern length of 8, a pattern width of 8, and a spacing of zero (except for "Rectangle," which I printed using a spacing of 3).

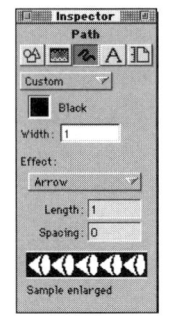

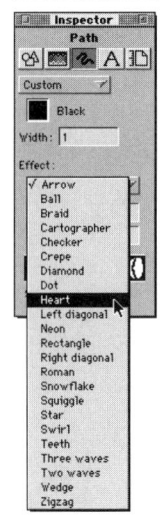

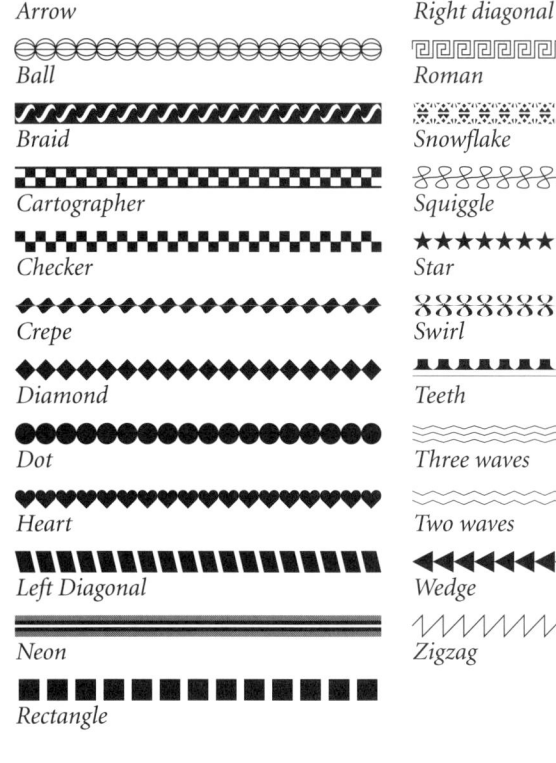

Arrow

Ball

Braid

Cartographer

Checker

Crepe

Diamond

Dot

Heart

Left Diagonal

Neon

Rectangle

Right diagonal

Roman

Snowflake

Squiggle

Star

Swirl

Teeth

Three waves

Two waves

Wedge

Zigzag

The appearance of custom strokes can vary a great deal, depending on what variables you enter in the Inspector.

Here's what the parameters control.

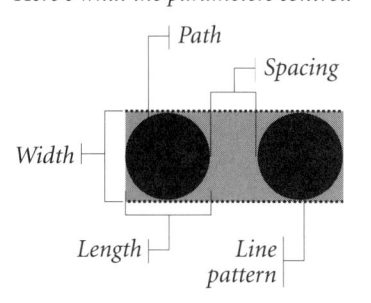

Path
Spacing
Width
Length
Line pattern

Example settings for the Braid custom stroke

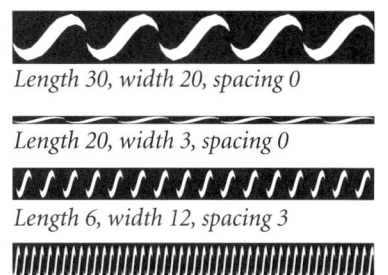

Length 30, width 20, spacing 0

Length 20, width 3, spacing 0

Length 6, width 12, spacing 3

Length 3, width 16, spacing 0

FIGURE 2-100
Patterned strokes

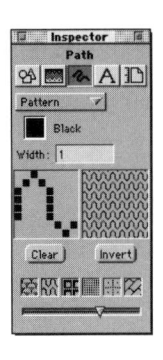

Choose a pattern from the scrolling display at the bottom of the dialog box, or click "Clear" to clear the current pattern and draw your own. Click "Invert" to invert the current pattern.

- You can't apply a halftone screen to patterned strokes.

- Patterned strokes are kinda ugly.

Patterned strokes are really intended to provide compatibility for imported PICTs drawn in MacDraw II. Some people feel more comfortable working with the patterned strokes than with the PostScript or custom stroke types, which is (in my opinion) unfortunate. If you're trying to make a stroke gray, apply a tint of black to the stroke. If you want to apply a stroke with a pattern to a path, use a custom stroke.

PostScript Strokes

When you choose PostScript from the Stroke Type popup menu in the Stroke Inspector, a large field appears at the bottom of the Inspector. In this field, you can enter up to 255 characters of PostScript code (you can also paste text into the field).

Don't press Return to break lines—FreeHand will think you're trying to apply the effect to the path (and won't enter a carriage return in the field, in any case). Separate your entries with spaces instead; PostScript doesn't need carriage returns to understand the code (see Figure 2-101).

Similarly, don't include the character "%" in your code—PostScript uses this character to denote comments, and will ignore any text following it (if you enter this character in the middle of your code, you'll probably cause a PostScript error).

PostScript strokes display on screen as a basic stroke of the width and color you specify. Your PostScript code can, of course, change the width or color of the stroke, if that's what you want.

While you can enter complete descriptions of PostScript strokes in this dialog box, you'll usually use it to call PostScript routines in

FIGURE 2-101
PostScript strokes

FreeHand enters this code by default; delete it before you type your code.

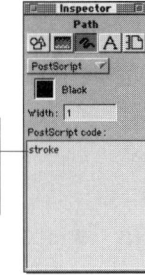

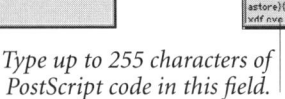

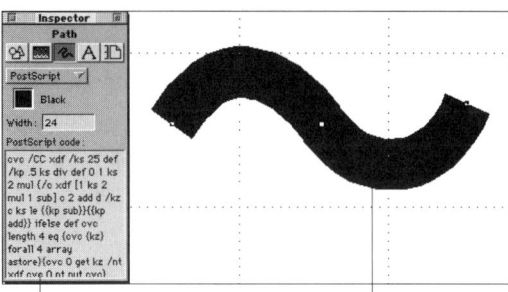

Type up to 255 characters of PostScript code in this field.

PostScript strokes look like this on your screen...

Note: You can't see the complete code for this PostScript stroke in this screen shot (some of it has scrolled out of the field). For a complete code listing, see Chapter 8, "PostScript."

...but print according to the code you enter.

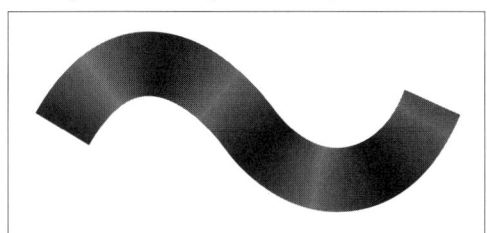

external UserPrep files. See Chapter 8, "PostScript," for more on passing values to external routines.

Editing Strokes

Once you've applied a stroke to a particular path, you can change the stroke using any of the following methods. Again, there's no "right" way to edit a stroke—which method is best and quickest depends on how you work and which palettes you have open at the time you want to change the stroke.

◆ Press Command-Option-L to display the Stroke Inspector, then make changes to the path's appearance in the Inspector.

◆ Choose one of the preset strokes from the Stroke Weights submenu of the Arrange menu.

◆ Choose Thicker or Thinner from the Stroke Weights submenu of the Arrange menu.

◆ Use the Color List to apply a color to the path (see Chapter 6, "Color," for more on applying colors using the Color List).

- Drag and drop a color swatch (from the Color List, the Color Mixer, the Tint palette, or the Inspector) onto the path (see Chapter 6, "Color," for more on drag-and-drop color).

- Click on a style name in the Styles palette.

Removing Strokes

To quickly remove a stroke from a path, use one of the following techniques.

- Select the path, then click None in the Color List (when Line is selected at the top of the Color List).

- Drag a color swatch from None in the Color List and drop it on the Line button at the top of the Color List.

- Drag a color swatch from None in the Color List and drop it on the path (see Chapter 6, "Color").

- Select the path, then display the Stroke Inspector and choose None from the Stroke Type popup menu.

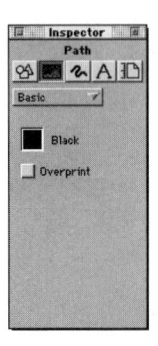

Fills

Just as strokes determine what the *outside* of a path looks like, fills specify the appearance of the *inside* of a path. Fills can make the inside of a path a solid color, or a graduated fill, or a pattern of tiny faces. Any closed (or composite) path you create can be filled.

You specify fills using the Fill Inspector. To display the Fill Inspector, press Command-Option-F. FreeHand features eight different fill types, which you can choose from the Fill Type popup menu—the popup menu at the top of the Fill Inspector.

Basic fills. Choose Basic from the Fill Type popup menu when you want to fill an object with a specific color (see Figure 2-102). Apply the color to your path by dragging a color swatch from the Color List (or the Color Mixer, or the Tint palette) into the color well in the Stroke Inspector (for more on applying colors to objects, see Chapter 6, "Color").

DRAWING 183

FIGURE 2-102
Applying basic fills

Select the path you want to fill, then choose Basic from the Fill Type pop-up menu.

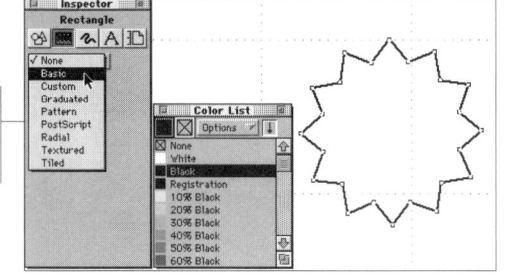

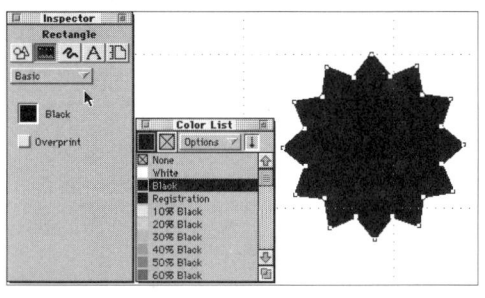

FreeHand fills the path with a basic fill of the current default color (in this example, Black).

To change the color of the fill, drag a color swatch from one of the color wells in the Color List (or from the Color Mixer or the Tints palette) and drop it in the color well in the Fill Inspector.

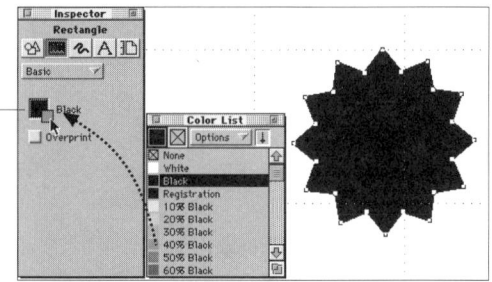

Alternatively, you could click on the color name in the Color List, or drag a color swatch onto the Fill button at the top of the Color List.

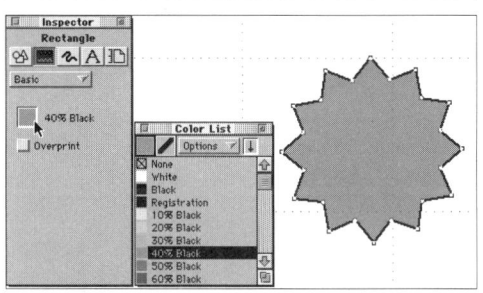

FreeHand applies the fill to the selected path.

Check the Overprint checkbox to specify that this fill overprints any underlying objects. If you don't check Overprint, the object will be knocked out of any underlying objects unless its ink color has been set to overprint. Depending on the colors you're using in your publication and the printing process you intend to use, this might not be what you want (see Figure 2-103).

184   REAL WORLD FREEHAND 5.0|5.5

FIGURE 2-103
Overprinting fills

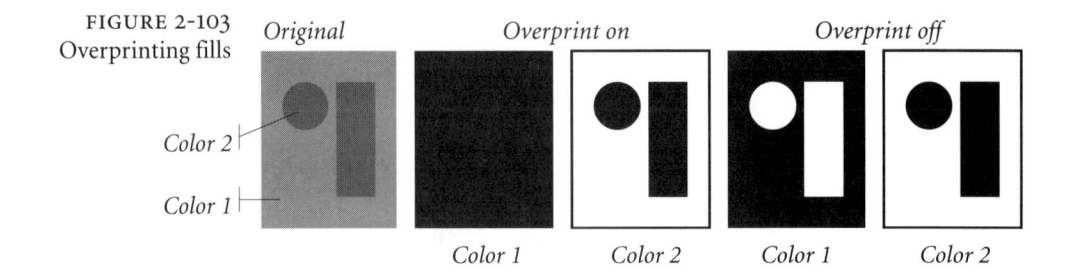

Original   *Overprint on*   *Overprint off*

Color 2

Color 1

Color 1   Color 2   Color 1   Color 2

Tip:
Dragging and
Dropping Basic
Fills

To change any fill to a basic fill, hold down Shift as you drop a color swatch onto a path. FreeHand fills the path with a basic fill of the color you dropped on the path (see Figure 2-104).

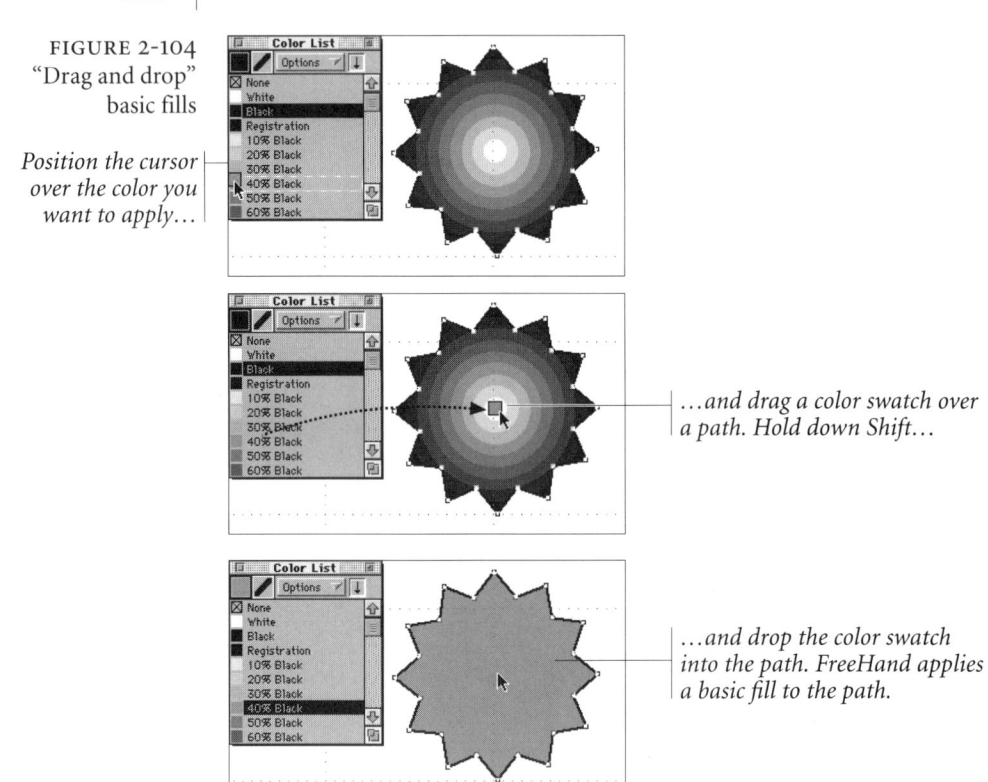

FIGURE 2-104
"Drag and drop"
basic fills

Position the cursor over the color you want to apply...

...and drag a color swatch over a path. Hold down Shift...

...and drop the color swatch into the path. FreeHand applies a basic fill to the path.

Custom fills. Choose Custom from the Fill menu to use one of FreeHand's special fills, such as Bricks, Noise, or Tiger Teeth. These fills are PostScript, so you they won't print on a non-PostScript printer (see Figure 2-105).

FIGURE 2-105
Custom fills

Black-and-White Noise

Bricks

Circles

Hatch

Noise

Random Grass

Random Leaves

Squares

Tiger Teeth

Top Noise

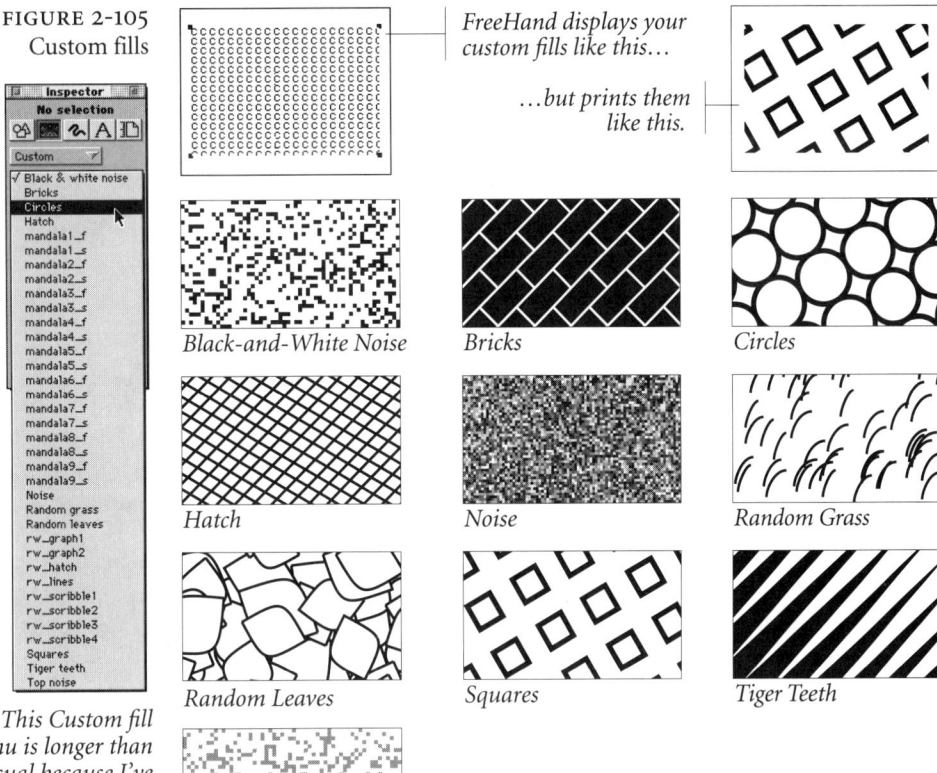

FreeHand displays your custom fills like this…

…but prints them like this.

Note: This Custom fill menu is longer than usual because I've added my own fills. To find out how to do that, see Chapter 8, "PostScript."

To apply a custom fill, follow these steps.

1. Select the path you want to apply the custom fill to.

2. Press Command-Option-F to display the Fill Inspector, if it's not already visible. Choose Custom from the Fill Type popup menu.

3. Choose a fill from the Effect popup menu in the Fill Inspector. Options for the specific fill you've chosen appear in the Fill Inspector. The number of parameters you can change varies from fill to fill.

4. Set the parameters for the fill (using the controls in the Inspector) and press Return to apply your changes.

Custom fills appear on screen as patterns of little Cs.

You can vary the appearance of the custom fills to a tremendous degree. For the Bricks fill, for example, you can specify the color, width, height, and angle of the "bricks" in the fill, as well as setting the color of the "mortar." Figure 2-106 shows how variables can dramatically change the appearance of a custom fill.

FIGURE 2-106
Changing variables
of custom fills

Variations on "Bricks"

Graduated fills. Choose Graduated to fill an object with a linear or logarithmic graduation from one color to another—an effect also known as a "fountain" or a "vignette." You can set the beginning and ending colors, and you can specify the type of graduation (linear or logarithmic) and the angle the graduation is to follow (see Figure 2-107).

You can't specify graduations between two spot colors (though you can specify graduations between two tints of the same spot color, or between a spot color and the default color "White"). As usual, there's a sneaky way around this limitation—see "Substituting Process Colors for Spot Colors" in Chapter 6, "Color."

A far more serious problem is that you can't set graduated fills to overprint, which makes it harder (maybe harder than it should be) to trap abutting graduated fills. To see how to do that, see "Trapping," in Chapter 6, "Color."

Finally, if you're considering using a graduated fill, you should take a look at "Blending," earlier in this chapter.

Tip:
Dragging and
Dropping
Graduated Fills

To change any fill to a graduated fill, hold down Control as you drop a color swatch into a closed path. FreeHand fills the path with a graduated fill, and sets the To color to the color of the swatch you dropped on the path. FreeHand sets the From color to the original color applied to the path. FreeHand determines the angle of the graduation from the point at which you drop the color swatch (see Figure 2-108).

DRAWING 187

FIGURE 2-107
Graduated fills

Select a path and choose Graduated from the Fill Type popup menu.

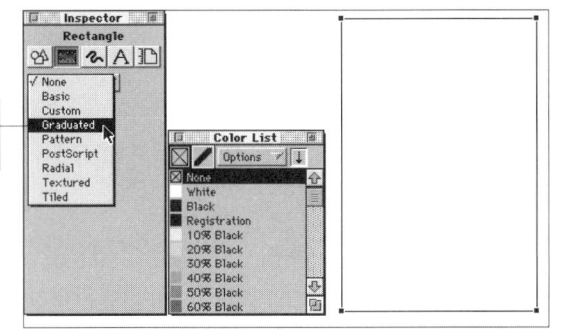

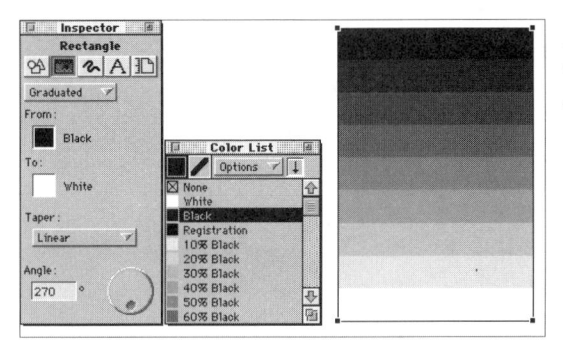

FreeHand applies a graduated fill to the path.

To change the appearance of a graduated fill, drag color swatches into the color wells in the Fill Inspector…

…or choose a different Graduated fill type…

…or change the angle of the fill.

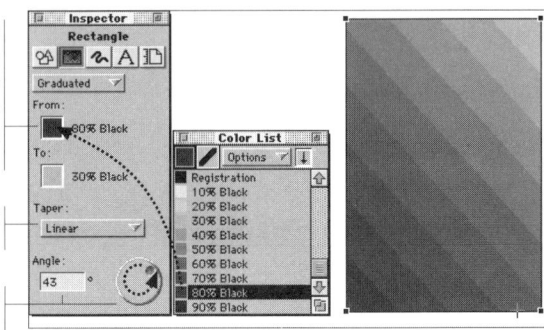

FIGURE 2-108
"Drag and drop" graduated fills

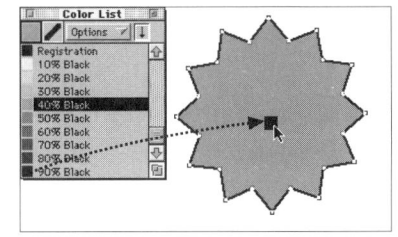

Hold down Control as you drop a color swatch into a path…

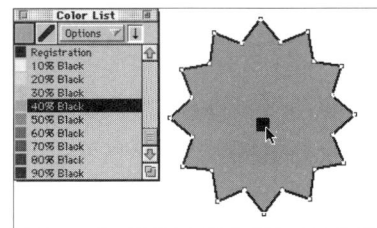

…and FreeHand applies a graduated fill to the path, using the color you dropped to set the fill's "To" color.

Patterned fills. Patterned fills have the same problems and limitations as patterned lines, discussed in "Patterned Lines," earlier in this chapter. I recommend that you don't use them.

PostScript fills. When you choose PostScript from the Fill menu, a large field appears at the bottom of the Fill Inspector (see Figure 2-109). PostScript fills work just like PostScript lines, described earlier in this chapter.

PostScript fills display on screen as a pattern of little PSes.

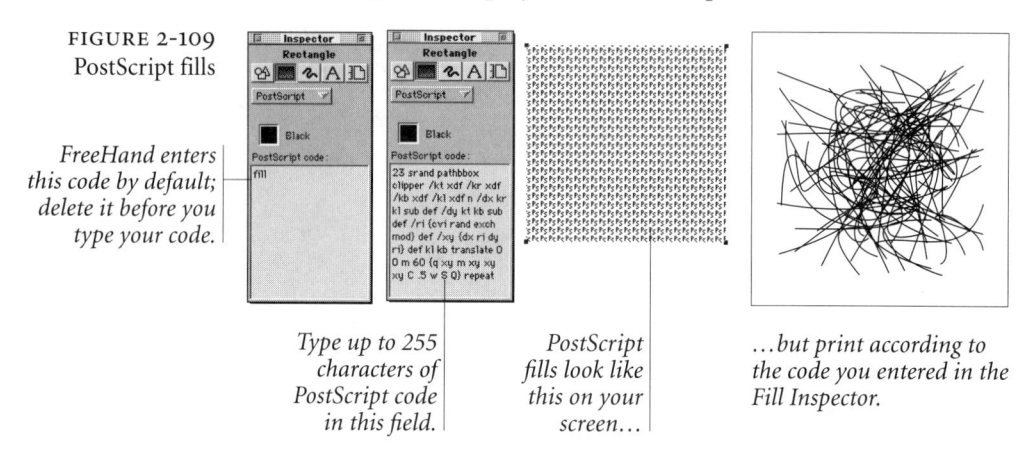

FIGURE 2-109
PostScript fills

FreeHand enters this code by default; delete it before you type your code.

Type up to 255 characters of PostScript code in this field.

PostScript fills look like this on your screen...

...but print according to the code you entered in the Fill Inspector.

Radial fills. A radial fill creates a concentric graduated fill from the center of an object to the outside of the object. By default, the center of a radial fill is placed at the center of the two most distant points in the object (see Figure 2-110). You can control the location of the center of a radial fill using the Locate Center control in the Fill Inspector—drag the handle around, and FreeHand repositions the center of the radial fill. Radial fills are subject to the same limitations as graduated fills.

Tip:
Dragging and
Dropping Radial
Fills

To change any fill to a radial fill, hold down Option as you drop a color swatch onto the path containing the fill. FreeHand fills the path with a radial fill, and sets the Inside color of the radial fill to the color of the swatch you dropped on the path. FreeHand sets the Outside color to the original color applied to the path. FreeHand positions the center point of the radial fill at the point at which you dropped the color swatch (see Figure 2-111).

DRAWING 189

FIGURE 2-110
Radial fills

Select a path and choose Radial from the Fill Type popup menu.

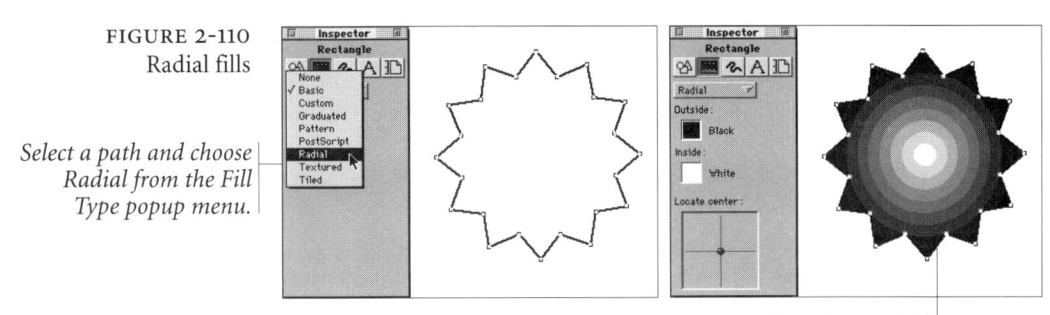

FreeHand applies a radial fill to the path.

To change the colors used in a radial fill, drag color swatches into the color wells in the Fill Inspector.

Change the location of the center point of the radial fill by dragging this control around.

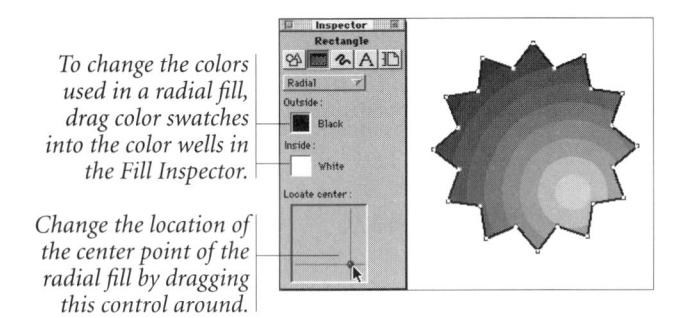

FIGURE 2-111
"Drag and drop" radial fills

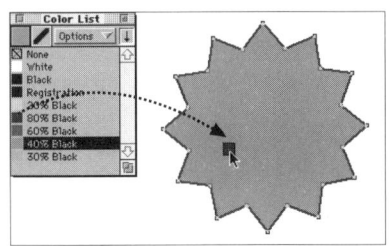

Hold down Option as you drop a color swatch inside a path...

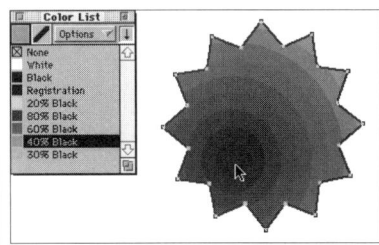

...and FreeHand applies a radial fill to the path, using the color you dropped to set the fill's Inside color. The point at which you dropped the color swatch becomes the center point of the fill.

Tiled fills. Tiled fills repeat a pattern of FreeHand objects inside a path; they're like the tiles you see in your kitchen or bathroom. Here's how to create a tiled fill (see Figure 2-112).

1. Create the objects you want to have repeated inside a path. You're creating one of the tiles you'll have in your tiled fill.

2. Copy the FreeHand objects to the Clipboard.

3. Select the path you want to apply the tiled fill to.

4. Press Command-Option-F to display the Fill Inspector. Choose Tiled from the Fill Type popup menu. The tiled fill attributes appear in the Fill Inspector.

5. Click the Paste In button in the Fill Inspector. This pastes the objects you copied to the Clipboard into the window next to the button.

6. Adjust the scale, offset, and angle of the tiles. If you want the objects in the fill to be rotated, skewed, scaled, or otherwise transformed, remember to check the Contents option in the Transform palette.

7. Press Return to apply the tiled fill.

FIGURE 2-112
Creating a tiled fill

Create the objects you want to use in your tiled fill and copy them to the Clipboard by pressing Command-C.

Select a path and press Command-Option-F to display the Fill Inspector. Choose Tiled from the popup menu.

Click the Paste In button, and FreeHand pastes the objects you copied into the Inspector.

Change the scale, angle, and offset as you want.

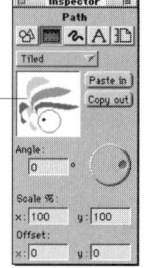

Press Return, and FreeHand applies the tiled fill.

Offset doesn't change the distance between tiles in a tiled fill—it changes the position at which FreeHand starts drawing the tiles (ordinarily, FreeHand calculates tile positions based on the lower-left corner of a page). Values you enter in the X field move the horizontal starting point of the tiled fill (positive numbers move the starting point to the right; negative values move it to the left);

values you enter in the Y field move the vertical starting point up (positive numbers) or down (negative numbers).

Tip:
Adding an offset between tiles

To add more space between tiles in a tiled fill, follow these steps (see Figure 2-113).

1. Draw a square around the original tile. Apply a fill and line of None to the square.

2. Select the square and the original tile and press Command-C to copy the objects to the Clipboard.

3. Display the Fill Inspector by pressing Command-Option-F, if it's not already visible.

4. Choose Tiled from the Fill Type popup menu (if the tiled fill options aren't already visible in the Fill Inspector).

5. Click Paste In.

The objects you copied to the Clipboard appear in the Fill Inspector. You'll see that the square you drew adds a margin around

FIGURE 2-113
Increasing the distance between tiles

Click the Copy Out button to copy the original tile to the Clipboard.

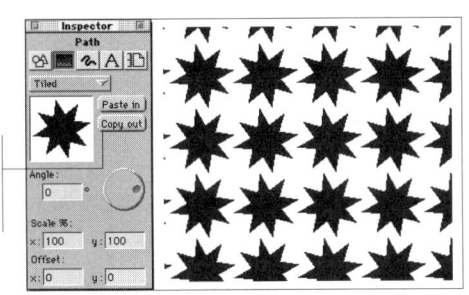

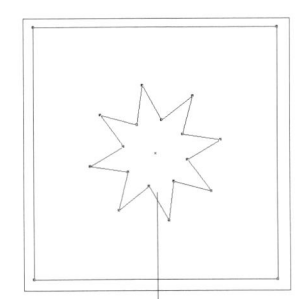

Paste the object into a publication and draw a box around it. Apply a fill and stroke of "None" to the box (shown here in keyline view). Copy the new tile to the Clipboard...

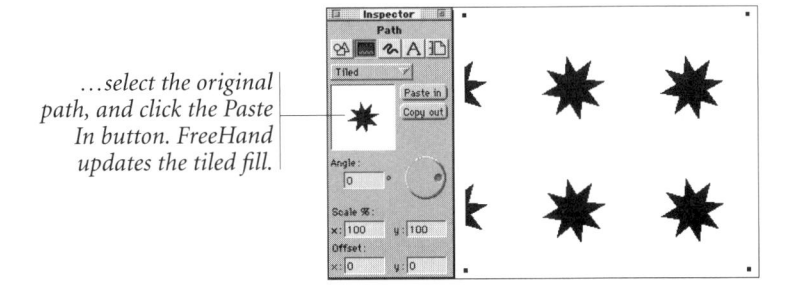

...select the original path, and click the Paste In button. FreeHand updates the tiled fill.

the object you're tiling, but doesn't print or obscure objects behind the tiled fill. Make the square larger or smaller to control the distance between tiles.

Tip:
Moving Paths Without Moving Tiles

Using the X and Y Offset fields to move a fill inside a path can be frustrating. Can't you just drag the path over the part of the tiled fill you want to see? Sure—here's how you do it (see Figure 2-114).

1. Press Command-M to display the Transform palette, if it's not already visible.

2. Click the Move button in the Transform palette.

3. Uncheck the Fills checkbox.

4. Drag the path to a new location.

FreeHand moves the path, but doesn't change the starting point of the tiled fill. You can also accomplish this task using the Transform palette (see Chapter 5, "Transforming," for more on moving a path without changing the appearance of its fills or contents).

FIGURE 2-114
Moving paths without moving fills

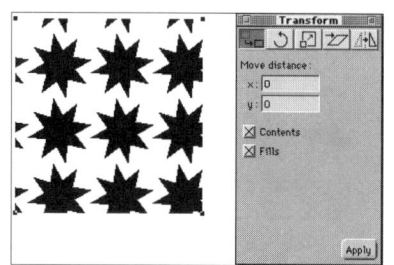

When you move a path with the Fills option checked...

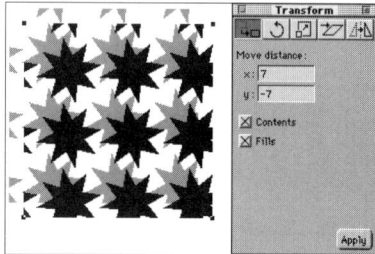

...the fill moves along with the path (original tiles shown in gray).

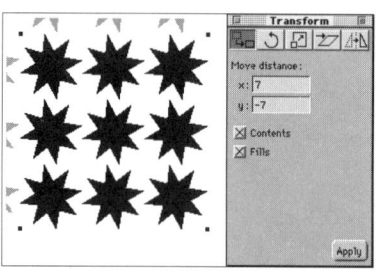

If you want the fill to stay where it is while the path moves, uncheck Fills (original path position shown in gray).

Textured fills. Choose Textured from the Fill menu to use one of FreeHand's textured fills, such as Denim, Burlap, or Coquille (see Figure 2-115). The textured fills are actually small bitmap images that FreeHand tiles inside a path—in older versions of FreeHand, you could see an obvious pattern in paths filled with the textured fills. These days, the pattern is a little less apparent, because FreeHand randomly rotates and flips the bitmaps as it creates the tiles.

Textured fills print with an opaque background—as if you'd drawn a shape behind the fill and colored it white. If you want textured fills to print with a transparent background, take a look at "Making Textured Fills Transparent," in Chapter 8, "PostScript."

FIGURE 2-115
Textured fills

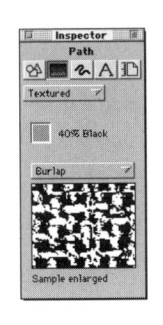

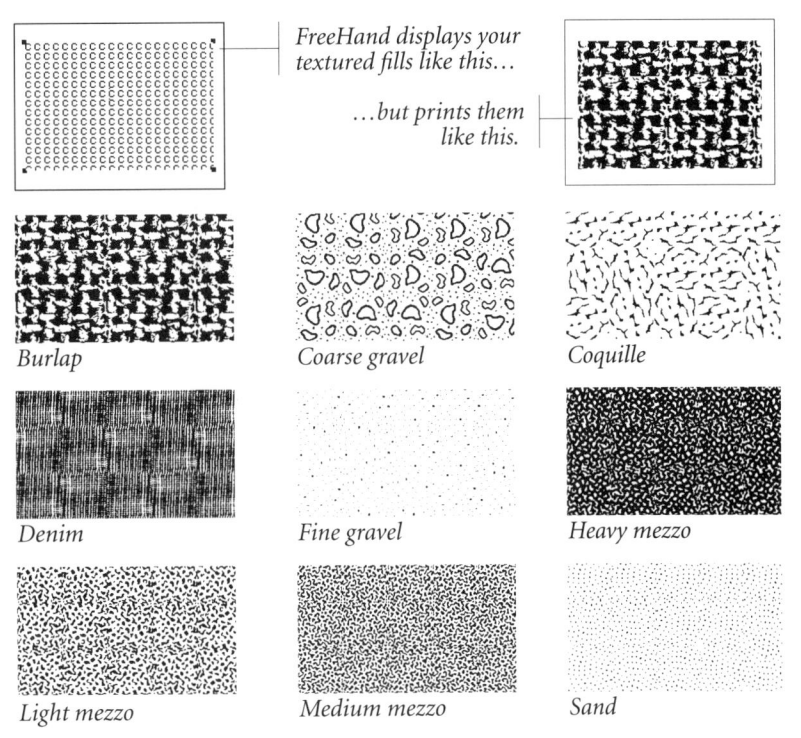

FreeHand displays your textured fills like this…

…but prints them like this.

Burlap

Coarse gravel

Coquille

Denim

Fine gravel

Heavy mezzo

Light mezzo

Medium mezzo

Sand

Editing Fills

Once you've applied a fill to a particular path, you can change the fill using any of the following methods.

- Press Command-Option-F to display the Fill Inspector, then make changes to the path's appearance in the Inspector.

- Use the Color List to apply a color to the path (see Chapter 6, "Color," for more on applying colors using the Color List).

- Drag and drop a color swatch (from the Color List, the Color Mixer, the Tint palette, or the Inspector) inside the path (see Chapter 6, "Color," for more on drag-and-drop color).

- Click on a style name in the Styles palette.

Removing Fills

To quickly remove a fill from a path, click None in the Color List when the Fill icon at the top of the Color List is selected, or drag a color swatch from None in the Color List and drop it on the Fill icon (Figure 2-116).

FIGURE 2-116
Removing a fill

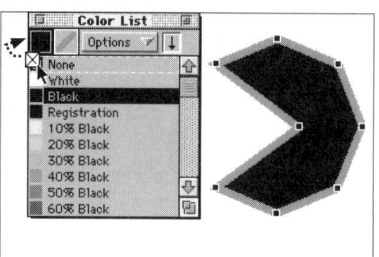

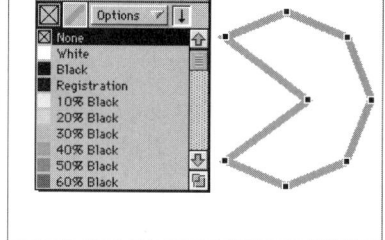

Drag a swatch from "None" into the Fill icon and drop it.

The fill is gone. The thrill might still be around, but the fill is gone.

Working with Graphic Styles

Styles are named collections of formatting attributes. What do I mean when I say "collections of formatting attributes"? I mean that the style includes all the formatting you can apply to an object. If you're using a two-point line that's colored 60 percent gray, you can create a style with those attributes (you can even name it "2-point 60% gray line") and apply it to every path you want to have those attributes, rather than going to the Fill Inspector, the Stroke Inspector, or the Color List every time you want to use that formatting.

In FreeHand 5, you can work with both graphic styles and text styles. Graphic styles apply strokes and fills; the text styles apply character and paragraph formatting. Because graphic styles and text styles work about the same way, I'll refer to either as "styles," and only call them "graphic styles" or "text styles" if there's some distinction I need to make.

When you format a path using the Stroke Widths submenu, or by choosing colors from the Color List, or by making changes in the Fill or Stroke Inspectors or the Halftone palette, or by dragging and dropping color swatches, you're formatting the path locally. We call this "local" formatting because the formatting applies to the selected path only, and is not explicitly shared with any other paths in your publication.

Style formatting, on the other hand, is global. When you apply a style to a path, FreeHand makes an association between that path and all the other paths formatted with that style. This means that you can change the style and have the changes you make applied to all the paths formatted with that style. This doesn't mean you lose flexibility—you can always apply local formatting to override the style formatting for styled paths.

Thinking About Styles

While styles are one of the most useful features of FreeHand, in my experience, as soon as you mention the word "styles," people start to panic.

There's no need to be scared—you're already thinking of the elements in your FreeHand publications as having styles. You think of each path as having a particular set of formatting attributes, and you think of groups of paths as having the same set of attributes ("These are all 12-point gray strokes"). FreeHand's graphic styles give you the ability to work with FreeHand the way you already think about your publications.

Use styles. Any time you find yourself choosing the same formatting attributes over and over again, you can create a style and dramatically speed up the process of creating your publication. More importantly, you can use more of your brain for doing your creative work, rather than trying to remember that this sort of path has this sort of a stroke, this sort of a fill, this color, this line width, and this halftone screen. Forget that! Set up a style and let FreeHand do that kind of thinking for you.

While styles encourage you to think ahead, they're also flexible; you can change all the paths tagged with a particular style at any time by simply editing the style's definition.

The Styles palette (see Figure 2-117) is the key to working with and applying styles. If the Styles palette is not visible on your screen, press Command-3 to display it. If the Styles palette is visible and you want to put it away, press Command-3.

FreeHand displays an icon next to each style name in the Styles palette, using different icons for text styles and graphic styles.

FIGURE 2-117
Styles palette

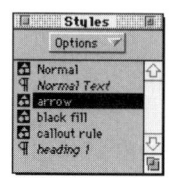

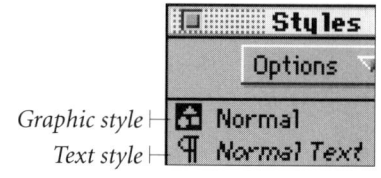

Graphic style
Text style

Creating Styles by Example

In FreeHand, the easiest way to create styles is by example. Once you've applied a set of attributes to a path using local formatting, you can turn that formatting into a style, which you can then apply to any other paths (see Figure 2-118).

1. Select the path with the attributes you want.

2. Choose New from the popup menu at the top of the Styles palette (if the Styles palette isn't currently visible, press Command-3 to display it). FreeHand adds a new style name to the Styles palette.

3. To give the style another name (FreeHand's default names—"Style 1," "Style 2," etc.—aren't very descriptive), double-click the style name in the Styles palette and type a new name. When you're through, press Return.

That's all there is to it. You've just created a style with the fill, line, color, and halftone attributes of the path you selected.

Tip: Stroke-Only and Fill-Only Styles

To make the style apply only to the stroke of a path, or only to the fill of a path, select the style name in the Styles palette and then choose "Edit Style" from the Styles palette's popup menu. FreeHand

DRAWING 197

FIGURE 2-118
Defining a new style

Select a path that has the formatting attributes you want.

Choose New from the Styles palette's popup menu.

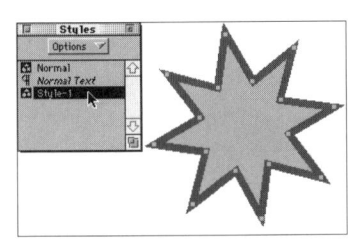

FreeHand creates a new style, applying the style to the selected path as it does so.

What's in a style? All of the settings for all of the controls in the Halftone palette, the Stroke Inspector, and the Fill Inspector are stored under one name in the Styles palette.

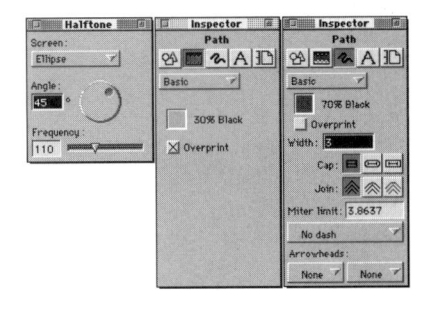

FreeHand's default style names aren't very descriptive, so you might want to change them.

Double-click the style name in the Styles palette.

Type a new name for the style.

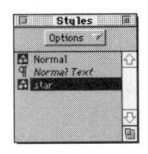

Press Return. FreeHand changes the name of the style in the Styles palette.

displays the Edit Style dialog box. Choose "Fill Attributes" from the Style Affects popup menu to create a fill-only style, or choose "Stroke Attributes" to create a stroke-only style (see Figure 2-119).

Tip:
Select One Example

When you're creating a style based on an example, make sure you select a single path before you define the style. If you select more than one path, there's a good chance the paths in your selection will have different formatting attributes. What happens then? FreeHand doesn't save the formatting for the attributes that differ (that is, if the selected paths have differing fills, FreeHand won't save the Fill attributes in the style you've created).

FIGURE 2-119
Fill-only and
stroke-only styles

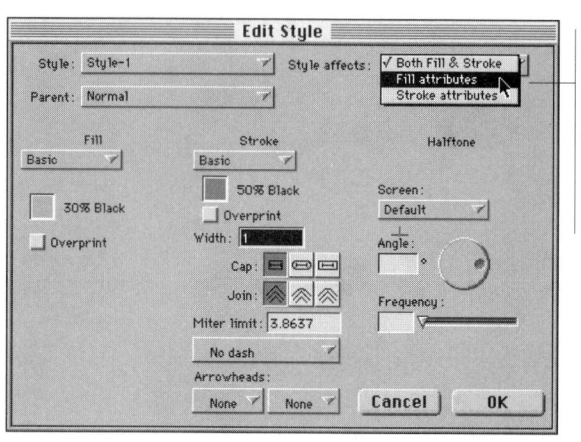

Choose "Fill attributes" to affect only the fill of paths you apply this style to, or choose "Stroke attributes" to affect only the stroke.

> **Tip:**
> **Halftone-Only Styles**
>
> You can use the above FreeHand behavior to your advantage to create "halftone-only" styles. Create two paths, applying different fill and stroke attributes to each path. Apply the same halftone settings to both paths. Select the two paths and choose "New" from the Styles palette's popup menu. FreeHand creates a style that applies only the halftone formatting. You can then use these halftone-only styles to apply specialized line screens to imported TIFF images (the halftone setting is the only part of a style definition that gets applied to TIFFs).

Creating Styles by Specifying Attributes

If you prefer creating styles by specifying formatting in a dialog box (instead of creating a style from an example path), FreeHand 5 gives you a way to do that (see Figure 2-120).

1. Deselect everything (press Command-Tab or click on an uninhabited area of the page).

2. Choose "New" from the Styles palette's popup menu. FreeHand creates a new style and adds it to the list of styles in the palette.

3. Without deselecting the style, choose "Edit style" from the Styles palette's popup menu. FreeHand displays the Edit Style dialog box.

4. If you want to base the style on some other style (other than the default style "Normal"), choose that style from the Parent popup menu. Note that choosing this option does

FIGURE 2-120
Defining a style by specifying attributes

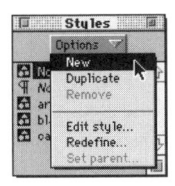

Choose New from the pop-up menu.

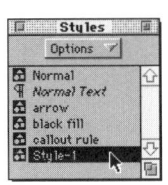

FreeHand creates a new style.

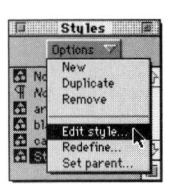

Choose Edit syle from the pop-up menu.

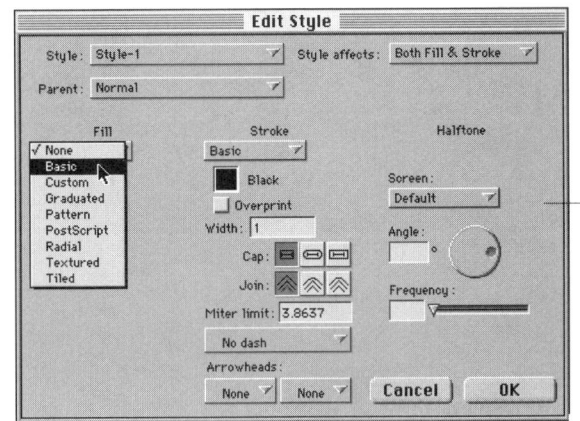

FreeHand displays the Edit Style dialog box. Set up the halftone, fill, and stroke for your style using the controls in the Edit Style dialog box. Press Return (or click the OK button) when you're done, and FreeHand applies the formatting to the new style.

not apply the parent style's attributes to the current style (see "Basing One Style on Another," later in this chapter).

5. If you want the style to apply only to the stroke or fill of paths, choose "Stroke Attributes" or "Fill Attributes" from the Style Affects popup menu. If you want the style to apply to both the fill and the stroke, choose "Both Fill & Stroke."

6. Set the fill, stroke, and halftone of the style using the corresponding sections of the dialog box (they work just like the Fill and Stroke Inspectors and the Halftone palette). When the style has the attributes you want, press Return or click the OK button to close the Edit Style dialog box.

7. If you want to change the name of the style, double-click the style name in the Styles palette, type a new name, and press Return.

Applying Styles

To apply a style, select the path you want to tag with the style, and then click on the style in the Styles palette. The path takes on all the formatting attributes of the style (see Figure 2-121). The path is now "tagged" with the style.

Alternatively, you can apply the style using the "drag and drop" method: drag the icon next to the style name out of the Styles palette, and drop it on a path. FreeHand tags the path with the style. Change the style, and you change the formatting of the path.

FIGURE 2-121
Applying styles

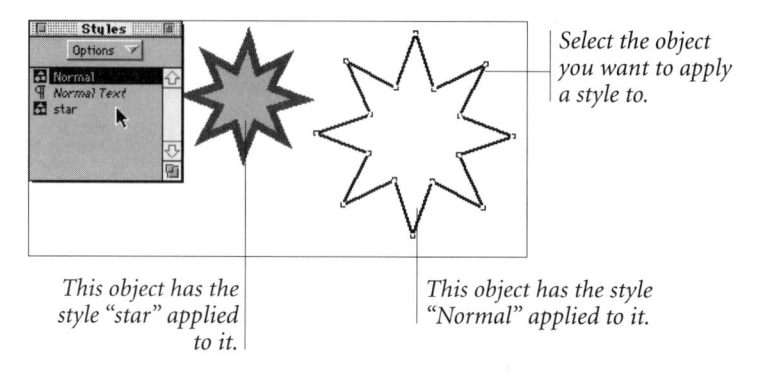

Select the object you want to apply a style to.

This object has the style "star" applied to it.

This object has the style "Normal" applied to it.

Click the style name in the Styles palette.

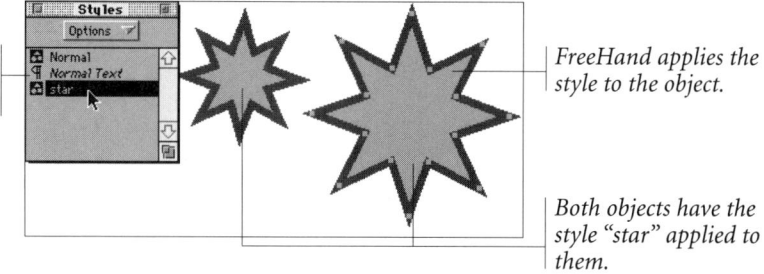

FreeHand applies the style to the object.

Both objects have the style "star" applied to them.

Redefining Styles To redefine a style, create or select a path with the style applied to it. Make local changes using the Fill and Stroke Inspectors and the Halftone palette. When the path looks the way you want it to, choose Redefine from the popup menu on the Styles palette. All of the paths formatted using that style change to reflect the changes you've just made (see Figure 2-122).

Basing One Style on Another Styles can inherit attributes from other styles. You can create a style that's just like an existing style except for some small difference, or create a style that's linked to any changes you make to an original style (color is a good example).

I call the original style the "parent" style and the inheriting styles "child" styles. When you change the properties of the parent style,

FIGURE 2-122
Editing styles

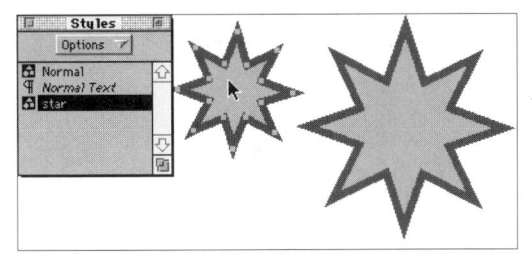

Select a path that's tagged with the style you want to redefine.

When you apply "local" formatting (that is, formatting independent of styles) to an object, FreeHand displays a "+" to the left of the style's name in the Styles palette.

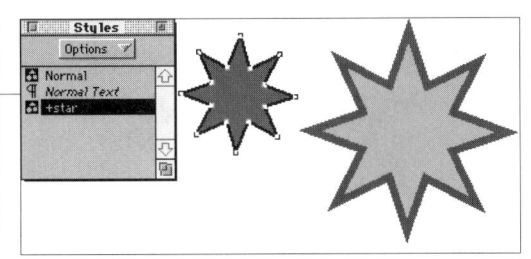

Change the path's fomatting (using any of the formatting techniques discussed earlier in this chapter).

Choose Redefine from the Styles palette's popup menu.

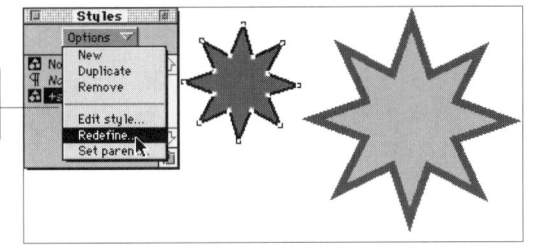

FreeHand displays the Redefine Style dialog box. Select the style you want to redefine (usually, it's the one applied to the current path) and press Return.

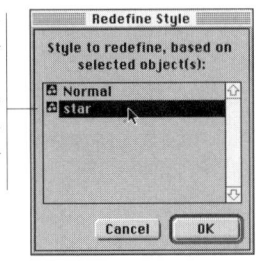

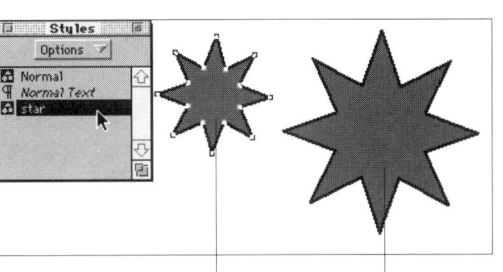

The formatting changes ripple through all of the paths tagged with the style you just redefined—even if they're not selected.

the changes you make ripple through the child styles. Child styles inherit changes only in the properties they share with their parent style. The attributes which differ between the parent and child styles remain the same.

People often have difficulty understanding the use and worth of parent and child styles—even to the point of calling attribute inheritance a bug. It's not a bug, it's a feature.

To create a new style that's based on the existing style, follow these steps (see Figure 2-123).

1. Select a path tagged with the style you want to base the new style on.

2. Make a change to the path's formatting (its fill, stroke, or halftone setting).

3. Choose New from the popup menu at the top of the Styles palette (if the Styles palette isn't currently visible, press Command-3 to display it). FreeHand adds a new style name to the Styles palette.

4. Double-click the default style name in the Styles palette and type a new name for the style, if you want. When you're done, press Return.

5. Choose Set Parent from the popup menu in the Styles palette. FreeHand displays the Set Parent dialog box.

6. Choose the parent style in the Set Parent dialog box and press Return to close the dialog box.

If you know what you're doing, you can use attribute inheritance to experiment—to try out new ideas quickly and easily. What would happen if all those red lines (of whatever line width and pattern) were blue? What would happen if all the paths you've filled with this tiled fill were filled with that graduated fill? The ripple-through effect of attribute inheritance from parent to child styles lets me ask "what if" questions quickly and easily.

Attribute inheritance also makes it easier for me to make last-minute production changes almost painlessly (there are no totally painless last-minute production changes). These are usually color changes. (Does anyone out there have a client/boss/whatever who never changes their mind about color after seeing the chromes? If so, could you please loan them to me?)

Duplicating Styles If you want to base one style on another, select the style you want to copy and choose Duplicate from the Styles palette popup menu. FreeHand creates a new style with the same formatting attributes

FIGURE 2-123
Basing one style
on another

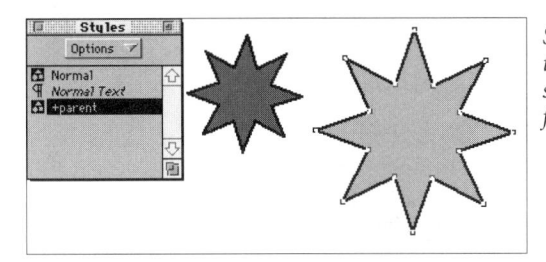

Select a path that's tagged with parent style and change its formatting.

Choose New from the Styles palette's popup menu to create a new style.

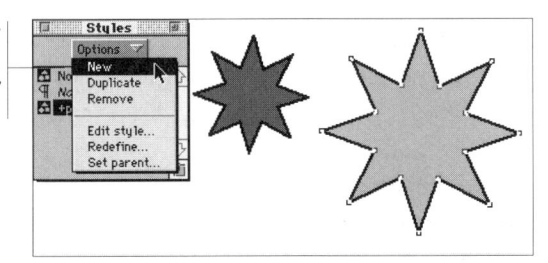

Choose Set Parent from the Styles palette's popup menu.

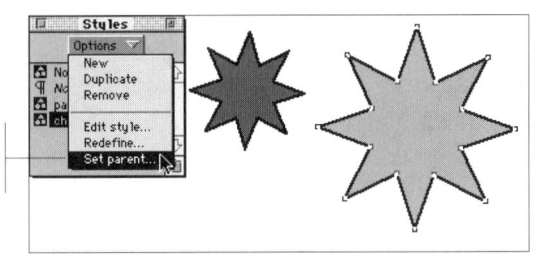

FreeHand displays the Set Parent dialog box. Select the style you want to base your new style on and press Return.

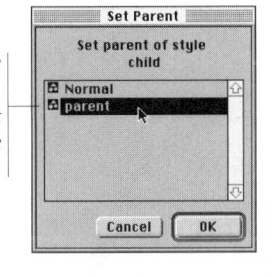

Once you've established a link between styles, changes to the parent style apply to any identical formatting attributes of the child style.

In this example, the strokes of the styles are the same, so FreeHand applies changes to the stroke of the parent to any paths tagged with the child style.

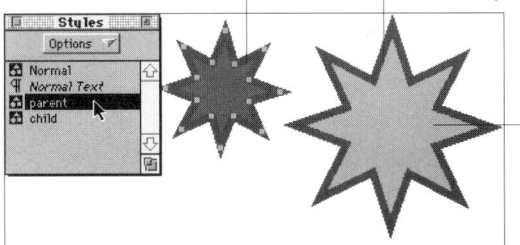

The child style's fill differs, and is unaffected by changes to the fill of the parent style.

as the style you selected. At this point, you can edit or redefine the style to make it different from its parent.

Styles and Local Formatting

You can always override the formatting for a styled path by selecting the path and making changes locally using the selections on the Attributes menu. When you've changed a styled path locally, the style name in the Styles palette appears with a "+" before it when you have the path selected. The "+" indicates that the path's style has been overridden by some sort of local formatting.

Attribute inheritance for paths which are both styled and have local formatting works like this: child styles still inherit changes in the properties they share with their parent style; the attributes which differ between the parent and child styles (including local formatting) stay the same when you change the parent style.

If you've overridden the formatting of a styled path with local formatting, and you want to reassert the path's original style, select the path and click on the style name in the Styles palette. The style overrides (wipes out) the local formatting, and the "+" disappears from the style name in the Styles palette (see Figure 2-124).

You can select more than one path with more than one sort of local formatting override and reassert the original style—select the paths and click on the style name in the Styles palette.

If you've locally formatted several paths with the same local formatting attributes and want to clear the formatting for each of

FIGURE 2-124
Overriding local formatting

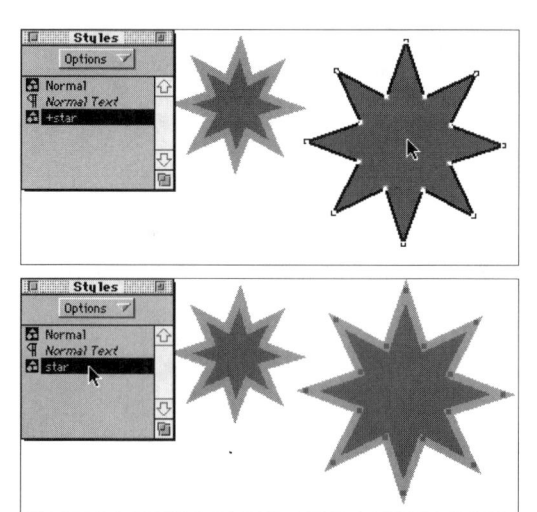

the paths without having to select each one and reassert the style, try this.

1. Select one of the locally formatted paths and choose Redefine from the popup menu in the Styles palette. This incorporates the local formatting into the style's definition.

2. Use local formatting to change the selected path to match the original style's definition. As you change the path's formatting, a "+" appears next to the style's name in the Styles palette.

3. Choose Redefine from the Styles palette's popup menu.

After you choose Redefine, all the paths—even those that had local overrides before you started this process—change back to the formatting specified by the style.

Note that you might have to go through this process several times if you have paths with different local formatting overrides.

Moving Styles from One Publication to Another

When you need to move styles from one publication to another, follow these steps.

1. Open the publication containing the style you want to move.

2. Select a path that's tagged with the style and press Command-C to copy the path to the Clipboard.

3. Open the publication you want to copy the style into.

4. Press Command-V to paste the path into the current publication. After you paste, the style name appears in the Styles palette. If you want, you can press Delete to get rid of the path you just pasted in. The style stays on the Styles palette.

If a style with the same name already exists in the target publication, it'll override the incoming style (the "home team" wins). The path you've pasted will be marked as if it had local formatting overriding the style.

Merging Styles

We can use FreeHand's "home team wins" rule to merge two styles into one style. Why would you want to merge two styles? If your publication needs to change from color to black and white, or from process color to spot color, you might want to change all the paths tagged with one style into another style.

If you have two styles you'd like to combine into a single style, follow these steps.

1. Select a path that's tagged with the style ("style 1") you want to end up with and copy it into another publication.

2. Change the name of the style to the name of the style you want to merge it with ("style 2").

3. Return to the original publication. Press Command-A to select everything in the publication.

4. Press Command-C to copy everything in the publication to the Clipboard.

5. Go to the second publication and press Command-V. FreeHand pastes all the objects on the Clipboard into the current publication, changing the definition of "style 2" as it does so.

Adding Styles to Your Defaults File

You can add styles to your FreeHand defaults template by opening the template, copying in elements having the styles you want, and then saving the file as a template. This way, the styles you've added will appear in every new publication you create.

Charting and Graphing

Because FreeHand works "by the numbers," it's fairly easy to create good-looking charts and graphs (I've always hated the dang things, myself). It might seem that the easiest way to get a chart or graph into your FreeHand publication would be to create one in Excel or Persuasion, then paste or place the chart into FreeHand. Because these charts are object-PICTs, FreeHand will convert them into FreeHand elements as they're pasted or placed.

The trouble with this method is that you often end up spending more time cleaning up the chart than you would if you were creating it from scratch. PICT-generating applications have weird ideas about how to draw things, generally using about three times as many elements as are necessary to draw any given picture. For more on importing object-PICT graphics, see "Importing PICTs" in Chapter 4, "Importing and Exporting."

The best method for more complex charts is to use the charting features in Illustrator (because you can open Illustrator files in FreeHand), but you can draw simple charts yourself in FreeHand.

Chart creation is best shown by example. Here are the basic steps you'll need to go through to create any chart.

- Choose a scale. For bar, column, and line charts, you set up the vertical and horizontal axes of the chart according to some scale—years, thousands of tons, or dollars—mapped into units of vertical and horizontal distance.

- Choose an equivalent unit of measure to represent the scale you've chosen. Once you know what the scale of your chart is, you can translate that scale into units of your measurement system. If the vertical axis of your chart is marked off in 10-year increments, pick some unit of measure as being equal to that scale. It doesn't matter what unit you choose as long as you're comfortable with the working size of the chart (remember, you can always scale the chart later, after you've got all the data points plotted). For a chart with a horizontal axis spanning 100 years in one-year increments, you'd better choose something small—like a point or .001 inch—to represent each year. If the same vertical axis were marked in 10-year increments, you'd do just as well choosing a larger unit of measure—a pica, or .5 inch.

- Set a zero point. If you're new to charts, this is where the horizontal and vertical axes of your chart meet.

- Draw the horizontal and vertical axes of your chart and mark them off in the increments you want with tick marks.

- Plot your data onto the chart using FreeHand's numeric movement features.

Bar and Column Charts

The only difference between bar charts and column charts is that column charts plot their data vertically and bar charts plot their date horizontally. You can use the same techniques to create either type of chart.

Imagine that you want to create a column chart showing how a particular organization's budget has grown over five years. You want to mark off the vertical axis in increments representing thousands of dollars; the horizontal axis in years. We have only a single data point for each year: $12,000 for 1985; $16,000 for 1986; $23,245 for 1987; $1,011 for 1988; $24,600 for 1989.

To create the chart, follow these steps (see Figure 2-125).

1. Choose a scale. For this example, each pica represents $1,000. Two picas represent each year on the horizontal scale. You could set the publication's Snap-to grid to picas to make the task of creating the chart a little easier.

2. Draw horizontal and vertical axes and set the zero point at their intersection.

3. Draw a box two picas wide by one pica tall using the Rectangle tool. Position the box to represent the budget amount for the first year.

4. Ungroup the box, select the two points along its top, and move the points down one pica. This positions the top two points of the box on the horizontal axis of the chart.

5. Press Command-M to display the Transform palette. Click the Move button at the top of the palette. Type "12" in the Y field to move the top of the box up 12 picas, a distance representing the $12,000 budget amount for 1985. Press the Apply button, and the top of the box moves to the point on the chart representing $12,000.

6. Clone the box from the first year across the other years, changing the position of the top of each box so that it matches the budget for that year. What about the data points that can't be expressed in even units of our measurement system, such as $23,245 for 1987? Simple. When you

FIGURE 2-125
Creating a column chart

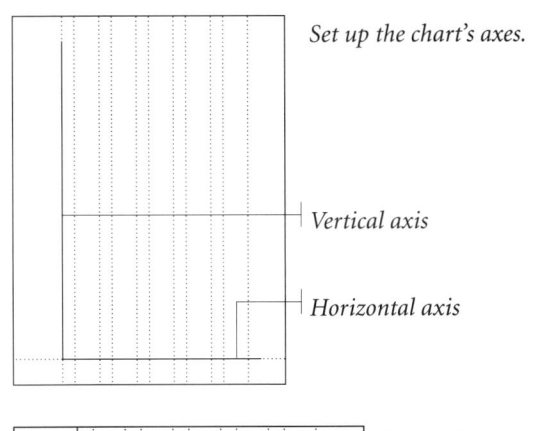

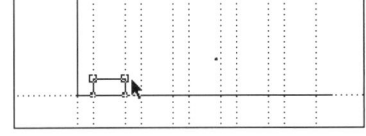

Set up the chart's axes.

Vertical axis

Horizontal axis

Draw a box for the first column, ungroup the box, and select the two top points. Use the Move palette to move the two points on top of the box down...

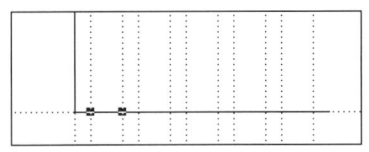

...so that they rest on the horizontal axis of the chart. Without deselecting the two points, use the Move palette again to move the top of the bar into position.

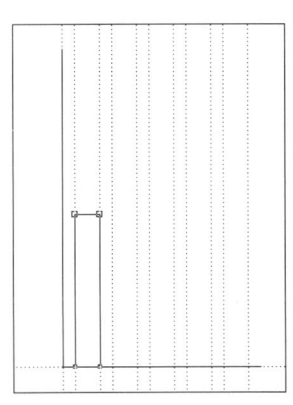

Once you've finished the first bar, use the same techniques to finish the other bars.

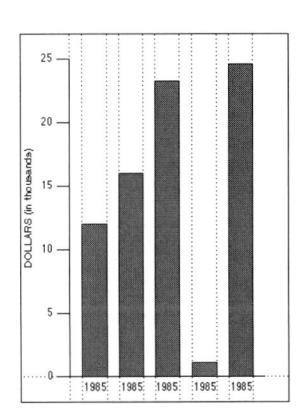

Finish the chart by adding labels and coloring the bars.

move those points vertically, type "23.245p" in the Y field in the Move section of the Transform palette.

7. Add labels and figures to the chart.

Stacked Bar and Stacked Column Charts

Stacked bar and stacked column charts break larger bodies of data into smaller parts, plotting those parts inside the area covered by the total. If you want to break down the budget amounts shown for the nonprofit organization from the previous example to show contributions from city, state, federal, corporate, and individual sources, you'd use a stacked column chart.

For the 1985 budget, the amounts contributed were:

$2,000 from the city
$1,600 from the state
$4,400 from the federal government
$4,400 from individuals

You'd go through the same Steps one through three as described in the previous scenario, and then create individual areas for each of the contributing sources to make up the column representing our $12,000 budget total. To do this, you'd follow these steps (see Figure 2-126).

1. Create a column representing the amount contributed by the city using the technique shown in Step four in the previous scenario. In this example, create a column representing the city's contribution of $2,000 moving the top of the column up two picas.

FIGURE 2-126
Creating a stacked column chart

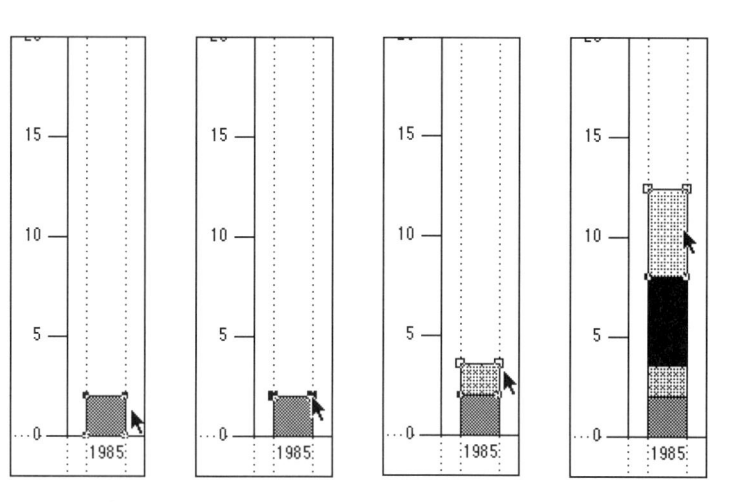

Create each part of the stacked bar chart using the moving and scaling techniques shown in Figure 2-125 (on the previous page).

2. Clone the column by pressing Command-=. Select the bottom two points of the cloned column. Press Command-M to display the Transform palette, if it's not already visible. The Y field of the Transform palette should appear filled in with the position of the top of the original column ("2"), so you can probably just press the Apply button to move the bottom of the cloned column to the top of the original column (if it doesn't, type "2" again in the Y field in the dialog box and press Return).

3. Without deselecting the points you moved, enter the distance representing the amount contributed by the state ("1.6p") in the Y field in the Transform palette. The bottom points you selected earlier now become the top points of a new column whose base rests precisely on the top of the column representing the amount contributed by the city.

4. Clone the column representing the state's contribution, and repeat the process of moving the bottom points on the cloned column twice to create the column representing the federal government's contribution.

5. Clone the column representing the federal contribution, and repeat the process of moving the bottom points on the cloned column twice to create the column representing contributions made by individuals in 1985.

6. Repeat this process for all the other years in the chart.

7. Add labels, figures, and a key to the chart.

Line and Area Charts

Line charts and area charts work about the same way a bar chart works—they plot data points along a horizontal axis. A line chart plots its data along a line, rather than on a bar or column. I still think of an area chart as being a line chart with fills, rather than listening to any of the people who've tried to convince me that the two types of charts are different. All I know is that you make them the same way in FreeHand.

Imagine you want to use a line chart to plot the budget of the same nonprofit organization used as an example in the two procedures above, over the same 5-year period. Once again, you want to mark off the vertical axis in increments representing thousands of dollars, and mark off the horizontal axis in years. You have a single data point for each year: $12,000 for 1985; $16,000 for 1986; $23,245 for 1987; $1,011 for 1988; $24,600 for 1989.

Set up your chart's scale by following Steps one through three in "Bar and Column Charts," and then follow these steps (see Figure 2-127).

1. Draw a path along the horizontal axis of the chart using the corner tool, placing a point along the horizontal axis every two picas (starting with a point placed at the zero point).

FIGURE 2-127
Creating a line chart

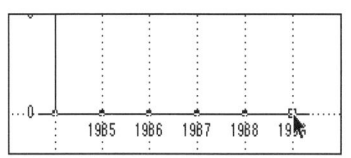

Set up the axes of your chart, select the corner tool and, and draw a path with a point at each horizontal increment. Then select the first point display the Move palette.

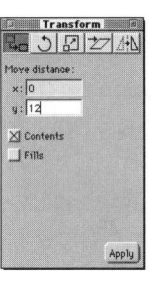

Move the point into position using the Move palette.

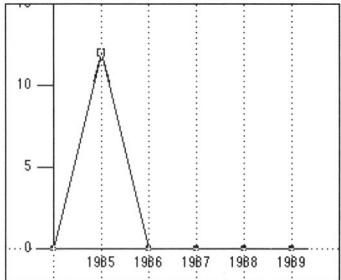

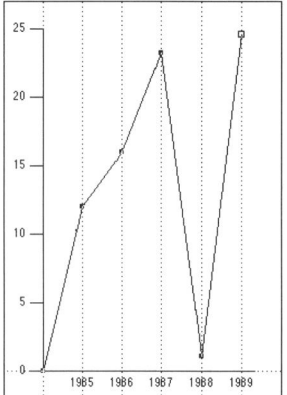

Repeat the process for each point on the line, and then finish the chart by adding labels or changing the line style or color.

2. Select the first point in the path.

3. Press Command-M to display the Transform palette. In the Move panel, type "12" in the Y field to move the point up 12 picas, a distance representing the $12,000 budget amount for 1985. The point moves to the vertical position on the chart representing $12,000.

4. Repeat the process for the four remaining points.

5. Add labels and figures to the chart.

If you wanted to make this line chart into an area chart, you'd make the line plotting the data points into the top edge of a filled path, as shown in Figure 2-128.

To show the amounts contributed by various sources, as we did using the stacked column chart, you'd use an area chart filled with different colors or tints, as shown in Figure 2-128.

FIGURE 2-128
Area charts

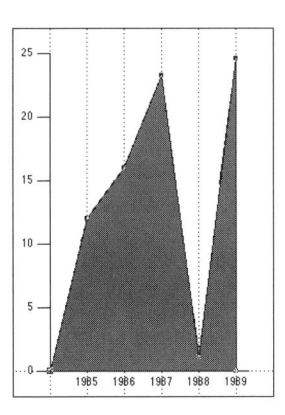

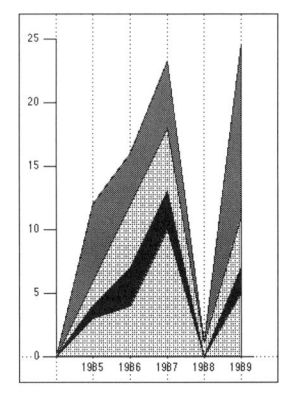

Area chart　　　　　　　　　*Area chart showing individual levels*

Pie Charts

Pie charts use degrees around a circle as their measurement system, rather than horizontal and vertical axes. Pie charts typically show parts of some total amount or percentage.

Getting there's half the fun.

If you wanted to show the contributions to our example non-profit agency's budget from 1985 as percentages in a pie chart, you'd first have to convert the raw numbers to percentages. This isn't hard: just divide the amounts by the total ($2,000 divided by $12,000 would give us 16 percent for the city's contribution). The other contributors would be 13 percent from the state, 36 percent from the federal government, and 36 percent from individual contributors. These figures have been rounded a bit, and they do total a little over 100 percent. Don't worry about it.

Now turn these percentages into degrees by multiplying each number by 3.6 (because 360 degrees is equal, in this case, to 100 percent). This multiplication produces 57 degrees from the city, 46 degrees from the state, 129 degrees from the federal government, and 129 degrees from individuals.

To create a pie chart, follow these steps (see Figure 2-129).

1. Set a zero point on your page.

2. Draw a horizontal line using the line tool, starting at the zero point. Press Command-E and choose None from the Line popup menu. Switch to Keyline mode by pressing Command-K so that you can see the path.

3. Clone the line (Command-=).

4. Double-click the rotate tool. The Rotate palette appears, if it's not already visible. In the Angle field, type "57." Press Tab to move to the X field and type "0." Press Tab again to move to the Y field and type "0." This tells FreeHand to rotate the line around the zero point you set. Press Return to rotate the line.

5. Select the two endpoints that overlap at the zero point and press Command-J to join the points. Press Command-Option-I to display the Object Inspector. Click the Closed option in the Object Inspector and press Return. FreeHand closes the path by drawing a line between the two points farthest from the zero point.

6. Clone the triangle. Select the point on the cloned triangle that's the farthest clockwise, considering the zero point as the center of a clock's face. Double-click the rotate tool. The Rotate palette appears, with 57 still entered in the Angle field. Type "0" in both the Horizontal and Vertical fields. This tells FreeHand to rotate the point around the zero point. Type the number of degrees for the next segment in

DRAWING 215

FIGURE 2-129
Creating a pie chart

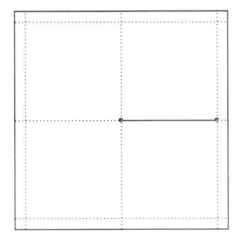

Set the zero point where you want to locate the center of your pie chart, then draw a line out from the zero point.

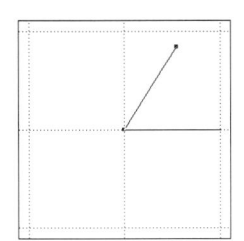

Clone the line, and select the point on the cloned line that's away from the zero point. Rotate the line around the zero point by 57 degrees.

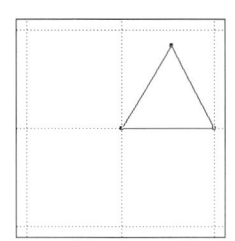

Join the two lines to make a path. Clone the triangle.

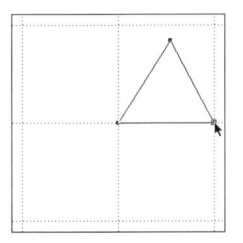

Select the point on the corner of the triangle that's in the same position as the endpoint of the original line.

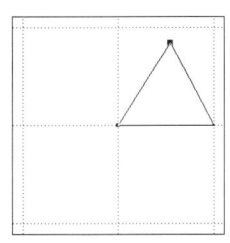

Press Command-, to repeat the rotation you used earlier.

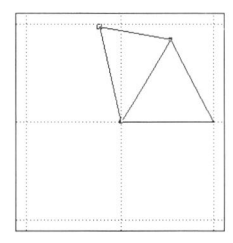

Without deselecting the point, use the Rotate dialog box to rotate the point 46 degrees.

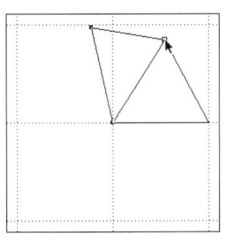

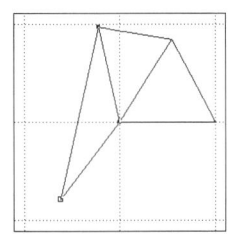

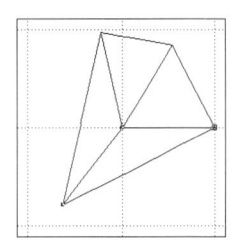

Repeat the process of cloning and rotating the triangles until you've plotted all of your data.

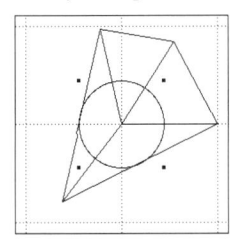

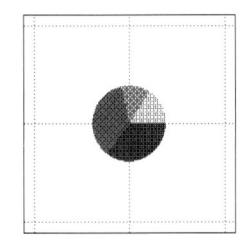

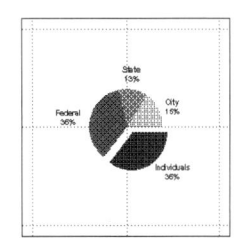

Draw a circle over the triangles. Color each triangle, and then use "Intersect" to create each pie wedge. Add labels, and you've got a pie chart.

the Angle field. In this example, this is the percentage contributed by the state government, 13 percent, or 46 degrees. Make sure that the center of rotation is still the zero point, and press Return. Repeat this process for the other two contributors.

7. Select the Ellipse tool, position the cursor over the zero point (look at the status bar to make sure you're on the zero point), hold down Option and Shift, and draw as large a circle as you can (without the edge of the circle extending past the outside edges of any of the triangles) at the center of the four triangles.

8. Use "Intersect" from the Path Operations submenu of the Arrange menu to create the pie wedges.

I admit that this isn't the most elegant process in the world—but it does work.

Perspective Projection

Perspective rendering (also known as central projection in the smoke-filled back rooms of the technical illustration bars where I used to hang out) is a drawing technology dedicated to rendering an image in space much the same way as our eyes see things. Perspective rendering came into vogue during the renaissance, and we haven't yet found a better way of representing our three-dimensional world on two-dimensional media (such as computer screens and paper).

Perspective rendering relies on models of the physical positions of these items.

- The eye of the observer
- The object or objects being viewed
- The plane of projection
- The vanishing point or vanishing points

Scared yet? Don't be—just have a look at Figure 2-130.

The whole point is understanding where objects fall inside a frame (also called the plane of projection) which lies between you and the objects. The objects exist between the plane of projection and one or more vanishing points. When you look at a photograph, you're looking at an exercise in perspective rendering, frozen in time, where the piece of film is roughly equivalent to the plane of projection.

When did this book become a drafting class? About the time I discovered I couldn't explain how to do this stuff in FreeHand without defining some terms.

FIGURE 2-130
How perspective rendering works

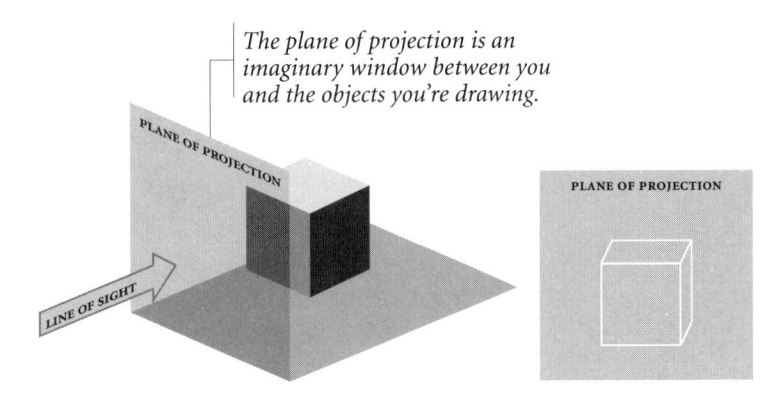

The plane of projection is an imaginary window between you and the objects you're drawing.

Purists will note that this is an isometric view.

What you see through the plane of projection.

Here's another way of looking at it.

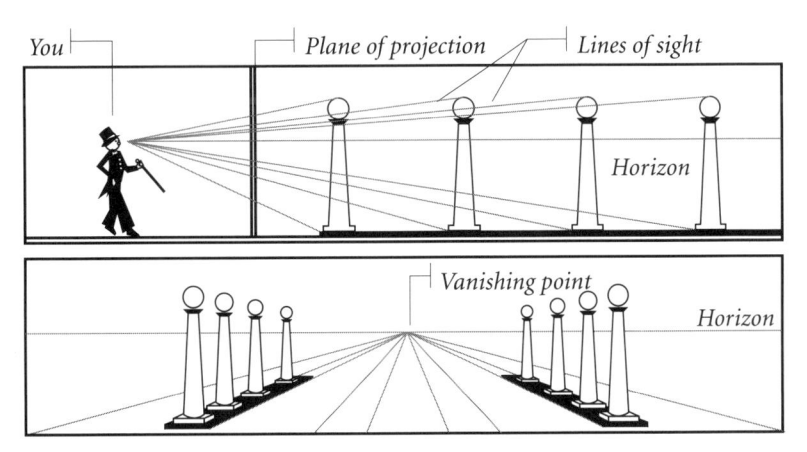

Single-View Perspective

Single-view perspective relies on a single vanishing point. You rarely see single-view perspective in the real world, because there's almost always more than one natural horizon in your field of view. The classic example of single-view perspective is that of a highway stretching into the distance on a perfectly flat plain (see Figure 2-131).

FIGURE 2-131
Single view perspective

Okay, so I added a few things.

To create guidelines for a single-view perspective in FreeHand, follow these steps (see Figure 2-132).

1. Designate a point as your vanishing point. Make this point your zero point. In most cases, this point should be around the vertical and horizontal center of your illustration. If it's not, you've got to ask yourself why you're not using multiview perspective.

2. Use the line tool to draw a horizontal line from the left edge of your publication to the zero point.

3. Press Command-= to clone the line.

4. Select the point on the cloned line that's farthest from the zero point and drag it some distance up or down on the page.

5. Press Command-D to repeat the clone and drag operation you've just performed. Continue pressing Command-D until you've created as many guidelines as you want. You'll probably have to adjust the endpoint from time to time to get the guidelines where you want them.

FIGURE 2-132
Creating a
perspective grid

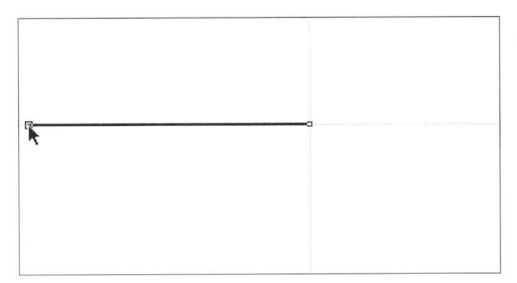

Draw a line.

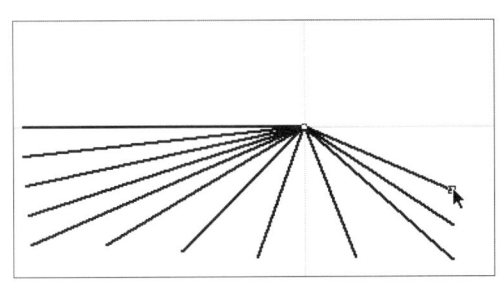

Clone the line. Select the endpoint of the cloned line and drag it to a new position.

Repeat the clone-and-drag sequence until you have all of the guidelines you want.

Once you've created all of the guides you want, send them to the Guides layer to convert them to guides.

6. Select all the lines you just drew and send them to the Guides layer. Now you can use them as drawing guides.

| Blending and Single-View Perspective | You can use blends as an aid to perspective rendering, particularly if you've got a shape that starts near the plane of perspective and extends toward the vanishing point. You'd draw the nearest and farthest cross-sections of the object, and then blend between the two cross sections, as shown in Figure 2-119. |

| Multiview Perspective | Multiview perspective is much more like the way we see the world, because it uses more than one vanishing point. You can use the single-view perspective grid building techniques in multiview perspective—you just use more than one grid (see Figure 2-120). |

FIGURE 2-119
Blending and perspective drawing

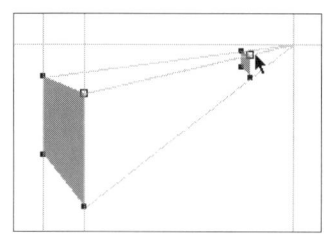

Select two reference points...   *...and blend.*

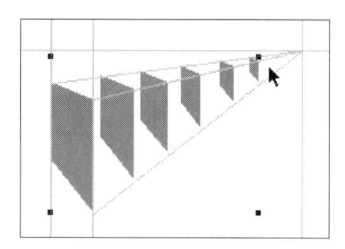

FIGURE 2-120
Multiview perspective

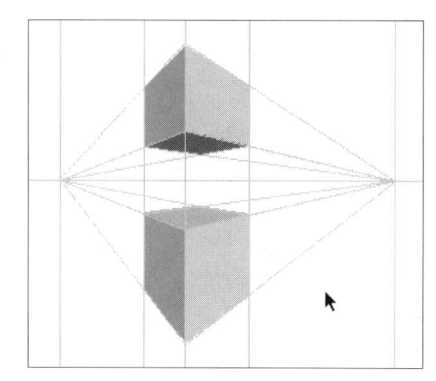

Multiview perspective depends on the use of more than one vanishing point.

In this example, I've moved the Guides layer to the front to better show the perspective guides.

Oblique Projection

Unlike perspective projection, oblique projection is nothing like the way we see objects. It's an abstraction that's good for keeping measurements intact for manufacturing drawings, and it's also a good way to render a 3-D shape quickly.

In oblique projection, one face of an object is always against the plane of projection, and the horizontal lines in that object are always drawn 90 degrees from the vertical (what we normally think of as horizontal). The horizontal lines on the other sides of the object are always drawn at the same angle, rather than at angles that converge on a vanishing point. In oblique projection, 45 degrees, 30 degrees, and 60 degrees are commonly used angles.

The next trick of oblique projection is that the scale of the lines and objects drawn away from the plane of projection isn't foreshortened as they recede from the viewer but are drawn to a single, fixed scale.

Just to add some historical color, oblique projections in which measurements away from the plane of projection are rendered at full scale are called cavalier projections, because they were often used for drawing fortifications in renaissance and medieval times. Half-scale renderings are called cabinet projections because they were used by furniture builders (see Figure 2-121).

FIGURE 2-121
Oblique projection

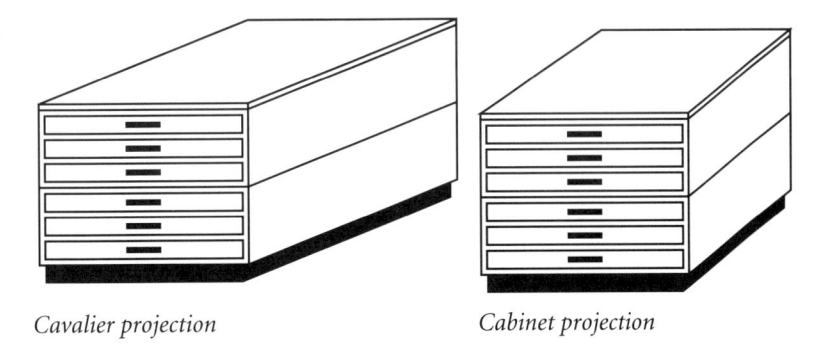

Cavalier projection   *Cabinet projection*

If you've been around the Macintosh-graphics community for long, you've seen lots of oblique projection—mainly because 45-degree lines offered the least jagged line you could get out of MacPaint. Early Macintosh artists created a style that's stuck with us—even now that we can draw smooth lines at any angle (see Figure 2-122).

FIGURE 2-122
Macintosh projection

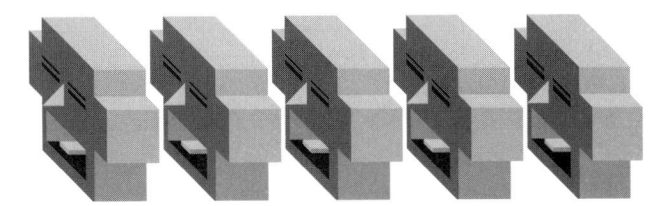

Creating Grids for Oblique Projection

Creating grids for oblique projection drawing is easy in FreeHand. You could, of course, simply draw a grid using the Line tool or the Rectangle tool, then rotate the grid and send it to the Guides layer. That works, but you won't get the benefit of snapping to the intersections of the grid (you'll snap to the lines, rather than to the lines' intersections).

I've got a technique I like better—I create a grid of objects that work well with FreeHand's Snap To Point option, rotate these objects and assign them to a layer of their own, then lock that layer. Why not send them to the Guides layer? Because objects on the Guides layer don't work with "Snap To Point," and that's the "snap"

FIGURE 2-123
Grid for 45-degree oblique projection

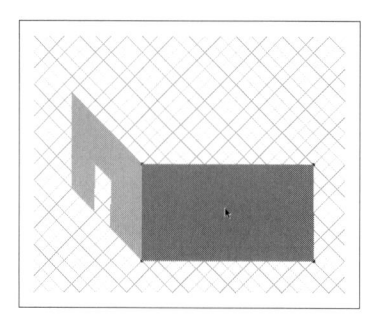

FIGURE 2-124
Grid for 30-degree oblique projection

Type "30" in the Constrain field in the Setup Inspector.

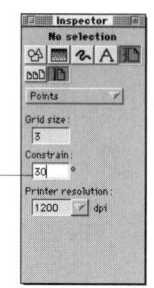

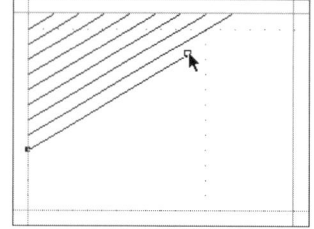

Hold down Shift to constrain lines as you draw them.

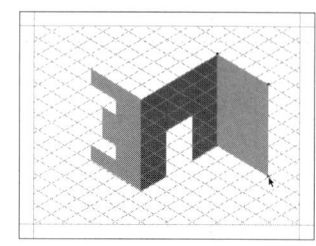

Draw objects, using your grid as a guide.

you want to use. For a demostration of how to create these "snap guides," see Figure 2-125.

FIGURE 2-125
Creating a grid of "snap guides"

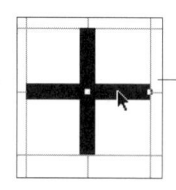

Create a "snap point" by drawing four lines. The lines should touch at the center of the point, but shouldn't be joined together.

Clone and move the points to create a grid.

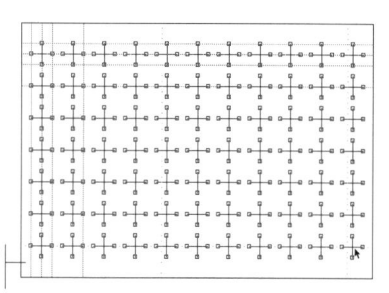

Rotate the grid to whatever angle you want to work with. In this example, I've tinted the objects making up grid to make it easier to see what I'm doing.

Turn on the Snap to Point option on the View menu.

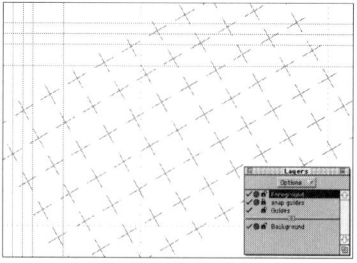

Send the grid to a layer, then lock the layer.

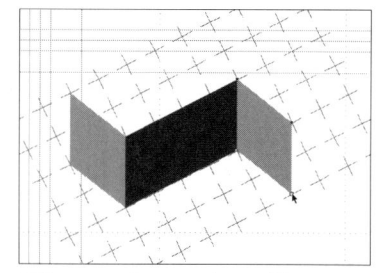

When you draw, points will snap to the "snap points" in the grid.

Axonometric Projection

I'm sure that there are plenty of drafters that'd argue this one with me, but I think of axonometric projection as being about the same as oblique projection. In axonometric projection, the faces of the object are rotated away from the plane of perspective by some pair of different angles.

There are three types of axonometric projection: isometric, dimetric, and trimetric.

Isometric projection In isometric projection, the object you're drawing has both of its primary axes rotated away from the plane of projection by the same angle (see Figure 2-126).

You can create grids for isometric projection using the techniques for creating oblique projections (described earlier in this chapter), but you'll use only the grid lines—and not the horizontal guides—to draw horizontal lines perpendicular to the major axes of the object.

Circles in isometric projection are rendered as ellipses.

FIGURE 2-126
Isometric projection

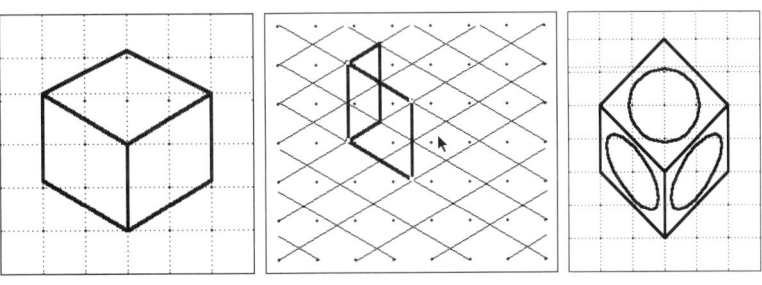

Horizontal lines in isometric projection

Circles become ellipses in isometric projection

Dimetric projection. In dimetric projection, the object you're drawing has both of its primary axes rotated away from the plane of projection by different angles (see Figure 2-127). For this type of projection, the grid you create should have one angle going from left to right, and another, different angle going from right to left.

Trimetric projection. You guessed it, in trimetric projection, the axes of the object you're drawing are rotated at three different angles

FIGURE 2-127
Dimetric projection

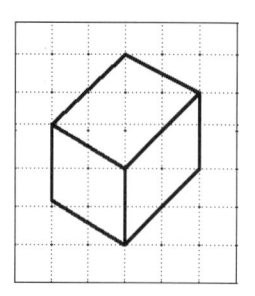

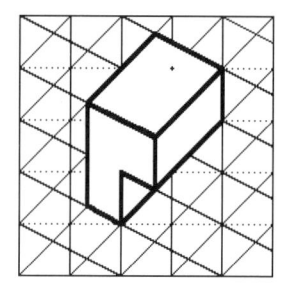

Grids in dimetric projection

from the plane of projection. I never really have figured out how trimetric projection differs from dimetric projection. Once again, you can create a grid that has one angle going from left to right, and another, different angle going from right to left.

Drawing Conclusions

Earlier in this chapter, I noted that I was confused by FreeHand's approach to drawing when I first encountered it. As I worked with the tools, however, I found that the parts of my brain that were used to using rapidographs (an obsolete type of pen used by the ancient Greeks), curves, and rulers quickly adapted to the new drawing environment. Eventually, I realized that this was the easier way to draw.

Then, after reading a related article in a tabloid at the supermarket, it dawned on me that the archaic methods I'd learned were nothing less than an extraterrestrial plot—forced on us in classical antiquity by evil space gods, to some cosmic purpose which I cannot—as yet—reveal.

Just keep at it.

Ruddigore

The Grand Duke

Iolanthe

CHAPTER 3
Text and Type

When you're lying awake with a dismal headache, and repose is taboo'd by anxiety, I conceive you may use any language you choose to indulge in, without any impropriety; for your brain is on fire—the bedclothes conspire of usual slumber to plunder you: first your counterpane goes, and uncovers your toes, and your sheet slips demurely from under you; then the blanketing tickles—you feel like mixed pickles—so terribly sharp is the pricking, and you're hot, and you're cross, and you tumble and toss till there's nothing 'twixt you and the ticking.
Then the bedclothes all creep to the ground in a heap, and you pick 'em all up in a tangle; next your pillow resigns and politely declines to remain at its usual angle! Well, you get some repose in the form of a doze, with hot eye-balls and head ever aching, but your slumbering teems with such horrible dreams that you'd very much better be waking; for you dream you are crossing the Channel, and tossing about in a steamer from Harwich—which is something between a large bathing machine and a very small second-class carriage—and you're giving a treat (penny ice and cold meat) to a party of friends and relations—they're a ravenous horde—and they all came on board at Sloane Square and South Kensington Stations.
And bound on that journey you find your attorney (who started that morning from Devon); he's a bit undersized, and you don't feel surprised when he tells you he's only eleven. Well you're driving like mad with this singular lad (by-the-by, the ship's now a four-wheeler), and you're playing round games, and he calls you bad names when you tell him that "ties pay the dealer;" but this you can't stand, so you throw up your hand, and you find your as cold as an icicle, in your shirt and your socks (the black silk with gold clocks), crossing Salisbury Plain on a bicycle; and he and the crew are on bicycles too—which they've somehow or other invested in—and he's telling the tale of the particulars of the company he's interested in—it's a scheme of devices, to get at low prices all goods from cough mixtures to cables (which tickle the sailors), by treating retailers as though they were all vegetables—you get a good spadesman to plant a small tradesman (first take off his boots with a boot-tree), and his legs will take root, and his fingers will shoot, and they'll blossom and bud like a fruit-tree—from the greengrocer tree you get grapes and green pea, cauliflower, pineapple, and cranberries, while the pastrycook plant cherry-brandy will grant, apple puffs, and three-corners, and Banbury's—shan't pay rent, and you're not very man, the taken by-the-bye while returning, and just as a stripe clothed that you awake with a shudder despairing—you're a regular wreck, with a crick in your neck, and no wonder you snore, for your head's on the floor, and you've needles and pins from your soles to your shins, and your flesh is a-creep, for your left leg's asleep, and you've cramp in your toes, and a fly on your nose, and some fluff in your lung, and a feverish tongue, and a thirst that's intense, and a general sense that you haven't been sleeping in clover; but the darkness has passed, and it's daylight at last, and the night has been long—ditto ditto my song—and thank goodness they're both of them over!

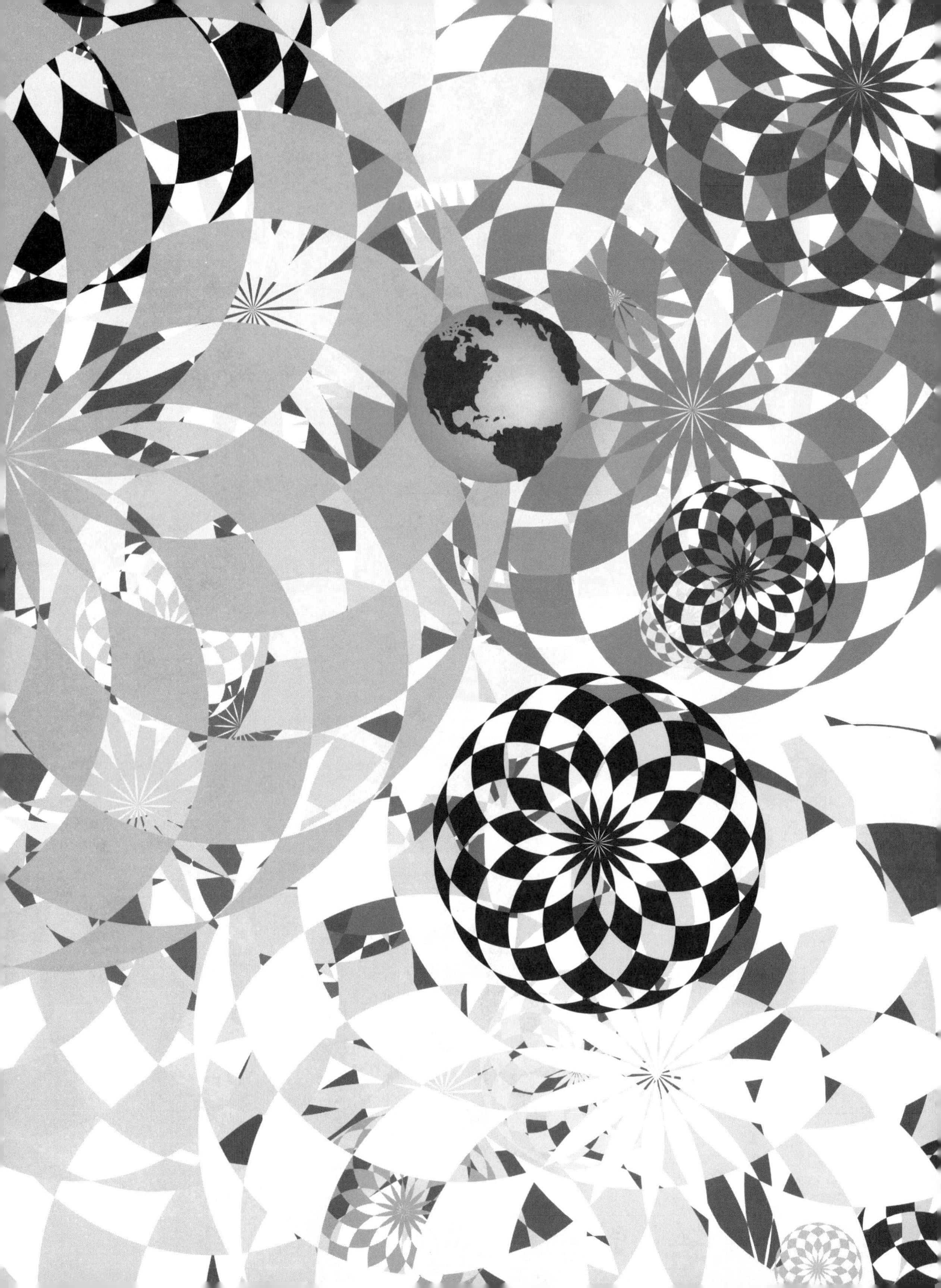

CHAPTER THREE   §   TEXT AND TYPE

Words.

Somehow, we can never quite get away from them. In academic circles, debate continues on whether we're born with the ability to understand language, or whether it's something we're taught. I don't know the answer, and, most of the time, I don't even know which side of the debate I'm on. What I do know is that language is the most important technology we humans have yet developed.

As I mentioned at the start of the last chapter, FreeHand serves the language of drawing very well. Does FreeHand neglect text in favor of points and paths, strokes, and fills? Not anymore—FreeHand 5 gives you almost all the text-formatting tools you could ever ask for (though I'm still asking for character styles and an XPress Tags import filter). If you consider Convert to Paths a character format, FreeHand provides more character-formatting flexibility than any page-layout program.

This chapter is all about working with text and type in FreeHand. Why do I say "text and type?" What's the difference? To me, "text" means content—the stream of words in a publication and how they're organized. "Type," on the other hand, means how the characters of text look—their font, size, color, and paragraph formatting.

There are areas of overlap between these definitions—for example, entering a column-break character (which is really text editing) forces text to the top of the next available column—which does change the appearance of the text. It gets confusing. I've tried to cover things in order: first create some text, then arrange it on the page, and then format it. In the last part of the chapter, I talk about various commands and procedures that change text into something that's not quite text: text that's bound to a path, or text that's been converted into paths.

Entering and Editing Text

Before we can work with text, we've got to create some. Select the Text tool from the toolbox (or press A), click or drag the tool in the publication window, and type (see Figure 3-1). FreeHand creates a text block and enters the characters you type in the text block. For FreeHand 3 users, this should be a thrill—no more trips to the Text dialog box to enter and edit text. (If you missed the Text Editor—as the dialog box is now named—in FreeHand 4, you'll be happy to know that it came back in FreeHand 5.)

If the New Default-Sized Text Containers Auto-Expand option in the Text Editing Preferences dialog box is turned off, clicking to create a text block creates a text block that's a fixed size (18 picas wide by 12 picas tall). If you've set your text containers to auto-expand, the text block increases in width as you add text. Instead of clicking to create a text block, drag the Text tool—when you do this, FreeHand creates a text block that's the width and height you specified by dragging (see Figure 3-2).

The text in a FreeHand publication exists inside text blocks, on paths, or inside paths (see Figure 3-3). You can even think of text blocks as a special kind of rectangle, or you can think of paths as

FIGURE 3-1
Entering text

To enter text, click or drag the text tool in the Publication window...

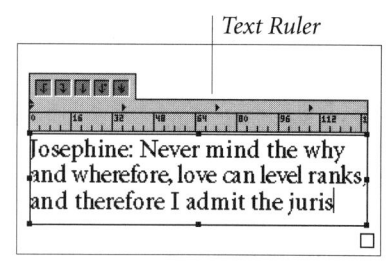

...and type. The tab ruler and tab icons appear at the top of the text block you've created.

FIGURE 3-2
Drag-creating
a text block

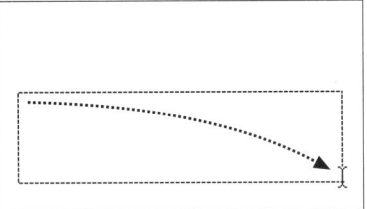

Drag the text tool on the page…

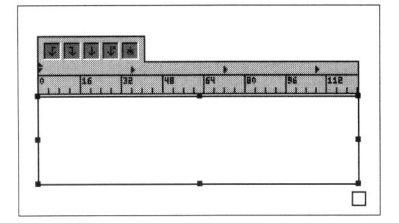

…and FreeHand creates a text block that's the width and height you specified by dragging.

FIGURE 3-3
Text blocks

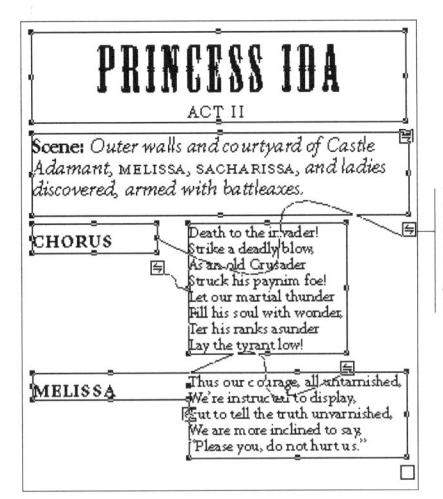

Link boxes attached to each text block show you if the text block is linked to any other text blocks. The goofy lines show you which text block it's linked to.

text blocks with certain weird properties. It's up to you. A text block can contain any number of different character formats, type effects, paragraph specifications, inline graphics, or colors.

Text blocks can contain up to 100 columns or rows (see Figure 3-4). When you flow text inside a path, on the other hand, you're limited to a single column and row. Columns break a text block into evenly-spaced horizontal sections. Rows break the text block up vertically. I call the area of intersection between a row and a column a "cell." You can think of each cell in a text block as a miniature text block, complete with margins.

Text blocks can be resized, reshaped, and manipulated in a variety of other ways, and we'll talk more about them in "Working with Text Blocks," later in this chapter.

When you create or select a text block, FreeHand displays three things around the text block: the Text Ruler, the text box's selection handles, and the Link box (see Figure 3-5).

FIGURE 3-4
Columns, rows, and cells

A column

A row

A cell

FIGURE 3-5
Text block controls

Tab icons

Text Ruler

Selection handles

Top handle

Corner handle

Text block border

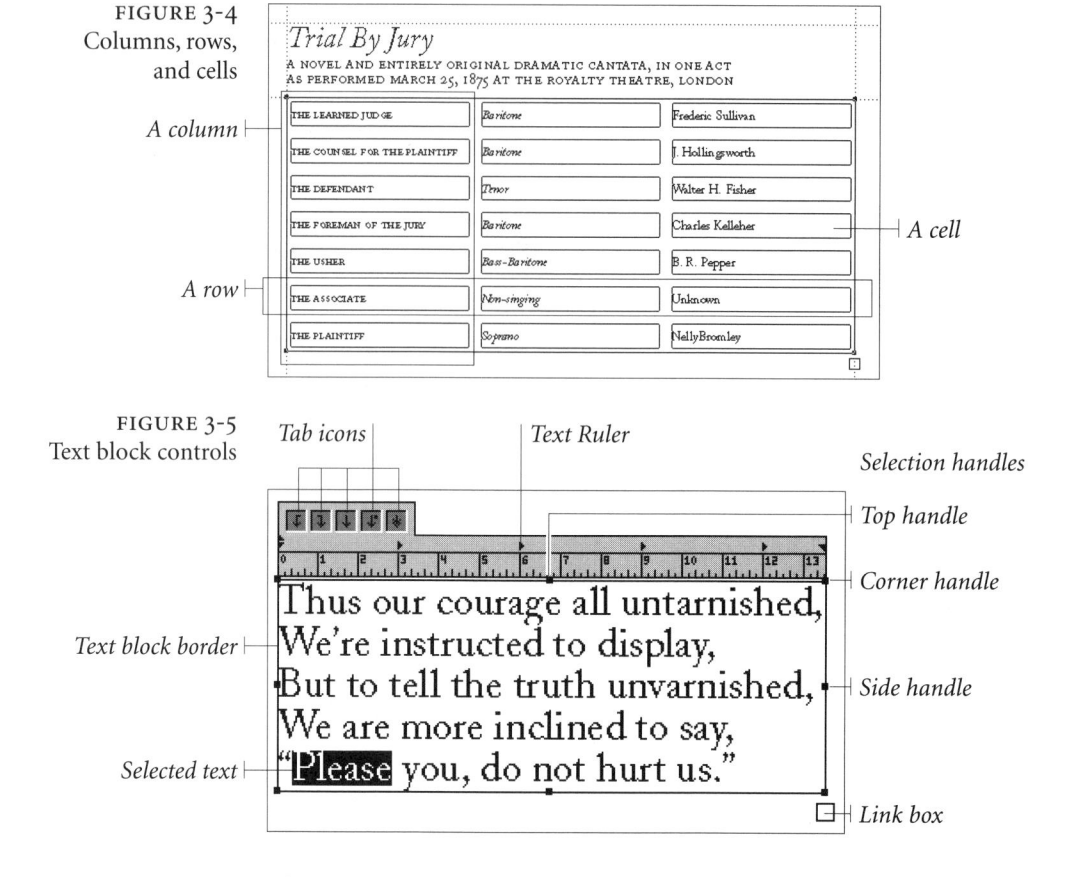

Side handle

Selected text

Link box

The Text Ruler. You use FreeHand's Text Ruler to set indents and tabs (see "Setting Indents and Tabs," later in this chapter). To display or hide the Text Ruler, press Command-\.

Tip:
Turning Off the Text Ruler

If you don't like looking at the Text Ruler and the selection handles as you edit text, you can turn them off by pressing Command-\ (or by choosing Text Rulers from the View menu). Now, when you select text with the Text tool, you won't see the Text Ruler or the boundaries of the text block (see Figure 3-6).

If you want to see the boundary of the text block, but don't want to see the Text Ruler, turn on the Show Text Handles When Text Ruler is Off option in the Text Editing Preferences dialog box.

Selection Handles. You can use the text block's selection handles to resize the text block, to change the formatting of the text inside the

FIGURE 3-6
Turning Off
the Text Ruler

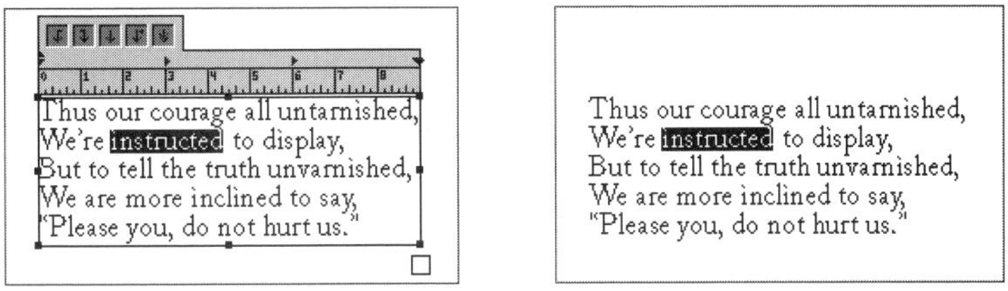

Text Ruler on.

Press Command-/, and the Text Ruler disappears. Press Command-/ again to bring it back

text block, and to turn auto-expansion on and off for the text block (see "Working with Text Blocks," later in this chapter).

When a text block is set to auto-expand horizontally, the selection handle on the right side of the text block displays as a hollow square (see Figure 3-7). When you've set a text block to auto-expand vertically, the bottom handle displays as a hollow square.

FIGURE 3-7
Selection handles
and auto-expanding
text blocks

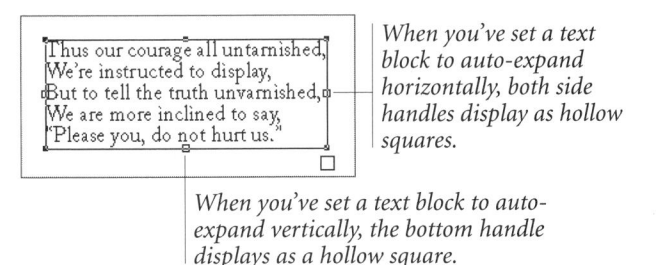

When you've set a text block to auto-expand horizontally, both side handles display as hollow squares.

When you've set a text block to auto-expand vertically, the bottom handle displays as a hollow square.

The Link box. The Link box, which appears below the lower-right corner of the text block, gives you the ability to link the text block to, or unlink the text block from, other text blocks or paths (see "Linking Text Blocks," later in this chapter).

If a text block contains more text than is currently displayed, you'll see a filled circle inside the text block's Link box. When a text block is linked to any other text blocks or paths, you'll see a link symbol in the text block's Link box (see Figure 3-8).

You can link text blocks to other text blocks, and to open or closed paths. In this book, I'll refer to all the text in a series of linked text blocks (including text that isn't in any text block), as a story. Text that doesn't fit within a series of linked boxes I call "overset," or "unplaced" text.

You don't have to add text to the text blocks you create—you can leave empty text blocks on your page until you have text to add

FIGURE 3-8
Link box icons

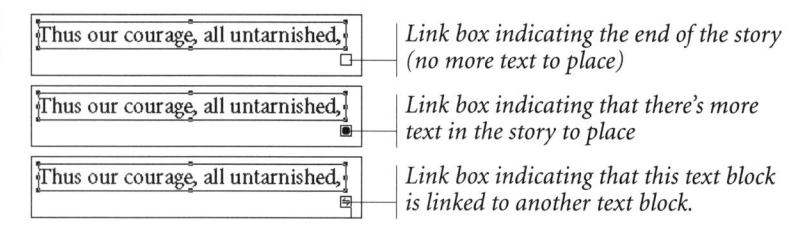

Thus our courage, all untarnished,	Link box indicating the end of the story (no more text to place)
Thus our courage, all untarnished,	Link box indicating that there's more text in the story to place
Thus our courage, all untarnished,	Link box indicating that this text block is linked to another text block.

to them (provided, of course, that these aren't auto-expanding text blocks, which disappear if you don't enter any text in them). This way, you can work on your publication's layout—including setting up links between text blocks—without necessarily having the publication's copy on hand.

Tip: Deleting Empty Text Blocks

If you've created more text blocks than you've used, you can get rid of all the empty text blocks in your publication by choosing "Delete Empty Text Blocks" from the Delete submenu of the Xtras menu.

If you don't see this menu choice, you haven't installed the Delete Empty Text Blocks Xtra. Locate this file on your original FreeHand installation disks (or CD-ROM), uncompress it using the Installer, and place it in the Xtras folder in your FreeHand folder.

If you see text blocks you thought were empty hanging around after this Xtra does its work, they're probably not really empty. FreeHand won't delete text blocks that have spaces, tabs, or other invisible characters in them, so you'll have to delete these yourself.

Tip: Applying Formatting to Text Blocks

When you want to apply the same formatting—character or paragraph—to all the text inside a text block, select the text block using the Pointer tool and then apply formatting using the Type Specifications palette (or the type-related sections of the Inspector). You don't have to select text with the Text tool to apply formatting.

Tip: Finding Empty Text Blocks

If you've lost track of an empty text block, switch to keyline view; FreeHand displays the boundaries of all text blocks when you're in keyline view.

Auto-expanding Text Blocks

One of the biggest new features in FreeHand 5 was auto-expanding text blocks—text blocks that expand horizontally or vertically as you add text to them (see Figure 3-9). FreeHand 5.5 adds a

FIGURE 3-9
Auto-expanding text blocks

Note: In FreeHand 5, horizontally auto-expanding text blocks are always left aligned. In FreeHand 5.5, auto-expanding text blocks use the alignment of the paragraphs they contain.

Click the Text tool to create an auto-expanding text block.

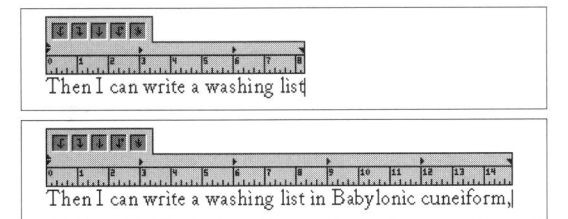

As you type, FreeHand enlarges the text block.

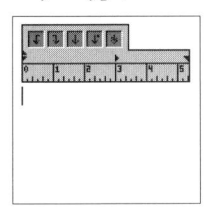

If you've set the text block to auto-expand vertically...

...FreeHand increases the height of the text block as you type.

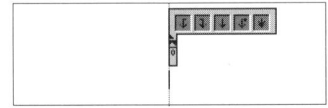

The paragraph alignment you've selected affects the way that the text block expands. In this example, the paragraph is centered...

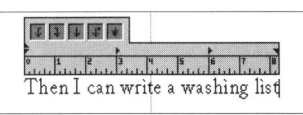

...which means that the text block expands equally to the left and to the right.

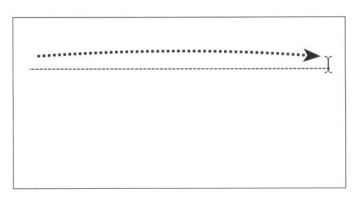

Hold down Control and drag the text tool horizontally...

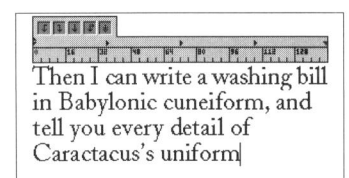

...and FreeHand creates a text block that auto-expands vertically.

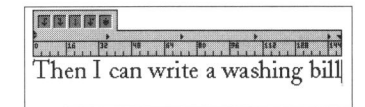

Hold down Control and drag vertically...

...and you get horizontal auto-expansion.

number of improvements to this feature. You can turn autoexpansion on and off for any text block, at any time. Here are a few things you should keep in mind when you're working with auto-expanding text blocks.

- You can't drag the text block's selection handles to change the width of text blocks you've set to auto-expand horizontally. When you do this, the text block snaps back to the width defined by the text in the text block.

- You can't change the height of vertically auto-expanding text blocks by dragging the text block's selection handles. Again, the height of an auto-expanding text block is determined by the text in the text block.

- In FreeHand 5, the text in text blocks you've set to auto-expand horizontally is always formatted as align left, regardless of the alignment you specify in the Alignment Inspector. In FreeHand 5.5, text blocks auto-expand according to the alignment of the paragraphs they contain.

If you turn on the New Default-Sized Text Containers Auto-Expand option in the Text Editing Preferences dialog box, any text block you create by clicking the Text tool will be set up to auto-expand horizontally and vertically (see "Text Editing Preferences" in Chapter 1, "FreeHand Basics").

To turn on auto-expansion for a text block, follow these steps (see Figure 3-10).

1. Select a text block with the Pointer tool.

2. Display the Object Inspector for the text block by pressing Command-Option-I. In the Object Inspector, you'll see two small icons to the right of the W(idth) and H(eight) fields.

3. Click the icon next to the W(idth) field to make the text block auto-expand horizontally; click the one next to the H(eight) field for vertical auto-expansion. As you click these icons, you'll see the text block expand in the direction you specified. Click them once to turn auto-expansion on; click the button again to turn auto-expansion off.

TEXT AND TYPE   235

FIGURE 3-10
Turning on auto-expansion

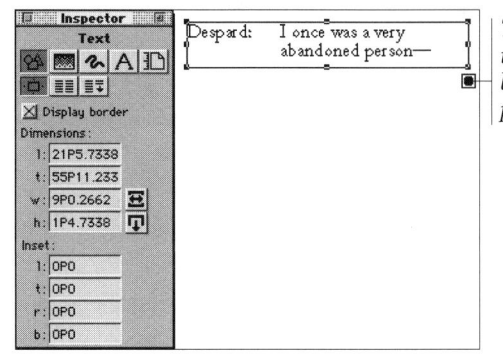

The Link box shows us that there's more text in this text block than we can see on the page.

Click the vertical auto-expansion button in the Object Inspector for the text block...

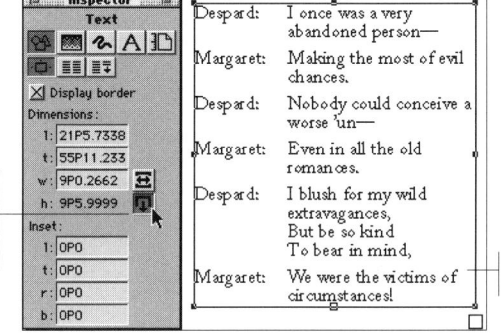

...and FreeHand expands the text block vertically.

Tip:
Auto-expanding Shortcuts

Double-click a side handle of a text block with the Pointer tool to turn horizontal auto-expansion on or off for the text block. Double-clicking the bottom handle on a text block turns vertical auto-expansion on or off (see Figure 3-11). If you're editing text and find that you want to change the expansion properties of a text block, hold down Command to switch to the Pointer tool, then double-click one of the text block's handles.

FIGURE 3-11
Auto-expanding shortcuts

Double-click the bottom handle to make the text block auto-expand vertically, or either of the side handles to make the text block auto-expand horizontally.

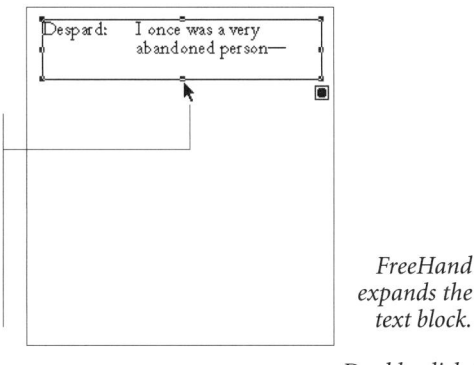

FreeHand expands the text block.

Double-click the handle again to turn off auto-expansion.

Entering and Editing Text with the Text Editor

If you'd rather enter or edit text using FreeHand's Text Editor, you can turn on the Always Use Text Editor option in the Text Editing Preferences dialog box (see "Text Editing Preferences" in Chapter 1, "FreeHand Basics"). When you do this, clicking (or dragging) the Text tool on the page displays the Text Editor—a moveable dialog box that's something like a little word processor inside FreeHand (see Figure 3-12). Cartographers in particular begged for the return of this feature after it was dropped in FreeHand 4.

FIGURE 3-12
Text Editor

Click this button to display the contents of the Text Editor in 12 point black text (this makes tiny text easier to edit)

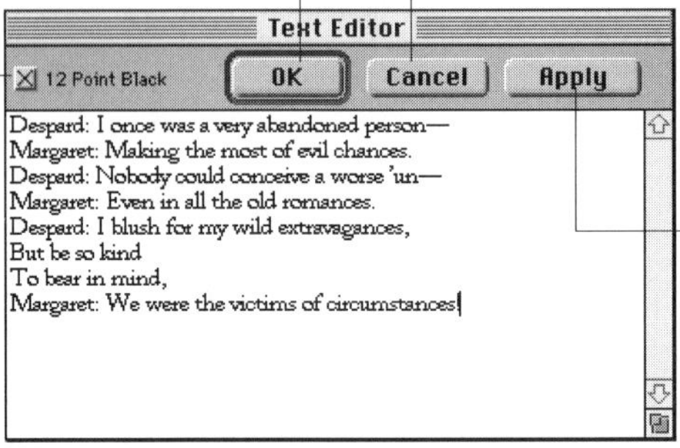

Click the OK button (or press Enter) to close the Text Editor and save your changes.

Click the Cancel button (or press Escape) to close the Text Editor without saving your changes.

Click the Apply button to apply your changes without closing the Text Editor.

In the Text Editor, you can view your text and its formatting (though the line breaks will probably differ from those you'll see when you close the Text Editor), or you can choose to view all the text in black at 12 point. Give your eyes a break and click the 12 Point Black option in the Text Editor when you're working with very small type, with pale-colored or white type, or other hard-to-see text.

If you want to see what the text you're entering or editing looks like without leaving the Text Editor, drag the Text Editor so that it's not obscuring the type you want to see, then click the Apply button. FreeHand applies any changes to the text or formatting you've made in the Text Editor.

When the Text Editor is open, you can apply formatting to both selected text and the current text block using any of FreeHand's formatting tools (the Object Inspector, Fill Inspector, Stroke Inspector, and all the different sections of the Text Inspector included).

Tip:
Closing the Text Editor

Pressing Enter closes the Text Editor. In earlier versions of FreeHand (excepting FreeHand 4, which had no Text Editor), I kept pressing Return, hoping it would close the dialog box. It doesn't—it simply enters carriage returns.

Tip:
Mixing Text Entry and Editing Methods

I like to do most of my text entry and editing on the page, but sometimes I like using the Text Editor dialog box—especially when I'm working with tiny or reversed type. Do I have to go to the Text Editing Preferences dialog box every time I want to create a text block using the Text Editor? Nope—if you hold down Option as you click the Text tool on the page, FreeHand displays the Text Editor dialog box.

You can also press Command-Shift-E to open the Text Editor immediately after you create or select a text block.

Moving the Cursor

When you're typing text into a text block, you shouldn't have to take your hands off the keyboard to move the cursor. While FreeHand's cursor movement shortcuts aren't perfect (it'd be great to have cursor movement keyboard shortcuts like those found in PageMaker or Word), they can come in handy (see Table 3-1). Hold down Shift as you press any of these shortcuts, and FreeHand selects text as you move the cursor.

TABLE 3-1
Cursor movement shortcuts

Press:	To move to:
Right Arrow	Next character
Left Arrow	Previous character
Up Arrow	Previous line
Down Arrow	Next line
Command-Right Arrow	Next word
Command-Left Arrow	Previous word
Command-Up Arrow	Previous line
Command-Down Arrow	Next line
Home	Beginning of story
End	End of text block

Tip:
Switch to the Text Tool by Clicking

Double-click a text block with the Pointer tool to position a text cursor at the end of the text block. This is the same as switching to the Text tool and clicking an insertion point at the end of the text, but it's quicker.

Selecting Text

As in most Macintosh word processing programs, holding down Shift as you press cursor movement keys selects text (Command-Shift-Right arrow, for example, selects the next word in the story). Also, as you'd expect, dragging a text cursor through text selects the text you drag over. In addition, you can use any or all of the following shortcuts.

- Double-click a word with the Text tool to select the word.

- Triple-click in a text block with the Text tool to select all the text in the current paragraph.

- Triple-click a text block with the Pointer tool to select all the text in story (same as triple-clicking with the Text tool).

- Press Command-A when you have a text insertion point active in a story to select all the text in the story.

Entering Special Characters

What makes a special character special? Is it innate, or is it the character's upbringing? In FreeHand, it's hard to tell—some of the characters listed on the Special Characters submenu of the Type menu are active—they "tell" FreeHand to break a line or a column at a specific place. Some of the characters on the list, on the other hand, enter a character that's really no different from any other text character you can type, except that it doesn't appear printed on your keyboard. Table 3-2 tells you what FreeHand's special characters do when you enter them in your text.

While you can use the Special Characters submenu of the Type menu to enter special characters in your text, I prefer typing the characters from the keyboard (after all, that's where my hands are when I'm working with text). Table 3-3 shows keyboard shortcuts for FreeHand's special characters.

TABLE 3-2
Special characters and what they do

Character:	What it does:
End of column	Tells FreeHand to break the text following that character, and start the next line of text at the start of the next available column in the story. If no column is available, FreeHand stores the text as overset text and displays a solid circle in the text block's Link box.
End of line	Breaks the line at the point you entered it (like a carriage return), but, unlike a carriage return, an end-of-line character doesn't start a new paragraph. End-of-line characters are great when you're working with tables.
Nonbreaking space	Keeps the words on either side of the character together, on the same line. If you don't want FreeHand to break a line between "H.M.S." and "Pinafore," for example, enter a nonbreaking space between the two words. This space expands or contracts based on the kerning, letterspacing, and wordspacing applied to the line it appears in.
Em space	A fixed space (that is, it doesn't change size depending on the surrounding kerning, letterspacing, and wordspacing) equal in width to the point size applied to the character. An em space set to a size of 12 points is 12 points wide.
En space	A fixed space equal to half an em space. A 12 point en space is 6 points wide.
Thin space	A thin space is equal to one tenth of an em space. A 12-point thin space is 1.2 points wide.
Em dash	A dash equal to the width of an em space.
En dash	A dash equal to the width of an en space.

TABLE 3-2
Special characters
and what they do
(continued)

Character:	What it does:
Discretionary hyphen	Or "dishy"—tells FreeHand that it can hyphenate the word at the point you enter the special character, if necessary. If FreeHand doesn't break the word, it doesn't display the hyphen. Whenever possible (that is, any time the character following the hyphenation point is anything other than a return or end-of-line character), use discretionary hyphens rather than entering a hyphen in your text.

TABLE 3-3
Typing special
characters

Special character:	What you press:
End of column	Command-Shift-Enter
End of line	Shift-Enter
Nonbreaking space	Option-spacebar
Em space	Command-Shift-M
En space	Command-Shift-N
Thin space	Command-Shift-T
Em dash	Option-Shift-hyphen
En dash	Option-hyphen
Discretionary hyphen	Command-hyphen

Checking Spelling

When I'm close to the end of a project, every word in the project looks misspelled. Is "dog" *really* spelled "d-o-g"? At that point in a project, I can't take anything for granted. While years of psychotherapy haven't gotten me past this last-minute panic, FreeHand's ability to check the spelling of the text in publications helps. (It doesn't help with my seeming inability to type any zip code other than "98103," on the other hand—the code for the area I've lived in for the last twenty years.)

To check the spelling of the text in all or part of your publication, press Command-Shift-G (or choose Spelling from the Type menu). FreeHand displays the Spelling palette (see Figure 3-13). You can control what and which text gets checked.

- To check the spelling of all the text in your publication, deselect everything (press Command-Tab), display the Spelling palette (if it's not already visible), and click the Start button.

- To check an entire story, select one of the text blocks in the story with the Pointer tool, display the Spelling palette, then click the Start button.

- To check the spelling in a range of text, select the text with the Text tool, display the Spelling palette (if it's not already visible), and click the Start button.

FIGURE 3-13
Checking spelling

If you've turned on the Show Selection option, FreeHand scrolls to display any suspect words it finds while checking spelling.

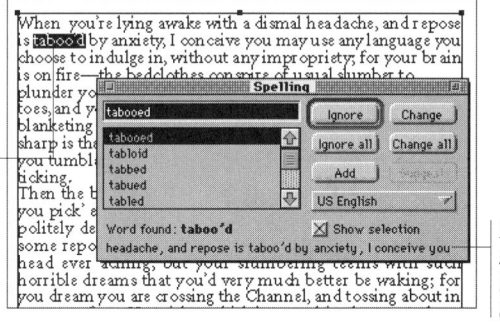

FreeHand always shows the suspect word here, regardless of the state of the Show Selection option.

As FreeHand processes the text, it selects words it thinks are misspelled (and displays the word, in context, at the bottom of the Spelling palette), along with a list of alternative spellings (if it can think of any). At the same time, it copies the most-likely alternative spelling (if any) into the Suggestion field.

If you've turned on the Show Selection checkbox in the Spelling palette, FreeHand displays suspect words as it selects them, scrolling your view of the document to make them visible, if necessary. If this option is turned off, you'll have to figure out where the word is, based on the text displayed at the bottom of the Spelling palette. What's the point of this option? Scrolling to display the suspect word is slower.

You can direct FreeHand to scan your text for repeated words ("the the") or for capitalization errors (a sentence starting with a lowercase character), using the Spelling Preferences dialog box (see "Spelling Preferences" in Chapter 1, "FreeHand Basics").

How does FreeHand know a word is misspelled? It doesn't, really. From FreeHand's point of view, words not found in the spelling dictionary or the user dictionary are misspelled. FreeHand, however, leaves the final decision up to you. Once FreeHand's encountered a misspelled word, the Spelling palette gives you a series of choices.

- Click the Ignore button to direct FreeHand to skip the selected word without changing it.

- If you see the word you're looking for in the list of suggestions, select it. FreeHand changes the text in the Suggestion list to match the word you selected.

- Click the Change button to change the selected word into the text displayed in the Suggestion list in the Spelling palette. If you've directed FreeHand to check for duplicate words, and FreeHand's found a duplicate word, this button becomes the Delete button: click it to remove one of the duplicate words.

- Click the Ignore All button to tell FreeHand to ignore other occurrences of the selected word for the rest of this FreeHand session (that is, until you quit FreeHand).

- Click the Change All button to change every occurrence of the selected word to whatever you've entered in the Suggestion list of the Spelling palette.

- Click the Add button to add the selected word to FreeHand's user dictionary (that's the word that's selected, not the alternative spelling displayed in the Suggestion list in the Spelling palette). How the word is entered in the user dictionary depends on the settings in the Spelling Preferences dialog box (see "Spelling Preferences" in Chapter 1, "FreeHand Basics").

**Tip:
Add Names to
Your User
Dictionary**

Okay, I mention this because I'm tired of FreeHand suggesting "Olive Cavern" whenever it encounters my name, but the truth is that very few names appear in FreeHand's dictionary. Save yourself a lot of mouse clicks ("Ignore," "Ignore," "Ignore!") in the Spelling palette by adding your name—and any other names you type often—to your user dictionary.

Finding and Changing Text

One of the most important and useful features in a word processor, text editor, or page layout application is the ability to find a particular string of text (a "string" being a series of characters) and change it to another string of text. Why is this so important? First, it helps you clean up text that's been typed by someone else (all those straight quotes and double dashes); second, it gives you a way to make last-minute text changes—which we all run into at one point or another—quickly and easily.

Setting the Range

How much, or how little, of the text in your publication do you want to search? To search all the text in a publication, deselect everything (press Command-Tab) before you start searching. To search an entire story, select one of the text blocks in the story with the Pointer tool before you search. To search a smaller amount of text, select the text with the text tool, then start searching.

Finding Text

First of all, I often need to find a word or phrase in a publication—I don't need to change it into another word or phrase, I just need to find it. That's where FreeHand's "Find" command comes in. To search for a string of text, follow these steps (see Figure 3-14).

1. Display the Find Text palette, if it's not already visible, by pressing Command-Shift-F.

2. Enter the text you want to find in the Find field. If you need to enter a special character (such as a tab, a carriage return, or an em space), choose the character from the Special popup menu next to the field.

FIGURE 3-14
Finding a string of text

Type the text you want to find in the Find field of the Find Text palette.

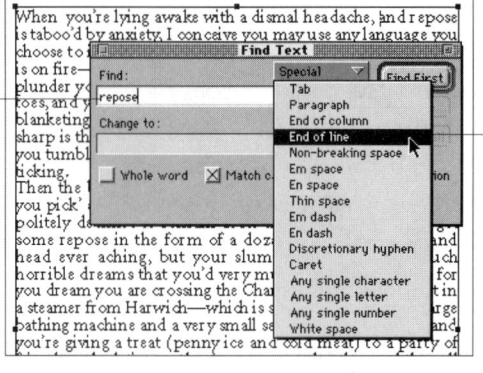

Enter any special characters you want to find using the Special popup menu.

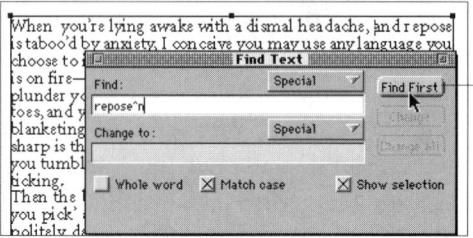

Click the Find First button to find the text you've entered in the Find field.

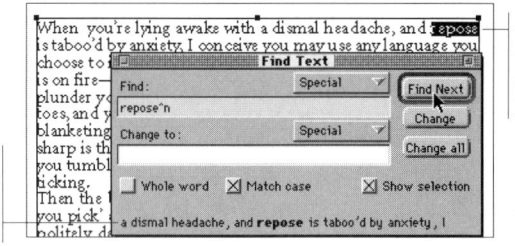

FreeHand displays the text you've found, in context, at the bottom of the palette.

If you've checked the Show Selection option, FreeHand scrolls to display the text you've found.

Click the Find Next button to find the next occurrence of the text.

If you want FreeHand to pay attention to the case of the characters you've entered (that is, you're looking for "Free-hand," not "FreeHand"), turn on the Match Case option. If you want FreeHand to only consider entire words that match the text you've entered (that is, you want "Free," but not "FreeHand"), turn on the Whole Word option.

3. Click the Find First button. FreeHand searches through your text until it finds the word (or pattern of characters) you entered.

If you've turned on the Show Selection option in the Find palette, FreeHand changes your view of the publication to display the text. If you're simply searching for a text string, leave this option on.

4. Once FreeHand finds the first occurrence of the text, the Find First button changes, becoming the Find Next button. To find the string of text again, click the Find Next button.

In the procedure above, I mentioned choosing special characters from the Special popup menu. If you'd rather type the special character yourself (I would), you can—by entering the character shown in Table 3-4. As you look at the table, note that capitalization counts—"^t," for example, finds a different character than "^T" would.

TABLE 3-4
Find and Change metacharacters

When you want to find/change:	Enter:
Tab	^t
Carriage return	^p
End of column	^d
End of line	^n
Non-breaking space	^S
Em space	^M
En space	^N
Thin space	^T
Discretionary hyphen	^-
Caret	^^
Any single character	^@
Any single letter	^*
Any single number	^#
White space	^w*

* "white space" is any space character following selected punctuation (:.!?), or any string of more than two space characters or tabs.

Changing Text Most of the time, you're looking for text so that you can change it. While FreeHand doesn't—yet—give you the ability to change the formatting of the text you find, you can change any string of text into any other string of text. To change text you find, follow these steps (see Figure 3-15).

FIGURE 3-15
Changing text

Enter the text you want to find in the Find field. In the Change To field, Enter the string you want to use to replace the text you find.

Click the Find First button.

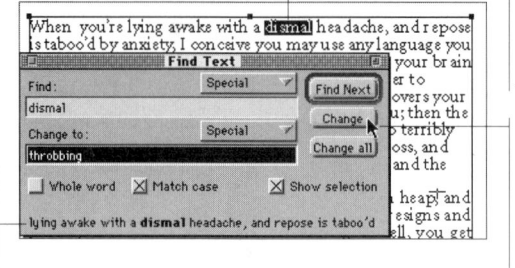

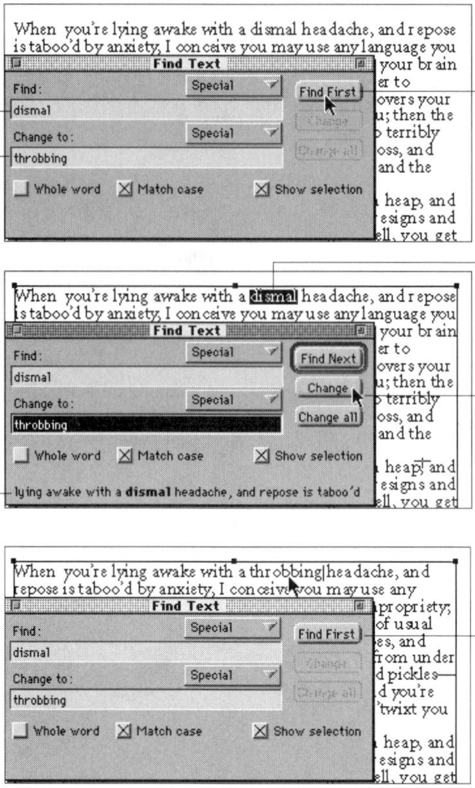

If you've checked the Show Selection option, FreeHand scrolls to display the text you've found.

FreeHand displays the text you've found, in context, at the bottom of the palette.

Click the Change button to change this occurrence of the found text, or click the Change All button to change every occurrence of the text.

FreeHand changes the text.

Click the Find First button again to find the next occurrence of the string you entered in the Find field.

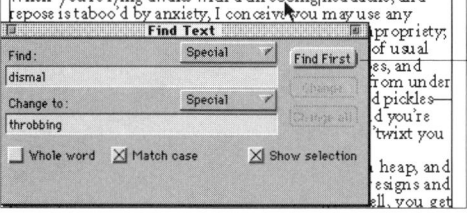

1. Display the Find Text palette and enter the string you want to search for in the Find field (for a more complete description, see "Finding Text," earlier in this chapter).

2. Enter the string you want to have replace the string you entered in Step 1 in the Change field. If you need to enter a special character, type it, or choose it from the Special popup menu next to the field.

3. If you want to view the text FreeHand finds (before you change it), turn on the Show Selection option and click the Find First button. FreeHand finds the string you entered. Click the Change button to change the text to the string you entered in the Change field. After you click the Change button, FreeHand finds the next occurrence of the string.

    If you want to change every occurrence, click the Change All button. FreeHand changes all the strings it finds.

TEXT AND TYPE 247

If you don't want to change this occurrence of the string, click the Find Next button. FreeHand finds the next occurrence of the string you entered in the Find field.

Tip:
"Find" and Formatting

What can you do when you need to apply a specific set of formatting attributes to a word in your publication? If you were using PageMaker or XPress, you'd be able to search for the word and apply formatting to it. While you can't do that in FreeHand, you can use FreeHand's ability to copy and paste formatting to do something very similar (see Figure 3-16).

1. Select some text that's formatted with the attributes you want.

2. Press Command-Option-Shift-C to copy the formatting attributes applied to the selected text.

FIGURE 3-16
Changing formatting with the Find Text palette

In this example, I've used wild card characters to search for all dollar amounts between $10.00 and $99.00.

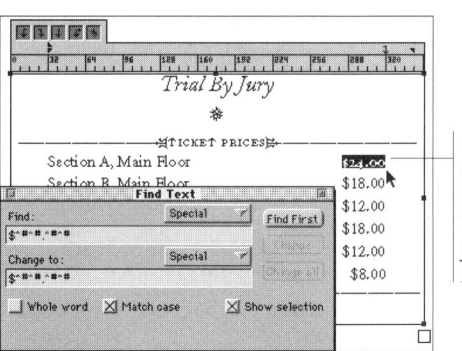

Once FreeHand finds the first occurrence of the text, format the text the way you want it (in this case, I've changed the font from Adobe Caslon Regular to Adobe Caslon Expert Regular).

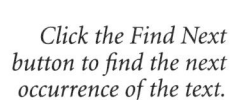

Click the Find Next button to find the next occurrence of the text.

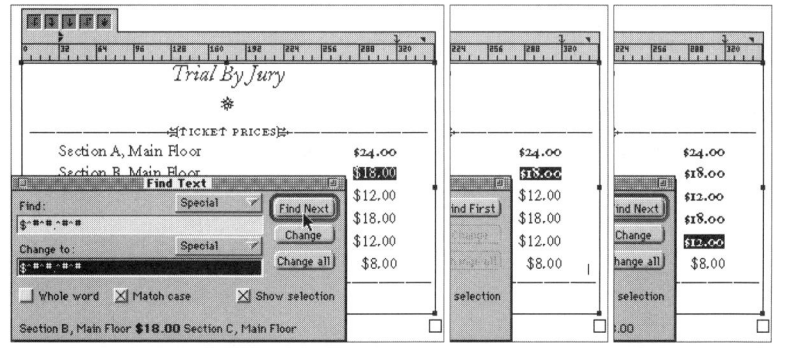

Work your way through the prices in the publication…

…formatting each price as you find it, then clicking the Find Next button to move to the next price.

3. Press Command-Shift-F to display the Find Text palette (if it's not already visible). Type the text you want to find in the Find field. Turn on the Show Selected option so that you can see what you're doing.

4. Click the Find First button. FreeHand finds and selects the first occurrence of the string.

5. Press Command-Option-Shift-V to paste the formatting attributes you copied. FreeHand formats the text.

6. Now you can work your way through the publication, clicking the Find Next button to find the string and applying the formatting you copied as you go.

Working with Text Blocks

Once you've created a text block, you can work with it just as you can anything else on the FreeHand page and pasteboard. You can rotate text blocks, scale them, reflect them, skew them, group and ungroup them, and apply colors to them. You cannot, however, paste objects inside the characters of a text block without first converting the text to paths (see "Converting Characters into Paths," later in this chapter).

Copying and Pasting Text

If you want to copy some text from an existing text block into a new text block, select the text using the Text tool, and then press Command-C to copy the text to the Clipboard. Press Command-Tab to deselect the current text block and press Command-V. FreeHand creates a new text block and pastes the text you copied to the Clipboard into it (see Figure 3-17).

If you want to copy the contents of a text block into another text block, select the first text block with the Pointer tool and press Command-C to copy (or Command-X to cut) the text block to the Clipboard. Press A to select the Text tool, and click an insertion in the second text block at the position you want to paste the text, then press Command-V to paste. FreeHand pastes the contents of the first text block into the second text block (see Figure 3-18).

FIGURE 3-17
Creating a new text block from existing text

Select the text you want to turn into an independent text block.

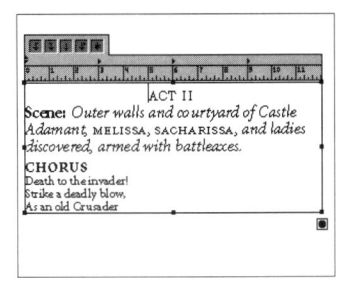

Cut the text to the Clipboard.

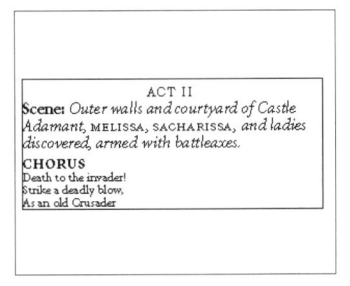

Press Command-Tab to deselect the text block.

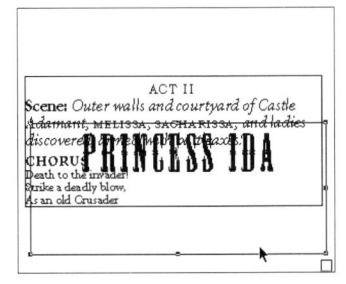

Paste the new text block into your publication.

FIGURE 3-18
Inserting text blocks

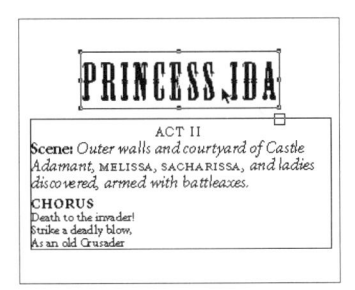

Select a text block with the pointer tool.

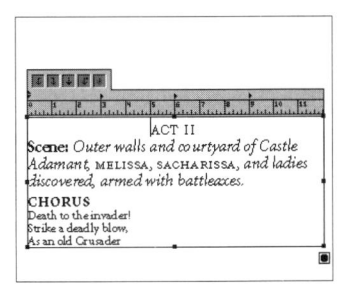

Cut or copy the text block to the Clipboard.

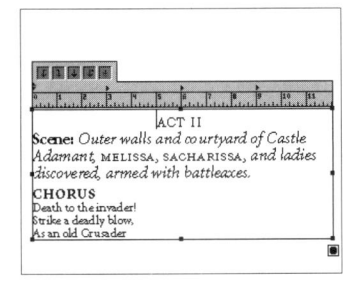

Click the text tool where you want to insert the text.

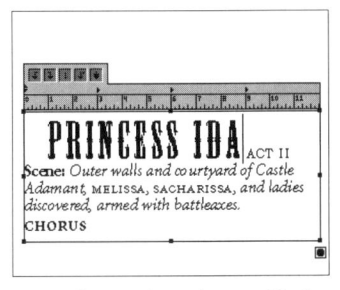

Paste the text into the text block.

Resizing text blocks. You can use the selection handles on a text block to resize the text block itself, resize the text inside the text block, change the kerning of the text, adjust the word spacing used inside the text block, and change the leading of all the lines inside the text block, as shown in Table 3-5 and Figure 3-19.

Changing the shape of a text block by dragging a corner handle recomposes the lines of text inside the text block. You don't have to enter carriage returns, end-of-line characters, or (don't even think about it!) tabs to break lines, unless you really want a line break at that specific point in your text, and want it there regardless of any changes you might make.

You can also use a text block's selection handles as a method of moving the text block. Why would you want to do this? It can sometimes be difficult to drag a text block into a precise position. It always seems to snap to the wrong grid mark or ruler guide (or the wrong side of the text block snaps to the grid). You can get around this by simply dragging one of the corner handles to the point you want to move the text block, then adjusting the other handles (see Figure 3-20).

TABLE 3-5
Working with text block handles

To do this:	Do this:
Resize the text block	Drag a corner handle
Resize the text block proportionally	Drag a corner handle while holding down Shift
Resize the text while resizing the text block	Drag a corner handle while holding down Option.
Proportionally resize the text and the text block	Drag a corner handle while holding down Shift and Option
Change the leading of text inside a text block	Drag the top or bottom handle of the text block*
Change the kerning of text inside a text block	Drag a side handle*
Adjust the wordspacing of text inside a text block	Hold down Option and drag a side handle*

*Only applies to a single-column text block

FIGURE 3-19
Working with text block selection handles

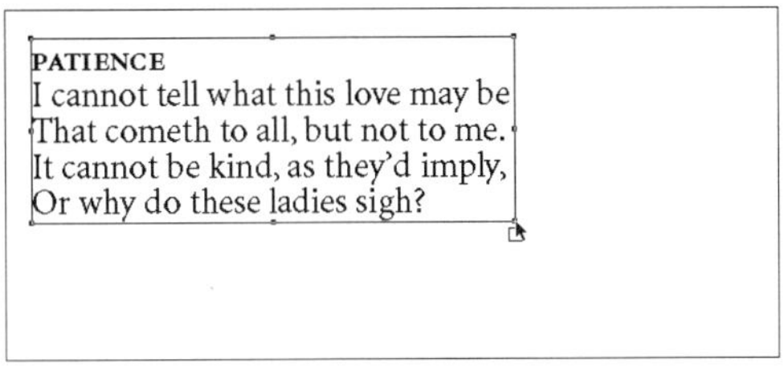

To change the size of the text block...

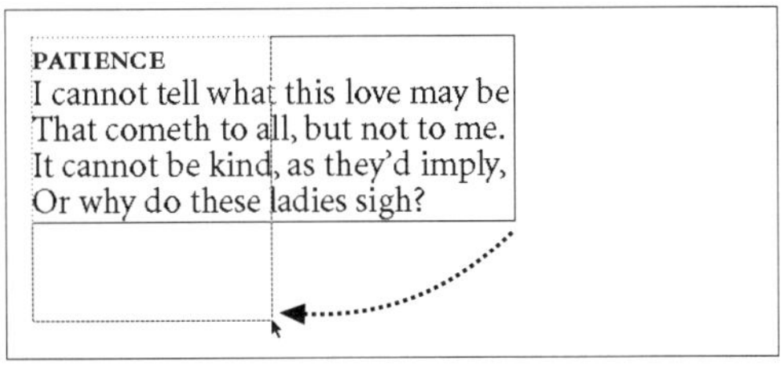

...drag a corner handle.

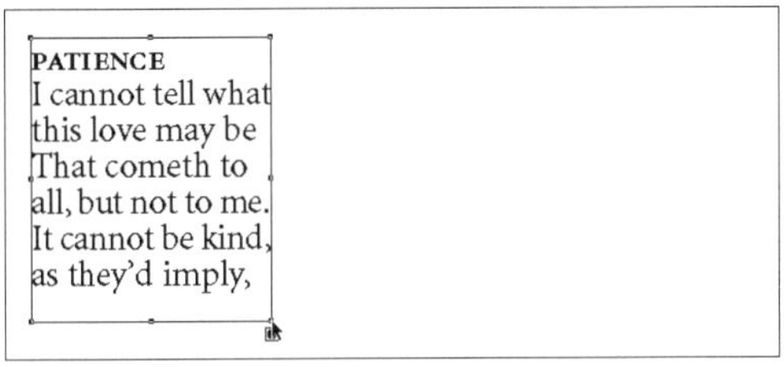

FreeHand resizes the text block, reflowing the text inside the text block to fit the new shape.

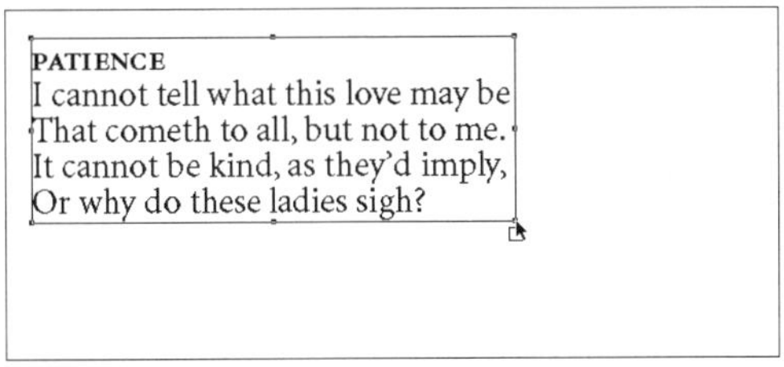

To change the size of the text inside a text block...

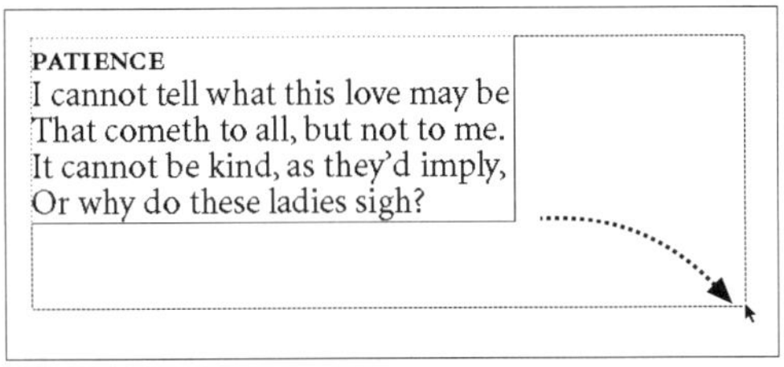

...hold down Option and drag a corner handle (hold down Shift and Option as you drag to resize the text proportionally).

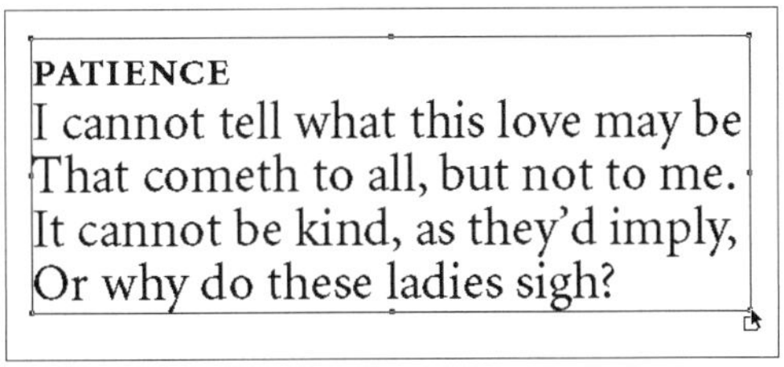

FreeHand resizes the text and the the block.

FIGURE 3-19
Working with text
block selection handles
(continued)

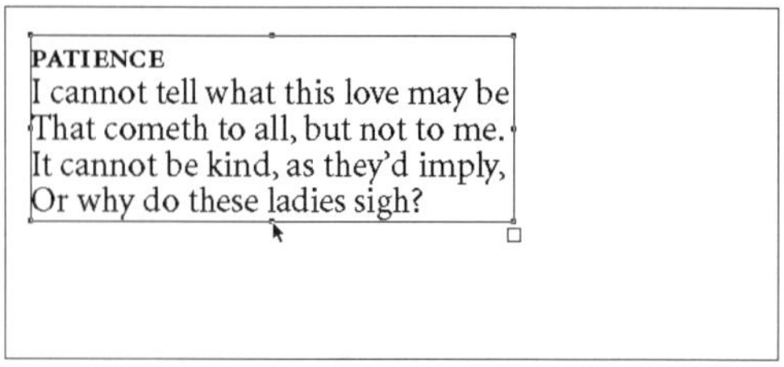

PATIENCE I cannot tell what this love may be That cometh to all, but not to me. It cannot be kind, as they'd imply, Or why do these ladies sigh?	To change the leading of the text in a text block...
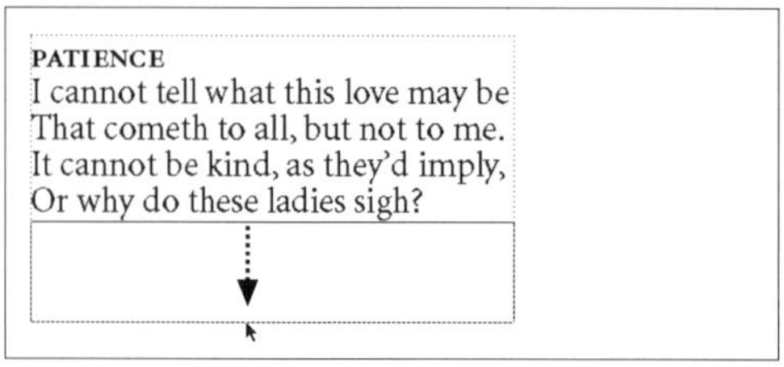 PATIENCE I cannot tell what this love may be That cometh to all, but not to me. It cannot be kind, as they'd imply, Or why do these ladies sigh?	...drag a bottom or top handle.
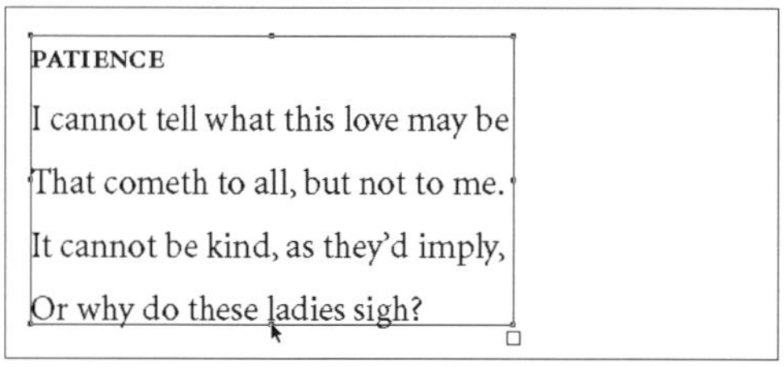 PATIENCE I cannot tell what this love may be That cometh to all, but not to me. It cannot be kind, as they'd imply, Or why do these ladies sigh?	FreeHand changes the leading of the text in the text block. In FreeHand 5.5, this even works with auto-expanding text blocks.
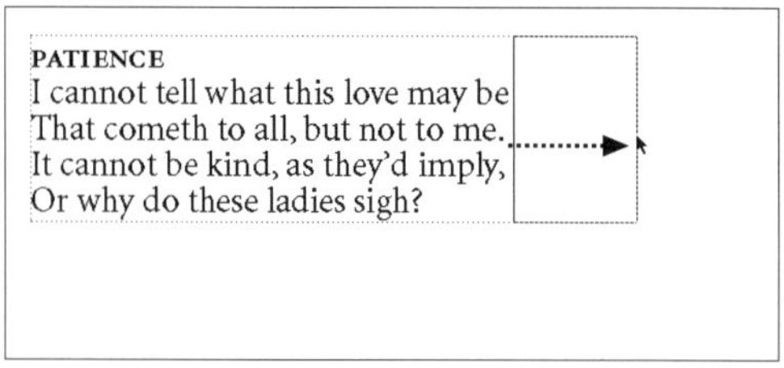 PATIENCE I cannot tell what this love may be That cometh to all, but not to me. It cannot be kind, as they'd imply, Or why do these ladies sigh?	To change the range kerning of text in a text block, drag a side handle.
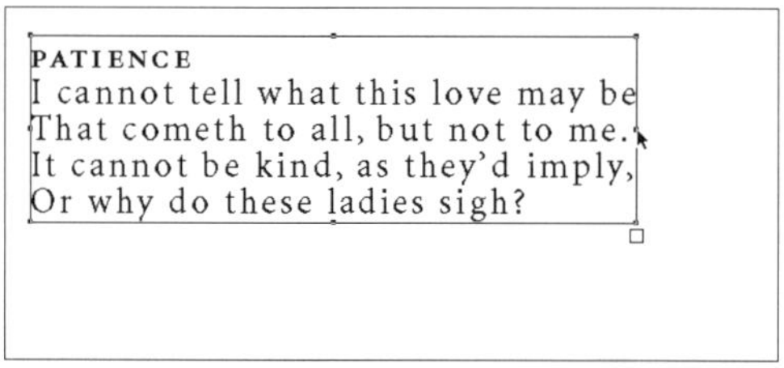 PATIENCE I cannot tell what this love may be That cometh to all, but not to me. It cannot be kind, as they'd imply, Or why do these ladies sigh?	FreeHand increases or decreases the range kerning of the text inside the text block. In FreeHand 5.5, this even works with auto-expanding text blocks.
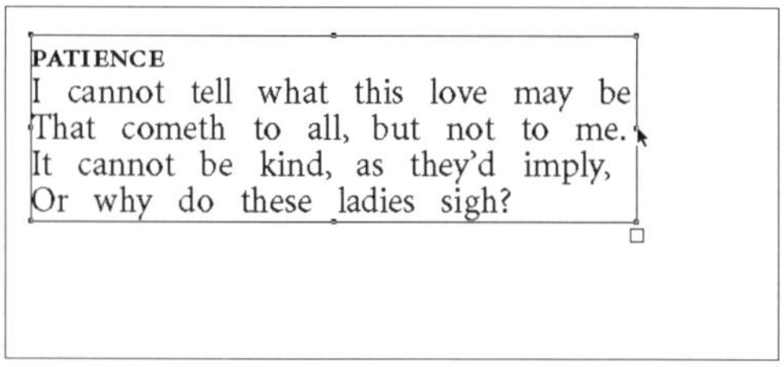 PATIENCE I cannot tell what this love may be That cometh to all, but not to me. It cannot be kind, as they'd imply, Or why do these ladies sigh?	Hold down Option as you drag a side handle, and FreeHand changes the wordspacing of the text in the text block.

FIGURE 3-20
Moving text blocks by dragging handles

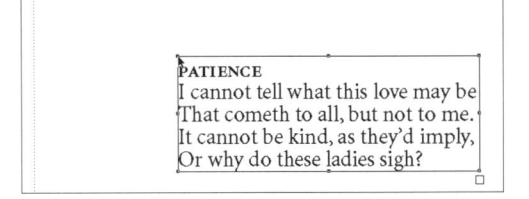

If you're having trouble moving a text block to a new location…

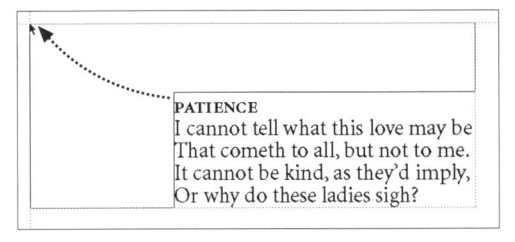

…drag a corner handle…

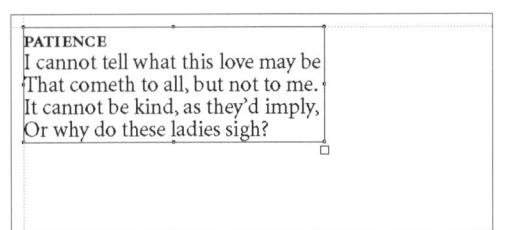

…and adjust the shape of the text block once you've got one corner where you want it.

Tip: Resizing Text Blocks Using the Inspector	If you want to make a text block a specific size, use the Inspector. Select the text block, then display the Object Inspector by pressing Command-Option-B (if the Inspector palette isn't currently visible, you'll have to press Command-I first). In the Object Inspector for the text block, enter the width and height you want for the text block in the W(idth) and H(eight) fields, and press Return to apply your changes. FreeHand sizes the text block to the dimensions you specified.
Tip: Making Text Blocks Transparent	When you click an insertion point in a text block, FreeHand makes the background of the text block opaque white, by default. If you want to see what's behind a text block (assuming that the text block doesn't have a fill applied to it), or if you want to see the text block's background color (if the text block has a fill applied to it), check Buffered Drawing in the Display Preferences dialog box (see Figure 3-21).

FIGURE 3-21
Seeing through text blocks

When you turn off "Buffered drawing" in the Display Preferences dialog box, FreeHand draws a white box behind the text block containing the cursor.

Turn "Buffered drawing" on, and you'll be able to see through the text block as you enter or edit text.

Tip:
Deselecting Text Blocks

When you're editing text, you can't press Tab to deselect the text block; pressing Tab just enters tab characters in the text block. Instead, hold down Command and press Tab, and FreeHand deselects the text block. Pressing Command-Tab does the same thing with any tool or object selected as Tab does, so I've gotten in the habit of pressing Command-Tab to deselect all objects. This way, I only have to remember one shortcut.

Linking Text Blocks

FreeHand's text blocks, like those found in PageMaker or XPress, can be linked together so that text can flow from one text block to another. By linking text blocks, you can create articles that flow over several magazine pages, for example. Linking and unlinking text blocks, like many other activities in FreeHand, is a drag-and-drop process (see Figure 3-22).

FIGURE 3-22
Linking text blocks

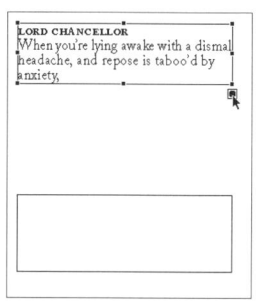

Position the pointer tool over a text block's Link box.

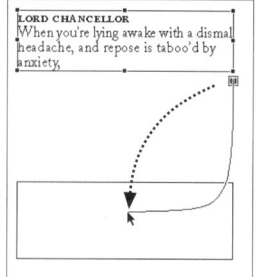

Drag a line out of the Link box and drop it into another text block (example shown in keyline for clarity).

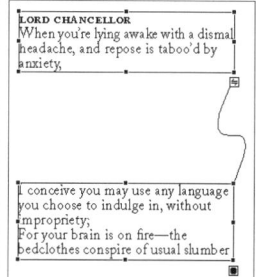

FreeHand links the two text blocks, flowing any overset text from the first text block into the second text block.

1. Select a text block.

2. Position the cursor over the Link box and drag a line to the interior of another text block.

3. Release the mouse button to drop the link. You've just linked the two text blocks.

4. To see the effect of the link between the text blocks, size the first text block so that it's too small to have all the text you entered. The text appears in the second text block you created.

Unlinking text blocks is just as easy—select the text block you want to unlink, and then drag a line from the Link box to an empty area on your page or pasteboard. Linked text, if any, flows back into the other text blocks in the selected story (see Figure 3-23).

FIGURE 3-23
Unlinking text blocks

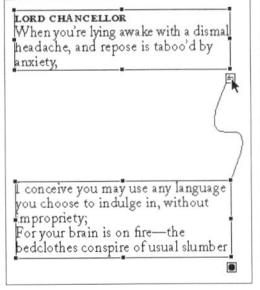

Position the pointer tool over a text block's Link box (examples shown in keyline view).

Drag a line out of the Link box and drop it on an empty area in the publication window.

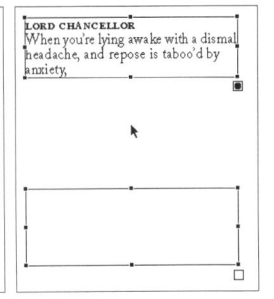

FreeHand unlinks the text blocks, storing any overset text in the first text block.

Alternatively, you can break a link between text blocks by deleting one of the text blocks. If the text block you deleted isn't the last text block in the story, FreeHand flows the text from the text block into the next text block in the story. If the text block you deleted is at the end of the story, FreeHand stores the text in the last text block in the story (as overset text).

Multicolumn and Multirow Text Blocks

A FreeHand text block can contain up to 100 rows and 100 columns. Any time you look at a FreeHand text block, you'll see at least one column and one row—you can't have fewer.

Multicolumn text blocks are pretty similar to those found in a variety of other programs, but multirow text blocks may take some getting used to. In essence, they let you set up any text block as a big table. You can think of each cell inside a text block as a smaller text block, with its own margins and border. All of the cells inside a text block have the same margin and border properties, and have whatever background fill you've applied to the entire text block.

How do you add rows and columns to FreeHand's text blocks? Use the Column Inspector (see Figure 3-24).

1. Select a text block using the Pointer tool.

2. Press Command-Option-R to display the Column Inspector (if it's not already visible).

3. In the Column Inspector, enter the specifications you want for your rows and columns. Columns divide the text block evenly—you can't have columns of unequal width in FreeHand 5 (unless you use wrapping tabs, as shown in "Setting Tabs," later in this chapter).

The height of the rows in a text block depends on the amount of text inside each row. You can make rows taller by adding end-

FIGURE 3-24
Multicolumn text blocks

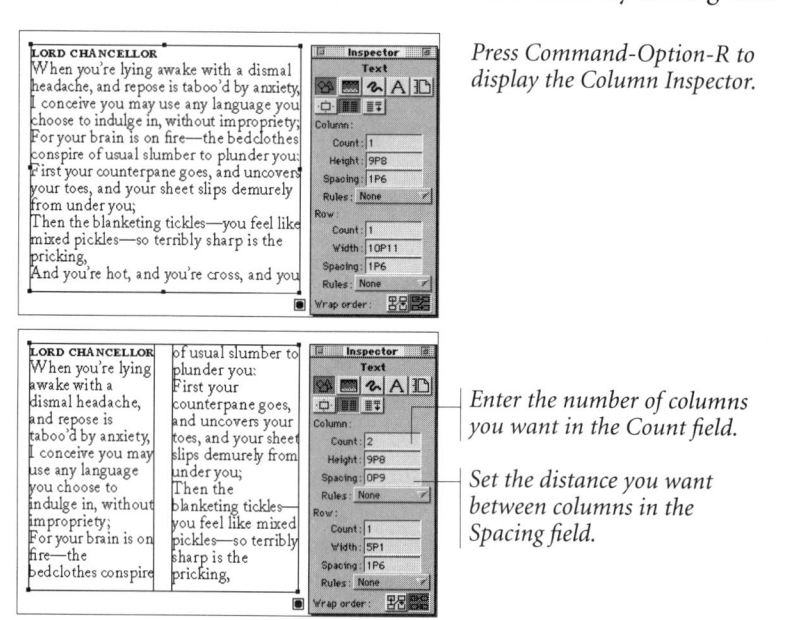

Press Command-Option-R to display the Column Inspector.

Enter the number of columns you want in the Count field.

Set the distance you want between columns in the Spacing field.

of-line characters in the text if you want. You can make rows taller by entering a number in the Column Height field that's larger than the height of the tallest cell in the text block (see Figure 3-25).

FIGURE 3-25
Controlling row height

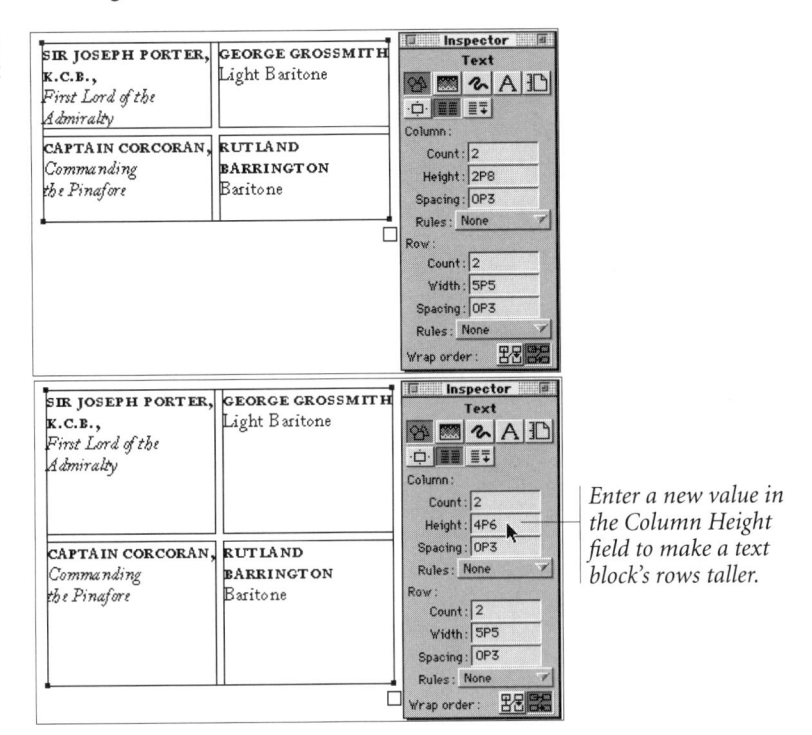

Enter a new value in the Column Height field to make a text block's rows taller.

If you'd rather work with columns of a specific width, you can specify the width of columns in FreeHand's text blocks using the Column Inspector. It's a little confusing: the Column section of the Inspector doesn't include a setting for width. Instead, it includes a setting for the height of the columns in the text block. You enter the column width in the Width field in the Row section of the Inspector (see Figure 3-26). This makes a little more sense when you're working with a multirow text block, such as one containing a table.

Note that, as you'd expect, changing the column widths (or row heights) of a text block also changes the width (or height) of the text block.

You can control the order in which FreeHand flows text inside the columns and rows in a text block using the buttons at the bottom of the Column Inspector (see Figure 3-27).

FIGURE 3-26
Specfiying column widths

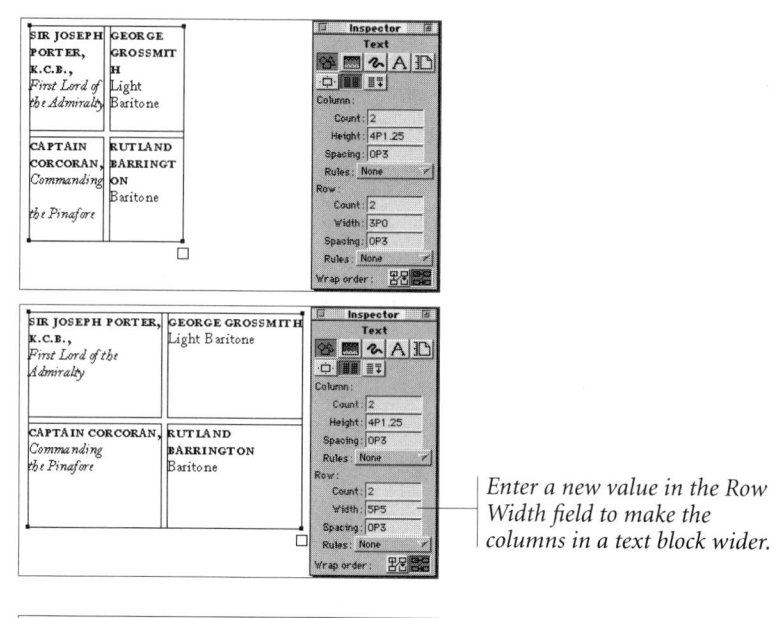

Enter a new value in the Row Width field to make the columns in a text block wider.

FIGURE 3-27
Text flow order

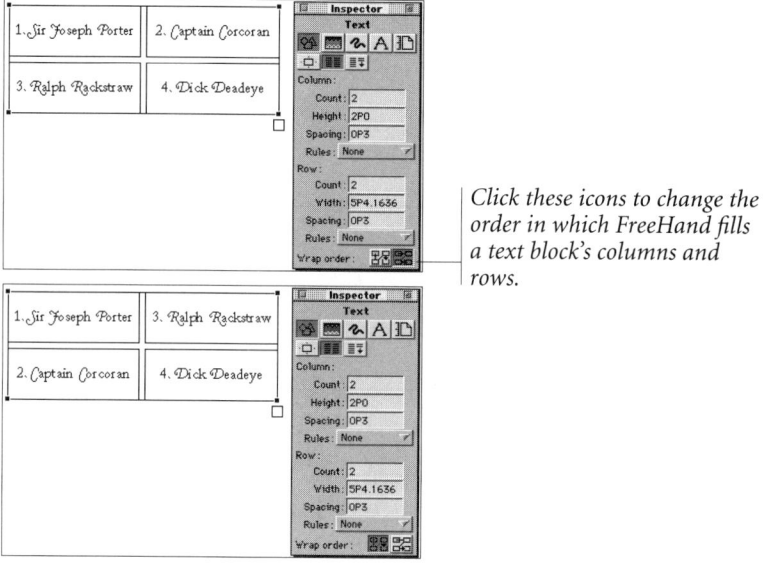

Click these icons to change the order in which FreeHand fills a text block's columns and rows.

Borders and Fills for Text Blocks

Here's how to add a border or a background fill to your text blocks (see Figure 3-28).

1. Select a text block using the Pointer tool.

2. Press Command-Option-I to display the Object Inspector.

FIGURE 3-28
Adding borders to text blocks

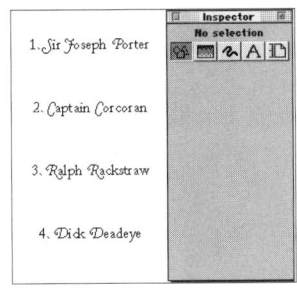

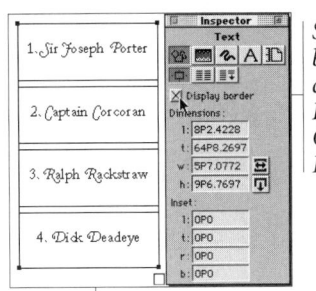

Select a text block and click Display Border in the Object Inspector.

Format the text block's border using the Fill Inspector and the Stroke Inspector.

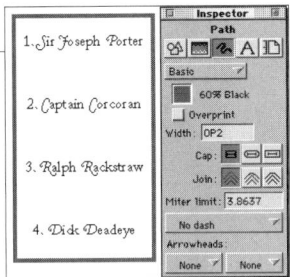

FreeHand displays the border (or borders, if you're working with a multicolumn or multirow text block).

3. Check the Display border option.

4. Format the border and the background fill of the text block using the Fill Inspector (press Command-Option-F) and the Stroke Inspector (press Command-Option-L).

You can also set the background fill of a text block by selecting the text block with the Pointer tool and then dropping a color swatch on it. For more on applying fills using drag-and-drop, see Chapter 6, "Color."

Adding Borders to Rows, Columns, or Cells

You use the popup menus in the Column Inspector to add rules around cells (the text areas created by the intersection of rows and columns) at either the column's full height (or the row's full width) or at the inset you've specified (the inset distances are the same as you specified for the entire text block). Confused? Take a look at Figure 3-29.

A few things about column rules:

- Column rules don't convert to paths when you convert the text block containing them (they disappear).

- In the Column section, choose Full Height if you want your column rules to extend to the top and bottom edges of the

FIGURE 3-29
Adding cell borders

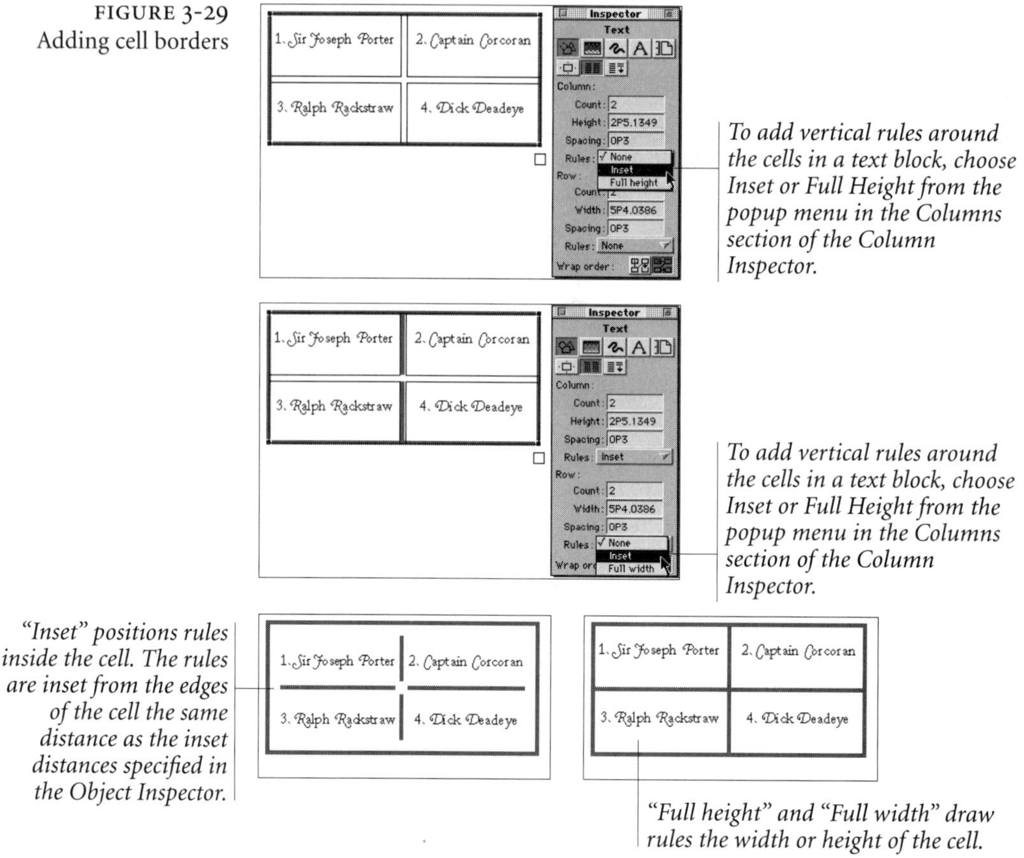

To add vertical rules around the cells in a text block, choose Inset or Full Height from the popup menu in the Columns section of the Column Inspector.

To add vertical rules around the cells in a text block, choose Inset or Full Height from the popup menu in the Columns section of the Column Inspector.

"Inset" positions rules inside the cell. The rules are inset from the edges of the cell the same distance as the inset distances specified in the Object Inspector.

"Full height" and "Full width" draw rules the width or height of the cell.

text block. Choose Inset if you want the column rules to stop inside the cell (the Inset distances—from each edge of the cell—are the same as the text block's margins).

♦ In the Row section of the Column Inspector, choose Full Width from the popup menu to make the rules attached to the rows of the text block extend to the right and left edges of your text block. Choose Inset if you want the rules to stop, in each cell, at the cell's margin.

To add borders to the rows and/or columns in a text block, follow these steps.

1. Select a multicolumn text block.

2. If the Column Inspector's not already open, display it by pressing Command-Option-R.

TEXT AND TYPE 261

3. Use the two Rules popup menus to choose the type of rules you want.

4. Press Return to apply your changes.

Tip: If You Can't See Your Text Block's Border

If you've applied a stroke to a text block and still can't see the border, make sure you've checked Display Border in the Object Inspector for the text block. If Display Border is checked, and you still can't see your border when you select the text block, check Buffered Drawing in the Display Preferences dialog box. If the border you've applied to a text block is smaller than one point wide, you won't see it when you have the text box selected—it's smaller than the text block boundary FreeHand displays when you select a text block (see Figure 3-30).

FIGURE 3-30
Displaying a text block's border

When you've applied formatting to a text block but it doesn't seem to be having any effect…

…you need to turn on the Display Border option in the Object Inspector. Note that turning this option on can make a text block's control handles difficult to see or select.

Tip: Balancing Columns

When you want to distribute your text evenly between a number of columns, so that each column contains the same number of lines of text, try this—check the Balance Columns field in the Copyfit Inspector (press Command-Option-C to display the Copyfit Inspector if it's not visible). FreeHand will try to put an equal amount of text in each column in the current text block (or story, if the text block's linked to other text blocks), while keeping in mind the other settings for the text in the text block (see Figure 3-31). The number you enter in *N* Lines Together in the Paragraph Inspector affects FreeHand's ability to balance columns.

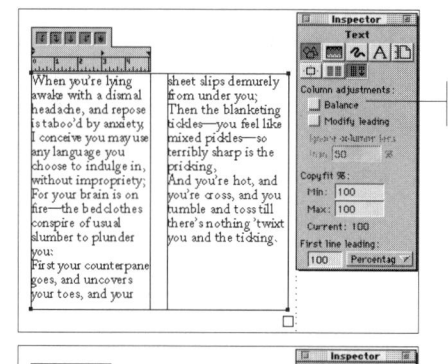

FIGURE 3-31
Balancing columns

When you check Balance Columns...

...FreeHand distributes the text in the story between the available columns.

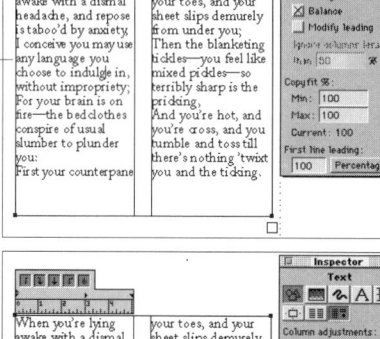

If you'd set the N Lines Together value for this paragraph to "2" (in the Paragraph Inspector), FreeHand takes that value into account when balancing the columns—in this case, it means the columns won't balance as well.

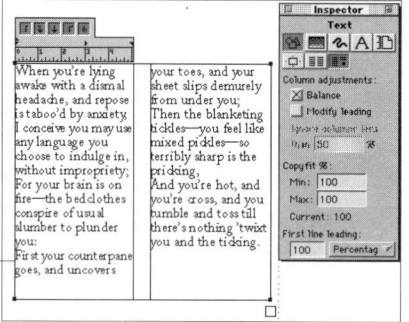

Character Formatting

Character formatting is all about controlling the way the individual letters, symbols, or punctuation of your text look. Font, type style, type size, color, leading, and text effect are all aspects of character formatting.

I refer to all formatting that can be applied to a selected range of text as "character" formatting, and refer to formatting that FreeHand applies at the paragraph level as "paragraph" formatting. Tab settings, paragraph rules, space above, and space after are examples of paragraph formatting. There are definite areas of overlap in these definitions, as well. Leading, for example, is really a property that applies to an entire line of text (FreeHand uses only one leading value for a line of text), but I'll call it "character" formatting, nonetheless.

In addition to these distinctions, FreeHand's paragraph styles can include character formatting, but apply to an entire paragraph. See "Working with Text Styles," later in this chapter.

First off, let me say that while there are loads of commands on the submenus of the Type menu, I usually set or change type specifications through the Type Specifications palette (see Figure 3-32). Why? Try selecting a font, type style, and size using the Font, Size, and Leading submenus a few times.

FIGURE 3-32
Type Specifications palette

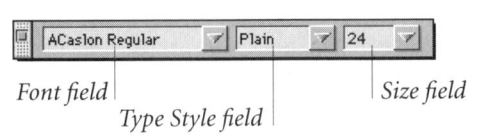

Font field
Type Style field
Size field

You set options in the Type Specifications palette by typing in the fields or by using the popup menus.

As soon as you're tired of that, display the Type Specifications palette (press Command-T if the Type Specifications palette isn't visible) and try the following steps (see Figure 3-33).

1. Press Command-~ to move to the Font field.

2. Type the first few letters of the font name you want (stop typing when FreeHand matches the font name).

3. Press Tab to move to the Type Style field.

4. Type "i" for Italic, "b" for bold, "p" for plain, or "boldi" for bold italic.

5. Press Tab to move to the Type Size field.

6. Type a number for the size of your type and press Enter to apply your changes. FreeHand formats the text as you've specified.

Even though the steps, when written down, sound like they'd take longer, they're much quicker—and your hands stay on the keyboard, ready to enter or select more text. Best of all, you don't have to follow those little arrows off the side of the menu and then

FIGURE 3-32
Changing type specifications

Select the text you want to format.

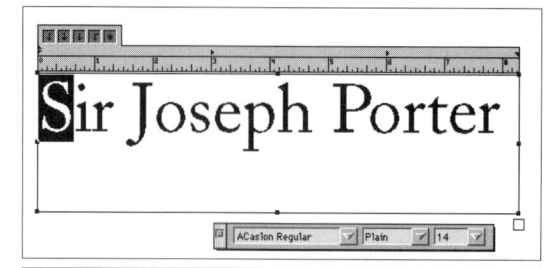

If the Type Specifications palette isn't already visible, press Command-T to display it.

Press Command-~ (this moves the cursor to the Font Selector field of the Type Specifications palette).

Type the name of the font you want to select, or choose a font from the popup menu.

If you're typing the font name, FreeHand tries to match the characters you enter to a font name on the list. As soon as it finds a match, it displays it in the Font Selector field.

In this example, I had to type quite a few characters to get the font name I wanted.

Press Return. FreeHand formats the selected characters using the font you've specified.

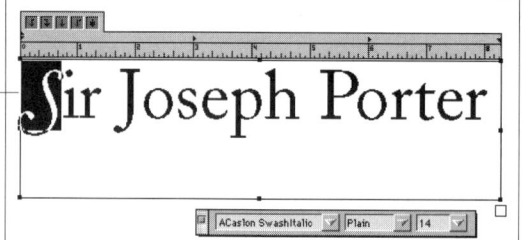

track down the number or name you want on the submenu that pops out.

Font To apply a particular font to text you've selected, type the name of the font you want in the Font field in the Type Specifications palette, or use the attached popup list of font names (or, if you prefer, choose the font name from the Font submenu of the Type menu). As you type, FreeHand displays the names of fonts in your system that match the characters you type. Once the font name you want appears in the field, you can stop typing. At that point, you can press Tab to move to the next field in the Type Specifications palette, or press Return to apply your font change.

**Tip:
Getting the Fonts
You Ask For**

This sounds pretty simple, but beware—imagesetters and other page layout programs can get confused if you specify the specialized screen font for bold, italic, or bold italic versions of a particular font (such as "I Times Italic"). Instead, specify the "base" (or "Roman," "Plain," "Normal," or "Regular") font name and apply the formatting attribute you want using the Type Style field in the Type Specifications palette.

This also makes changing fonts easier—you can change from one font to another and retain any formatting you've done using type styles. For example, you could change a text block from Utopia Regular to Bodoni Book without losing italics you'd applied to individual words or characters (their font would change, but their type style wouldn't).

How can you tell which of the screen fonts are the specialized versions? This gets very tricky. To specify Times Bold, for example, you want to choose Times, and then make it bold by choosing "Bold" from the Style popup menu, rather than choosing the screen font "B Times Bold." Stone Serif, on the other hand, contains two bold weights: Semibold and Bold. When you make the roman screen font for Stone Serif ("1StoneSerif") bold, you get Stone Semibold. To get bold, you need to choose the roman screen font for Stone Serif Bold ("B1StoneSerifBold").

If, on the other hand, you're working with a font family with a large number of different "base" fonts—Adobe Caslon, for example—it gets more confusing (see Figure 3-34). Adobe Type Reunion can help you a lot in cases like this (for more on Adobe Type Reunion, see Appendix A, "System"). But watch out for font changes if you open the publication on a machine that doesn't have ATR running.

There's nothing for it but to experiment with the fonts you've got. If you're getting substituted fonts (usually Courier or Times) when you're trying to print a bold, italic, or bold italic version of a font, you've probably chosen the specialized screen font. Try choosing the roman version of the font, applying the type style you want, and printing again.

FIGURE 3-34
Fonts and how they appear on your menus

If you're using Adobe Type Reunion (ATR) or merged font families, your font list will look something like this (if you're using merged font families but aren't using ATR, you won't see the submenu of type styles).

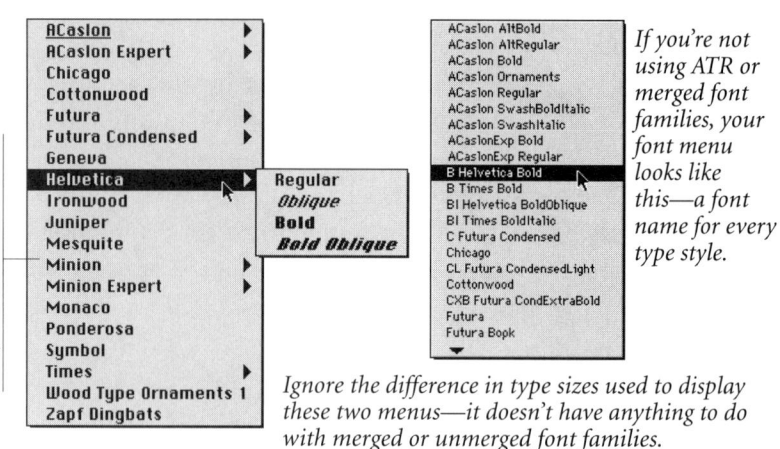

If you're not using ATR or merged font families, your font menu looks like this—a font name for every type style.

Ignore the difference in type sizes used to display these two menus—it doesn't have anything to do with merged or unmerged font families.

Why does this happen? It's history, really—the history of type on the Macintosh. See "Managing Fonts," in Appendix A, "System."

Tip:
Don't Be
Compulsive

When you select text that has more than one font, type style, or size applied to it, the fields in the Type Specifications palette corresponding to those attributes go blank. Don't let this worry you—and don't fill in the fields, unless you really want to apply uniform formatting to your selection (see Figure 3-35). If you leave those fields blank, FreeHand doesn't alter those attributes at all.

When you select text that's displayed using a substitute font (because you don't have the font loaded on your system; see "Font Substitution," later in this chapter), FreeHand leaves the Font field of the Type Specifications palette blank. Again, don't enter anything in the field unless that's what you really want to do.

FIGURE 3-35
Mixed type specifications

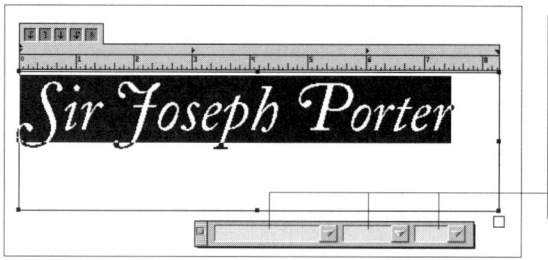

The selected text contains differing fonts, type styles, and type sizes, so FreeHand leaves the fields in the Type Specifications palette blank.

Tip:
Programming
QuicKeys to
Select Fonts

I set up QuicKeys (see Appendix A, "System") to select frequently used fonts (once again, this is to avoid submenus and popups). It's easy to remember that Control-Option-Z changes the font to Zapf Dingbats, or that Control-Option-P selects Perpetua (or Palatino, or whatever you like). It's easier to program QuicKeys to choose fonts from the Font submenu of the Type menu than the Font popup menu on the Type Specifications palette. Follow the steps below to set up a font-choosing QuicKey.

1. Open QuicKeys (it's usually Command-Option-Return, since that's the default).

2. Choose Menu Selection from the Define menu.

3. Pull down the Font submenu of the Type menu and select the font you want.

4. Assign a key to your new Menu Selection QuicKey.

Font substitution. When you open a FreeHand publication containing fonts that aren't currently loaded in your System, FreeHand displays the Missing Fonts dialog box (see Figure 3-36), which tells you what fonts you're missing, and also lets you substitute fonts for the missing fonts. Press Return to substitute Courier for all missing fonts.

FIGURE 3-36
Missing fonts dialog box

FreeHand lists the missing fonts here.

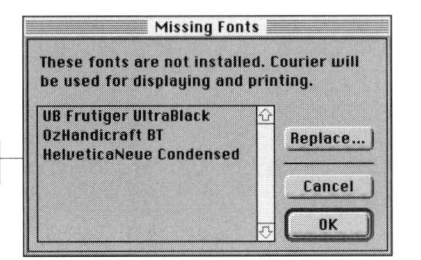

Press Return to use Courier, or press the Replace button...

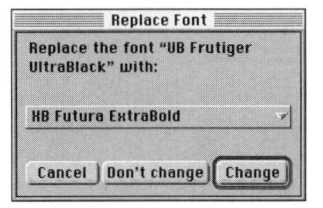

...and FreeHand displays the Replace Font dialog box, where you can replace missing fonts with specific fonts you have installed on your system.

FreeHand temporarily applies a different font to the characters formatted with the missing font. By "temporarily," I mean that the publication retains the information about what font was originally applied to the text. What's the use of that? Let me use an example.

Suppose you lay out a publication on your machine at the office, save it, and take it home for the evening. At home, you open the publication—and FreeHand warns you that you're missing "Oz Handicraft," a font you have on the machine you have at your office. You substitute Courier for Oz Handicraft, and make a few changes to an illustration in your publication. You then—without applying any font changes to the text—save your publication.

Note that FreeHand does not apply the spacing of the original font to the substituted font (as PageMaker, for example, does). This means that all the text you formatted using the font changes position, usually to the point that the line breaks in your publication change. When this happens, I avoid making any formatting changes to the text. I might enter new copy, or edit the existing copy, but it's pointless to do any kerning or text-block adjustment when you're working with substituted fonts.

The next day, you open the publication on the Macintosh at your office. Because you haven't applied any permanent font changes to your text, FreeHand formats and displays the text in its original font, Oz Handicraft.

If you don't want to work with substituted fonts, you need to load the required fonts. If you're working with Suitcase or Master-Juggler (see Appendix A, "System"), you can close the publication, load the fonts, then reopen the publication. If you're loading and unloading fonts by moving them to and from the Fonts folder, you need to quit FreeHand, move the fonts, then restart FreeHand.

Obviously, loading the font is better than working with substitute fonts. If you hadn't wanted that font, you wouldn't have used it in the first place.

Tip: Use an Ugly Font	When I have to use FreeHand's font substitution, I substitute Zapf Chancery for the missing font—I'd never use it for anything else, and it stands out from all the other text in the publication.
Tip: SuperATM and Font Substitution	If you're running SuperATM, have turned on its font substitution feature, and open a publication containing missing fonts, you won't see the Missing Fonts dialog box; instead, SuperATM will create a substitute font for the missing fonts and FreeHand will display the text in that font. The advantage is that line breaks are more likely to stay the same. The disadvantage is that if you forget to load the real font, you can run into some serious problems when you take the file to your imagesetting service bureau.

You can keep SuperATM from substituting fonts by turning off the Substitute for Missing Fonts option in SuperATM's control panel. Once you turn ATM's font substitution off, you can delete the 1.4-meg ATM Font Database file from your System folder.

Type Style To apply a type style to text, type "p" for plain, "i" for italic, "b" for bold, or "boldi" for bold italic in the Type Style field in the Type Specifications palette, or choose a type style from the attached popup list (or choose a type style from the Style submenu of the Type menu). If a font doesn't have an alternate type style (bold, italic, or bold italic), FreeHand grays the name of the type style in the menus (see Figure 3-37).

When you try to type the name of a type style that's not available in the Type Style field, FreeHand beeps.

After you've chosen the type style you want, press Tab to move to the Size field, or press Return to apply your changes.

FIGURE 3-37
Grayed-out type styles

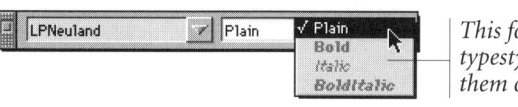

This font doesn't have these typestyles, so FreeHand grays them out.

Size Type the point size you want in the Size field in the Type Specifications palette, or choose a size from the attached popup menu. If you're directly entering the size, you can specify it in .0001-point increments. You can also change the size of the type in a text block by stretching the text block (see "Working with Text Blocks," earlier in this chapter).

After you've entered the size you want, press Return to apply your changes.

Tip:
Bumping Text Up or Down in Size You can make selected text larger or smaller, in one-point increments, using the keyboard. To make selected text larger by one point, press Command-Shift-period. To make it smaller by one point, press Command-Shift-comma.

Tip:
Greeking Remember that greeking—whether the type is displayed or drawn as a gray bar—is set in the Preferences dialog box. If you make the type smaller (at the current magnification) than the threshold you

set in the Display Preferences dialog box, it'll appear as a gray bar (see "Preferences" in Chapter 1, "FreeHand Basics.")

Leading

Text characters—usually—sit on an imaginary line, which we call the baseline. Leading (pronounced "ledding") is the vertical distance from the baseline of one line of text to the next text baseline. In FreeHand, leading is measured from the baseline of the current line of text to the baseline of the line of text above (see Figure 3-38). When you increase the leading in a line of text, you push that line farther from the line above it, and farther down from the top of the text block.

FreeHand's Paragraph Inspector offers three different leading methods: Extra, Fixed, and Percentage.

Extra leading method. When you choose Extra from the Leading Type popup menu, FreeHand adds the point size of the largest character of text in the selection to the value you enter in the Leading field. If, for example, you wanted to add four points of leading between each line of type, you'd choose Extra and enter "4" in the Leading field. When you change the size of the characters, the distance between the baselines changes, even though the leading value you've entered remains the same.

Fixed leading method. With Fixed leading, FreeHand sets the leading of the selected lines of text to the value you enter in the Leading field. Fixed is the most precise leading method, because you'll always get the leading value you enter, regardless of the size of the selected text. You can enter a leading value in .0001-point increments.

Percentage leading method. When you choose Percentage from the Leading Type popup menu, FreeHand uses a leading value that's a percentage of the size of the selected text, based on the largest point size in the selection. Again, your leading will change if you change the size of the text. This may, or may not be, what you want.

You can set any leading amount using any one of the three leading methods. That said, however, I admit that I only use the

FIGURE 3-38
Leading

Leading is the vertical distance between baselines of type.

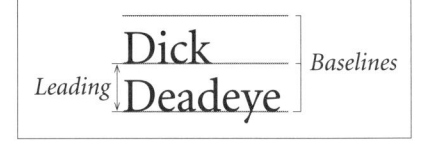

When you use FreeHand's Extra leading method, FreeHand adds the value you enter in the Leading field to the point size of the largest character in the line to calculate the leading for the line.

If want 24 points of leading, and you're working with 18-point text, enter "6" in the Leading field.

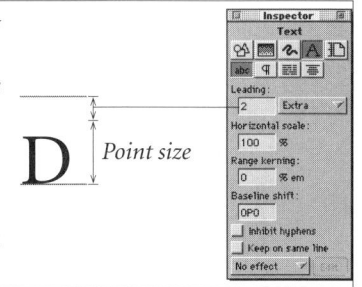

When you use the Fixed leading method, FreeHand uses the value you enter in the Leading field for the leading of the line.

If you want 24-point leading, enter "24" in the Leading field.

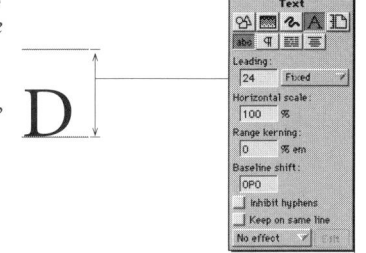

When you're using the Percentage leading method, FreeHand sets the leading based on the percentage of the largest size of type in a line.

If you want 24 point leading, and you're working with 18-point type, enter "133" in the Leading field.

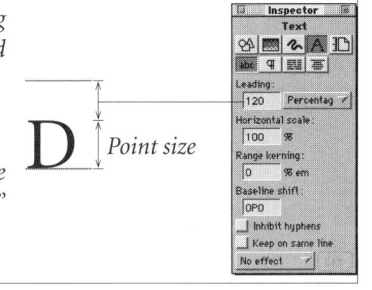

Fixed leading method. I like knowing the distances between the baselines of the text in my text blocks, without having to do any multiplication or addition. I also believe that leading shouldn't—necessarily—have anything to do with the size of the characters in the line. Fixed is the only leading method that doesn't change as I change type sizes.

Regardless of the leading method you're using (Fixed, Percentage, or Extra), the largest leading in the line predominates to the next line break. If the character containing the larger leading flows to a new line, the leading moves with it (see Figure 3-39).

FIGURE 3-39
The largest leading in a line predominates

This character has a larger leading than the other characters in the line.

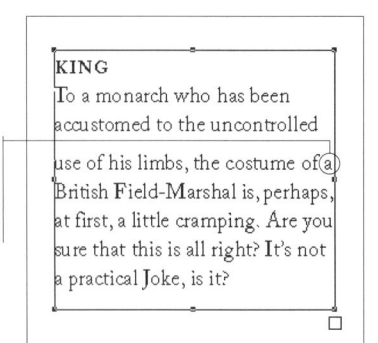

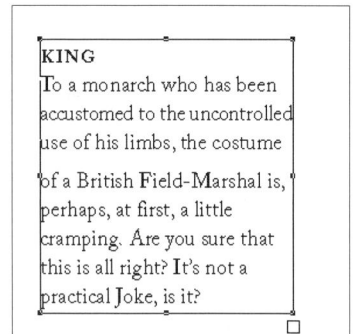

When the character with the larger leading moves to another line (if, for example, the width of the text block changes, as in this example), the larger leading is applied to that line.

Baseline Shift

Sometimes, you need to raise the baseline of a character or characters above the baseline of the surrounding text. You can't do this by changing the leading setting of the characters (remember, the largest leading in the line predominates). Instead, you use the Baseline Shift field in the Character Inspector (see Figure 3-40).

FIGURE 3-40
Baseline shift

Select the character or characters you want to shift…

You can also press Option-Up Arrow to shift the baseline of the selected text up one point, or press Option-Down Arrow to shift it down one point.

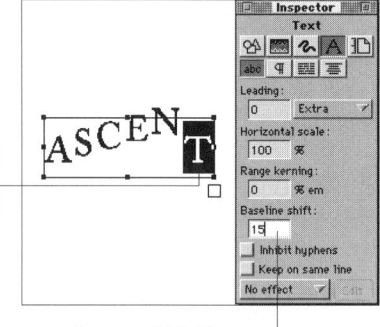

Enter a shift distance (positive numbers move the baseline up, negative numbers move it down) in the Baseline Shift field.

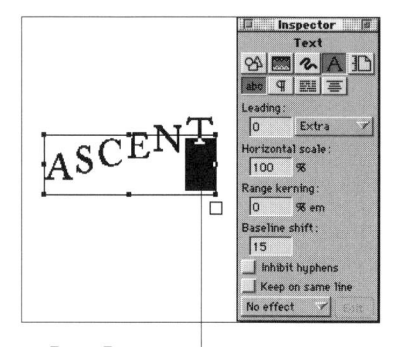

Press Return or Enter, and FreeHand shifts the baseline of the selected character or characters.

Enter an amount in the Baseline shift field to shift the baseline of the selected text by that amount. As you'd guess, positive values move the selected text up from the baseline; negative values move the selected text down from the baseline.

Tip:
Baseline Shift Keyboard Shortcut

You can apply baseline shift using your keyboard. To do this, select some text and press Option-Up Arrow to move the baseline of the text up (each keypress moves the text up one point), or Option-Down Arrow to shift the baseline down one point.

First line leading

Because I like to position and align text blocks by snapping their tops to ruler guides or the grid, it's important to me to know where the first baseline in a text block falls relative to the top of the text block.

To set the distance from the top of the text block to the first baseline, display the Inspector (press Command-I if the Inspector isn't already visible) and then press Command-Option-C. At the bottom of the Copyfit section of the Object Inspector, you'll see a section controlling first line leading.

FreeHand offers three methods: Percent, Fixed, and Extra.

- ◆ Percent uses a percentage of the height of the text in the first line of the text block.

- ◆ Extra adds an amount equal to the height of the first line in the text block plus some measurement you enter.

- ◆ Fixed uses the leading value that you enter, regardless of the size of the characters in the line.

I only use Fixed—I can enter a precise leading value, and not worry about the leading changing because I've added a drop cap or other enlarged character. If I want the baseline of the first line of text in a text block to fall twelve points from the top of the text block, I enter 12 (see Figure 3-41).

If you enter zero using the Fixed first baseline method, Free-Hand does just what it should: it hangs the characters of the first line of text out of the top of the text block, and positions the zero point of that line of text at the top of the text block. If you set your

FIGURE 3-41
Setting the first baseline

The trouble with the "Extra" and "Percentage" first line leading methods.

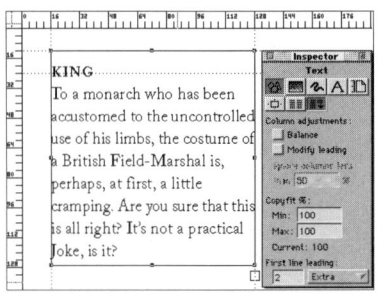

"Extra" first line leading method. Where does the baseline fall (get out your calculator)?

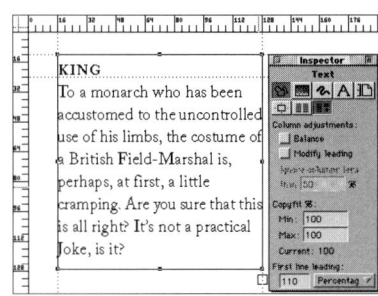

"Percentage" first line leading method. Where does the baseline fall?

Use the "Fixed" first line leading method—it's easy to get the baseline right where you want it.

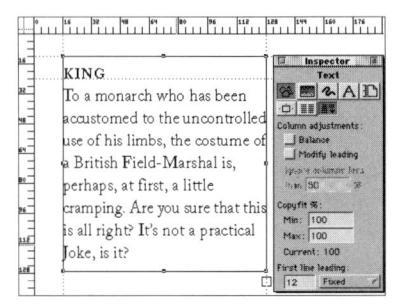

"Fixed" first line leading method. The baseline falls precisely where you want it (in this example, 12 points from the top of the text block).

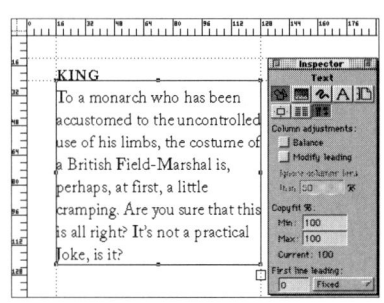

If you choose "Fixed" and enter zero, the first baseline falls exactly at the top of the text block. Don't tell any software engineers you know how to do this.

text blocks up this way, you'll be able to snap the baseline of the first line of text in a text block to a ruler guide. Since the baseline is at the top of the text block, the characters in the first line hang out of the top. This is sometimes just what you need, even though it's the eventuality the other leading methods were designed to prevent (for some reason, software engineers *hate* it when text hangs out of text blocks).

**Tip:
If Your Leading Looks Funky**

If your leading looks odd inside a text block that should have only one leading setting, select the text block and press Command-Option-T to display the Character Inspector (if it's not already visible). If the Leading field is blank, you've somehow gotten another leading setting inside the text block. Either re-enter the proper leading value, or move your cursor through the text block until you find which character is carrying the rogue leading value (you'll see it in the Character Inspector).

Applying Colors to Text

Characters in FreeHand's text blocks can be filled or stroked with any color. While text blocks can be filled or stroked with any of FreeHand's fills (see "Borders and Fills for Text Blocks," earlier in this chapter), you can apply only Basic fills and strokes to text (if you convert the characters to paths, of course, you can format them as you would any FreeHand path).

The Color List Shows Container Color and Color List Shows Text Color options in the Colors Preferences dialog box specify which part of a text block—the block itself, or the text it contains, respectively—sets the colors displayed in the Color List, the Fill Inspector, and the Stroke Inspector. These options also control *which part* of the text block is affected when you apply a color to it. Turn on the Color List Shows Text Color option, and FreeHand applies any color changes you make to the text in the text block.

FreeHand offers several ways of applying color to text and to text blocks—try them and see which methods work best for you.

Filling text. To apply a fill to selected text inside a text block, follow these steps (see Figure 3-42).

1. Select the text you want to color using the Text tool.

2. Click on a color name in the Color List. FreeHand applies a basic fill of the color you clicked to the selected text.

Select the text and display the Fill Inspector, and you can set whether the text overprints or not (for more on overprinting, see "Trapping," in Chapter 6, "Color").

You can also use the Fill Inspector to apply a color fill to text.

1. Use the Text tool to select the text you want to fill.

2. Press Command-Option-F to display the Fill Inspector, if it's not already visible.

3. Choose Basic from the Fill Type popup menu in the Fill Inspector (the other fill types have no effect on text).

4. Click on a color in the Color List. Check Overprint in the Fill Inspector if you want the fill to overprint objects behind it. FreeHand applies the basic fill to the text you selected.

FIGURE 3-42
Applying color to text

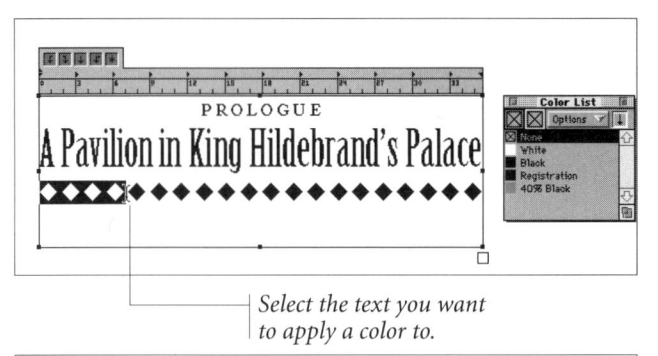

Select the text you want to apply a color to.

Click a color name in the Color List. FreeHand applies the color to the selected text.

To apply a color to text using the drag-and-drop method, follow these steps (see Figure 3-43).

1. Select the text you want to color using the Text tool.

2. Drag a color swatch from a color well (ideally, from the Color List) and drop it on the selected text. Or drop the color swatch on the Fill icon at the top of the Color List.

FreeHand applies a basic fill of the color you dropped to the selected text.

To apply a color to all the text in a text block, turn on the Color List Shows Text Color option in the Colors Preferences dialog box,

FIGURE 3-43
Applying color to text using the drag-and-drop method

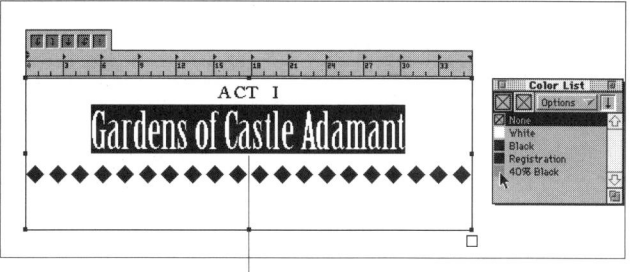

Select the text you want to color.

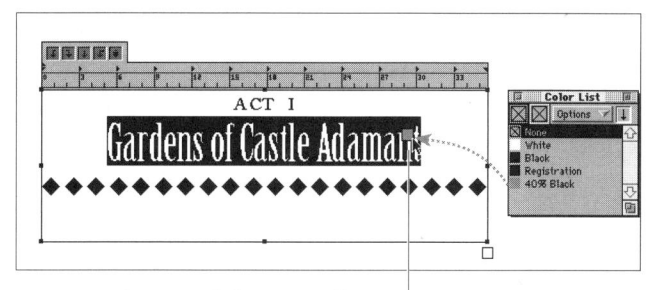

Drag a color swatch from one of the color wells in the Color List and drop it on the selected text.

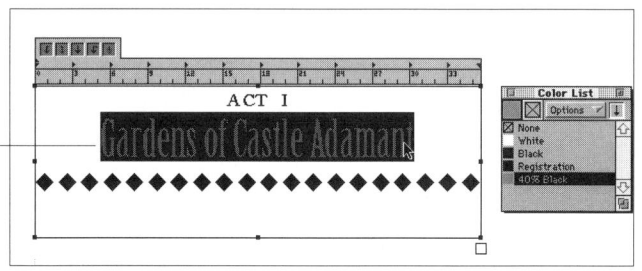

FreeHand applies the color to the fill of the selected text.

then click on the color in the Colors List. FreeHand applies the color to all the text in the text block.

Alternatively, you can use the drag-and-drop method to color all the text in a text block—select all the text, drag a color swatch from a color well, and drop it on a character in a text block. FreeHand applies the color to all the text in the text block (see Figure 3-44).

Stroking text. I keep running into people who think that you have to convert text characters to paths before you can apply a stroke to them. You don't—as far as basic strokes and fills go, FreeHand treats text characters as if they are paths.

FIGURE 3-44
Another way to apply a color using the drag-and-drop method

Drag a color swatch from one of the color wells in the Color List…

…and drop it onto a character.

FreeHand applies the color to all of the text in the text block.

To apply a stroke to text using the Stroke Inspector, follow these steps (see Figure 3-45).

1. Select the text you want to stroke.

2. Press Command-Option-L to display the Stroke Inspector, if it's not already visible.

3. Choose Basic from the Stroke Type popup menu in the Stroke Inspector (the other stroke types have no effect).

FIGURE 3-45
Applying a stroke to text

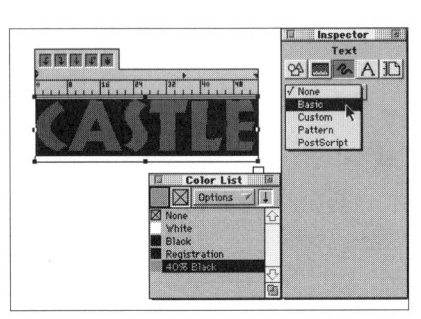

Select the text, then apply a basic stroke using the Stroke Inspector—just as you would if you were applying a stroke to a path.

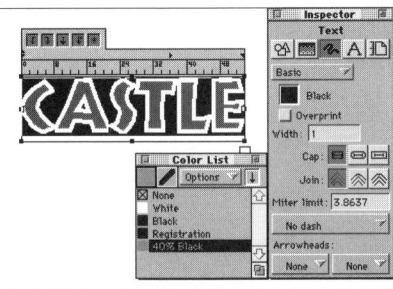

TEXT AND TYPE 279

4. Click on a color in the Color List. Check Overprint in the Stroke Inspector if you want the stroke to overprint objects behind it (including the character's fill, if any).

To apply a stroke to text using the drag-and-drop method, follow these steps (see Figure 3-46).

1. Select the text you want to stroke using the Text tool.

2. Drag a color swatch from a color well (ideally, from the Color List) and drop it on the Stroke icon at the top of the Color List.

FreeHand applies a basic stroke of the color you dropped to the selected text. Use the Stroke Inspector to set the width of the stroke, if necessary.

FIGURE 3-46
Applying a color stroke to text using drag-and-drop

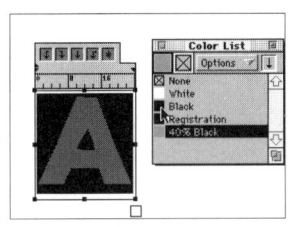

Select the text you want to apply a stroke to.

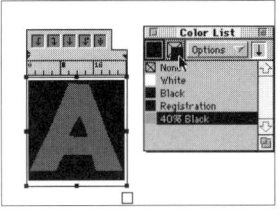

Drag a color swatch from the Color List...

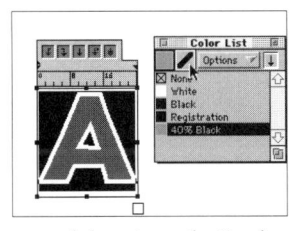

...and drop it on the Stroke button in the Color List.

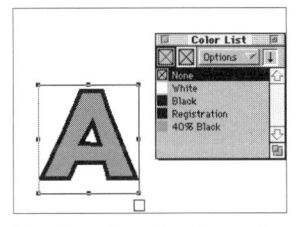

FreeHand applies the stroke to the selected text, using the default stroke width.

Tip:
Graphic Styles and Text Blocks

Given that you can apply strokes and fills to text using the Fill and Stroke Inspectors, you'd think you could apply graphic styles to text, as well. Unfortunately, FreeHand doesn't work that way. When you select text with the Text tool and apply a graphic style, Free-Hand applies the fill, stroke, and halftone properties of the style to the text block itself—not to the text contained in the text block. FreeHand does this regardless of the setting of the Color List Shows Text Color option in the Colors Preferences dialog box.

You can, however, specify text color as an attribute of a text style. See "Working with Text Styles," later in this chapter.

| Tip: Avoid Fuzzy Type | Even the most skilled color separators will tell you to avoid applying a process-color tint build to fine hairlines and text smaller than about 14 points (12 points for bold). It's difficult, even on the very best presses (or even the best-maintained imagesetters and film processors) to keep small type and fine lines in register, so it ends up looking fuzzy in your printed publication. So use spot colors for fine lines and type. If you're stuck, try to find a process color which gives you 80 percent of cyan, magenta, or black, and try to apply it to a sans serif face; it's less likely to look fuzzy. |

Stretching Characters Horizontally

Enter a value in the Horizontal Scale field in the Character Inspector to create expanded (wider) or condensed (narrower) versions of your type (see Figure 3-47). Before I became too old and tired, I used to argue that these aren't true expanded or condensed fonts, which involve custom-designed, hand-tuned character shapes and spacings, but never mind.

FIGURE 3-47
Scaling characters horizontally

A   A   A   A   A   A   A
40% 60% 80% 100% 120% 140% 160%

You can also change the horizontal scaling of type by dragging the selection handles of text blocks (see "Working with Text Blocks," later in this chapter).

Text Effects

Text effects are just that—special effects for type. They're generally for creating eye-catching display type. To apply one of FreeHand's text effects, select some text and choose an effect from the Text Effects popup menu at the bottom of the Character Inspector. Press Enter, and FreeHand applies the text effect to the text you've selected. If you can't see the text effect, make sure that Display Text Effects is checked in the Display Preferences dialog box. If Display

Text Effects is checked and you still can't see the text effect, are you sure you're not in keyline view? (Text effects don't display in keyline view.)

The rules drawn by the Highlight, Underline, and Strikethrough text effects interact with FreeHand's paragraph rules. See "Paragraph Rules and Text Effects," later in this chapter.

Highlight. When I designed Guy Kawasaki's book *Database 101* for Peachpit Press, I wanted a text effect that would look like someone had gone through the book highlighting words and phrases with a thick felt marker. I didn't want to have to draw a box behind every piece of text needing this effect, so I hacked my copy of PageMaker so text formatted with the "Strikethru" type style would print as a solid gray bar behind the text. What's this got to do with FreeHand? One of the new text effects introduced in FreeHand 5 does the same thing—and you don't even have to write any custom PostScript code.

When you want to place a rule (of any thickness) behind your text, select the text, then choose "Highlight" from the Text Effects popup menu. FreeHand applies the Highlight text effect (see Figure 3-48). By default, the Highlight effect adds a light gray rule with a thickness of the height of the selected text (taking that value from the largest character in the selection). The rule is vertically centered around a position one-fourth of the height of the text from the baseline of the text (taking that value from the largest leading value in the selection).

FIGURE 3-48
Highlight text effect

When you apply the Hightlight effect to text, FreeHand draws a rule behind the text, simulating the effect of a "highlighter" pen.

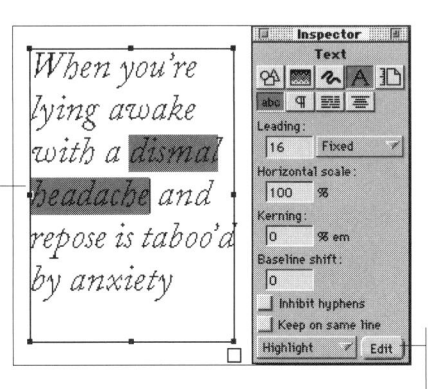

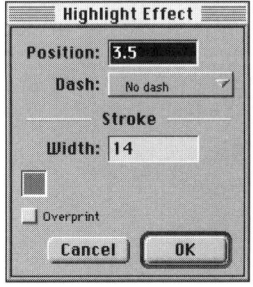

Click the Edit button, and FreeHand displays the Highlight Effect dialog box, where you can edit the effect.

You can adjust the width of the rule, its color, and its dash pattern (yes, you heard that right) by selecting the text and clicking the Edit button at the bottom of the Character Inspector. FreeHand displays the Highlight dialog box.

- The Position field in the Highlight dialog box sets the vertical center of the rule FreeHand draws behind your text, measured from the baseline of the text. You can enter positive or negative numbers in the Position field.

- The Dash popup menu sets the dash pattern for the rule. As in the Stroke Inspector, you can create and edit your own dash patterns if you don't see the pattern you want—hold down Option and choose one of the patterns on the menu.

- The value you enter in the width field sets the width of the rule.

- The color well sets the color of the rule, and works just like any other color well in FreeHand (don't let the dialog box fool you—you can drag color swatches into this color well as you would any other).

- The Overprint checkbox gives you the ability to set the rule to overprint.

Inline. Remember Trace Edges from MacPaint? Inline does much the same thing—drawing outlines around solid characters. To set the number and thickness of the outlines, click the Edit button at the bottom of the Character Inspector. FreeHand displays the Inline Effect dialog box (see Figure 3-49).

FIGURE 3-49
Inline text effect

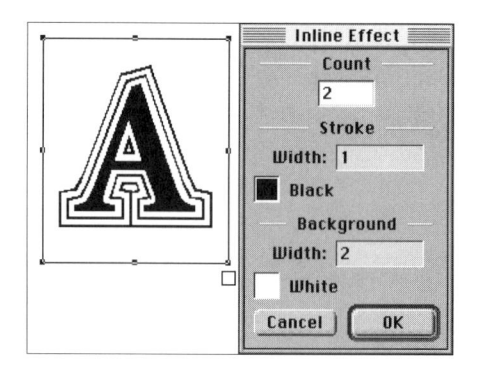

Shadow. Use Shadow to apply a drop shadow to the selected text. This drop shadow is offset to the right and below the text it's applied to (see Figure 3-50). The distance that the drop shadow is offset is based on the size of the characters. The drop shadow is set to 50 percent of the color of the selected text.

FIGURE 3-50
Shadow text effect

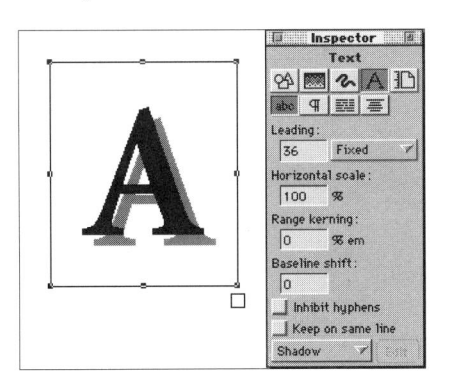

Strikethrough. The Strikethrough text effect is identical to the Highlight text effect, except the default position, width, and color of the rule it creates differ. Strikethrough adds a rule behind your text with a position setting of 6, a line weight of 1, and the color Black (see Figure 3-51).

After you've applied the Strikethrough text effect, you can change the appearance of the rule by clicking the Edit button at the bottom of the Character Inspector. See the discussion of the Highlight text effect, earlier in this chapter, for more on the options in the Strikethrough dialog box.

Figure 3-51
Strikethrough effect

When you apply the Strikethrough effect to text, FreeHand draws a rule through the text.

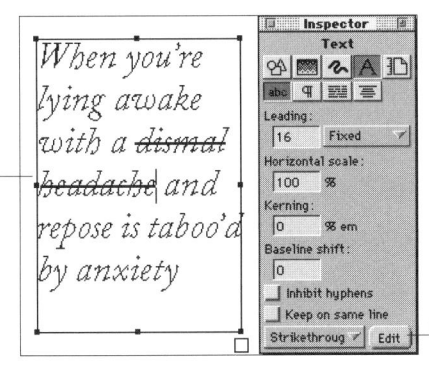

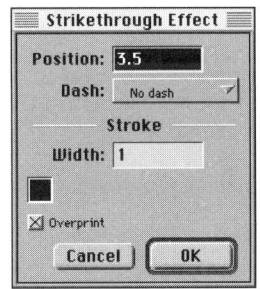

Click the Edit button, and FreeHand displays the Strikethrough Effect dialog box, where you can edit the effect.

Underline. The Underline text effect is (you guessed it) the same as Highlight and Strikethrough, but has different default settings for position, width, and rule color. For the Underline text effect, these are set to -2, 1, and Black, respectively (see Figure 3-52).

After you've applied the Underline text effect, you can change the way the underline looks by selecting the text and clicking the Edit button at the bottom of the Character Inspector. See the discussion of the Highlight text effect, earlier in this chapter, for more on the options in the Underline dialog box.

FIGURE 3-52
Underline effect

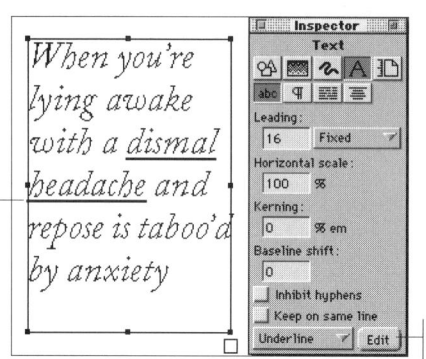

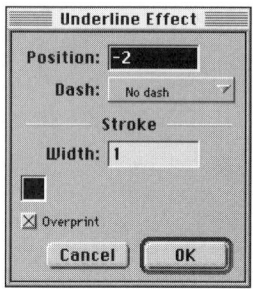

When you apply the Underline effect to text, FreeHand draws a rule beneath the text.

Click the Edit button, and FreeHand displays the Underline Effect dialog box, where you can edit the effect.

Zoom text. Zoom text creates a string of characters that appear to recede toward a vanishing point. You see zoom text all the time in television commercials, usually for furniture and carpet dealers' goin' out of business/liquidation/oncoming recession sales.

Use this one with caution, though, and it can be a useful tool (see Figure 3-53). To control the distance, offset, and color range

FIGURE 3-53
Zoom text effect

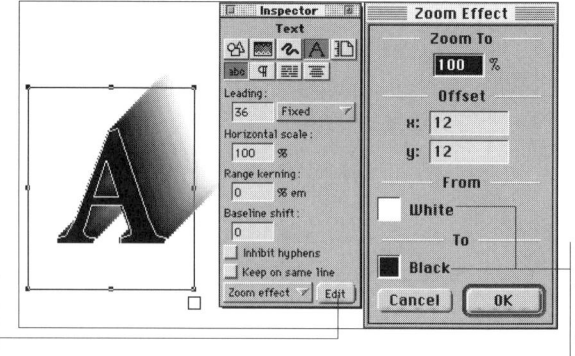

Click the Edit button to display the Zoom Effect dialog box.

Printed example

You can drop color swatches into the color wells in the Zoom Effect dialog box.

of the Zoom Effect, click the Edit button at the bottom of the Character Inspector. FreeHand displays the Zoom Effect dialog box, where you can specify the size of the most distant character in the zoom, the offset of that character, and the change in color from one end of the zoom to the other. If you're using process colors, or are zooming from one spot color to white or a tint of the same spot color, you can even zoom from one color to another.

**Tip:
Bounding Boxes
and Zoom Text**

If you're exporting text which has the Zoom text effect applied to it, make sure that the bounding box of the EPS is large enough to accommodate the full extent of the zoomed text. These days, FreeHand handles this pretty well, but, if you're having problems with your text effect getting clipped off in your EPSes, you'll have to fix it yourself. The easiest way to do this is to draw a no-line, no-fill box around the text that extends to the edge of the effect.

**Tip:
In Search of the
Elusive Macron**

The Macintosh character set includes many interesting and useful diacritical marks, but it doesn't include the one you need if you're working with clients in Korea (and other Pacific-Rim countries): the macron. If you've looked in a dictionary, you've seen this mark everywhere—it's used to denote a long vowel sound (like the "O" in "Olav").

In FreeHand 5, you can create a "fake" macron by using the Highlight, Underline, or Strikethrough text effects. All you need to do is set the rule these effects create to something that matches the size of the character you're attaching it to, then set the position of the rule so that it falls above the character (see Figure 3-54).

FIGURE 3-54
Creating a macron

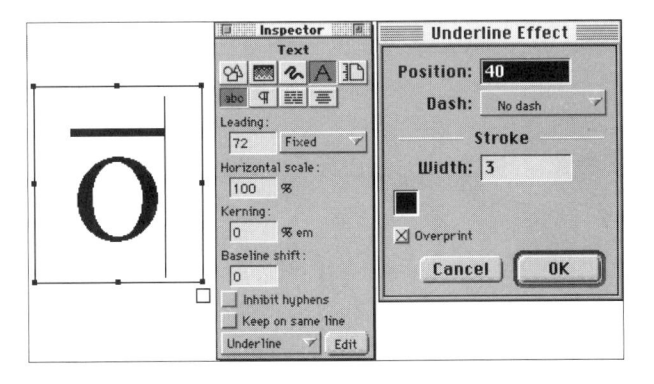

Tip:
Text on a Path and Text Effects

When you apply the Highlight, Strikethrough, or Underline text effect, the effect applies to any space characters in the selected text. If you then bind the text to a path, however, the effect doesn't apply to the spaces (see Figure 3-55). This may or may not be what you're looking for. If you want the effect to apply to spaces in text you've bound to a path, you can enter non-breaking spaces (press Option-Spacebar)—FreeHand always applies the effect to them.

FIGURE 3-55
Text effects and "Bind text to path"

Normal spaces create a gap in the text effect.

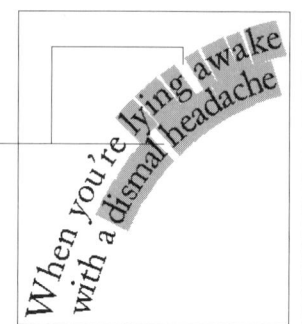

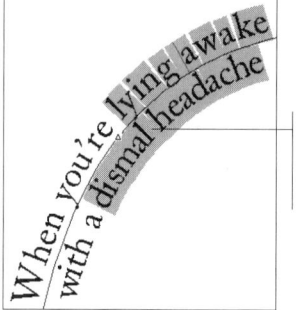

FreeHand always applies text effects to non-breaking spaces.

Kerning

Kerning brings characters closer together horizontally, or (these days) moves them farther apart (once, kerning meant only *decreasing* the space between characters) by fine increments (see Figure 3-56). FreeHand kerns in percentages of an em, and can kern in increments as fine as .0001, or .01 percent, of an em. Just as a reminder: an em is equal to the size of the type in the line. An em space in 24-point type is 24 points wide. You can use kerning to add up to 10 ems (1000%) or subtract two ems (-200%) of space.

While some "conventional" (that is, expensive, dedicated, obsolete) typesetting systems kern in absolute increments (fractional points, generally), most current typesetting systems (desktop and otherwise), kern in units relative to the size of the type. Practically, this means that you can make the type larger or smaller and retain the same relative amount of kerning.

FIGURE 3-56
Kerning

Unkerned text

Kerned text

TEXT AND TYPE 287

You can kern any amount of text in FreeHand—from an individual character pair to all the character pairs in all the text blocks in a publication.

To kern a pair of characters, position the text cursor between the two characters and either press keyboard shortcuts (see Table 3-6) or enter a kerning value in the Kerning field of the Character Inspector (see Figure 3-57). Enter positive values in the Kerning field to move the characters farther apart; enter negative numbers to move them closer together.

TABLE 3-6
Kerning keyboard shortcuts

To kern:	Press:
.1 em (10 percent) closer	Command-Option-Shift-Left Arrow
.01 em (one percent) closer	Command-Option-Left Arrow
.1 em (10 percent) apart	Command-Option-Shift-Right Arrow
.01 em (one percent) apart	Command-Option-Left Arrow

FIGURE 3-57
Kerning a pair of characters

Position the cursor between the characters you want to kern.

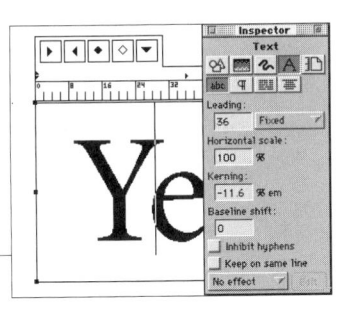

The Kerning field shows you any kerning that's already in effect between the characters.

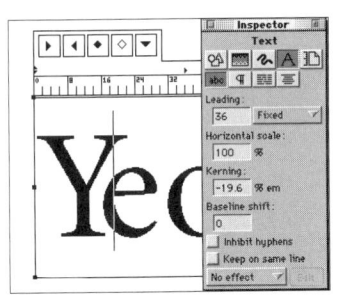

Press keyboard shortcuts to kern the characters. As you kern, the Kerning field shows you the kerning amount.

To kern a range of text, select some text—select text with the Text tool, or select a text block (or blocks) using the Pointer tool—and then press keyboard shortcuts or enter a value in the Kerning field (Figure 3-58).

Range kerning is often referred to as "tracking," but tracking is actually something very different. Range kerning adjusts intercharacter spacing by a set amount (.5 percent of an em, for example), regardless of the size of the type. Tracking, on the other hand, adjusts intercharacter spacing by different amounts for

FIGURE 3-58
Kerning a range of characters

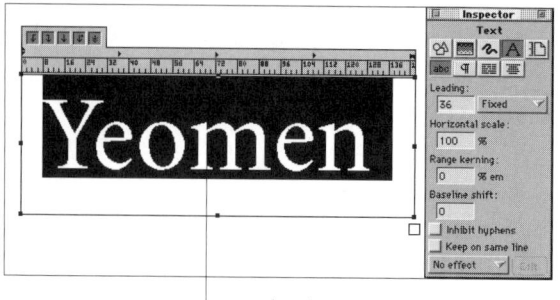

Select the range of text you want to kern.

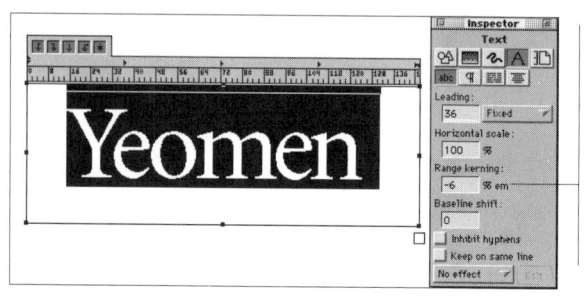

Enter a kerning amount in the Range Kerning field and press Return, or press keyboard shortcuts. FreeHand kerns the selected range of text.

different type sizes. For example, 12-point text in a particular font might be adjusted by one-half of a percent of an em, while 48-point type of the same face might be adjusted by -2 percent of an em. FreeHand doesn't offer a tracking feature (yet).

Paragraph Formatting

What's a paragraph? FreeHand's definition is simple—a paragraph is any string of characters that ends with carriage return or an end-of-column character (see "Entering Special Characters," earlier in this chapter, for an explanation of end-of-column characters).

When you apply paragraph formatting, the formatting applies to all the characters in the paragraph. Paragraph alignment, indents, tabs, spacing, and hyphenation settings are all examples of paragraph formatting.

You don't have to select all the text in a paragraph to apply paragraph formatting. To select a paragraph, all you have to do is click an insertion point in the paragraph. To select more than one paragraph for formatting, drag the cursor through the paragraphs you want to format—the selection doesn't have to include all the text in the paragraphs, it only has to *touch* each paragraph.

If you want to select all the paragraphs in a text block for formatting, select the text block with the Pointer tool. If you want to select all of the paragraphs in a story, triple-click one of the text blocks in the story with the Pointer tool (or click the Text tool on one of the text blocks in the story) and then press Command-A (for Select All).

Alignment

Click the buttons in the Alignment Inspector (press Command-Option-A to display the Inspector if it's not already visible) to set the alignment of the selected paragraphs. You can align paragraphs in the usual ways—Right (also known as "rag left"), Left (also known as "rag right"), Center, and Justify (see Figure 3-59). Free-Hand 4 dropped FreeHand 3's kooky Vertical alignment feature, probably because no one was using it.

FIGURE 3-57
Aligning paragraphs

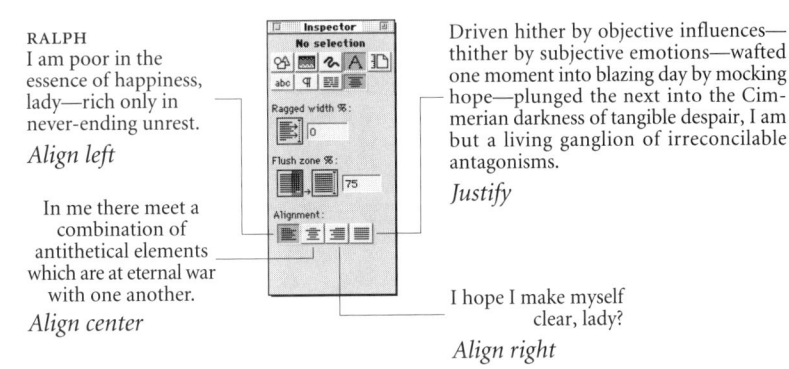

RALPH
I am poor in the essence of happiness, lady—rich only in never-ending unrest.
Align left

In me there meet a combination of antithetical elements which are at eternal war with one another.
Align center

Driven hither by objective influences—thither by subjective emotions—wafted one moment into blazing day by mocking hope—plunged the next into the Cimmerian darkness of tangible despair, I am but a living ganglion of irreconcilable antagonisms.
Justify

I hope I make myself clear, lady?
Align right

Tip:
Forced Justification

Sometimes, you want to justify a single line of text—for example, when you want to spread a heading across the width of a column. When you select the text and click the Justify button in the Alignment Inspector, nothing happens. What gives? When you justify a paragraph, FreeHand sets the last line of the paragraph flush left, ragged right. This is good, because (most of the time) you don't want the last line of the paragraph stretching all the way across the column.

How can you get your text to stretch across the column? Use the Flush Zone setting (see Figure 3-60).

1. Select the paragraph.

2. Display the Alignment Inspector, if it's not already visible, by pressing Command-Option-A.

3. Enter "0" in the Flush Zone field (and click the Justify button if the paragraph isn't already justified).

4. Press Return to apply your changes. FreeHand spreads the line of text across the column.

FIGURE 3-60
Forced justification

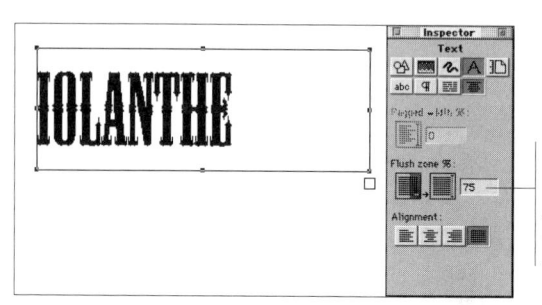

This text is justified, but doesn't spread out to fill the column...

...because the width of the line is less than the percentage of the column width set in the Flush Zone field.

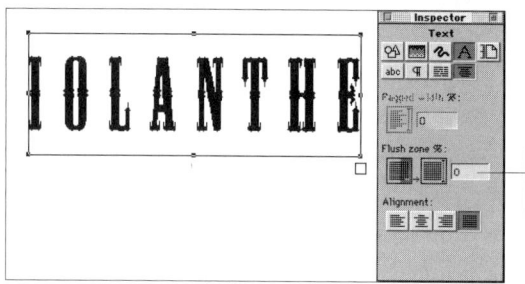

To spread the text across the column, enter zero in the Flush Zone field.

Tip:
Unjustified Justification

You may know people who call align right "right justify," or align left "left justify." Feign ignorance until they correct themselves. As you know, justification means to spread a line from one margin to the other, so there can't be anything called "right justify" or "left justify."

Tip:
QuicKeys for Alignment

Because other page-layout programs use keyboard shortcuts Command-Shift-R for right alignment and Command-Shift-L for left alignment, Command-Shift-C for centered text, and Command-Shift-J for justified text, consider adding these keyboard shortcuts with QuicKeys. You'd create a Sequence QuicKey that does just what you'd do—press Command-Option-A to display the Alignment Inspector and click the alignment icon you want.

If you do this, you'll have to redefine some of FreeHand's default keyboard shortcuts—Command-Shift-J, for example, usually means Split Element.

Spacing

Now that FreeHand has paragraph formatting features, you're faced with a dilemma you didn't have to face in previous versions of the program. I call it the text composition balancing act. Word- and letterspacing, hyphenation, alignment, and the values you enter for Ragged Width and Flush Zone (in the Alignment Inspector) *all* interact, with FreeHand using each setting to compose the best-looking text it can.

What do I mean by "the best-looking text"? It's more than a little subjective. In general, I think that the right edges of your left-aligned type shouldn't be too ragged (that is, there shouldn't be extreme variation in the widths of the lines in a paragraph), and the word- and letterspacing inside lines of justified text shouldn't be noticeably tight or loose, or vary too much from line to line.

I do know three, entirely objective things about spacing text in FreeHand.

- What constitutes "good spacing" varies from font to font and line width to line width. There is no "master" spacing setting that will work every time.

- FreeHand's default settings will not produce good text spacing and hyphenation for all fonts and all column widths.

- It's up to you to space your text the way you like it. The best thing you can do for the appearance of the type in your FreeHand publications is to experiment until you see what you like.

When FreeHand composes a line of text, it has to make decisions—decisions about where to hyphenate words, and about how much type to fit on a line. FreeHand needs your help in these tasks; it can't figure out what sort of spacing is appropriate for your text.

You use the Spacing Inspector and the Alignment Inspector to give FreeHand spacing guidelines.

To display the Spacing Inspector, press Command-Option-S (see Figure 3-61). The percentages you enter in the Spacing Inspector apply to all selected paragraphs.

FIGURE 3-61
Spacing Inspector

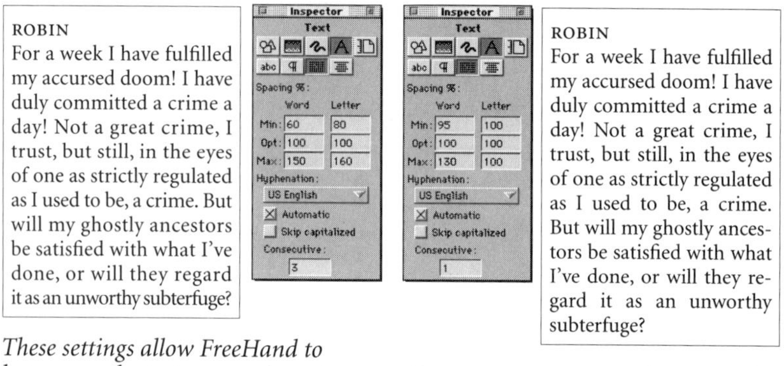
ROBIN
For a week I have fulfilled my accursed doom! I have duly committed a crime a day! Not a great crime, I trust, but still, in the eyes of one as strictly regulated as I used to be, a crime. But will my ghostly ancestors be satisfied with what I've done, or will they regard it as an unworthy subterfuge?
Inspector
Text
abc
Spacing %:
Word
Letter
Min: 60
80
Opt: 100
100
Max: 150
160
Hyphenation:
US English
Automatic
Skip capitalized
Consecutive:
3
Inspector
Text
abc
Spacing %:
Word
Letter
Min: 95
100
Opt: 100
100
Max: 130
100
Hyphenation:
US English
Automatic
Skip capitalized
Consecutive:
1
ROBIN
For a week I have fulfilled my accursed doom! I have duly committed a crime a day! Not a great crime, I trust, but still, in the eyes of one as strictly regulated as I used to be, a crime. But will my ghostly ancestors be satisfied with what I've done, or will they regard it as an unworthy subterfuge?

These settings allow FreeHand to letterspace the text—sometimes too much (the last line is way too tight).

These spacing settings tell FreeHand to increase or decrease wordspacing, and leave letterspacing alone.

What are the percentages in the Spacing Inspector based on? What does 100 percent mean? FreeHand bases word- and letter-spacing percentages on values specified in the font itself, by the font designer. These values represent the designer's vision of the ideal spacing for the font, and they're different for every font. You don't need to agree with these values—both word spacing and letter spacing for the font Utopia Regular, for example, seem extremely wide to me—you just need to know that they're where FreeHand gets its ideas about how to space the font.

All of this means that there aren't any "perfect" spacing values that work for all fonts, line widths, and alignments. What can you do? There's nothing for it—you have to work with each font (and, frequently, each publication) until you come up with spacing settings that look good to you. After awhile, you'll develop a "feeling" for certain fonts, and you'll be able to space them well without even thinking about it.

What spacing values should you start with? For non-justified type, set everything to 100 percent to start with, and then work from there. For justified type, start experimenting with word spacing percentages of 95, 100, 120 (that's Minimum, Optimum, and

Maximum, respectively), and letterspacing percentages of 100, 100, 100. I prefer letting FreeHand word space up to 180 percent before I even think about using letterspacing.

Ragged Width. When FreeHand varies word- and letterspacing in non-justified type, it's just trying to make your text match the value you entered in the Ragged Width field (in the Alignment Inspector). The percentage you enter in the Ragged Width field sets the minimum width for lines in non-justified paragraphs (see Figure 3-62). Smaller values produce paragraphs with more ragged edges (the right edge, in left-aligned text; the left edge in right-aligned text); larger values produce text with more uniform edges.

FIGURE 3-62
Ragged width and spacing

What's the difference between these two examples? Take a look at the second and third lines in each. In the example above, Free-Hand has increased the letterspacing to make the shorter lines fill the line; in the example below, we've encouraged FreeHand to leave the letterspacing of those lines alone.

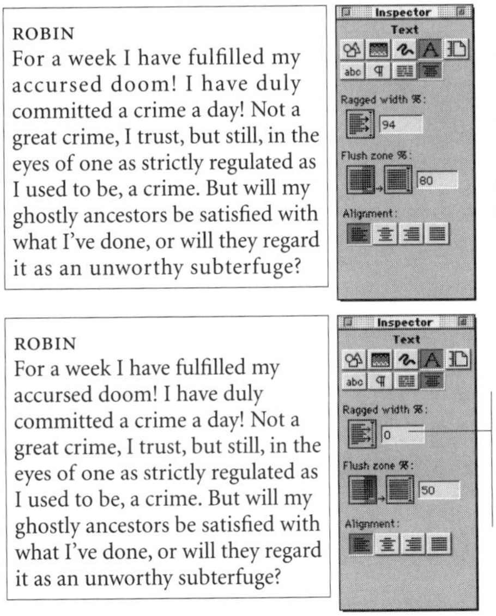

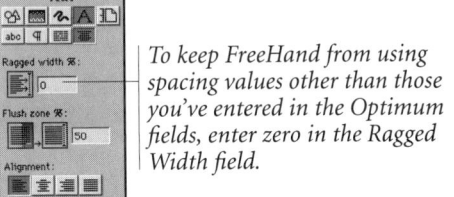

ROBIN
For a week I have fulfilled my accursed doom! I have duly committed a crime a day! Not a great crime, I trust, but still, in the eyes of one as strictly regulated as I used to be, a crime. But will my ghostly ancestors be satisfied with what I've done, or will they regard it as an unworthy subterfuge?

ROBIN
For a week I have fulfilled my accursed doom! I have duly committed a crime a day! Not a great crime, I trust, but still, in the eyes of one as strictly regulated as I used to be, a crime. But will my ghostly ancestors be satisfied with what I've done, or will they regard it as an unworthy subterfuge?

Why does spacing sometimes vary when you're working with nonjustified copy? Shouldn't FreeHand space the text according to the percentages you've entered in the Optimum fields in the Spacing Inspector?

That depends on what you've entered in the Alignment Inspector's Ragged Width field.

To keep FreeHand from using spacing values other than those you've entered in the Optimum fields, enter zero in the Ragged Width field.

If you're setting non-justified text, and want FreeHand to leave your word and letter spacing alone (that is, to use the percentages you entered in the Optimum fields in the Spacing Inspector), enter "100%" for Ragged Width.

FreeHand is—as far as I know—alone among page-layout programs in that its minimum and maximum settings for word spacing and letterspacing apply to paragraphs of any alignment. This only happens when you've entered a value larger than zero in the Ragged Width field.

Flush Zone. The percentage you enter in the Flush Zone field controls the spacing of the last line of a justified paragraph. The question FreeHand's asking is: "If the last line in your paragraph gets within a certain distance of the right side of the column, should I justify it?" When you enter anything less than "100%" in the Flush Zone field, you're specifying the line width—expressed as a percentage of the width of the column—at which you want FreeHand to start justifying text (see Figure 3-63).

In my opinion, you should set Flush Zone to either "100", to leave the last lines of justified paragraphs alone (that is, flush left, ragged right), or "0", to force-justify a single line of text (see "Forced Justification," later in this chapter). I have, however, met people whose typographic opinions I respect who set their Flush Zone to 95 percent.

FIGURE 3-63
Flush Zone

GHOSTS
We spectres are a jollier crew than you, perhaps, s   u   p   p   o   s   e   !

Flush Zone set to 20

GHOSTS
We spectres are a jollier crew than you, perhaps, suppose!

Flush Zone set to 100

Enter a percentage in the Flush Zone field to tell FreeHand how to justify the last line of a justified paragraph. Most of the time, you can leave it set to 100.

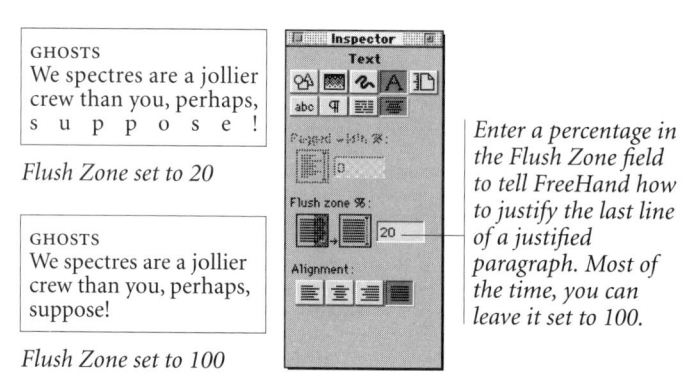

Hyphenation

Another key factor in the spacing of your text is hyphenation—when and where FreeHand can break words in order to compose lines of text as you've specified using the spacing settings (see Figure 3-64). Like spacing, hyphenation settings are very subjective, and what "looks good" varies from person to person and publication to publication.

FreeHand's hyphenation controls are very simple.

♦ Use the language popup menu to choose the dictionary you want to use.

♦ Check Automatic to use the hyphenation points defined in the hyphenation dictionary. Automatic has no bearing on any discretionary hyphens you've entered.

FIGURE 3-63
Hyphenation

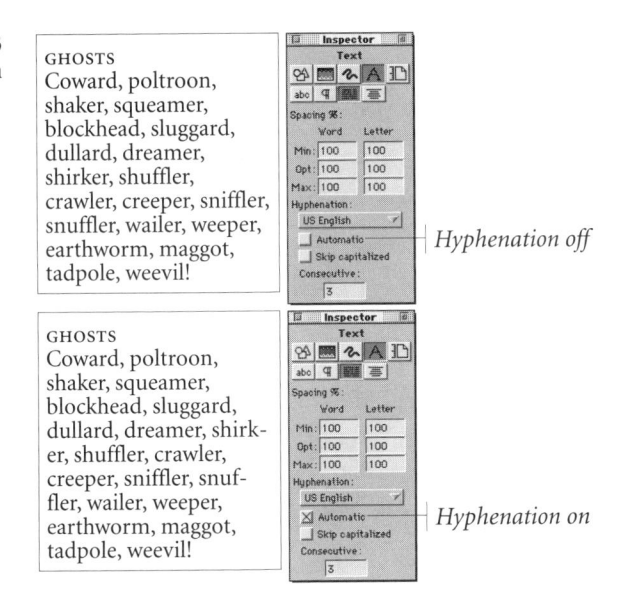

GHOSTS
Coward, poltroon, shaker, squeamer, blockhead, sluggard, dullard, dreamer, shirker, shuffler, crawler, creeper, sniffler, snuffler, wailer, weeper, earthworm, maggot, tadpole, weevil!

⎯ *Hyphenation off*

GHOSTS
Coward, poltroon, shaker, squeamer, blockhead, sluggard, dullard, dreamer, shirker, shuffler, crawler, creeper, sniffler, snuffler, wailer, weeper, earthworm, maggot, tadpole, weevil!

⎯ *Hyphenation on*

- Check Skip Capitalized to tell FreeHand not to break words typed with initial capital letters, such as names (where would you break "Kvern"?) or acronyms ("SPECTRE").

- Enter a number in the Consecutive field to set the number of consecutive hyphens you'll allow in a paragraph. The larger the number you enter here, the less difficult it'll be for FreeHand to obey your spacing settings. I usually enter "1", unless I'm working in an extremely narrow column, because I hate seeing stacks of hyphens at the right edge of columns of type.

Paragraph Indents

FreeHand's paragraphs can be indented from the left and right sides of the column using the Left and Right fields in the Paragraph Inspector. You can enter positive or negative numbers in either field. Enter positive numbers to push the edges of the paragraph in from the edges of the column it occupies; enter negative numbers to push the edges of the paragraph beyond the column's edges (see Figure 3-65).

In addition, there's a special indent, First, that applies to the first line of the paragraph alone. The value you enter in First sets the distance between the first-line indent and the left indent, and can be positive or negative. You can even enter a first-line indent that causes text to hang outside the text block (see Figure 3-66).

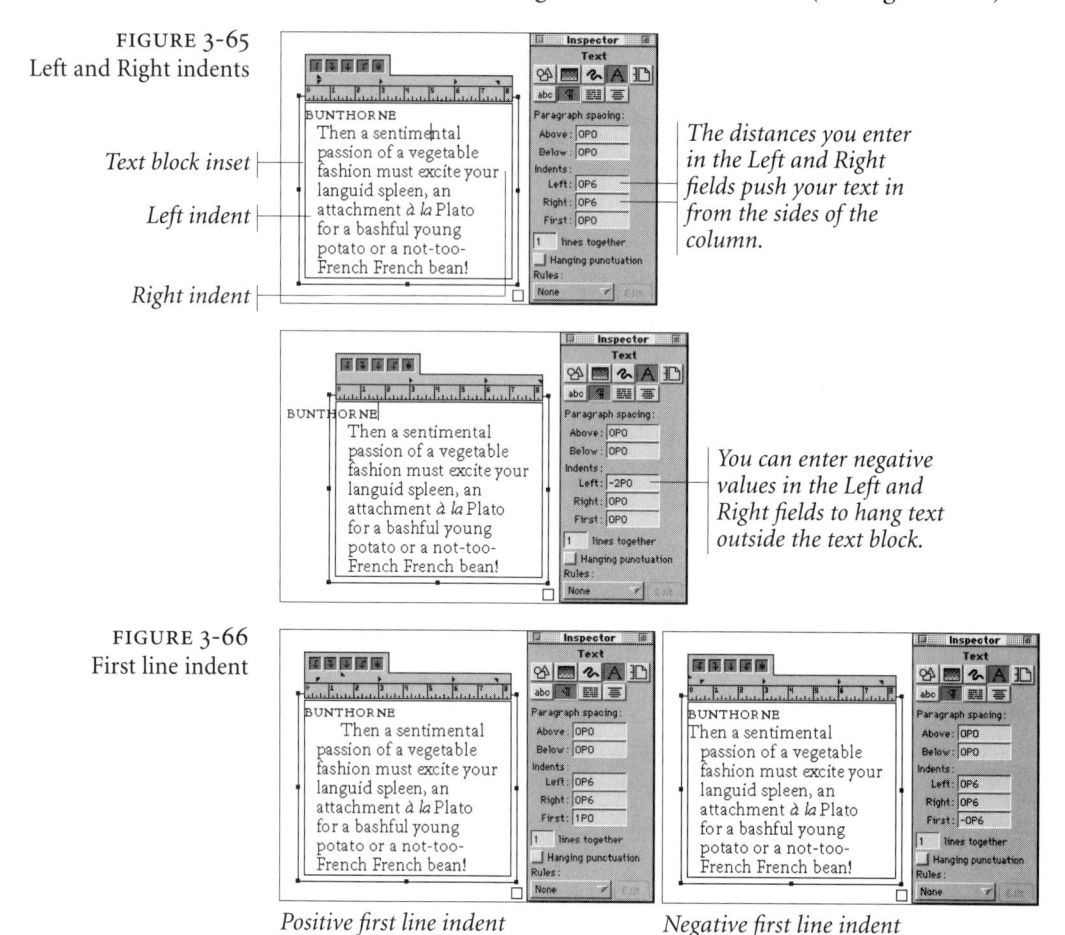

FIGURE 3-65
Left and Right indents

Text block inset
Left indent

Right indent

The distances you enter in the Left and Right fields push your text in from the sides of the column.

You can enter negative values in the Left and Right fields to hang text outside the text block.

FIGURE 3-66
First line indent

Positive first line indent   *Negative first line indent*

Hanging Punctuation

Because we don't "see" punctuation when we're reading, a line beginning (or, in some cases ending) with punctuation (especially quotation marks) doesn't look like it aligns with other lines in the surrounding text. It's a kind of typographic optical illusion. To compensate, typographers since Gutenberg have "hung" punctuation—moving the punctuation slightly beyond the edge of the text column. (Gutenberg also changed the spelling of words to fit his justification scheme—just as we do today when we're in a hurry or desperate.)

You can think of FreeHand's hanging punctuation as something like a special, negative indent for a specific line. In fact, you can hang punctuation manually using FreeHand's right and left paragraph indents—just enter the distance you want the punctuation to extend beyond the edge of the text box. When text reflows, however, you have start again from scratch.

FreeHand gives you an easy way to apply hanging punctuation that automatically adjusts as text reflows (see Figure 3-67). Hanging punctuation applies to ' ' " " . , ; : ` -

FIGURE 3-67
Hanging punctuation

"Oh, a private buffoon is a light-hearted loon, if you listen to popular rumor."

Normal punctuation

"Oh, a private buffoon is a light-hearted loon, if you listen to popular rumor."

Hanging punctuation

1. Type some text that begins with a quotation mark.

2. If the Paragraph Inspector isn't already visible, display it by pressing Command-Option-P.

3. Without deselecting the text block you created, check the Hanging Punctuation checkbox. Watch as FreeHand hangs the quotation mark outside the text margins of the text block, which produces a better visual alignment. FreeHand does this any time one of the special characters appears at the left or right edge of a text block or column.

You can't set the distance the special characters hang outside the text block, and you can't add characters to the list of characters hanging punctuation affects.

Tabs Tabs (which we knew as "tab stops" when we used typewriters—that is, sometime before we came down from the trees) define what FreeHand does when it encounters a tab character in your text, and you use tabs to control the horizontal position of text in your text blocks. FreeHand's Text Ruler features left, right, center, decimal, and wrapping tabs (see Figure 3-68).

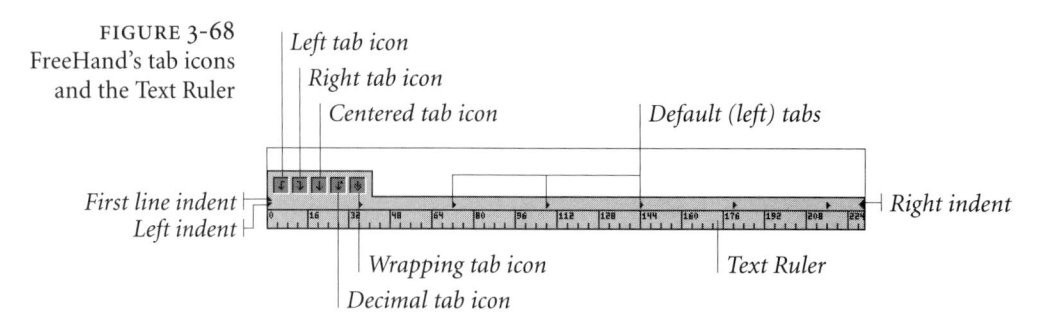

FIGURE 3-68
FreeHand's tab icons and the Text Ruler

Left tab icon
Right tab icon
Centered tab icon
Default (left) tabs
First line indent
Left indent
Right indent
Wrapping tab icon
Decimal tab icon
Text Ruler

You can also use FreeHand's tab ruler to set indents—this is handy, because indents and tabs often work together.

A few things about tabs:

- Use tab characters and tabs, not spaces, to add horizontal space in your lines of text.

- Tabs apply to entire paragraphs—you can't have different tabs inside a single paragraph.

- Don't force line breaks using tab characters—use returns, end-of-column, or end-of-line characters when you want a line to break in a specific place.

- Use tabs and indents to create hanging indents—not carriage returns and tab characters (or, worse, spaces).

Left, Right, and Center tabs. FreeHand's left, right, and center tabs are the same as the basic tabs you'll find in any word processor (see Figure 3-69).

Left tabs push text following a tab character to a specific horizontal location in a column, and then align the text to the left of the tab.

Right tabs push text to a location and then align the text to the right of a tab character.

Center tabs center a line of text at the point at which you've set a tab character.

Decimal tabs. Decimal tabs push text following a tab character so that any decimal point you've entered in the text aligns with the point you set the tab (see Figure 3-70). If there's no decimal in the text, FreeHand treats the decimal tab as a right tab.

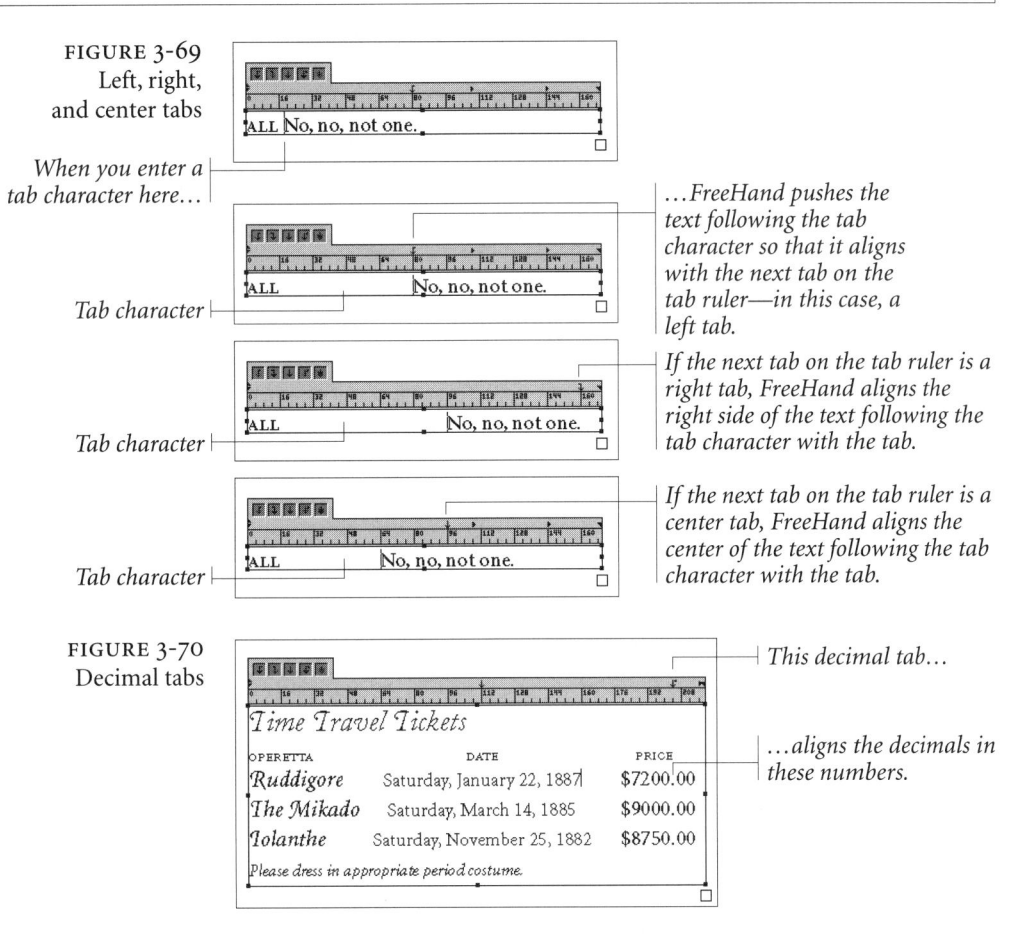

FIGURE 3-69
Left, right,
and center tabs

When you enter a
tab character here...

Tab character

Tab character

Tab character

...FreeHand pushes the
text following the tab
character so that it aligns
with the next tab on the
tab ruler—in this case, a
left tab.

If the next tab on the tab ruler is a
right tab, FreeHand aligns the
right side of the text following the
tab character with the tab.

If the next tab on the tab ruler is a
center tab, FreeHand aligns the
center of the text following the tab
character with the tab.

FIGURE 3-70
Decimal tabs

This decimal tab...

...aligns the decimals in
these numbers.

Wrapping tabs. Wrapping tabs create a column inside a column of your text block (see Figure 3-71). Wrapping tabs are unique to FreeHand—no other page layout or illustration program has anything like them. Wrapping tabs are great for creating columns within columns, or for creating columns of unequal widths inside a text block (columns set with the Column Inspector always divide a text block evenly).

Setting tabs. To set a tab, follow these steps (see Figure 3-72).

1. Select the text you want to format.

2. If you haven't already entered tab characters in the text, enter them.

FIGURE 3-71
Wrapping tabs

Wrapping tabs create a column inside a column of text.

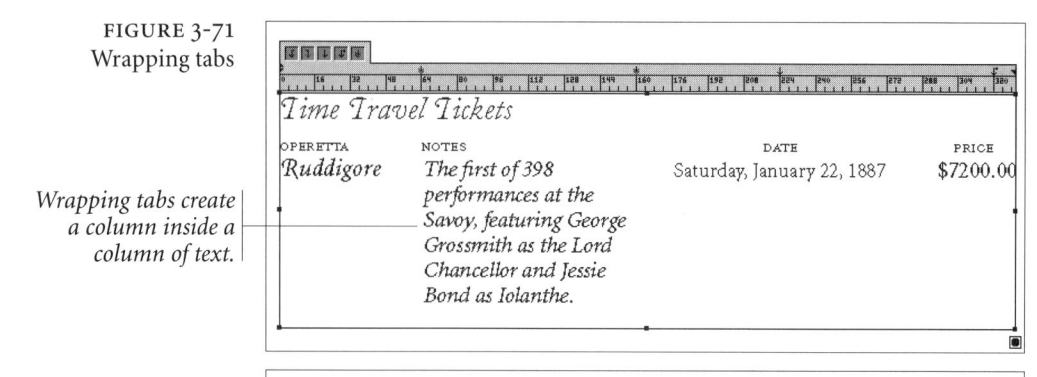

When you position a single wrapping tab at the left or right margin, FreeHand creates a column. It's as if the margin is another wrapping tab.

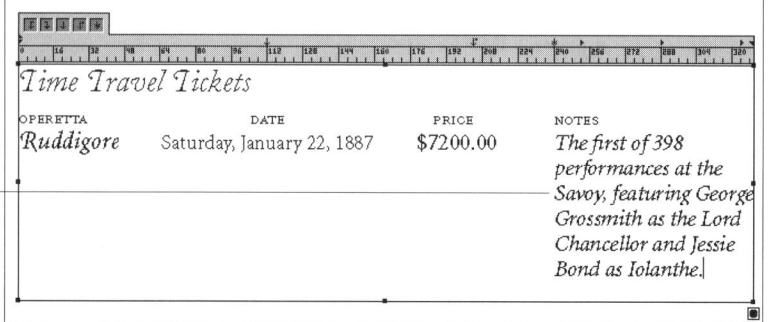

3. Drag a tab icon for the type of tab you want to set onto the tab ruler. As you drag, the Info Bar shows you the position of the tab icon.

4. When the tab icon reaches the position at which you want to set the tab, drop it onto the ruler.

To change a tab's position, drag the tab on the tab ruler (see Figure 3-73).

To change a tab's alignment, drag a tab of the alignment you want onto the tab's position (see Figure 3-74). You've got to drop the new tab icon precisely on the old one, or you'll end up with two tabs on your tab ruler right next to each other.

To remove a tab, drag the tab icon off the tab ruler and drop it on your page or pasteboard (see Figure 3-75). Note that this doesn't remove any tab characters you've typed in your text, though it does make them behave differently.

Creating a hanging indent. As in both Word and PageMaker, you create a hanging indent by dragging the left margin icon to the

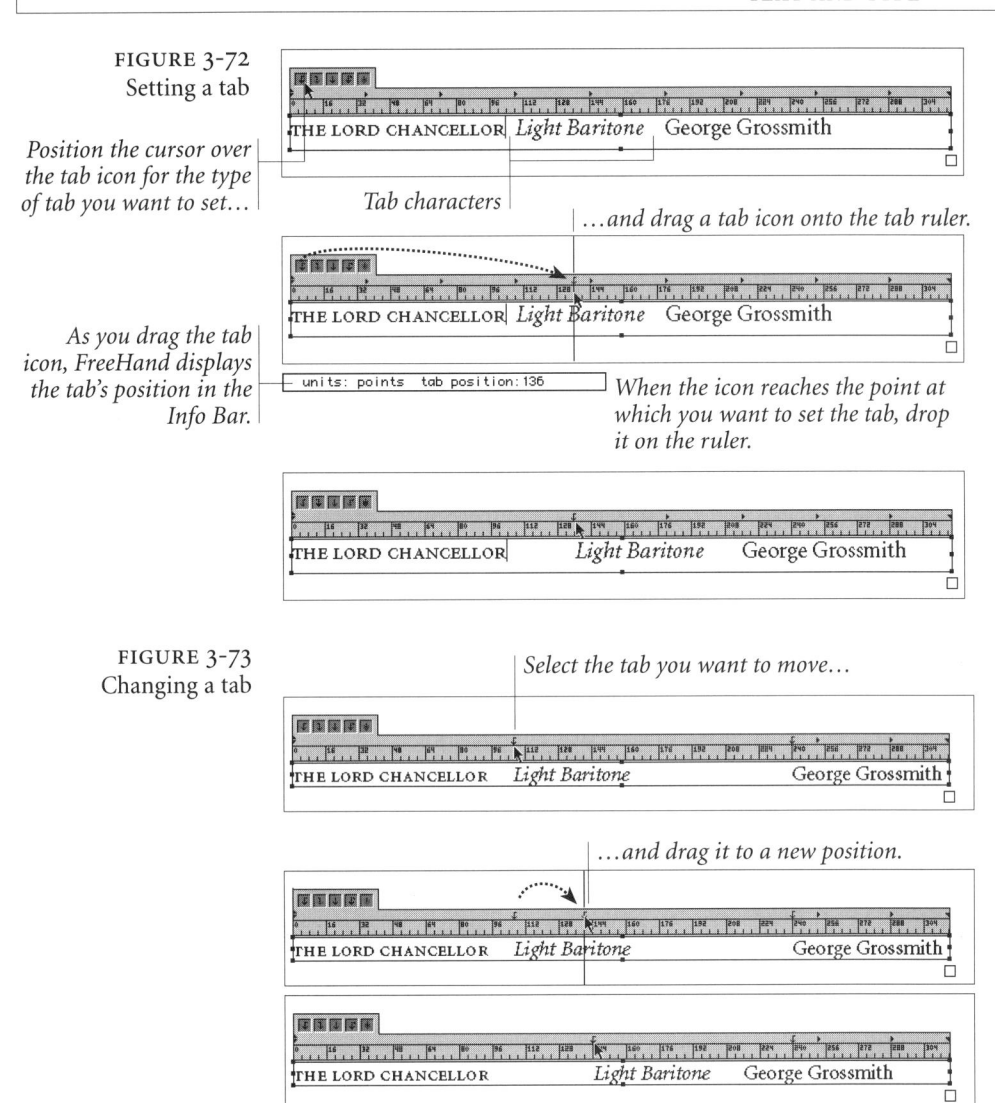

FIGURE 3-72
Setting a tab

Position the cursor over the tab icon for the type of tab you want to set...

Tab characters

...and drag a tab icon onto the tab ruler.

As you drag the tab icon, FreeHand displays the tab's position in the Info Bar.

When the icon reaches the point at which you want to set the tab, drop it on the ruler.

FIGURE 3-73
Changing a tab

Select the tab you want to move...

...and drag it to a new position.

right of the first-line indent icon, then setting a left tab at the same position as the left margin icon (see Figure 3-76).

**Tip:
Hanging Side Heads**

Headings that appear in a column next to text (such as the heading for this tip) are difficult to create in most publishing or word processing software (only Corel Ventura Publisher features an automated method for creating hanging side heads). Using FreeHand's wrapping tabs, it's easy, as shown in Figure 3-77.

FIGURE 3-74
Changing
tab alignment

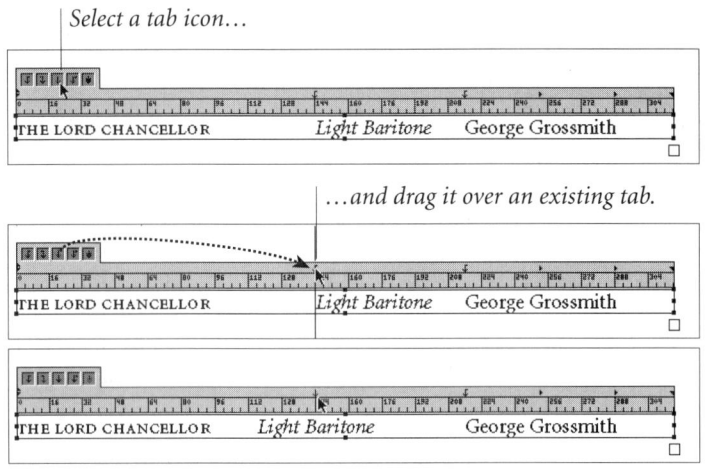

Select a tab icon...

...and drag it over an existing tab.

FreeHand changes the tab's alignment.

FIGURE 3-75
Removing a tab

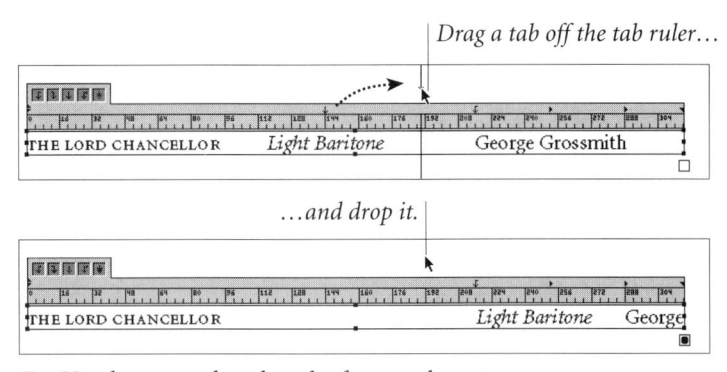

Drag a tab off the tab ruler...

...and drop it.

FreeHand removes the tab and reformats the text.

Setting Tabs with the Edit Tab Dialog Box

Another way to set tabs is to use the Edit Tabs dialog box. It's also the only way to specify tab leaders—repeating characters that fill the space taken up by a tab. To set a tab using the Edit Tabs dialog box, follow these steps (see Figure 3-78).

1. Click the Text tool in a text block. Display the Text Ruler, if it's not already visible, by pressing Command-/.

2. Double-click the area immediately above the ruler (the place where you see tabs you've set and any of FreeHand's remaining default tabs). FreeHand displays the Edit Tabs dialog box.

FIGURE 3-76
Creating a
hanging indent

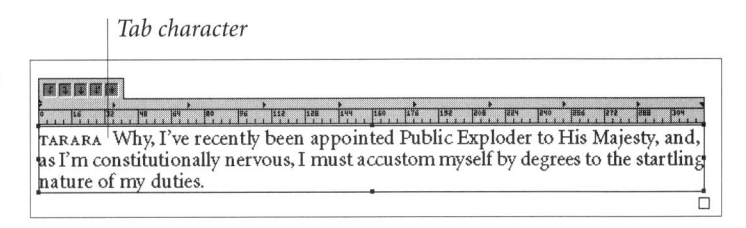

Tab character

Set the indent for the body of the paragraph by dragging the left indent and first line indent icons.

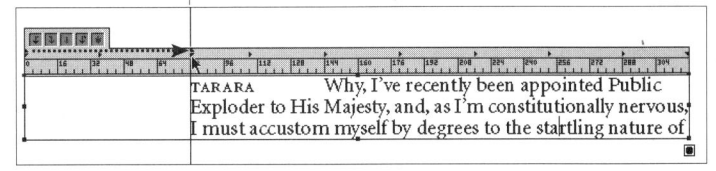

Set the hanging indent by dragging the first line indent icon to the left of the left indent icon.

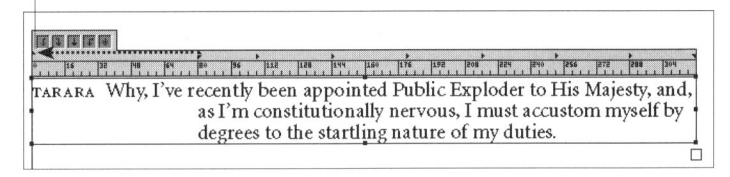

Position a left tab at the same location as the left indent icon.

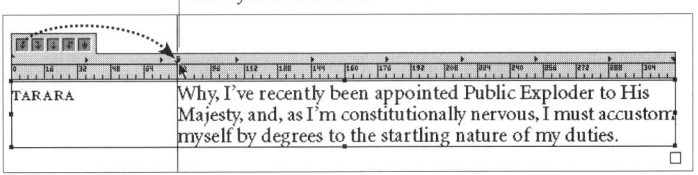

3. Type a tab position in the Position field.

4. Choose a tab alignment from the Alignment pop-up menu.

5. If you want to use a tab leader, type the character you want to use for your leader in the Leader field, or choose one from the pop-up menu attached to the field. Note that you can enter more than one character in the Leader field, but FreeHand uses only the first character you type.

6. Press Return (or click the OK button) to set the tab.

FIGURE 3-77
Creating hanging side heads

Position two wrapping tabs.

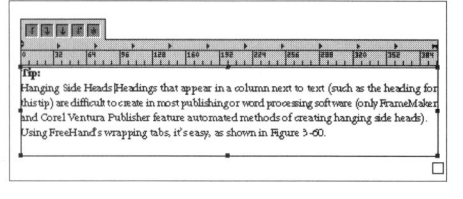

Enter two tab characters between the side head and the paragraph it accompanies.

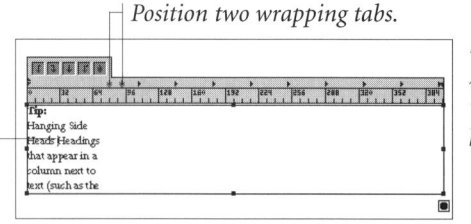

The space between the wrapping tabs defines the "gutter" between the side head and the body text.

This tab makes text wrap between it and the left margin.

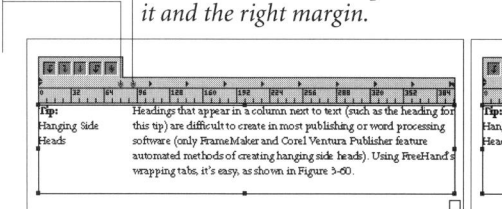

This tab makes text wrap between it and the right margin.

If you enter only one tab character, text wraps inside the two wrapping tabs, creating a very narrow column.

To edit a tab, double-click a tab marker in the Text Ruler. FreeHand displays the Edit Tab dialog box. Edit the tab's position, leader, or alignment as you would if you were creating the tab.

Tip: Make These Tabs Like Those

When you want to make a series of selected paragraphs have the same tab settings as the first paragraph in the selection, hold down Option and click above the ruler in the Text Ruler. FreeHand applies the tab settings of the first line to the rest of the selection (see Figure 3-79).

Spacing Before and After Paragraphs

To increase or decrease the amount of space above or below a paragraph, enter a value (distance) in the Above or Below field in the Paragraph Inspector (press Command-Option-P to display the Paragraph Inspector, if it's not already visible) and press Return. FreeHand adds the space above or below the paragraph, as you specified (see Figure 3-80).

You can enter positive or negative numbers in the Paragraph Spacing fields. Enter a negative number in the Above field, and

FIGURE 3-78
Setting a tab with the
Edit Tabs dialog box

Select the paragraphs you want to format.

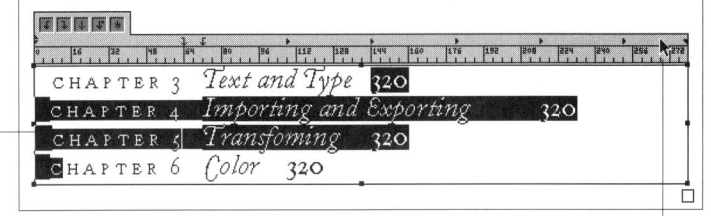

Double-click the Text Ruler.

FreeHand displays the Edit Tab dialog box.

In this example, I'm setting a right tab at the right edge of the text block (which I know is 280 points wide).

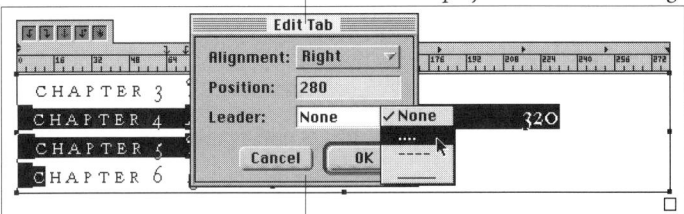

Choose an alignment, position, and tab leader (if you want one) for the tab.

Press Return to add your new tab to the Text Ruler.

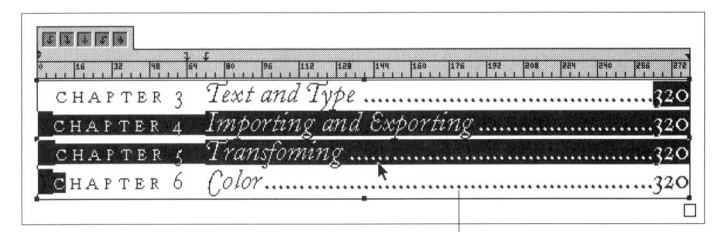

Tab leader characters

FreeHand moves the paragraph up—even to the point where the paragraph hangs out of the top of the text block or collides with the paragraph above. Enter a negative number in the Below field, and FreeHand moves the following paragraph up in the text block. I haven't found any limit to the numbers you can enter in these fields—either positive or negative.

Controlling Widows

Everyone has a different definition for the meaning of the typographic terms "widow" and "orphan." To me, a "widow" is a single line of a paragraph at the top or bottom of a page or column, and an "orphan" is when a paragraph ends with a single, short word on a line by itself. To FreeHand, a "widow" is a single line of a paragraph at the top of a text block or column. I don't know what it thinks an "orphan" is.

FIGURE 3-79
Applying the same tab settings to a series of paragraphs

Select the paragraphs you want to format, making sure that the start of the selection touches some part of the paragraph containing the tab settings you want to use.

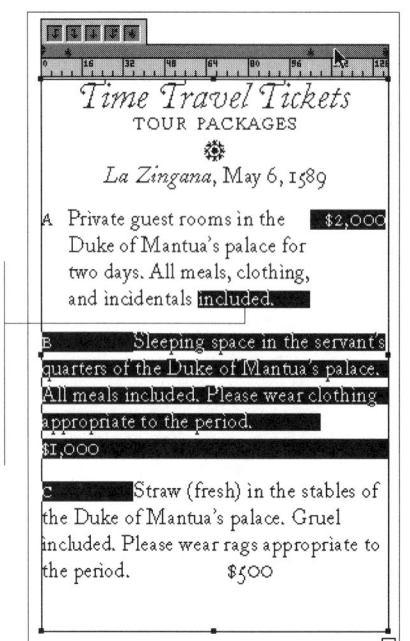

Hold down Option and double-click the area above the ruler in the Text Ruler…

…and FreeHand applies the tab settings of the first paragraph in the selection to all of the other paragraphs in the selection.

FIGURE 3-80
Vertical spacing around paragraphs

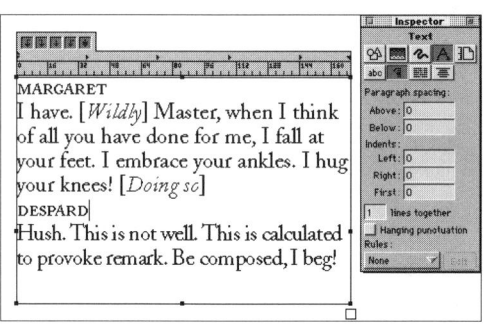

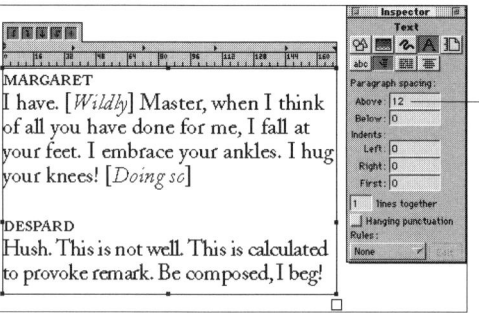

Enter a value in the Above field to add space before a paragraph.

The *N* Lines Together field in the Paragraph Inspector controls the way FreeHand breaks a paragraph between columns or linked text blocks. When you enter "1" here (the default), you're telling FreeHand that it's free to break paragraphs however it sees fit. When you enter "2," or a larger number, FreeHand always breaks paragraphs so that two (or more) lines of the paragraph appear at the top of the next text block (see Figure 3-81).

FIGURE 3-81
Keeping lines together

With "1" entered in the N *Lines Together* field, FreeHand leaves the first line of this paragraph at the bottom of the column.

If you enter "2" in the N *Lines Together* field…

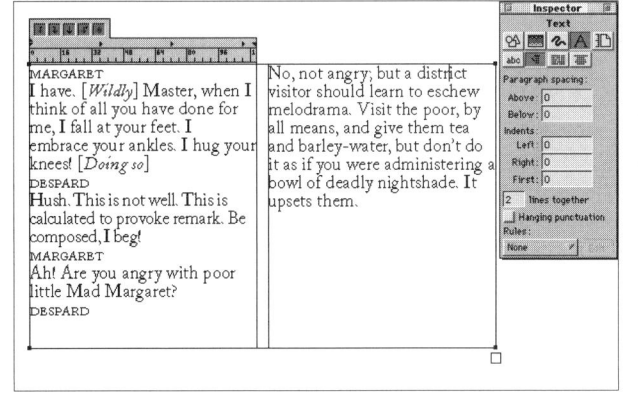

…*FreeHand pulls the first line of the paragraph to the top of the next column.*

Paragraph Rules

In the old days, we had to add rules between paragraphs manually, dragging the rules around every time the text changed. Many of today's page layout applications feature rules you can attach to a paragraph, which then move with the paragraph as the text reflows. FreeHand features a limited version of this feature (compared, at least, to PageMaker and Quark XPress).

To attach a rule to a paragraph, position the text cursor inside the paragraph, press Command-Option-P to display the Paragraph

Inspector, choose a rule type (Centered or Paragraph) from the popup menu at the bottom of the Inspector, and press Return. Centered rules are centered in the column or text block; Paragraph rules have the same alignment as the paragraph they're attached to (see Figure 3-82).

FIGURE 3-82
Paragraph rules

Move the cursor to the paragraph you want to attach a paragraph rule to.

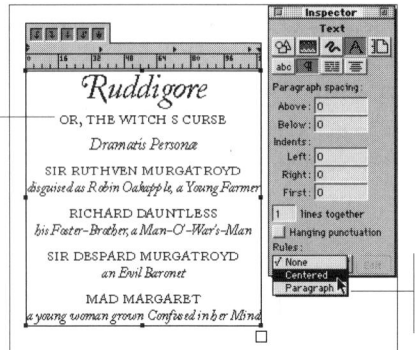

"Centered" rules are centered on the paragraph or the column. "Paragraph" rules use the alignment of the paragraph they're attached to.

Choose a paragraph rule option from the Rules popup menu.

FreeHand attaches a rule to the paragraph.

If you don't see a rule, you haven't applied a stroke to the text block. Use the Stroke Inspector to apply a stroke to the text block.

FreeHand vertically centers paragraph rules between the bottom of the last line of the current paragraph and the top of the first line of the following paragraph.

Click the Edit button, and the Paragraph Rule Width dialog box appears.

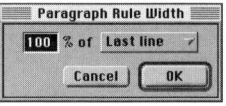

Paragraph rule spanning the column.

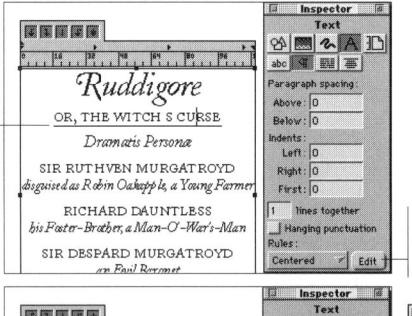

Choose whether you want the paragraph rule to span the width of the text (that is, the last line of the paragraph it's attached to) or the width of the column.

A few notes about paragraph rules:

◆ You can't select paragraph rules by clicking on them with the Pointer tool.

◆ When you convert text to paths, any paragraph rules selected with the text are not converted—they disappear.

- FreeHand vertically centers paragraph rules in the space between the their paragraph (the paragraph where you specified the rule) and the following paragraph, taking leading, paragraph space before, and paragraph space after into account.

- FreeHand strokes the paragraph rules with the stroke that's applied to the text block. You can't apply different strokes to a text block's border and to the paragraph rules within that text block (you can, however, uncheck Display Border in the Object Inspector and draw a path around the text block—it's easier than drawing paragraph rules, most of the time).

Tip:
Paragraph Rules and Text Effects

The rules drawn by the Highlight, Strikethrough, and Underline text effects print *over* any paragraph rules (see Figure 3-83). You can think of a text block as having (at least) three internal layers, with paragraph rules at the back, text at the front, and rules drawn by text effects in between.

FIGURE 3-83
Paragraph rules, Highlight, Strikethrough, and Underline

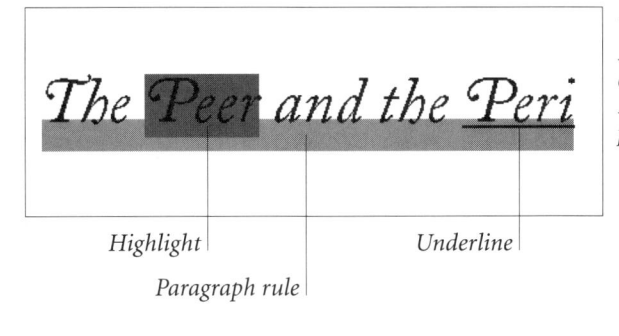

The rules in Freehand's text effects print over FreeHand's paragraph rules.

Highlight

Paragraph rule

Underline

Working with Text Styles

When you think about the text in your publication, chances are good you're thinking of each paragraph as being a representative of a particular *kind* of text. You're thinking, "That's a headline, that's a subhead, and that's a photo caption." Chances are also good that you're thinking of those paragraphs as having certain formatting attributes: font, size, color, and leading.

That's what text styles do—they bundle all those attributes together and make it possible for you to apply them to text with a single click. But there's more—if you then change your mind about the formatting, you can edit the style, and all the text with that style applied to it (that is, "tagged" with the style) is reformatted automatically.

Text styles work about the same way as graphic styles do—see "Working with Graphic Styles" in Chapter 2, "Drawing"—but they can save you even more time. What makes me say this? Think about it—FreeHand has far more controls for text formatting than it does for formatting paths. Once you've created a text style for a specific kind of text, you'll never have to go through the Type Specifications palette, Character Inspector, Paragraph Inspector, Spacing Inspector, or Alignment Inspector again to format that text—unless, of course, you want to apply a local formatting override to your styled text, which you're always free to do.

Global versus Local Formatting

I just mentioned "local" formatting. What am I talking about? The key to understanding text styles is understanding the difference between style-based formatting and local formatting.

Local formatting is what you get when you select text and apply formatting directly, using the Type Specifications palette and the different sections of the Type Inspector. When you apply formatting using text styles from the Styles palette, on the other hand, you're applying "global" formatting (that is, formatting specified by the selected style).

You can tell if there's local formatting applied to a styled paragraph by looking at the Styles palette. Click the text tool in a styled paragraph, and you'll see a "+" after the style name if the paragraph contains local formatting (see Figure 3-84).

FIGURE 3-84
Global and local formatting

The "+" next to the style name in the Styles palette shows that the selected character doesn't conform to the style's formatting—it's formatted "locally."

Note: FreeHand marks text styles by putting a paragraph symbol (¶) next to the style name in the Styles palette.

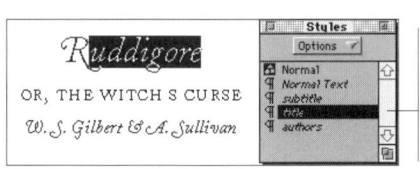

This selection, on the other hand, gets its formatting from the selected style. All of the other text tagged with this style shares the same "global" formatting attributes.

Styles Are More than Formatting

When you apply a style to a paragraph (which I call "tagging" a paragraph with a style), you're doing more than just applying the formatting defined by the style. You're telling FreeHand *what the paragraph is*—not just what it looks like, but what role it has to play in your publication. Is the paragraph important? Is it an insignificant legal notice in type that's intentionally too small to read? The style says it all.

The most important thing to remember when you're creating and applying styles is that tagging a paragraph with a style creates a link between the paragraph and all other paragraphs tagged with that style, and between the paragraph and the definition of the style. Change the style's definition, and watch the formatting and behavior of the paragraphs tagged with that style change to match.

Creating a Text Style

The easiest way (in my opinion) to create a text style is to use local formatting to format a paragraph, then create a new style based on that paragraph (see Figure 3-85).

1. Select a formatted paragraph.

2. Display the Styles palette (press Command-3).

3. Choose "New" from the Styles palette's popup menu. FreeHand adds a new text style to the list of available styles in the Styles palette. This style includes all the formatting applied to the selected paragraph. If you want to change the name of the style, double-click the style's name in the Styles palette, type the name you want, and press Return.

That's all there is to it—you've created a text style, and FreeHand has applied the style to the selected paragraph (text styles pay no attention to the status of the Auto-Apply Style to Selected Objects option in the Expert Editing Preferences dialog box—see "Expert Editing Preferences" in Chapter 1, "FreeHand Basics"). If you had more than one paragraph selected, FreeHand either takes the formatting of the first paragraph in the selection or takes the formatting common to all the paragraphs in the selection, depending on your settings in the Build Paragraph Styles Based On section of the Text Editing Preferences dialog box (see the corresponding section in Chapter 1, "FreeHand Basics").

FIGURE 3-85
Creating a style by example

Use local formatting to format a paragraph.

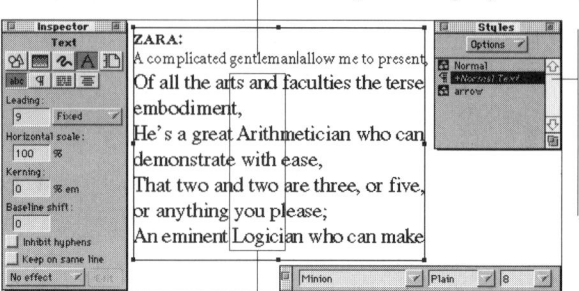

The "+" next to FreeHand's "Normal" style shows that you've overridden the style's default formatting.

These paragraphs are formatted with FreeHand's default style, "Normal."

Click the Text tool inside the example paragraph and choose New from the Options popup menu on the Styles palette.

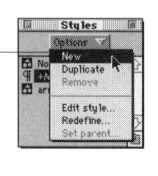

FreeHand adds a new style to the Styles palette. This style contains all of the formatting of the example paragraph.

Click the style name in the Styles palette to apply the style to the example paragraph.

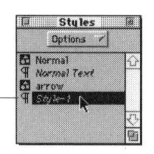

When you create a style, FreeHand assigns a default name to the style. To change the name, double-click the style name, type a new name, and press Return or Enter.

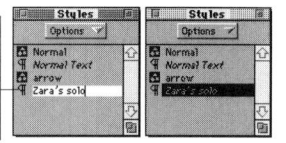

To apply the new style to other paragraphs, select the paragraphs...

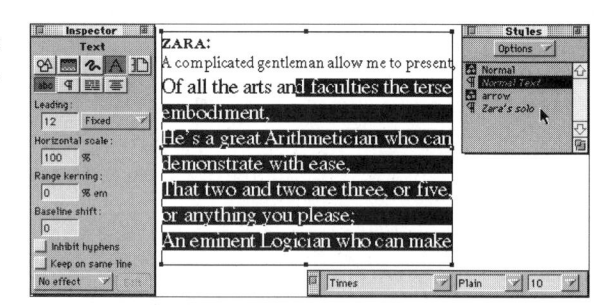

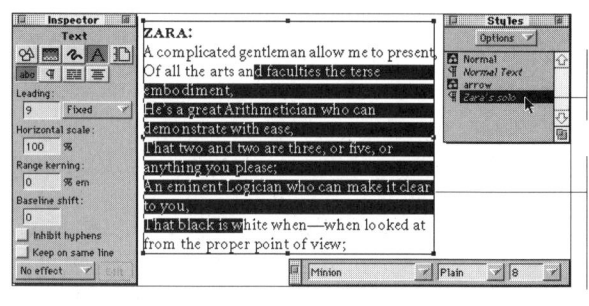

...and click the style name in the Styles palette.

FreeHand applies the style's formatting to all of the selected paragraphs.

TEXT AND TYPE 313

If you've selected more than one paragraph, and you've turned on the Build Paragraph Styles Based On Shared Attributes option in the Text Editing Preferences dialog box, any of the formatting attributes that aren't shared between the selected paragraphs are omitted from the style's definition.

If you prefer, you can create a text style by entering text formatting for the style in a dialog box that's similar to the text formatting controls (see Figure 3-86).

1. Choose "New" from the popup menu in the Styles palette. FreeHand creates a new text style and adds it to the list of styles in the palette. If you like, you can change the style name by double-clicking the name, typing a new name, and pressing Return.

FIGURE 3-86
Creating a style by specifying attributes

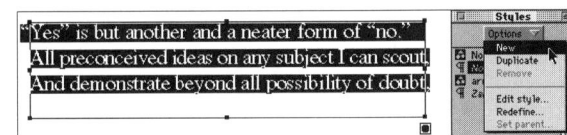

Choose New from the Options menu at the top of the Styles palette.

FreeHand creates a new style and adds it to the Styles palette. At this point, the style's formatting is identical to that of "Normal."

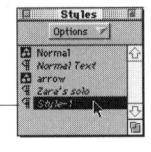

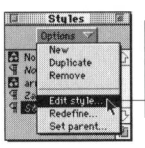

Select the new style name and choose Edit Style from the Styles palette's Options menu (or hold down Option and click the style name in the Styles palette).

FreeHand displays the Edit Style dialog box.

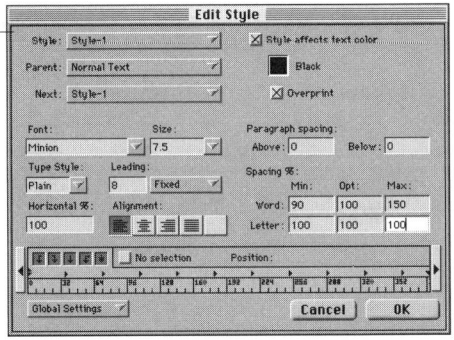

Set the formatting attributes you want for the style using the controls in the Edit Style dialog box. When you're done, click the OK button.

FreeHand applies the formatting to any paragraphs tagged with the style.

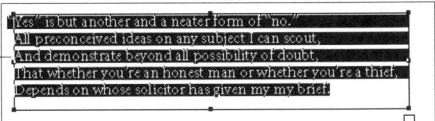

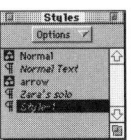

2. Hold down Option and click the style name in the Styles palette. FreeHand displays the Edit Style dialog box. In this dialog box, you'll see most (but not all) of FreeHand's text formatting controls.

3. Work your way through the Edit Style dialog box, setting the options as you want them for your new style. When everything looks the way you want it to, press Return to close the dialog box.

Creating a style this way is a little bit more awkward than simply basing a style on an example paragraph, but it does offer a couple of advantages.

- You can set the parent style of a style as you create the style. For more on creating hierarchies of styles, see "Basing One Style on Another" in Chapter 2, "Drawing"—everything I said there about graphic styles also applies to text styles.

- You can direct FreeHand to apply—or not apply—a color as part of the style, using the Style Affects Color checkbox.

- You can specify the "next" style (that is, the style you get when you enter a carriage return at the end of a paragraph while you're entering text).

- You can set tabs on the Text Ruler at the bottom of the Edit Style dialog box. This may or may not be an advantage; I only mention it because I've met at least one person who likes setting tabs "without all that pesky text in the way."

Applying a Text Style

Once you've created a style, you'll probably want to apply it to a paragraph. To apply a text style to a paragraph, select the paragraph with the Text tool (all you have to do to select the paragraph is click the Text tool in it; you don't have to drag the cursor through the text to select all the text in the paragraph), then click the style name in the Styles palette. FreeHand applies the style to the text (see Figure 3-87).

If you want to apply a text style to all the paragraphs inside a text block, select the text block with the pointer tool and click the

FIGURE 3-87
Applying a style to text

Click the Text tool in the paragraph you want to apply a style to (or drag through a series of paragraphs—you don't have to select the entire paragraph).

Click the style name in the Styles palette. FreeHand applies the style to the selection.

style in the Styles palette. As you'd expect, this also applies the style to any paragraphs in other, linked, text blocks that start or end in the selected text block.

You can also apply styles using the same sort of "drag-and-drop" technique as you use to apply colors to objects—position your cursor over the icon (¶) to the left of the style name in the Styles list, then drag. As you drag, FreeHand displays an icon representing the text style (does this make it a "style swatch"? I don't know!). Drop the icon on the text you want to tag with the style (see Figure 3-88).

FIGURE 3-88
Applying styles with drag-and-drop

Drag the paragraph icon from the styles palette and drop it on top of the paragraph you want to format.

FreeHand applies the style to the paragraph you dropped the paragraph icon on.

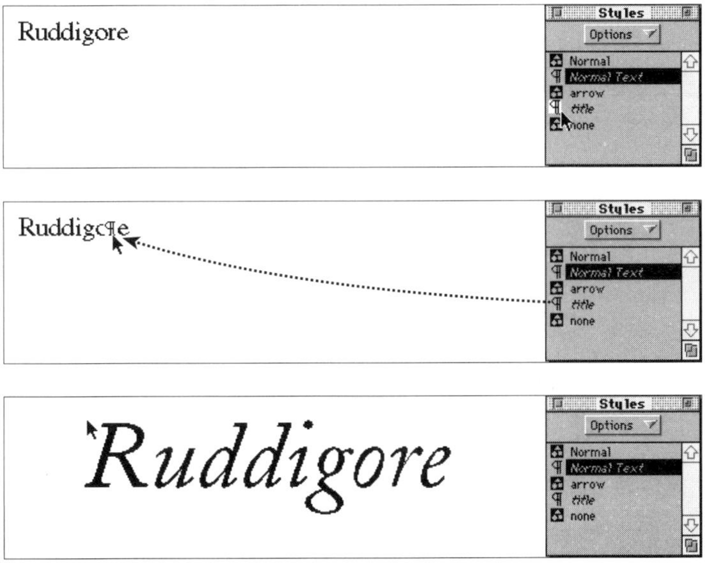

If you're using the drag-and-drop technique, the extent of the text you're applying the style to depends on settings in the Text Editing dialog box. If you've turned on the Drag and Drop a Paragraph Style to Change a Single Paragraph option, only the paragraph directly under the icon when you release the mouse button is affected. If you've turned on the Drag and Drop a Paragraph Style to Change the Entire Text Container (I've got to talk the FreeHand engineers into shorter titles for their controls), on the other hand, the style affects the text block you dropped it on (and the beginnings or ends of any paragraphs beginning or ending inside the text block).

Editing Styles

After you've created a style, you can edit the style's formatting and behavior—its *definition*. To edit a style by example, follow these steps (see Figure 3-89).

1. Select a paragraph tagged with the style, then format it the way you want.

2. Choose "Redefine" from the popup menu at the top of the Styles palette. FreeHand displays the Redefine Style dialog box. Select the style you want to redefine from the list—usually, the style you want to redefine (the one you selected and edited) is selected. Press Return.

3. FreeHand updates the style based on the paragraph attributes you've selected, changing any other paragraphs tagged with the style as it does so.

If you'd rather change a style by entering specifications, follow these steps (see Figure 3-90).

1. Hold down Option and click the style name you want to edit in the Styles palette. FreeHand displays the Edit Style dialog box.

2. Make changes to the controls in the Edit Style dialog box. When you're done, press Return to close the dialog box and apply your changes to the style. FreeHand updates all the paragraphs tagged with the style.

TEXT AND TYPE 317

FIGURE 3-89
Editing a style

This paragraph is tagged with the style "title."

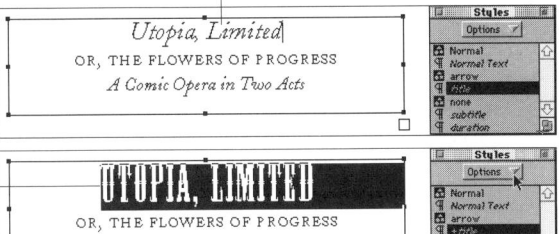

Format the paragraph using local formatting (in this example, I've changed the font, type style, range kerning, and size).

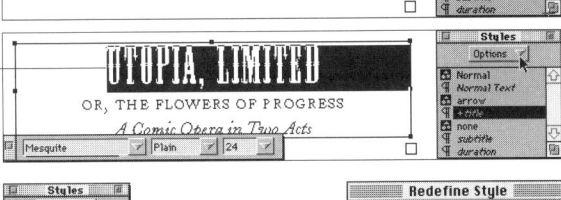

Choose Redefine from the Style palette's Options menu.

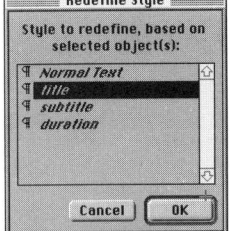

FreeHand displays the Redefine Style dialog box. Most of the time, the selected style is the one you want to redefine, so you can simply press Return.

FreeHand changes the formatting of all of the paragraphs tagged with the redefined style.

FIGURE 3-90
Editing a style using the Edit Styles method

Select the style you want to edit and choose Edit Style from the Styles palette's Options menu (or hold down Option and click the style name in the Styles palette).

FreeHand displays the Edit Style dialog box. Make any formatting changes you want (if you can—not all formatting attributes are supported by the Edit Style dialog box), then click the OK button.

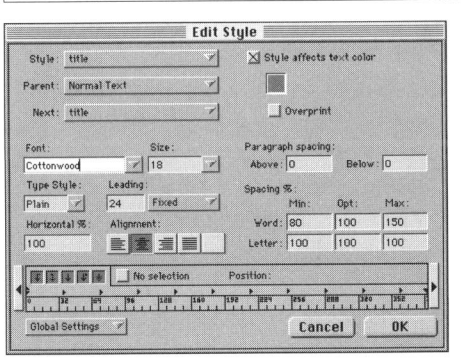

FreeHand changes all of the paragraphs tagged with the style you edited.

Tip:
Creating a Text Style Mask

Hang on, this one's pretty twisted. I haven't yet thought of a use for the FreeHand behavior I'm about to describe, so I can't give you an example of why you'd want to take advantage of it. I do believe, however, that you *might* someday be in a position to use it. So make a mental note of it and file it away. It strikes me that this is the kind of thing that could save your neck in a last-minute production crunch. You never know what'll turn up. If you've turned on the Build Paragraph Styles Based on Shared Attributes option in the Text Editing Options dialog box (see "Text Editing Preferences" in Chapter 1, "FreeHand Basics"), FreeHand looks at all the paragraphs in a selection as it builds a style definition. If, during this process, FreeHand encounters a difference between the selected paragraphs' formatting, it won't set the corresponding attribute in the style's definition.

Okay, that's a little obscure. Let's say you've selected two paragraphs, and that the only difference between those paragraphs is the size of the type. Choose "New" from the popup menu in the Styles palette, and FreeHand creates a style that, when applied, won't affect the size of the type in the paragraphs you're applying it to. If you look at the style's definition in the Edit Style dialog box, you'll see that the Size field is blank.

Is this a bug? I don't think so—in fact, I think it lets you do some useful things. Think about it—you can create styles that apply only a font and a color, or only spacing settings. I call these "partial styles," or "style masks," because they don't cover all the features of a normal text style. As it turns out, there's an easy way to create styles that affect only a few of a paragraph's formatting attributes (see Figure 3-91).

1. Create a style with formatting attributes you'll never use. I mean it—make it 71.05 point Zapf Chancery bold, with a paragraph space before of minus 24 points and a color of "Aromatic Puce." Go all out—set up the paragraph so that *every attribute* is set to something so repellent that you'd rather die than be caught using it in a publication. Name this style "pariah" (or whatever you like), and save it in your FreeHand defaults template (see "Setting Defaults" in Chapter 1, "FreeHand Basics").

FIGURE 3-91
Creating a style mask

Create a style with attributes so hideous or unlikely that you know you'll never use them.

What makes this style a pariah?

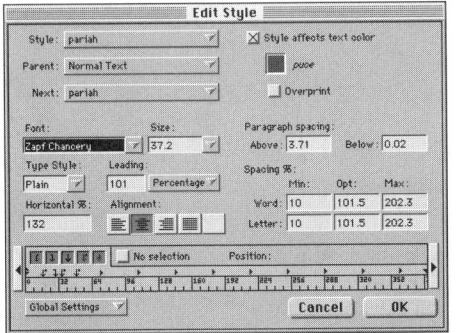

Lots of things.

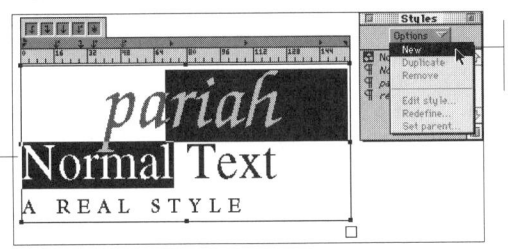

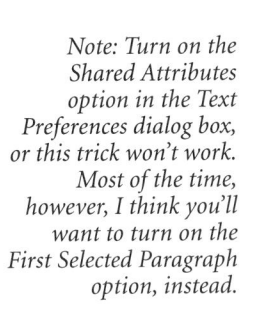

Choose New from the Styles palette's Options menu.

Select two paragraphs: one tagged with the "pariah" style, one tagged with FreeHand's default style "Normal."

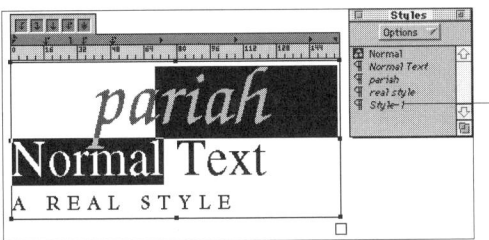

FreeHand creates a new style based on the shared attributes of the two styles.

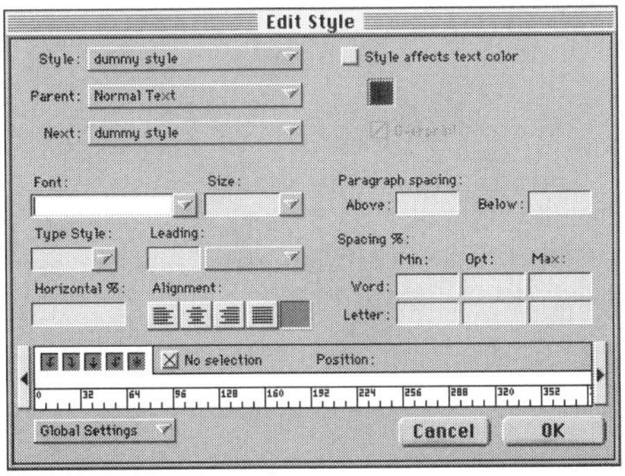

Note: Turn on the Shared Attributes option in the Text Preferences dialog box, or this trick won't work. Most of the time, however, I think you'll want to turn on the First Selected Paragraph option, instead.

Which is to say: nothing.

At this point, you've created a style mask. When you want to apply some set of attributes without applying local formatting, make changes to this style's definition and apply this style to the paragraphs you want to format. It's crazy, but it might save you time when you're desperate.

2. When you want to create a style mask, create two paragraphs. Tag one paragraph with the default "Normal" style. Tag the other paragraph with the style you created in Step 1.

3. Select both paragraphs and choose "New" from the popup menu in the Styles palette. FreeHand creates a style that has—are you ready for this?—no attributes set, because none of the attributes in the two paragraphs match.

4. Hold down Option and click the style name of your new, worthless style in the Styles palette. FreeHand displays the Edit Style dialog box. Every attribute you see in the Edit Style dialog box should be blank.

5. Set the attributes you want the style to apply (and set only those attributes). Press Return to close the Edit Style dialog box.

At this point, you've got a style that applies some, but not all, attributes when you tag a paragraph with it. Why use this style instead of local formatting? First, it applies to an entire paragraph (which may or may not be what you want). Second, you can apply more than one attribute at once (if all you're doing is applying a single attribute, you might be better off using local formatting).

Here's another approach. Suppose you want a style that's identical to another style, but leaves one or two attributes undefined. That is, you want a new style that applies all the formatting of an existing style except, for example, leading. The following steps show you the quickest way I've found to do this.

1. Deselect everything (press Command-Tab) and, in the Styles palette, select the name of the style you want to base your new style on.

2. Choose "Duplicate" from the popup menu in the Styles palette. FreeHand creates a copy of the selected style.

3. Hold down Option and click the new style in the Styles palette. FreeHand displays the Edit Style dialog box.

4. Change the attributes you want to leave undefined in the partial style you're creating.

5. Create two paragraphs. Apply the first (base) style to one paragraph, and apply the second (copied) style to the other. Select both paragraphs.

6. Choose "New" from the Styles palette's popup menu. FreeHand creates a new style, leaving the attributes the two paragraphs share undefined. Now you can delete the style you created in Step 2.

At this point, you've got a style that's identical to the first style (the one you selected in Step 1), but has a "hole" or two in it. You can apply this style to paragraphs in your publication, knowing that doing so won't disturb the existing formatting corresponding to the attributes you changed in Step 4.

Automatic Copyfitting

When you've got to make your text fit into a particular space, there are several things you can do. I've arranged your options, from best to worst (in my opinion), in the following list.

- Edit the text.

- Range kern the text.

- Reduce or increase the size, leading, and inter-paragraph spacing of the text.

- Use FreeHand's automatic copyfitting features (essentially an automated method of performing the previous step).

What if you can't edit the text, and there's too much text to range-kern into the space you have available? At that point, you're stuck, and the only thing you can do is to add or remove space and/or increase or decrease type size until your copy fits in your publication. The best way to do this is to try different combinations of type size, leading, and interparagraph spacing. The disadvantage is that this "hit and miss" method takes time—and sometimes time is that last thing you have. Sometimes, FreeHand's automatic copyfitting might be just what you need.

To use FreeHand's automatic copyfitting, follow these steps (see Figure 3-92)

1. Select a text block.

2. Press Command-Option-C to display the Copyfit Inspector.

3. Check the Modify Leading checkbox if you want FreeHand to change the leading as it tries to fit your text.

4. In the Ignore Columns Less Than N% field, enter a number. Entering "0" tells FreeHand to fit all the columns in the story equally, which is probably what you want. If not, experiment with values until you get what you want (sorry, you're on your own with this one).

5. Enter minimum and maximum percentages in the Max and Min fields. The value you enter in the Min field specifies how small you'll let FreeHand make the type (as a percentage of the type's current size); Max specifies how large FreeHand can make the type to fit it in the text block.

6. Press Return to apply your changes.

FreeHand changes the type size and leading of the lines in the selected story so that the text vertically fills all the text blocks in the story.

A few things about copyfitting:

♦ When you select a text block for copyfitting, FreeHand applies copyfitting changes to any text blocks linked to that text block. That is, copyfitting applies to entire stories, not just to individual text blocks.

♦ When you check Modify Leading in the Copyfit Inspector, you're telling FreeHand that it can decrease or increase the leading in the selected story. When FreeHand changes the leading in a story, it changes all the leading by the same percentage.

♦ The Min and Max fields in the Copyfit Inspector set the minimum and maximum percent change in type size

TEXT AND TYPE 323

FIGURE 3-92
Automatic copyfitting

There's too much text in this story to fit in this text block. For whatever reason, the text has to fit in the text block, and we can't edit it. What can we do?

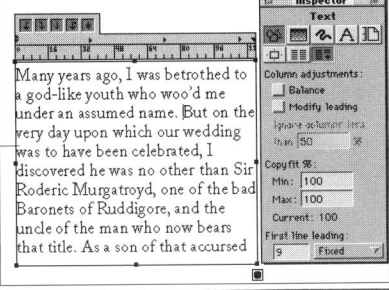

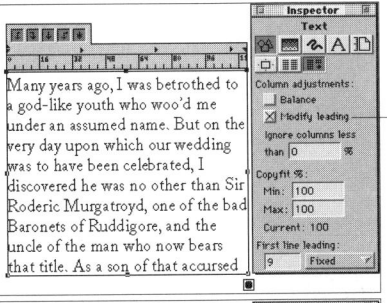

Check the Modify Leading checkbox to tell FreeHand to try to fit the text by changing the leading. In this case, FreeHand changes the leading, but still can't make all of the text fit. In my experience, "Modify Leading" works best when you're trying to fill a text block.

Direct FreeHand to make the text fit by changing its size using the Min and Max fields. In this example, I told FreeHand it could make the text as small as 80% of its original size.

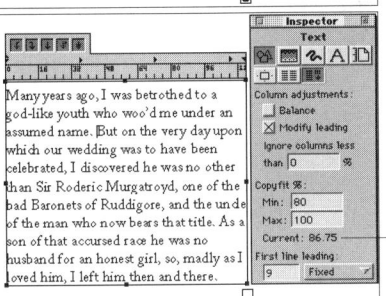

FreeHand reduces the size of the text in the story to make it fit in the text block.

This (non-editable) field displays the current text reduction (or enlargement).

FreeHand can use to try to fit the story in the space you have available. Like Modify Leading, this control changes all the type in your text block by a fixed amount. To leave the size of your text alone, enter "100%" in both fields.

♦ The Current percentage (displayed below the Max field) shows you the current scaling of the text in the story, if any. What's the use of this? If FreeHand's been unable to copyfit a story, it's probably because the percentage you entered in the Min field is too large. If you see that the Current percentage is the same as the minimum or maximum percentage, and the text still doesn't fit in the space available, you know that you have to lower the percentage in the Min field or increase the percentage in the Max field.

Joining Text to a Path

One of FreeHand's signature features is the ability to place text along paths of any shape or length. To join text to a path, select some text, press Shift and select a path, and then press Command-Shift-Y (or choose Bind to Path from the Type menu). FreeHand joins your text to the path (see Figure 3-93).

Once you've joined text to a path, you select the text and the path as you'd select any other text—select the Text tool and drag it through the characters you want to select, double-click to select a word, or triple-click to select all the text on the path. Selecting the path itself can be a little more difficult, but switching to Keyline view can make it easier to see and select the path.

If you want to unjoin, or split, the text from the path, select the path and choose Remove From Path from the Type menu. The text and the path become separate objects again.

FIGURE 3-93
Joining text to a path

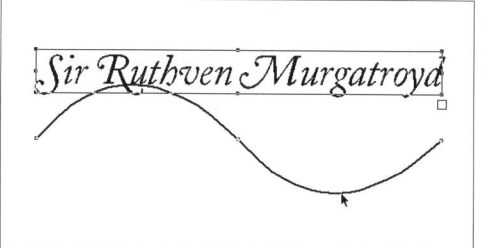

Select some text, select a path, and press Command-Shift-Y...

...and FreeHand binds the text to the path.

To edit text that's been bound to a path, drag the text tool through it, just as you'd do to select any other text on your page (FreeHand 3 users note—no more trips to the Text dialog box).

Joining text to a path is a great—if somewhat overused—feature. It's often confusing, though. People have a hard time understanding why the text they've just joined to a path falls where it does on the path. There are a few simple rules to keep in mind when you're joining text to a path.

- Text joins the path according to the alignment of the text block; left-aligned text starts at the first point in the path, right-aligned text starts at the last point on the path, centered text is centered between the first and last points, and force-justified text is spread out over the whole length of the path.

- If the path is shorter than the first line of text, the excess text gets shoved off the end of the path.

- The first line (that is, text in a text block up to the first carriage return) of text in the text block you join to the path gets joined to the top of the path; the second line of text gets joined to the bottom of the path.

- Justified text will bunch up when joined to a path that's shorter than the text.

If you're confused, I understand. Take a look at Figure 3-94 (on the next page).

In the Object Inspector, you can set the way that the text you've joined to a path follows that path. The Top and Bottom popup menus in the Object Inspector control the way that the baseline of your text aligns to the path (see Figure 3-95), and the Orientation popup menu controls the way that your text follows the path (see Figure 3-96).

The system (the Top and Bottom popup menus) takes some getting used to—particularly if you're a FreeHand 3 user. The weirdest thing is that if you choose None from both the Top and the Bottom popup menus, FreeHand doesn't display any text on the path at all. If the text you've bound to the path is linked to any other text, FreeHand flows the text into the next text block in the story. This is all perfectly logical, but it still took me months to understand it.

FIGURE 3-94
Joining text and text alignment

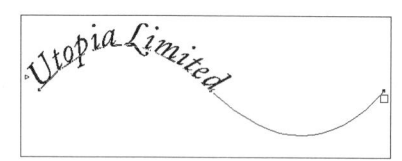

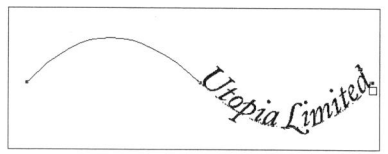

Align left

Align right

First point in the path

Note: You can always adjust the position of type on a path by dragging the position triangle—the little triangle that appears at the text's alignment point (at the left edge of the text for left-aligned text, at the center for centered text, etc.). As you drag the triangle, FreeHand changes the position of text on the path.

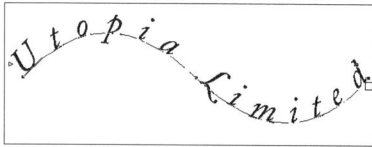

Align center

Justify

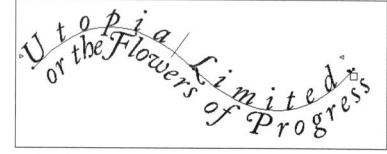

FreeHand composes as much text on a path as it can (according to the settings in the Spacing Inspector), then stores the rest as overset text.

The first paragraph of text in a text block joins to the top of the path; the second paragraph of text joins to the bottom of the path. If you join more than two paragraphs of text to a path, the other paragraphs are stored as overset text.

FIGURE 3-95
Baseline alignment options for text on a path

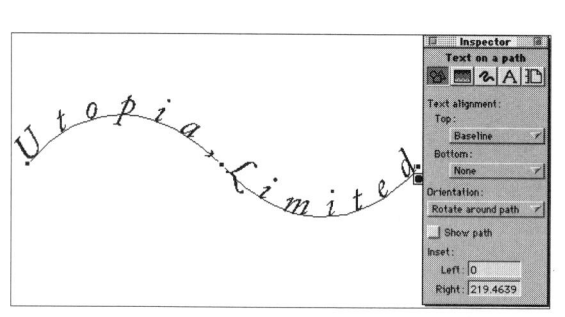

Choose "Baseline" to align the baseline of the text with the path.

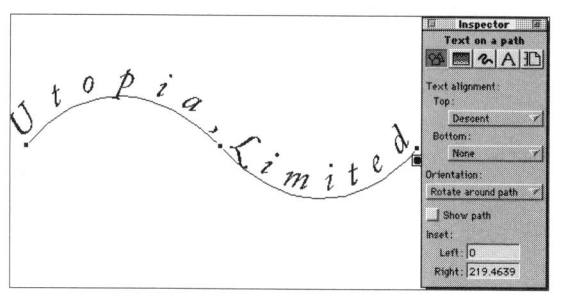

To align the bottoms of the characters to the path, choose "Descent."

TEXT AND TYPE 327

FIGURE 3-95
Baseline alignment
options for text
on a path
(continued)

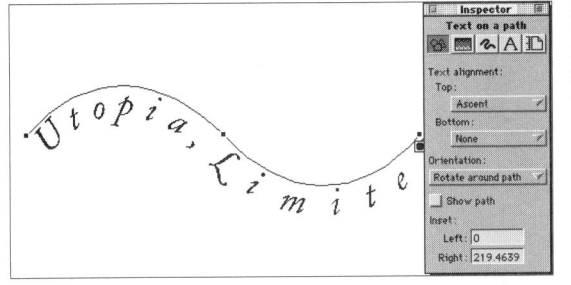

To align the tops of the characters to the path, choose "Ascent."

FIGURE 3-96
Controlling the
orientation of text
on a path

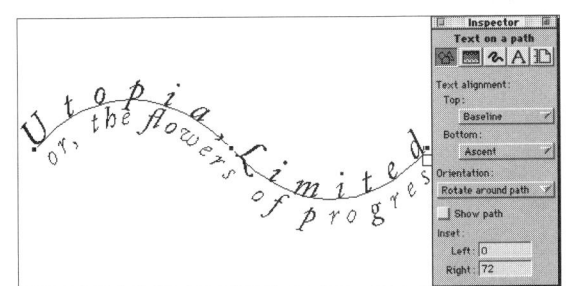

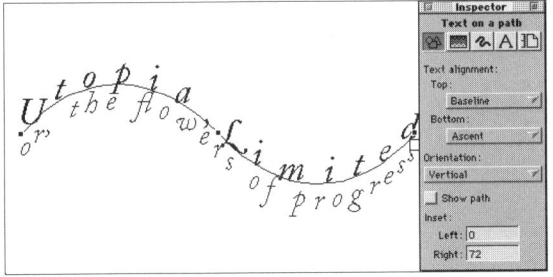

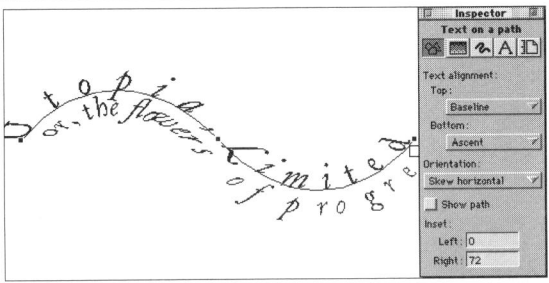

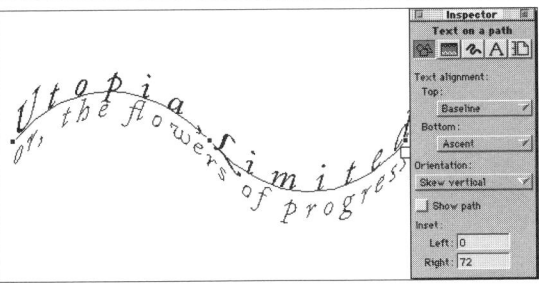

Beyond these options, the Show Path option makes the path a visible and printing path. You can alter the stroke and color of the path as you would any other path.

Tip: Autoskewing Text

The Skewing tool (see "Skewing" in Chapter 5, "Transforming") is lots of fun, but this trick is even more fun. When you need to make some text appear as if it's on a plane that's rotated away from the plane of the page, follow these steps (see Figure 3-97).

1. Draw a path using the Line tool.
2. Type some text.
3. Select the text and the path.
4. Press Command-Shift-Y to join the text to the path.

FIGURE 3-97
Autoskewing text

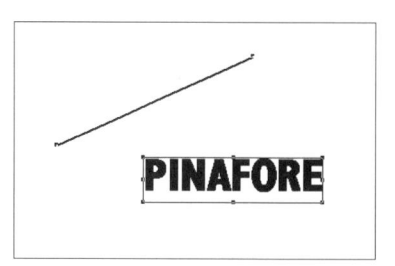

Select the text and the line.

Press Command-Shift-Y to join the text to the line. Press Command-Option-I to display the Object Inspector.

Choose Skew Vertical from the Orientation popup menu and press Return.

Why you (might) want to do stuff like this

5. Press Command-Option-I to display the Object Inspector.

6. Choose Ascent from the Top popup menu, and choose Skew Vertical from the Orientation popup menu. Press Return to apply your changes.

7. Now you can skew the text by dragging either end of the path anywhere you want.

Flowing Text Inside Paths

When you need a text block that's not rectangular, you can flow text inside a closed path of any shape. To flow text inside a path, follow these steps (see Figure 3-98).

1. Select the text block containing the text you want to flow inside the path.

2. Shift-select the path you want to flow the text inside (this only works with closed paths).

3. Select Flow Inside Path from the Type menu (or press Command-U). FreeHand flows the text in the text block inside the path.

FIGURE 3-98
Flowing text inside a path

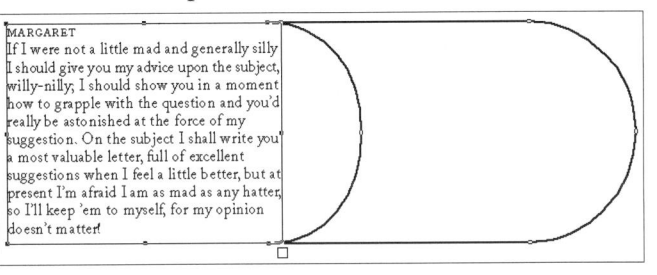

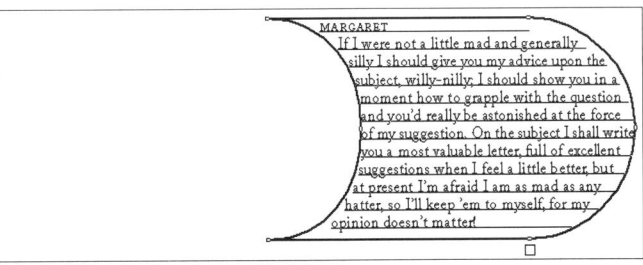

If you flow a multicolumn text block inside a path, FreeHand converts it to a single column.

When you flow text inside a path, you won't be able to scale the text, or change its leading, kerning, or word spacing, by dragging the corner handles of the text block. In fact, you won't see the selection handles of the text block at all—only those of the path. When you drag the corner handles of the path, FreeHand reflows the text inside the path as if you'd dragged a corner handle (that is, line breaks change, but the type formatting remains the same).

To remove text from the inside of a path, choose Remove From Path from the Type menu. FreeHand separates the path and the text block, and places them on your page as individual objects.

Tip:
The Quick Way to Flow Text Inside a Path

If you want to flow text inside a path, and you haven't already created the text block, here's a quick way to get text inside a path. Select the path, press Command-Shift-U (or choose Flow Inside Path from the Type menu), and start typing text (see Figure 3-99). FreeHand flows the text you type inside the path.

FIGURE 3-99
Typing text into a path

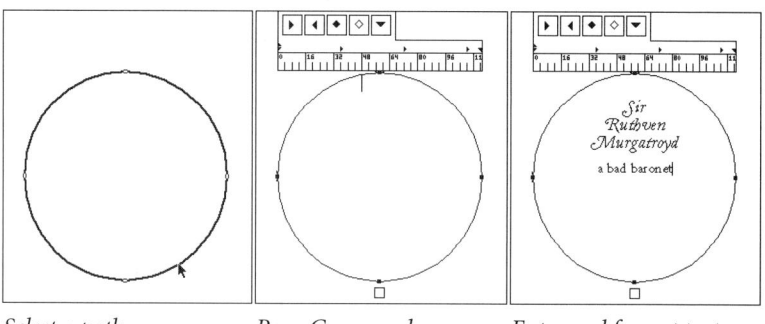

Select a path.

Press Command-Option-U. FreeHand positions a cursor inside the path.

Enter and format text as you would in any text block.

Wrapping Text around Objects

Wrapping text around an object is something like the opposite of flowing text inside a path. In the former, you want text to stay inside a path; in the latter, you want to keep text out of—or away from—an object. To wrap text around an object, follow these steps (see Figure 3-100).

TEXT AND TYPE

FIGURE 3-100
Wrapping text around an object

Select the object you want to wrap text around and bring it to the front (in this example, I've selected the circle). Press Command-Shift-W...

...and FreeHand displays the Text Wrap dialog box.

Enter the standoff distances you want for your text wrap and press Return.

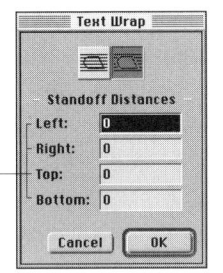

FreeHand wraps text around the object.

1. Place a basic shape or path on top of a text block that contains a few paragraphs of text. If the text block's in front of the object, the text won't wrap around the object.

2. Select both the text block and the path.

3. Press Command-Shift-W (or choose Text Wrap from the Arrange menu). FreeHand displays the Text wrap dialog box.

4. Click the wrap icon (the one on the right) and press Return (or click the OK button) to close the dialog box. FreeHand wraps the text in the text block around the object.

You can apply a text wrap to any single object in FreeHand, including other text blocks. If you want to apply a text wrap to all the objects in a group, subselect (hold down Option to subselect objects inside groups) the objects in the group and apply a text wrap to them.

Converting Characters into Paths

When you work in graphic design, you frequently need to alter characters of type for logos or packaging designs. For years, we dreamed about the ability to turn type into paths we could edit. Finally, applications such as FreeHand and Illustrator added the feature.

You can convert characters from just about any font (TrueType, PostScript Type 1 and Fontographer PostScript Type 3 fonts) for which you have the printer (outline) font into freeform paths.

Once you've converted the characters into paths, you lose all text editing capabilities, but you gain the ability to paste things inside the character outline, to apply lines and fills that you can't apply to normal text (including tiled, graduated, radial, or PostScript fills), and to change the shape of the characters themselves.

To convert characters into paths, select the text block or text blocks you want to convert, and then choose Convert to Paths from the Type menu. FreeHand converts the characters into paths (see Figure 3-101).

When you first convert characters into paths, all the converted characters are grouped together. To work with an individual character, choose Split Element from the Element menu. If FreeHand runs out of memory while converting the characters to paths, try

FIGURE 3-101
Converting text to paths

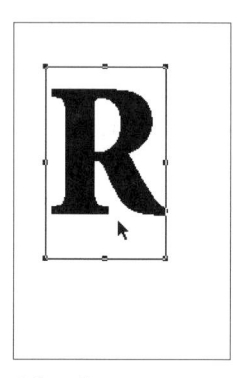

Select the text you want to convert to paths.

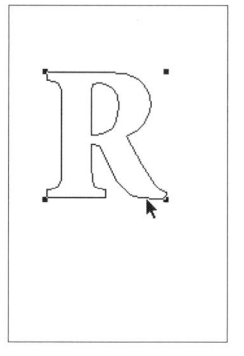

Press Command-Shift-P (or Choose Convert to Paths from the Type menu). FreeHand converts the characters to paths...

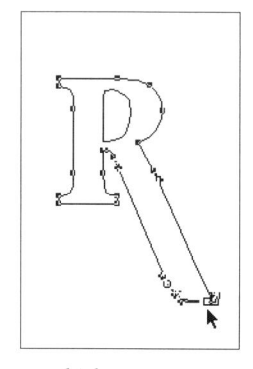

...which you can edit as you would any other path.

selecting fewer characters and trying again (or increase the amount of RAM available to FreeHand; see "Increasing Free-Hand's RAM Allocation" in Chapter 1, "FreeHand Basics").

When you convert characters containing interior space (such as "P," or "O") into paths, FreeHand turns them into composite paths (see "Composite Paths" in Chapter 2, "Drawing"). This is handy. Not only are multiple-part characters (such as i, é, and ü) treated as single paths, but characters with interior paths (such as O, P, A, and D) are transparent where they should be, and fill properly (see Figure 3-102).

You can always make the characters into normal (that is, not composite) paths, if you want, by selecting the character and choosing Split Element from the Element menu.

FIGURE 3-102
Text converted into composite paths

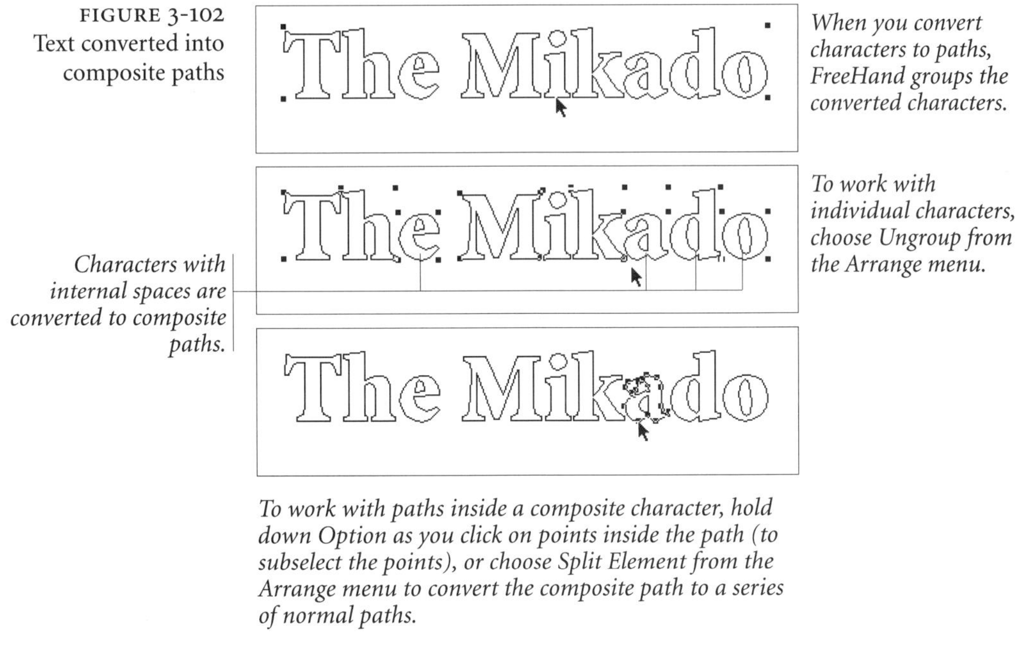

When you convert characters to paths, FreeHand groups the converted characters.

To work with individual characters, choose Ungroup from the Arrange menu.

Characters with internal spaces are converted to composite paths.

To work with paths inside a composite character, hold down Option as you click on points inside the path (to subselect the points), or choose Split Element from the Arrange menu to convert the composite path to a series of normal paths.

Tip:
If Your Characters Won't Convert

If you weren't able to convert the text into paths, make sure that you have the outline (printer) fonts and that they're somewhere FreeHand can find them (See Appendix A, "System"). If you don't have the outline fonts, FreeHand won't be able to convert your text into paths.

**Tip:
Don't Worry
About Down-
loadable Fonts**

If you've exported FreeHand files containing lots of downloadable fonts as EPS, then imported them into other page-layout applications, you've probably had trouble getting the EPS to print with the proper fonts. For whatever reason, EPS graphics and downloadable fonts don't mix very well.

So why bother with fonts at all? Instead, you can convert all your text to paths (though this might not work for zoom text and other text effects) before you export your publication as an EPS (clearly, this isn't going to work if your publication contains lots of text). This way, the application that's printing your EPS doesn't have to worry about getting the downloadable fonts right. Your EPSes will print faster, too.

**Tip:
Justifying
Character
Outlines**

Here's something that happens to me all the time: I convert a force-justified line of characters into paths, and then I find that I need to make them fill a different horizontal distance. Instead of creating a new text block, formatting and force-justifying it, and then converting the characters to paths again, you can follow these steps (see Figure 3-103).

1. Drag the first character of the line to the left edge of the space you want to spread the text across.

2. Drag the last character of the line to the right edge of the of the space you want to fill.

3. Select all the characters in the line.

4. Press Command-Shift-A to display the Alignment palette, if it's not already visible.

5. Choose Distribute Widths from the Horizontal popup menu in the Alignment palette.

FreeHand distributes the characters you selected across the width defined by the first and last character in the line. If the text contains more than one word, you'll have to adjust the word spacing manually, and then use the Alignment palette again to distribute the characters in each word—but it's still quicker than the alternative methods.

TEXT AND TYPE | 335

FIGURE 3-103
Justifying character outlines

You've converted some characters to paths, and, later, realize you want them to fill a wider (or narrower) column. What can you do?

Select the converted characters.

Ungroup the paths.

Drag one character to the width you want to fill.

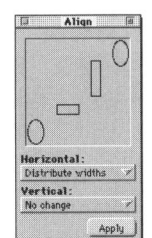

Select all the characters and press Command-Shift-A to display the Alignment palette (if it's not already visible).

Choose Distribute Widths from the Horizontal popup menu and click Apply to distribute the characters.

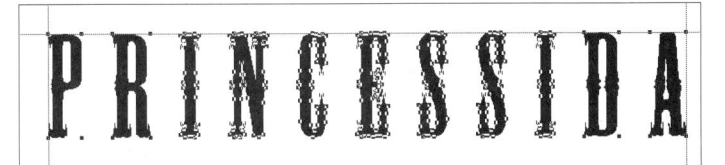

FreeHand spreads the characters to fill the line.

If there are spaces in the text, you'll have to adjust the positions of the characters, then redistribute the characters inside each word.

Tip:
Making Type Glow

When you want to add a glowing outline to your type, follow these steps (see Figure 3-104).

1. Convert the text to paths.

2. Press Command-= to clone the paths.

3. Apply a stroke to that cloned paths. This stroke width should be two times the width of the glow you want to create, and should be the color you want for the outside of the glow effect.

4. Press Command-B to send the cloned paths behind the original paths.

5. Apply a stroke to the original paths. This stroke should be the color you want for the inside of the glow effect.

FIGURE 3-104
Creating glowing type

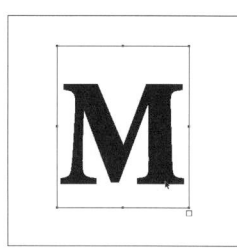

Select the text.

Convert the text to paths.

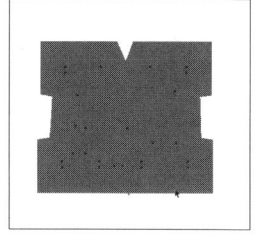

Ungroup the converted paths, clone them, and then apply a thick, colored stroke to the cloned paths.

Printed example

Send the cloned paths to the back. Apply a thin stroke to the original characters.

Select corresponding points on the original characters and clones (sometimes, it'll be hard to see what's selected)...

...and press Command-Shift-E to blend the paths.

6. Character by character, blend the original paths with their corresponding background paths. For characters with internal spaces (such as "O"), you'll have to split the paths and then blend the interior spaces separately.

Inline Graphics

One of my favorite new features in FreeHand 5.5 is the ability to paste a FreeHand object—any kind of FreeHand object—inside a text block. Once there, the object behaves (more or less) like a character of text. I call these embedded objects "inline graphics."

What's so great about inline graphics? They come in handy when you want to keep a corporate logo next to the corporation's address, regardless of where that address flows as the text before the address expands or contracts during editing. Or you want to put a box around a paragraph and have the box travel with the paragraph. Inline graphics also give you a way around some of the limitations of FreeHand's paragraph rules.

Creating an inline graphic

Creating an inline graphic is simple. Cut or copy the object you want to convert to an inline graphic to the Clipboard, then click the Text tool inside a text block and paste. FreeHand pastes the object from the Clipboard into the text block (see Figure 3-105).

FIGURE 3-105
Creating an inline graphic

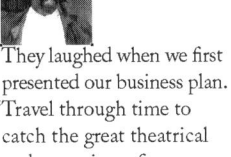

Select the object you want to paste into a text block and cut or copy it to the Clipboard.

Click the text tool in a text block.

Paste the object into the text block. You've just created an inline graphic.

Working with Inline Graphics

Inline graphics can take some getting used to. For starters, here are a few things you should keep in mind as you're working with inline graphics.

- When you paste an object into a text block, that object behaves just as if it were a character of text. Inline graphics respond to changes in size, leading, kerning, and horizontal scaling.

- When you select multiple objects and paste them into a text block, FreeHand groups the objects together (that is, they don't become separate inline graphics).

- Inline graphics transform (skew, scale, rotate, and flip) when you transform the text block.

- Inline graphics appear as black dots in the Text Editor (see Figure 3-106).

FIGURE 3-106
Inline Graphics in the Text Editor

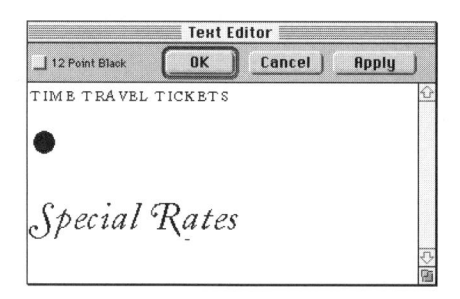

Removing inline graphics. To remove an inline graphic from a text block, select the graphic with the text tool and press Delete.

Extracting inline graphics. To turn an inline graphic back into an independent object, convert the text block containing the inline graphic to paths. You might want to copy the inline graphic to its own text block before you do this.

Adjusting the text wrap of inline graphics. When you create an inline graphic, FreeHand applies a default text wrap to the graphic. You can't turn the text wrap of an inline graphic off (you can, however, set the text wrap so that text overlaps the inline graphic). To edit the text wrap, follow these steps (see Figure 3-107).

FIGURE 3-107
Adjusting the Text Wrap of Inline Graphics

When you paste an object into a text block as an inline graphic, FreeHand assigns a leading value that puts the bottom of the graphic on the baseline of the text.

This inline graphic is in a paragraph by itself.

In this example, I'll show you how to drop the inline graphic behind this text—once that's done, we'll have a background image that follows the text it surrounds.

Assign a fixed leading value to the inline graphic.

Set a baseline shift for the graphic. In this case, I've chosen a baseline shift equal to the height of the graphic.

When you adjust the leading and baseline shift amount, the selection sometimes looks strange (in this case, it doesn't even look like the inline graphic is still selected). Don't worry about it.

How did I know the height of the graphic? It's right here in the Type Specifications palette.

Select the inline graphic with the Text tool and click the Edit button at the bottom of the Character Inspector.

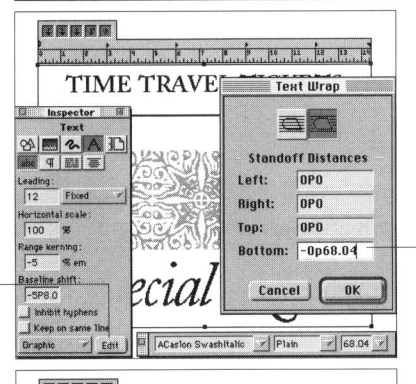

FreeHand displays the Text Wrap dialog box. Enter a negative value in the Bottom field (in this example, I've entered the height of the graphic).

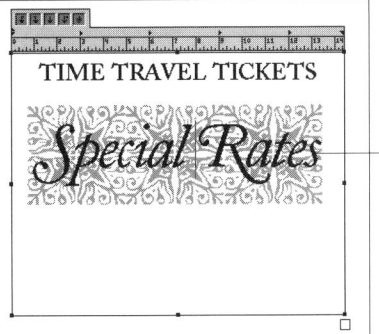

FreeHand positions the inline graphic behind the text.

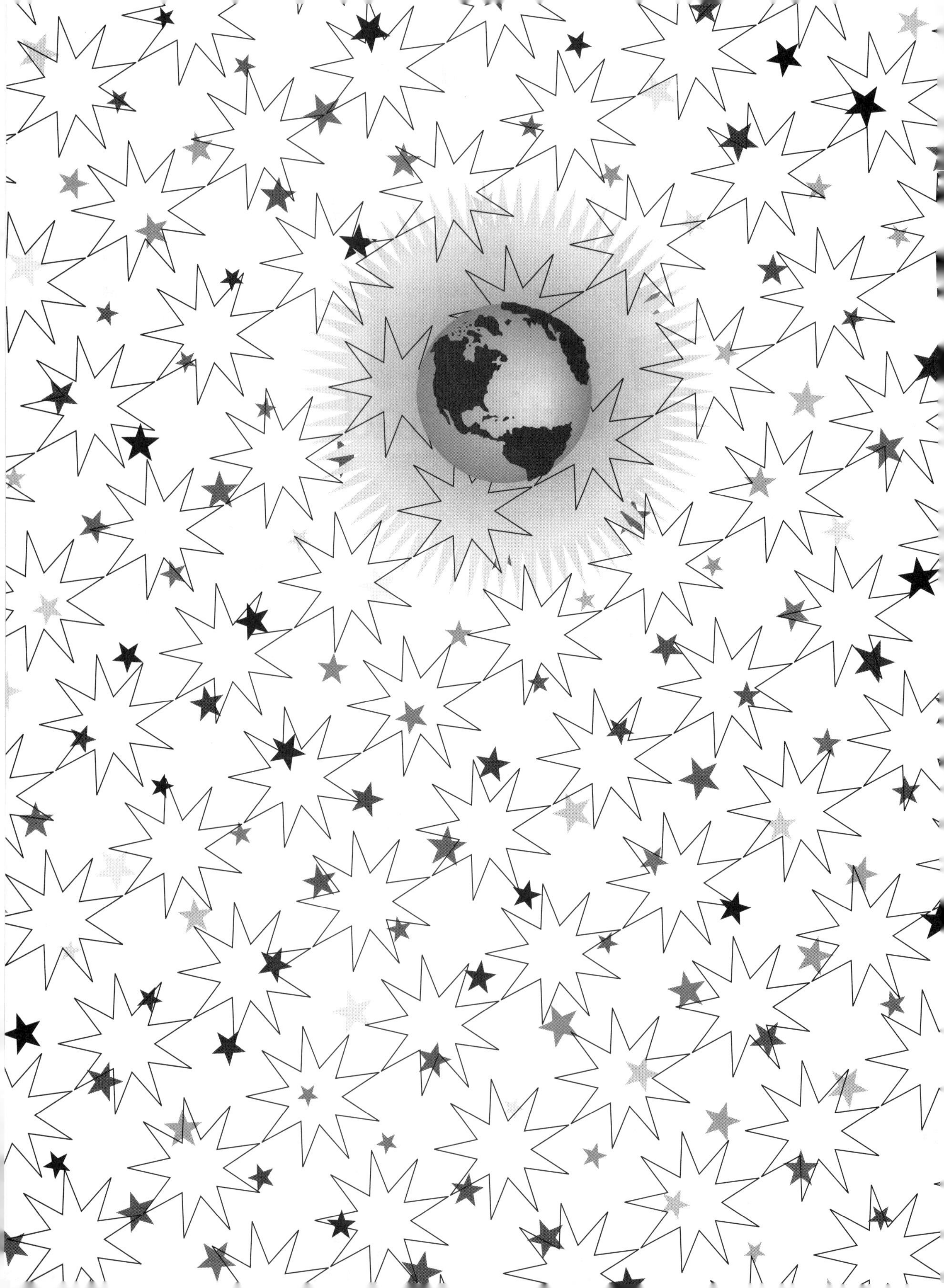

CHAPTER FOUR ❧ IMPORTING AND EXPORTING

Someday
you'll need something FreeHand's drawing and typesetting abilities can't give you. You'll need to edit color TIFFs, or to do 3-D rotation and rendering. Other applications do these things better than FreeHand does. But once you've done the work you need to do using some other application, you can bring the files you create into your FreeHand publication. And you can export your FreeHand publications in forms that can be used in other page-layout and drawing programs.

There's a big difference between opening a file and importing, or "placing," a file. When you open a file, FreeHand converts the file's contents into objects that behave like FreeHand's own paths, text, and imported graphics. When you import, or "place" a file, you won't be able to edit the contents of the file, though you will be able to move, scale, rotate, reflect, and skew it.

FreeHand can open EPS files saved in most Adobe Illustrator formats (FreeHand now supports Illustrator 1.1, Illustrator 88, Illustrator 3.0, Illustrator 5.0, and Illustrator 5.5 formats), from other PostScript drawing programs, and you can import place (as opposed to import) any EPS file.

If you've turned on the Convert Editable EPS When Placed option in the Importing/Exporting Preferences dialog box, FreeHand converts some EPSes to editable FreeHand objects when you place them (see "Importing/Exporting Preferences" in Chapter 1, "FreeHand Basics").

You can use word processors and page-layout programs to enter and format text and then place the formatted text in FreeHand as RTF (Rich Text Format—a Microsoft text-only format capable of describing anything, including text formatting and graphics, in a Microsoft Word document). You can import text-only (ASCII) files from text editors and databases. You can scan an image in either color or grayscale, edit it with an image-editing program, then place it in FreeHand, and use it as part of your FreeHand publication—including generating color separations when you print. You can also create graphics in other drawing programs, and open or place them into FreeHand.

FreeHand 5.5 also reads Adobe Acrobat PDF files—which means you can take a PDF created by almost any application, open it in FreeHand, and edit it. As you'll see, this makes PDF a great format for getting pages out of other page layout programs (such as PageMaker or XPress) and into FreeHand.

FreeHand's no slouch at exporting graphics for use in other applications—FreeHand's exported EPS formats can be imported into every major page-layout or illustration program and combined with text and graphics created in those programs. For FreeHand 3 users, there's a special treat—you can create EPS files you can open in FreeHand—no more keeping two versions of the same file on your tired hard disk. And, if exporting as an EPS doesn't work, there are several ways to export object-PICT graphics (with attached PostScript, so you won't lose any details or PostScript effects) to applications that don't support EPS import.

Want to put your FreeHand publication online, or send it to a client for an approval? If you've got the Acrobat Distiller, it's easy to make a FreeHand PostScript file into a PDF.

Last, but not least, you can export text from a FreeHand publication as either RTF or text-only files.

Importing Anything

It doesn't matter what kind of file you're importing; it always works the same way (see Figure 4-1). If all you want to know is how to get a file into your publication, read the next procedure and skip

IMPORTING AND EXPORTING   345

FIGURE 4-1
Placing any file

Press Command-Shift-D (or choose Place from the File menu). FreeHand displays the Place Document dialog box.

Double-click a file name in the Place Document dialog box (or select a file name and press Return)...

...and FreeHand displays a loaded Place Gun.

Click the Place Gun on your page...

...and FreeHand places the file.

Alternatively, you can drag the Place Gun...

Hold down Shift as you drag to scale the object proportionally as you place it.

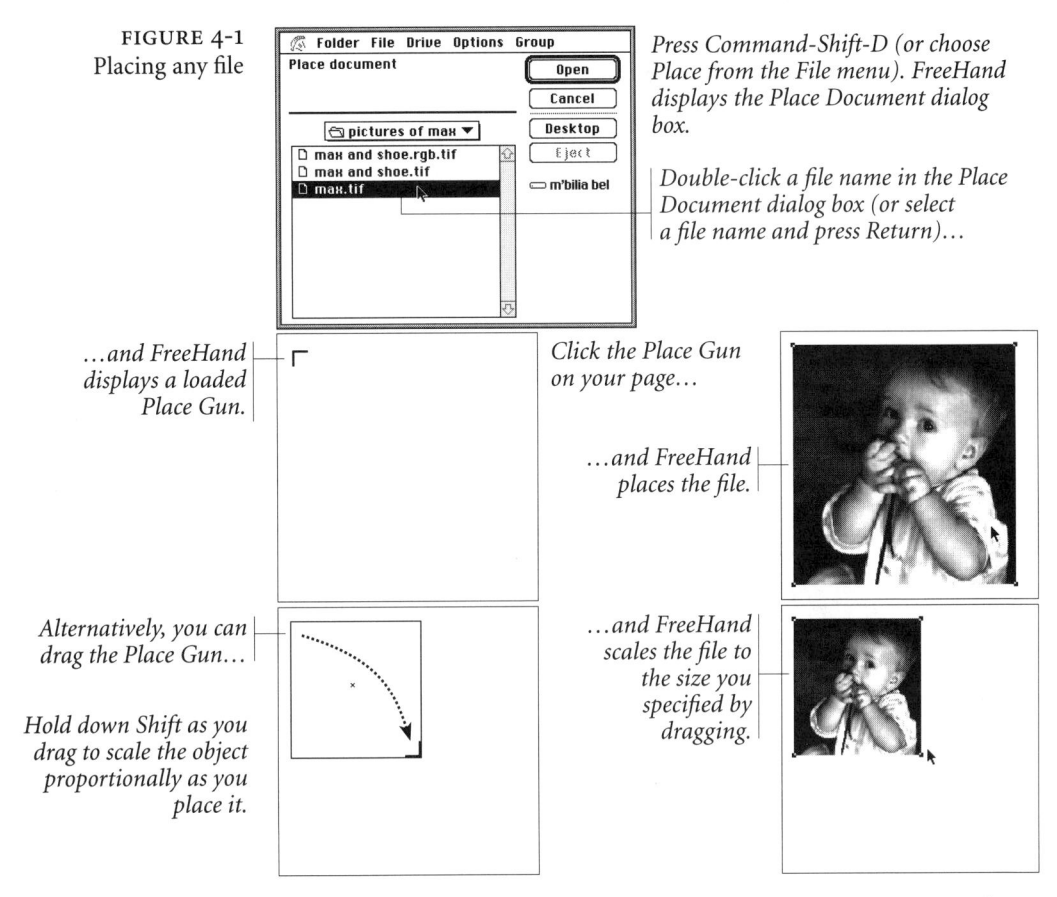

...and FreeHand scales the file to the size you specified by dragging.

the rest of the chapter. If you really want to know all the tricks to working with the different file types, read on!

1. Press Command-Shift-D (or choose Place from the File menu). FreeHand displays the Place Document dialog box.

2. Choose a file and click the OK button (or press Return). The cursor changes into an icon, which I call a Place Gun.

3. Click the Place Gun on your page (or on the pasteboard), and FreeHand imports the file you selected. Instead of clicking, you can drag the Place Gun to size the file (whether it's a graphic file or a text file) as you place it. Hold down Shift as you drag, and FreeHand sizes incoming graphics proportionally, or, if you're importing text, creates square text blocks.

About Graphic File Formats

FreeHand can import a wide range of graphic file formats, including Adobe Illustrator EPS formats, Adobe Streamline files, grayscale and color TIFFs, EPS files, paint-type images, and PICT type graphics. From FreeHand's point of view, there are certain limitations and advantages to each of these file formats.

Just to refresh everybody's memory, here are a few quick definitions, rules, and exceptions regarding graphic file formats.

First, each Macintosh file contains information on the type of file it is (the "file type") and what application was used to create it (the "creator"). Both the file type and creator are stored as distinct, four-letter codes. You can view or edit these using programs such as Apple's free ResEdit, PrairieSoft's DiskTop, or DeBabelizer. We don't have to worry too much about the creator, but the file type code makes an enormous amount of difference in how FreeHand deals with the file.

PNTG and TIFF

File types PNTG and TIFF are bitmap, or image, formats which store their pictures as matrices (rows and columns) of pixels, each pixel having a particular gray or color value (also known as a gray depth, color depth, or bit depth).

PNTG-type graphics are also called paint-type graphics (because they are in the format created by the venerable MacPaint). Each pixel in a paint-type graphic has a value of either one or zero, on or off, black or white. One-bit TIFFs, often called bilevel TIFFs, work the same way.

Pixels in grayscale TIFF images are typically stored as values between zero and 255, which means that each pixel in these images can be one of 256 possible color (or gray) values—that's an eight-bit, grayscale TIFF. Color images can use over 16 *million* possible different values per pixel—that's a 24-bit color TIFF.

PICT and EPS

File types PICT and EPS store their pictures as sets of instructions for drawing graphic objects. Because of this, they're often called "object-oriented," which you shouldn't confuse with the "object-oriented programming" you hear so much about these days. The drawing instructions say, "Start this line at this point and draw to that point over there"; or, "This is a polygon made up of these line segments." The instructions contain values for fills and colors: "This polygon is filled with a specific gray level."

The main difference between these two formats is that the instructions in PICT graphics are expressed in QuickDraw, which is the language your Macintosh uses to draw lines, images, and characters on its screen; while the instructions in EPS graphics are written in PostScript, the language your PostScript printer uses to make marks on paper. PostScript is a far richer language for describing graphic objects.

Because the EPS graphics aren't written in the Macintosh's display language, they often carry a TIFF (bitmapped) or PICT (bitmapped or object) rendition along as a screen preview of their contents. FreeHand saves its EPS previews as object PICTs, unless you've turned on the Bitmap PICT Previews option in the Importing/Exporting Preferences dialog box (see "Importing/Exporting Preferences" in Chapter 1, "FreeHand Basics"). Bitmap PICT previews are usually smaller than object PICT previews, and almost always redraw faster in other applications—but they give you a less accurate view of the contents of an EPS.

How does FreeHand create this image? Remember that FreeHand can convert its internal database into QuickDraw (what you see on the screen) or into PostScript (what FreeHand sends to your PostScript printer). Once the file's exported as an EPS, it's not in FreeHand anymore, so FreeHand can't convert it into QuickDraw commands for your screen display. When you choose to export an EPS as Macintosh EPS, FreeHand generates and attaches a QuickDraw (PICT) version of the graphic to the PostScript code.

Here are the exceptions to the above descriptions.

- Some PICT files contain only bitmaps (I call these "bitmap-only PICT" files to differentiate them from "object PICT" files, such as those created by MacDraw). Because of problems and limitations associated with image PICT files (FreeHand can't color-separate them, and has trouble printing them), FreeHand converts them to TIFF data as you import them and embeds the data in your publication file.

- Object-PICT files can contain bitmapped images. FreeHand converts the images stored inside object PICTs to TIFF on import, as noted above.

- EPS files can also contain bitmapped images.

FreeHand can open or import both image- and object-PICT files. When you import a PICT, FreeHand converts the file to a group of FreeHand objects you can position on your page. When you want to create a new file containing only the objects in the PICT file, use Open. Once the PICT files have been converted, you can work with them as you would any other FreeHand element.

FreeHand can also directly open a number of EPS file types. You can open all files saved in the Adobe Illustrator formats (any of them). If you can't open an Illustrator EPS file, it's probably because it's been saved in an Illustrator format newer than version 5.5. When this happens, you can open the file with Illustrator and save it in one of the Illustrator formats FreeHand can open. If you don't need to edit the contents of the file, you can always add it to your publication using Place (though there are great reasons not to do this, as shown in "XXX," later in this chapter).

When you open an EPS file (as opposed to placing it), the objects in the file are converted into FreeHand elements and can be edited as you'd edit any FreeHand element.

Most graphics applications can save their files in more than one file format, and almost every illustration or page-layout application can write at least one file format that FreeHand can read. If you're having trouble placing or opening a file, try opening it again in its original application (or another application that can read its original file type) and save it in a file type FreeHand can read.

FreeHand can import or open the following file types.

- Aldus FreeHand 2.0 through 4.0

- Macromedia FreeHand 5.0 (including 5.01 and 5.02)

- Adobe Illustrator 1.1, Adobe Illustrator 88, Adobe Illustrator 3.0, Adobe Illustrator 5.0, and Adobe Illustrator 5.5

- EPS (including DCS and DCS2)

- TIFF

- PICT and PICT2

- Text only, or ASCII text

- Rich Text Format (RTF)

- Adobe Acrobat Portable Document Format (PDF)

Some programs are real "Swiss Army knives," and can open and save files in lots of different formats. Photoshop, for example, can open and save files in a dozen different bitmap formats. If you're working in a studio that has to deal with files from MS-DOS systems and/or dedicated computer-graphics workstations, Photoshop is a great program to have around even if you use it for nothing more than file conversions.

In addition, FreeHand 5.5 can use Photoshop's plug-ins for acquiring a variety of different graphic formats (such as Compuserve GIF images). See Appendix A, "System."

There are several different file-conversion programs on the market that can make it easier to convert an unreadable image file into a file type that FreeHand can read, but the best by far is DeBabelizer. For more on DeBabelizer, see Appendix A, "System."

Tip:
There's Always Pasting...

If the application you're trying to get something out of isn't able to save in any format FreeHand can read, try copying elements out of it and pasting them into FreeHand. This will sometimes work when all else fails.

Importing Object PICTs

FreeHand imports PICT graphics created by charting programs (such as Adobe Persuasion or Microsoft Excel), PICT graphics created by drawing programs (MacDraw), and PICT tables created by Microsoft Word or Aldus Table Editor. Don't I mean the *Adobe* Table Editor? Nope—I mean the Aldus Table Editor included with PageMaker 4.2 (and still at large). *Adobe* PageMaker 6 includes the *Adobe* Table Editor, which can write EPS files (and is therefore covered in "Importing EPS Graphics," later in this chapter).

As you open or place these files, each of the elements in the original illustration is converted to a FreeHand element. Often, it'll seem like you've got two or three times as many elements as you need. This is just because PICT has weird ideas about how to draw things (see Figure 4-2).

FIGURE 4-2
"Extra" elements in converted PICT

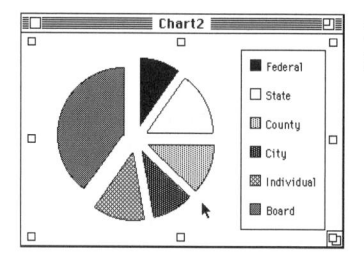

This chart looks fine in Excel (more or less)...

Each filled object becomes at least two paths (one for the line; one for the fill). In this example, each line segment is a separate path.

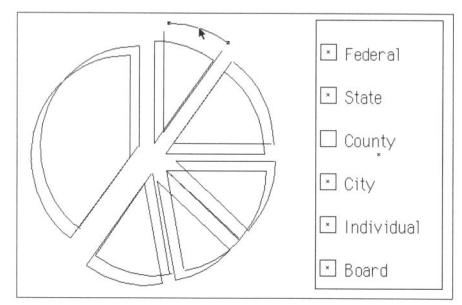

...but when you paste it into FreeHand you see that it has far more objects than you'd think it would.

Tip: Before you import that PICT...

Before you place or open an object-PICT file, make sure you've checked the Convert PICT Patterns to Grays option in the Importing/Exporting Preferences dialog box. This way, the nasty patterns that PICT drawing applications use to represent shades of gray will get converted into what they should be—shades of gray—as you import them.

Importing Charts from Microsoft Excel and Adobe Persuasion

Both Excel and Persuasion have good charting features, and you can bring their charts into FreeHand with a minimum of fuss. To save a chart created in Persuasion, go to the slide containing the chart and choose Export from the File menu. Choose PICT from the Format popup menu, type a name for your chart, and press Return to export the chart. Now you can open and convert the chart with FreeHand (see Figure 4-3).

Excel can't export its charts as PICTs, so you'll have to copy them to the Clipboard, and then paste them into FreeHand. When

IMPORTING AND EXPORTING 351

FIGURE 4-3
Exporting a slide
from Persuasion

In Persuasion, go to the slide you want and choose Export from the File menu.

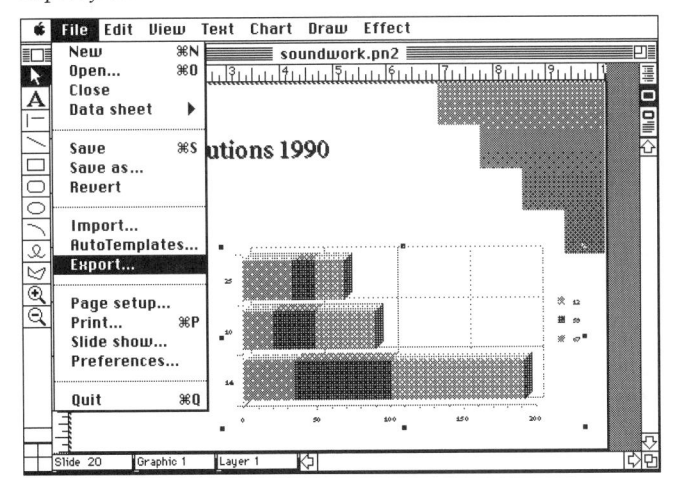

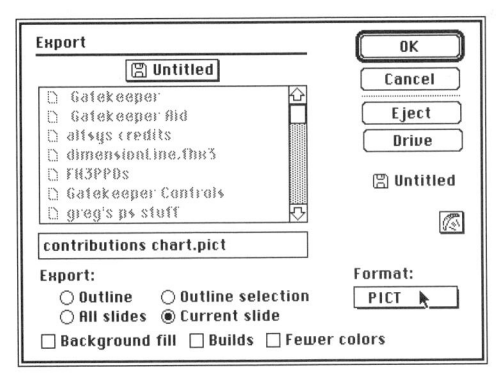

Type a name for your chart and choose PICT.

When you open the chart, FreeHand converts the PICT objects into FreeHand elements.

You can edit the converted objects as you would any FreeHand elements.

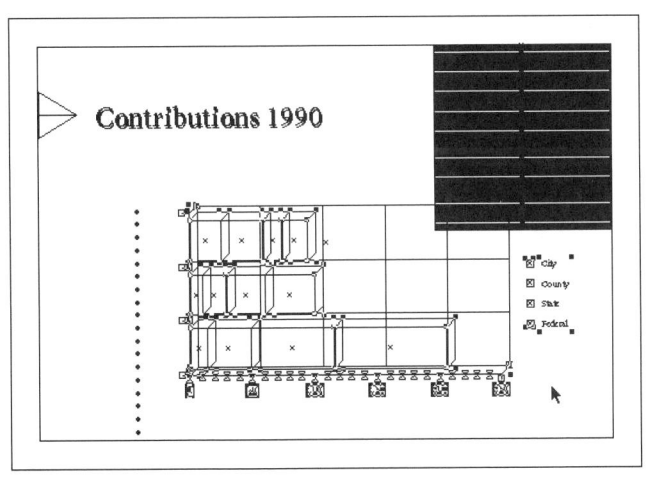

you paste the chart into FreeHand, the objects in the chart are converted into editable FreeHand elements.

Tip: For Fewer Converted Objects

Before you export (or copy) your chart from a PICT-type charting program, set the line widths of the filled objects in the chart to None (or whatever the equivalent is in the program you're using). When FreeHand converts PICTs, a line means one object, and a fill means another object. Because you always end up deleting all the lines and then applying a line to the filled object, doesn't it make sense to get rid of the lines before exporting the PICT?

Importing PICTs from CAD Programs

Because most Macintosh CAD programs are capable of saving their drawings in the PICT format, it's easy to bring engineering or architectural drawings into FreeHand. Why would you want to take the drawings out of their native CAD program? Macintosh CAD programs are great at rendering precise views of an object or building, but they're just not that good at making a drawing sexy or handling type in a professional manner. Often, versions of the drawings for marketing and technical illustration need the PostScript drawing features found in FreeHand.

To get objects out of your CAD program and into FreeHand, export or save your drawing as a PICT and then open and interpret the PICT file with FreeHand. If your CAD program can't save as PICT, you can still get the drawing into FreeHand by copying the objects out of the drawing program and pasting them into FreeHand.

There are a few things about converted CAD drawings you need to keep in mind (see Figure 4-4).

- FreeHand converts each line segment into a closed path.

- Arcs and ellipses are often converted into sets of closed paths made up of single straight line segments.

- Line joins will often miss, particularly where lines meet arcs.

The good news, however, is that you've still got the fundamental shape of the object you want. Once the objects are in a FreeHand publication, you can do as much—or as little—clean-up as you want or have time for.

FIGURE 4-4
Imported CAD drawing

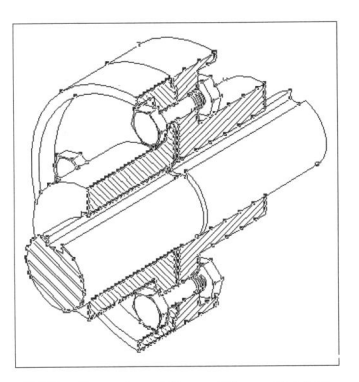

CAD drawing (from VersaCAD) pasted into FreeHand

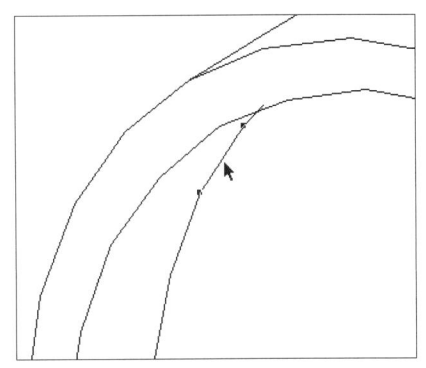

When you zoom in on the imported drawing, you'll see that all of the curves in the drawing are rendered as straight, closed paths.

Working with TIFFs

FreeHand can place and separate color TIFF images, and TIFF printing has been improving steadily since FreeHand 2. I mention FreeHand 2 because I've met several FreeHand users with habits left over from that version of the program. They don't dare apply a color to a grayscale TIFF, or paste a TIFF inside a path, because they're afraid their publications will take forever to print (or won't print at all). FreeHand's TIFF printing improvements make it possible to use those features in your publications.

If you prefer separating your color images before final production, or if you prefer another program's separations, you can pre-separate your color images, then save them as CMYK EPSes or TIFFs and place them in FreeHand.

Halftones

Commercial printing equipment can only print one color per printing plate at one time. We can get additional "tints" of that color by filling areas with small dots; at a distance (anything over a foot or so), these dots look like another color. The pattern of dots is called a halftone (for more on digital halftoning and commercial printing, see Chapter 6, "Color").

We use halftones to print the different shades inside photographs. The eye, silly and arbitrary thing that it is, tells our brain that the printed photograph is made up of shades of gray (or color)—not different patterns of large and small dots.

TIFFs, Screen Frequency, and Resolution

Let me introduce you to the TIFF balancing act. It goes like this: for any printer resolution (in dots per inch, or dpi) there's an ideal screen frequency (in lines per inch, or lpi)—a frequency that gives you the largest number of grays available at that printer resolution. If you go above this screen frequency, you start losing gray levels.

To find the line screen that'll give you the largest number of grays for your printer's resolution, use this equation.

number of grays = (printer resolution in dpi/screen ruling in lpi)^2+1

If the number of grays is greater than 256, the number of grays equals 256. PostScript has a limit of 256 gray shades at any resolution, for any printer.

So if you want 256 grays, and your printer resolution is 1270 dpi, the optimum screen ruling would be around 80 lpi.

What if you want to use a higher screen frequency? Something's got to give—and, usually, what gives is resolution. When you print at higher imagesetter resolutions, you can use much higher line screens before you start losing grays.

There's another part to the balancing act—the resolution of your scanned images.

It's natural to assume that by scanning at the highest resolution available from your scanner you can get the sharpest images. This bit of common knowledge, however, doesn't hold true for grayscale or color images; for these, scan at no more than twice the screen frequency you intend to use. Higher scanning resolutions do not add any greater sharpness, but the size of your image files increases dramatically. To determine the size of an image file, use this equation.

file size in kilobytes = (dpi^2 × bit depth × width × height)/8192 (bits in a kilobyte)

Bit depth is eight for an eight-bit image, 24 for an RGB color image, and 32 for a CMYK image.

There's one guy I know who always complains about the size of the TIFF files he's working with. He told me the other day about a color magazine cover that took up 60 MB on his hard drive. I didn't say anything, but I think he's overscanning. Here's why—if the size of his image is 8.5 x 11 inches, he's using a 150 lpi screen, and he's working with an RGB image, his file should be 21.4 MB (because $300^2 \times 24 \times 8.5 \times 11/8192=24653.3$—divide the result by 1024 to get megabytes). If he's working with a CMYK TIFF, his file size should be $300^2 \times 32 \times 8.5 \times 11/8192=32871.1/1024$, or 32.1 MB—still nowhere near the file size he's griping about.

Ideally, you should scan at the same size as you intend to print the image. Resolution changes when you change the size of the image, so if your scanner won't create an image at the size you want, you can compensate for the effect of resizing the image in FreeHand using this equation.

(original size/printed size) × original (scanning) resolution = resolution

If you'd scanned a three-by-three-inch image at 300 dpi and reduced it to 2.25 inches square (a reduction of 75 percent), the resolution of the image is 400 dpi.

Tip: Scanning Line Art

If you're scanning line art, save the files as bilevel TIFFs rather than as grayscale. You'll save lots of disk space, and your line art TIFFs will be just as sharp as they'd be if you saved them as grayscale TIFFs. Also, scan your line art at the highest resolution you can get out of your scanner. Line art, unlike grayscale and color images, does benefit from increased resolution, because you're not creating halftones.

Tip: Increasing Line Art Resolution

Sometimes, your scanner can't scan at a high enough resolution to give you a good scan of line art. This is especially true when you're scanning those great, copyright-free engravings from Dover's clip art books. In this case, try this trick, which I stole (with permission) from Steve Roth and David Blatner's excellent *Real World Scanning and Halftones* (also from Peachpit Press; see Appendix C, "Resources," for an address). This process produces a bilevel image at twice the resolution of your scanner.

1. Scan the image as grayscale at the highest optical resolution your scanner offers.

2. Resample the image to twice its original resolution using Photoshop (or other image editing program).

3. Sharpen the image.

4. Select Threshold from the Map submenu under the Image menu. Drag the arrow back and forth to adjust the break point for black and white. Click OK.

5. Convert the image to a bilevel TIFF and save it.

TIFF Controls   When you select a paint-type graphic, bilevel TIFF, or grayscale TIFF file, FreeHand adds six controls to the Object Inspector: the Edit and Links buttons, Scaling percentage fields, the Transparent checkbox, and a color well (see Figure 4-5).

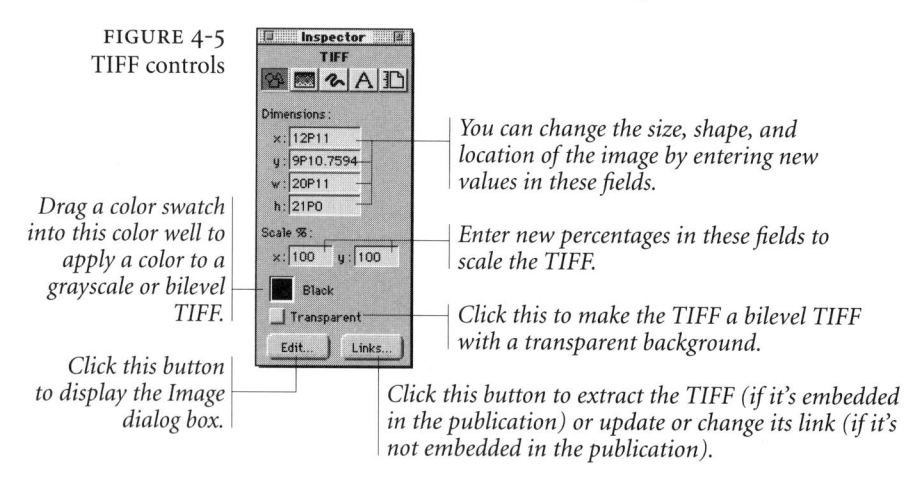

FIGURE 4-5
TIFF controls

You can change the size, shape, and location of the image by entering new values in these fields.

Drag a color swatch into this color well to apply a color to a grayscale or bilevel TIFF.

Enter new percentages in these fields to scale the TIFF.

Click this to make the TIFF a bilevel TIFF with a transparent background.

Click this button to display the Image dialog box.

Click this button to extract the TIFF (if it's embedded in the publication) or update or change its link (if it's not embedded in the publication).

Scaling percentage fields. To change the width or height of an imported image, enter new scaling percentages in the X (horizontal scaling) or Y (vertical scaling) fields.

Image color well. To apply a color to a grayscale or bilevel TIFF, drag a color swatch into the color well (or you can drop a color swatch on the TIFF itself). You can't use these controls with a color TIFF, so FreeHand grays them out when you have a color TIFF selected.

Transparent. When you check the Transparent box in the Object Inspector, the white areas of a TIFF become transparent (see Figure 4-6). If you choose this option when you've got a grayscale

FIGURE 4-6
Making the background of a TIFF transparent

Paint-type graphics set to Black and White have an opaque background.

Click Transparent, and you'll be able to see through the background of the image.

TIFF selected, FreeHand converts the TIFF to a bilevel TIFF. It'll seem like you've lost some image information, but don't worry—you can always uncheck Transparent again and all your grayscale information will reappear.

Ordinarily, FreeHand treats the background of a grayscale or bilevel TIFF as an opaque white box the size of the TIFF's selection rectangle. This differs from PageMaker, where bilevel TIFFs are always transparent (unless you choose Gray or Screened in PageMaker's Image Control dialog box) and grayscale TIFFs are always opaque (unless you choose Black and White in the Image Control dialog box).

Tip:
Set Bilevels to Transparent for Faster Printing

Bilevel TIFFs (and paint files) set to Transparent print four times faster than the same images set to Black and White. Why? To make a long story short, it has to do with conformance to the OPI specifications. If you need an opaque background, why not draw a box with an opaque fill behind the transparent image?

Links. Click the Links button to update or change the link to an imported graphic, or to extract an embedded graphic (see "Working with Links," later in this chapter).

Working with the Image Dialog Box

When you click the Edit Image button in the Object Inspector, FreeHand displays the Image dialog box (see Figure 4-7), where you can change the brightness, contrast, and (in a very rudimentary way) the gray map for the image.

FIGURE 4-7
Image dialog box

The Image dialog box isn't modal; you can drag it out of your way if you need to see an image behind it.

Gray level presets

Click to increase brightness

Click to decrease brightness

Click to increase contrast

Gray level bars

Click to decrease contrast

The dialog box above is for a grayscale TIFF. If you select a bilevel TIFF or a paint-type graphic, the gray level bars show that there are only two gray levels in the image.

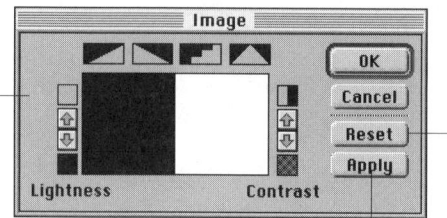

Click the Reset button to reset the image's gray levels to the default gray map (it's the same as clicking the first gray level preset).

If you make changes to the gray level bars, the Apply button becomes active. Click it to apply your changes to the image. By clicking the Apply button, you can see your changes without closing the Image dialog box.

Lightness and Contrast. The Lightness slider controls the brightness of the entire image. Increase the brightness of the image by clicking the up arrow; decrease the brightness of the image by clicking the down arrow. Note that clicking on the arrow changes the position of the gray slider bars (see Figure 4-8).

If you want to increase the contrast of the image, click the up arrow above Contrast. If you want to decrease the contrast of the image, click the down arrow. As you click on the arrow, the slider bars in the window to the left of Contrast move (see Figure 4-9).

FIGURE 4-8
Changing lightness

Default lightness

Image darkened by pressing on the down arrow in the Lightness control

FIGURE 4-9
Changing contrast

Default contrast

Increased contrast

Gray level sliders. Each slider inside the Image dialog box applies to $1/16$ of the gray levels in the image, so each slider in four-bit TIFF equals one gray level (there are 16 possible gray levels in a four-bit TIFF); each slider in an eight-bit TIFF represents 16 adjacent gray levels, because there are 256 possible gray levels in an eight-bit TIFF. The gray level bars control gray levels from the darkest to the lightest in your image as they go from left to right. Slide a gray level bar up to increase the lightness of all the pixels with that group of gray levels; slide it down to decrease their lightness (see Figure 4-10).

FIGURE 4-10
Working with gray level bars

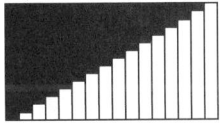

Default gray levels

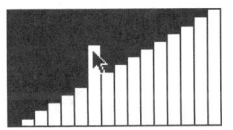

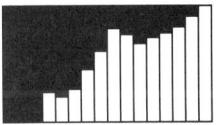

You can adjust individual gray bars until you've achieved the effect you want.

Gray level presets. The Image dialog box contains four default settings for the grayscale slider bars: Normal, Negative, Posterize, and Solarize (see Figure 4-11). Clicking the Normal icon returns the image control settings for the TIFF to the position they were in when the TIFF was first imported. Clicking the Negative icon inverts all the grayscale slider bar settings from their Normal setting.

FIGURE 4-11
Gray level presets

Normal   *Negative*   *Posterize*   *Solarize*

Posterize maps all the gray levels in the TIFF to four gray levels. Solarize maps all the gray levels to a kind of bell curve. This produces an effect similar to the photographic effect "solarization," which is produced by exposing photographic film to light before developing the film.

Reset. Click the Reset button to undo any changes you've made in the Image dialog. Clicking Reset returns the gray bars to their default position—the "normal" ramp.

Apply. Click Apply button to see what the changes you've made in the Image dialog box look like without having to close the Image dialog box (remember, you can drag the dialog box around to get a better look at the TIFF).

Resizing Images to Your Printer's Resolution

Paint-type images and bilevel TIFFs often use regular patterns of pixels to represent gray areas in the image. You can see these patterns of black and white pixels in the scroll bars in most Macintosh applications. You'll also see them if you're scanning and saving images as "halftones" from most popular scanner software (see Figure 4-12).

When you print graphics containing these patterns, you'll often get moiré patterns in the patterned areas (see Figure 4-13).

Purists will argue that these aren't true moiré patterns, and state that moiré patterns are created by the mismatch of two (or more) overlapping screens. While it's true we have only one overlay, we nevertheless have two overlapping, mismatching screens—the resolution of the image and the resolution of the printer. Both are matrices of dots.

When the resolution of the image you're trying to print and the resolution of the printer don't have an integral relationship (that

FIGURE 4-12
Pixel patterns representing grays

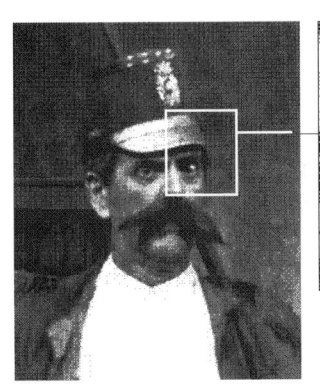

Paint-type graphics and bilevel TIFFs often use patterns of black and white pixels to represent grays.

FIGURE 4-13
Moiré patterns

Moiré patterns

Not resized to printer resolution

Resized to match printer resolution

is, when the printer resolution divided by the image resolution equals other than a whole number), some rounding is going to have to occur, because your printer can't render fractional dots. When this happens, parts of pixels get cut off or added to make up the difference (see Figure 4-14).

Instead of figuring out the scaling percentages for each bilevel image you're working with, take advantage of FreeHand's "magic stretch" feature, which resizes images to match the resolution of your target printer.

Hold down Option as you resize an image and the image snaps to sizes that have an integral relationship with the selected printer resolution. Hold down Shift and Option as you size the graphic both to size the graphic proportionally and to match the printer's resolution (see Figure 4-15).

Where do you set the printer's resolution? Enter a value in the Printer Resolution field in the Setup Inspector that matches the

FIGURE 4-14
Integral and non-integral resolutions

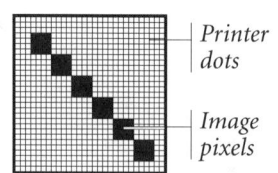

Printer dots

Image pixels

Your printer can't print fractional dots—they're either on or off. When your image pixels and printer dots have an integral relationship (4:1 in this example), the printer can match your image's pixels.

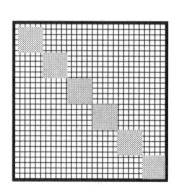

When the image pixels don't match your printer's resolution, the printer has to guess which printer dots it should turn on or off...

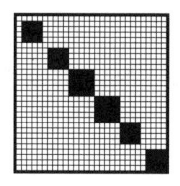

...which distorts your image.

FIGURE 4-15
Magic-stretching an image

Point at a corner of an image, hold down Option-Shift...

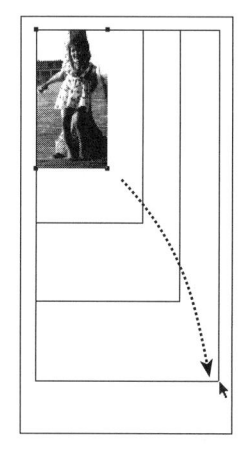

...and drag. The image snaps to possible sizes as you drag.

When you've reached the size you want, stop dragging.

resolution of the printer you'll be use for the *final* printing of the publication (not the resolution of your proof printer).

The value you enter in the Printer Resolution field does not affect the actual resolution of your printer; it's just there to give FreeHand a value to use when calculating magic stretch sizes.

Magic stretching doesn't improve the printing of grayscale or color TIFFs—even though they'll snap to the same sizes—and it doesn't have any effect on object-PICT or EPS graphics.

Cropping TIFF Images

If you're used to PageMaker's Cropping tool, and are looking for a similar tool in FreeHand, you're out of luck—there isn't one. Instead, however, you can use FreeHand's Paste Inside feature to

IMPORTING AND EXPORTING 363

crop your image. It's better than the Cropping tool anyway. When you want to use just part of a TIFF image in your FreeHand publication, try this (see Figure 4-16).

1. Size the TIFF to the size you want.

2. Draw a path around the part of the TIFF you want to use.

3. Select the TIFF and press Command-X.

4. Select the path and press Command-Shift-V (or choose Paste Inside from the Edit menu). FreeHand pastes the TIFF inside the path.

While I'm on the topic of cropping images, I should mention that it's better to create your images in your scanning or image-editing software so that you don't have to crop. When you crop an image, the parts of the TIFF you can't see don't just go away; FreeHand still has to keep track of the entire TIFF, which means slower screen redraw and printing.

FIGURE 4-16
Cropping a TIFF

Draw a path around the area you want to crop.

Cut the TIFF image to the Clipboard, then select the path and paste the image inside the path.

Tip:
Adjusting Cropping

If you just need to make a minor adjustment to the way you've cropped a TIFF, try this (see Figure 4-17).

1. Select the cropped TIFF.

2. Press Command-M to display the Transform palette, if it's not already visible. If the Move panel of the Transform palette isn't already visible, click the Move icon to display it.

FIGURE 4-17
Adjusting cropping

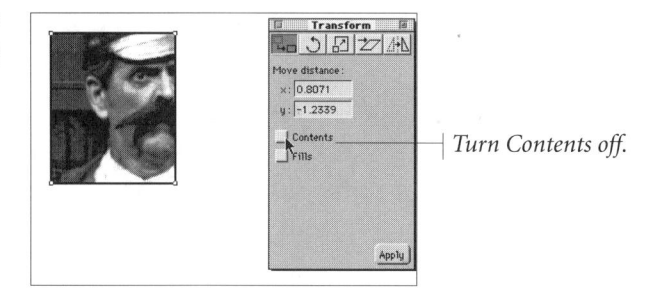

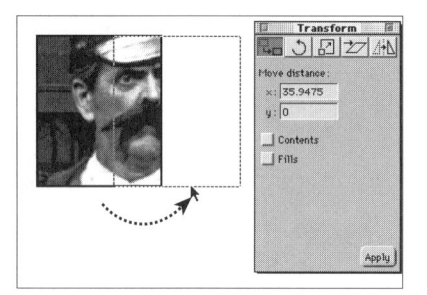

Turn Contents off.

Drag the path to a new location.

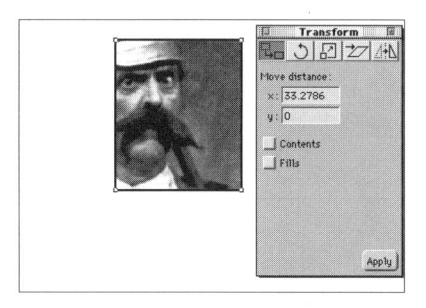

FreeHand moves the path, but leaves the path's contents in their original position. To move the path back to its original position, turn Contents on again, so that the TIFF moves with the path.

3. Uncheck Contents, then drag the path (or move the path using the X and Y fields in the Transform palette). Free-Hand moves the clipping path without changing the position of the TIFF inside the clipping path.

Creating an Outline Mask for a TIFF Image

Something that people often miss when they think about cropping images in FreeHand is that the path you're using to crop the image can be any size or shape. You can paste TIFFs inside ellipses, characters, or totally freeform paths. This comes in handy when you've got to pull a particular object out of a placed TIFF file. Trace the part of the TIFF you want, cut the TIFF to the Clipboard, and paste it inside the shape you've just drawn (see Figure 4-18).

FIGURE 4-18
Creating an
outline mask

Draw a path around the parts of the image you want (it helps to send the image to the background before tracing).

Paste the image into the path. You can adjust the points on the path to change the cropping of the image.

Voilà! Instant outline mask. Note that you can adjust the cropping by dragging individual points on the clipping path to get it just right, and that you can stroke the path to trap the image if you need to (for more on trapping images, see Chapter 6, "Color"). Just for fun, go ask your local prepress outfit what they'd charge to do this.

Creating a Vignette Mask for a TIFF Image

Here's another photographic effect that used to cost a bundle—creating a vignette. What's a vignette? It's where a photo progressively lightens as it approaches the edge of some shape (traditionally, an ellipse) until the photographic material is entirely white at the point at which it reaches the edges of the shape. Think of the photos of your 19th-century ancestors—they're probably vignettes.

While this technique is still going to be cheaper than doing the same thing photographically, it's going to take some time to print, especially on an imagesetter. It's also much easier to do using Photoshop (or other image-editing application), and should only be done in FreeHand in desperation. Still, desperation is what this book's about. The process is illustrated in Figure 4-19.

1. Draw a path around the part of the TIFF that you want to leave unchanged. This area is the center of the vignette effect. The TIFF should extend for some distance beyond this area in all directions.

FIGURE 4-19
Creating a vignette

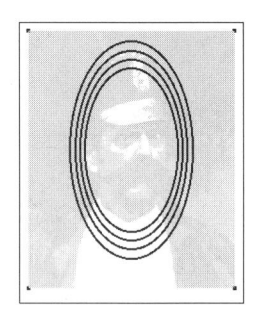

Create several paths.

Create several clones of the image. Paste the images into the paths, pasting the lightest image into the largest path.

2. Cut the TIFF to the Clipboard and paste it inside the path.

3. Clone the clipped TIFF.

4. Scale the cloned clipping path so that it's larger than the original clipping path (in the example shown above, I scaled each path in the vignette so that it was 105 percent of its original size).

5. Select the cloned clipping path and choose Cut Contents from the Edit menu. FreeHand places the TIFF on top of the path.

6. Without deselecting the TIFF, apply a color to the TIFF so that it's lighter than the original TIFF. In our example, I made each TIFF 10 percent lighter than the previous one.

7. Cut the TIFF to the Clipboard, select the cloned path, and choose Paste Inside from the Edit menu to paste the TIFF inside the path.

8. Send the path to the back, or to another layer that's behind the original clipping path.

9. Repeat steps 3 through 8 until all or nearly all the color values inside the TIFF are white.

When you work through this procedure, you end up with a stack of cropped images, with the TIFFs inside each clipping path getting lighter and lighter as they get farther and farther from the center of the vignette.

It's occurred to me that you could probably produce the same effect using the Lightness control in the Image dialog box instead of coloring each TIFF a lighter shade. I used colors because it's easier to control the amount of a color—there's no numeric way to adjust lightness. Another point is that you can do this technique much faster if you work in Keyline view—you don't have to spend any time redrawing the TIFF. Finally, you can probably do a better job of this in an image-editing program.

Preseparating Color TIFFs

If you prefer the color separations of color TIFF images created by some other program—Adobe Photoshop comes to mind—to the separations created by FreeHand (see Color Figure 10 for a comparison), you can preseparate color TIFFs into CMYK and place them in FreeHand as EPS, DCS, or TIFF files.

EPS files created this way contain all the information the color-separating application would have sent to a printer to create color separations of an image. DCS is a variation of EPS, and stores the color-separated image as five files (one for each color, plus a "header" file that's the part you work with). CMYK TIFF contains the separated image data, but doesn't contain any special halftoning information.

When you place the preseparated file in FreeHand and print the publication, FreeHand separates the file as the original application would have.

The following steps show how you'd preseparate an RGB image using Adobe Photoshop.

1. In Photoshop, make sure that your separation settings are the way you want them. Switch to CMYK mode, and Photoshop separates the image.

2. Choose Save As. In the Save As dialog box, choose "EPS" or "TIFF" from the File Format popup menu. Click the Save button. If you select "EPS," the EPS Options dialog box appears. If you choose "TIFF," the TIFF Options dialog box appears.

3. In the EPS Options dialog box, pick a screen preview from the list of preview options, choose either ASCII or Binary as your encoding scheme (binary files are smaller), and check

the Include Halftone Screens and Include Transfer Functions options (if you want to include Photoshop's screening). Check the Desktop Color Separation option if you want to use the DCS method of storing the file as five separate files. Press Return to save your image as an EPS file.

If you're saving your file as a TIFF, you've got fewer options. Choose the Macintosh or MS-DOS option for the TIFF's image data (you'll probably want to use "Macintosh"). Check the LZW Compression option if you want to compress the TIFF as you save it. (FreeHand has no trouble with LZW-compressed TIFFs from Photoshop, so you might as well compress the file.) Press Return to save your file as a CMYK TIFF.

Running Photoshop Plug-Ins

In FreeHand 5.5, you can run Photoshop plug-ins (also known as filters) on TIFF (or bitmap PICT, for that matter) images you've placed in your publication. FreeHand can't run *all* Photoshop filters—the Unsharp Mask filter, for example, isn't supported, for example (which is a pity, because it's the most important one), but most of the special effects filters, such as the Page Curl plug-in from Kai's Power Tools, work well.

How do you use the Photoshop plug-ins? First, you've got to set them up. Copy an alias of the plug-ins (from your Photoshop Plug-Ins folder) to the Xtras folder in the FreeHand folder. Restart FreeHand, and you'll see Photoshop plug-ins on the submenus of the Xtra menu. When a filter is intended for use on bitmap images, FreeHand puts "[TIFF]" in front of the plug-in's name on the menu.

To run a Photoshop plug-in on an image, follow these steps (see Figure 4-20).

1. Select the image.

2. Choose one of the plug-ins from the Xtras submenus. Some plug-ins simply run, some display a dialog box. If the plug-in you've chosen does display a dialog box, adjust the dialog box controls, then click the OK (or whatever) button to apply the effect.

FIGURE 4-20
Applying a Photoshop Filter to an Image

Select an image.

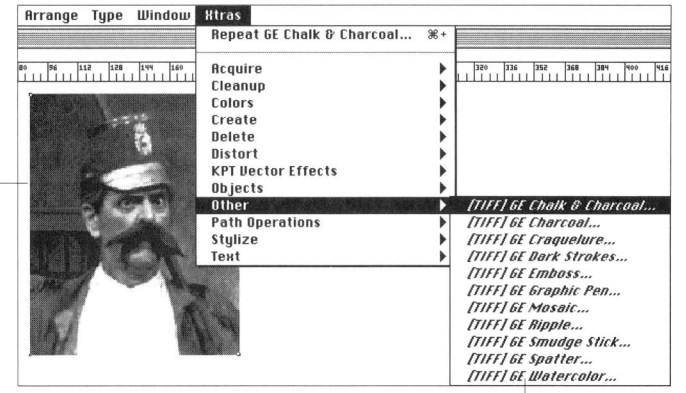

Choose a Photoshop filter from the Xtras menu. Note FreeHand adds "[TIFF]" before the names of filters that work on images.

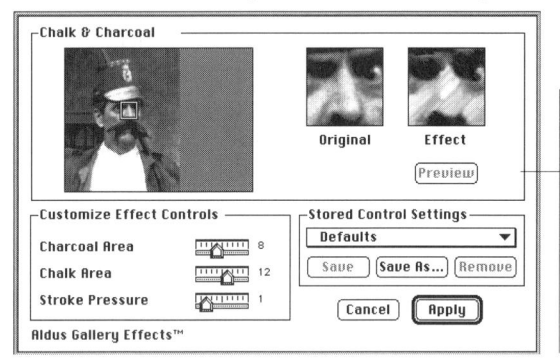

Make any changes you want in the filter's dialog box (if it has one). In this example, I've used a plug-in from the Adobe (my package still says "Aldus") Gallery Effects package.

FreeHand applies the effect to the selected image.

Note: When you run a Photoshop filter on an image that's linked to your publication, FreeHand embeds an altered copy of the image in the publication. This increases the size of the publication. If you want to store the image externally, use FreeHand's "Extract" feature.

Running Photoshop plug-ins on images in FreeHand requires lots of RAM. You can make more RAM available by turning off the Buffered Drawing option in the Redraw Preferences dialog box (see "Redraw Preferences" in Chapter 1, "FreeHand Basics"), or you can quit FreeHand and increase the application's RAM allocation (see "Changing FreeHand's RAM Allocation" in Appendix A, "System"), then restart FreeHand and try again.

After you're run a Photoshop plug-in, you can repeat the effect on any other image you select by pressing Command-Shift-+ (or by choosing Repeat *plug-in name* from the top of the Xtras menu).

When you run a Photoshop filter on an image that's linked to an external file (rather than embedded in the FreeHand publication, FreeHand creates a copy of the image, embeds it in the Publication, and applies the filter to the copy of the image. If you want to store the image externally, you can extract the image, then link to the new file (see "Extracting Embedded Images," later in this Chapter).

Tip:
Why Don't I See All My Plug-Ins?

Some of Photoshop's plug-ins don't work in FreeHand—some, in fact, make FreeHand crash. To see a list of incompatible plug-ins, take a look at the file named Disabled Plug-Ins in the Xtras folder inside the Macromedia folder in your Preferences folder (which is inside your System folder).

If you see a plug-in that you've just *got* to use on this list, and have installed the plug-in (or its alias) in your Xtras folder, you can try running it (don't say you weren't warned). Delete the plug-in's name from the list, then save the file (make sure you save the file as text-only). When you restart FreeHand, you'll see the plug-in on the Xtras menu. Select an image and give it a try.

One item on the list that I'd like to see working is the TWAIN Acquire plug-in (TWAIN is a standard for software that controls scanners—I've heard it stands for "Technology Without An Interesting Name"). I have been told that the TWAIN Acquire, TWAIN Select Source, and TWAIN TIF files that come with Photoshop 3.0.4 work with FreeHand 5.5, but I haven't seen it, myself. If you have these files, you might try removing the two TWAIN plug-ins from the list in the Disabled Plug-Ins file, and then try running the plug-ins. If they work, you'll be able to control your scanner from inside FreeHand.

Tip:
Acquiring Images with Quick Edit

One very handy Photoshop plug-in is the Quick Edit Acquire plug-in. With the Quick Edit plug-in, you can crop images as you place them. To import part of an image, follow these steps (see Figure 4-21).

1. Choose Quick Edit from the Acquire submenu of the Xtras

FIGURE 4-21
Acquiring Images
with Quick Edit

If you've moved the Photoshop Quick Edit plug-in (or its alias) into the Xtras folder, you can use Quick Edit to import parts of TIFF images. Choose Quick Edit from the Acquire submenu of the Xtras menu...

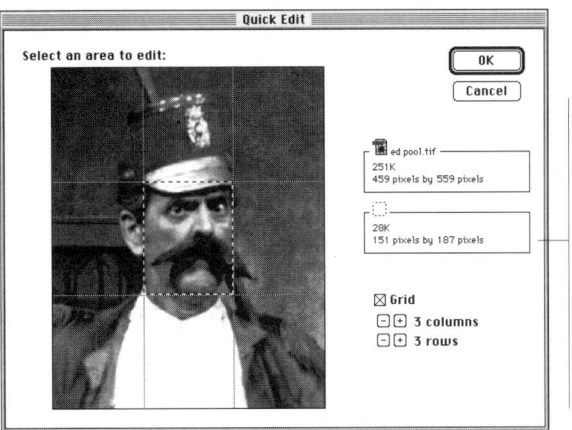

...and choose a file from the standard file dialog box. Once you've selected a file, FreeHand displays the Quick Edit dialog box. Select the part of the TIFF you want to import and press Return.

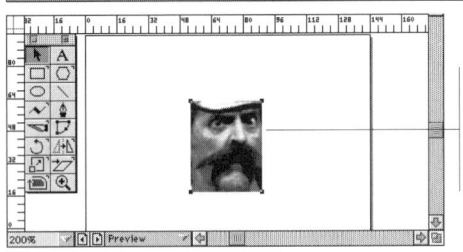

Click or drag the Place icon to import the image. When you import part of a TIFF using Quick Edit, FreeHand embeds the TIFF in the publication.

menu (assuming that you've copied the Quick Edit plug-in or its alias into FreeHand's Xtras folder). FreeHand displays the Quick Edit dialog box.

2. Select the part of the image you want to import (drag a rectangular selection over the area in the preview window).

3. Press Return (or click the OK button). FreeHand displays the TIFF place icon.

4. Click the place icon to import the part of the image you selected.

When you use the Quick Edit plug-in, FreeHand embeds the section of the image you select in your FreeHand publication. If you want to work on the cropped image outside of FreeHand, or if you want to link to the image, you can extract the image and save it as a TIFF file (see "Extracting Embedded Images," later in this chapter).

Importing EPS Graphics

If you work with other programs that can export files as EPS, or if you write your own PostScript programs, you can import those files into FreeHand and combine them with text and graphics you've created in FreeHand. You have the choice of placing EPS files as imported graphics or—with some EPS formats—converting the graphic into FreeHand objects.

What happens when you place an EPS? That depends on the application that wrote the EPS, and on the setting of the Convert Editable EPS When Placed option in the Importing/Exporting Preferences dialog box (see "Importing/Exporting Preferences" in Chapter 1, "FreeHand Basics").

- If the EPS is a format that FreeHand can open (FreeHand or Illustrator), *and* the Convert Editable EPS When Placed option is turned on, FreeHand converts the placed EPS to editable FreeHand elements.

- If FreeHand can't convert the EPS format, or if the Convert Editable EPS When Placed option is turned off, FreeHand imports the EPS as a graphic. In this case, you won't be able to edit the content of the EPS.

Another preference setting, the Embed TIFF/EPS upon Import Rather than Link option in the Expert Import/Export Preferences dialog box, controls whether FreeHand links to external EPS files, or whether those EPS files are embedded in the FreeHand publication. See "Linking and Embedding," later in this chapter. Here are a couple things to keep in mind, however.

- If both the Embed TIFF/EPS upon Import Rather than Link option and the Convert Editable EPS When Placed option are turned on, FreeHand converts the objects in editable EPS to FreeHand objects when you place the file.

- If the Embed TIFF/EPS upon Import Rather than Link option is turned on and the Convert Editable EPS When Placed option is turned off, FreeHand embeds the EPS in your publication file when you place the file.

If You See an "X" Instead of a Graphic

When you import an EPS graphic (and you're not in Keyline mode), if you see a box with an "X" through it, instead of a screen preview, you've imported a file that doesn't have a screen preview attached. The file contains the dimensions of the graphic, and it'll probably print correctly, but there's nothing for you to look at as you lay out your page. This happens in these scenarios.

- There's not enough memory to display the preview. Increase FreeHand's application size (see "Increasing FreeHand's RAM allocation" in Chapter 1, "FreeHand Basics"), or close some publications.

- There was too little memory available to create the screen preview when FreeHand (or other application) created the EPS file. If you're placing a FreeHand EPS, think again: wouldn't it be better to paste that graphic into the current publication instead of placing it?

- The graphic has no screen preview attached. This happens if the file is a PostScript program written by an application that doesn't support preview images, or if the file was created using a word processor, or if the person creating the EPS saved it without a screen preview. This also happens if you've edited a normal EPS with a word processor and have not reattached the screen preview PICT. See "Converting FreeHand 3 EPS Files to Illustrator 1.1 EPS Format" below on editing old EPS graphics with a word processor.

If you can't get by without a screen preview, see the section "Working with PDF," later in this chapter.

Importing FreeHand EPS

If you've turned the Convert Editable EPS When Placed option off in the Importing/Exporting Preferences dialog box, placing a FreeHand EPS in a FreeHand publication is a silly thing to do. Think about it—why do you want to import FreeHand objects in a state that you can't edit? Instead, either turn on the Convert Editable EPS option and place the EPS, or paste the FreeHand elements from another FreeHand publication.

There's more to it than editing, however—when you create a FreeHand EPS, the EPS includes all the PostScript code needed to print the EPS correctly *outside* FreeHand. This EPS information makes the file take far longer to print when you're printing from *inside* FreeHand (see Figure 4-22).

FIGURE 4-22
Importing FreeHand
EPS versus pasting
FreeHand objects

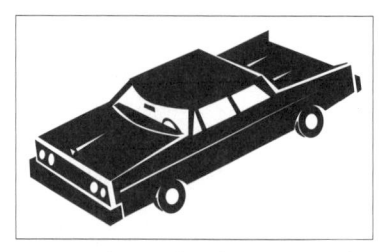

FreeHand EPS placed in FreeHand. Processing time: 34 seconds

FreeHand elements pasted from one publication to another. Processing time: two seconds

To make sure this doesn't happen to you, turn on the Convert Editable EPS When Placed option in the Importing/Exporting Preferences dialog box (see "Importing/Exporting Preferences" in Chapter 1, "FreeHand Basics").

If you're placing the EPS because you want to deal with the objects as a single graphic, why not group them?

Importing Illustrator EPS

If I had to choose between FreeHand and Illustrator, I'd take FreeHand. In fact, I don't use Illustrator much these days, though it's an excellent program. But I do know lots of people who swear by Illustrator, and I know even more people who strongly prefer using both. Luckily, the path from Illustrator to FreeHand is clear. FreeHand can open or place EPS files created by Illustrator (all versions through 5.5, at the time of this writing).

When you open an Illustrator EPS, FreeHand converts the paths and type into FreeHand elements. If you place an Illustrator EPS, FreeHand displays the screen-preview image (if there is one) and treats the file as an imported graphic—you can transform it, but you can't edit its contents.

When you open an Illustrator EPS, some of Illustrator's features are converted; some aren't.

Paths. FreeHand imports paths in Illustrator EPSes just as they were drawn in Illustrator. FreeHand converts Illustrator points into curve points whenever possible, though points defining sharp angles or sudden changes of curve direction are converted into corner points. As points are converted, FreeHand adds handles to each converted point so that the path matches the path you drew in Illustrator.

Text. FreeHand converts Illustrator text into FreeHand text blocks. Typically, the Illustrator text is converted one line at a time, though any changes in type style or font will create new text blocks, as will any kerning (including automatic kerning pairs). If the EPS was saved in the Illustrator 1.1 format, each line of text will be an individual text block.

Color. Process colors you've defined in Illustrator are imported as you defined them, but the color names don't appear in your Colors palette. To add colors from a converted Illustrator file to your Color List, follow the steps described in "Adding Colors from Illustrator" in Chapter 6, "Color."

Blends. Illustrator blends are often made up of separate objects, so you can't change the blend once you've imported it except by deleting the intermediate blend steps and blending again.

Complex Paths. Compound paths you've created using Illustrator's Make Compound command are converted to FreeHand's composite paths. ("Composite path" and "compound path" are just two ways of saying the same thing.)

Creating Your Own EPS Graphics

You can create EPS graphics using a word processor or LaserTalk (see Appendix A, "System," for more on LaserTalk), but you've got to remember two things.

- ◆ If it doesn't print when you download it, it won't print after you've placed it in FreeHand. Always test every change you make in your word processor by downloading the text file to the printer and seeing what you get before you place the file in FreeHand, or at least before you take the FreeHand file to a service bureau.

- ◆ When you edit an EPS graphic with a word processor and save it in the text-only (ASCII) format, you break the link between the PostScript text part of the EPS and the screen preview PICT resource. You can use ResEdit to rejoin the two parts of the EPS, provided you don't overwrite the original file.

Why would you want to create your own EPS graphics? There are lots of things you can do with PostScript that FreeHand doesn't do (yet). See Chapter 8, "PostScript," for some examples and more on creating your own EPS graphics.

Creating Invisible EPS Graphics

I often want to use full-page EPS backgrounds but I can't stand waiting for the background's screen preview to redraw every time I do something. In FreeHand, of course, the easiest thing to do is to set the layer the background's on to be invisible. But if you're creating a FreeHand EPS background to place in some (other) page-layout program, you need this trick (see Figure 4-23).

FIGURE 4-23
Creating an invisible EPS graphic

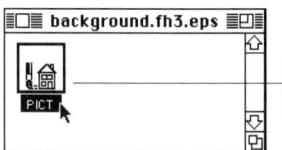

Locate and open the EPS file using ResEdit.

Once the file's open, double-click on the PICT resource class icon.

ResEdit displays the EPS file's screen-preview image. Select the image and press Delete.

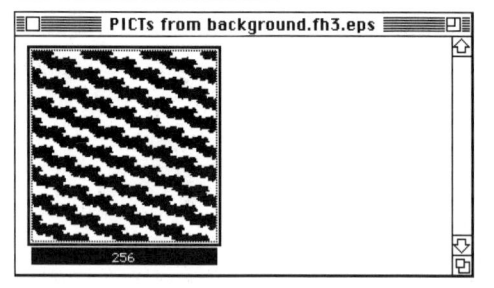

Press Command-K to create a new PICT resource.

Press Command-I to display the Info dialog box. Type "256" in the ID field.

Press Command-S to save your work, and quit ResEdit.

When you place the EPS file, you won't see the screen preview, but it'll print just as it did before.

1. Open the EPS file with ResEdit (for more on ResEdit, see Appendix A, "System").

2. Open the PICT resource.

3. Choose Clear from the Edit menu.

4. Press Command-K to create a new PICT resource.

5. Make sure that the new PICT has a resource ID of 256 by pressing Command-I and typing 256 in the ID field in the Info window that appears.

6. Press Command-S to save the file, and quit ResEdit.

Now, when you place the edited EPS file, you'll get a transparent bounding box that's the size of the graphic, but no screen preview will appear, and it won't take any time to redraw the image. The image will print out, though.

Creating Visible, Nonprinting Graphics If you want to place a graphic on the page, but don't want it to print, the best thing to do is to move it to some nonprinting layer. Use this trick when you want to create a FreeHand EPS to import into a page-layout program, and want the contents of the graphic to display but not print.

1. Open a copy of the EPS file with a word processor.

2. Delete everything in the document from the line that begins with "%%BoundingBox:" to the line that says "%%EndDocument" and save the file as text-only.

3. Launch ResEdit.

4. Locate and open the text file you just created. When ResEdit asks if you want to add a resource fork to the file, click OK.

5. Open the original EPS file and select the PICT resource class.

6. Copy the PICT resource class out of the original EPS file and paste it into the resource listing for the text file.

7. Press Command-S to save the file, and quit ResEdit.

Why would anyone want to do this? It's handy to be able to place nonprinting notes ("type headline here") in page-layout programs. Sometimes people want to lay out and proof their publications without having to take the time to print the EPS.

Linking and Embedding

In FreeHand, you can choose to embed (that is, store) imported graphics in your FreeHand publication, or you can choose to link to them. When you link to a graphic, FreeHand creates a low resolution screen preview of the graphic, and uses that preview to draw the image on your page.

When you print, FreeHand includes data from linked graphics in the stream of PostScript it's sending to your printer or to disk. This means that you need to take any linked graphics with you when you want to print your publication at an imagesetting service bureau.

If you've turned on the High Resolution TIFF Display option in the Redraw Preferences dialog box, FreeHand refers to the external TIFF files when you change your view of the imported graphic, using image data in the file to give you a better view of the image.

Which method should you use? It's up to you. When you embed graphics, your publication size increases, but you don't have to keep track of the original files. When you link to externally-stored graphics, your publications will be smaller, but you'll have to keep track of more than one file.

In some cases, FreeHand automatically embeds graphics in your publications.

- If you turn on the Embed TIFF/EPS upon Import Rather than Link option in the Expert Import/Export Preferences dialog box, FreeHand always embeds TIFF and EPS graphics you place. If you've turned on the Convert Editable EPS When Placed option in the Importing/Exporting preferences dialog box, editable EPSes are converted to FreeHand objects when you place them—EPSes in formats that can't be edited are embedded.

- If you apply a Photoshop filter to a linked image, FreeHand embeds an altered copy of the image in your publication.

- If you place a bitmap PICT image, FreeHand converts the image to a TIFF and embeds the TIFF file in your FreeHand publication.

- If you acquire an image with the Photoshop QuickEdit plug-in.

When you select an imported graphic and display the Object Inspector, you'll see the Links button at the bottom of the Inspector. The Links button, along with the two preferences settings mentioned above, is the key to controlling linked graphics in your FreeHand publications.

Click the Links button in the Object Inspector, and FreeHand checks the status (is the file stored internally or externally? is the file still around? has it been modified recently?) of the graphic. If the graphic is embedded in the publication, FreeHand displays the Links dialog box (see Figure 4-24). If the graphic is linked, you'll see the Set Link dialog box (that's what I call it, anyway; it's a standard file dialog box where you can update or change your link—see Figure 4-25).

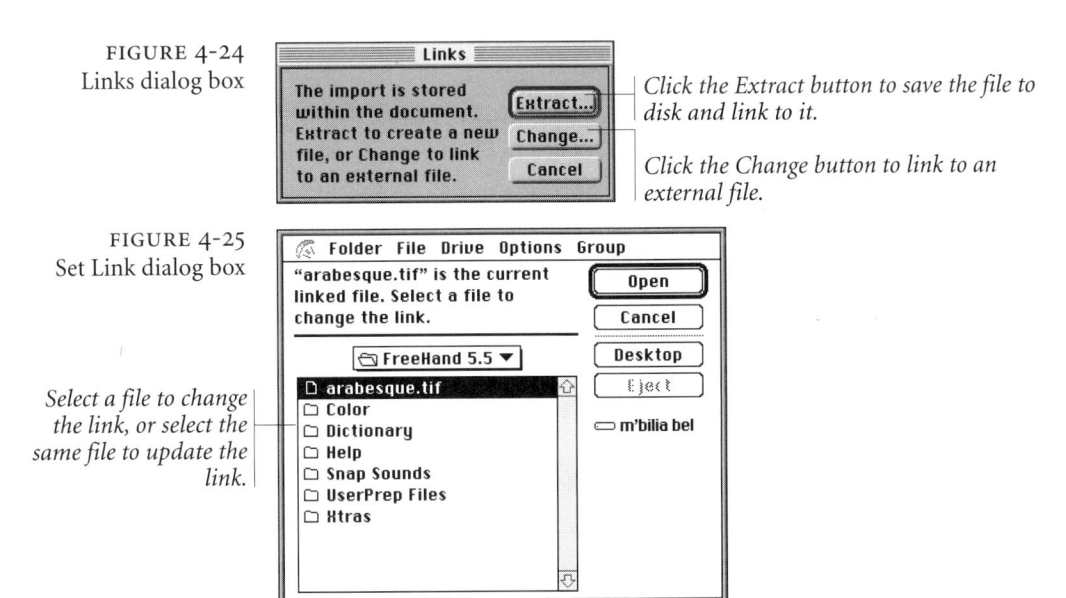

FIGURE 4-24
Links dialog box

Click the Extract button to save the file to disk and link to it.

Click the Change button to link to an external file.

FIGURE 4-25
Set Link dialog box

Select a file to change the link, or select the same file to update the link.

To replace an embedded graphic with a linked file, follow these steps.

1. Select the embedded graphic.

2. Display the Object Inspector (press Command-Option-I).

3. Click the Links button at the bottom of the Object Inspector. FreeHand displays the Links dialog box.

4. Click the Change button. FreeHand displays the Set Link dialog box.

5. Select the file you want to link to and press Return (or click the OK button). FreeHand replaces the selected embedded graphic with the external file. If you want, you can link to the original external file (the one you embedded earlier).

To embed a linked graphic, follow these steps.

1. Display the Expert Import/Export Preferences dialog box (choose Preferences from the File menu, then click Import/Export in the Expert Preferences section of the list).

2. Turn on the Embed TIFF/EPS Upon Import Rather Than Link option and press Return to close the dialog box.

3. Place the linked file again. FreeHand embeds the file in your publication. Adjust the size and position of the graphic so that it matches the original.

Extracting Embedded Graphics

Because FreeHand can embed graphics in its publications, you also need some way to get them *out* again. In FreeHand 5.5, you can export, or "extract" graphics embedded in FreeHand publications. This is a good thing, because, as you'll recall, FreeHand often embeds graphics (see "Linking and Embedding," earlier in this chapter).

To extract an embedded graphics file, follow these steps (see Figure 4-26).

IMPORTING AND EXPORTING   381

FIGURE 4-26
Extracting an
embedded graphic

*If you've applied a
Photoshop filter (in
this example, the KPT
Vortext Tiling plug-in)
to a TIFF, FreeHand
embeds a copy of the
image in your
publication, then runs
the filter on the copy.*

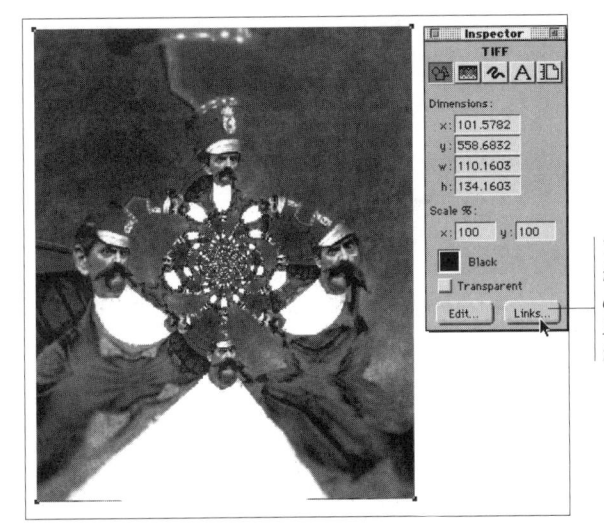

*To extract the
image, select it,
display the Object
Inspector, and click
the Links button.*

*FreeHand displays the
Links dialog box.*

*Note: If FreeHand
doesn't display
this dialog box, the
image is linked, not
embedded, so there's
no need to extract it.*

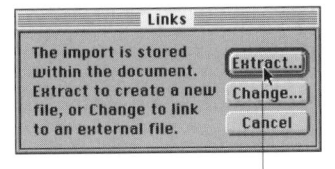

Click the Extract button.

*Select a volume and
folder, then type a
filename for your
extracted file.*

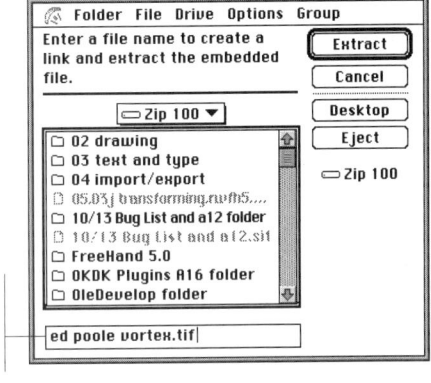

1. Select the embedded graphic.

2. Display the Object Inspector (press Command-Option-I) and click the Links button at the bottom of the Inspector. If the graphic you selected is embedded in the publication, FreeHand displays the Links dialog box.

3. Click the Extract button. FreeHand displays the Extract dialog box (again, this is what I call it—it doesn't really have a title).

FreeHand saves the embedded graphic. If you've selected an image, FreeHand saves the file as an RGB TIFF. If you've selected an EPS, FreeHand simply writes the EPS to disk.

Importing Text

After I'd finished producing the documentation for FreeHand 2 at Aldus, FreeHand's product manager asked me what one feature I'd like to see in FreeHand 3. "Give me a Text Place Gun," I said. In FreeHand 4, I finally got my wish (though I doubt it had much to do with my request). In FreeHand 5, you can import, format, and edit both formatted (RTF) and unformatted (text-only) text files.

Importing Text-Only Files

Word-processing programs, databases, spreadsheets, and almost all other applications speak one common language—they can all save their documents as text-only, or ASCII files. Text-only files don't include any formatting information—no font, size, leading, or paragraph spacing—they're just characters.

Sometimes you want to save files as text-only to strip out any formatting that's been applied to them (usually, you do this because the person who entered the text applied formatting you don't want). Sometimes text-only is the only kind of file an application can write. Either way, you can import the text files into FreeHand and format them there.

The only real trick to working with text files has do with where they come from. Often, text files generated by applications running on other platforms (you know, DOS/Windows boxes, Sun Workstations, and NeXT machines) or from online services (such as Compuserve and the Internet) are full of weird characters, or, most often, have carriage returns at the end of every line in a paragraph. In general, you need to run these text files through a conversion utility before you place them in FreeHand. I use Apple File Exchange (part of Apple's basic system software) and McSink (a shareware text editor) to convert text files. For more on text file conversion utilities, see Appendix A, "System."

Tip: Inserting Text into an Existing Text Block

When you're placing a text file in FreeHand, you can't choose to insert the text into an existing text block (unlike PageMaker, where you have the option of either inserting the incoming text in existing text, or of replacing the existing text with the incoming text). So you have to place the text, then copy text out of the new text block and paste it into the original text block. The following steps show you the least-painful method I've come up with for doing this (see Figure 4-27).

1. Drag-place the text file in your FreeHand publication (drag-placing means you can keep the text block small). After you place the file, FreeHand selects the new text block.

2. Press Command-X to cut the text to the Clipboard.

3. Click the Text tool where you want to insert the text, or, if you want to replace all the text in a story, triple-click one of the text blocks in that story with the Pointer tool.

4. Press Command-V to paste the text you copied to the Clipboard. FreeHand inserts the text in the text block (or text blocks).

Using this technique, you can set up your text blocks *before* you have any text to place in them. It gives you something to do while you're waiting for someone else to finish writing or editing the text—a handy thing, especially if you're laying out a magazine or newspaper in Freehand.

FIGURE 4-27
Inserting text in an existing text block

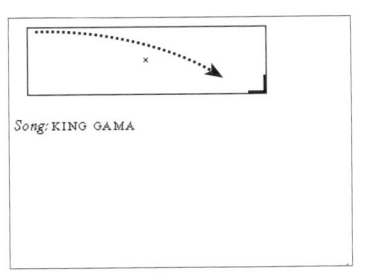

Drag-place the text.

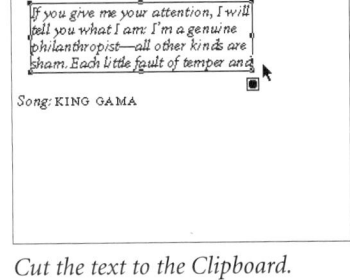

Cut the text to the Clipboard.

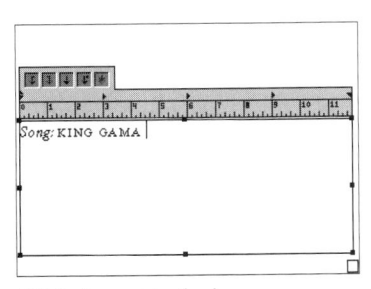

Click the text tool where you want to insert the text.

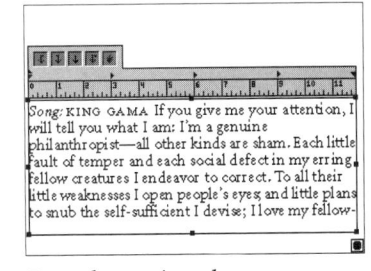

Paste the text into the story.

Importing RTF Being able to import text-only files is wonderful, but what if you need to import formatted text from your word processor or page layout application? That's where Microsoft's Rich Text Format (RTF) comes in. Technically, RTF isn't a file format—RTF files are saved as text-only format—it's a specific way of organizing text inside a file. RTF files contain text codes and values capable of describing anything and everything that can appear in a Microsoft Word document. The best way to understand how RTF works is to look at a sample RTF file, created by FreeHand (see Figure 4-28). This example file shows almost all the text formatting FreeHand can import or export from an RTF file.

FIGURE 4-28
FreeHand RTF file

```
{\rtf1\mac{\fonttbl{\f3\fnil Times;}{\f4\fnil Bembo;}}
{\colortbl\red0\green0\blue0;\red0\green0\blue0;\red158\green48\blue0;}
\deftab720\pard \li0 \ri0 \fi0 \sb0 \sa0 \fs48 \f4 \cf1 \ql \sl-200 RTF Test
Document\par
\pard \li0 \ri0 \fi0 \sb0 \sa0 \fs20 \f4 \cf1 \ql \sl-200 {\b bold}\par
\pard \li0 \ri0 \fi0 \sb0 \sa0 \fs20 \f4 \cf1 \ql \sl-200 {\i italic}\par
\pard \li0 \ri0 \fi0 \sb0 \sa0 \fs20 \f4 \cf1 \ql \sl-200 {\b \i bold italic}\par
\pard \li0 \ri0 \fi0 \sb0 \sa0 \fs20 \f4 \cf1 \ql \sl-200 {\up6 baseline shift up}\par
\pard \li0 \ri0 \fi0 \sb0 \sa0 \fs20 \f4 \cf1 \ql \sl-200 {\dn6 baseline shift
do}{\dn6 wn}\par
\pard \li0 \ri0 \fi0 \sb0 \sa0 \tqr\tx2162 \fs20 \f4 \cf1 \ql \sl-200 \tab right
tab\par
\pard \li0 \ri0 \fi0 \sb0 \sa0 \tqr\tx727 \fs20 \f4 \cf1 \ql \sl-200 \tab left tab\par
\pard \li0 \ri0 \fi0 \sb0 \sa0 \tqc\tx1322 \fs20 \f4 \cf1 \ql \sl-200 \tab center
tab\par
\pard \li0 \ri0 \fi0 \sb0 \sa0 \tqdec\tx2162 \fs20 \f4 \cf1 \ql \sl-200 \tab decimal
tab.\par
\pard \li0 \ri0 \fi0 \sb0 \sa0 \fs20 \f4 \cf1 \ql \sl-200 align left text\par
\pard \li0 \ri0 \fi0 \sb0 \sa0 \fs20 \f4 \cf1 \qr \sl-200 align right text\par
\pard \li0 \ri0 \fi0 \sb0 \sa0 \fs20 \f4 \cf1 \qc \sl-200 centered text\par
\pard \li0 \ri0 \fi0 \sb0 \sa0 \fs20 \f4 \cf1 \qj \sl-200 justified text\par
\pard \li0 \ri0 \fi0 \sb120 \sa0 \fs20 \f4 \cf1 \ql \sl-200 {\expnd20 range
k}{\expnd20 er}{\expnd20 ned text}\par
\pard \li0 \ri0 \fi0 \sb120 \sa0 \fs20 \f4 \cf1 \ql \sl-200 space above\par
\pard \li0 \ri0 \fi0 \sb0 \sa1440 \fs20 \f4 \cf1 \ql \sl-200 space below\par
\pard \li720 \ri0 \fi0 \sb0 \sa0 \fs20 \f4 \cf1 \ql \sl-200 left indent\par
\pard \li720 \ri0 \fi0 \sb0 \sa0 \fs20 \f4 \cf1 \ql \sl-200 right indent\par
\pard \li0 \ri0 \fi240 \sb0 \sa0 \fs20 \f4 \cf1 \ql \sl-200 first line indent\par
\pard \li0 \ri0 \fi0 \sb0 \sa0 \fs20 \f4 \cf1 \ql \sl-200 end of \line line character
\par
\pard \li0 \ri0 \fi0 \sb0 \sa0 \fs20 \f4 \cf1 \ql \sl-200 dis\-chy\par
\pard \li0 \ri0 \fi0 \sb0 \sa0 \fs20 \f4 \cf2 \ql \sl-200 color\par
\pard \li0 \ri5330 \fi0 \sb0 \sa0 \fs48 \f4 \cf1 \ql \sl-480 {\shad shadow}\par
\pard \li0 \ri5330 \fi0 \sb0 \sa0 \fs48 \f4 \cf1 \ql \sl-480 {\outl outline}\par
\pard \li0 \ri5330 \fi0 \sb0 \sa0 \fs48 \par }
```

One of the peculiarities of RTF is that it repeats local formatting for each paragraph, even if the formatting hasn't changed between paragraphs, ass you can see in the sample. This is just how RTF, as defined by Microsoft, works. If you leave out the repetition for a paragraph, FreeHand formats the text using the default text formatting when you import the file.

If you look at a Microsoft Word RTF file, you'll see a lot more information at the start of the file than you see in Figure 4-28—most of it, from FreeHand's point of view, useless. Word, when it writes an RTF file, includes every font that's currently installed in your system in the font table (the section in the RTF file beginning with "\fonttbl"), whether that font is used in the document or not (FreeHand includes only the fonts you've actually *used*, which makes more sense to me).

Following the font table, most RTF files will include a color table ("\colortbl"), and sometimes a table containing the styles defined in the document ("\stylesheet"). Table 4-1 shows the RTF codes you'll see and use most often.

A few notes about RTF files:

- Most measurements in an RTF file are in *twips*, or twentieths of a point (.05 point). Type size is measured in half-point increments. If you export FreeHand text containing measurements finer than a twip (a leading value of 10.12, for example), or type sizes finer than half a point (10.7, for example), FreeHand rounds to the nearest twip, or half point, respectively.

- Type styles and baseline shift are typically enclosed in "curly" brackets (for example: "{\b \i bold italic}")—the brackets mark the beginning and end of the formatting.

- Wrapping tabs are not supported by RTF.

- Column breaks are not supported by RTF.

- Horizontal scaling of text is not supported by RTF.

- Text colors are imported as unnamed, process colors (they're represented as RGB colors in the RTF file, but they're converted to CMYK as FreeHand imports the file).

TABLE 4-1
Frequently used RTF codes

Code:	What it means:
\s*n*	Style number. This won't make any difference to FreeHand, but you might see it in RTF files generated by other applications. In addition, RTF files generated by applications which support paragraph styles, such as PageMaker, QuarkXPress, and Microsoft Word, will have a table (like the RTF font table or color table) at the start of the document listing the styles and style names used in the document.
\f*n*	Font number. The number of the font in the font table at the start of the RTF document.
\fs*n*	Font size in half points
\b	Bold
\i	Italic
\sl-*n*	Leading. For some reason, both FreeHand and Word put a "-" in front of the leading amount.
\li*n*	Left indent
\ri*n*	Right indent
\fi*n*	First line indent
\tx*n*	Tab position
\cf*n*	Text color. The number of the color determined by the color's position in the color table at the start of the RTF document.
\par	Carriage return
\ql	Left alignment
\qr	Right alignment
\qj	Justified alignment
\qc	Centered alignment
\tqr	Right-aligned tab
\tql	Left-aligned tab
\tqc	Center tab

TABLE 4-1
Frequently used
RTF codes (continued)

Code:	What it means:
\pard	Start of a new paragraph (you can think of "\par" and "\pard" as a carriage return/line feed combination—it's what they might be if you transfer this RTF file to a DOS/Windows PC. On the Macintosh, of course, all you really need is "\par," but FreeHand adds "\pard" because that's how the RTF specification says it's done).
\tqdec	Decimal tab
\tx*n*	Tab position (always follows "\tqr," "\tql," "\tqc," or "\tqdec")
\'*n*	Special character expressed as a hexadecimal number
\up*n*	Baseline shift up (sometimes superscript)
\dn*n*	Baseline shift down (sometimes subscript)
\-	Discretionary hyphen
\tab	Tab character
\deftab	Distance between default tabs
\line	End-of-line character
\~	Nonbreaking space
\shad	Shadow text effect
\outl	Stroked text
\expnd*n*	Range-kerning amount
\sb*n*	Space above.
\sa*n*	Space below.
\fnil, \froman	Alternate fonts—RTF includes its own font substitution scheme. "\froman" and "\fswiss" tell Word on DOS/Windows PCs to use Times (or even "TmsRmn") or Helvetica instead of the original font, if the original font's not found. FreeHand always uses "\fnil,"—no substitution.

- FreeHand doesn't support case changes you can specify in a word processor or page layout application. When FreeHand imports an RTF file containing "\caps" (all capitals) or "\scaps" (small capitals), it ignores the codes and draws the text as it was typed (small caps will appear in lowercase).

- FreeHand doesn't support the type styles Strikethrough and Underline. FreeHand imports text coded with the RTF codes "\strike" (strikethrough), or "\ul" (underline) without those formatting attributes.

- FreeHand doesn't import style definitions in RTF files, and doesn't export style definitions when you export files as RTF.

- Hidden text ("\v"), table of contents markers ("\tc'), and index entries ("\xe" and "\:") are stripped out of RTF files on import into FreeHand.

- FreeHand doesn't support graphics (PICT, EPS, or TIFF) embedded in RTF files.

- FreeHand's text effects aren't supported by RTF, and FreeHand does not export then when you create an RTF file.

- RTF codes specifying page layout information, such as page headers and footers, explicitly specified paragraph positions, or page margins, are stripped out of the RTF file on import into FreeHand.

Importing Text Tagged with XPress Tags

Part of the "Real World" tradition of this book is the idea that you might, someday, have to convert files from one format to another using nothing but a text editor. For example, let's say you're stranded in the middle of the Sahara, you have a file that's been exported from QuarkXPress as an XPress Tags (Quark's text-only equivalent to RTF) file you need to import into FreeHand, and you don't have a copy of QuarkXPress (if you did, you could export the text as RTF, a format FreeHand understands). Do you wait until a passing caravan offers you the use of their copy of XPress, or do you roll up your sleeves and convert the file yourself?

Now that your forearms are bare, take a look at Table 4-2, which shows the RTF equivalents for commonly-used XPress Tags.

You can automate most or all of this conversion process using the incredible search-and-replace utility Torquemada the Inquisitioner. For more on Torquemada, see Appendix A, "System."

TABLE 4-2
Converting XPress Tags to RTF

Attribute:	XPress Tag:	RTF equivalent:
Plain	<P>	\plain
Bold	<B>	\b
Italic	<I>	\i
Outline	<O>	\outl
Shadow	<S>	\shad
Baseline shift up/superscript	<+> (or <b*n*>)	\up
Baseline shift down/subscript	<-> (or <b-*n*>)	\dn
Font	<f"name">	\f*n* (Where *name* is the name of the font in your system and *n* is the number of the font in your font table.)
Type size	<z*n*>	\fs*n* (multiply the XPress Tag specified font size by 20 to convert it to twips.)
Color	<c"name">	\cf*n* (Where *name* is the name of the color in your XPress publication and *n* is the number of the color in your RTF color table.)
Left align	<*L>	\ql
Right align	<*R>	\qr

TABLE 4-2
Converting XPress
Tags to RTF
(continued)

Attribute:	XPress Tag:	RTF equivalent:
Center	<*C>	\qc
Justify	<*J>	\qj
Return	<\n>	\par
End-of-line character	<\d>	\line
Dischy	<h>	\-
Paragraph format	<*p(*n*, *n*, *n*, *n*, *n*, G or g>	The values in the tag specify left indent, first-line indent, right indent, leading, space before, and space after, respectively (so you'd convert them to twips by multiplying them by 20, and then use \li *n*, fi *n*, ri *n*, \sl-*n*, \sb *n*, and \sa *n* to render them in RTF syntax. "G or g" specifies whether the paragraph is locked to XPress' baseline grid, and has no RTF counterpart.
Tabs	<*t(*n*, *n*, "character")>	The first value in the tag is the tab's position, the second value is the tab's alignment (where 1=center, 2=right, 3=decimal, and 4=left), followed by the tab's leader *character*. In RTF, you'd set the tab's alignment first using \tqr, \tql, \tqc, or \tqdec, and then set the position (again, convert the value in the XPress Tag file to twips by

TABLE 4-2
Converting XPress
Tags to RTF
(continued)

Attribute:	XPress Tag:	RTF equivalent:
Tabs (continued)		multiplying by 20) using \tx *n*. FreeHand doesn't have tab leaders, so you can omit the leader character.
Kerning or range kerning	<k*n*> or <t*n*>	Convert the values in the tags to twips by multiplying them by .0005 (each increment is $^1/_{200}$ of an em), then multiplying them by the current type size, and then dividing by 20 to convert to twips. An XPress Tag value of 4000, in 24-point text, therefore, is equal to an RTF value of two, because 4000 × .0005 × 24/20 = 2.4 (which we round down, because you can't have fractional twips).

Tip:
Learning more about RTF

If you want to learn more about RTF, you can get a copy of the RTF specification (the specification is updated every few months) by writing to: Microsoft Corporation, Department RTF, 16011 NE 36th Way, Box 97017, Redmond, Washington, 98073-9717.

Exporting

All of the tricks shown earlier in this chapter for importing data from other applications make it clear that FreeHand's good at importing. But what about exporting? FreeHand supports four EPS export formats (Generic, MS-DOS, Macintosh, and a new one, Photoshop EPS) and all current Adobe Illustrator formats. You can Copy FreeHand elements out of FreeHand, creating an object PICT with attached PostScript that can be pasted into just about anything. You can also export as PICT (don't), PICT2 (don't, unless you have to), and you can export the text in your publication as text-only (without formatting) or as RTF (with formatting).

Something you should understand about exporting: unless you choose to include your original FreeHand file in one of the EPS formats (check Include FreeHand document in EPS when you're exporting the file), *the file is going to change.* I don't mean that objects in the EPS are going to move around, or change color, or anything like that. What I mean is that the layers, styles, and other attributes of a typical FreeHand document are going to be lost. Everything will look the same, but the structure of the file will be different.

That's not—necessarily—a bad thing. I mention it here because I don't want you to be surprised the night before a deadline.

When you export a FreeHand page as PICT or PICT2, its appearance will change significantly (objects will *move*—PICT is a less accurate format than EPS, and rounding errors do occur when you save files as PICTs). If you save the file in any of the Adobe Illustrator formats, you'll lose features specific to FreeHand, such as graphic styles and wrapping tabs.

In all the cases mentioned, you'll be able to open and edit the file again. If you export the file as EPS and don't include the FreeHand page inside the EPS, you might not even be able to open the EPS.

Finally, you can render objects in your FreeHand publication to a bitmap PICT file. If you don't own Photoshop, it's the easiest way to convert FreeHand elements to a bitmap image.

The first half of this chapter covered how to get from there to here. Here's the dope on how to get from here to there. Exporting works the same way for any type of file, as shown in the following steps (see Figure 4-29).

1. Choose Export from the File menu (or press Command-E). FreeHand displays the Export Document dialog box.

2. Choose a file format from the Format popup menu.
   If you choose any of the Adobe Illustrator formats, EPS formats, or PICT formats, FreeHand displays page export options at the bottom of the dialog box. You can export any or all of the pages in your publication as EPS. If you

FIGURE 4-29
Exporting a file

Type a name for the file you're exporting.

Check this option to make it possible for FreeHand to open the EPS in the future.

FreeHand's export options

Choose a file type from this popup menu.

Set the range of pages you want to export here.

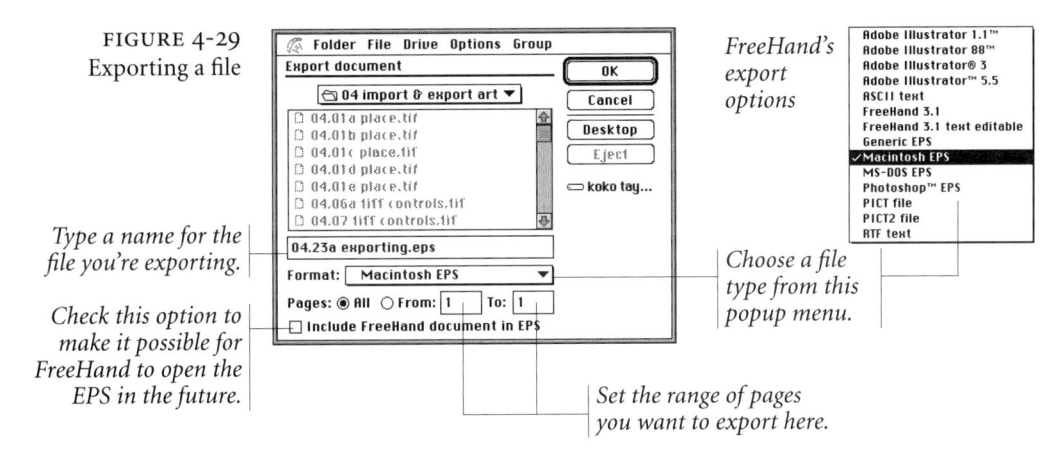

When you export more than one page, FreeHand creates separate files and numbers them sequentially "filename1.eps", "filename2.eps", etc.)

select a range of pages, FreeHand creates one EPS file for each page you export.

If you choose any of the EPS formats, you can include the FreeHand page in the EPS file by checking Include FreeHand Document in EPS. The FreeHand file that's included in the EPS is exactly the same file as FreeHand creates when you save the file, so all your layers and styles are available when you open the EPS. (Note that you can't include the FreeHand document in any of the Adobe Illustrator formats.)

When you export text (as ASCII text or RTF), FreeHand includes all of the text in the publication in the exported file. If you want to export some, but not all, of the text in your publication, copy the text to a new publication, and export it from there.

3. Type a name for your file and direct it to the folder and volume you want.

4. Press Return to export the file.

That's all there is to the mechanics of exporting a file. Now, on to the fun stuff—the details.

Creating EPS Graphics

Actually, exporting EPS graphics is what most people think of when they think of using FreeHand with other applications. It's only because of the twisted orientation of this book (that FreeHand is your main publishing program for short, complex documents) that exporting FreeHand elements appears in this chapter as a kind of afterthought.

EPS Output Options. Before you export a file as EPS, choose Output Options from the File menu. FreeHand displays the Output Options dialog box (see Figure 4-30). These options affect both printing and EPS export.

- Check Include Invisible Layers when you want to print all the foreground layers in the publication.

- Check Split Complex Paths to make paths containing graduated, radial, and tiled fills—or paths you've pasted other objects inside—easier to print. Don't check this option if you're exporting an EPS containing a large TIFF you've pasted inside a path—it can cause the TIFF to download over and over again, increasing your printing time dramatically.

- ASCII Encoding and Binary Data determine how FreeHand saves any imported TIFF images. Unless you're directly connected to your printer via serial cable, you should click Binary Data—images saved as Binary Data are more compact and are quicker to transmit to your printer.

- If you're taking your EPS to an OPI (Open Prepress Interface) system, such as Kodak's Prophecy, click "None (OPI comments only)". Since you'll be linking to another version of the image, your FreeHand file need only contain the location and size of the image, and doesn't need to contain the image data.

- If you plan to print the EPS from an application that can't separate RGB TIFFs, check Convert RGB TIFF to CMYK. PageMaker and QuarkXPress can both separate RGB TIFFs, and do a better job of it than FreeHand, so you should leave this option off if you're going to those applications.

FIGURE 4-30
Output Options
dialog box

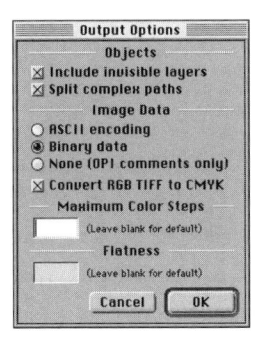

- If you're printing to a color prepress system, or a continuous-tone film recorder, enter 256 in the Maximum Color Steps field. This limits the number of shades of color FreeHand uses to render blends and graduated and radial fills. These devices can only print so many colors at once.

- For faster printing, enter a value above zero in the Flatness field (for more on flatness, see "Thinking Like a Line" in Chapter 2, "Drawing"). You can safely enter up to "3" with no noticeable change in your publication's printed quality on most printers and imagesetters.

Incredible as it might sound, the Output Options dialog box is one of the most important new features in FreeHand. In previous versions, you could set global flatness for a publication only when you were printing from FreeHand—you couldn't set the flatness for all the paths in an EPS without editing the EPS in a word processor. Similarly, the Split Complex Paths feature affected only FreeHand printing, not EPS files exported from FreeHand.

Embedding FreeHand files in EPS graphics. When you check Include FreeHand Document in EPS in the Export Document dialog box, FreeHand writes the FreeHand page you're exporting into the EPS file. When I first heard of this feature, I assumed that FreeHand attached the file to the EPS as a resource (like the PICT screen preview). Not so—FreeHand exports a special version of the file as text, and embeds it in the text of the EPS file (that is, in the file's data—not resource—fork). When you place the EPS in another program, the text version of the FreeHand file gets sent along to your printer when you print.

What good is this? In versions of FreeHand prior to version 4, you had to keep two versions of a FreeHand file on your disk—the EPS, which you could import into other programs, and the original FreeHand file, which you could open and edit in FreeHand. In FreeHand 5 (as in FreeHand 4), you can choose to store one file, which you can use in other programs, and which can be opened and edited by FreeHand.

When you use a word processor to open an EPS file that's been exported with Include FreeHand document in EPS checked, you'll see the line "%%BeginAGDEmbeddedDoc: version 1.0," lots of gibberish, and the line "%%EndAGDEmbeddedDoc." What is that stuff? It's your FreeHand page, saved as text. You can leave it alone or throw it away—it's up to you. If you can't stand the idea that you're sending your printer more bytes that are absolutely necessary (these extra characters do take a little time to transmit from your Macintosh over your network to your printer), by all means delete the text. Don't throw it away if you want to open the EPS file again in FreeHand, of course.

Tip:
Breaking a Multi-Page Publication into Single Pages

When you want to create a new publication from a single page of a multipage publication, you could make a copy of the file and then delete all the pages you don't want, or you can export the page as an EPS, checking Include FreeHand Document in EPS as you do so. You can then open the EPS file and save the page as a separate FreeHand document, complete with the styles, layers, and colors you defined in the original publication.

Generic EPS. When you need to create an EPS file containing the PostScript required to print the FreeHand publication you've created, but don't want the file to have a screen preview attached, choose Generic EPS from the Format popup menu.

If you place a Generic EPS file in FreeHand, you'll see a box with an "X" through it. There's a way to add a screen preview to a Generic EPS file, as described in "Creating a Screen Preview for EPS Graphics," earlier in this chapter.

Use Generic EPS when you're exporting a FreeHand graphic for use in a non-Macintosh, non-MS-DOS system (if you're preparing a graphic that'll be placed in a FrameMaker publication on a Sun workstation, for example), or if you just don't want to bother with a screen image. The Generic EPS file is a straight text file.

Macintosh EPS. A Macintosh EPS file is a PostScript text file with a PICT resource attached to it. When you place the EPS file in FreeHand or any other Macintosh program that can import EPS, the PICT is what you see on your screen.

MS-DOS EPS. Because MS-DOS files are structurally different from Macintosh files in that they're data files only (there's no concept of different forks for data and resources in the MS-DOS or Windows world) MS-DOS EPS files have a TIFF image of the graphic embedded in the file as hexadecimal data.

If you're exporting a FreeHand file as MS-DOS EPS, don't forget to use a file name your MS-DOS system can understand (eight characters or fewer), and add the extension ".eps" to the file name. Most MS-DOS applications have no way of knowing what type a file is without the extension.

Photoshop EPS. In FreeHand 5.0, the best way to rasterize a FreeHand file (that is, convert it to a bitmap) was to export the file using one of the Adobe Illustrator export formats. The whole trick is getting Photoshop to recognize the EPS—Photoshop couldn't see or recognize FreeHand EPSes. That's what the Photoshop EPS format does—it makes an EPS Photoshop can recognize.

The Photoshop EPS format is an Illustrator format (as far as I can tell, it's pretty close to the Illustrator 3.0 format), and has the limitations of that format—including lack of support for TIFF images. See "Exporting Publications in Adobe Illustrator Format." later in this chapter.

FreeHand, TIFFs, and PageMaker 6

A funny thing happened after FreeHand broke up with Aldus and started dating Macromedia (for more on this soap opera, see the Introduction): PageMaker stopped printing TIFFs in FreeHand EPS files. I don't think that Adobe (PageMaker's new master) did this on purpose (and I'm not a believer in conspiracy theories)—but, nevertheless, it happened. I do know, however, what causes the problem, and I do know how to fix it.

Here's the deal. When FreeHand writes coordinates into an EPS, it bases the coordinate system used in the EPS on the FreeHand pasteboard, rather than on the coordinate system of the individual page. Every time you've printed spreads, or printed objects off your page, you benfit from this behavior. FreeHand includes the PostScript operator "translate," along with the appropriate location of the lower-left corner of the current page. This effectively resets the coordinate system of the page—and it's an entirely legitimate PostScript programming practice, regardless of the misleading and incorrect note in the PageMaker ReadMe file.

Trouble is, PageMaker's OPI reader doesn't know about it, and assumes that all EPSes have a coordinate system starting at the lower-left hand corner of the page. This wouldn't be bad—except the option activating the OPI reader for EPS graphics is buried in a hidden dialog box, and it's *on* by default.

What happens? When you place a FreeHand EPS containing TIFFs in PageMaker, PageMaker won't print the TIFFs (unless the FreeHand page was positioned at the lower-left corner of the FreeHand pasteboard when you exported it). The EPS prints, but the TIFFs disappear.

How you fix this problem depends on whether you're using an OPI system or not. If you're not, and simply want to print the TIFFs in your FreeHand EPSes to an imagesetter, follow these steps (see Figure 4-31).

1. When you're ready to place the EPS in PageMaker, hold down Shift as you click the OK button in the Place Document dialog box. PageMaker displays the EPS Import Filter dialog box.

2. Uncheck the Read Embedded OPI Image Links option and press Return to place the EPS.
   If you're working with an EPS that's already been placed in a PageMaker publication, replace the EPS with the original EPS file, making the change in the EPS Import Filter dialog box as you replace the file.

If you *are* using an OPI system, and want to link to high-resolution images, drag the FreeHand page containing the FPO (or low

FIGURE 4-31

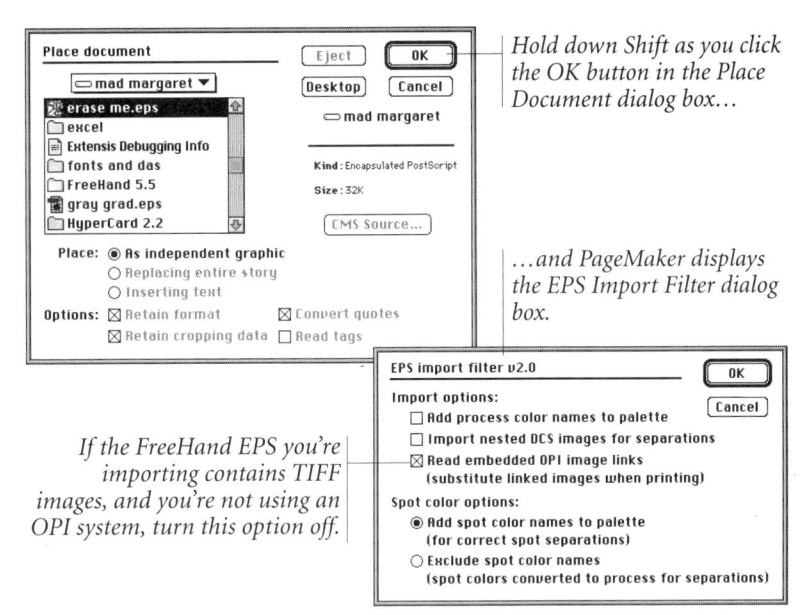

PageMaker's Hidden EPS Options

Hold down Shift as you click the OK button in the Place Document dialog box...

...and PageMaker displays the EPS Import Filter dialog box.

If the FreeHand EPS you're importing contains TIFF images, and you're not using an OPI system, turn this option off.

resolution) images to the lower-left corner of the FreeHand pasteboard, then export the page as EPS. This way, the coordinate system in the EPS will match PageMaker's expectations, and you'll be able to use the positioning information in the EPS. In this case, you can turn on the Read Embedded OPI Image Links option in the EPS Import Filter dialog box.

Exporting Publications in Adobe Illustrator Format

When you export your FreeHand file in the Adobe Illustrator 5 or Adobe Illustrator 5.5 file format, several things happen.

- You lose all style information. The objects on your page are all formatted using local formatting—their appearance doesn't change.

- Illustrator doesn't support the import of TIFF images, so any TIFF images in your FreeHand publication are omitted from the Illustrator file.

- Multicolumn and multirow text blocks are converted to linked, single-column text blocks.

- Any Custom or PostScript line or fill effects you've used in your FreeHand publication are omitted from the exported Illustrator file. You just get the paths.

In addition to the above problems, several other things happen when you export files in the Adobe Illustrator 3 file format.

- You lose all layer information. The appearance of the objects on your page won't change (that is, they'll still be stacked up in the same order), they just won't be assigned to layers.

- Graduated and radial fills get rendered as Illustrator blends—versions of Illustrator prior to Illustrator 5 didn't feature graduated and radial fills.

When you export to Adobe Illustrator 88 or Adobe Illustrator 1.1 format, a few other things happen (in addition to the changes described for the Adobe Illustrator 3 format).

- Composite paths are converted to individual paths.

- The text blocks in your FreeHand publication are converted to single-line text blocks in the exported Illustrator 88 file.

Tip: Breaking Text Blocks into Single Lines

A friend of mine needed to break all of the text in a text block into separate text blocks, each text block containing a single line of text. He didn't want to copy and paste the text (it was a large text block, containing captions he wanted to position on a map). He asked me if I had any idea how he could do this.

I told him to export the text block in the Illustrator 88 format, then open the file he'd exported in FreeHand. Sure enough, his text block had been broken into many smaller text blocks, each one containing a single line of his text.

Copying: Another Way to Export

There's another way to get objects out of FreeHand, and this one doesn't involve the Export dialog box—copying. There's not much to it: select the objects you want to use in another application and press Command-C (or choose Copy from the Edit menu). Switch to the other application and paste. Use this technique when you want to use a FreeHand graphic in an application that can't import EPS files, but can handle PICTs. FreeHand attaches PostScript code to the object PICTs it copies to the Clipboard, so the graphic will print correctly when printed on a PostScript printer.

Note some points about copying.

- ◆ The screen image that results when you copy a graphic to another application is not as good as the image FreeHand adds to an EPS file when you're exporting a file as EPS.

- ◆ Graphics that you copy to another application do not include any downloadable fonts, and it's often difficult to get the fonts to download from whatever application you've pasted the graphics into; so be prepared to manually download fonts if you're using these graphics. Or you can convert type to paths before copying.

- ◆ When you copy objects out of FreeHand, FreeHand copies the objects as PICT (with attached PostScript), RTF, AGD1 (native FreeHand format), and ASCII (or text-only). When you paste the Clipboard's contents into another application, that application pastes the data in the format it likes best. For more on which data types get sent to the Clipboard, see "Expert Import/Export Preferences" in Chapter 1, "FreeHand Basics."

Placing FreeHand Graphics in Page-Layout Programs

If you need to produce documents longer than a few dozen pages, you're going to have to look to a page layout program. Luckily, you can take your FreeHand illustrations with you. There are a few tricks and twists to this process.

Bounding boxes. You'll note that FreeHand's bounding boxes are sometimes just a little bit larger than the edges of the graphic, or that the graphic is not positioned inside the bounding box the way you'd like it.

What's going on? According to Adobe's EPS specification, EPS bounding box measurements should be expressed in integers (such as 100, 612, or 792). In FreeHand 3, Altsys engineers, with their usual mania for accuracy, used EPS bounding boxes accurate to $1/10,000$ of a PostScript point (which meant you'd see numbers such as 100.0125, 612.0005, or 792.9999 in FreeHand 3 EPS files). Most applications don't observe the fractional part of the EPS bounding box when they create a box to put the graphic in, so you could lose up to half a point (more or less) around the boundary of your graphic.

All of this changed with FreeHand 4, whose EPS bounding boxes are expressed in integers. I actually believe that the more accurate way is the better way, but this is, after all, the "real world," and we've got to get along with other applications.

If you're using FreeHand 5 and the edges of your exported EPS graphics seem to be getting clipped off when you place them in other applications, you've run into a new bounding box bug that's unrelated to the above discussion. Updating to FreeHand 5.01 fixes this problem (the updater is available on CompuServe or from Macromedia—see Appendix C, "Resources"). This problem is fixed in FreeHand 5.5.

If you're having this problem, and don't have time to update your copy of FreeHand before your next deadline, draw a box around the graphics you're exporting, making the box a little larger than the objects it encloses. Set the line and fill of the box to None, and export the EPS.

EPS files and downloadable fonts. You've probably heard that EPS graphics include any downloadable fonts used in the file. It's not necessarily true—sometimes EPS files contain the fonts; sometimes they only list the fonts.

When your page-layout program's printing, it creates the image of the page in your printer's memory by starting with the objects on the page that are the farthest to the back (actually, I'm only certain of this for PageMaker and QuarkXPress). When the application starts to print an EPS graphic, it reads the fonts listed in the EPS and downloads any needed fonts to your printer.

This does not guarantee that the fonts will still be in the printer's memory when they're called for inside the EPS, because a lot can happen between the start of the file (when your page layout program downloads the font) and whenever the font is needed.

Your page-layout application cannot manage the printer's memory once you're inside the EPS—only before and after your printer processes the EPS. By contrast, when you're printing objects you've created using your page-layout program's tools, your page-layout application manages font downloading and printer memory on an object-by-object level—it can always download another copy of the font if necessary.

If you've got an older printer with one megabyte of RAM, like a LaserWriter or LaserWriter Plus, it's much more likely that this will be a problem, because it's much more likely that your page-layout program will have to flush the downloadable font out of the printer's RAM to make room to print something else. It's also something you'll sometimes run into when you're printing to an imagesetter, because the higher resolution of imagesetters also means that these printers will run short of RAM.

If you have enough RAM in your printer, or if your printer has a hard disk, manually download the fonts to your printer. This guarantees they'll print, and your file will print faster, too.

Tip:
Importing Named Process Colors into QuarkXPress

When you import a FreeHand EPS into a QuarkXPress picture box (in version 3.3), XPress adds the spot colors used in the EPS to its list of colors, but doesn't add any named process colors you might have used in the graphic. You can add them yourself, or follow these steps.

1. Select the named process color in the Color List and choose Duplicate from the Color List's popup menu. FreeHand adds a duplicate of the color to the Color List.

2. Select the duplicate color and choose Make Spot from the popup menu.

3. Apply the new spot color to an object on your page.

4. Export the page as an EPS.

5. Import the EPS into XPress. XPress adds the spot color to its color list.

6. Delete the EPS.

7. Convert the spot color to a process color. Now you can apply the named process color to other elements in your XPress publication.

In a review of a previous version of this book, the reviewer commented that this method might result in shifts in the color's definition—something you definitely don't want. While that's true for spot colors defined in FreeHand using the RGB, HLS, or Apple color models, we're working with named process colors (which I assume you've defined using the CMYK model).

I haven't seen any changes in color definitions when I use this method, but the reviewer is right—you've got to watch out when you're converting from process to spot colors, or when you're moving colors from one application to another.

Converting FreeHand 3 EPS Files to Illustrator 1.1 EPS Format

It's going to happen to you someday. You'll need to edit an old FreeHand 3 graphic and will have only an EPS version of the file—not the original file. Here's what to do. First, try opening the EPS with FreeHand—it can open some simple FreeHand 3 EPS files.

If that didn't work, you'll just have to give up and start re-creating the illustration—unless you know how to translate FreeHand's EPS file into an Illustrator 1.1 format EPS file. Once it's in Illustrator 1.1 format, you can open it in either Illustrator or FreeHand.

Before you go any further, please note that this section doesn't deal with FreeHand 4 or 5 EPS files—only those EPSes created by FreeHand 3.0, 3.1, and 3.1.1. The instructions provided here won't work with FreeHand 4 or 5 EPSes.

If you have FreeHand 5.5 *and* the Adobe Acrobat 2.1 Distiller, you can skip the rest of this section—a much easier solution to your problem is covered in "Working with PDF," later in this chapter.

The best way to learn about the differences between the two formats is to take a look at the EPS files written in them.

1. Create a file in FreeHand and export it as an Illustrator 1.1 EPS.

2. Export the same file as Generic EPS.

3. Open both files with a word processor and compare them. You'll start seeing similarities and differences almost at once.

Focus on the parts of the files between the "%%EndSetup" comment and the "%%PageTrailer" comment. These are the parts that describe points, paths, and other objects. Table 4-3 shows the significant part of two EPS files describing the same path. Note

TABLE 4-3
Illustrator and FreeHand syntax compared

Note: While each column in this table describes the same object, it is not a line-by-line comparison.

Illustrator 1.1 version:	FreeHand version:
0 i 0 J 0 j 1 w 4 M []0 d[]	0 d
%%Note:	3.863708 M
192 1044 m	1 w
192 -252 L	0 j
N	0 J
-342 480 m	0 O
954 480 L	0 R
N	0 i
-342 336 m	false eomode
954 336 L	[0 0 0 1] Ka
N	[0 0 0 1] ka
336 1044 m	vms
336 -252 L	u
N	234 468 m
0 G	234 324 L
192 480 m	378 324 L
192 336 l	378 324 378 406 327 382 C
336 336 l	276 358 285 362 285 362 C
336 418 285 394 v	278 400 L
234 370 243 374 y	378 413 L
236 412 l	378 468 L
336 425 l	234 468 L
336 480 l	4 M
192 480 l	s
s	U
	vmr

that these lines show the same object, but that the line on the right does not necessarily match the line on the left.

First of all, note that the coordinate systems differ slightly. In this case the Illustrator coordinate system starts 42 points farther along the horizontal axis and 12 points earlier along the vertical axis than the FreeHand coordinate system. Differences in coordinate systems will vary between publications. In this case, "192 480 m" ("m" is for *moveto*) in the Illustrator file equals "234 468 m" in the FreeHand EPS.

In general, don't worry about differences in coordinate systems; the point is to get the objects into one program or the other. You can always adjust their positions once you've opened the file.

The first thing you need to do to convert a FreeHand EPS file into an Illustrator 1.1 format EPS file is to edit the file's header. To do that, follow these steps.

1. Open the file with your word processor. If you're using Microsoft Word, hold down Shift as you choose Open from the File menu, press Shift-F6, or select Open, and then select All Files from the List Files of Type popup menu. The first six lines of the file should look like this (the words shown in italics will vary—don't worry about them).

   ```
   %!PS-Adobe-2.0 EPSF-1.2
   %%Creator: FreeHand
   %%Title: filename
   %%CreationDate: date and time
   %%BoundingBox: x1 y1 x2 y2
   %%DocumentProcSets: FreeHand_header 3 0
   ```

2. Change the line beginning with "%%DocumentProcSets" to look like this:

   ```
   %%DocumentProcSets: Adobe_Illustrator_1.1 0 0
   ```

3. Delete the line beginning with

   ```
   "%%DocumentSuppliedProcSets:".
   ```

4. Leave the line beginning with "%%ColorUsage:" as it is.

5. Delete the line beginning with "%%FHPathName:".

6. Leave the line "%%EndComments" as it is.

7. Select from the line beginning with "%%BeginProcSet:" to the end of the line "%%EndProcSet" and delete the selection. Leave the two lines following ("%%EndProlog" and "%%BeginSetup").

8. Select from the beginning of the line "FHIODict begin" to the start of the line "%%EndSetup" and delete the selection. Type two lines between "%%BeginSetup" and "%%EndSetup" as follows.

```
Adobe_Illustrator_1.1 begin
```

The text you see between the line "%%EndSetup" and the line "%%Trailer" is the body of your FreeHand EPS file. Table 4-4 shows you how to convert paths, while Table 4-5 covers converting text objects.

Text is tricky. You'll usually have to guess for *alignment* and *kerning*, and you'll have to derive *horizontalScale* from the *size* specified in FreeHand, because FreeHand's already done all the positioning and scaling before exporting the file as EPS. Still, I've had good luck moving text back and forth.

TABLE 4-4
Converting from FreeHand to Illustrator syntax

If you see this in a FreeHand EPS:	Convert it to:	What it does:
[ ]0d	[ ]0d	The numbers between the brackets set the dash pattern, if any, of the path. In this example, the line's not dashed, so the array inside the brackets is empty. For a dashed line, the code would look something like "[2 1]0d" for a two-unit-on, one-unit-off dashed pattern. This code is the same as PostScript's *setdash* operator.

If you see this in a FreeHand EPS:	Convert it to:	What it does:
x M	*x* M	The number before this code sets the miter limit of the path. This code is the same as the PostScript *setmiterlimit* operator.
x w	*x* w	The number before this code sets the width of the path, in points. This shortcut is the same as the PostScript operator *setlinewidth*.
x i	*x* i	The number before this code sets the flatness of the path. "i" is the same as the PostScript operator *setflat*.
x j	*x* j	The number before this code sets the line join of points inside the path. 0 = miter joins; 1 = round joins; 2 = beveled joins. This code is the same as the PostScript operator *setlinejoin*.
x J	*x* J	The number before this code sets the line cap style. 0 = butt caps; 1 = round caps; 2 = projecting caps. This code is equivalent to the PostScript operator *setlinecap*.
x1 y1 m	*x1 y1* m	Moves to the specified point. This code is the same as the PostScript operator *moveto*.

TABLE 4-4
Converting from FreeHand to Illustrator syntax (continued)

TABLE 4-4
Converting from
FreeHand to
Illustrator syntax
(continued)

If you see this in a FreeHand EPS:	Convert it to:	What it does:
x1 y1 L	*x1 y1* l	Draws a line to the specified point and places a curve point (a "smooth" point in Illustrator parlance) with no curve control handles extended at that point. If you want to place a corner point, use "L" instead of "l". This code is the same as the PostScript operator *lineto*.
x1 y1 x2 y2 x3 y3 C	*x2 y2 x3 y3* v or *x1 y1 x3 y3* y	Sets a curve point and control handles. If *x1 y1* in the FreeHand version equals the previous point (usually *x1 y1* L), then convert it to a "v"; otherwise, convert the curve point to a "y".
s	s	Close and stroke the current path with the predefined line weight, miter specifications, and color. Exactly the same as the PostScript operator *stroke*.
b	b	Close the current path, and then fill and stroke the path with the predefined line weight, miter specifications, and colors.
[*c m y k*] Ka	*c m y k* K	Sets the fill color. 80C0M10Y10K would be written as .8 0 .1 .1 K.

TABLE 4-4
Converting from
FreeHand to
Illustrator syntax
(continued)

If you see this in a FreeHand EPS:	Convert it to:	What it does:
[*c m y k*] ka	*c m y k* k	Sets the stroke color. 20C5M0Y0K would be written as .2 .5 0 0 k.
x O	Delete this line	
x R	Delete this line	
Vms	Delete this line	
Vmr	Delete this line	
Vmrs	Delete this line	
U and u	U and u	"u" indicates the start of a group, "U" indicates the end of a group. You can delete these if you want.

TABLE 4-5
Converting text

FreeHand:	Illustrator:
%%IncludeFont: *fontName*	/_*fontName size leading kerning alignment* z
MacVec 256 array copy /*fontNumber* /|_____*fontName* dup RF findfont def { *fontNumber* [*size* 0 0 *leading* 0 0] makesetfont *x y* m 0 0 32 0 0 (*textString*) ts } [*c m y k*] sts	[*horizontalScale* 0 0 1 x y]e* (*textString*)t T

* Use "e" for text that's filled but not stroked, "o" for text that's both filled and stroked, and "r" for text you want stroked but not filled. These options use the current fill and stroke settings—see Table 4-3, above, for more information on setting strokes, fills, and colors. Table 4-6 shows an example of text set in FreeHand 3 and Illustrator 1.1 formats.

TABLE 4-6
Text conversion example

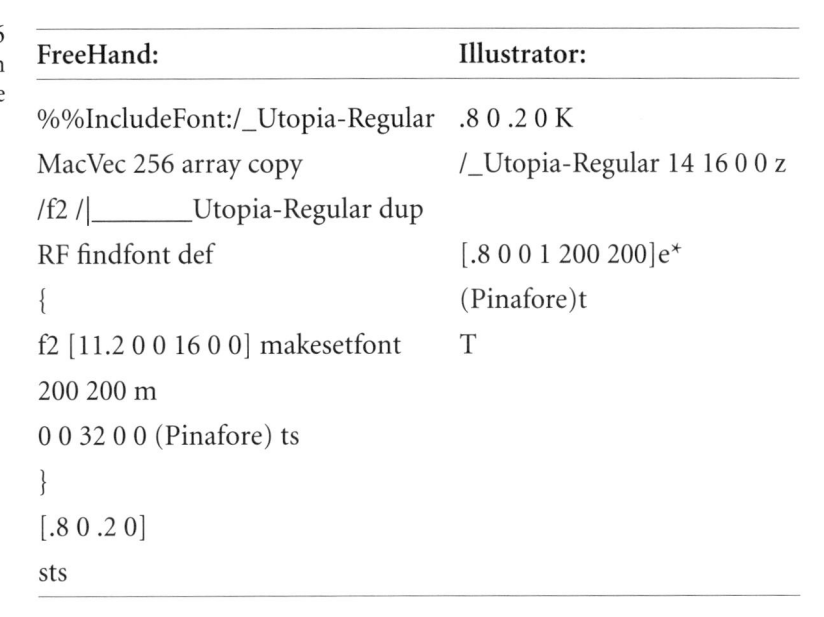

FreeHand:	Illustrator:
%%IncludeFont:/_Utopia-Regular	.8 0 .2 0 K
MacVec 256 array copy	/_Utopia-Regular 14 16 0 0 z
/f2 /|_____Utopia-Regular dup	
RF findfont def	[.8 0 0 1 200 200]e*
{	(Pinafore)t
f2 [11.2 0 0 16 0 0] makesetfont	T
200 200 m	
0 0 32 0 0 (Pinafore) ts	
}	
[.8 0 .2 0]	
sts	

Once you've reached the line "%%Trailer" you've finished converting the body of the file. Select through the line "%%Trailer" to the end of the file and delete the selection. Type in the Illustrator 1.1 codes for the end of the file as shown below.

```
%%PageTrailer
%%Trailer
_E end
%%EOF
```

Save the file as Text Only. Try opening it with Illustrator. If you've made a mistake, Illustrator displays a dialog box containing a hint (see Figure 4-32). FreeHand displays a dialog box telling you you've made an error, but doesn't give you the hint.

Make a note of what Illustrator thinks is wrong with the file, return to the file, and try to fix it.

FIGURE 4-32
Illustrator's hint

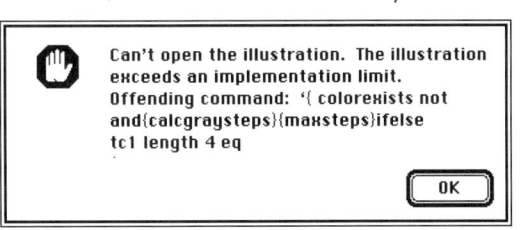

Can't open the illustration. The illustration exceeds an implementation limit.
Offending command: '{ colorexists not and{calcgraysteps}{maxsteps}ifelse tc1 length 4 eq

OK

Rasterizing FreeHand Objects

When you want to turn something you've drawn in FreeHand into a bitmap, you use the Create PICT Image Xtra or Photoshop. Why would you want to turn FreeHand objects into a bitmap? Because, if you do, you'll be able to run Photoshop filters on them, or take them into a painting program for editing. Finally, there's the Macromedia angle—you might want to use them in a Director presentation.

Using the Create PICT Image Xtra

If you don't have Photoshop, or if you simply don't want to leave FreeHand, you can rasterize objects in your publication using the Create PICT Image Xtra.

This technique works best with grayscale or black-and-white graphics, because FreeHand converts the color values in the objects you rasterize to RGB values in the bitmap it creates. This can cause color shifts in the objects (relative to other objects in the publication), and it means you've got to convert the values to CMYK again to print separations of the image.

The cool thing is that you can turn anything, *anything* in your FreeHand publication into a bitmap—provided you have enough RAM to create the image (if you don't have enough RAM, see "From FreeHand to Photoshop," later in this chapter). Once the PICT image is created and embedded in your publication, you can extract it, saving it as a TIFF (see "Extracting Embedded Graphics," earlier in this chapter).

To turn FreeHand objects into a bitmap (that is, rasterize them), follow these steps (see Figure 4-33).

1. Select the objects you want to rasterize.

2. Choose PICT Image from the Create submenu of the Xtras menu (or click the corresponding button in the Operations palette). FreeHand displays the Create PICT Image dialog box.

    This is the place where you have to make some tough decisions. Choosing to use more colors, or a higher resolution makes you image look better, but also makes the conversion process take longer.

IMPORTING AND EXPORTING   413

FIGURE 4-33
Rasterizing Objects
with the Create PICT
Image Xtra

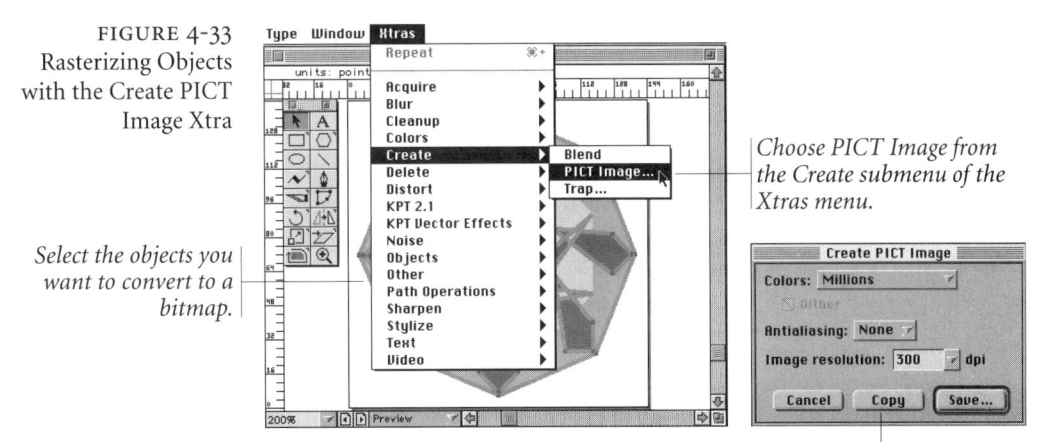

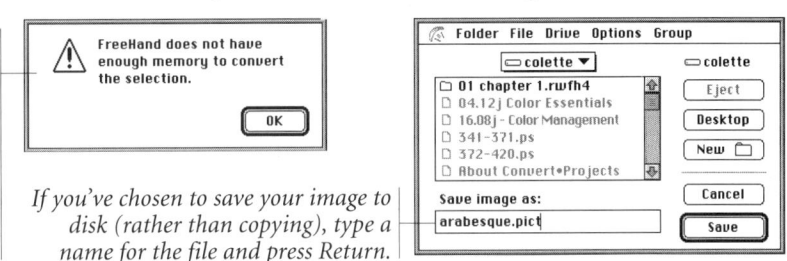

Choose PICT Image from the Create submenu of the Xtras menu.

Select the objects you want to convert to a bitmap.

FreeHand displays the Create Pict Image dialog box. Adjust the controls in the dialog box, then click Copy (to copy the image to the Clipboard) or Save (to save the image to disk).

Rasterizing FreeHand objects uses up lots of memory, so don't be surprised if you see this alert. You'll have to export the selected objects as a Photoshop EPS, then rasterize the EPS using Photoshop.

If you've chosen to save your image to disk (rather than copying), type a name for the file and press Return.

Unless you are creating an image for use in a Director presentation, I suggest you turn the Dither option off. When FreeHand converts FreeHand objects to a PICT Image, and you're using 256 colors or fewer, FreeHand dithers the colors in the image. If you're using Thousands or Millions of colors, Dither is unavailable.

Turn the Antialiasing option on if you want FreeHand to smooth the edges of the paths you're rasterizing. Usually, you use antialiasing when you're preparing files for online distribution—antialiasing rarely looks good in print.

Tip:
Bypassing the
Create PICT
Image dialog box

If you know that the last settings in the Create PICT Image dialog box are the same settings you want to use, you can skip the Create PICT Image dialog box by holding down Shift as you choose PICT Image from the Create submenu of the Xtras menu. When you do this, FreeHand creates a PICT image of the selected objects and copies the image to the Clipboard.

From FreeHand to Photoshop

The Create PICT Image Xtra often runs out of RAM when you're trying to rasterize FreeHand objects, particularly when you've chosen a large number of colors ("Thousands" or "Millions") and a high resolution. Sometimes, you won't be able to convert the objects you want.

If you own Photoshop, however, you can use it to rasterize FreeHand objects. The following steps show you how (see Figure 4-34).

1. Export the file you want to rasterize using the Photoshop EPS format.

2. Start Photoshop, if it's not already running, and open the EPS file you created. Photoshop displays the EPS Rasterizer dialog box (the title of this dialog box varies from version to version).

3. Choose the options you want in the EPS Rasterizer dialog box and press Return. Photoshop rasterizes the objects in the file.

Once you've converted the file to a bitmap image, you can set it up for color separation, if necessary, or apply effects to it with Photoshop's plug-ins.

FIGURE 4-34
Opening FreeHand Files in Photoshop

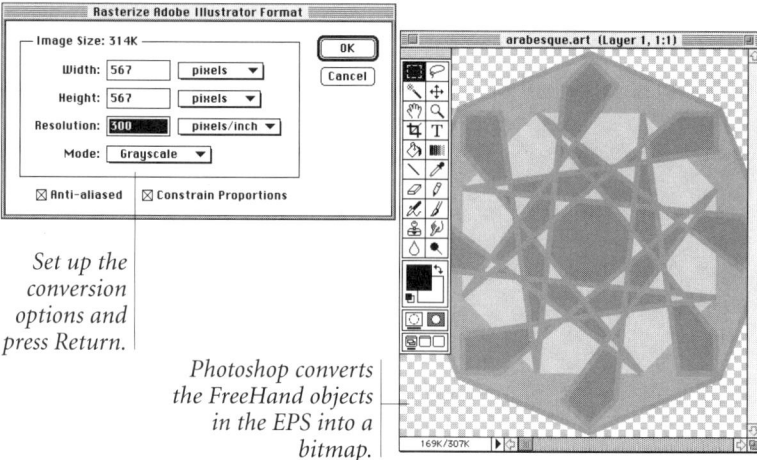

When you're ready to export the FreeHand objects you want to rasterize, choose Photoshop EPS as your export format.

When you open an EPS, Photoshop displays the Rasterize Adobe Illustrator Format dialog box.

Note: Photoshop won't rasterize images you've placed in your FreeHand publication (no, not even images saved in the EPS format).

Set up the conversion options and press Return.

Photoshop converts the FreeHand objects in the EPS into a bitmap.

Publishing and Subscribing

One of the features that appeared in System 7 is Publish and Subscribe—a way of linking data between applications. With Publish and Subscribe, you can import a chart from Excel into a Word document in such a way that the graphic in the Word document updates when you change the chart in Excel. It's an alternative to the usual export-and-then-import process, and features the ability to open the originating application (Excel, in the above example) from the subscribing application (Word).

I don't use Publish and Subscribe, myself—I find the process of saving files and importing them using Place easier to work with. I have been told that Publish and Subscribe is most useful when you need to update FreeHand graphics placed in multiple documents, or when you want to be able to launch FreeHand from an application containing a FreeHand EPS (though you can do this without using Publish and Subscribe; see "Linking to PageMaker," later in this chapter).

When you make a file available to Publish and Subscribe, you're "publishing" an "edition," and the application the file came from is called the "publisher." When you import the edition file, the application you're using is called the "subscriber." Just to make things a bit confusing, the edition file, once placed in your subscribing application, is also called the "subscriber."

FreeHand can act as both a publisher and a subscriber. To subscribe to an edition file, follow these steps (see Figure 4-35).

1. Publish the file (precisely how you do this differs from application to application, but it's usually the Create Publisher menu item under the Edit menu).

2. Switch to FreeHand and choose Subscribe To from the Editions submenu of the Edit menu.

3. In the Subscribe To dialog box, select the edition file you want to subscribe to and click OK. FreeHand changes the cursor into a Place Gun.

4. Click (or drag) the Place Gun in the publication window to position the edition file you're subscribing to.

FIGURE 4-35
Subscribe To
dialog box

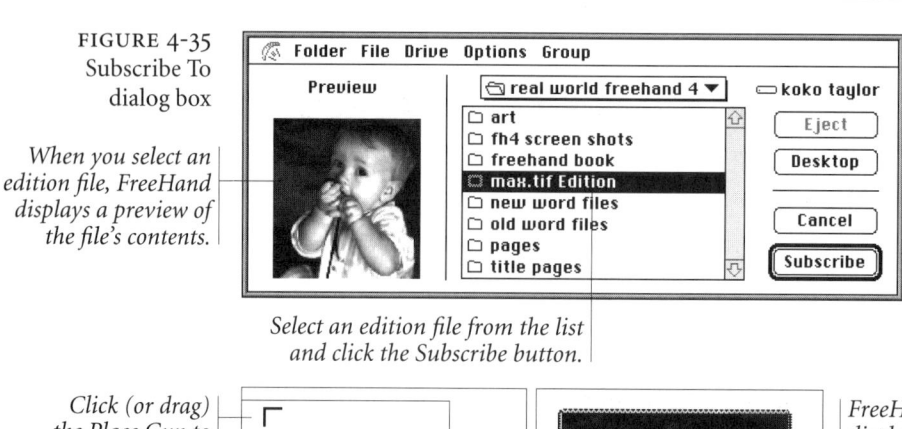

When you select an edition file, FreeHand displays a preview of the file's contents.

Select an edition file from the list and click the Subscribe button.

Click (or drag) the Place Gun to place the file.

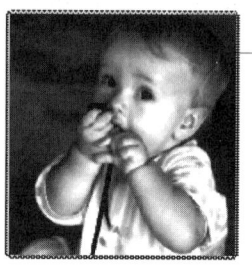

FreeHand displays a patterned border around edition files.

When you're subscribed to an edition, you can set the update options for that edition—do you want it to update (change) when and if the edition file changes? Do you want to update the edition now? Do you want to stop your subscription to the edition? To do any or all of these tasks, choose Subscriber Options from the Editions submenu of the Edit menu. FreeHand displays the Subscriber Options dialog box (see Figure 4-36).

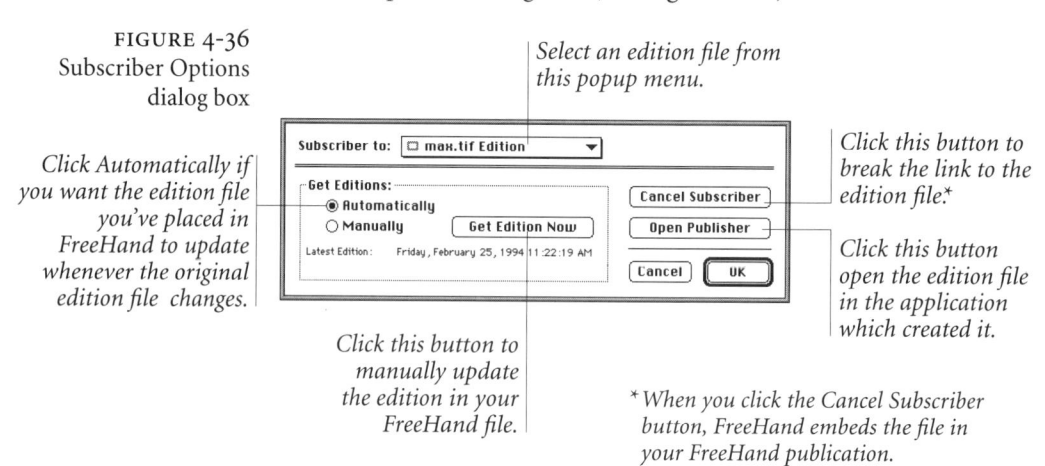

FIGURE 4-36
Subscriber Options
dialog box

Click Automatically if you want the edition file you've placed in FreeHand to update whenever the original edition file changes.

Select an edition file from this popup menu.

Click this button to break the link to the edition file.*

Click this button open the edition file in the application which created it.

Click this button to manually update the edition in your FreeHand file.

*When you click the Cancel Subscriber button, FreeHand embeds the file in your FreeHand publication.

IMPORTING AND EXPORTING 417

To publish an edition, follow these steps (see Figure 4-37).

1. In FreeHand, turn to the page you want to publish as an edition file. FreeHand publishes whole pages only—you can't publish selected items.

2. Choose Create Publisher from the Editions submenu of the Edit menu. FreeHand displays the Create Publisher dialog box.

3. In the Create Publisher dialog box, you can choose to publish your edition as either an EPS or a PICT file. Unless the application in which you're planning to place the edition file can't accept EPS graphics, use EPS, rather than PICT.

4. Enter a name for your edition file and press Return. FreeHand publishes the file, making it available to any application that supports Publish and Subscribe.

FIGURE 4-37
Publishing an edition

Create the objects you want to publish.

Choose Create Publisher from the Editions submenu of the Edit menu.

FreeHand displays the Create Publisher dialog box.

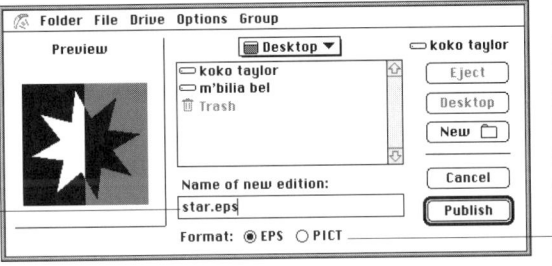

Type a name for your edition file here.

Choose an edition file format (choose EPS, unless you'll be printing to a non-PostScript printer, or know that the subscribing application can't subscribe to EPS).

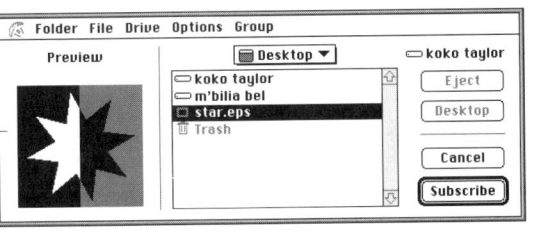

Here's your edition file, as seen from PageMaker's Subscribe To dialog box.

You can choose to update an edition you published with FreeHand (and, potentially, the way that edition appears in all subscribing documents), or cancel an edition, from FreeHand. To do this, choose Publisher Options from the Editions submenu of the Edit menu. FreeHand displays the Publisher Options dialog box.

If you're in FreeHand and you want to edit an edition file in its originating application, choose Edit Original from the Editions submenu of the Edit menu. Your Macintosh switches to the application (if it's running) or locates and launches the application (if it's not), and then opens the edition file in that application.

Keep the following things in mind when you're working with Publish and Subscribe.

- When you subscribe to an edition that's been published as a PICT or as an EPS, FreeHand doesn't convert the file to FreeHand elements (as it would if you placed the file). It acts like an imported graphic.

- You can't apply text wrap to a subscriber.

- Instead of the usual selection handles, edition files display a dotted border when you select them in your FreeHand publication. When you cancel a subscription to a particular edition, the file displays normal selection handles.

When you want to delete an edition file published by FreeHand, thereby breaking the link between the edition and all subscribing documents, choose Subscriber Options or Publisher Options from the Editions submenu of the Edit menu. In either dialog box, click the Cancel Publisher button. FreeHand deletes the edition file. When you do this, the appearance of your subscribing publications doesn't change—they'll still contain the edition file, just as if you'd placed it.

Tip: Linking to PageMaker

PageMaker and FreeHand have their own link—when you hold down Option and double-click a selected FreeHand EPS in a PageMaker publication, PageMaker switches to FreeHand (if it's running), or launches FreeHand (if it's not running), and opens the original file (or the EPS file, if the EPS file contains the FreeHand file). When you save the file from FreeHand, FreeHand exports the file and updates the EPS in your PageMaker publication.

Managing Linked Files

When you link to a TIFF or EPS file, FreeHand doesn't include the file in your publication, but establishes a link between the publication and the imported file. Linking means you don't have to store two copies of the original file—one on disk, and one in your FreeHand publication—which saves disk space.

When you move a linked file, or change its name (including any changes you might make to the name of the folder you've stored it in—or the volume you've stored it on), you break the link between the file and any FreeHand publication you've placed it in. You can also break the link when you move the publication file to another volume.

When you do this, FreeHand displays a box where the linked graphic would appear in your publication (see Figure 4-38). Don't worry—FreeHand maintains the link information. This means you can still link the file, once you find it.

If FreeHand can't find a linked file when you're opening a publication, it looks in the folder containing the illustration for the linked file. If FreeHand doesn't find the linked file there, it displays the Locate File dialog box (see Figure 4-39). Use the Locate File dialog box to locate and link to the file.

If you can't find the original file, you can close the Locate File dialog box without linking to a file. Locate the original file, and put it inside the same folder as the publication, and FreeHand updates the link (unless you're in keyline mode, you'll see the image replace the placeholder in the publication window).

FIGURE 4-38
Losing links

When you move, delete, or rename a linked file, FreeHand displays a box where the file appeared in your publication.

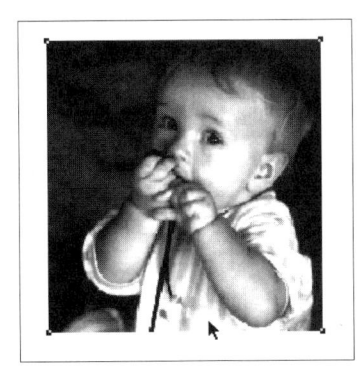

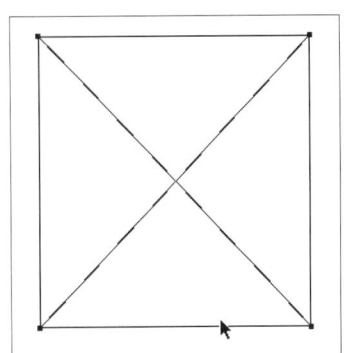

FIGURE 4-39
Locate File dialog box

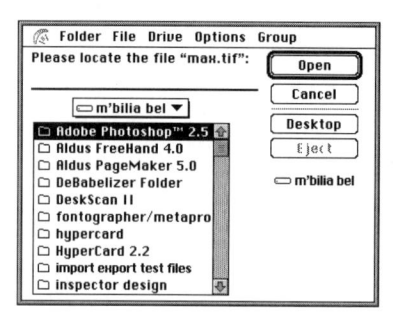

Tip:
Losing Links on Purpose

I work on my FreeHand documents at my office and at home. When I need to work on a FreeHand publication at home, I frequently leave linked TIFF images behind, and take just the FreeHand publication file. This means that I can still work on any text or paths in the file, but that I don't have to carry the TIFF files around (also, working with TIFFs on my slow home machine is pretty painful). I can even change the position and size of the TIFF placeholders. When I open the file back at my office, FreeHand re-links to the TIFFs.

Working with PDF

FreeHand 5.5 can open Adobe Acrobat Portable Document Format files (or PDF), turning the contents of the files into editable FreeHand objects as it does so. Many of you have gotten the idea that PDF is great for putting publications on the World Wide Web, or for creating other sorts of online publications. Many of you, on thinking this, have to stifle a yawn whenever the topic comes up. Sure, it's a great format for that pie-in-the-sky "paperless office" stuff, but what's it got to do with the world of ink-on-paper where most of us spend our time?

I'll tell you. PDF isn't just for online publications. It makes a great format for moving laid-out pages from one publishing application to another—what's usually called an "interchange format" (RTF is another example of an interchange format). Having FreeHand read PDF files makes it easy to take a page you laid out in PageMaker, or XPress, and open it in FreeHand. The conversion won't always be perfect, but it'll often be close.

For the most part, creating a PDF file is a two-step process. First, you print a publication to disk as PostScript, then you run the PostScript file through the Acrobat Distiller (which is a limited PostScript interpreter—see Appendix A, "System"). The Distiller saves the rendered PostScript file as a PDF. This is how you'd create a PDF from a FreeHand publication.

There's no trick to opening a PDF—you open it as you would any FreeHand publication. Once you've opened a PDF, however, there are a few things you should look for.

- Bookmarks, annotations, and thumbnails in PDF files are not converted when you open the PDF.

- If some or all of the fonts used in a PDF file aren't available, you'll have to substitute fonts (just as you would if you'd opened a FreeHand publication containing fonts FreeHand can't find on your system)

- Text will sometimes be broken into short "runs" of text—creating a new text block for every change in formatting. You can combine these text blocks as you would any FreeHand text blocks.

- If each page of a converted PDF file appears as a single object, the elements on the page have probably been enclosed by a clipping path. Select each page and press Command-Shift-X (or choose Cut Contents from the Edit menu) to remove the elements from the clipping path.

The Best of All Possible Worlds

Can you get there from here? When you're working with FreeHand, you can almost always export or save files in a form you can use in another program, and you can usually produce files in other programs you import or open using FreeHand.

There are definitely bumps in the road—PageMaker's confused EPS Import filter, for example. Sometimes, you've got to go through an intermediate program—such as the amazing DeBabelizer—to convert files from one format to another (particularly if the files came from another type of computer).

Someday, we'll have a more complete, universal, and sophisticated file format for exchanging publications. I'd like to think that Adobe Acrobat's PDF would be that format, but few applications, as I write this, both read and write PDF. When the great day arrives, we'll be able to take page layouts from FreeHand to PageMaker to Photoshop—using each program for what it's best at—without losing any formatting.

And the streets will be paved with gold, mounted beggars will spend the day ducking winged pigs, and the Seattle Mariners will win the World Series.

CHAPTER

Transforming

5

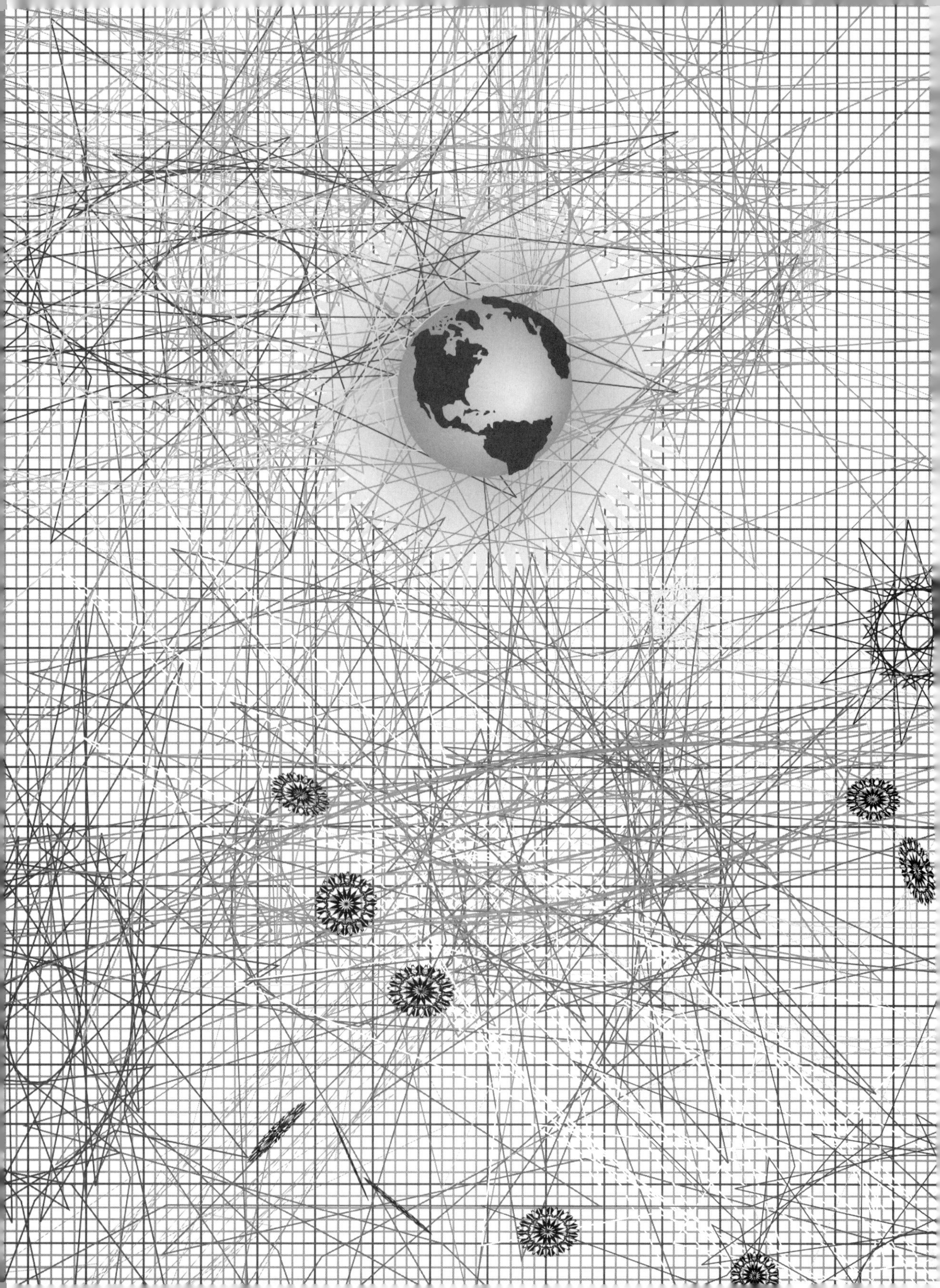

CHAPTER FIVE ❧ TRANSFORMING

In the previous chapters, I've covered the process of creating FreeHand elements. This chapter talks about what you can do with those elements once you've drawn, typed, or imported them. The process of rotating, reflecting, skewing, scaling, cloning, or moving objects is called *transformation*.

Many of the topics in this chapter have been touched on in the preceding chapters—mainly because everything you can do in FreeHand is interconnected. In the old days, software was entirely linear or modal: one had to proceed from this screen to that screen following a particular sequence of steps. These days, software is extremely nonlinear and nonmodal (that is, you can do things many different ways in many different orders), and, therefore much harder to write about. Your purchase of this book will make my time at Looney Farm that much more pleasant. Thank you.

Transformations are the key to using FreeHand efficiently. I don't know how many times I've seen people laboriously drawing and redrawing shapes when they could have been using the Clone, Rotate, and Reflect commands to accomplish the same ends faster and with far less trouble. Any time you can see a similarity between the shapes on one side of an object and another, you should be thinking about reflection. Any time you see an object that's made up of the same shape rotated around a center point, you should be thinking about rotation. Start looking at the paths you draw as patterns of clones and transformations, and you'll be a long way toward becoming a FreeHand wizard.

Like the Inspector, the Transform palette has several different subpanels (for moving, rotating, scaling, skewing, and reflecting objects). I refer to each panel as a separate palette: the Move, Rotate, Scale, Skew, and Reflect palettes. This beats saying "the Rotate panel of the Transformation palette."

In addition to the operations corresponding to the transformation tools, I think of several other FreeHand features as "transformations." Specifically, I include clipping paths (using Paste Inside), locking objects, and alignment and distribution. You'll find these topics at the end of the chapter.

There are two ways to transform any object on a FreeHand page. After you select an object, you can drag using the specific transformation tool, or you can type numbers in the Transform palette (see Figure 5-1). There's no "right" or "best" way to do transformations—you can experiment with the different methods and see which you like best. I change methods depending on the situation (and my mood).

If that's all there is to transforming, then what's in the rest of this chapter? Homespun philosophical insights guaranteed to make this book a checkout counter bestseller? Nope. As you might expect, there's more to transforming objects than meets the eye. The rest of the chapter covers the down-and-dirty details.

Grouping and Transformation

When you transform a group, FreeHand transforms all the lines and fills inside the group proportionally, unless you've checked Transforms As Unit (which you'll find in the Object Inspector for the group). Check this option if you want to transform the line weights and fills inside the group nonproportionally, resulting in an effect that resembles perspective drawing (see Figure 5-2).

When you ungroup objects you've transformed with Transform As Unit turned on, any lines and fills applied to those objects revert to their undistorted appearance.

Transformation Shortcuts

As you think about transforming objects, keep in mind two of FreeHand's most important keyboard shortcuts: Command-, (comma) and Command-D.

Command-, means "transform it again"; it performs the previous transformation you used (see Figure 5-3). You don't even have

TRANSFORMING 427

FIGURE 5-1
Transforming
anything

*Transforming objects
by dragging*

Rotation tool

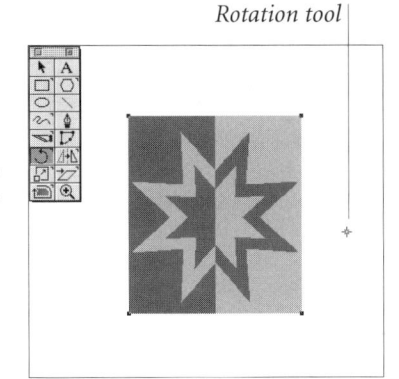

Axis of transformation

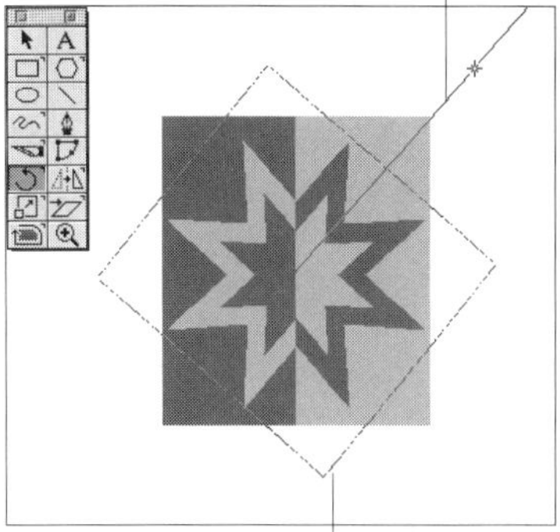

Keyline preview of
transformation.

Select the object you want to transform, then select the transformation tool you want to use. In this example, I've selected the Rotation tool.

Drag the transformation tool in the Publication window. As you drag, FreeHand displays a preview of the transformed object.

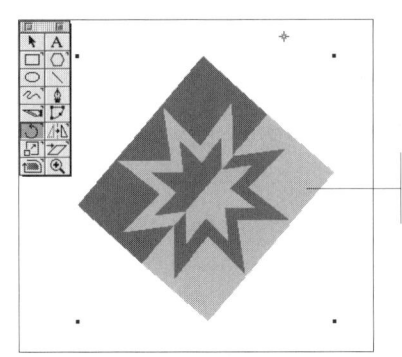

When the object looks the way you want it to, stop dragging. FreeHand transforms the object.

*Transforming objects
using the Transform
palette*

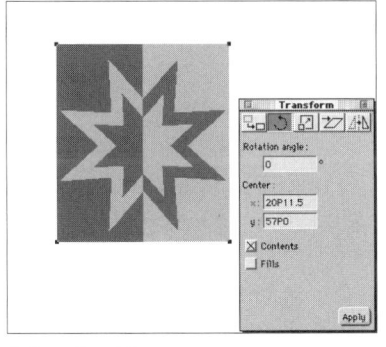

Select the object you want to rotate and press Command-M to display the Transform palette. Click the buttons at the top of the palette to display the transformation you want. In this example, I'm using the Rotate palette.

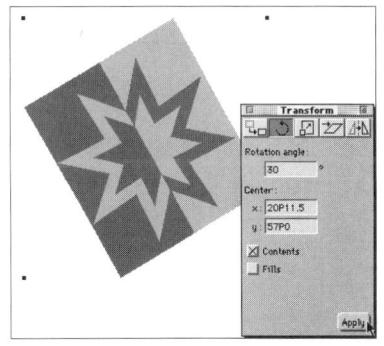

Enter the values you want in the Transform palette (in this example, the Rotate palette), check any appropriate checkboxes (they vary from palette to palette), and click the Apply button (or press Return).

FIGURE 5-2
Transforming groups

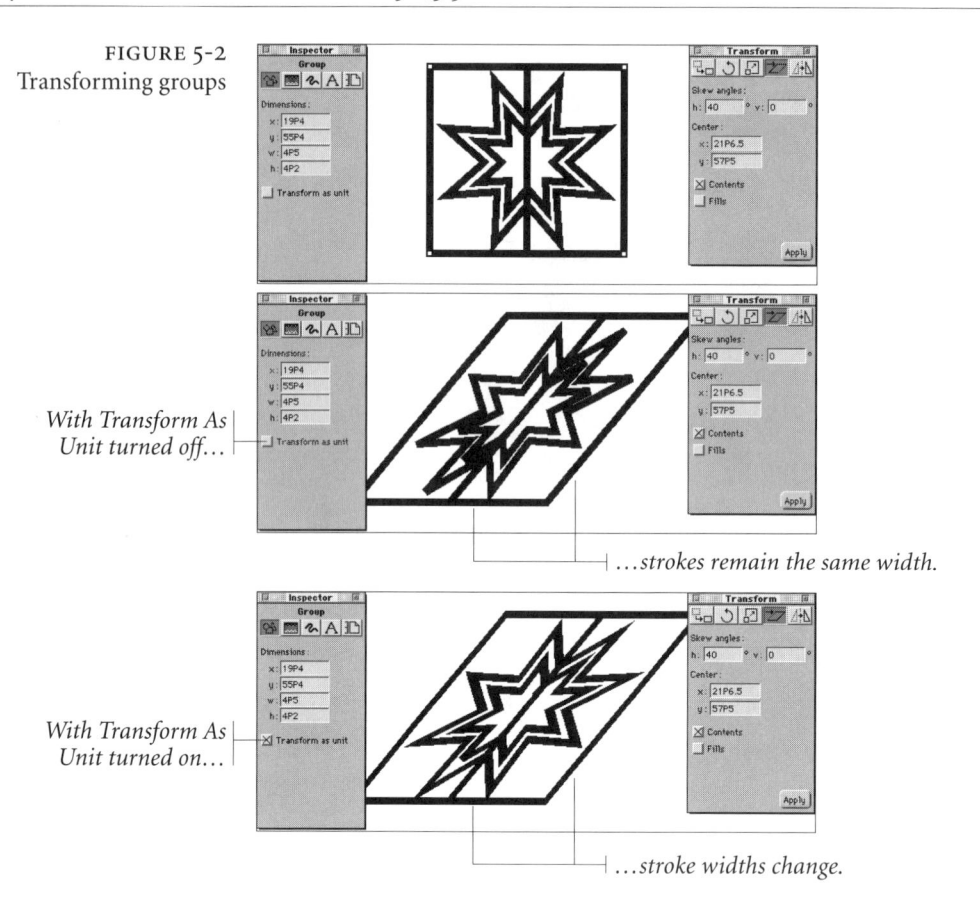

With Transform As
Unit turned off...

...strokes remain the same width.

With Transform As
Unit turned on...

...stroke widths change.

FIGURE 5-3
Transform again

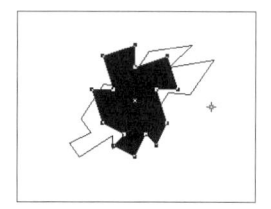

Transform an object (in this example, I'm skewing the object using the Skewing tool).

Press Command-comma, and FreeHand applies the most recent transformation again.

to have the same object selected as the one you originally transformed—you can transform an object, select a different object, and then transform that object using the same settings.

Command-, is great for experimentation, because just by pressing the keyboard shortcut you can ask, What if I moved it a little bit more? or What if I skewed it a little bit more? If you don't like what you've done, press Command-Z to undo it.

If you haven't done any transformations lately, Command-D actually does what the menu item (Duplicate) says—it duplicates the object, placing the duplicate at a slight distance from the original object. Most of the time, however, Command-D means, "Clone it and transform it again," and performs the most recent transformation while cloning the currently selected object. You can use Command-D to do all kinds of things (see Figure 5-4).

Note that the transformation (whatever it was) persists until the next transformation. That is, if you rotate something, drag out some ruler guides, copy something to the Scrapbook, then select an object and press Command-, FreeHand rotates the object as you specified in the earlier transformation—*even if it's not the same object you originally transformed.*

FIGURE 5-4
Clone and transform again

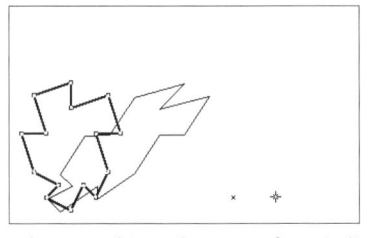

Clone an object, then transform it (in this example, I've skewed the clone of the object using the Skewing tool).

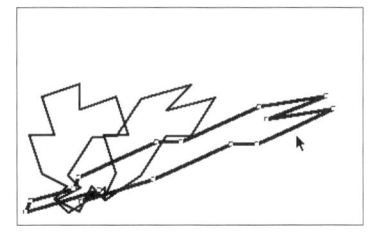

Press Command-D, and FreeHand clones the selected object and applies the last transformation to it.

Moving

Moving an object from one place to another is probably the task you do most often in FreeHand. There are four ways to move objects in FreeHand.

- Dragging the objects with the Pointer tool.

- Entering values in the Move palette.

- Changing coordinates in the Object Inspector.

- Pressing the arrow, or "nudge" keys.

Moving Path Contents and Fills

Check the Contents box when you want objects that you've pasted inside a path to move with that path (see Figure 5-5). Check Fills to move the fill you've applied to the path (see Figure 5-6)—though it only makes a difference when you're moving paths filled with tiled fills. If you don't want the paths' contents or fill to move, uncheck the appropriate checkbox (or checkboxes).

Note that these checkboxes affect movement whether you're using the Move palette to move objects or not.

These checkboxes have no effect on objects other than paths.

FIGURE 5-5
Moving contents

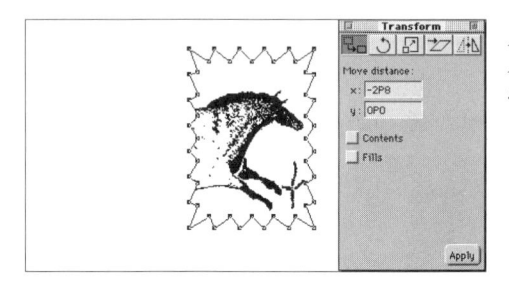

In this example, I'll use the Move palette to move the selected path to the left.

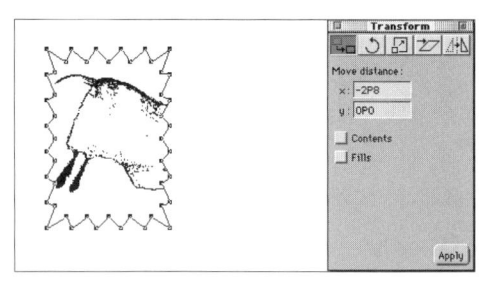

With Contents off, objects you've pasted inside a path don't move when you move the path.

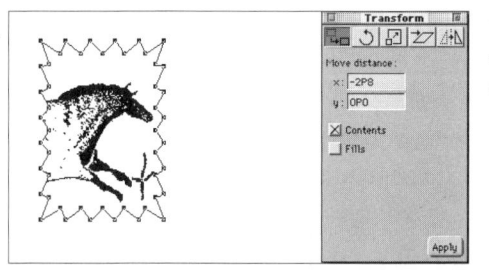

With Contents turned on, objects you've pasted inside a path move with the path.

Tip: Moving Selected Points

When you drag some, but not all, of the points on a path, FreeHand doesn't move objects you've pasted inside the path, regardless of the state of the Contents checkbox in the Move palette. This comes in handy when you need to adjust a path you've used to crop a TIFF image (see Figure 5-7).

FIGURE 5-6
Moving fills

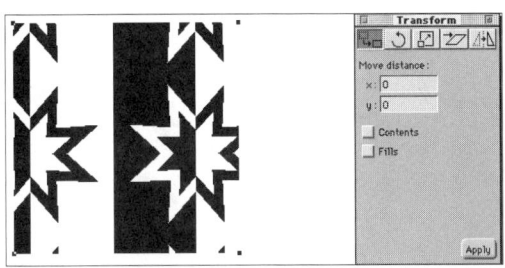

In this example, I'll use the Move palette to move the selected path to the right.

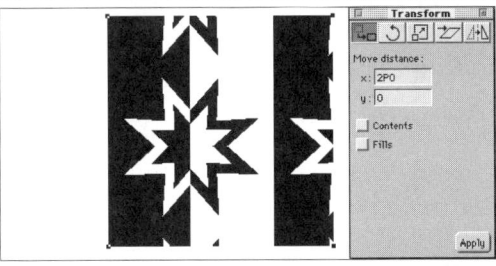

With Fills off, the path's tiled fill doesn't move with the path.

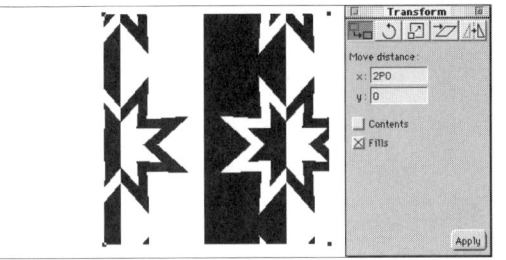

With Fills turned on, the tiled fill moves as you move the path.

FIGURE 5-7
Moving selected points

Regardless of the setting of the Contents checkbox in the Move palette, moving points does not move the contents of the path (unless, that is, you select all of the points in the path).

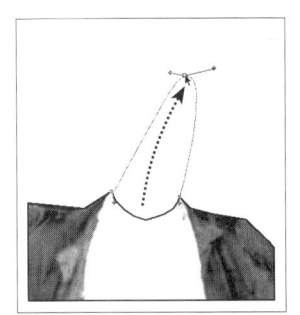

This is a good thing, because it makes it easy to edit paths you've used to crop TIFFs.

Tip:
A Trick that No Longer Works

In FreeHand 3, you could select and move all the points in a path without moving the path's contents, regardless of the state of the Contents checkbox in the Move dialog box (in FreeHand 3, all the controls in FreeHand's Transform palette were found in separate dialog boxes). When you select and move all the points in a path, FreeHand moves—or doesn't move—the contents of the path, depending on the state of the Contents field in the Move palette.

The good news, however, is that the control is no longer buried—it's in the Move palette, where you can always check the setting before you move a path (the original tip was great, because it saved you a trip to a dialog box).

Moving by Dragging

FreeHand's just like any other Macintosh program—if you want to move something, select the object with the Pointer tool and drag.

Tip:
Dragging Things Quickly Versus Dragging Things Slowly

If you select something and immediately start dragging, you'll see only a box the shape of the object's selection rectangle. If, on the other hand, you hold down the mouse button for a second before dragging, you'll see the object as you drag it (whether this works for multiple selected objects or not depends on the setting you've entered in the Preview Drag field in the Editing Preferences dialog box; see "Setting Preferences" in Chapter 1, "FreeHand Basics").

Dragging quickly is great for snapping objects into position by their outlines; waiting a second before dragging is best for seeing things inside a selection as you position them on the page (see Figure 5-8).

FIGURE 5-8
Seeing objects as you drag them

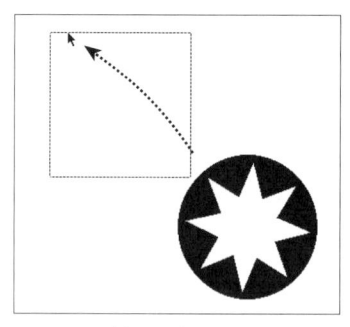

Drag quickly, and you'll see only an outline of the objects.

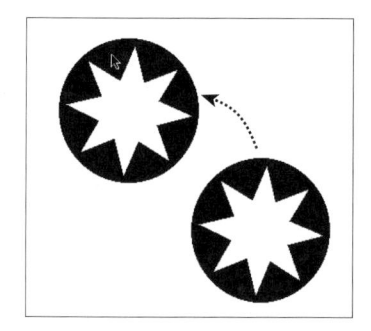

Pause a second before you start dragging, and you'll see the objects.

Tip:
Seeing What
You Drag

To make FreeHand show you a screen display of the object you're dragging—no matter how many objects you've selected and no matter what the setting of the Preview Drag preference—tap the Option key before you start dragging (that is, after you've pressed the mouse button down, but before you've moved the mouse). Wait for FreeHand to draw the objects you've selected, and then drag the objects. As you drag, FreeHand displays the objects.

Tip:
Constraining
Movement

Holding down Shift as you drag elements constrains their movement to 45-degree angles (just as in almost every other Macintosh graphics application), which makes it easy to drag objects only horizontally or vertically. FreeHand adds another wrinkle, however: the axis from which those 45-degree increments are derived can be set to present any angle (see "Constraining Tools" in Chapter 1, "FreeHand Basics").

Moving "By the Numbers"

When I need precision, I always move objects by entering numbers in the Move palette (see Figure 5-9). And it's not just because I'm a closet rocket scientist; it's because I don't trust a 72-dpi screen, even at 800 percent magnification (at 256k percent magnification, I'm still skeptical). You shouldn't either, when it comes to fine adjustments in your FreeHand publication.

1. Select the object you want to move.

2. Display the Transform palette, if it's not already visible (you can double-click any of the transformation tools in the toolbox to display the palette, or press Command-M). Click the Move icon button at the top of the Transform palette to display the Move palette, if necessary.

3. Enter values in the fields. Type positive numbers to move objects up (toward the top of the screen) or to the right; type negative numbers to move them down or to the left).

4. Set the Contents and Fills checkboxes the way you want them (see "Moving Contents and Fills," earlier in this chapter).

5. Press Return (or click the Apply button). FreeHand moves the selected object.

FIGURE 5-9
Moving with
the Move palette

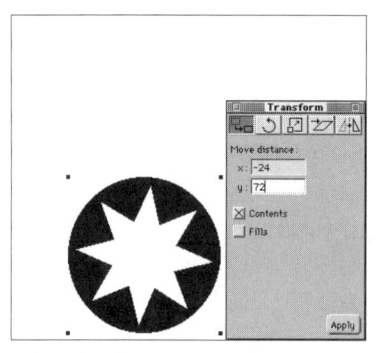

Select the object you want to move and type distances in the Move palette.

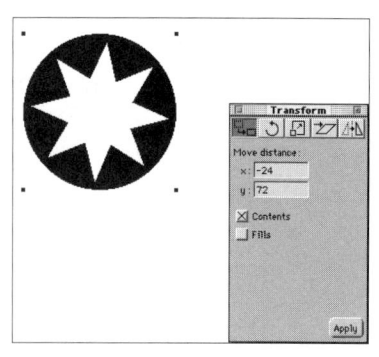

Click the Apply button, and FreeHand moves the object the distance and direction you specified.

Moving Objects with the Inspector

The X and Y fields in the Object Inspector aren't only there to show you where the object is; you can use them to move the object to a specific location on your page. To move the object to a new location, type coordinates in the X and Y fields (remember, coordinates are measured from the current position of the zero point, and specify the location of the lower-left corner of the selected object), and press Return (see Figure 5-10).

If you're looking at the Object Inspector, and you don't see the X and Y fields, you're looking at an ungrouped path. Group the path, and the fields appear in the Object Inspector. You can always ungroup the path after you've moved it.

FIGURE 5-10
Moving with
the Object Inspector

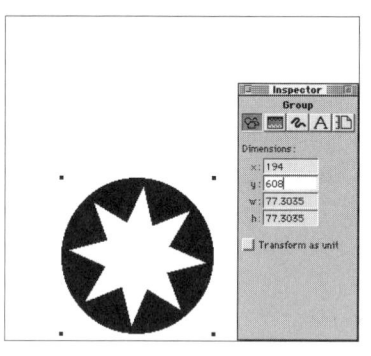

Enter the coordinates at which you want to position the lower-left corner of the object in the X and Y fields of the Object Inspector and press Return.

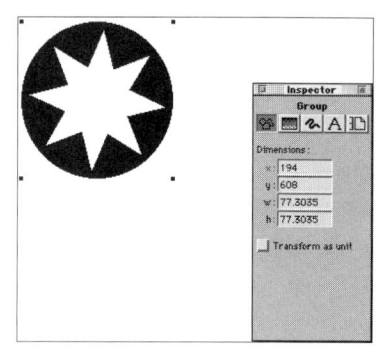

FreeHand moves the object to the new coordinates.

Moving by Pressing Arrow Keys

As if dragging by eye and specifying coordinates weren't enough movement options, FreeHand also sports "nudge" keys. Select an element and press one of the arrow keys, and the element moves in that direction in the increments you set in the Cursor Key Distance field in the Editing Preferences dialog box (see "Setting Preferences" in Chapter 1, "FreeHand Basics").

Scaling

In FreeHand, you can change the size of objects using any of the following techniques.

- Dragging the Scaling tool on the page.
- Entering values in the Scale palette.
- Dragging a selection handle with the Pointer tool.
- Changing values in the Object Inspector.

In addition, you can change the size of text boxes by changing the size of the column heights and row widths in the Column Inspector (see "Multicolumn and Multirow Text Blocks" in Chapter 3, "Text and Type").

Scaling Contents, Fills, and Lines

When you scale a path, you can choose to scale the path's contents (that is, whatever you've pasted inside the path), or the fill and stroke you've applied to the path. To scale these items, check the Contents, Fills, or Lines boxes, respectively, in the Scale palette (see Figure 5-11). To keep the paths' attributes from scaling as you scale the path, uncheck the appropriate box or boxes.

Using the Scaling Tool

When you want to scale an object until it "looks right," use the scaling tool (see Figure 5-12).

1. Use the Pointer tool to select the object you want to scale.
2. Select the Scaling tool from the toolbox.

FIGURE 5-11
Scaling path attributes

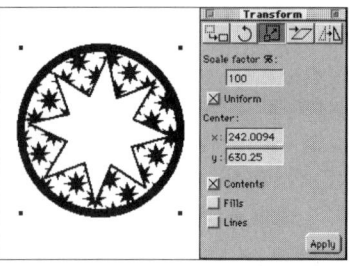

Original object before scaling

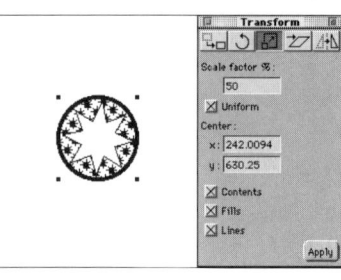

When you check the Fills and Lines boxes, FreeHand scales those path attributes as it scales objects.

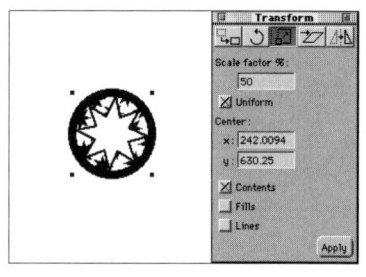

When you uncheck Fills and Lines, FreeHand does not scale any strokes or fills as it scales objects.

FIGURE 5-12
Using the Scaling tool

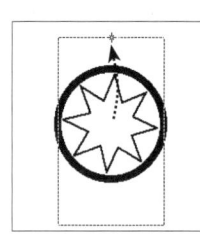

To scale an object vertically, select the object and drag the Scaling tool up (to make the object larger) or down (to make the object smaller).

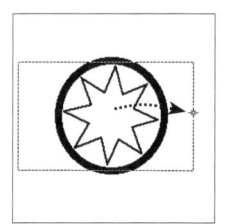

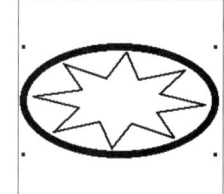

To scale an object horizontally, select the object and drag the Scaling tool to the left (to make the object smaller) or to the right (to make the object larger).

To proportionally scale an object, select the object and hold down Shift as you drag the Scaling tool.

To scale from an object's center, hold down Control as you drag the Scaling tool.

3. Position the Scaling tool at the point around which you want to scale. Most of the time, you'll want to hold down Control to scale an object around its center.

4. Drag the Scaling tool horizontally to scale the object's width, or drag vertically to scale the object's height. Dragging diagonally sizes the object's width and height. Hold down Shift as you drag to scale the object proportionally.

    If the object you're scaling is a paint-type graphic or a bilevel TIFF, you can hold down Option and Shift to scale the object both proportionally and to the printer's resolution (which you set in the Target Printer Resolution field in the Setup Inspector; see "Using the Setup Inspector" in Chapter 1, "FreeHand Basics").

5. When the object's the size you want it, stop dragging.

Using the Scale Palette

When you know you want to make an object larger or smaller by an exact percentage, use the Scale palette (see Figure 5-13).

1. Select the object you want to scale.

2. Display the Scale palette (if it's not already visible, double-click the scaling tool in the toolbox).

FIGURE 5-13
Using the Scale palette

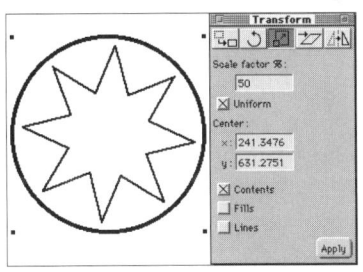

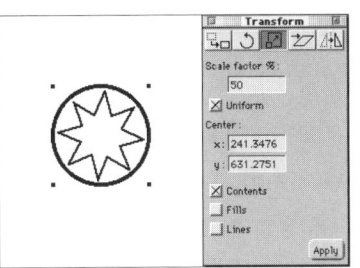

Select the object you want to scale and type a percentage in the Scale Factor % field.

If you want to scale an object non-proportionally, uncheck Uniform.

Press Return (or click Apply), and FreeHand scales the object.

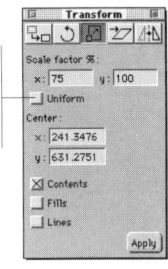

3. Uncheck Uniform if you want to scale the object's width and height by different percentages (leave Uniform checked to scale both dimensions by the same percentage).

4. Set the Contents, Fills, and Lines checkboxes the way you want them (see "Scaling Contents, Fills, and Lines," earlier in this chapter).

5. Enter percentages in the Scale Factor field (or, if you're scaling width and height separately, enter percentages in the X and Y fields).

6. Press Return to scale the object.

Tip: Resetting the Center of Scaling

If you want to use the Scale palette to resize an object around its center point, and see that the coordinates in the X and Y fields in the Scale palette aren't at the center of the object (it's easy to accidentally set them to other coordinates—all it takes is clicking the scaling tool on the page), you can reset them to the object's center.

Click on the object with the Pointer tool (hold down Command to turn the current tool into the Pointer tool, if necessary), and FreeHand enters the coordinates of the object's geometric center in the X and Y fields.

Tip: Picking a Point to Scale Around

Suppose you want to enlarge or reduce an object, but you want the lower-left corner of the object to stay in its original location (that is, you want the object to grow up, and to the right). If you know the location of the point you want to scale around, you can enter that point in the Scale palette—but I rarely go to all that trouble—I simply click the Scaling tool on that point (being careful, as I do so, that I don't drag the tool). FreeHand enters the coordinates of the point I click on in the X and Y fields in the Scale palette.

Tip: Positioning Objects by Setting the Zero Point

One of the easiest ways to set the center of transformation is to position the zero point where you want the center of the object to fall, and then enter "0" in the Horizontal and Vertical fields in the Center options section of the Scale dialog box. It's easier than entering "23.0476" and "47.135" (for example).

Scaling with the Pointer Tool

As in any other Macintosh drawing or page-layout application, you can change the size of objects by dragging their corner handles with the Pointer tool (see Figure 5-14). As you drag, the object you're dragging gets larger or smaller. Hold down Shift as you drag to resize the object proportionally.

I confess: I use this method far more often than I use the Scaling tool (mainly because I can switch to the Pointer tool from any tool by holding down Command, while there's no keyboard shortcut for the Scaling tool).

When you resize a rectangle, ellipse, or grouped path by dragging a selection handle, FreeHand doesn't resize anything you've pasted inside the object, regardless of whether Contents is checked in the Scale palette.

Tip: Resizing from an Object's Center

Hold down Option as you drag a selection handle to resize an imported graphic, group, rectangle, or ellipse from its center point. This trick doesn't work for ungrouped paths.

FIGURE 5-14
Scaling objects by dragging selection handles

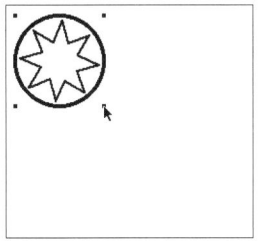

With the Pointer tool, position the cursor over a corner handle...

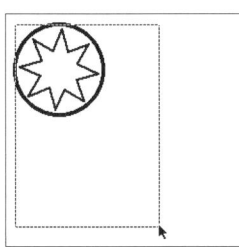

...and drag to scale the object.

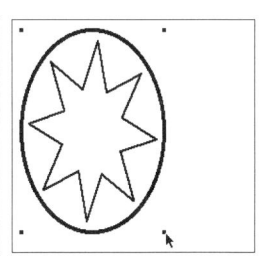

When the object is the size and shape you want, stop dragging.

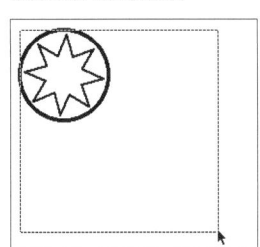

To scale an object proportionally, hold down Shift as you drag a corner handle.

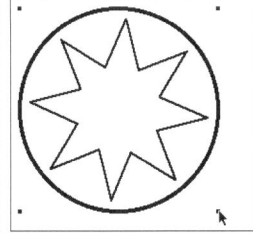

To scale a group, imported graphic, or basic shape from its center point, hold down Option as you drag.

Scaling with the Object Inspector

When you select an object other than an ungrouped path, that object's width and height appear in the W and H fields in the Object Inspector (to see the width and height of a path, first select the path and press Command-G to group it). To change the object's width or height, enter new values in these fields, and press Return. FreeHand changes the size of the object.

I find this feature particularly useful when I'm working with rectangles I've drawn with the Rectangle tool. I use rectangles a lot when I'm laying out a page, and I usually know what size they need to be, so I use the Object Inspector to set their width and height. Doing that is often easier than drawing them to precisely the right size.

Rotating

Some applications (such as PageMaker) store the original orientation and angle of objects on their pages. To these applications, rotation is an absolute measurement—the current angle of an object always refers to that object's original rotation angle (usually zero degrees). In FreeHand, rotation is a relative—the object's current angle of rotation is always considered to be zero degrees, regardless of any previous rotation.

This approach has advantages and disadvantages. You can't rotate an object back to its original state by giving it a rotation angle of zero, as you can in PageMaker (in FreeHand, a rotation angle of zero means the object doesn't rotate at all). In FreeHand, however, you can always rotate the object another 12.5 degrees, without adding that value to the object's existing rotation angle to derive the angle you enter (as you would in PageMaker).

You can always rotate an object back to its original angle, provided you keep track of how far you've rotated it away from that angle.

Using the Rotation Tool

To rotate an object "by eye," follow these steps (see Figure 5-15).

1. Select the object you want to rotate.

2. Select the Rotation tool from the toolbox.

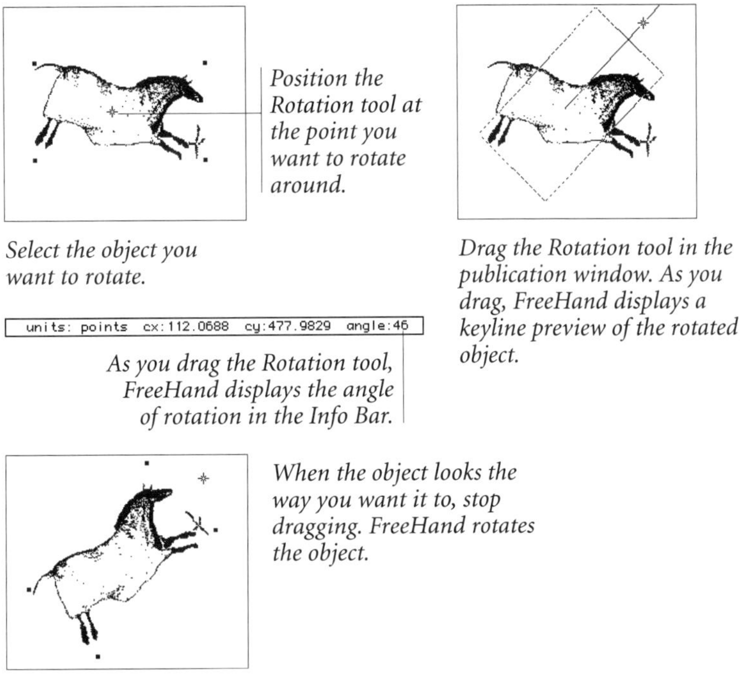

FIGURE 5-15
Rotating an object using the Rotation tool

Position the Rotation tool at the point you want to rotate around.

Select the object you want to rotate.

Drag the Rotation tool in the publication window. As you drag, FreeHand displays a keyline preview of the rotated object.

As you drag the Rotation tool, FreeHand displays the angle of rotation in the Info Bar.

When the object looks the way you want it to, stop dragging. FreeHand rotates the object.

3. Position the Rotation tool at the point where you want to put the center of rotation. Hold down Control to set the center of rotation at the center of the object.

4. Drag the Rotation tool. As you drag, FreeHand displays the angle of rotation in the Info Bar.

5. When the object looks the way you want, stop dragging.

Using the Rotate Palette

To rotate an object using FreeHand's Rotate palette, follow these steps (see Figure 5-16).

1. Select the object you want to rotate.

2. Display the Rotate palette (if it's not already visible, double-click the Rotation tool in the toolbox).

3. If you're rotating a path, make sure that the Contents and Fills checkboxes are set the way you want them (see "Rotating Contents and Fills," later in this chapter).

FIGURE 5-16
Rotating an object
"by the numbers"

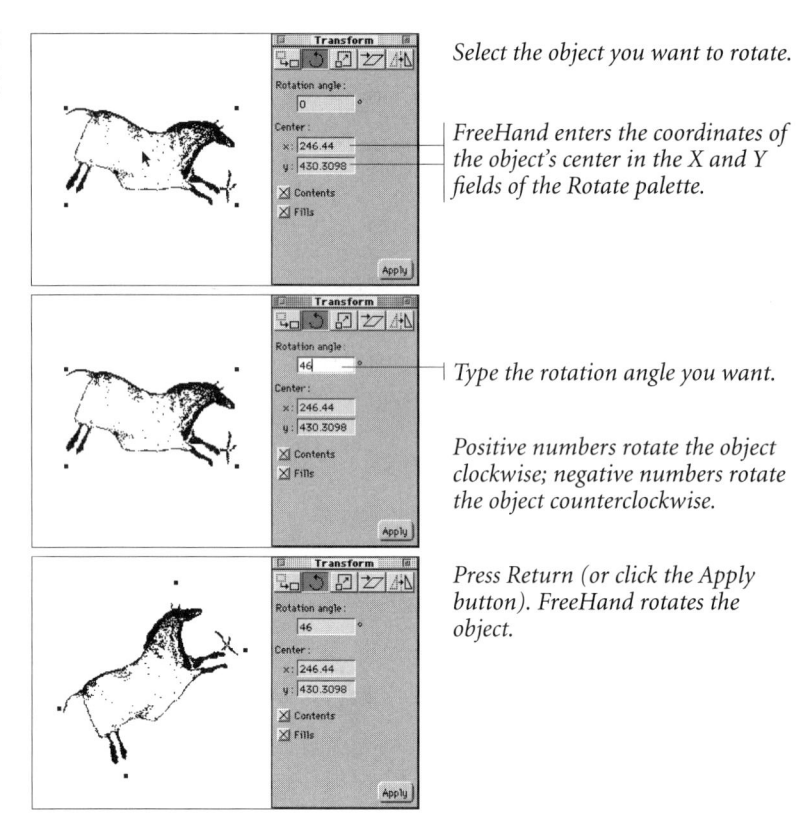

Select the object you want to rotate.

FreeHand enters the coordinates of the object's center in the X and Y fields of the Rotate palette.

Type the rotation angle you want.

Positive numbers rotate the object clockwise; negative numbers rotate the object counterclockwise.

Press Return (or click the Apply button). FreeHand rotates the object.

4. Enter values in the Rotation angle field.

    FreeHand's Rotate palette isn't picky. You can enter positive numbers (such as "45"), negative numbers (such as "-270"), and absurd numbers (such as "478") in the Rotation Angle field. Positive rotation angles rotate the selected object clockwise; negative values rotate the object counterclockwise. You enter rotation angles in .1 degree increments.

5. Press Enter (or click the Apply button in the Rotate palette) to rotate the object.

Tip:
Rotating Around a Specific Point

When you're rotating an object using the Rotate palette, it's easy to get it to rotate around its center. What if, instead, you want to rotate the object around some other point?

You can always enter the coordinates of the location you want to rotate around in the X and Y fields in the Rotate palette, but wouldn't it be nice to click on a spot on the page, as you can when you're rotating using the Rotation tool?

You can: just click the Rotation tool on the page before you enter anything in the Rotate palette. Don't drag the Rotation tool, and don't click too quickly—I find it takes a second for the palette to update. When the X and Y fields in the palette change to match the current location of the cursor, release the mouse button and press Command-` to move your cursor to the Rotation Angle field. Enter an angle and press Return to rotate the object. FreeHand rotates the object around the point you specified by clicking.

Rotating Multiple Selected Objects

When you rotate more than one object (in this sense, I'm counting groups as a single object), the objects rotate around a single point (see Figure 5-17). This point can be their joint geometric center, the point where you started dragging the Rotation tool, or a point you specified in the Rotate palette. They don't all rotate around their individual center points.

FIGURE 5-17
Rotating multiple objects

When you rotate multiple objects in FreeHand...

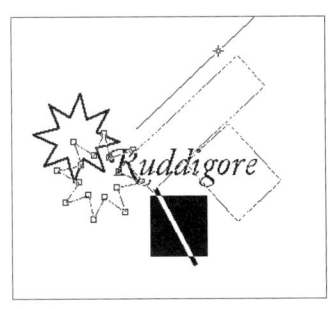

...they rotate around a single center of rotation.

Like this: Objects rotated around a single point.

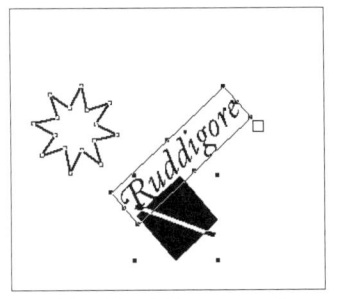

Not like this: Objects rotated around their individual centers.

Rotating Contents and Fills

You can choose to have a path's contents (objects you've pasted inside the path) or fills rotate with the path as you rotate the path (see Figure 5-18). To rotate the path's contents, check the Contents checkbox in the Rotate palette before you rotate the path. To rotate the path's fill, check Fills.

Rotating a fill doesn't change the screen angle of any halftone screen you've applied to the fill (you control screen angles using the Halftone palette).

FIGURE 5-18
Rotating contents and fills

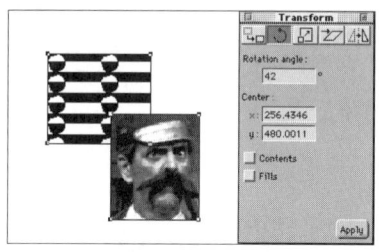

In this example, I'll use the Rotate palette to rotate two paths. One path is filled with a tiled fill; the other has a scanned image pasted inside it.

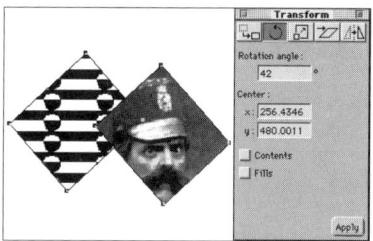

With Contents unchecked, objects you've pasted inside a path don't rotate when you rotate the path. Turn Fills off, and tiled fills won't rotate when you rotate the path.

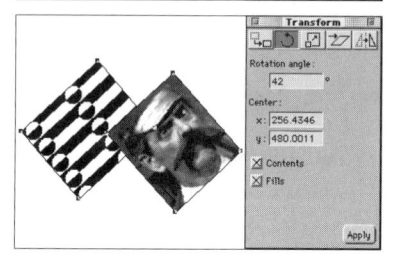

Turn on Contents, and objects inside paths rotate with the paths. When you want tiled fills to rotate with the path, turn on Fills.

Rotating Selected Points

You don't have to select all the points in a path to apply rotation to that path; you can rotate some or all of the points. What possible use is this? Look at Figure 5-19.

Rotation and Path Direction

While you're rotating things, remember that the direction, or winding, of rotated paths does not change (for more on PostScript path direction, see "Thinking Like a Line" in Chapter 2, "Drawing")—it still starts from the same point as it did before you rotated it (see Figure 5-20).

TRANSFORMING 445

FIGURE 5-19
Rotating selected points

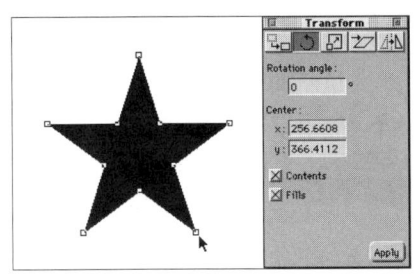

Select some, but not all, of the points on a path.

The selected points rotate...

...the unselected points stay in their original positions.

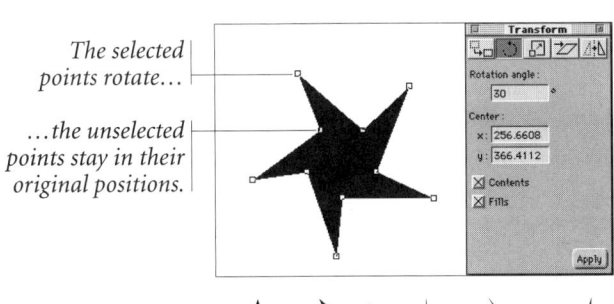

Rotate the selected points.

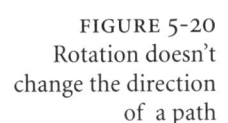

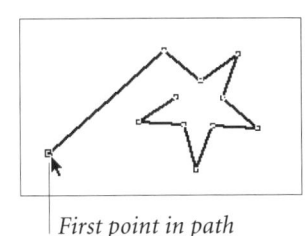

FIGURE 5-20
Rotation doesn't change the direction of a path

First point in path

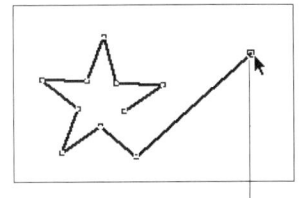

First point in path

Even though you've rotated this path 180 degrees...

...the first point in the path remains the same.

Rotation and Perspective Drawing

You can use rotation and scaling to create isometric projections of 3-D objects in FreeHand (for more on perspective drawing, see "Perspective Projection" in Chapter 2, "Drawing"). The following steps show you how (see Figure 5-21).

1. Create an orthographic view of the object (also called a plan view: front, top, and side views of the object).

2. Select the top view of the object. Display the Rotate palette. Type "90" in the Rotation Angle field and press Return. FreeHand rotates the top view of the object 90 degrees.

FIGURE 5-21
Rotating and scaling create an isometric projection

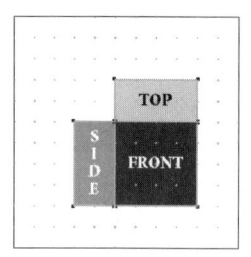

Draw the front, side, and top of an object.

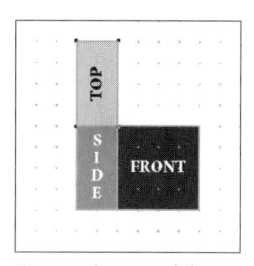

Rotate the top of the object 90 degrees.

Rotate all three objects -45 degrees.

Scale the top and front vertically by 57.735 percent.

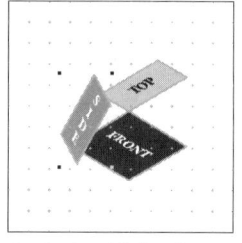

Scale the side horizontally by 57.735 percent.

Rotate the front 60 degrees.

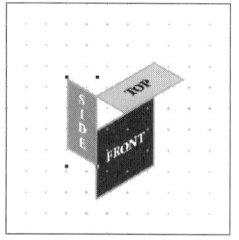

Rotate the side 30 degrees.

Snap all the pieces together.

3. Select all three views of the object. Display the Rotate palette. Type "-45" in the Rotation Angle field and press Return. FreeHand rotates the top view of the object 45 degrees counterclockwise.

4. Deselect the side view (keep the top and front views selected). Display the Scale palette (double-click the scale tool in the toolbox). With the Uniform box checked, enter "57.735" in the Scale Factor field and press Return. FreeHand scales the top and front views.

5. Select the side view and deselect the front and top views. Uncheck Uniform in the Scale palette. Type "57.735" in the X field and press Return. FreeHand scales the side view horizontally.

6. Select the front view of the object. Display the Rotate palette. Type "60" in the Rotation Angle field and press Return. FreeHand rotates the front view 60 degrees clockwise.

7. Select the side view. Type "30" in the Rotation Angle field and press Return. FreeHand rotates the side view 30 degrees clockwise.

8. Snap the three pieces of the object together, and you've got an isometric projection of the object. You can enhance the 3-D effect of the projection by shading the sides of the object, if you want.

Reflecting

Reflection flips a selected object or objects across a specified axis. When we're drawing, we very often work with paths which are mirror images of each other around an axis. FreeHand's reflection tool makes it possible for us to work the way we think.

You can reflect selected objects by dragging the Reflection tool, or by entering values in the Reflect palette.

Using the Reflection Tool

To reflect an object "by eye," follow these steps (see Figure 5-22).

1. Select the object you want to reflect.

2. Select the Reflection tool from the toolbox.

3. Move the cursor to the point where you want to place the axis of reflection.

4. Drag the object across the axis of reflection (as you drag, FreeHand displays a dotted line showing the axis of reflection). Hold down Control as you drag to locate the

center of reflection at the center of the object. Hold down Shift as you drag to constrain the reflection angle to 45-degree angles. As you drag, FreeHand displays the angle of reflection in the status bar.

5. When you're through reflecting the object, stop dragging. FreeHand reflects the object as you've specified.

FIGURE 5-22
Reflecting objects using the Reflection tool

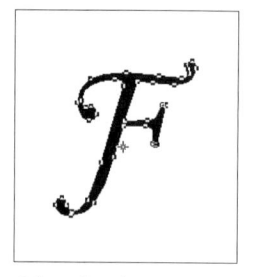

Select the object you want to reflect.

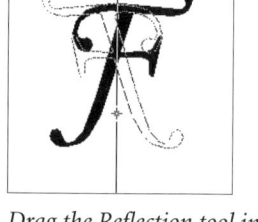

Drag the Reflection tool in the publication window. The point where you start dragging determines the axis around which FreeHand reflects the object.

As you drag, FreeHand displays the angle of reflection in the Info Bar...

...and displays a preview of the reflected object.

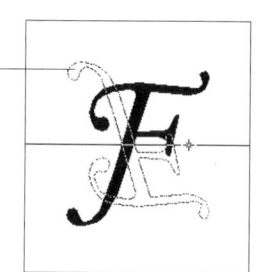

Hold down Shift and drag toward the top or bottom of the publication window to reflect the object across its vertical axis. Hold down Shift and drag left or right to reflect the object horizontally.

Using the Reflect Palette

Most of the time, I know precisely how I want to reflect an object, so I use the Reflect palette (see Figure 5-23). Come to think of it, I don't think I ever use reflection to do anything other than flip objects across their vertical or horizontal axes. More candidates for keyboard shortcuts....

To reflect an object using the Reflect palette, follow these steps.

1. Select the object you want to reflect.

2. If the Reflect palette isn't already visible, display it by double-clicking the reflection tool in the toolbox.

3. Set the Fills and Contents checkboxes the way you want them (see "Reflecting Contents and Fills," later in this chapter).

4. Type the values you want in the Reflect Axis field (enter "90" to reflect the object across its vertical axis, "180" to reflect the object across its horizontal axis). Positive values entered in the Reflect Axis field reflect the selected object counterclockwise; enter negative values to reflect the object clockwise.

5. Press Return. FreeHand reflects the object as you specified.

FIGURE 5-23
Reflecting contents and fills

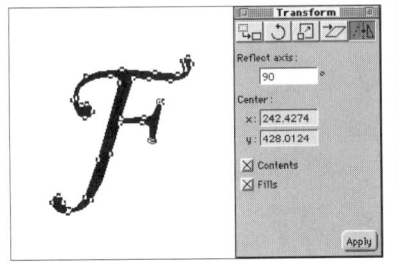

Select the object you want to reflect, type an angle in the Reflect Axis field of the Reflect palette...

...and press Return (or click the Apply button). FreeHand reflects the selected object across the axis you entered.

Reflecting Contents and Fills

When you're reflecting a path, you can choose to reflect the path's contents (what's pasted inside the path) or fills as you reflect the path (see Figure 5-24). To reflect path contents, check Contents. To reflect the path's fill, check the Fills box.

Reflection and Path Direction

Reflection changes the winding, or direction, of reflected paths (for more on PostScript path direction, see "Thinking Like a Line" in Chapter 2, "Drawing"). The path still starts from the same point as it did before you reflected it, but the path's direction now goes the opposite direction (see Figure 5-25).

FIGURE 5-24
Reflecting contents and fills

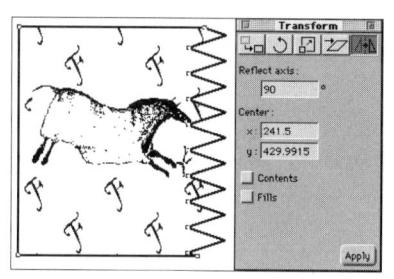

In this example, I'll use the Reflect palette to reflect a path containing both a tiled fill and an image.

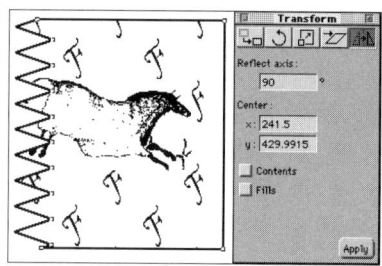

With the Contents and Fills checkboxes off, FreeHand reflects the path, but doesn't reflect the object pasted inside the path or the path's tiled fill.

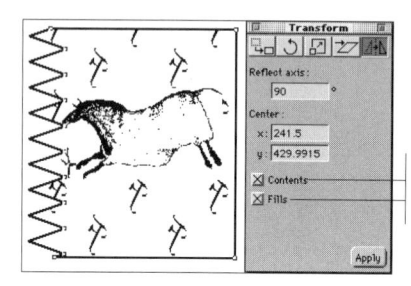

With the Contents and Fills checkboxes turned on, FreeHand reflects the image and the tiled fill.

FIGURE 5-25
Reflection and path direction

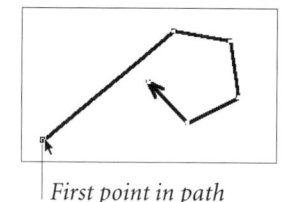

First point in path

First point in path

Before reflection, this path winds clockwise.

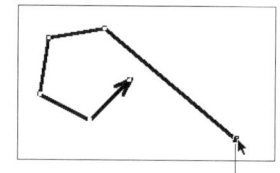

After reflection, the path winds counterclockwise.

Skewing

Skewing an object makes it appear that the plane the object's resting on has been rotated. It's good for creating perspective effects.

Skewing is hard to get used to at first, because vertical skewing seems to affect the horizontal lines in an object, while horizontal skewing affects the vertical lines in an object. It's just something you'll have to get used to (see Figure 5-26).

Using the Skewing Tool

Follow these steps to skew an object by eye (see Figure 5-27).

1. Select the object you want to skew.

TRANSFORMING 451

FIGURE 5-26
Horizontal and vertical skewing

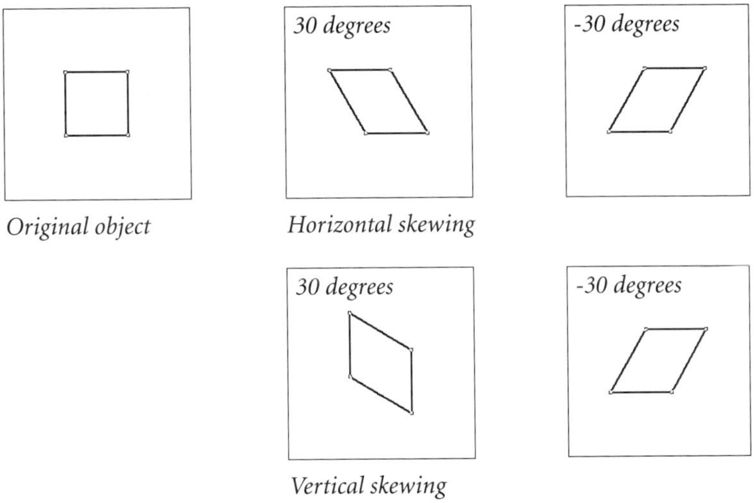

Original object

30 degrees *-30 degrees*

Horizontal skewing

30 degrees *-30 degrees*

Vertical skewing

FIGURE 5-27
Skewing an object by eye

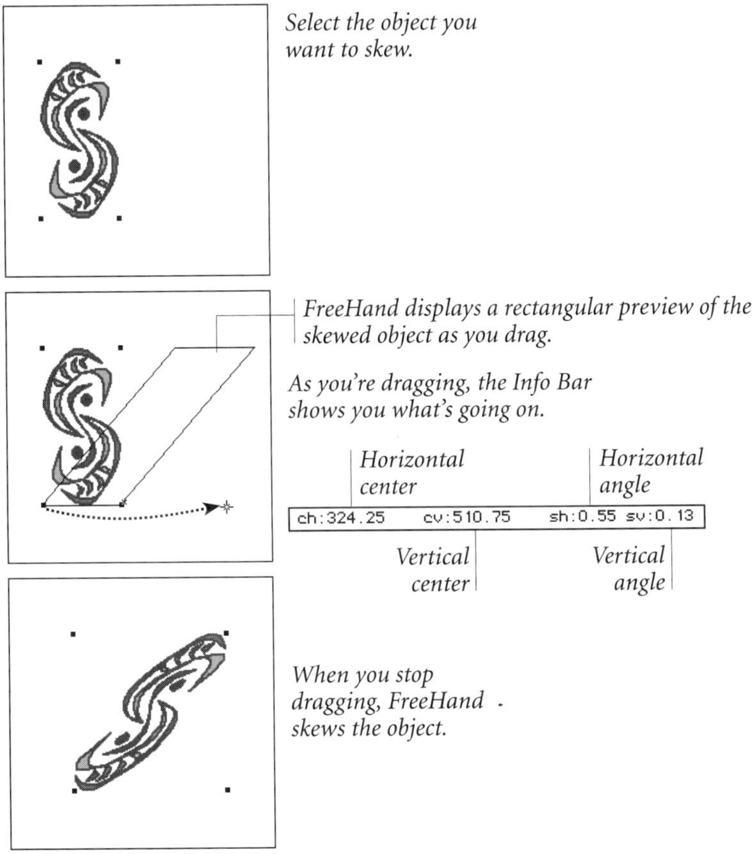

Select the object you want to skew.

Position the cursor to define the center point you're skewing around and drag the cursor in the publication window.

FreeHand displays a rectangular preview of the skewed object as you drag.

As you're dragging, the Info Bar shows you what's going on.

| Horizontal center | Horizontal angle |

`ch:324.25   cv:510.75   sh:0.55 sv:0.13`

| Vertical center | Vertical angle |

Hold down Shift as you drag to constrain the skewing to either vertical or horizontal.

When you stop dragging, FreeHand skews the object.

2. Choose the Skewing tool from the toolbox.

3. Position the cursor where you want the skew to start.

4. Drag the Skewing tool to skew the object. As you drag the cursor, the skewing angles display on the status bar.

5. When the object looks the way you want it, stop dragging.

Using the Skew Palette

To skew an object using the Skew palette, follow these steps (see Figure 5-28).

1. Select the object you want to skew.

2. Display the Skew palette by double-clicking the Skewing tool in the toolbox, if necessary.

3. Set the Contents and Fills checkboxes (see "Skewing Contents and Fills," later in this chapter).

4. Enter skewing angles in the H (horizontal) and V (vertical) fields in the Skew palette.

5. Press Return (or click the Apply button in the Skew palette) to skew the selected object.

FIGURE 5-28
Skewing with the Skew palette

Select the object you want to skew.

Enter skewing angles in the H (for horizontal) and V (for vertical) fields.

Check the Contents box if you want FreeHand to skew any objects pasted inside the path when it skews the path.

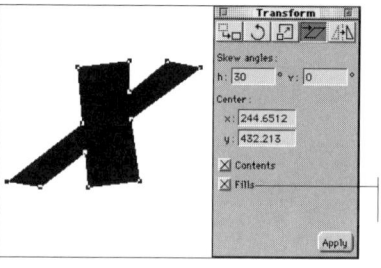

Press Return (or click the Apply button), and FreeHand skews the selected object.

Check the Fills box if you want FreeHand to skew the path's fill.

TRANSFORMING 453

Skewing Contents and Fills

If you want to skew a path's contents (objects you've pasted inside the path) as you skew the path, check the Contents box. To skew the path's fill, check Fills.

Skewing and Perspective Drawing

If you survived the parts of Chapter 2, "Drawing," covering perspective, oblique, and axonometric projections, here's your reward: skewing is a fantastic way to automate drawing oblique and axonometric projections. In many cases, these simple projections can substitute for (much more complicated) perspective rendering. The following steps show you how to create an oblique projection of an object (see Figure 5-29).

1. Draw the orthographic views (top, side, and front) of an object.

2. Select the side view of the object.

FIGURE 5-29
Skewing to create an oblique projection

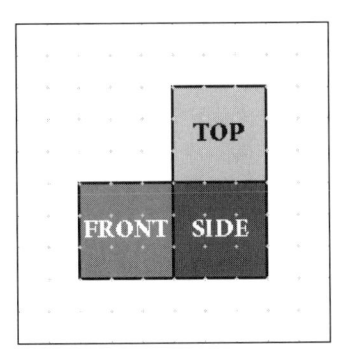

Draw the top, front, and side of the object.

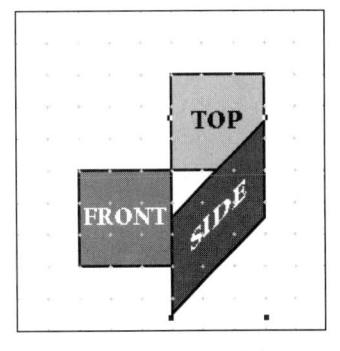

Select the side view and skew it 45 degrees vertically.

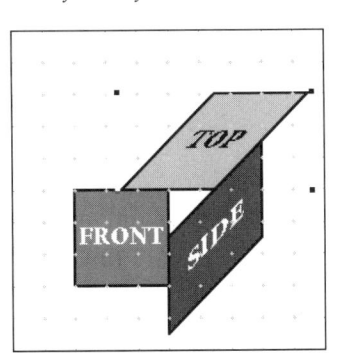

Select the top view and skew it -45 degrees horizontally.

Snap the three views together.

3. Display the Skew palette (if the palette's not visible, double-click the Skewing tool in the toolbox). Type "45" in the V field and press Return. FreeHand skews the front view of the object.

4. Select the top view of the object.

5. Type "-45" in the Horizontal field and press Return. FreeHand skews the top view.

6. Snap all the objects together, and, voilà, you've got an oblique projection.

Skewing is also a great help in creating axonometric views of an object. Axonometric views differ from oblique views in that they're both skewed and scaled, and that the front view is skewed away from the plane of perspective.

Creating Clipping Paths

Another of FreeHand's basic transformations is Paste Inside—the ability to use any path as a clipping path for any object or objects. Paste Inside has already gotten some coverage in Chapter 2, "Drawing," but here's more. Clipping paths are the key to three other FreeHand techniques.

- Cropping imported graphics (this technique is covered in Chapter 4, "Importing and Exporting").

- Trapping objects which cross color boundaries (this technique is covered in depth in Chapter 6, "Color").

- Creating transparency and translucency effects.

Clipping paths are also just plain fun. Be aware, however, that clipping paths increase the complexity of your publication by an order of magnitude as far as the PostScript interpreters in printers and imagesetters are concerned. This doesn't mean they should be avoided! Just remember that publications containing clipping paths will take longer to print, and may produce overtime charges at your imagesetting service bureau. In other words, make sure that the effect you hope to achieve by using clipping paths is worth the added expense and time.

Use the following steps to create a clipping path (see Figure 5-30).

1. Draw, type, or import an object.

2. Draw a path on top of the initial object.

3. Select the original object and press Command-X to cut it to the Clipboard.

4. Select the first object and press Command-Shift-V (or choose Paste Inside from the Edit menu). The parts of the second object which fell within the first object's area appear inside the first object.

What happens when you use Paste Inside more than once for the same clipping path? Each successive Paste Inside places the contents of the Clipboard on top of any objects already inside the

FIGURE 5-30
Creating a clipping path

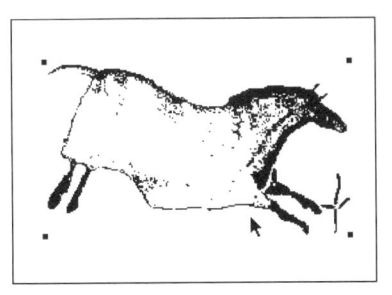

Draw, type, or import something...

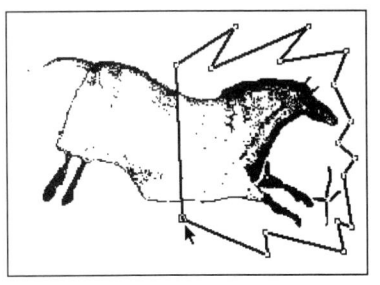

...and draw a path on top of it. Select the original object and cut it to the Clipboard.

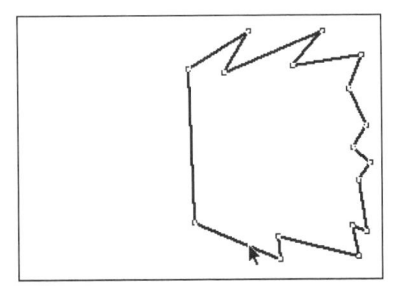

Select the path...

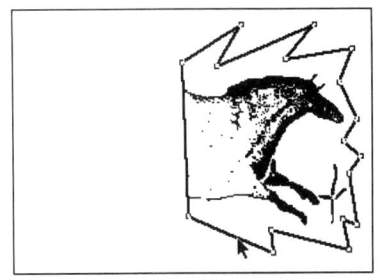

...and choose Paste Inside from the Edit menu. FreeHand pastes the object inside the path.

clipping path. You'll still be able to see any objects not obscured by opaque lines or fills (see Figure 5-31).

If you need to edit the objects you've pasted inside a path, or if you want to remove them, select the object that contains them and choose Cut Contents from the Edit menu (or press Command-Shift-X). The objects which had been pasted inside the path you selected are pasted on top of the path you cut them from (see Figure 5-32). The objects retain the stacking order they had inside the path (the last object pasted inside it on top).

FIGURE 5-31
Multiple Paste Insides

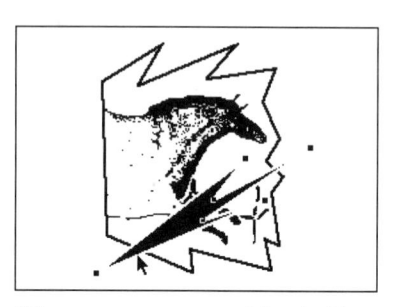

When you paste a new object inside a clipping path that contains other objects...

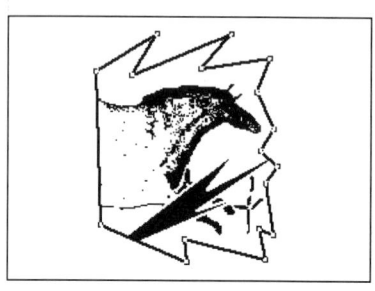

...FreeHand pastes the new object on top of the other objects already inside the path.

FIGURE 5-32
Removing objects from inside a clipping path

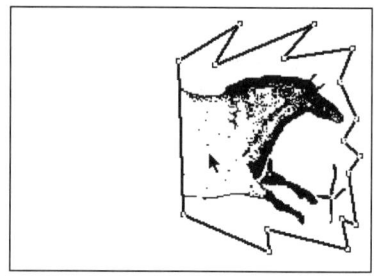

Select the clipping path...

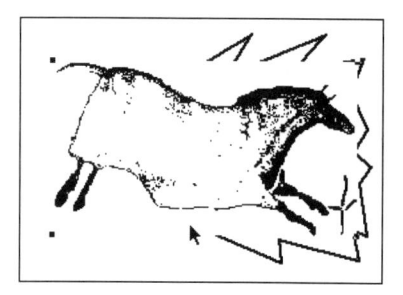

...and choose Cut Contents from the Edit menu. FreeHand pastes the path's contents on top of the path.

Using Paste Inside to Crop Imported Images

FreeHand lacks a tool analogous to PageMaker's Cropping tool, but you can simulate the behavior of the Cropping tool using FreeHand's Paste Inside feature. Actually, the ability to create clipping paths of any shape in FreeHand is more powerful and flexible than PageMaker's Cropping tool (which crops only in rectangles).

For more on cropping images, see "Cropping TIFF Images" in Chapter 4, "Importing and Exporting."

Creating a Color Change Where an Object Crosses a Color Boundary

Here's an effect that we used to sweat over in the dark days when everything was done with a copy camera, hot wax, cold beer, and a knife. Suppose you have some black text that crosses from a white background onto a black background. If the edge of the black background is a straight line, the effect is pretty easy to create. But if the edge of the black background is a curved or jagged line, it's nearly impossible to create this effect using a copy camera. With FreeHand, it's so easy that a number of power users I know have missed it (see Figure 5-33).

1. Create your type.
2. Create the black background object.

FIGURE 5-33
Changing colors as you cross a color boundary

Create two paths. Fill one with black; fill the other with white. Create a text block that crosses both paths. Color the text block black.

Clone the text block and cut the clone to the Clipboard. Select the white shape and choose Paste Inside from the Edit menu.

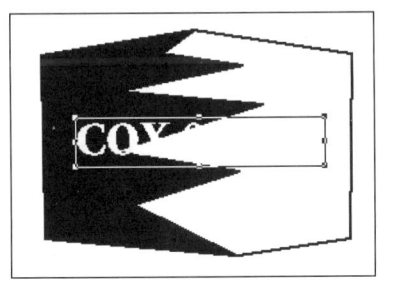

Select the text block and color it white.

Cut the white text block. Select the black shape and choose Paste Inside from the Edit menu.

3. Position the type and the black background object in the alignment you want.

4. Clone the text block.

5. Color the clone of the text block white and press Command-X to cut it to the Clipboard.

6. Select the black object and press Command-Shift-V (or choose Paste Inside from the Edit menu). FreeHand pastes the white text block inside the black object. Can't see it? Select the black text block and send it to the back.

Note that this same trick works just as well for colored text and a colored background, and that, by extension, it works for multiple adjacent color fields which have multiple overlapping objects which change color as they pass through the different color fields. For an example of this trick, refer to the color section of this book. And don't forget to trap!

Creating the Illusion of Transparency Using Clipping Paths

Have you ever wondered why you can't just select a FreeHand element and click an option that makes the object transparent? (You can, of course, for placed images, but that's not what I'm talking about.) When PostScript fills an object, it assumes that the fill is opaque. FreeHand, being a child of PostScript, adheres to this assumption, but also gives you a number of ways to fool PostScript into rendering objects that look transparent.

When an object passes behind some transparent or translucent plane, it changes color—sometimes very subtly. To simulate this effect in FreeHand, clone the partially obscured object and change the colors of the cloned objects from their original colors. Then paste those objects inside the transparent or translucent object (see Figure 5-34).

You can use this optical illusion to simulate the effect of viewing an object through a number of simple transparent/translucent planar surfaces. The main difficulty of rendering transparency and translucency in two-dimensional work is that you walk a fine line. If the color shift is too great, it'll look like you've created another object; if the color shift is too slight, it won't look like an object's transparent. Transparency is harder to simulate than translucency.

FIGURE 5-34
Creating transparent objects

This object is colored 20-percent gray, and has lightened copies of the background objects pasted inside it.

Creating three-dimensional transparency is both easier and more difficult. It's easier because color shifts and perspective shifts around three-dimensional objects provide more cues to the eye and so are more easily simulated; it's more difficult because you've got to figure out what those shifts are to be able to simulate them.

Once again, you'll have to look at my example and figure out how the techniques I use work with the publication and effect you're creating (see Figure 5-35).

FIGURE 5-35
Creating three-dimensional transparent and translucent effects

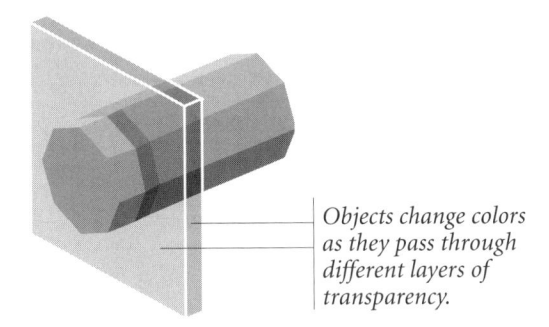

Objects change colors as they pass through different layers of transparency.

Creating Transparent Text

An effect you see very often, especially in television video advertising, is that of a character or word superimposed on an image where the characters are wholly or partially transparent. Here's how you can you achieve this effect in FreeHand (see Figure 5-36).

1. Place an image.

2. Create some type and position it over the image. Without deselecting the text block, choose Convert to Paths from the Type menu. FreeHand converts the characters to paths.

FIGURE 5-36
Transparent text above an image

Create some type on top of an image you've placed.

Convert the text to paths, then paste a lightened clone of the image inside the text.

3. Select the image and press Command-= to clone the image. Without deselecting the cloned image, display the Object Inspector (press Command-Option-I) and click the Edit button at the bottom of the Inspector. FreeHand displays the Image dialog box. Change the image's gray levels so that it's about half as dark as the original image. When you're through changing the gray levels, press Return to close the Image dialog box.

4. Press Command-X to cut the altered image.

5. Select the text (which is now a composite path) and press Command-Shift-V (or choose Paste Inside from the Edit menu).

FreeHand pastes the altered image inside the characters. This produces the illusion that you're looking through transparent text. You can enhance this illusion by cloning the type and offsetting the clone slightly from the original text to create a drop shadow, and then pasting another clone of the original image inside the drop shadow.

Locking Objects

In a previous edition of this book, I mentioned locking objects only once, in the section on alignment and distribution. It's the way I was brought up—out in the mountains in Idaho we never locked anything (our car keys spent the night, undisturbed, in the ignition switches of our cars). I view the difficulties of urban living as the result of a large-scale conspiracy of keys and locks.

In FreeHand, locking an object means that you can't transform it or change its appearance. You can still select the object, and you can copy it or clone it, but you can't do anything to it.

To lock an object, select the object and press Command-L (or choose Lock from the Arrange menu). When you select a locked object, you'll see a lock icon in the info bar.

To unlock an object, press Command-Shift-L (or choose Unlock from the Arrange menu).

Aligning and Distributing

For most people, MacDraw ushered in the era of object alignment. You could align the left, right, top, bottom, or center of selected objects. It was the greatest. I spent whole afternoons just aligning things. You couldn't do that in MacPaint.

FreeHand, which counts MacDraw as one of its forebears, also features object alignment. FreeHand aligns objects based on the rectangular area each object takes up, which I'll call the object's bounding box. The selection handles of the object show you the object's bounding box (to see the bounding box of a path, group the path). Note that imported EPS graphics and TIFF files can have bounding boxes that have nothing to do with the actual content of the graphic (see Figure 5-37).

FreeHand's object alignment capabilities include both Align, which does exactly what you'd expect; and Distribute, which means, "Evenly arrange the selected objects inside the selection rectangle formed by the objects." Align and Distribute can be used at the same time; you can, for example, vertically align objects while horizontally distributing them.

FIGURE 5-37
Object bounding boxes

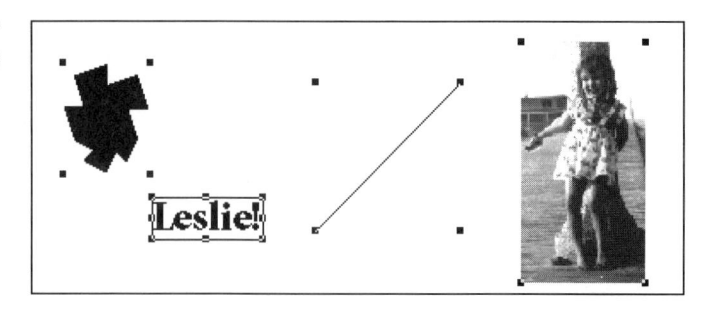

Aligning Objects

When you've selected the objects you want to align, press Command-Shift-A to display the Align palette, pick an alignment using the popup menus, and then click the Apply button in the palette (pressing Return doesn't work, for some reason). FreeHand aligns the selected objects as you've specified (see Figure 5-38).

Tip: Locking as an Adjunct to Alignment

If any of the selected objects is locked, FreeHand aligns objects based on that object's position (see Figure 5-39). If more than one of the selected objects is locked, FreeHand bases alignment on the object nearest the alignment specified (that is, the topmost locked object for Top alignments, the leftmost locked object in Left alignments, etc.).

I use this technique all the time—and it's virtually the only reason I lock individual objects. When I want to protect part of my publication from accidental editing, I usually put that part of the publication on a layer and lock that layer. Unlocking a layer is easier than tracking down individual, locked objects.

Tip: Centering Text Vertically

When you want to center text vertically inside an object, simply choosing to align by object centers doesn't usually work. Why? Because the alignment is based on the size of the text block—not on the size of the text.

Convert the characters to paths, however, and the bottom of the path will truly be the bottom of the character and the characters align properly to the center of the object (see Figure 5-40).

Distributing Objects

Have you ever wanted to space a bunch of objects at even distances from each other (from each other's centers, at any rate) across a particular horizontal measurement? If you have, FreeHand's Distribute feature should make your day.

TRANSFORMING 463

FIGURE 5-38
Aligning objects

Select all of the objects you want to align and/or distribute.

Press Command-Shift-A to display the Align palette, if it's not already visible.

Pick an alignment from the Horizontal and Vertical popup menus and click the Apply button.

FreeHand aligns (and/or distributes) the objects.

FIGURE 5-39
Locking and alignment

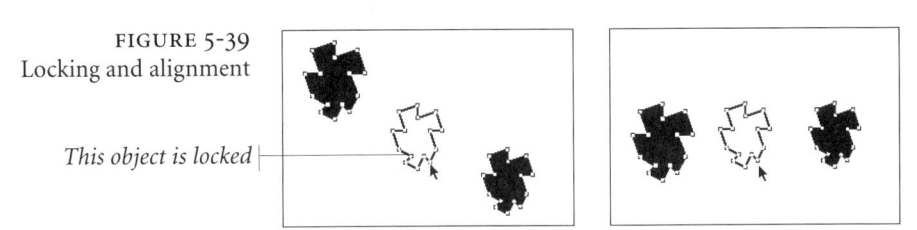

This object is locked

Align the tops of these objects, and they'll align to the top of the locked object—even if it's not the topmost object selected.

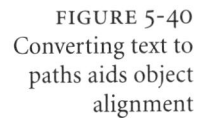

FIGURE 5-40
Converting text to paths aids object alignment

Alignment is based on the top and bottom of the text block, so you can end up with extra space below the text.

If you convert the text to paths, it'll be aligned based on the actual height of the characters.

To distribute objects, select the objects, press Command-Shift-A to display the Align palette, select the alignment and distribution options you want from the popup menus, and then click the Apply button in the palette. FreeHand aligns and distributes the objects as you've specified (see Figure 5-41).

FIGURE 5-41
Distributing objects

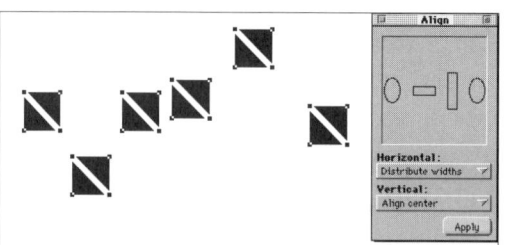

Select the objects you want to distribute, set up the distribution and alignment you want in the Align palette, and click the Apply button.

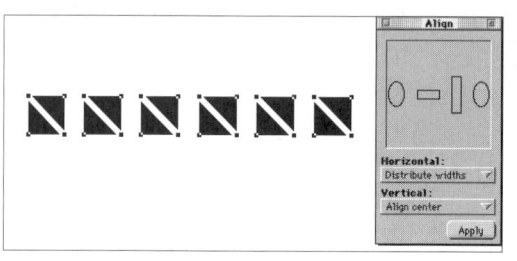

FreeHand distributes the selected objects.

Transformation Xtras

Two of the tools in the Xtra Tools palette (press Command-Shift-K to display the palette, or choose Xtra Tools from the Other submenu of the Window menu) transform FreeHand paths: the Fisheye Lens tool and the 3-D Rotation tool.

Fisheye Lens Tool

The Fisheye Lens tool distorts paths, changing the path so that it looks like you're viewing the path through (you guessed it) a fisheye, or "wide angle," lens. The Fisheye Lens tool has no effect on imported graphics.

To use the Fisheye Lens tool, select a path (or paths), select the tool from the Xtra Tools palette, and drag the tool over the paths. As you drag, FreeHand extends an ellipse (hold down Shift as you drag to make it a circle) behind the tool. This ellipse sets the area the Fisheye Lens tool affects. When you stop dragging, FreeHand applies the effect (see Figure 5-42).

TRANSFORMING 465

FIGURE 5-42
Using the Fisheye Lens tool

If the Xtra Tools palette isn't already visible, display it by pressing Command-Shift-K.

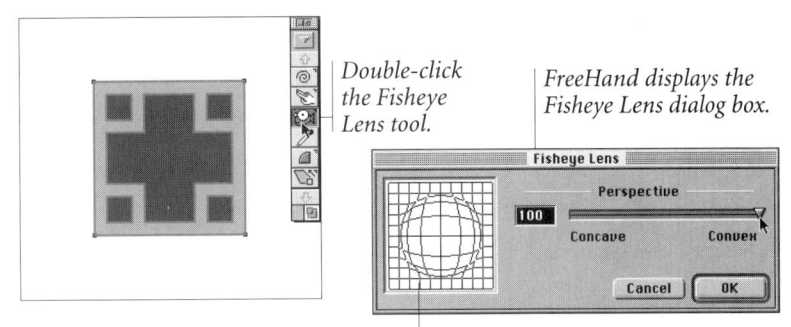

Double-click the Fisheye Lens tool.

FreeHand displays the Fisheye Lens dialog box.

As you make changes in this dialog box, FreeHand displays a preview of the effect in this window.

Change the Fisheye Lens effect by dragging the slider or entering a new value in the field.

Drag the Fisheye Lens tool over the objects you want to distort. As you drag, FreeHand extends an ellipse from the point at which you started dragging—this indicates the area the effect will apply to.

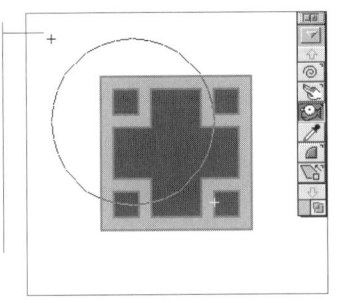

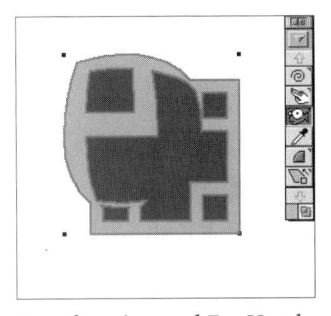

Stop dragging, and FreeHand distorts the area you selected.

To set options for the Fisheye Lens tool, double-click the tool in the Xtra Tools palette. FreeHand displays the Fisheye Lens dialog box. Change the effect of the Fisheye Lens tool by dragging the Perspective slider (or entering a number in the field). FreeHand shows you a preview of the effect.

3D Rotation Tool

The 3D Rotation Tool applies several transformations at once—mostly scaling, skewing, and rotation—to make paths look as if they've been rotated away from the plane of the page. The 3D Rotation tool has no effect on imported graphics (TIFFs or EPSes).

To use the 3D Rotation tool, select a path (or paths), select the tool from the Xtra Tools palette, and drag the tool. As you drag, FreeHand extends a line from the point at which you started dragging (or the point you specified in the 3D Rotation dialog box). In addition, FreeHand displays a preview of the transformed state of the path. Stop dragging, and FreeHand applies the effect to the path (see Figure 5-43).

FIGURE 5-43
Using the 3D Rotation tool

If the Xtra Tools palette isn't already visible, display it by pressing Command-Shift-K.

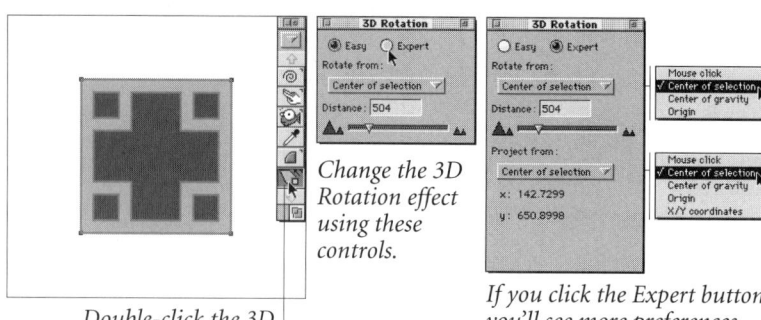

Double-click the 3D Rotation tool.

Change the 3D Rotation effect using these controls.

If you click the Expert button, you'll see more preferences.

As you drag the 3D Rotation tool, FreeHand displays a preview of the effect.

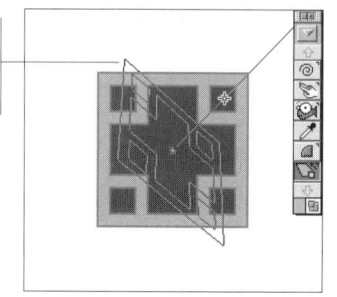

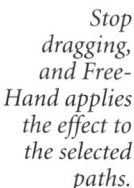

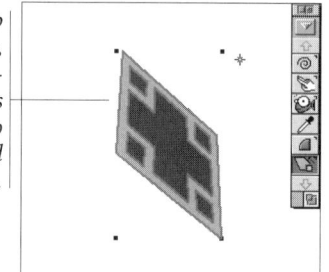

Stop dragging, and Free-Hand applies the effect to the selected paths.

My Life Was Transformed

All around you, every day, things are changing from one thing to another. Fuzzy caterpillars turn into moths. Clark Kent jumps into a phone booth and emerges as Superman. Democrats turn into Republicans (I understand it's part of their mating cycle). Werewolves stalk the moors under the full moon. The bat on page 155 is, by day, a harmless graphic designer with prominent canines. These transformations are all everyday, natural, phenomena.

I didn't understand this when I first approached FreeHand's transformation tools. The tools seemed alien, awkward, and I didn't use them very much. Then, one day, I saw them as extensions of the way I already thought about drawing. Now, I use them more than I use the drawing tools.

Make FreeHand's transformation tools an integral part of how you work with the program, and you'll have their powerful, almost magical forces on your side. And that means you'll have more time for other things. Like howling at the moon.

CHAPTER

Color

6

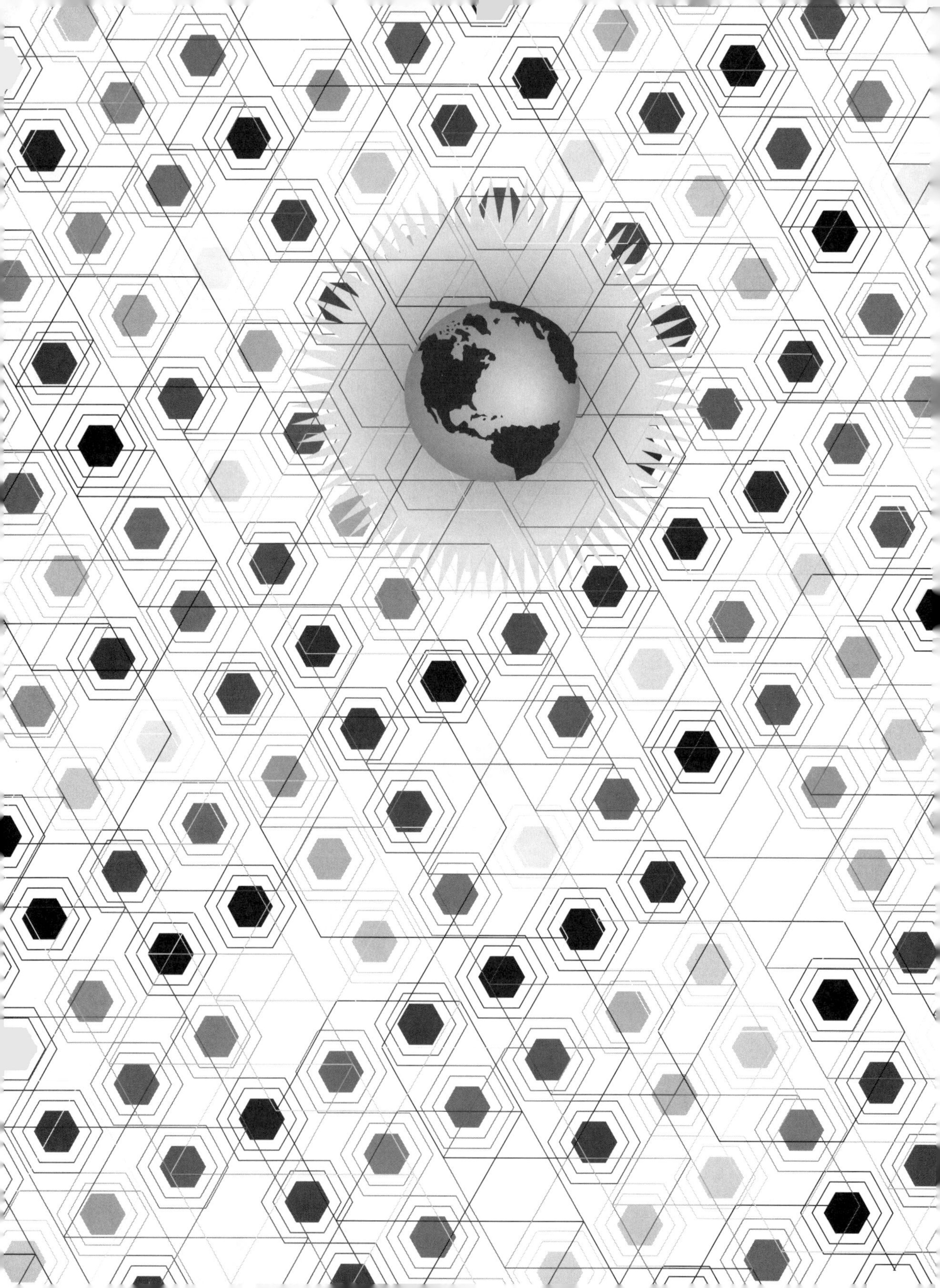

CHAPTER SIX — COLOR

I remember drawing things when I was a kid. I enjoyed drawing with a pen or pencil, but I didn't really get excited until someone got out the crayons. Or the finger-paints. Or the watercolors and brushes. Drawing black lines on paper was fun, but that color stuff was *what it was all about*.

Color communicates, telling us things about the object bearing the color. Without color cues, we'd have a hard time guessing the ripeness of a fruit or distinguishing a poisonous mushroom from an edible one. And many animals would have a hard time figuring out when to mate, or with whom.

We associate colors with human emotions: we are green with envy; we've got the blues; we see red. Colors affect our emotions, as well. Various studies suggest that we think best in a room of one color, or relax best in a room of another color.

What does all this mean? Color's important. A rule of thumb in advertising is that a color advertisement gets something like ten times the response of a black-and-white ad.

FreeHand's always been one of the best desktop-publishing tools for creating color publications. So what's new?

Rearranging Furniture. In FreeHand 4, tints had their own palette, the Tints palette. These days, you specify tints using the Tints panel of the Color Mixer. It's the same set of controls, but it's one less palette to worry about. See "The Color Mixer," later in this chapter.

The Return of the Spread Size Field. Now you see it, now you don't. And then you see it again. FreeHand 3's "automatic trapping" (the Spread Size field in the Print Options dialog box) disappeared in FreeHand 4, but returned in FreeHand 5. In the previous edition of this book, I assured you that you wouldn't miss it—but apparently, some of you did (or maybe the comparative features list that every software marketer has to do looks better with another checkmark), so it's back (in the Print Options dialog box). Now that you know it's there, do your best to ignore it. Why? Let's just say it's not a good way to create traps for your publication—the Trapping Xtra is far better. See "Trapping," later in this chapter, and the discussion of the Spread Size field in "FreeHand Printing Options" in Chapter 7, "Printing."

"Automatic" Trapping. Have a couple of simple paths you know need to be trapped, but don't want to go to the expense (in time and money) of having your service bureau trap your publication using TrapWise? Don't have the time or the inclination to create the traps yourself? FreeHand's Trap Xtra might save your day. Using this Xtra, you can create traps for paths formatted with basic strokes or fills, or type you've converted to such paths. See "Trapping," later in this chapter.

Color Manipulation Xtras. In FreeHand, you've always had a great deal of control over the color of an object, but, historically, you've had that control over one object at a time, or over a set of objects with the same color attributes. If you wanted to increase the amount of cyan in a series of differently colored objects, on the other hand, you were stuck—you'd have to do it one object at a time. FreeHand 5's color manipulation Xtras apply color changes to all the objects in a selection—automating this previously laborious process. See "Color Xtras," later in this chapter.

Color Printing

It's impossible to discuss creating and using colors in FreeHand without talking a little about printing. If you already know about color printing, feel free to skip ahead, though you'll miss all the jokes if you do. Everyone else should note that this is a very simple explanation of a very bizarre and complex process.

The Printing Process

After you've printed your FreeHand publication to film and delivered it to your commercial printer (I like to walk in through the loading dock), your printer takes your film and uses it to expose (or "burn") a photosensitive printing plate. The surface of the plate has been chemically treated to repel ink (it's "hydrophilic"). When the printing plate is exposed, the image areas from your film become able to accept ink (or "hydrophobic"). Once the plate's been exposed, your printer attaches the printing plate to the cylinder of a printing press.

As the cylinder holding the plate turns, the parts of it bearing your image become coated with ink, which is transferred (via another, rubber covered cylinder—the offset cylinder) to the paper. This transfer is where we get the term "offset," as in "offset printing," because the plate itself does not touch your paper.

Printing presses put ink on paper one ink color at a time. Some presses have more than one printing cylinder (also called a printing "head" or "tower") and can print several colors of ink on a sheet of paper in one pass through the press, but each printing cylinder carries only one color of ink. We can make it look like we've gotten more than one color of ink on a printing plate by using screens—patterns of dots that, from a distance, fool the eye into thinking it sees a separate color (see Figure 6-1).

FIGURE 6-1
Black and...gray?

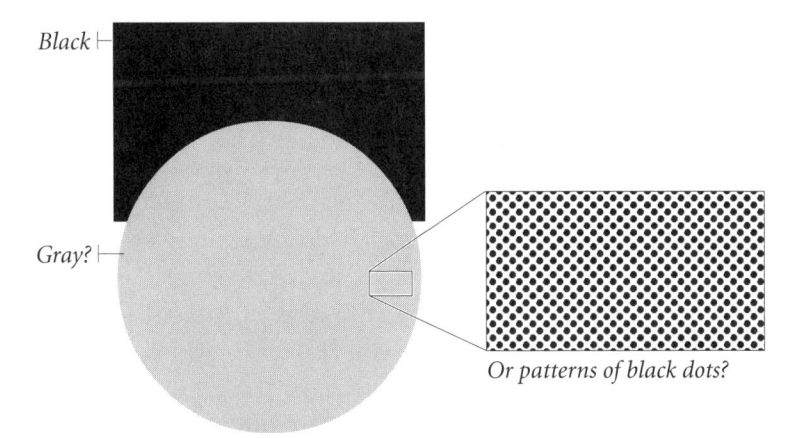

Black

Gray?

Or patterns of black dots?

Spot and Process Inks

Spot-color printing is simple: your commercial printer mixes inks to get exactly the color we want, then loads the press with that mixture of inks. Sometimes, we'll use "tint builds"—screens of spot inks printed on top of each other—to create a new color without using another ink. In process-color printing, tint builds are where it's at; we use overlapping screens of four inks (cyan, magenta, yellow, and black) to simulate a large part of the visible color spectrum. If everything's gone well, the dots of the different colored inks are placed near each other in a pattern called a rosette (see Color Figure 6 on the color pages for an example of a rosette).

Process-color printing can't simulate all the colors our eyes can see (notably metallic and fluorescent colors), but it can print color photographic images. Spot colors can print any color you can make with pigments, but can't be used to print color photographic images. Technically, you *can* print color photographs using spot colors, but—unless you were very careful—you'd end up either compromising color-matching in the photographs, or printing more than four inks.

New Screening Technologies

Recently, some companies have been experimenting with color separation methods that do not produce rosettes.

Flamenco screening. One method (sometimes called "Flamenco" screening) prints all process inks at the same screen angle and line screen, producing a grid of color dots. Once again, the eye reads these juxtaposed dots of the four process inks as colors. While this method can produce good-looking images that lack moiré patterns at fairly low screen frequencies, higher screen frequencies often show severe color shifting from one part of the image to another. In effect, it's a huge moiré pattern.

Flamenco screening is mostly used in the newspaper industry.

Stochastic screening. Another method, stochastic, or Frequency Modulation (FM), screening avoids halftoning altogether. Stochastic screening converts grayscale and color information into high-resolution dithered bitmaps (shades of MacPaint!). When you print bitmaps you've applied colors to (that is, cyan, magenta, yellow, and black) on top of each other, the eye sees more colors—just as it does when you print rosettes. It's like a Seurat painting.

As I'm writing this (in June 1995), imagesetter manufacturers have begun to offer stochastic screening hardware and software for their RIPs under various tradenames (Agfa's, for example, is called Crystal Raster). Third parties have also released software that works with software RIPs running on desktop computers.

You don't have to print to a specially-equipped imagesetter to experiment with stochastic screening—you can do it (or something like it) yourself, using Photoshop and FreeHand. See "Do-It-Yourself Stochastic Screening," later in this chapter, for more information on separating color images using stochastic screening—we'll use Photoshop's diffusion dither.

Or you can purchase a stochastic screening application, such as Icefields, from Isis Imaging, and screen your images yourself. For more on Icefields, see "Stochastic Screening Without an Imagesetter," later in this chapter.

Hi-Fi color. You'll often hear stochastic screening mentioned in the same breath as a new process-color printing method, high-fidelity color (usually called "hi-fi" color). The most popular current hi-fi color scheme uses seven inks—cyan, magenta, yellow, orange, green, violet, and black—to simulate more of the visible spectrum than can be simulated using four-color process printing. (Other schemes use six or eight colors, or a different set of seven inks.) The idea's still the same—put dots close together, and people see more colors than you've printed. In any case, you don't have to use hi-fi color to use stochastic screening.

The samples of hi-fi color I've seen have been very impressive—the technique makes it possible to print fluorescent, metallic, and intense colors that would be impossible to print using conventional four-color process printing.

As I write this book, very few commercial printers are set up to do hi-fi color (in fact, you can probably count on your fingers the number of printers in North America equipped to print seven colors in a single pass through the press). The technology is on the horizon, however, and it's getting closer. Is it the next "revolution" in printing? Will all commercial printers be using hi-fi color in five years?

I have no idea.

Color in FreeHand

Now that you know all about color printing, it's time to get down to specifying colors in your FreeHand publication.

The colors you work with in your publication correspond to the inks you'll use to print your publication. When you create, edit, or import a color in FreeHand, you're working with a single ink, or a tint of that ink, or a set of inks (a "tint build") which, when printed, optically blend together to produce the color.

How you specify colors affects what you can do with objects you apply the colors to. You can blend between objects with different process colors applied, or create graduated or radial fills from one process color to another. You can't do that with spot colors (well, actually, you *can*, but FreeHand turns all the intermediate blend steps into process colors)—though you can go from one spot color to white, black, or another tint of that same spot color.

When it comes time to print, the ink list (in the Print Options dialog box) displays the inks needed to print the colors you've defined in your publication. If you've defined process colors, you'll see the process inks (cyan, magenta, yellow, and black) in the ink list. If you've defined spot colors, you'll see the spot inks associated with those colors in the ink list. Unlike in some other applications, you can't select an ink and convert it to a process color from the Print options dialog box; you have to return to the publication window and use the Color List when you need to do that.

Spot Color or Process Color or Both?

Whether you use spot colors, process colors, or both depends on the needs of your specific publication—which has to do with your printing budget, your communications goals, and, most importantly, your mood. If you plan to use color photographs in your publication, you're going to have to use at least the four process inks. If you're printing on a tight budget, you'll probably want to use one or two inks.

When you're creating a color, you're offered a variety of choices: is the color a spot color, a process color, or a tint? If you don't yet know how your publication will be printed, don't worry too much about whether a color is defined as a spot or process color—you can always change it later. It's much easier to go from spot to process than the other way around.

Is What You See Anything Like What You'll Get?

Any time you're working with colors, refer to printed samples of the colors, rather than looking at the colors on your screen. Remember that, unlike the paper you'll be printing on, your screen is backlit, so it displays colors very differently from what they'll look like when printed.

If you're using uncoated paper, look at samples of the ink (spot color) or ink mix (process color) printed on uncoated stock. If you're using coated paper, look at examples printed on coated paper. If you're using a colored paper, try to find an example of the ink printed on a colored paper—though these examples are much harder to find.

If you're working with Pantone (or PMS) colors, Pantone makes a line of swatch books showing their colors printed as spot colors and books of process color conversions of their colors; they're printed on both coated and uncoated stocks, and although they're kind of expensive, they're not as expensive as pulling a job off of a press because you didn't like the press check. They're downright cheap if you consider what it must cost to print them.

Though I know everybody does it, I would never use Pantone spot colors (the ones you find in the Pantone library) to specify a process color. The Pantone Matching System is a spot-color specifying system, and the colors don't convert to process colors particularly well because you can't make any given hue just using process colors (see the discussion earlier in this chapter). Still, Pantone has included the process color conversions for these colors (as seen in their *Process Color Imaging Guide*) in the definition of these spot colors.

Don't trust color PostScript printers to give you an accurate simulation of what the colors in your publication are going to look like when they're printed by your commercial printer. They simply lack the resolution and color range to produce good process colors (and bear in mind that, because most color PostScript printers print using something akin to the process-color method, your spot colors will be converted to process colors during printing).

When you need to create a color proof of your publication, but aren't yet ready to have your commercial printer set up their press to print a sample for you, use one of the color proofing processes (such as Chromalin or Press Match) to create your proofs from the film you've gotten out of your imagesetter. Imagesetting service bureaus frequently offer color proofing as part of their business. Some of these proofing processes can give you a proof on the paper you're intending to use, or can give you transparent overlays that you can place on top of your selected paper to get an idea of what your publication will look like when printed.

Controlling Your Color-Viewing Environment

If it's important to you that what you see on your screen looks as much like what the printed version of your publication as possible, there are a few rules you need to follow.

- Use a monitor and video card capable of displaying 24-bit color. Eight-bit color, as built into the Macintosh IIci, IIsi, and Centris series, is simply not going to do the trick. Neither is the 16-bit color you'll find on most Quadras.

- Calibrate your monitor. Radius and Tektronix, for example, make color monitor calibrators that work with FreeHand's onscreen display of colors. Find the one that works with your monitor and use it.

- Control the lighting around your monitor and keep it consistent when you're working. Just about everyone agrees that the fluorescent lighting used in most of our office buildings is the worst possible lighting for viewing colors. Turn it off, if you can, and rely on incandescent lighting (desk lamps with one sort of bulb or another) to light your work area. If you can't turn it off, try getting some "full spectrum" (or "amber") fluorescent tubes to install above your monitor. These also reduce eye strain.

- Control the lighting of the area where you'll be viewing your color proofs. Ideally, you'd have a room or small booth equipped with "daylight" (or 5,000-degree Kelvin) lamps—but few of us can afford the money or space required.

Why is lighting important? Basically, the temperature of the light affects what a color "objectively" looks like. You can't assume ideal-viewing conditions, but you have to work in them to be able to do consistent work.

These rules have been passed on to me by people who are serious about color, and whose opinions I respect. But, this being a "Real World" book, I have to point out that these conditions are difficult to achieve. My Macintoshes run in eight-bit or 16-bit color 98 percent of the time, and their monitors have never been anywhere near a calibration system. The lights above my desk are fluorescent tubes—and white ones, at that. And as for having a special booth or room for viewing color proofs—hah!

To compensate, I base my design decisions on printed examples of spot and process colors and pay little attention to what's on the screen except to remind me of what colors I've put where. When I get a color proof, I look at it in several different lighting environments: outdoors, indoors under typical fluorescent lighting, and indoors under typical incandescent lighting. These are, after all, the conditions under which people will be viewing it.

Color Models

FreeHand lets you define colors using any of four color models—CMYK, RGB, HSB, and HLS. Which one should you use? Read on.

Spot colors. If you're working with spot colors, it doesn't matter what color model you choose, and it really doesn't matter what the color looks like on the screen, as long as you let your commercial printer know what color of ink they need to use to print your publication. How do you know what ink to use? If you use Pantone colors (the most likely scenario), you can tell them the PMS color number. If you don't, it's trickier, but your printer can help you match the color you want to an ink they can mix.

Process colors. If you're working with process colors, *specify your color using the CMYK color model or a CMYK color-matching system*, or be ready for some nasty surprises when your publication gets printed. Once again, look at a printed sample of the process color, and enter the values given in the sample book for the color. It might seem too obvious to state, but don't enter other CMYK values unless you want a different color!

Tints. In addition, if you're trying to create a tint of an existing color (process or spot), use the Tints section of the Color Mixer—don't try to approximate the right shade by mixing colors. You can base your tint on a spot color, a process color, or another tint. Don't base your tints on other tints unless you want to lose your mind. What's a 20-percent tint of a 67-percent tint of a 45-percent tint of PMS 327?

FreeHand's Color Libraries

FreeHand supports the most frequently used color-matching systems in the graphic arts industry. There's nothing magical about these color libraries—they're just sets of agreed-upon industry standards. You can create these colors yourself, and name them however you like (and for process-color work, that's what we do—choosing colors and entering tint percentages from a process-color swatch book). And using canned spot colors means you don't have to figure out what color specifications will simulate the spot ink on your screen and your color printer.

- DIC. A spot-color specifying system corresponding to inks manufactured by Dainippon Ink and Chemicals, Inc. It's something like a Japanese version of Pantone—and not seen frequently in North America or Europe—except in printing subsidiaries of Japanese printers. Still, it's a nice set of colors, which you might want to use if you can get a printer to match them.

- Focoltone. A process-color specification system (mostly used in Europe). Colors in the Focoltone library are organized in sets of colors with common percentages of at least one process color. The idea is to create a library of colors that, when applied to objects, are easy to trap, or don't need trapping at all.

- Pantone. The basic set of spot-color inks manufactured by Pantone, Inc. These inks are the industry standard for spot color in the North American printing business (as always, ask your commercial printer).

- Pantone Process. A set of Pantone process-color tint builds. These colors have no relation to the Pantone spot colors.

- Toyo. A spot-color library for matching inks from the Toyo Ink Manufacturing Company, Ltd., and corresponding to their Toyo 88 Color Guide ink sample book. Like DIC, Toyo is primarily used in Asian countries, and isn't seen much in Europe or North America.

- TruMatch. A process-color specifying system featuring small percentage changes from one process color to another. Their swatch book is often preferred over any of the others by designers for specifying process color.

You can create your own color libraries by exporting colors from FreeHand, or you can create them yourself using a word-processing program (or a spreadsheet, or a database—anything that can write text-only—or ASCII—files). See "Creating Color Libraries," later in this chapter.

FreeHand's Color Controls

You create and add colors using two palettes—the Color List and the Color Mixer. FreeHand's color wells and color swatches are the key to using either palette.

Drag and Drop Color

Most color-related procedures in FreeHand involve dragging a color swatch from one color well to another. What's a color swatch? What's a color well? Take a look at Figure 6-2. As you'll see in the procedures in this chapter, color wells and color swatches are the key to working with color in FreeHand.

Color List

The most important of the three color palettes is the Color List (see Figure 6-3). You use the Color List to import colors from color libraries, export colors to color libraries, name colors, apply colors, duplicate colors, and convert colors from spot to process (or from process to spot).

Fill and Stroke buttons. At the top of the Color List, just below the palette's title bar, you'll see the Fill and Stroke buttons. These aren't labelled in any way, but the Fill button is the one on the left (here's

480   REAL WORLD FREEHAND 5.0|5.5

FIGURE 6-2
Color wells and
color swatches

Color wells

Color well

Color well

Color wells

Color well

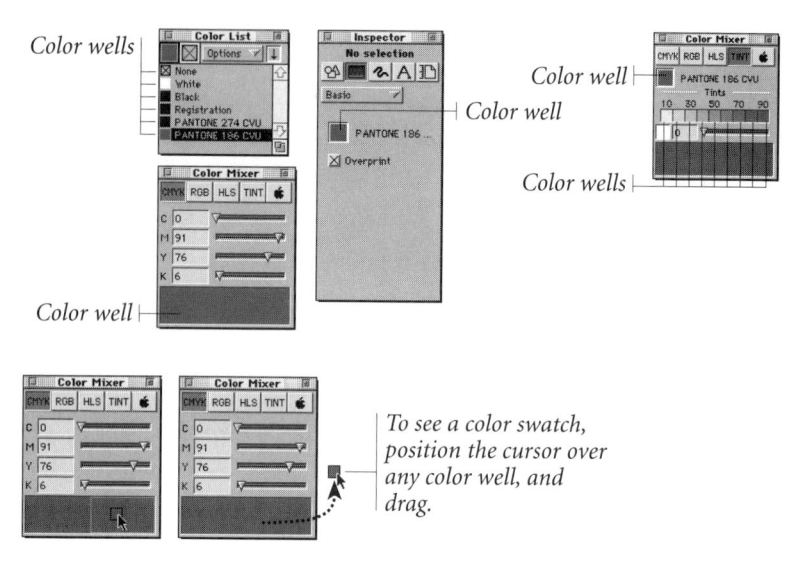

To see a color swatch,
position the cursor over
any color well, and
drag.

FIGURE 6-3
Color List

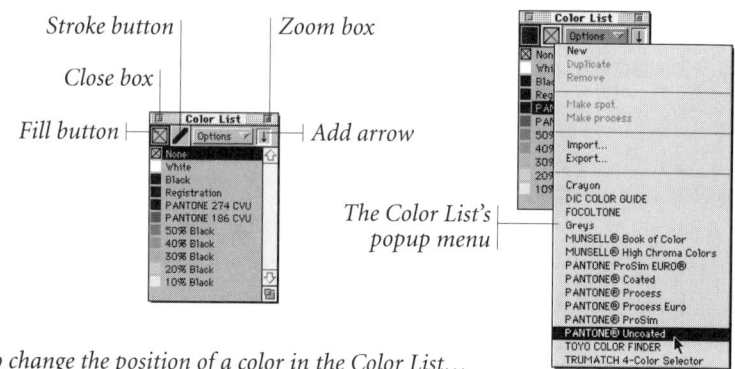

Stroke button

Zoom box

Close box

Fill button

Add arrow

The Color List's
popup menu

To change the position of a color in the Color List…

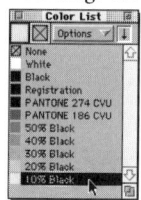

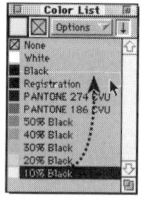

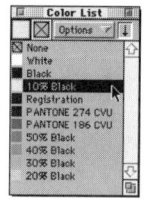

Select the color…   …and drag it up or   When the color's where you
                     down in the Color List.   want it, stop dragging.

proof that FreeHand's user interface, while easy to use, is hard to write about). When you want to work with an object's fill, click the Fill button; to work with an object's stroke, press the Stroke button. FreeHand shows you which button is active by displaying a black border around the button.

The Color List popup menu. The Color List's popup menu, to the right of the Fill and Stroke buttons, is what you use to duplicate colors, delete colors, choose color libraries, and convert colors from one color type (spot or process) to another.

The Add arrow. The Add arrow is another unnamed feature of the Color List. It's to the right of the popup menu—a little box with an arrow in it. Ordinarily, you add colors to the Color List by dropping color swatches into the open area at the bottom of the list. If you can't see the an open area, drop the swatch on the Add arrow. FreeHand adds the color to the end of the list.

For more on adding new colors to the Color List, see "Creating New Colors," later in this chapter.

Changing the order of the colors in the Color List. To change the order in which colors appear in the Color List, point at a color name and then drag the color name up or down in the Color List. Once you've got the color where you want, drop it. This can be handy when you've got a long list of colors and want to position the most-used colors near the top of the palette.

Tip: The Quick Way to Display the Color List	If you can't see the Color List, double-click any color well (in the Inspector, or in the Color Mixer, for example). FreeHand displays the Color List. This shortcut is a toggle—if the Color List is already visible, double-clicking a color well closes the Color List.
The Color Mixer	You use the Color Mixer to create and edit the colors you use in your publications. The Color Mixer gives you four different color models to choose from: CMYK, RGB, HLS, Tint, or HSB (also known as the Apple color model or Color Picker). To display the controls for a color model, click the corresponding button in the Color Mixer (see Figure 6-4).
Tip: The Quick Way to Display the Color Mixer	To display the Color Mixer, double-click one of the color wells in the Color List. FreeHand displays the Color Mixer, and loads it with the color definition of the color you clicked. If the Color Mixer is already visible, but loaded with another color definition, triple-click a color well in the Colors List.

FIGURE 6-4
Color Mixer

RGB model

HLS model

Tints

Drag a color swatch into this color well...

...and FreeHand generates tints of the color, in 10-percent increments.

Click the buttons in the Color Mixer to change the color model you're using.

Don't drag the color swatch into this color well. If you do, FreeHand gets confused.

Type a percentage here for a custom tint (or drag the slider).

CMYK model

Apple Color Picker

Double-click a color swatch and FreeHand displays the Color Mixer, loaded with that color.

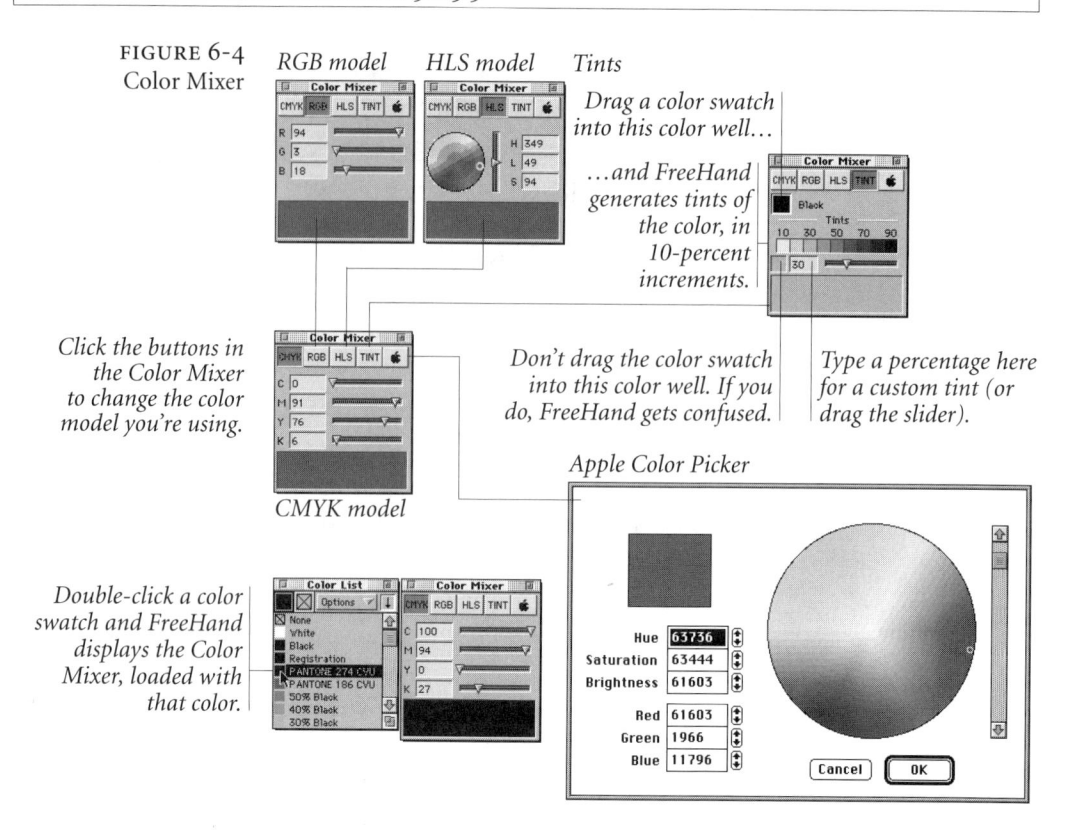

Tip:
The Quick Way to Load the Color Mixer with a Color

When you want to edit a color, but your wrist is too tired to drag a color swatch from a color well (in the Color List, Fill Inspector, or elsewhere) into the Color Mixer, triple-click any color well filled with the color. FreeHand hides, then displays the Color Mixer. When the Color Mixer returns, it's loaded with the color you clicked.

If you want to add a color from a TIFF image, use the Eyedropper tool (see "Color Xtras," later in this chapter).

Creating and Adding Colors

Now that you know what the tools are, you're probably wondering how they work. FreeHand 3 users sometimes find the process of creating colors in FreeHand 4 and 5 more difficult than the process they're used to. I think that creating and editing colors is somewhat quicker, overall, in FreeHand 5 than in previous versions of

FreeHand—but you have to get used to the tools and learn the "tricks." Read on.

Adding Colors from a Color Library

Most of the time, you'll be adding colors from FreeHand's color libraries. Why should you do this? Because your commercial printer wants you to (when they talk in their sleep, they call out Pantone numbers), and because it's the quickest way to add a named color to your publication. To choose a color from a color library, follow these steps (see Figure 6-5).

1. Display the Color List (if it's not already visible, press Command-9).

2. Choose a color library from the popup menu at the top of the Color List. FreeHand displays the Library dialog box.

3. Pick a color by clicking on one of the color swatches in the Library dialog box. To select more than one color, hold down Shift as you click on the color swatches. You can also

FIGURE 6-5
Adding a color from a color library

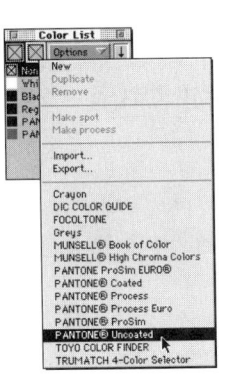

Type the name or number of the color you want here, and FreeHand selects the color. This saves you the trouble of scrolling through the list of colors.

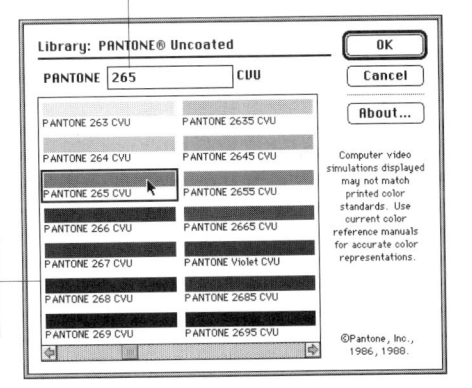

Hold down Shift as you click on colors to select more than one color at a time from the list.

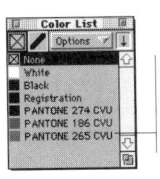

After you click OK to close the Library dialog box, FreeHand adds any color (or colors) you've selected to the Color List.

hold down Shift and drag the cursor to select a series of adjacent colors (in fact, you can Shift-drag through the entire library to select all the colors in the library).

4. Press Return (or click the OK button). FreeHand closes the Library dialog box and adds the selected color or colors to the Color List.

Tip:
Leave the Color Name Alone

If you're working with Pantone spot colors, don't rename the color unless you're working with one of the applications that names PMS colors differently from FreeHand (see "Keep Your Color Names Straight," below). Just stick with the color name that's entered in the Name field when you select the PMS color. This way, when you print, you can turn on the Separation Names option in the Print options dialog box and the color name will print on the correct color overlay. Your commercial printer has a pretty good idea what "PMS 327 CV" means, but might go mad trying to guess what you meant by naming a color "angry spam."

Then again, if you know you're going to be using a PMS ink but don't know which one, you can always name the color "Spot Color" or some such, and tell the printer which ink to use when you hand over the job.

Tip:
Why Import Colors?

What's the difference between importing colors using the Import command and choosing a listed library? The libraries shown on the menu are the ones FreeHand found in the Color folder in your FreeHand folder. If you've stored a library somewhere else, you can retrieve colors from it using Import. You might want to store your color libraries somewhere else to keep the popup list shorter.

Tip:
Keep Your Color Names Straight

If you're using FreeHand to create EPS graphics containing spot colors that will be placed in a publication created by another application, and you want to color-separate from that publication, make sure that your spot color names match between FreeHand and the other application. Color separation programs are as literal-minded as every other piece of software, so when you're separating a publication containing the spot colors "OceanBlue" and "Ocean_Blue" you can expect to get two overlays. Since you only want all the spot-color items to come out on one overlay, keep your color names consistent between documents. Make sure they're identical—right down to capitalization and punctuation.

This is especially true when you're working with Pantone colors, because different applications use different names for the same Pantone colors.

Note that all of this makes no difference whatever if you're converting these colors to process colors as you separate the file.

Creating a Color   To create a new color, follow these steps (see Figure 6-6).

1. Display the Color List (if you can't see the Color List, press Command-9).

2. Double-click a color swatch in the Color List to display the Color Mixer, if it's not already visible.

3. Pick a color model by clicking the buttons at the top of the Color Mixer. If you're working on a publication that you'll be printing using process colors, use the CMYK color model. If you're creating a custom spot color (have you talked with your commerical printer about this?), it really doesn't matter which color model you use.

FIGURE 6-6
Creating a new color

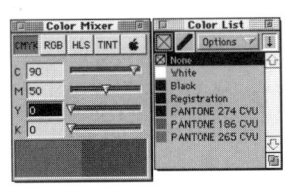

Add arrow

Display both the Color List and the Color Mixer. Specify a new color using the Color Mixer.

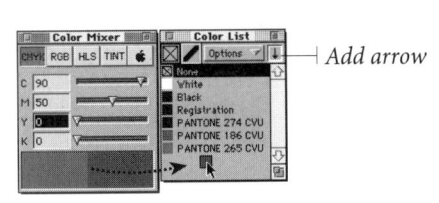

Drag a color swatch from the Color Mixer and drop it into an empty area in the Color List (or on the Add arrow).

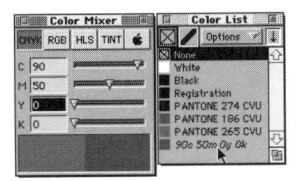

FreeHand adds the new color to the Color List, and assigns the color a default name.

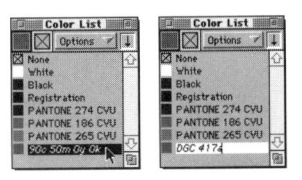

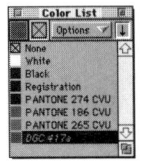

To change the color name, double-click the name in the Color List, type the new name you want, and press Return.

4. If you're using the CMYK or RGB color model, specify your color by entering numbers in the fields or sliding the sliders. If you're using the HSB or Apple Color Picker, click on a point in the color picker those models display. If you're using the Tints panel of the Color Mixer, click on one of the color wells for the tint percentage you want, or enter a percentage in the Tint Percentage field.

5. Drag a swatch of the color from the color well at the bottom of the color mixer onto the Add arrow at the top of the Color List (or drag the swatch into an empty area at the bottom of the Color List). FreeHand adds the color to the Color List, assigning it a default color name as it does so. You might have to scroll the list of colors to see the new color (it'll appear at the bottom of the list).

6. If you want to change the color's name, double-click on the color name in the Color List, type the new name for your color, and press Return. If you want, you can hide the Color Mixer by double-clicking a color swatch in the Color List.

Tip:
Keep Your Color Definitions Straight

If you're using FreeHand to create EPS graphics containing named process colors, and want import the EPS into another application and print color separations from there, make sure that your color specifications match between FreeHand and the other application. PageMaker imports the named process colors, so you're safe there—but QuarkXPress 3.3 doesn't import named process colors from an EPS (XPress does import named spot colors).

Once again, you can't rely on your screen display, because different applications display colors differently. Make the CMYK settings for your named process colors identical from one application to another, and you can count on their printing identically when you separate the publication.

Creating Color Libraries

FreeHand can read two different types of color libraries—binary files, which are stored in a proprietary format, and text files, which are saved as text-only. Binary files generally have the file extension ".BCF," and text-only files have the extension ".ACF." If you create your own color libraries, you can use any file name you want, but I'd advise you to stick with FreeHand's file extensions.

Exporting color libraries. You create binary color libraries when you export colors from FreeHand. To do that, follow these steps (see Figure 6-7).

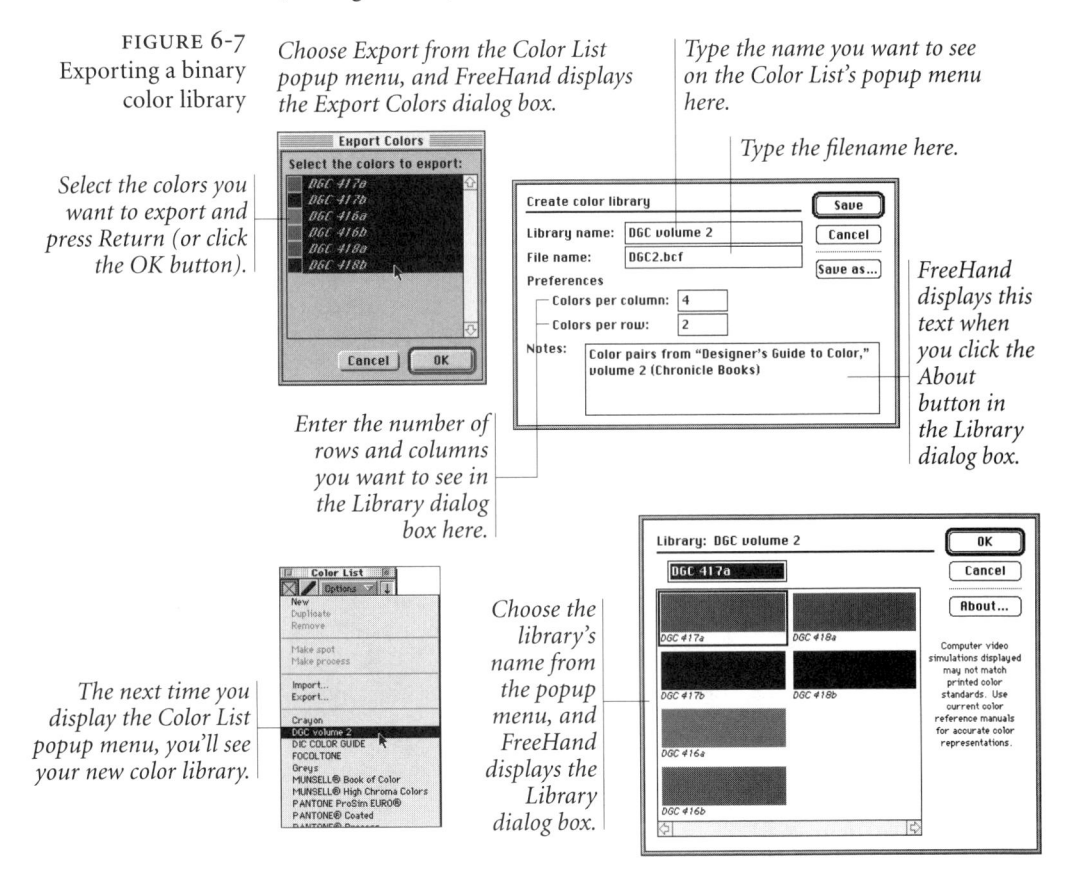

FIGURE 6-7
Exporting a binary color library

Choose Export from the Color List popup menu, and FreeHand displays the Export Colors dialog box.

Type the name you want to see on the Color List's popup menu here.

Select the colors you want to export and press Return (or click the OK button).

Type the filename here.

FreeHand displays this text when you click the About button in the Library dialog box.

Enter the number of rows and columns you want to see in the Library dialog box here.

The next time you display the Color List popup menu, you'll see your new color library.

Choose the library's name from the popup menu, and FreeHand displays the Library dialog box.

1. Choose Export from the Color List's popup menu. FreeHand displays the Export Colors dialog box.

2. Select the colors you want to export from the list in the Export Colors dialog box and press Return. FreeHand exports the colors you've selected.

Creating color libraries using a word processor. You can edit an existing color library (such as "CrayonLibrary.acf") to create a new color library using any word processor that can save files as text-only (ASCII). If you're working from a process-color swatch book, here's your chance to enter lots of colors at once.

Color library files begin with the following text (items you enter are shown in italic). Table 6-1 shows what the different lines mean.

```
ACF 1.0
library name
LibraryVersion: number
Copyright: © your name here
AboutMessage: your message here
Names: Partial or Full
Rows: number of rows
Columns: number of columns
Entries: number of entries
Prefix: prefix you want for the colors in the library
Suffix: suffix you want for the colors in the library
Type: Process, Spot, or Mixed
Models: color models
PreferredModel: preferred color model
Data:
```

TABLE 6-1
Color Library Keywords

Keyword:	What it means:
Library name	The name of the library as you want it to appear on the Color List's popup menu. Your library's name can be up to 31 characters long.
LibraryVersion	Enter a number here to represent the version number of your library. You can leave this line blank if you want.
AboutMessage	The message you want to see when you click the About button in the Library dialog box.
Names	Enter "Full" to display names with their suffixes and prefixes attached (see "Suffix" and "Prefix," later in this table), or "Partial" to display only the names of the colors. If you're insane, you can even enter "None", which means you won't see any color names in the Color List.

TABLE 6-1
Color Library
Keywords
(continued)

Keyword:	What it means:
Rows	The number of vertical color swatches FreeHand displays in the Library palette. Larger numbers mean smaller swatches; smaller numbers mean bigger swatches. Enter a "1" to produce the tallest possible color swatch.
Columns	The number of horizontal swatches FreeHand displays in the Library palette. Enter a "1" to produce the widest possible color swatch.
Entries	The total number of colors in the library.
Prefix	Any text you want to appear before your color names in the Color List.
Suffix	Any text you want to appear after your color names in the Color List.
Type	The type of colors contained in the library. You can enter "Process", "Spot", or "Mixed".
Models	A list of the color models used in the library. You can enter "CMYK" and "RGB".
PreferredModel	Enter "CMYK" or "RGB" here—it doesn't seem to make any difference to FreeHand. If you're creating a color library to use with PageMaker, on the other hand, the value you enter here determines which color model PageMaker's Edit Color dialog box displays when you edit the color.

After you create the library header, enter your color definitions as shown below, where *colorname* is the name you give the color and *cyan*, *magenta*, etc. are the color percentages for the color model being used (where 1.0 = 100 percent).

```
percentageC percentageM percentageY or percentageK
process or spot
colorname
```

For example

```
0 0 0 .1
Process
10% Gray
```

If you want to define a color using the RGB color model, enter the RGB values as shown below. Enter each of the component colors ("Red", "Green", and "Blue") using a scale where "65535" equals 100 percent of that color and "0" equals zero percent.

```
Red Green Blue
spot
colorname
```

For example

```
65535 65535 0
Spot
10% Gray
```

When you're through adding colors to your color library, save the file as text-only (ASCII), giving the file the extension ".acf." An example of a very short color library is shown in Figure 6-8.

Importing Colors from PageMaker

Because it's so important to have your spot-color names—or your process-color specifications—match, it's great to be able to import objects from PageMaker into FreeHand and add the color names and specifications used in PageMaker to your Color List.

Most of the time, it's easiest to pick the colors you want from a color library—FreeHand and PageMaker can use the same color libraries. If you're working with lots of custom spot colors (i.e., colors that didn't come from a color library), follow these steps to bring those spot colors into FreeHand.

1. Create spot colors in PageMaker.

2. Save one page containing objects with the colors you want to bring into FreeHand to disk as an EPS file. (In PageMaker, press Command-P to display the Print dialog box, enter the page number you want to print in the Range field, click the Options button, then use the controls in the Print Options dialog box to print the page to disk as an EPS file.)

FIGURE 6-8
A very short color library

```
ACF 1.0
Short
LibraryVersion: 1.0
Copyright: ©Olav Martin Kvern
AboutMessage: Why did you click that button?
Names: Partial
Rows: 2
Columns: 2
Entries: 4
Prefix:
Suffix:
Type: Process
Models: CMYK
PreferredModel: CMYK
Data:
.4 0 .2 .5
ColorPair 1a
.6 .4 .5 .5
ColorPair 1b
0 .1 0 .7
ColorPair 2a
.7 .6 .3 .5
ColorPair 2b
```

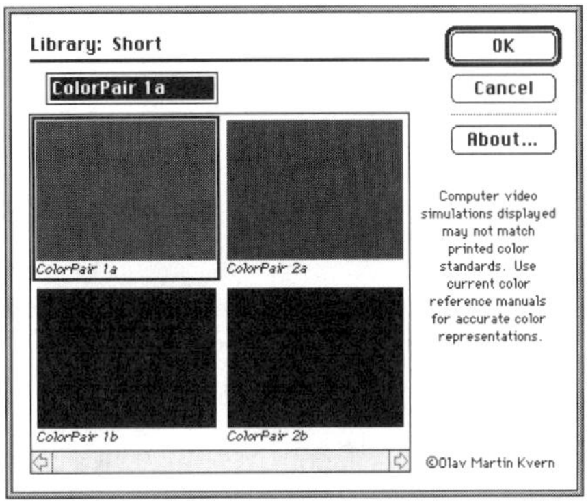

3. In FreeHand, press Command-Shift-D (or choose Place from the File menu).

4. Locate and select the EPS file you just printed to disk and press Return. FreeHand displays a loaded Place Gun. Click the gun to place the PageMaker EPS. As FreeHand places the EPS file, it adds the colors defined in the PageMaker EPS to the Color List.

You can take color names and definitions created in FreeHand back to PageMaker—when you import a FreeHand EPS file, PageMaker updates the Colors palette with any named colors in the placed EPS.

When you import an EPS from PageMaker or QuarkXPress, FreeHand doesn't import the named process colors defined in the EPS. Process-colored objects in the the EPS separate correctly when you print, but the name of the color doesn't get added to the Color List. If you want to use these colors in your FreeHand publication, you'll have to either re-create them in FreeHand, or follow these steps.

1. Convert the named process colors you want to import into FreeHand to spot colors in PageMaker or XPress.

2. Export an EPS containing examples of the colors.

3. Place the EPS in FreeHand. The spot color names appear in the Color List. You can delete the placed EPS, if you want.

4. Convert the imported spot colors to process colors (select each color and choose Convert to Process from the Color List popup menu).

Adding Colors from Illustrator

You can't name process colors in Adobe Illustrator, so when you open or place EPS files created in Illustrator, FreeHand's Color List doesn't update with any custom process colors you've used in the Illustrator file.

If you've placed the EPS file, there's not much you can do to get the color specifications from the Illustrator file into FreeHand; you'll have to recreate the colors from scratch. Remember that you've got to make the color definitions identical to have the colors match when you separate the publication.

If you've opened and converted the EPS file, on the other hand, you can add the colors to your Colors palette.

1. Ungroup the converted Illustrator EPS.

2. Select an object in the converted graphic that's filled with the color you want to add to your Color List.

3. Press Command-Option-F to display the Fill Inspector.

4. Drag a color swatch from the Fill Inspector's color well to an empty area in the Color List (or drop it on the Add arrow at the top of the Color List).

5. Double-click on the name of the color in the Color List, type a new name for the color, and press Return to change the color's name.

Importing Colors from Other Applications

In general, you can import spot-color definitions from any other application that supports named colors by creating an EPS file containing the spot colors you want, and then placing the EPS in

FreeHand. The named colors in the EPS file appear in the Colors palette. At that point, you can delete the EPS graphic, if you want.

If you edit the properties of a color you've imported with an EPS graphic, don't expect the changes you've made to affect the color definitions inside the EPS—they won't. The colors inside the EPS are, in effect, locked.

If you imported the EPS only to get the color definitions and have deleted the EPS, there's no problem. If you've imported an EPS, edited the colors that are imported with the EPS, and applied the edited colors to FreeHand objects, you can expect the colors inside the EPS and the colors of the FreeHand objects to separate differently. If they're spot colors, you'll end up with (at least) an extra overlay. If they're process colors, colors that should look the same will look different.

Editing Colors

To edit a color, follow these steps (see Figure 6-9).

1. If the Color Mixer isn't already visible, double-click the color well in the Color List for the color you want to edit. Once the Color Mixer is visible, drag a color swatch from the color well in the Color List into the large color well at the bottom of the Color Mixer. The Color Mixer fills in with the specifications of the color you selected.

2. Drag the color sliders or type numbers in the fields (if you're using the CMYK or RGB color models). If you're using the Apple or HSB color models, pick a color in the color wheel.

3. When the color has the specifications (or appearance) you want, drag a color swatch from the color well in the Color Mixer to the color well in the Color List.

Converting Spot Colors to Process Colors

Sometimes you need to change a color you've specified as a spot color into a process color. Your budget's expanded, you've got a sweetheart deal from your commercial printer, your client/boss/

FIGURE 6-9
Editing a color

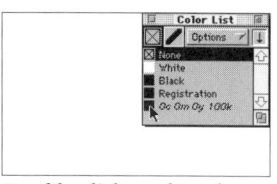

Double-click on the color you want to edit in the Color List.

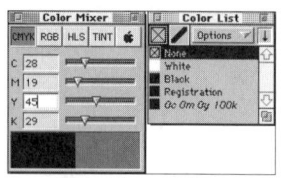

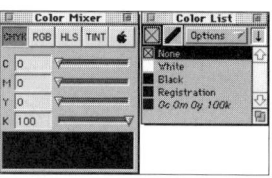

FreeHand displays the Color Mixer.

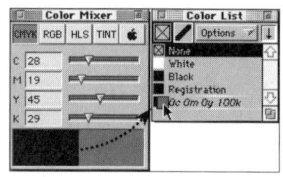

Use the fields or sliders in the Color Mixer to adjust the color.

Drag a color swatch from the Color Mixer and drop it on the color well of the color you're editing in the Color List.

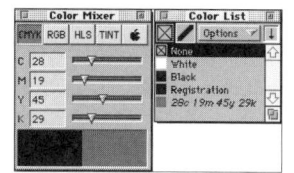

FreeHand updates the color.

whatever just *has* to have a color photograph—something happens so that you find you have to change your publication's color printing method from spot color to process color. Here's what you do (see Figure 6-10).

1. Select the color in the Color List.

2. Choose Make Process from the Color List's popup menu.

FreeHand converts your spot color to a process color. The process colors will rarely match the spot color—this is partly because the conversion process isn't perfect, but it's mostly because process color can't simulate the range of colors you can print with spot color inks (especially, as I've noted elsewhere, Pantone inks). Tweak the new process color until it looks the way you want, or until it matches the specs in your process color swatch book.

When you convert a Pantone spot color into a process color, FreeHand uses the CMYK percentages listed in Pantone's *Process Color Imaging Guide.*

FIGURE 6-10
Converting spot colors
to process colors
(and vice versa)

Select the spot color you want to change.

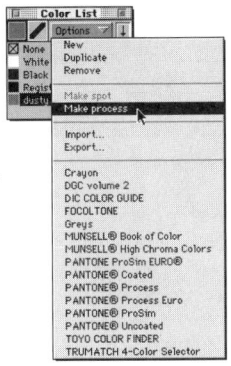

Choose Make Process from the popup menu.

FreeHand converts the spot color to a process color (and italicizes the color name in the Color List).

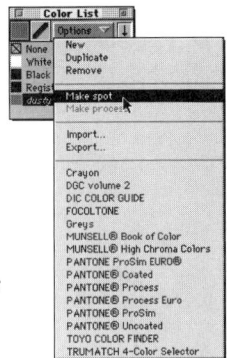

To turn a process color into a spot color, select the color and choose Make Spot from the popup menu.

Tip:
Changing from one library color to another

You've just changed your mind—you want all the "PANTONE 192 CVU" in your publication to change to "PANTONE 274 CVU" You can, of course, change the name and color specifications of "PANTONE 192 CVU" to match "PANTONE 274 CVU"—though it's easy to make an error typing the name. Or you could tell your commercial printer that the film overlay labelled "PANTONE 192 CVU" should be printed as "PANTONE 274". But what if you're compulsive (I know you're out there), and really want to change the one color to another, precisely as it's listed in the color library? First deselect everything (press Command-Tab), and then follow these steps (see Figure 6-11).

1. Add (or import) the new color from a color library.

2. Double-click the name of the color you just added.

3. Press the Left Arrow or Right Arrow key, then drag the cursor to select the color name (for some reason, double-clicking on the name doesn't work). Press Command-C to copy the color name to the Clipboard.

4. Drag a color swatch from the new color's color well into the color well of the color you want to change. If you're editing a library color, FreeHand asks if you want to replace the color. You do, so click OK. FreeHand changes the color specifications of the color.

FIGURE 6-11
Changing from
one library color
to another

Create a new color, then select the new color's name and press Command-C to copy it to the Clipboard.

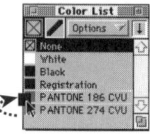

Drag a color swatch from the new color to the original color's color well. If you're working with a library color, FreeHand asks if you want to redefine the color. You do; so click OK.

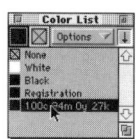

Remove the new color from the Color List.

Double-click the original color's name and press Command-V to paste the color name from the Clipboard.

Press Return. FreeHand updates the color name.

5. Delete the new color.

6. Double-click the name of the original color.

7. Press Command-V to paste the color name you copied earlier, then press Return. FreeHand changes the name of the color in the Color List.

Applying Colors

Once you've selected an object, you can use any of the following techniques to apply a color to the object (see Figure 6-12).

- Click the Fill or Stroke button and then click on a color in the Color List. FreeHand applies the color to the object's fill and/or (if it's a path or a text block) stroke.

- Drag a color swatch from the Color List to the Fill or Stroke button at the top of the Color List.

- Drag a color swatch from any color well and drop it on an object. If you drop the swatch inside a closed path, Free-Hand applies the color to a path's fill. If you drop the swatch on the path, FreeHand applies the color to the object's stroke.

- Drag a color swatch from any color well and drop it into the color well in the Fill or Stroke Inspector and press Return. FreeHand applies the color to the fill or stroke of the object.

COLOR 497

FIGURE 6-12
Applying colors

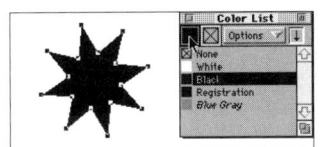

Select an object. Click the Stroke or Fill button...

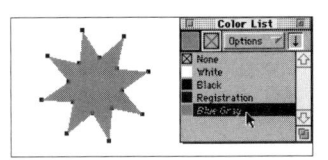

...and click a color name. FreeHand applies the color to the selected object.

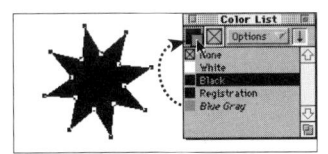

Select an object. Drag a color swatch from a color well...

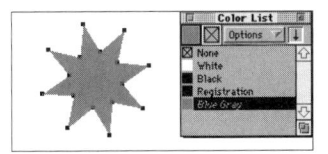

...and drop it on the Fill or Stroke button. FreeHand applies the color.

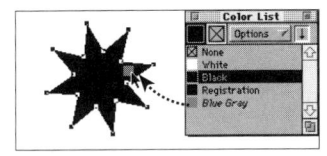

Drag a color swatch from a color well...

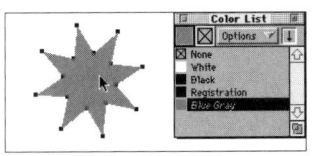

...and drop it on top of an object (the object need not be selected).

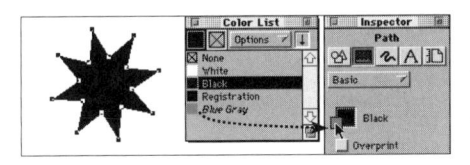

Select an object. Drag a color swatch from the Color List (or the Tints palette, or the Color Mixer) and drop it in the color well in the Fill (or Stroke) Inspector.

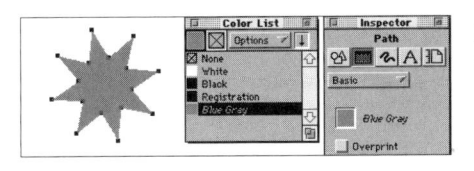

Press Return, and FreeHand applies the color.

Applying Colors to Text

You can apply a fill or stroke to the characters of text in your publication. To apply a color to text, select the text with the Text tool and apply a color using any of the techniques described in the previous section. What happens when you select the text block with the Pointer tool and apply a color depends on the setting of the Color List Shows option in the Colors Preferences dialog box (see "Colors," in Chapter 1, "FreeHand Basics").

Applying Colors to Groups

You can apply a color to a group, changing the stroke and fill of all the objects inside the group. There are some odd wrinkles to this.

- Objects inside the group with any basic fill or a fill of None will be filled with a basic fill of the color you apply.

- Patterned fills are colored with the color you apply, but remain patterned fills (you shouldn't be using these anyway, as explained in "Fills" in Chapter 2, "Drawing").

- Graduated and radial fills change so that the color you've applied to the group is their starting color.

- Tiled and PostScript fills are unaffected.

You can still subselect objects inside the group and change their color and fill specifications, regardless of any color you've applied to the group.

Applying Colors to Imported Graphics

FreeHand separates imported EPS graphics according to the color definitions inside the EPS, so applying a color to an EPS image has no effect.

You can apply colors to paint-type graphics, bilevel TIFFs, and grayscale TIFFs. When you print, FreeHand separates the image (or prints it as tints of a spot color, if you've applied a spot color to it). Applying a color to a color TIFF has no effect on the way that TIFF is separated by FreeHand.

Creating Duotones

Contrary to what you may have heard elsewhere, a single grayscale TIFF with two process inks applied to it does not a duotone make. It doesn't even make a "fake" duotone—which you create by printing a grayscale image on top of a tint of an ink.

The trouble is, I haven't found two people who agree on how to create a duotone. Some people change the screen frequency of the image for one color. Some people enhance the highlights in the image that prints on the overlay for the more dominant color and enhance the shadows in the image that prints on the overlay for the subordinate color. Some people do both. And so on.

Inside this book, I'm the absolute dictator, and I say that a duotone is created by printing two slightly different TIFFs on top of each other. The TIFF for the more dominant color in the color scheme has had its shadows enhanced; the TIFF for the subordinate color has had its highlights enhanced. By "enhanced," I mean that the darkest five percent (or so) of the pixels in the image become black and that the lightest five percent become white. The darkest—or lightest—areas in the image seem to spread out slightly. The screen frequencies and screen angles are the same for the two TIFFs.

If you have Photoshop, of course, you can use it to create your duotones. But if you don't, read on.

To create duotones using only FreeHand, follow these steps (see Figure 6-13 and Color Figure 8).

1. Place the grayscale TIFF you want to print as a duotone.

2. Enhance the shadows in the image. To do this, display the Image dialog box (select the TIFF and click Edit in the Object Inspector), then decrease the contrast and lightness of the image.

3. Clone the image, then enhance the highlights in the image. To do this, use the Image dialog box to increase the contrast slightly, then increase the lightness of the image.

4. Apply with the dominant color you intend to use to create the duotone to the image you edited in Step 2. Apply with the duotone's subordinate color to the image you edited in Step 3.

5. When you print the publication, print the ink colors you've applied to the TIFFs one color at a time, starting with the color of whichever TIFF is on top. Once that overlay's printed, bring the other TIFF to the top of the stack (remember that you can Control-click through the stacked objects to select it) and print the other color used to create the duotone. When plates are made from the two overlays, the TIFFs overprint each other, producing a real duotone. I won't say this produces great duotones, but it does work.

Why couldn't you just stack up the TIFFs and use ink-level overprinting commands to make them overprint? You can, if you modify your copy of FreeHand as shown in "Overprinting TIFFs" in Chapter 8, "PostScript." To see what this effect looks like, see Color Figure 5 in the color pages in this chapter.

FIGURE 6-13
Creating duotones

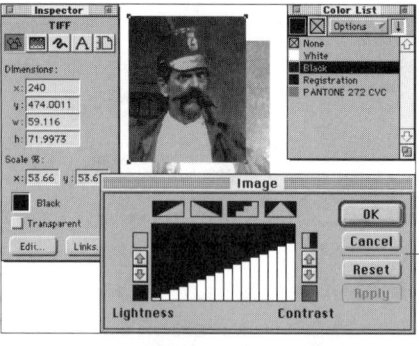

Create two copies of the image. Place the two images on top of each other in FreeHand (in this example, I've offset the images so that you can see what's going on). Color the images different colors.

Use the Image dialog box to decrease the lightness and contrast of the darker image.

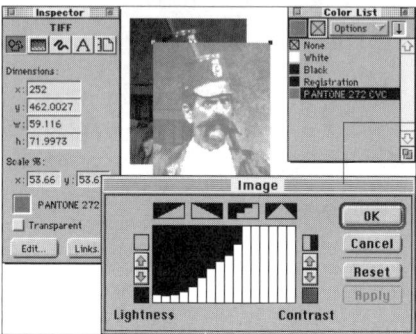

Use the Image dialog box to increase the lightness and contrast of the lighter image.

Print the two color plates separately, bringing each image to the front as you print the corresponding ink.

Removing Colors To remove a color, select the color name in the Color List and choose Remove from the popup menu attached to the Color List. If there are other colors in the publication based on the selected color (tints, mostly), or if there are objects with that color applied to them, or if the color is used in a style's defintion, FreeHand complains that that color is in use somewhere in the publication and cannot be removed. Locate the objects or colors containing the color you want to remove and (for objects) change their colors or (for tints) remove them.

This is something of a bother. FreeHand should make it easier to merge or change all of one color to another color. Until that feature's added, it's something you've got to be aware of.

Copying Colors If you need to copy a color or set of colors from another FreeHand publication into the current publication, just open the source publication, select some objects with those colors applied, copy them out of the source publication and into the target publication. Remember FreeHand's "home team wins" rule—any colors in the target publication with names the same as those of the incoming colors override the incoming color definitions.

Color Xtras

FreeHand comes with several Xtras dedicated to working with color in your publication—you'll see them on the Colors submenu of the Xtras menu. (If you don't see them there, you'll have to install them—see "Installing Xtras" in Appendix B, "Your FreeHand Installation.") In addition, you'll find the Unused Named Colors Xtra on the Delete submenu of the Xtras menu and the Eyedropper tool on the Xtra Tools palette.

Many of these Xtras (Color Control, Desaturate Colors, Saturate Colors, Lighten Colors and Darken Colors, to be exact) create new process colors when you use them. So you can't expect to use them in your spot-color publications (instead, use the Tints panel of the Color Mixer to create lighter or darker tints of spot colors). Note, too, that these Xtras don't change the color definitions in the Color List, and don't add the new colors they create to the Color List. To add the colors to the Color List, use the Name All Colors Xtra (see "Name All Colors," later in this chapter).

Color Control

Do you ever need to add a percentage of some color to a series of objects? I've seen it happen: the client looks at the color proofs, then in an authoritative voice says, "Add 15 percent yellow to this character's face." You know that the character's face is made up of several dozen blended objects and graduated fills, and you start to panic at the thought of changing the colors of so many objects (and this always happens close to a deadline). You can stop sweating—the Color Control Xtra gives you a way to change the colors applied to any number of selected objects (see Figure 6-14).

1. Select the objects whose colors you want to change.

2. Choose "Color Control" from the Colors submenu of the Xtras menu. FreeHand displays the Color Control dialog box.

FIGURE 6-14
Color Control Xtra

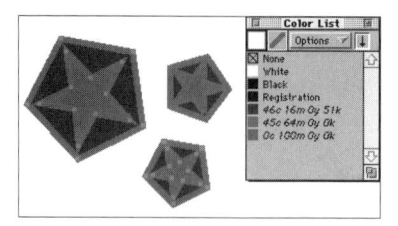

If you want to change the color definitions for an object or objects...

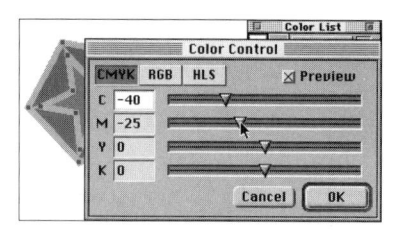

...choose Color Control from the Color submenu of the Xtras menu. Choose a color model and adjust color values.

If you've turned on the Preview option, FreeHand shows you the effect of your changes.

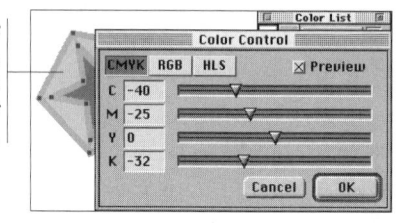

When the objects look the way you want them to...

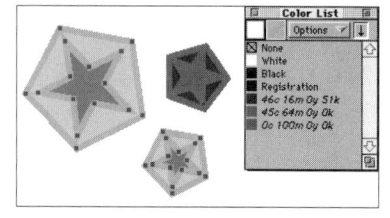

...press Return to close the Color Control dialog box. Note that FreeHand does not add the edited colors to your Color List.

3. Click the button corresponding to the color model you're working with, then make changes to the slider settings (drag the sliders or enter new percentages in the attached fields). If you've turned on the Preview option, you'll see the result of your changes on the selected objects.

4. When the colors look the way you want them to, press Return (or click the OK button) to apply your changes.

Darken Colors

When you choose "Darken Colors" from the Colors submenu of the Xtras menu, FreeHand makes the colors applied to the selected objects a little darker. What's that mean? Well, if you're using the CMYK color model, FreeHand adds three percent to the values of cyan, magenta, and yellow applied to the selection, and adds two percent to the color's black percentage. If you're using the RGB model, FreeHand subtracts five percent from each base color's setting. If you're using the HLS model, FreeHand subtracts five from the Lightness value of the color. And, finally, if you're using the Apple color model, FreeHand subtracts 6553 from the Brightness value of the color.

COLOR PAGE 1

COLOR FIGURE 1
Overprinting and knockouts

Objects colored with spot color 1 set to knock out (Overprint box unchecked).

Spot color 1 plate

Spot color 2 plate

Color 1 knocks out color 2

Objects colored with spot color 1 set to overprint (Overprint box checked).

Spot color 1 plate

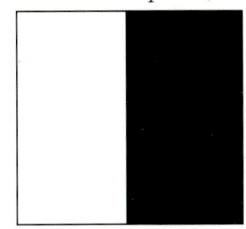

Spot color 2 plate

Color 1 prints over color 2

COLOR FIGURE 2
Trapping an open path

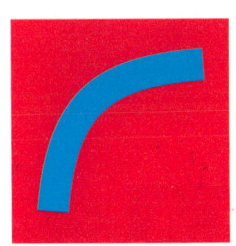

This cyan path needs to be trapped.

To create a spread, clone the path, and then increase the width of the cloned path. Set the cloned path to overprint.

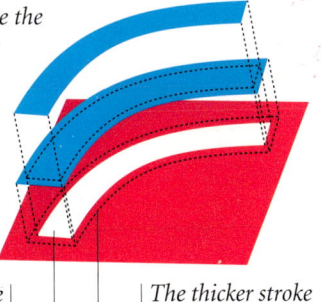

The thinner stroke knocks out objects behind it.

The thicker stroke overprints objects behind it.

To create a choke, clone the path and then decrease the stroke width of the cloned path. Set the original path to overprint.

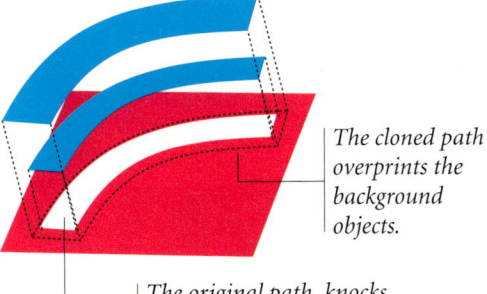

The cloned path overprints the background objects.

The original path knocks out objects behind it.

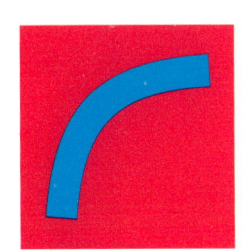

Trapped path

COLOR PAGE 2

COLOR FIGURE 3
Trapping closed paths and text

Unless I've been very lucky, you'll see the paper showing through around the cyan circle in this example. To prevent the paper from showing, you need to trap the object.

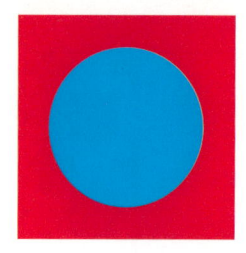

Select the object you want to trap and press Command-Option-L to display the Stroke Inspector. There, add a stroke to the object by choosing Basic from the Stroke Type popup menu.

Enter a value in the Width field that's twice the width of the spread you want, and check Overprint.

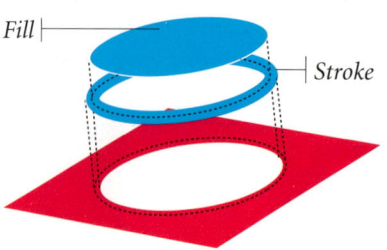

Fill | Stroke

When you print, the the stroke of the ellipse overprints the background rectangle, while the fill knocks out. This creates a spread.

To create a choke, apply an overprinting stroke the color of the background rectangle to the ellipse.

Here's the trapped version of the example.

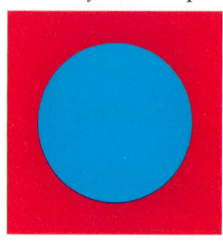

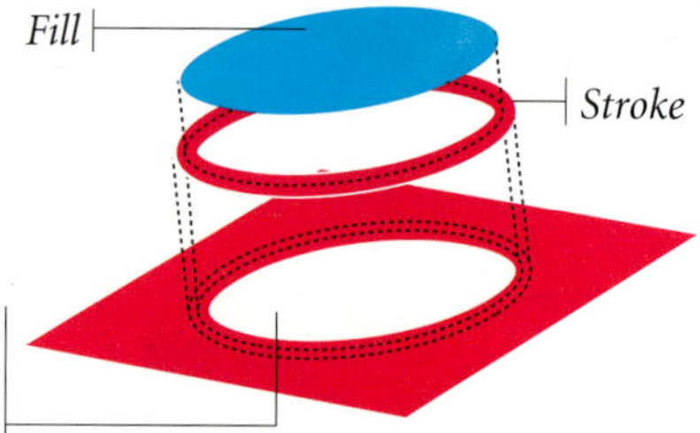

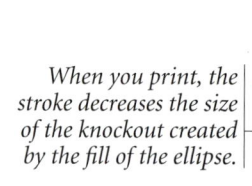

Fill | Stroke

When you print, the stroke decreases the size of the knockout created by the fill of the ellipse.

UTOPIA
LIMITED
Not trapped

Again, unless I've been lucky, you'll see the paper showing through around these characters. That means that this text needs to be trapped.

UTOPIA
LIMITED
Trapped using a spread

This stroke overprints the background objects, creating a spread. Unless I've been very unlucky, you won't see the paper showing around the edges of these characters.

UTOPIA
LIMITED
Trapped using a choke

The stroke decreases the size of the knockout behind the text, creating a choke.

COLOR PAGE 3

COLOR FIGURE 4
Trapping graduated fills

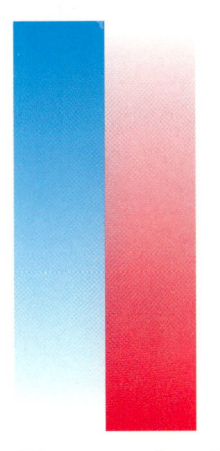

When two graduated fills abut, you run the risk of having the paper show through between the fills.

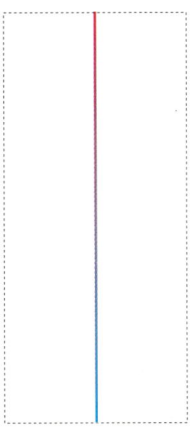

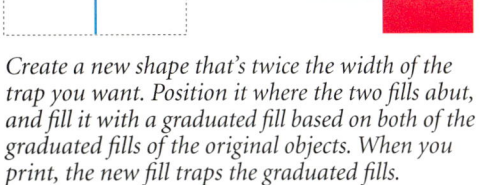

Create a new shape that's twice the width of the trap you want. Position it where the two fills abut, and fill it with a graduated fill based on both of the graduated fills of the original objects. When you print, the new fill traps the graduated fills.

COLOR FIGURE 5
TrapWise trapping

You shouldn't even think of trapping this manually.

TrapWise displays a preview of the spreads and chokes it uses to trap the file. (This screen shot is from the Windows version of TrapWise).

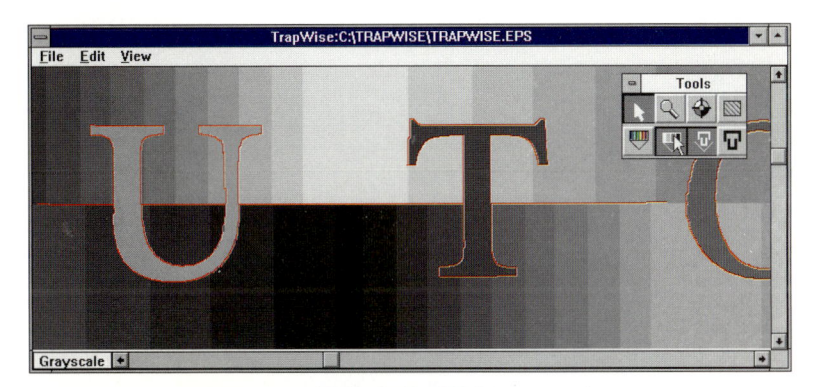

Example EPS trapped by TrapWise.

COLOR PAGE 4

COLOR FIGURE 6
Rosettes

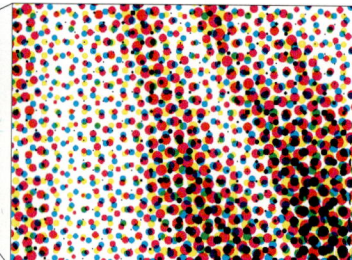

Rosettes for an area of flat color: 10C 10M 10Y 10K (ugly, but good for demonstration purposes).

COLOR FIGURE 7
Creating tint builds

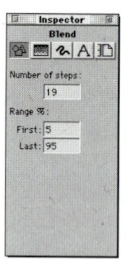

You can quickly create palettes of tints using FreeHand's Blend command.

To see the color definition for a tint, drag a color swatch from the Fill Inspector's color well into the Color Mixer's color well.

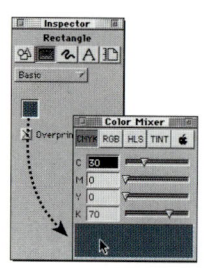

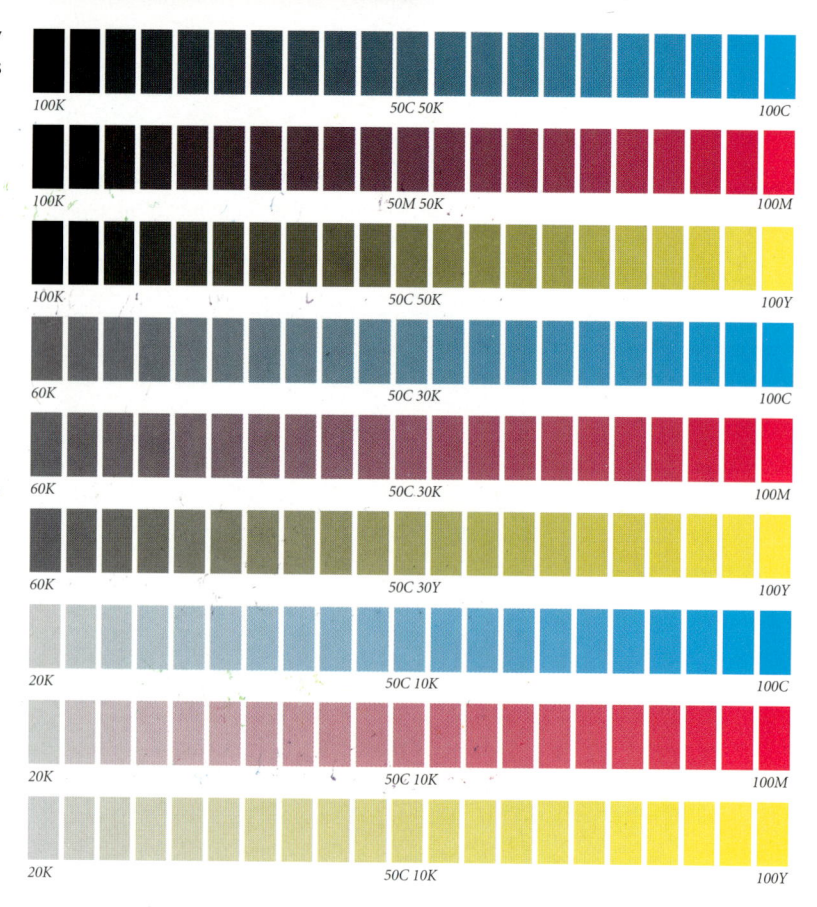

COLOR PAGE 5

COLOR FIGURE 8
Duotones

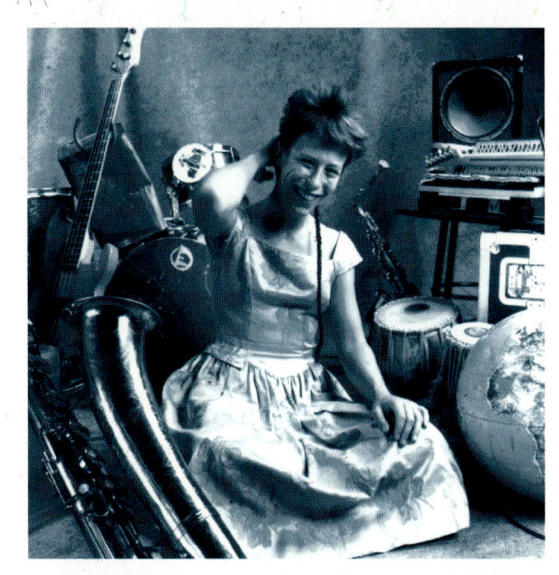

FreeHand duotone. Two overlapping TIFFs colored with different colors (cyan and black) and with different settings in FreeHand's Image dialog box.

Photoshop duotone.

Photographs of Amy Denio by Roger Schreiber

Two "fake" duotones

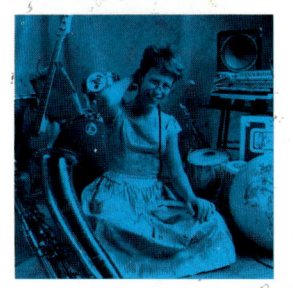

100 percent cyan background  *50 percent cyan background*

COLOR PAGE 6

COLOR FIGURE 9
Color Examples

FreeHand's Neon custom stroke effect is great—but you can't see it on your screen. Here's a way to create glowing lines you can see on your screen.

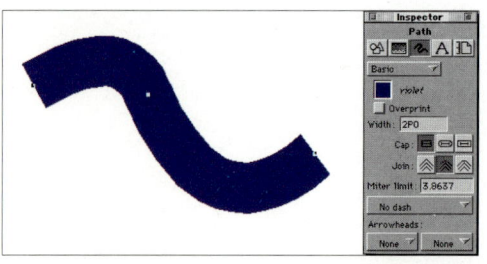

Draw a path.

Assign a thick stroke weight to the path that's the color of the outside of the "glow" you want to create.

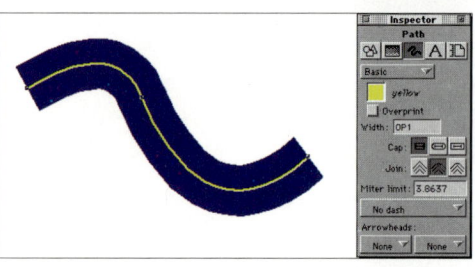

Clone the path.

Assign a thin stroke weight to the cloned path. This stroke should be the color you want for the inside of the "glow" effect.

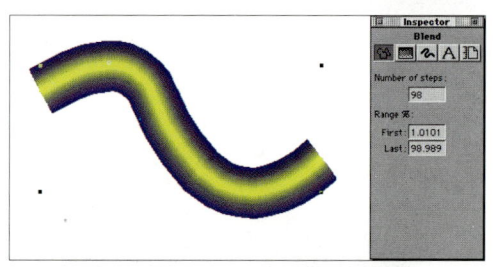

Blend the two selected paths.

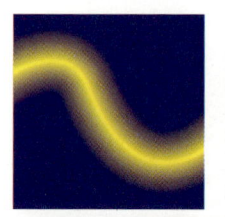

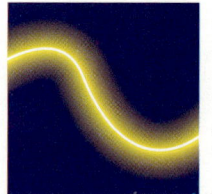

For an effect that looks more like a neon lighting tube, blend from white to the glow color, then blend from the glow color to the background color.

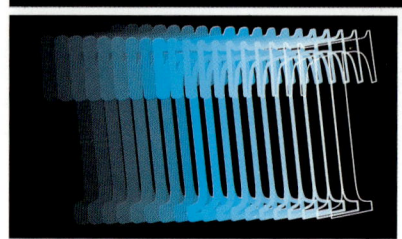

Each "neon" character above is composed of two blends. One blend goes from white to a color; the other goes from that color to black.

COLOR PAGE 7

COLOR FIGURE 10
Separating color images

Example RGB TIFF separated by FreeHand.

Example color TIFF separated by Photoshop, saved as an EPS, and printed from FreeHand (you could also save the file as DCS from Photoshop).

COLOR PAGE 8

COLOR FIGURE 11
Printing color images using random dither patterns

If you look closely at these images, you won't see rosettes—you'll see overlapping, random dither patterns (in this example, I've used a 600 dpi diffusion dither from Photoshop.

This technique is also called "stochastic" screening, and my version of it is still at an extremely experimental stage (it looked pretty good in the last edition, but I have no idea what it will look like this time).

COLOR FIGURE 12
Stochastic screening

Real stochastic screening (as opposed to the "fake" stochastic screening shown above) created by Icefields from Isis Imaging (at 800 dpi).

What about tints? You'd think FreeHand would increase the percentage of the base color when you apply this Xtra, but it doesn't. Instead, the Xtra changes the color components of the tint, effectively creating a new, unnamed color. Which means you should use the Tints panel of the Color Mixer when you want to make tints lighter or darker, rather than using this Xtra.

Desaturate Colors
According to my dictionary, "saturation" of a color is its "vividness of hue." If I were someone other than who I am, I'd probably leave it at that, or simply tell you to run the Xtra and see what happens to your color definitions. Maybe we'd both be better off.

As I understand it, saturation is a measurement of the amount of the primary colors (red, blue, and green, the colors we *see*, not the various color models we use to *simulate* them on a computer monitor or printing press). Saturated colors have a lot of one or two primary colors in them. When we desaturate a color in FreeHand, we're simulating the removal of some amount of the third primary color from the color we've defined.

In practical terms, that means that FreeHand changes the percentages of cyan, magenta, yellow, and black in the colors applied to the selected objects. The percentages changed, however, vary for each component color, and vary depending on the color definition.

The percentage of cyan changed in a color defined as 80C 40M 0Y 30K, for example, differs from the percentage changed in a color defined as 80C 0M 100Y 10K—even though the original percentage of cyan in the two colors is the same. In general, desaturating colors *removes* percentages from each component color, but that's not always the case. (In our example colors, for instance, eight percent is *added* to the percentage of magenta in the second color.) Run the Desaturate Colors Xtra enough times, however, and you'll reach zero percent for all component colors.

Lighten Colors
The Lighten Colors Xtra works just like the Darken Colors Xtra in reverse. If you're using the CMYK model, the Lighten Colors Xtra decreases the percentages of cyan, yellow, magenta, and black applied to the selected objects. If you're using the RGB, HLS, and HSB models, FreeHand decreases the base color components used in the colors applied to the selection.

Name All Colors Have you applied colors to objects from the Color Mixer (rather than applying them using the Color List)? If so, the Name All Colors Xtra can save you when your client decides to change their corporate colors as you're getting ready to imageset their new brochure. Choose "Name All Colors" from the Colors submenu of the Xtras menu, and FreeHand adds all the colors you've used in your publication to the Color List—including any colors generated by blending (that is, the colors applied to the intermediate object in a blend). Each color shows up in the list only once (see Figure 6-15). If you've chosen the Use CMYK Names option in the Colors Preferences dialog box, FreeHand creates a name based on the CMYK definition of the color; if you've chosen "Use RGB Names," FreeHand assigns a name based on the RGB values of the color (see "Colors Preferences" in Chapter 1, "FreeHand Basics").

FIGURE 6-15
Naming unnamed colors

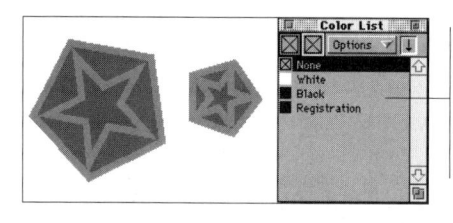

What's wrong with this picture? There are paths on the page, and they've obviously had colors applied to them, but no colors (apart from the default colors) appear in the Color List.

Choose Name All Colors from the Colors submenu of the Xtras menu, and FreeHand adds every color used in the publication to the Color List.

Randomize Named Colors You guessed it—the Randomize Named Colors Xtra randomly changes the color values in all named colors in a publication. Of what possible use is this? I don't know about you, but I need shaking up from time to time. When my creative process gets stuck in a rut, I find that introducing some random element sometimes gives me the inspiration I need. Choose "Randomize Named Colors" from the Colors submenu of the Xtras menu, and watch FreeHand redefine your colors. The results are generally hideous, but might give you the creative jolt you need.

This Xtra also makes for a good practical joke to pull on your fellow FreeHand users while they're away from their machines for a minute or two, but don't tell anyone I said so (it can, of course, be undone).

Saturate Colors
When you run the Saturate Colors Xtra, you increase the saturation of the colors in the objects you've selected. What's saturation? I'm glad you asked—take a look at "Desaturate Colors," earlier in this chapter.

Sort Color List by Name
Having trouble finding a color you know you named "Aardvark" or "Zymurgy" because there are so many colors in your Color List? Choose "Sort Color List by Name" from the Colors submenu of the Xtras menu, and FreeHand alphabetizes the color names in your Color List (see Figure 6-16).

FIGURE 6-16
Alphabetizing color names

If you're having trouble locating a color in your Colors List...

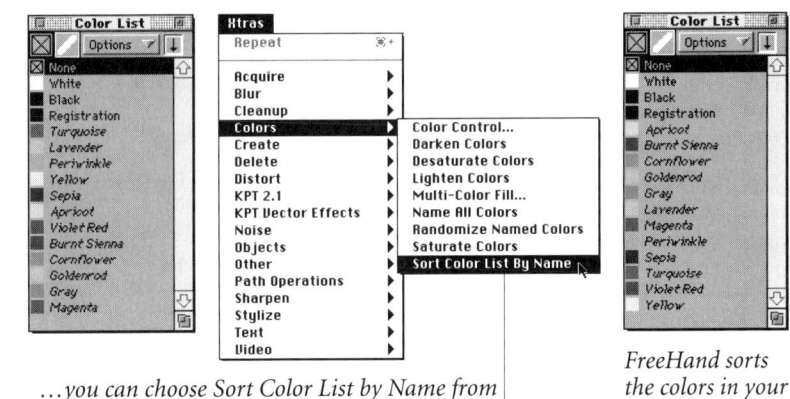

...you can choose Sort Color List by Name from the Color submenu of the Xtras menu.

FreeHand sorts the colors in your Color List.

Delete Unused Named Colors
Is your Color List longer than it should be? Filled with dozens of named colors you were "trying out" but then decided against? To shorten your Color List, choose "Unused Named Colors" from the Delete submenu of the Xtras menu, and FreeHand will remove all the colors it finds in the Color List that aren't applied to an object or used in a style definition.

Eyedropper Tool
In my career as a graphic artist, I've matched colors to shoes, shirts, horses, grapes, jewelry, lawnmowers, and a host of other items (not to mention things I can't mention in a family publication). I used to do this by comparing printed swatches of ink to

photographs or to the item itself. These days, I'd use the Eyedropper tool to pull a color out of a scanned image of the photograph.

The Eyedropper tool is one of FreeHand's Xtras, and appears on the Xtra Tools palette (press Command-Option-K to display the Xtra Tools palette, if it's not already visible). Select the Eyedropper tool, then point at an object on your page or pasteboard with the tip of the tool. Hold down the mouse button, and a swatch of the color of the pixel immediately beneath the tip of the Eyedropper tool appears, stuck to your cursor. Drag this color swatch to an empty area in the Color List (or to the Add arrow at the top of the Color List), then drop it. FreeHand adds a new color to your Color List, basing the color on the color value of the pixel you clicked on (see Figure 6-17).

Obviously, you'll get better results if you turn on the High Resolution TIFF Display option in the Redraw Preferences dialog box (see "Redraw Preferences" in Chapter 1, "FreeHand Basics"). Also, if the image is RGB instead of CMYK, you get FreeHand's idea of what the resulting CMYK values will be after separation; this won't be accurate unless FreeHand does the separations.

The current bit depth setting of your monitor has no effect on the Eyedropper tool—it gets the color definition from the object's color definition.

FIGURE 6-17
Eyedropper tool

Select the Eyedropper tool from the Xtra Tools palette.

Position the end of the Eyedropper tool over the color you want to acquire (in this case, I've pointed at a pixel in an image, but you can point the Eyedropper tool at any object on a FreeHand page). Drag the Eyedropper tool, and a color swatch appears.

Drop the color swatch into the Colors List, or into any color well, or onto a path or object.

You can also drag the color swatch to any color well, or drop it on objects to apply the color to them. If you're loading the Eyedropper tool with a color from a path, or from an object (such as a grayscale TIFF) that you've applied a named color to, FreeHand loads the Eyedropper tool with the named color (which you can then apply to other objects).

Creating Spot-Color Tint Builds

When you're working with spot-color publications, you often want to create tint builds (also known as stacked screens) of the colors you're working with to broaden the range of colors in your publication. Since you can't create a color containing percentages of two or more spot colors (20-percent black and 60-percent PMS 327, for example), it'd seem, at first glance, that you're stuck. You're not, though, as the following exercise demonstrates.

1. Open a new publication and add a spot color (create your own, or use one from the Pantone spot-color library). If one doesn't already exist, create a 20-percent tint of black.

2. Draw a rectangle.

3. Without deselecting the rectangle, fill it with the spot color you created in step 1. Set the rectangle's stroke to None.

4. Clone the rectangle by pressing Command-=.

5. Fill the clone with the 20-percent tint of black.

6. Press Command-Option-F to display the Fill Inspector. Check Overprint to make the rectangle overprint.

That's all there is to it. When you print, the gray rectangle overprints the spot-color rectangle, creating a combination of the two spot colors. Unfortunately, you can't see the tint build onscreen or on color printouts; you just see the color of the frontmost object. The next section shows another means to the same end.

Using Blending to Create Process-Color Tint Builds

Here's a trick I use to create a palette of tint builds for my publications (see Figure 6-18).

1. Draw a rectangle, fill it with 100-percent cyan, magenta, or yellow, and set the rectangle's stroke to None.

2. Clone the rectangle, move it away from the original rectangle, and fill it with 100-percent black.

3. Select both rectangles, press Command-U to ungroup them, and select a blend reference point on each rectangle. Press Command-Shift-B (or choose Blend from the Path Operations submenu). FreeHand blends the rectangles.

   Display the Object Inspector by pressing Command-Option-I. Type the number of tint builds you'd like to create

FIGURE 6-18
Creating a palette of tint builds

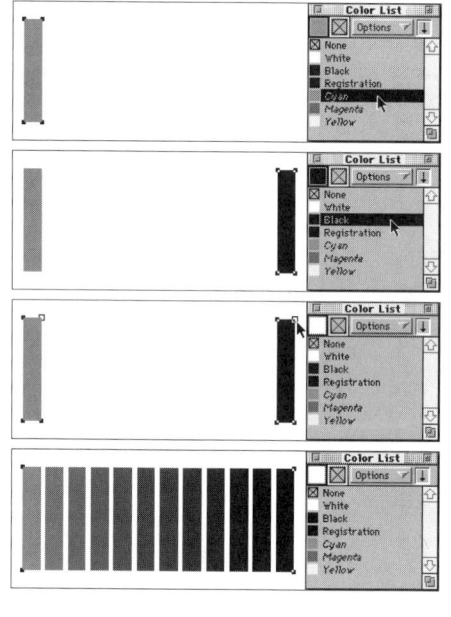

Draw a rectangle and fill it with 100-percent cyan, magenta, or yellow.

Clone the rectangle and drag the clone away from the original rectangle. Color the clone 100-percent black.

Press Command-U to convert the rectangles to paths. Select a point on each path press Command-Shift-B to blend the rectangles.

Adjust the number of blend steps using the Object Inspector. Ungroup the blend (press Command-U twice) and select a rectangle that's filled with a color you like.

Display the Fill Inspector.

Drag a color swatch from the color well in the Fill Inspector to an empty area in the Color List (or to the Add arrow).

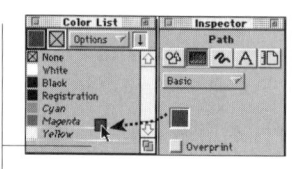

FreeHand adds the color to the Color List. You can change the name of the color, if you want, by double-clicking on the color name, typing a new name, and pressing Return.

in the Number of Steps field and press Return to change the blend. The intermediate objects in the blend are colored with tints. These new colors do not appear in your Colors palette.

4. Ungroup the blended objects.

5. Select an object filled with one of the colors you want and press Command-Option-F to display the Fill Inspector. The color well in the Fill Inspector displays the color of the path you selected.

6. Drag a color swatch from the color well to the Add Arrow at the top of the Color List. FreeHand adds the color to your list of colors (change the name of the color, if you want).

7. Repeat steps 5 and 6 until you've defined all the colors you want.

Substituting Process Colors for Spot Colors

Blending's a great way to create a set of tint builds, but blending one spot color into another produces blended objects that are filled with process color simulations of the original spot colors. This makes it tough to quickly create a set of spot-color tint builds in FreeHand. What to do? Substitute process colors for your spot colors. But what if you want to see something like the spot color you're working with on screen, instead of looking at cyan, magenta, or yellow?

The following procedure shows you how to change the on-screen display of a process color to match that of a spot color.

1. Choose a Pantone color in the Color List.

2. Drag a color swatch from the color well for the Pantone color into the large color well at the bottom of the Color Mixer.

3. Click the RGB button in the Color Mixer.

4. Write down the Red, Green, and Blue percentages for your spot color. Multiply each percentage by 65535 and write the numbers down. Close the dialog box.

Example: PMS 299 CV = 15R 56G 75B *or* 9830.25R 36699.6G 49151.25B

5. Choose Preferences from the File menu. The Display Preferences dialog box appears.

6. Click the Calibrate button. The Display Color Setup dialog box appears.

7. Click the swatch of color you're using to substitute for your spot color. The Apple Color Picker dialog box appears.

8. Type the numbers you derived in the Red, Green, and Blue fields and close all the dialog boxes.

Your process color now matches (or comes close to matching) your spot color.

When you change the color display options via the Preferences dialog box, the changes remain in effect until you change them again. They're not stored in the individual publications. This means you'll have to change the color display options again when you want to display a normal process-color publication. You can make a QuicKey to reset your color display options. Create a QuicKey sequence containing the QuicKeys shown in Table 6-2.

Now that you've got onscreen correspondence, you can create stacked screens to your heart's content using individual process colors as substitutes for individual spot colors.

Trapping

A trap is a method of overlapping abutting colored objects to compensate for the imperfect registration of printing presses. Because registration, even on good presses with good operators, can be off by a quarter point or more, abutting elements in your publication may not end up abutting perfectly when the publication is printed by your commercial printer. What happens then? The paper stock shows through where you don't want it to show (see Figure 6-19).

Do I need to tell you what happens if you take your work to a less skilled printer? Or to a press that's badly out of register or run

COLOR 511

TABLE 6-2
Reset color display QuicKey

QuicKey:	QuicKey contents:	What it does:
Menu/DA	Preferences	Selects Preferences from the File menu.
Button	Color	Clicks Color in the Preferences list.
Button	Calibrate	Clicks the Calibrate button in the Preferences dialog box.
Click	120, 54*	Clicks the Cyan color swatch in the Display color setup dialog box.
Text	ΔΔΔ0Δ65535Δ65535**	Enters the correct (in my opinion; you might want to enter something else) values for screen display of cyan.
Literal	Enter	Closes the Apple Color Picker dialog box.
Click	37, 202*	Clicks the Magenta color swatch in the Display color setup dialog box.
Text	ΔΔΔ65535Δ0Δ65535**	Enters the values for screen display of magenta.
Literal	Enter	Closes the Apple Color Picker dialog box.
Click	204, 201*	Clicks the Yellow color swatch in the Display color setup dialog box.
Text	ΔΔΔ65535Δ0Δ65535**	Enters the values for screen display of yellow.
Literal	Enter	Closes the Apple Color Picker dialog box.
Literal	Enter	Closes the Display color setup dialog box.
Literal	Enter	Closes the Preferences dialog box.

* These coordinates might be slightly different on your system.

** Δ indicates a tab character in the QuicKeys Text dialog box. Where you see a Δ, just press Tab.

FIGURE 6-19
Why you need to trap

Color 1
Color 2

When you don't trap, you can end up with paper showing through where it shouldn't.

When you trap, you enlarge (or shrink) the objects so that they'll overlap a little bit when they print—regardless of the paper stretching or shifting on the press.

by turkeys? Disaster. Also, some printing processes, notably silkscreening, require larger traps than others. In any case, talk with your commercial printer regarding the tolerances of their presses and/or operators.

Before I start describing trapping techniques in FreeHand, you ought to know that the best technique is one you find outside FreeHand—use Adobe TrapWise. TrapWise can trap your publications better than you can, and, if you use TrapWise, you don't even have to think about trapping. I'll provide descriptions of what you can do to trap your files, but I'll say at the outset—find a service bureau that'll trap your files with TrapWise, and save yourself time and trouble. For more on TrapWise, see Appendix A, "System."

If you can't, or don't, want to use TrapWise, you don't have to trap every potential registration problem yourself—you can use FreeHand's Trap Xtra. It does a good job of trapping objects formatted using basic fills or strokes. I'm still going to describe how to do the trapping yourself, then I'll talk about the Trap Xtra. I do this because I believe that you should know how to add and subtract, multiply and divide before you ever use a calculator.

Object-Level Overprinting

The key to trapping, in FreeHand and elsewhere, is in controlling which objects—or which parts of objects—print on top of other objects as the printing press prints your publication. While choosing to overprint entire inks can be handy (especially overprinting black), you really need to control the overprinting characteristics of individual objects to make trapping work (see Color Figure 1).

Luckily, you can. Any FreeHand path can be specified as an overprinting object (that is, it won't knock a hole in any objects behind it when you print), regardless of the object's color. The controls for object-level overprinting are found in the Fill Inspector and the Stroke Inspector (see Figure 6-20).

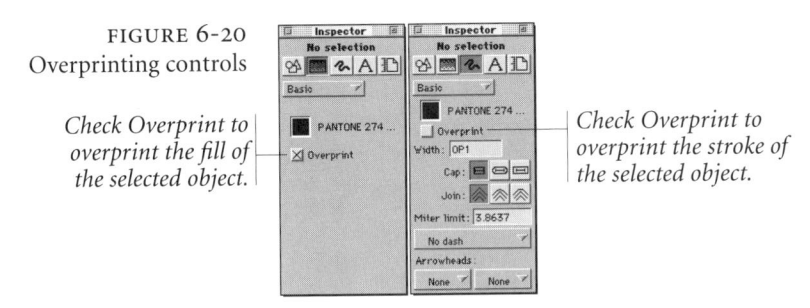

FIGURE 6-20
Overprinting controls

Check Overprint to overprint the fill of the selected object.

Check Overprint to overprint the stroke of the selected object.

Ink-Level Overprinting

In FreeHand's Print Options dialog box, you can choose to knock out or overprint an entire ink (see Figure 6-21). I find I usually overprint all inks, and knock out selected paths using the Overprint checkboxes in the Fill and Stroke Inspectors.

Object-level overprinting settings override ink-level overprinting settings for individual objects.

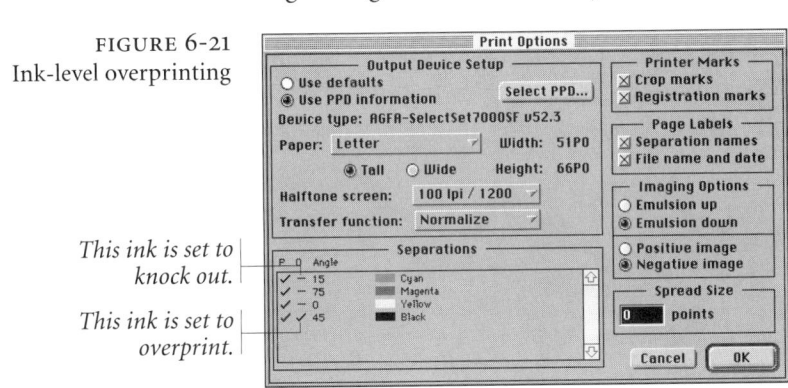

FIGURE 6-21
Ink-level overprinting

This ink is set to knock out.

This ink is set to overprint.

Manual Trapping

The keys to trapping in FreeHand are the Overprint checkboxes in the Fill Inspector and the Stroke Inspector. These controls, in combination with FreeHand's Paste Inside command, provide incredible manual trapping flexibility.

When you're working with FreeHand's trapping features, you'll be creating *spreads* (outlines of objects, in the same color as the object, that are slightly larger than the object itself) and *chokes* (outlines of the object that are the same color as the underlying object's color). Spreads make the object larger so that the edges of the object print over the underlying object; chokes make the area knocked out of the underlying object smaller than the outline of the foreground object.

Use chokes when the foreground object is a darker color than the background object, and use spreads when the foreground object is lighter. In other words, trap from light colors into darker colors. Sound subjective? It is. I use chokes when I'm trapping type—text characters often look distorted when you use spreads (the eye is very critical when it comes to text).

Spot-Color Trapping

In most cases, it's more important to trap abutting color fields in spot color publications than it is in process color publications. Why? Because when you're working with process colors, you've almost always got some kind of dot between objects (cyan, magenta, yellow, or black), so you're less likely to see the tell-tale paper-colored lines showing a poor trap (see Figure 6-22).

The easiest way to demonstrate how spot-color trapping works is to show you some examples. As you work through these examples, you'll trap an ellipse into a rectangle by manipulating the color, width, and overprinting specifications of the path that surrounds the ellipse. First, draw the colored objects.

FIGURE 6-22
Spot-color trapping and process-color trapping

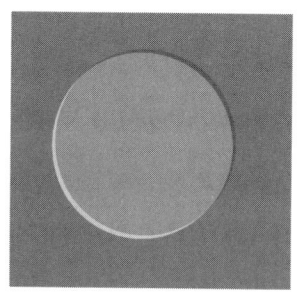

When you're trapping process colors, there's almost always some color value—dots—on one of the other plates...

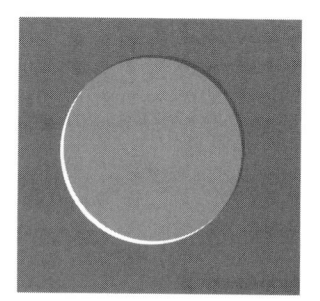

...while in spot-color trapping, there's usually not.

1. Create a rectangle. Fill the rectangle with a spot color (in these instructions, I'll call this color "Color 1"). Set the rectangle's stroke to None.

2. Draw an ellipse on top of the rectangle. Make sure that the ellipse is entirely inside the rectangle. Fill the ellipse with a different color from that of the rectangle (I'll call this color "Color 2"). Set the stroke of the ellipse to None.

3. Save the file.

Creating a spread. The ellipse needs to be trapped, or you'll run the risk of having paper-colored lines appear up around the ellipse when you print the publication. You can either spread or choke the ellipse, or both.

To spread the ellipse, follow these steps (see Color Figure 3).

1. Select the ellipse.

2. Press Command-Option-L to display the Stroke Inspector.

3. In the Stroke Inspector, choose Basic from the Stroke Type popup menu, set the line color to "Color 2" (the color of the ellipse), type a line width for your trap in the Width field. Finally, check the Overprint box and press Return.

The line width you enter in the Width field should be equal to twice the trap amount—if you enter "2", you'll get a stroke of one point on either side of the path, because PostScript lines grow out from the line's center. If your commercial printer has asked for a trap of .5 points, enter "1" in the Width field.

When you print, the ellipse is larger than the hole that's knocked out of the background rectangle, which means that the outside of the ellipse slightly overprints the background rectangle. You've just created a spread.

After you're through looking at the objects, or printing, choose Revert from the File menu and revert to the version of the file you saved earlier. This way, you're ready for the next procedure.

Creating a choke. To choke the ellipse, follow these steps (see Color Figure 3).

1. Select the ellipse.

2. Press Command-Option-L to display the Stroke Inspector.

3. In the Stroke Inspector, choose Basic from the Stroke Type popup menu, set the line color to "Color 1" (the color of the background rectangle), type a line width for your trap in the Width field. Finally, check the Overprint box and press Return.

When you print, the hole that's knocked out of the background rectangle is slightly smaller than the ellipse. This way, the outside of the ellipse slightly overprints the background rectangle. You've just created a choke.

Choose Revert from the File menu to get the file ready for the next procedure.

Trapping across color boundaries. The techniques described above work well as long as objects don't cross color boundaries. If the objects do cross color boundaries (especially going from a color background to a white background), it's too obvious that you've changed the shapes of the objects. What do you do?

1. Drag the ellipse so that it's partially outside of the rectangle.

2. Clone the ellipse by pressing Command-=.

3. Without deselecting the cloned ellipse, press Command-Option-L to display the Stroke Inspector.

4. In the Stroke Inspector, choose Basic from the Stroke Type popup menu, set the stroke color to "Color 1" (the color of the background rectangle), enter a stroke width for your trap in the Width field. Finally, check the Overprint box and press Return to apply your changes.

5. Press Command-X to cut the ellipse to the Clipboard.

6. Select the background rectangle and choose Paste Inside from the Edit menu.

7. Select the original ellipse and press Command-B to send it to the back.

At this point, the ellipse you pasted inside the rectangle spreads slightly, while the part of the ellipse outside of the rectangle remains the same size and shape (see Color Figure 3).

Choose Revert from the File menu to get ready for the next trapping example.

What happens when the object you need to trap overlaps more than one other, differently colored object? In this case, you can run into trouble. The trap you use for one background color might not be the trap you want to use for the other. You might want to spread one and choke the other, depending on the colors you're using.

In these cases, you use the same basic techniques described above for all of the overlapping objects. Try it (see Color Figure 3).

1. Draw another new rectangle (I'll call it Rectangle 2) so that it partially overlaps the original rectangle (which I'll call Rectangle 1). Create a third spot color ("Color 3") and apply it to the rectangle's fill. Set the rectangle's stroke to None. Drag the ellipse so that it partially overlaps both rectangles.

2. Select Rectangle 2 and press Command-= to clone it. Without deselecting the clone, press Command-Option-L to display the Stroke Inspector.

3. In the Stroke Inspector, choose Basic from the Stroke Type popup menu, set the line color to "Color 1" (the color of the background rectangle), enter a line weight for your stroke in the Width field, and check the Overprint box. Press Return to apply the stroke.

4. Select the ellipse and repeat step 3. Make sure that the clone of the ellipse is in front of the clone of the rectangle, then select both of the clones you've created and press Command-X to cut them to the Clipboard.

5. Select Rectangle 1 and choose Paste Inside from the Edit menu. You've just created chokes for the ellipse and Rectangle 2 at the points they overlap Rectangle 1.

6. Select the Ellipse and press Command-= to clone it. Change the stroke of the cloned ellipse as directed in step 3. Press

Command-X to cut the new clone to the Clipboard. Select Rectangle 2 and choose Paste Inside from the Edit menu. The ellipse is now choked where it overlaps Rectangle 2.

Trapping Lines The trapping techniques above work well for filled paths, but what about lines? After all, you can't apply two different line properties to a single line. Instead, you clone the line and make the width of the cloned line larger or smaller to achieve the spread or choke you want. One of the lines overprints; the other line knocks out.

Follow these steps to spread a line (see Color Figure 2).

1. Draw a rectangle. Create a spot color and fill the rectangle with it.

2. Draw a line inside the rectangle. Create another spot color and apply it to the line. Do not set this line to overprint.

3. Select the line and press Command-= to clone the line.

4. Press Command-Option-L to display the Stroke Inspector. Increase the width of the line by twice the amount of spread you need (remember, PostScript lines grow out from their centers) and check the Overprint box to make the stroke overprint.

That's all there is to it. The original line knocks a hole in the background rectangle, and the clone of the line spreads to just a little bit beyond the edges of the knockout.

To choke the line, follow these steps (see Color Figure 2).

1. Draw a rectangle. Create a spot color and fill the rectangle with it.

2. Draw a line inside the rectangle. Create another spot color and apply it to the line. Set this line to overprint.

3. Select the line and press Command-= to clone the line.

4. Display the Stroke Inspector. Decrease the width of the line by twice the amount of choke you need, and leave the Overprint box unchecked.

5. Hold down Control and select the original line. Press Command-F to bring it to the front.

This time, the cloned line is narrower than the original line, and knocks out an area that's slightly smaller than the original line, creating a choke.

If the line you need to trap crosses a color boundary, follow the same steps described above for trapping paths: clone the line, edit the line, cut the line, select the background object, choose Paste Inside, and send the original line to the back.

Trapping Text Text is usually the element in a publication that needs trapping the most. For whatever reason, it's easier to notice poor trapping around text than around other elements. At the same time, traps that are too large distort the shapes of the characters you're trapping. It's especially a problem with small type, especially serif type.

Here's how to create a spread for text (see Color Figure 3).

1. Draw a rectangle, create a spot color ("Color 1"), and apply it to the rectangle.

2. Type a text block. Position the text block on top of the rectangle so that it's entirely within the area occupied by the rectangle.

3. Create a second spot color ("Color 2") and apply it to the text in the text block.

4. While the text is still selected, press Command-Option-L to display the Stroke Inspector. Enter the width you want (remember, it's two times the amount of trap you want) in the Width field. Check the Overprint box and press Return.

The next example shows how you can choke text by making the shape the characters knock out of the background a little bit smaller than the characters themselves.

1. Draw a rectangle, create a spot color ("Color 1"), and apply it to the rectangle.

2. Create a text block. Position the text block on top of the rectangle so that it's entirely within the rectangle.

3. Create a second spot color ("Color 2"). Select all the text in the text block and click on "Color 2" in the Color List. FreeHand applies a fill of "Color 2" to the text.

4. Without deselecting the text, press Command-Option-L to display the Stroke Inspector. Enter the width you want for the trap in the Width field. Check the Overprint box and press Return.

If text crosses color boundaries, use the techniques described earlier for trapping overlapping paths.

Tip: Type and Black Ink

Type that's specified as 100-percent black always overprints, regardless of the settings you've made in the Fill and Stroke dialog boxes or in the ink list in the Print Options dialog box. You probably want 100-percent black text to overprint most of the time, but what if you don't? Create a color that's specified as 99-percent black and apply it to the text you want to knock out of whatever is behind it. 99-percent black works just like every other color. It can be set to knock out or overprint as you want, and it'll look just like 100-percent black.

Advanced Spot-Color Trapping

All of the trapping techniques demonstrated above assume that you're working with solid (that is, 100 percent) spot colors. What happens when you're working with tints of spot colors, and what happens when you're working with graduated or radial fills?

When you're working with tints, you simply use the above procedures, substituting the tints for the colors specified for the overprinting strokes you're using to create traps. When you're trapping graduated and radial fills, on the other hand, things get complex.

Trapping Spot-Color Graduated Fills

When graduated fills abut in your spot color publications, you need to provide for some sort of trapping between the two fills, or you'll end up with your paper color showing through between the fills. Apart from using TrapWise (see "Trapping with TrapWise," later in this chapter), the simplest thing to do is to set one or both spot colors to overprint, and then overlap the graduated fills by some small amount (something less than one point).

If you can't, or don't want to, overprint the spot colors you've used in your graduated fills, life gets harder. You'll have to create a pair of blends—one in each spot color—that mimic your graduated fills and position them where the graduated fills abut. Why create blends? Remember that each intermediate object in a blend is a solid color, or tint, and can be set to overprint.

Once again, I'll show you how to do this by leading you through a series of steps. You'll probably run into more complex examples of abutting graduated fills than the one shown in this example, but you can use these techniques for all situations in which spot color graduated fills abut (see Color Figure 4).

1. Draw two abutting rectangles.

2. Create two spot colors ("Color 1" and "Color 2").

3. Fill one of the rectangles with a graduated fill going from "Color 1" to white. Fill the other rectangle with a graduated fill going from white to "Color 2".

Next, you'll set up the objects for the blend.

1. Create two squares that are the width of the trap you want to use. Position one rectangle at either end of the point where the two graduated fills abut.

2. Fill one of the squares with "Color 1", and fill the other one with a zero-percent tint of "Color 1".

3. Set both squares to overprint using the Fill Inspector.

4. Select the same point on each of the small squares you've just created. It's probably easier to do this in Keyline view. If you can't select a point, ungroup the squares and try again.

5. Choose Blend from the Path Operations submenu of the Arrange menu. FreeHand blends the selected squares. Does the blend fill the distance from one of the objects to the other without any gaps? If not, display the Object Inspector for the blend, increase the number of blend steps, and press Return to close the dialog box and apply the new blend. Keep increasing the number of steps until there are no gaps in the blend.

6. Clone the original squares. Repeat the process substituting "Color 2" for "Color 1" in the blend.

When you print, the blended objects print over the area where the graduated fills abut, spreading the two graduations into each other. This technique brings up a point—if you can trap blends, and can't trap graduated fills, why not just use blends for all the graduated fills you need to trap? Why not, indeed. See "The Golden Rules" in Chapter 7, "Printing," for more on why you should use blends instead of graduated fills.

Trapping Spot-Color Radial Fills

After all the trouble we had to go through to create a trap for adjacent spot-color graduated fills, you'd think radial fills using spot colors would be more difficult. Luckily, that's not the case all the time. When you create a radial fill inside an object, you can simply add an overprinting stroke to the object containing the radial fill that's the color of the background object, thereby creating a choke.

Where things get ugly is in those cases where two radial fills abut each other. When that happens, try this trick.

1. Clone the objects containing the radial fill.

2. Set the fill of the clone to None, and stroke it with a one-point line that's the color of the outermost value of the radial fill (if you went from white to "Color 1", as we did in our example, you'd set the line's color to "Color 1"). Set the line to overprint.

3. Select the other object containing a radial fill and clone it.

4. Set the fill of the clone to None, and stroke it with a one-point line that's the color of the outermost value of the radial fill (if you went from white to "Color 2", as we did in our example, you'd set the line's color to "Color 2"). Set the line to overprint.

5. Cut the clone of the second object.

6. Select the first object you created and choose Paste Inside from the Edit menu.

7. Select the object you created in step 2 and cut it to the Clipboard.

8. Select the second object and choose Paste Inside from the Edit menu.

Process-Color Trapping

Process-color trapping is a bit simpler than spot-color trapping, because it's usually less critical that process-colored elements have traps (as simulated in Figure 6-22, earlier in this chapter), but it can be far harder to figure out exactly what color to make the stroke for a process-colored object. And when you're talking about trapping two process-colored graduated fills, watch out!

Simple Process-Color Trapping

In process-color trapping, you've got to make your overprinting strokes different colors from either the background or foreground objects. Why? Because process colors have a way of creating new colors when you print them over each other. It's what they do best.

As in the spot-color trapping section above, I'll demonstrate process-color trapping techniques by example. First, create a couple of objects.

1. Create a rectangle that's filled with "Color 1", which is specified as 20C 100M 0Y 10K.

2. On top of this rectangle, draw an ellipse and fill it with "Color 2", which is specified as 0C 100M 50Y 0K.

3. Select both objects and set their stroke to None.

4. Save the file.

The ellipse needs to be trapped, or you run the risk of having cyan-colored lines showing up around the ellipse when the publication is printed—which could happen if the cyan and yellow plates aren't in good register, or if your paper stretches. Whether you spread or choke the ellipse depends on its color. If the ellipse is darker than the background rectangle, choke the ellipse. If the ellipse is a lighter color than the background rectangle, spread the ellipse. In this case, the ellipse is a lighter color, so you'll use a spread. To spread the ellipse, follow these steps.

1. Create a new process color containing only those colors in "Color 2" having higher values than "Color 1". Quick quiz: what component colors in "Color 2" have higher values than their counterparts in "Color 1"? If you said 50Y, you're the lucky winner. Specify a new color: 0C 0M 50Y 0K.

2. Select the ellipse.

3. Press Command-Option-L to display the Stroke Inspector.

4. In the Stroke Inspector, choose Basic from the Stroke Type popup menu.

5. Drag a swatch of "Color 3" into the color well in the Stroke Inspector.

6. Type the width you want for your stroke in the Width field. It should be twice the width of your desired trap. Finally, check the Overprint box and press Return.

When you print, all the areas around the ellipse have some dot value inside them, and the new colors created where the objects abut won't be too obvious.

Choose Revert from the File menu to get ready for the next example.

What if the ellipse were the darker color? If it were, we'd have to choke it. To choke the ellipse, follow these steps.

1. Select the ellipse and fill it with "Color 1". Select the rectangle and fill it with "Color 2".

2. Create a new color ("Color 3") that contains only the largest color component in "Color 1". That's 100M, so "Color 3" should be specified as 0C 100M 0Y 0K.

3. In the Stroke Inspector, choose Basic from the Stroke Type popup menu, set the line color to "Color 3", type the width of the trap you want in the Width field. Finally, check Overprint in the line section of the dialog box and press Return.

When you print, the stroke you applied to the ellipse guarantees that there's no gap around the ellipse, even if you run into registration problems when you print the publication.

Complex Process-Color Trapping

What if the ellipse in the examples given above was not completely contained by the underlying rectangle? What if, in fact, only half of the ellipse passed into the rectangle?

You don't want to make the entire ellipse larger, so limit the spread and choke of the ellipse to the area inside the underlying rectangle by using the Paste Inside techniques shown in the section on spot color trapping earlier in this chapter.

Trapping Process-Color Graduated and Radial Fills

If you've gotten this far, call me the next time you're in Seattle and I'll buy you a beer at The Trolleyman. You've mastered the basic trapping techniques for spot and process colors, and you're ready to trap abutting process-color graduated and radial fills.

Create an object which covers the area where two process-color graduated fills abut and fill this object with a graduated fill. The colors in this graduated fill are derived from the colors used in the abutting graduated fills underneath it. Once again, I'll demonstrate the technique by having you work through an example, and once again we'll start by creating some objects.

1. Create two side-by-side, abutting rectangles.
2. Fill one rectangle with a graduated fill that goes from "Color 1" (25C 30M 0Y 20K) to "Color 2" (70C 20M 0Y 0K) at 90 degrees. Fill the other rectangle with a graduated fill that goes from "Color 3" (0C 80M 45Y 0K) to "Color 4" (0C 20M 60Y 0K) at 270 degrees.
3. Select both rectangles and set their strokes to None.
4. Draw a new rectangle over the abutting edges of the rectangles. Make the new rectangle the height of the existing rectangles, and make it twice as wide as the trapping amount you want. Center it horizontally over the line where the two rectangles abut.
5. Create two new process colors ("Color 5" and "Color 6"). "Color 5" should contain the highest color components from Color 1 and Color 3 (the two colors at the tops of the original rectangles): 25C 80M 45Y 20K. "Color 6" contains the largest color components from "Color 2" and "Color 4": 70C 20M 60Y 0K.

6. Fill the new rectangle with a new graduated fill going from "Color 5" to "Color 6" at 270 degrees.

It's harder to come up with a precise way to trap radial fills containing process colors, because unless the object with the radial fill is a perfect circle and the center of the fill is in the center of the circle, it's hard to know what color is at the edge of the radial fill. And it's almost never the same color all the way around the outside of the path.

So here's the sleazy way. Stroke the radial fill with an overprinting line containing about 20 percent of the background color. This way, there are at least some dots in any out-of-register areas. If you come up with a better way to trap process-color radial fills, please let me know.

Trapping Imported Images

Because you can place color TIFF images in FreeHand, you can run into some truly hairy trapping situations. What happens when you need to cut out part of a color TIFF and place it on a process-color background? This isn't actually as scary as it sounds. Just follow the instructions in the section "Cropping TIFF Images" in Chapter 4, "Importing and Exporting," to construct a clipping path for the TIFF, and then stroke the path with an overprinting line that's the same color as the background colors.

In this case, if the object passes over several color boundaries, avoid pasting both the TIFF and the path containing it into the underlying objects—it'll never print. Instead, clone the path, choose Cut Contents from the Edit menu and delete the extra TIFF. Then fill the new object with white, stroke it with your overprinting line (choke), and paste it inside the underlying object. Then place the original clipped TIFF above the area you've just choked.

Using the Trapping Xtra

If you need to trap a path that you've formatted using a basic stroke or fill, you can use FreeHand's new Trap Xtra. You're still going to need to know a lot of the manual techniques I outlined earlier—mostly for text you don't want to convert to paths—but the Trap Xtra can take care of many (maybe even most) misregistration problems you're likely to encounter in a FreeHand publication.

To use the Trap Xtra to add traps between overlapping or abutting paths, select the paths and choose "Trap" from the Create submenu of the Xtras menu. FreeHand displays the Trap dialog box (see Figure 6-23). Fill in the dialog box and press Return, and FreeHand creates traps for the objects you've selected.

FIGURE 6-23
Trap Xtra

Select the objects you want to trap and select Trap from the Create submenu of the Xtras menu.

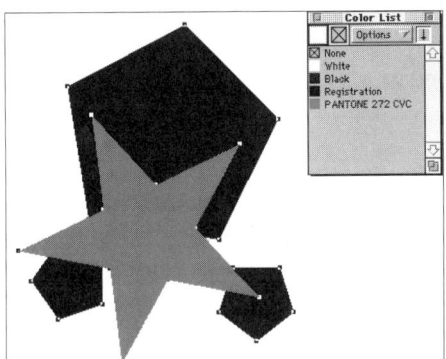

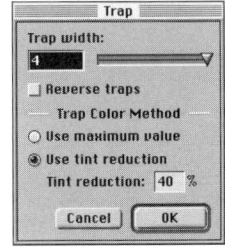

FreeHand displays the Trap dialog box. Set up your trapping by adjusting the controls here.

Note: I've used an absurdly large trap to make the process a little clearer.

FreeHand traps the objects.

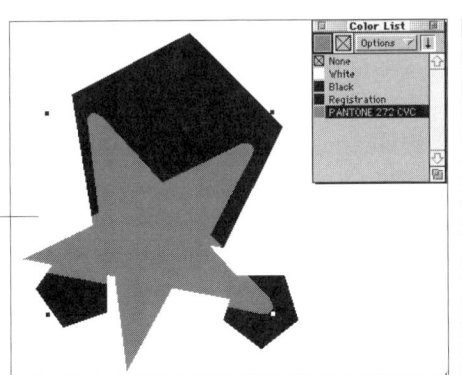

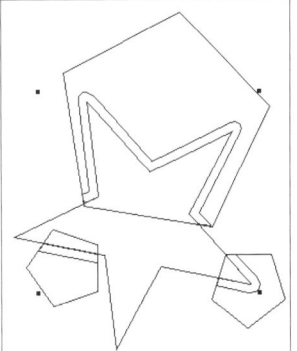

In Keyline view, you can see the trapping paths.

Trap Width. Enter the amount you want to trap the overlapping objects in this field (or move the slider until the value you want appears in the field). As I've been saying, this amount should be the amount your commercial printer says they need for their presses. In this case, you don't have to double the trapping amount—the Xtra takes care of that for you as it creates the traps.

Reverse Traps. When you check the Reverse Traps checkbox, you force FreeHand to spread traps it would normally choke, and choke traps it would normally spread. Use this option when you want to force a "darker" object to spread into a "lighter" object (ordinarily, FreeHand would choke behind the darker object). Why would you want to do this? Because the color definitions we use for objects—which is where FreeHand gets its ideas about the relative lightness and darkness of colors—might not match the properties of the inks we're using to print a publication. If the background ink is a fluorescent or metallic spot color, you probably want other inks to spread into the spot color (metallic and fluorescent spot inks are both more opaque and brighter than other inks). Alternatively, if you're working with a varnish, you'll probably want to spread the varnish into all other inks.

Trap Color Method. When FreeHand creates a new color to use for a process color trap, you can choose to trap using a color that's the sum of the difference between the abutting colors (turn on the Use Maximum Value option), or you can choose to decrease the ink percentages of that color (turn on the Use Tint Reduction option and enter a value in the Tint Reduction *n*% field). Most of the time, you should check the Use Tint Reduction option—traps created with lighter colors are less obvious.

Separating Color Images

FreeHand can separate color TIFFs (both CMYK and RGB) you've placed, and can also separate DCS and EPS preseparated images. In my opinion, the fastest and best method is to use a color-separation program such as Photoshop or Adobe PrePrint Pro to create a CMYK TIFF, an EPS file, a DCS 2.0 file, or a set of DCS 1.0 files, and place the separated image in FreeHand.

Why not just place an RGB TIFF in FreeHand? The color-separation programs have controls for correcting and improving color images. FreeHand really has very few tools for working with the content of color images. Like none, now that I think of it.

Still, FreeHand's separations of RGB images aren't bad (as long as you've done a decent job of correcting them and sharpening them in advance)—take a look at Figure 10 in the color pages to see an example.

Preseparating Color Images

If you want to separate your color images using Photoshop (or Fractal Design's Painter, or Adobe PrePrint Pro, or any other program capable of saving color separations in the EPS/DCS format) and then place the preseparated image in FreeHand, you can save the file as either a single EPS file, a single DCS 2.0 file (if you're using PlateMaker in Photoshop), or as DCS (five linked files).

If you save the image as a single EPS or DCS 2.0 file, place the entire file in FreeHand. If you save the image as DCS 1.0, place the DCS header file (it's the one without a C, M, Y, or K extension on its file name). In either case, when you separate the image with FreeHand, the separations will be the same as if you'd printed the separations directly from Photoshop. You might like FreeHand's separations better, though. Take a look at the side-by-side FreeHand, Photoshop, and PrePrint separations in the color section of this book (see Color Figure 10).

Which EPS preseparation method should you use? Saving the file as a single EPS or DCS 2.0 makes a large file, but saving as DCS 1.0 creates five files you've got to look after. The four DCS 1.0 separation files (the ones with C, M, Y, or K in their file names) have to be in the same folder as the DCS 1.0 header file, or FreeHand won't be able to find them to print.

FreeHand and OPI

Open Prepress Interface (OPI) is a standard for links between desktop systems and dedicated color prepress systems, such as those manufactured by Kodak, Scitex, Hell, and Crosfield. OPI concerns imported images (TIFFs and paint-type graphics) only.

When you export an EPS from FreeHand, the EPS contains OPI information (a set of PostScript comments) that these systems need to be able to work with the file. OPI comments are most important if you're going to do something like drop a Scitex-separated color image into a FreeHand publication.

To be entirely frank, I'm not sure it's worth it. For my purposes, separations created using FreeHand, Photoshop, and/or Adobe PrePrint Pro and an imagesetter can produce excellent quality in the 150-lpi-and-under range, which is where I do most of my work. If you want better than 150 lpi, OPI might be better for you.

Additionally, if you're working with very large images, or if you're working with a large number of images, you might want to have your prepress or imagesetting service bureau store and manage the files for you (while you take lower-resolution "For Position Only" images to work with on your Macintosh). Then, when you take your files to the service bureau to produce film, use OPI to link to the stored images.

Do-It-Yourself "Stochastic" Screening

Warning! This section is still under construction! Use the techniques described here with extreme caution (and, I might add, at your own risk). I've only just started figuring this out myself, but had to share it with you.

You can separate your own color images using the "stochastic" screening I described at the start of the chapter, using Photoshop (or any other image-editing program capable of creating a CMYK TIFF). You don't need to print on an imagesetter equipped with a special (and expensive) RIP, and you don't need to find a press capable of printing incredibly small dots. You can print on garden-variety imagesetters, at low resolutions, and then print on whatever presses you normally use.

Here's the deal—you can split the channels of a CMYK TIFF, save each channel as a separate diffusion dither (that is, as a bilevel bitmap), stack the dithered images up in FreeHand, applying colors to them as you do.

What are the advantages? There aren't any regular patterns in the dithered images, so you don't have to worry about moiré patterns. Images look sharper, because halftone cells actually blur the focus of an image slightly. You can print at lower resolutions (to get a fine linescreen for a halftoned image, you've got to print at resoultions of 2,400 dpi or higher—but you can print dithered images at 1,200 dpi). The dithered images print faster (they're just bilevel bitmaps), and they don't take any time for FreeHand to separate (as an RGB TIFF would).

What are the disadvantages? Dither patterns are more obvious in areas of flat color than halftone screens. It's still a somewhat experimental technique, and your commercial printers might look askance at it.

To separate a CMYK TIFF using "stochastic" screening, follow these steps (see Figure 6-24).

COLOR 531

FIGURE 6-24
Do-it-yourself stochastic screening

Open the TIFF you want to separate. If you haven't already converted it to CMYK, or done any color correction or sharpening, do it now.

Display the Channels palette (choose Channels from the Windows menu). Choose Split Channels from the Channels palette's popup menu (the commands are a little different in Photoshop 3—this is in Photoshop 2.5).

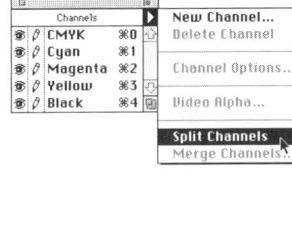

Photoshop displays the four, separate channels.

For each channel, choose Bitmap from the Mode menu. Photoshop displays the Bitmap dialog box.

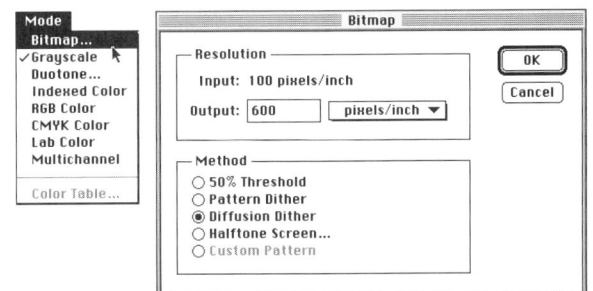

Enter a resolution for the dithered image (the range from 400–600 dpi seems most promising). Press Return (or click OK)…

…and Photoshop converts the grayscale image (this channel) to a bilevel bitmap. Save the bitmap. Repeat this process for the other three channels.

Stack the four bitmaps on top of each other in FreeHand. Set the bitmaps to Transparent using the Object Inspector. Apply the appropriate process color to each image, and print.

1. Open the TIFF with Photoshop. Set up your separation options as you normally would using the various setup dialog boxes in the Preferences submenu.

2. Select CMYK from the Mode menu.

3. Choose Split Channels from the Mode menu. Photoshop creates a separate grayscale TIFF for each channel (that is, each channel now shows what would be printed on each separation).

4. Choose Bitmap from the Mode menu. Photoshop displays the Grayscale to Bitmap dialog box. Click the Diffusion Dither button, and enter a resolution for the dithered bitmap you want to create.

    Most presses (and papers) have no problem printing the dots in bitmaps in the range of 400 dpi to 600 dpi (I like 600 dpi best, but you've got to experiment). Why not make a bitmap at imagesetter resolution—say, 2,400 dpi? Because your press won't be able to print the dots making up the image (ask your printer if their press can hold a one-percent spot in a 300-lpi screen, and you'll get the idea—the dots are just too small).

5. Save each of the bitmaps.

6. Place the four bitmaps on top of each other in FreeHand, coloring each one the appropriate process color. As you import and color each bitmap, check the Transparent box in the Object Inspector. Make sure that the bitmaps are all the same size and in the same position.

When you print separations of your publication, FreeHand prints the dithered bitmaps on separate pages (or pieces of film). When you make a color proof, or print your your publication on a press, you'll see the image.

I've only started using this technique—there are about a million details that I still need to work out (for example, separation settings that work well for conventional halftoning don't really work for this technique).

Most people working with stochastic screening see it as a high-end printing method—they're working with presses that can hold 300 lpi halftone screens. I don't see it that way at all. I think this technique would be best for people working at 150 lpi and under, on cheaper papers (like newsprint).

For an example of a color image separated using this technique, see Color Figure 11 in the color pages.

Stochastic Screening Without an Imagesetter

If you're like me, you looked at early examples of FM screening from Agfa's Crystal Raster system and got excited. Here, at last, was clarity, improved color depth, and a lack of moiré patterns. On further reflection, however, I realized that the dots produced by Crystal Raster were far too small to be printed on anything but the highest-quality, best-maintained, and most expensive printing presses around.

Here's the deal. The dots produced by the initial version of Agfa's Crystal Raster are, at their *largest*, around 20 microns (a micron is *one millionth* of a meter, or around $1/25,000$ of an inch) in diameter. In terms of a conventional halftone, that's only a little bit bigger than a *one-percent* halftone dot at 150 lines per inch. Ask your average commercial printer if their presses can consistently reproduce (or "hold") a dot that small. Once they stop laughing, they'll tell you they can't. If they're honest.

So the key to making FM screening useful to most of us is controlling minimum dot size—and this need is apparently being addressed by Agfa and Linotype-Hell in new revisions of their systems. However, in my opinion there's another flaw in these systems: they're "RIP-based"—they're circuit boards (containing hardware and software) that attach to an imagesetter's RIP (or "raster image processor"—the part of the imagesetter that turns the PostScript commands sent by your page layout or illustration program into the bitmap that the imagesetter prints).

This approach has several disadvantages. The add-on boards are expensive, which means you'll pay more for imagesetting time (as imagesetting service bureaus attempt to recoup the expense of the equipment). The RIP-based FM screening systems also tend to be an "all-or-nothing" approach—it's difficult (if not impossible) to mix FM and conventional halftone screening methods on a single page (again, I expect future revisions of the products will remedy this).

RIP-based FM screening systems also usually require that the imagesetter they're attached to be calibrated for the fine dots these systems produce, rather than for conventional halftones. This means, in practical terms, that imagesetting service bureaus who want to move to a RIP-based FM screening system have to dedicate an entire imagesetter to the output of FM-screened jobs.

A better approach—so much better that many manufacturers are now adopting it—is to do the processing using commercially available software on a general-purpose computer (such as a Macintosh or a Windows-compatible). This approach features several advantages:

- You can produce FM versions of your separated images yourself, on your own computer.

- You can apply FM screening to photographic images (where you want it) while leaving any EPS graphics or text on your page for conventional halftoning.

- You're not using expensive imagesetter RIP time to process images.

- FM screening software tends to be less expensive than imagesetter RIP hardware upgrades.

- You can build the calibration needed for your FM screens into your separations, rather than having to calibrate the imagesetter for FM screening.

- You can match the size of the dots you're printing to the characteristics of the press you're printing on.

I've been experimenting with an FM-screening program called Icefields, from Isis Imaging. Icefields is a stand-alone software package that runs on a Macintosh or Power Macintosh, and it's so easy to use it's almost frightening. All you need to do is choose an imagesetter resolution, pick a screening resolution, set the grayscale compensation for the imagesetter you're using (this is a particularly nice feature), and open an image (one you've scanned, color corrected, and saved as a grayscale or CMYK TIFF). Icefields then creates a file (or set of files, for a color image—Icefields saves in the DCS format) containing an FM-screened version of the image. To print the file, place it in your page layout or illustration program and print as you normally would. Color Figure 12 shows an image separated using Icefields.

Here are a few things to keep in mind when you're working with FM screening:

- Film you've created using FM methods must be the film you use to make your printing plates. In other words, you can't expect your printer to make another copy of your film, for whatever reason, as they prepare your job for printing.

- You can't enlarge or reduce the image once you've created the final version of it. Enlarging or reducing the FM dots either makes them too big (so they're obtrusive) or too small (which means they won't print).

- Some imagesetter-based screening systems will try to apply a halftone screen to the FM-screened image. You don't want this, so turn off the screening system when you print.

- The usual techniques for getting a sharper image from a digital halftone don't apply. Ordinarily, you want to slightly oversharpen a scanned image (using the Unsharp Mask filter in Adobe Photoshop, for example); when you use FM screening, this sharpening looks unnatural. Remember, you're sharpening to overcome the fuzziness imposed by the halftone screen; you don't need to worry about that when you're working with FM screening.

- Because halftones tend to desaturate (or reduce the color intensity) of a color image, people have taken to increasing the color saturation of their images before creating separations. FM screening produces more saturated colors than halftoning, so you don't need to adjust color saturation. If anything, you might want to *reduce* the color saturation of your images when you're using FM.

Color Me Gone

When you're working with color, take it easy. Experimenting with color printing (like doing your color separations using dithered bitmaps from Photoshop) can cost lots of money. Every now and then, however, you'll find a commercial printer who wants to learn about this crazy desktop stuff—and who will run your experiments on unused parts of other jobs.

As you work with commercial printing, always remember that you're at the mercy of a series of photochemical and mechanical processes—from your imagesetter through the printing press—that, in many ways, haven't changed since the turn of the century (if that recently).

Temperature, humidity, and ambient static electricity play large roles in the process, and the people who operate these systems are at least skilled craftspeople; at best, artists. Ask them as many questions as they'll answer, set your job up the way they want it, and then sit back and watch your job come off the press.

CHAPTER 7

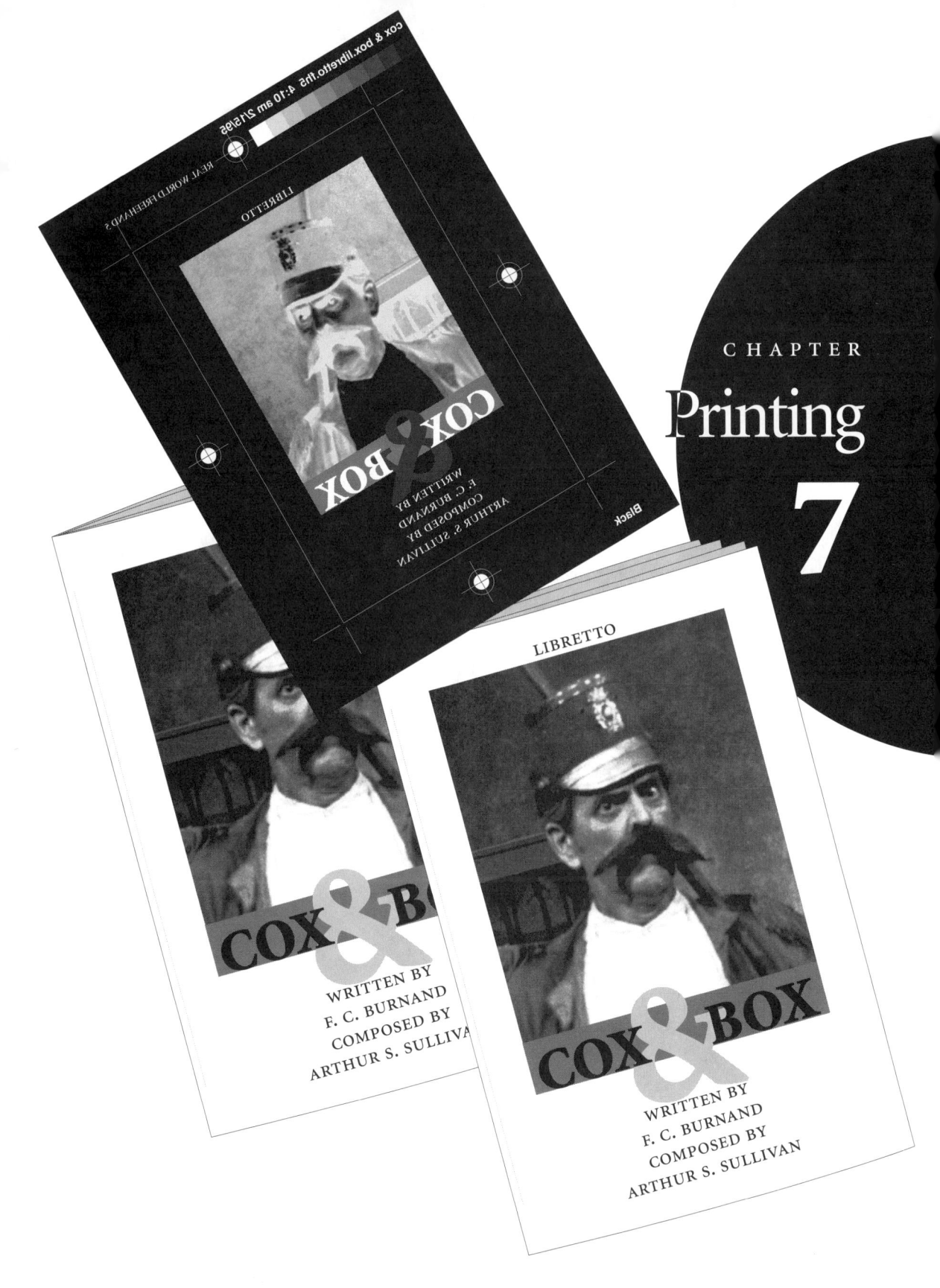

Printing

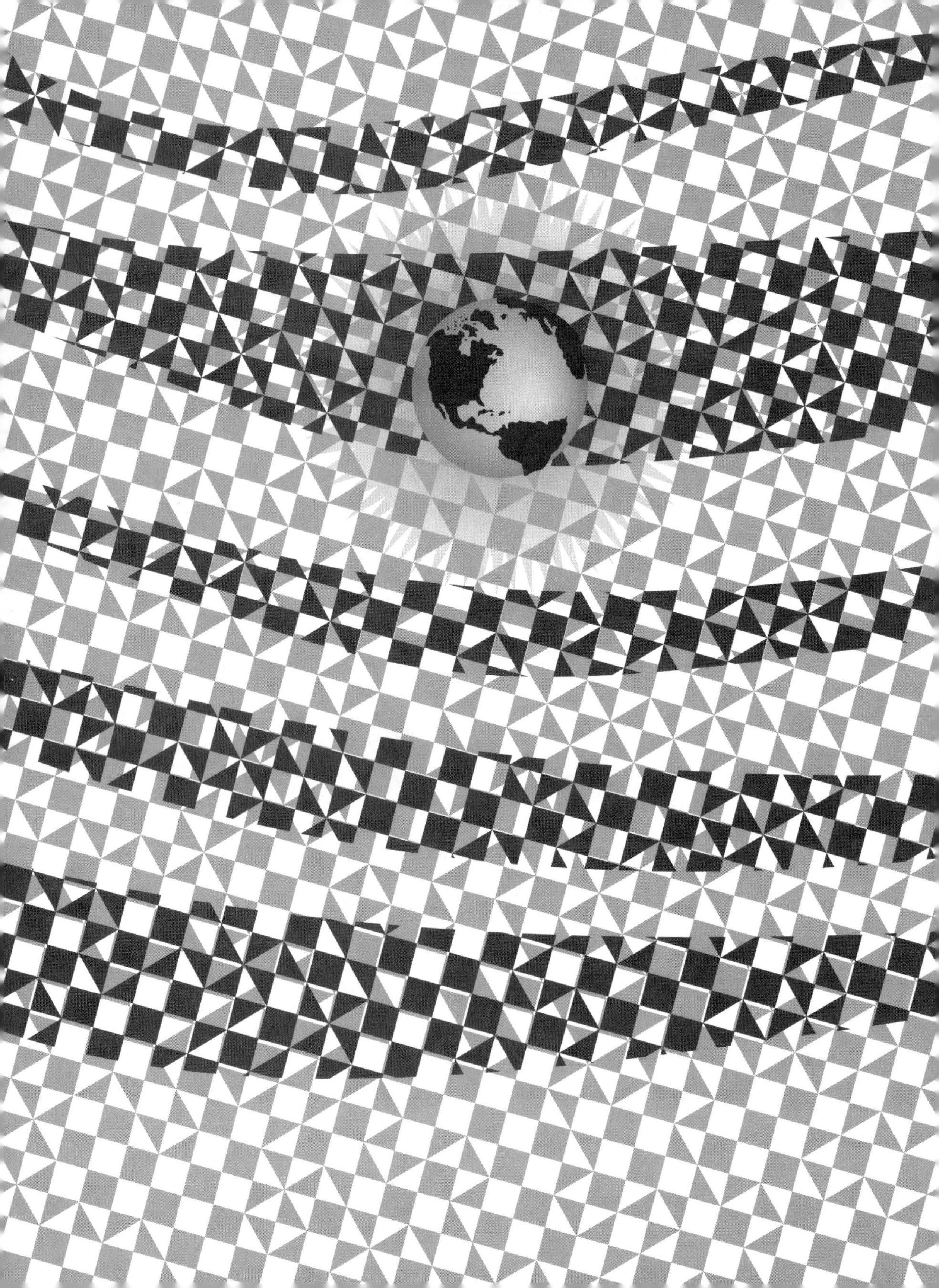

CHAPTER SEVEN ❧ PRINTING

Clay. Roll a carved cylinder over a flat sheet of wet clay, and the carvings on the cylinder are transferred—in reverse—to the surface of the clay. Once the clay hardens, the marks are there to stay.

The ancient Mesopotamians noticed this. They figured that by carving characters on the cylinders in reverse they could transfer them to the clay tablets. Roll the cylinders over several tablets, and you've made several copies of the symbols on the cylinders. They were a bureaucratic bunch, and covered their tablets with bills of lading, legal contracts, nondisclosure agreements, and other rules and regulations.

They invented printing.

We've improved on this process a little bit since then.

We found that, by smearing ink over the surface of the cylinder (or over the tablets, for that matter), we could transfer the images on the clay cylinder to that new stuff—the white sheets of beaten, bleached papyrus reeds the Egyptians made. It was easier to carry than the tablets.

Later, somebody came up with moveable type, and scribes the world over lamented the decline in the quality of written materials. The romance novel followed closely on the heels of this technological advance. Printing—the ability to make dozens, hundreds, thousands, millions of copies of an image—flourished.

Printing, ultimately, is what FreeHand is all about. Everything you do in FreeHand is directed toward the production of a mechanical (whether an illustration or a publication) for printing.

The FreeHand Print Dialog Box

When you press Command-P, FreeHand displays the Print dialog box (see Figure 7-1). Never mind that it says "Printer '*printername*'" instead of "Print." It's the Print dialog box and everybody knows it. Similarly, you'll see two Print Options dialog boxes in FreeHand—one from FreeHand itself (which appears when you click the Print button in the Print dialog box); one from the printer driver (which appears when you click the Options button in the Print dialog box). I'll refer to FreeHand's as the "Print Options dialog box," and call the other one the "LaserWriter Print Options dialog box."

The options you see in some of these dialog boxes might differ somewhat. In this chapter, I'm assuming you're using LaserWriter 8.0 (or above—sometimes known as PSPrinter) for your printer driver, and all the descriptions in this chapter are based on that driver. Most things, however, are the same or similar in earlier versions of the LaserWriter printer driver.

If you're still using an earlier version of the driver because you were scared by the bugs in LaserWriter 8.0, you might reconsider—most of the problems seem to be fixed in LaserWriter version 8.1.1 (and newer versions). The biggest problem remaining, in my opinion, is that most applications spool *their entire print job* to disk *before sending anything to the printer*. As I write this, PageMaker is the only application that's been updated to behave sensibly with LaserWriter 8.

Copies

Enter the number of copies of the page you want to print here. You can print up to 999 copies of your publication.

Tip: Printing More Than 999 Copies

Honest, I get asked about this, so here it is. If you need to print more than 999 copies of your publication, print your publication to disk as PostScript (see "Printing PostScript to Disk," later in this chapter), entering "999" in the Copies field of the Print dialog box. Open the PostScript file you've just created with a text editor, and search for "/copies 999 def." Once you've found this string, just replace "999" with the number of copies you want and save the file as text-only. Then download the PostScript file to your (long-suffering) printer.

FIGURE 7-1
Print dialog box

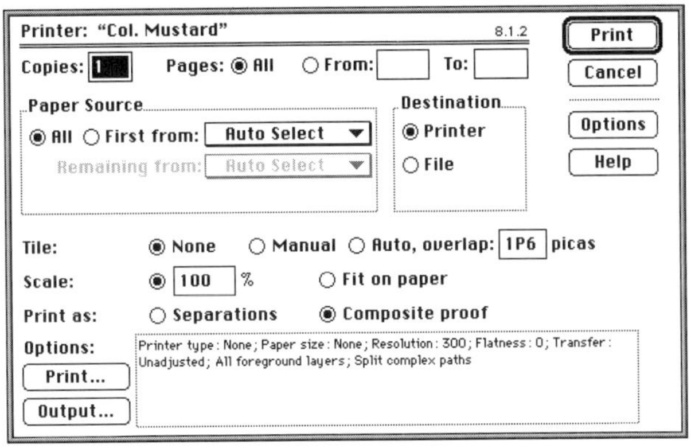

Pages
Enter the range of pages you want to print from your publication. Remember, pages in FreeHand are numbered relative to their position on the pasteboard—if you've moved pages around, your pages might be numbered differently from the last time you printed.

Paper Source
Where's the paper coming from? Some printers have multiple paper bins. You choose the one you want here.

Destination
Most of the time, you'll click Printer to send the pages to your printer. If you want to print your publication (or pages from your publication) to disk as PostScript, click File. When you do this, the Print button in the upper-right corner of the Print dialog box changes to Save. When you've set all the printing options you want (including the ones in the Output Options dialog box), click the Save button. The Create File dialog box appears.

Type a name for your PostScript file in the field, select the options you want at the bottom of the dialog box, and press Return (or click the OK button) to save your file to disk as PostScript.

Format. Choose PostScript Job from the Format popup menu. Don't use the EPS options on this popup menu to create EPS files; use Export from the File menu instead (for more on exporting EPS files, see Chapter 4, "Importing and Exporting"). Files created using the EPS options on this popup menu are larger and print less reliably than EPS files created using Export.

The ASCII and Binary options are overridden by the settings in FreeHand's Output Options dialog box.

If you know that the printer you'll be sending the file to is equipped with a Level 2 PostScript RIP, choose Level 2 Only. Otherwise, choose Level 1 Compatible.

Font Inclusion. If you know that the printer you'll be sending the file to has the fonts you've used in your publication, or if you plan to send the fonts as separate files (if, for example, you're taking your file to an imagesetting service bureau and plan to give them copies of the fonts you've used in the publication), choose None from the Font Inclusion popup menu.

Choose All to include all the fonts you've used in the publication in the PostScript file you create. If you do this, you won't have to worry about font substitution—but your PostScript file will take up more disk space (each font adds around 40 K to the file's size).

To save all fonts except Courier, Helvetica, Symbol, and Times, choose All But Standard 13 from the Font Inclusion popup menu.

Tile Use Tile when your pages are larger than the maximum page size of your printer. Auto Tile splits the pages in your publication into as many parts as FreeHand thinks are necessary; Manual Tile lets you tell FreeHand what size the individual tiles should be.

Auto Tile. When you choose automatic tiling, FreeHand bases the tile on the current printer's page size, and starts tiling from the lower-left corner of the page. Note that this is different from PageMaker, which measures down and to the right from the zero point when tiling.

The measurement you enter in the Overlap *N* points field is the amount of the image that's duplicated between adjacent tiles. This feature comes in handy when you're printing using a printer that won't run the image out to the edge of the paper (like most laser printers).

Manual Tile. When you choose Manual Tile, FreeHand prints a tile—a page the size of the current paper size—based on the location of the zero point on the current page.

Manual Tile is generally better than Auto Tile, because FreeHand's automatic tiling has no idea what's in your illustration, and can't, therefore, make decisions about where the seams between the tiles should fall. When you tile manually, you can make sure that the edges of the tiles don't fall across any fills (especially graduated and radial fills). When the edge of a tile falls across anything with a halftone screen, it's difficult—if not impossible—to piece the two tiles together. It's much easier to join lines and solid fills, and you should do your manual tiling with that in mind. Even if you have to make more tiles, it's better to tile across simple lines and solid fills.

Tip: Printing Spreads with Manual Tiling

When you want to print more than one FreeHand page on a single sheet of paper (or piece of imagesetter film), follow these steps (see Figure 7-2).

1. Position the pages next to each other on the pasteboard. The pages don't have to touch, but the dimensions of the area of the pages, including any bleed areas or gaps between pages, can't exceed that of the paper size you'll be printing on. The pages can be side-by-side, or on top of each other, or arranged in whatever anarchic fashion you see fit.

2. Choose Fit All from the Magnification submenu of the View menu. FreeHand fits all the pages in your publication in the publication window.

3. Make the page that's closest to the upper-right corner of the pasteboard the active page by clicking on the thumbnail of the page in the Document Inspector.

4. Reset the zero point so that it's at the lower-left corner of the lower-left page in the group of pages you want to print (or the lower-left corner of its bleed area, if any).

5. Press Command-P to display the Print dialog box. Use the Print Options and Output Options dialog boxes to specify the way you want the publication printed (it's especially important to set the page size you want in the Print Options dialog box). Finally, in the Print dialog box, enter the page number of the active page (see Step 3) in the From and To fields, and select click Manual to turn on manual tiling.

6. Print your publication. FreeHand prints one tile, starting at the point you set in Step 4. If your paper size is large enough, FreeHand prints the spread.

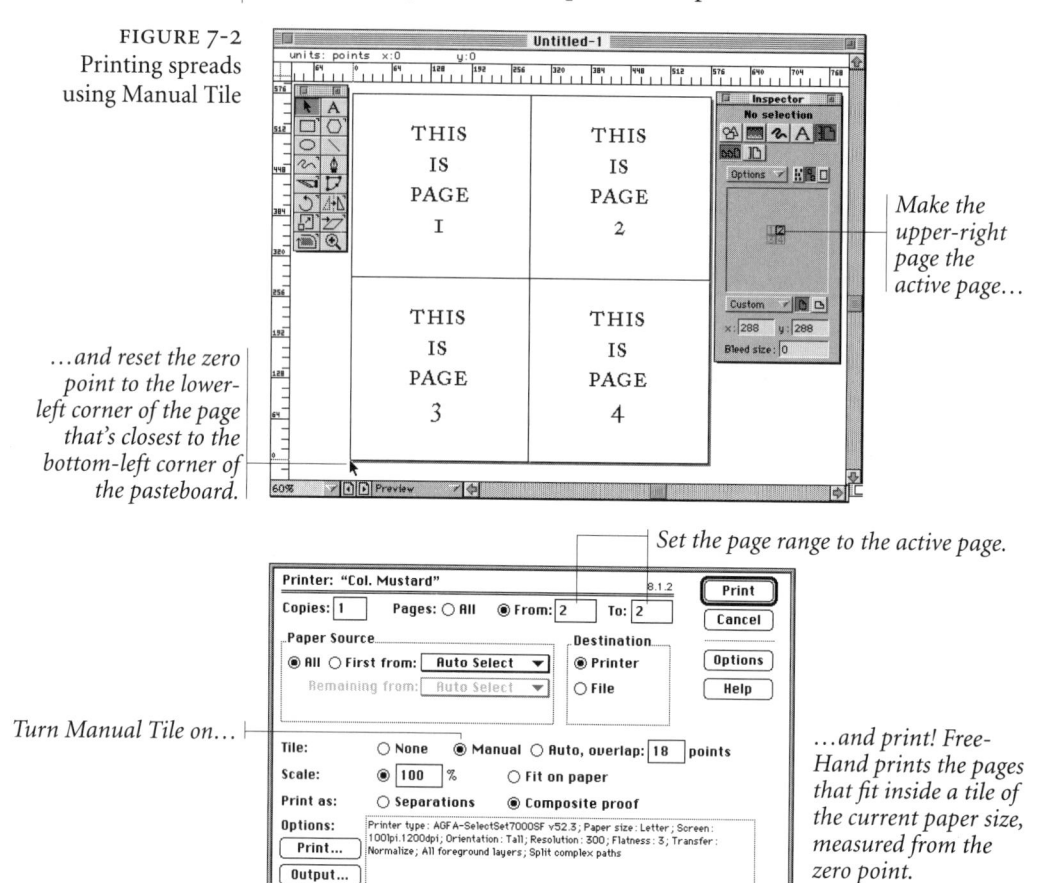

FIGURE 7-2
Printing spreads using Manual Tile

Make the upper-right page the active page…

…and reset the zero point to the lower-left corner of the page that's closest to the bottom-left corner of the pasteboard.

Set the page range to the active page.

Turn Manual Tile on…

…and print! FreeHand prints the pages that fit inside a tile of the current paper size, measured from the zero point.

Scale Enter a scaling value from 10 percent to 1,000 percent of the publication's original size (in one-percent increments). The Fit On Paper option scales the page automatically to the largest size that'll fit on the selected paper size.

Print Options Click the Separations option when you want to print color separations of your publication (which inks print depends on the specifications you've entered in the Print Options dialog box), and click the Composite proof option when you want to print all your colors as black and shades of gray, or when you want to print a color proof of your work on a color PostScript printer.

Printing and Page Setup

Because you're creating a publication that'll be printed on an existing PostScript printer, you've got to pay attention to the page sizes that are available. It might be too obvious to state, but if you can't print it, it's of no use to you.

You could tile your publication, but tiling only works in a few cases. Can you imagine grafting a bunch of halftoned images together? Or graduated fills? On negative film? You get the idea: it's impossible. Don't even try tiling unless you can set it up so that the edges of the tiles don't bisect anything containing a halftone screen.

That brings us back to paper sizes.

Page Size and Paper Size — When I talk about page size, I'm talking about the page size you've defined for your publication using the Document Inspector. This page size should be the same as the page size of the printed piece you intend to produce. "Paper size" means the size of the paper as it comes out of your printer or imagesetter. There can be a big difference between these two sizes. Try to print your publication on a paper size that is no larger than the publication's page size, unless you need printer's marks (crop marks and registration marks). For more on page size and paper size, see "Paper Size," later in this chapter.

Tip: Paper Size and Printer Marks — If you need printer's marks (crop marks or registration marks), print your publication on a paper size that is larger than your publication's page by about 60 points in either dimension.

Page Orientation and Paper Orientation — You set the orientation of your *page* in the Document Inspector by clicking either the Tall or Wide radio button (or, if you're working with a custom page size, by entering values in the X and Y fields). You set the orientation of the *paper* you're printing to by clicking either the Tall or Wide button in the Print options dialog box.

What do these two orientation settings have to do with each other?

If you create a tall page and print it to a normal orientation, wide paper size, expect the top and bottom of your publication to get clipped off. Ditto for a wide page size printed to a normal orientation, tall paper size.

Always print tall pages to tall paper sizes, and wide pages to wide paper sizes—even when you're printing to a transverse page size (see Figure 7-3).

- If you need to print a wide publication down the length of an imagesetter's paper roll (because it's too wide for the width of the roll), use a wide, transverse orientation paper size.

- If you want to save paper on the imagesetter's roll and speed up printing time, print tall page sizes to transverse paper sizes (provided that the page size isn't taller than the width of the imagesetter's paper roll). As always, ask your imagesetting service bureau what they want you to do.

FIGURE 7-3
Page orientation and paper orientation

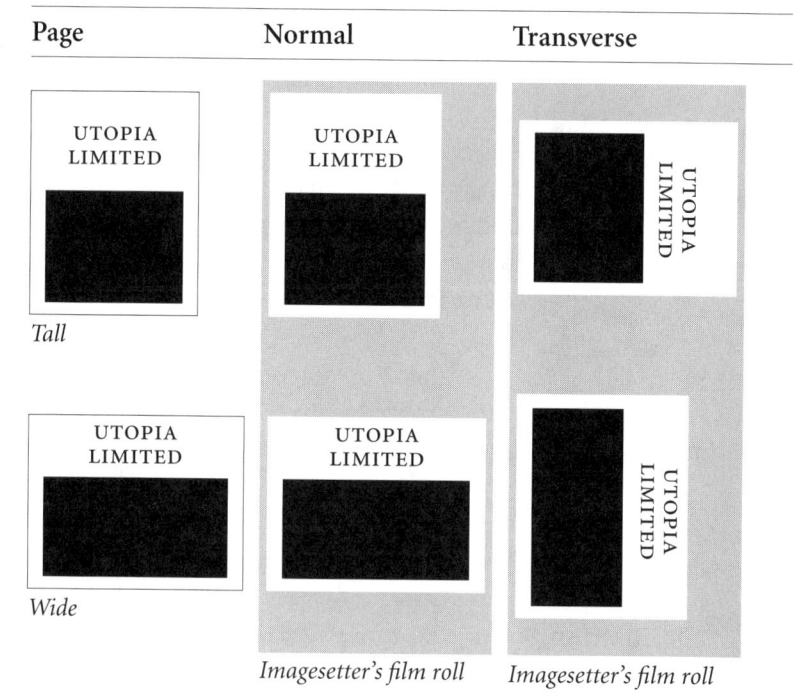

Printing Signatures

FreeHand's 222-by-222-inch maximum page size is large enough that you can arrange whole press sheets for many common presses, laying out and printing multiple pages in a single FreeHand publication (see Figure 7-4). To see how to print multiple pages on a single sheet of paper, see the tip "Printing Spreads with Manual Tiling," earlier in this chapter.

FIGURE 7-4
Press sheet

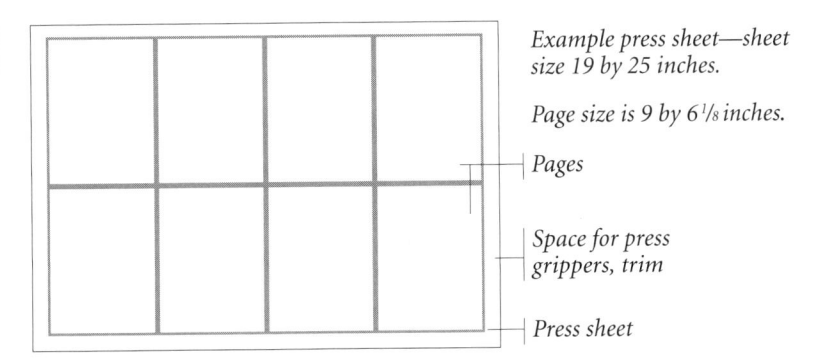

Example press sheet—sheet size 19 by 25 inches.

Page size is 9 by 6 1/8 inches.

Pages

Space for press grippers, trim

Press sheet

Signatures can be a real brain-twister. The object of creating a signature is to get pages onto a press sheet in such a way that your commercial printer can fold and cut the sheet so that it starts on the first page of the signature and ends on the last page. This means you have to position the correct pages in the right places and in the right orientations on both the front and back of the signature. Figure 7-5 shows how it works for a very simple signature.

You should try to leave ¼ inch for trim on each end of the signature and ½ inch on each side of the signature for color bars and for the press' grippers. Also, if your pages have bleeds, make sure you add ⅛ inch to all four sides of the page to accommodate the bleeds.

You'll still have to find some way of printing your signatures—very few imagesetters can handle paper sizes as large as you'll want for signatures (the largest image area I know of right now is a 30-by-40-inch single sheet). Table 7-1 shows some typical press sheet sizes and typical page sizes you can get out of them. Talk to your commercial printer about the sheet sizes their presses are capable of handling.

Don't despair if no imagesetters in your area can handle these sheet sizes. The most important thing about understanding how

FIGURE 7-5
Setting up a simple signature

After you print, fold, and cut this press sheet, you've got an eight-page signature, with the pages in the correct order.

```
┌─────────┬─────────┐        ┌─────────┬─────────┐
│  PAGE   │  PAGE   │        │  PAGE   │  PAGE   │
│    8    │    1    │        │    2    │    7    │
├─────────┼─────────┤        ├─────────┼─────────┤
│  PAGE   │  PAGE   │        │  PAGE   │  PAGE   │
│    5    │    4    │        │    3    │    6    │
│ (upside)│ (upside)│        │ (upside)│ (upside)│
└─────────┴─────────┘        └─────────┴─────────┘
    Front of sheet                Back of sheet
```

Allow some space for press grippers, color bars, folding, cutting, etc. (ask your commercial printer how much).

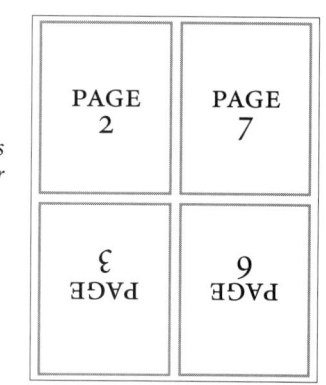

many of what size pages make up a press sheet is that you set up your publication to match sizes that don't waste too much paper. This isn't a comment about saving the environment—I've found it's cheaper by far to design for certain press sheet sizes.

In addition, commercial printers do lots of their printing on smaller sheet sizes. Table 7-2 shows some typical paper sizes you can use on smaller presses. You can fit signatures on these paper sizes, as well.

TABLE 7-1
Common press sheet sizes and signatures

Sheet size	19 x 25	23 x 29	23 x 35	25 x 38	26 x 40
Image area	18 x 24½	22 x 28½	22 x 34½	24 x 37½	25 x 39½

Pages per sheet						
3	18 x 8⅛	22 x 9½	22 x 11½	24 x 12½	25 x 13⅛
4	18 x 6½	22 x 7⅛	22 x 8⅝	24 x 9⅜	25 x 9⅞
4	9 x 12¼	11 x 14¼	11 x 17¼	12 x 18¾	12½ x 19¾
6	9 x 8⅛	11 x 9½	11 x 11½	12 x 12½	12½ x 13⅛
8	9 x 4⅞	11 x 7⅛	11 x 8⅝	12 x 9⅜	12½ x 9⅞
10	9 x 6⅛	11 x 5 11⁄16	11 x 6⅞	12 x 7½	12½ x 7⅞
15	3 9⁄16 x 8⅛	4⅜ x 11	4 ⅜ x 11	4¾ x 12½	5 x 13⅛
16	4½ x 6⅛	5½ x 7⅛	5½ x 8⅝	6 x 9⅜	6¼ x 9⅞

All dimensions in inches

TABLE 7-2 Typical sheet sizes for smaller presses	Text weights	Cover weights	Bond
	19 x 25	20 x 26	8½ x 11
	23 x 29	23 x 35	17 x 22
	23 x 35	26 x 40	22 x 34
	25 x 38		24 x 38

All dimensions in inches

You need to be absolutely certain you want to do this and that you know what you're doing before you try it. Make folded dummies of the signatures you want to use, and make sure that all the pages, front and back, fall where you want them to. When in doubt, leave it to the pros at your printer.

FreeHand Printing Options

FreeHand's Print Options dialog box is where you control what paper size you're printing to, which (if any) printer marks you want, and which inks you want to print, among other things. You get to the Print Options dialog box when you click the Print button in the Print dialog box (see Figure 7-6).

Because I find that I almost always have to go to the Print Options dialog box before I print, I've set up a QuicKey that takes me to the Print Options dialog box when I press Command-P.

Printer Type Click the Select PPD button to choose the PostScript Printer Description file (PPD) for your printer. If no PPD matches your printer's make and model, choose "General" or "Color General" (if you're printing to a color PostScript printer).

Paper Size When you choose a PPD, the available paper sizes for your printer appear in the Paper popup menu, including any custom paper sizes you've added to this PPD (see "Adding Custom Page Sizes to PPDs" later in this chapter).

Always choose a paper size that's at least the size of your publication's pages. If you're printing a publication that needs crop and

FIGURE 7-6
Print Options
dialog box

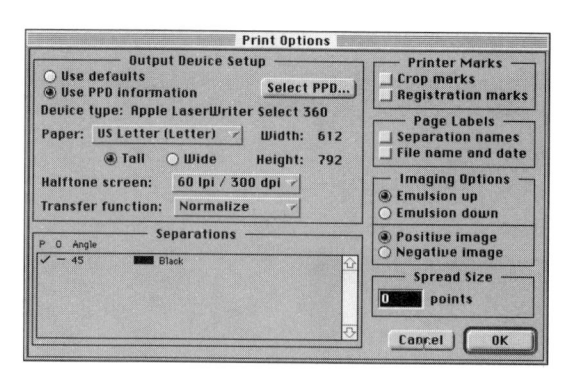

registration marks (collectively known as printer's marks; see "Crop Marks" and "Registration Marks," later in this chapter) printed off the page, or if parts of your publication bleed (extend beyond the edge of the publication page), you'll need to choose a paper size that's larger than your publication's page size to accommodate the printer's marks and/or the bleed.

If you've chosen an imagesetter PPD, another option, Other, appears on the popup menu. When you choose Other, FreeHand displays the Paper size dialog box, in which you can type whatever paper size you want. Remember, however, that the values you enter here need to take the width of the imagesetter's paper roll into account. Enter a width value greater than the width of the imagesetter's paper roll and you'll get a "limitcheck" error when you try to print.

Tip:
Update to
FreeHand 5.0.1
or Higher

If you haven't yet updated to FreeHand 5.0.1, 5.02, or 5.5, do it before you try printing to a custom paper size with a wide orientation on an imagesetter. FreeHand 5.0 would sometimes (depending on your printer and the method you used to specify your page size) crop off parts of your pages. To get a copy of the FreeHand 5.0.1 updater, look in the Macromedia forum on CompuServe, or call Macromedia customer service (see Appendix C, "Resources").

Tip:
Line Screens and
Transverse Page
Orientation

When you choose one of the transverse page sizes/orientations from the Paper size popup menu, FreeHand rotates the publication 90 degrees when printing. Halftone screens you've applied to specific objects in your publication are not rotated, which can mess things up if you're using a coarse screen like a line screen for special effects. If the direction of the halftone screen you've applied is important to your design, you can either add 90 degrees to the screen angles applied in your publication, or you can print to one of the normal-orientation page sizes.

Halftone Screen Choosing a screen frequency for your publication can be difficult. Higher frequency screens produce smoother-looking tints, but increasing screen ruling can also result in a loss of grays—depending on the resolution of the printer. And there's a limit to how fine a screen frequency you can print with various printing methods and paper stocks. If you don't have enough gray levels available on your printer, your publications print with noticeable banding and posterization. Lower screen frequencies can provide more gray levels, but also look coarser. What to do? Try using this equation to determine the number of grays you'll get from the screen ruling and printer resolution you've chosen.

number of grays = (printer resolution in dpi/screen frequency in lpi)2+1

The key to this equation is that "number of grays" can't be greater than 256—that's the maximum number of grays a PostScript printer can render.

You can work the equation another way; maybe this one's more useful.

screen frequency = square root of(16*printer resolution)

Other people like to use this equation.

required resolution = screen frequency * 16

If you come up with a line screen that's too coarse for your taste, think about it—is your publication one where you can sacrifice a few grays for a finer screen?

Transfer Function This option specifies how the printer's tint densities correspond to the tint densities you specify. Why do we need this? Because gray levels printed on 300-dpi printers look very different from the same gray levels printed on 2540-dpi printers (in general, lower percentages of gray, especially 10 percent, look darker at lower resolutions). If you choose Default, FreeHand prints exactly the density you've specified, without reading any of the gray level adjustment information from the PPD.

Ordinarily, Default is the best choice for most tasks. If you want to compensate for the differences between printers with different resolutions (to get a more accurate proof), use Normalize, which reads gray-level compensation information from the PPD.

Posterize creates special effects by converting the available gray levels into just four gray levels. Posterize works about the same way as the Posterize image preset. See "Bilevel and Grayscale TIFFs and Image control" in Chapter 4, "Importing and Exporting," for more on posterization. I can't think of any reason to use this, but that doesn't mean you're similarly impaired.

Printer Marks

Check Crop Marks to print lines, printed outside the area of your page, that define the area of your page. If your paper size is not larger than your page size, FreeHand won't print your crop marks.

When you check the Registration marks checkbox, FreeHand prints little targets around the edge of your page for your commercial printer to use when they're lining up, or registering, your color separations for printing. If your paper size is smaller than your page size, FreeHand won't print registration marks.

Page Labels

When you check the Separation Names checkbox, FreeHand prints the name of each ink color for each separation or overlay on each printed sheet. This way, you'll have an easier time telling the magenta overlay from the cyan overlay. If you're printing a composite, FreeHand prints the word Composite.

Check File Name and Date to print the file name and date on your publications on each page—this makes it easy to tell which of several printed versions is the most current. It can also make it easier for your commercial printer to tell which pieces of film in a stack of separations go together (it's easy for you to tell, but put yourself in their shoes for a minute). If the paper size is smaller than the page size, FreeHand won't print the file name and date.

Imaging Options   Use the Image Options to print a negative of your publication or to choose whether your publication prints emulsion up or emulsion down.

In the United States, most printers prefer getting their film negative, emulsion down, unless they've got stripping to do, in which case they prefer it emulsion up. Many non-North American printers—those in Japan, Hong Kong, Singapore, Italy, Switzerland, and elsewhere—like their film positive, emulsion down. Everything looks the same in the end; it's just a different standard. Printers vary a lot, though, so the best way to find out which way you should print your publication is to ask your commercial printer how they'd like to receive the film.

Separations   I call the list that appears in the Separations section of the Print Options dialog box the "Ink List." The Ink List is where you determine how the inks in your publication are printed; only color definitions and object-level overprinting instructions are more important (see Figure 7-7). All of the inks used in your publication are included in the Ink List. If you've used any spot colors, they appear; and cyan, magenta, yellow, and black appear if you've specified any process colors in the document.

Using the Ink List, you can control whether an ink prints, and whether that ink overprints (though object-level overprinting instructions will override the settings in this dialog box for the objects they're applied to).

Suppress printing of an ink. To keep an ink from printing, click the checkmark to the left of the ink's name (in the column headed with a "P").

What happens when you have objects containing percentages of process inks and turn off one of the inks? Simple enough—you don't get any of that ink. Turning an ink off doesn't affect any of the other inks in the object.

Turning an ink off doesn't affect that ink's knockout/overprinting settings. If the ink was set to knock out other inks, it'll still knock them out—whether you print it or not.

FIGURE 7-7
Ink List

FreeHand lists the inks used in the publication in the Separations section (which I call the Ink List) of the Print Options dialog box.

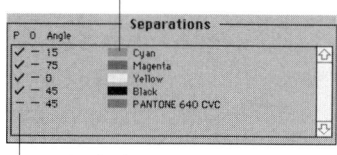

Uncheck this column to keep an ink from printing.

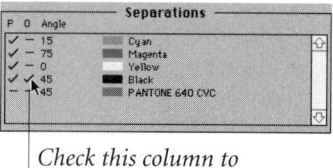

Check this column to make an ink overprint.

Overprinting inks. To make an ink overprint, click in the column headed with an "O." A check appears in the column, indicating that the ink is set to overprint. To make the ink knock out, click the checkmark—it'll turn back into a dash, indicating that the ink knocks out.

Overprinting an ink. The Overprint ink option makes all the objects with the selected ink applied to them overprint anything that's behind them. Any object-level overprinting instructions override this setting for the objects they're attached to.

Process colors bring up some interesting questions. If you've got an object that's colored 60C 30M 0Y 10K on top of an object that's colored 10C 40M 10Y 0K, what ink percentages do you get in the areas where the objects overlap? It's simple—the process colors on top win. Even if you set cyan to overprint, you'll still get 10-percent cyan in the areas where the top object overprints the bottom object.

To see what overprinting looks like, refer to the Color Figure 1 in the color pages in Chapter 6, "Color."

Screen angles. The screen angle that's shown in the Ink List comes from the PPD file you've selected. These are the imagesetter manufacturers' optimized screen angles, which help prevent moirés from occurring, so you shouldn't alter these unless you have a really good reason to do so. Still, if you want to change the angle, double-click the angle in the Ink List, then type a new angle in the Screen Angle field FreeHand displays.

If you've applied a halftone to an individual object using the Halftone palette, that halftone setting overrides the settings in the Print Options dialog box.

Output Options

It was frustrating—in FreeHand 3, you could set the flatness of all the paths in your document when you printed, but you couldn't do the same when you created an EPS of the same paths. Other printing controls, such as the ability to suppress printing of invisible layers, didn't apply to EPS files you created.

FreeHand 5 puts many of the controls that used to be in FreeHand 3's Print Options dialog box in the Output Options dialog box (see Figure 7-8). The settings in the Output Options dialog box apply to both files you print and files you save as EPS.

To display the Output Options dialog box, click the Output button in FreeHand's Print dialog box.

FIGURE 7-8
Output Options dialog box

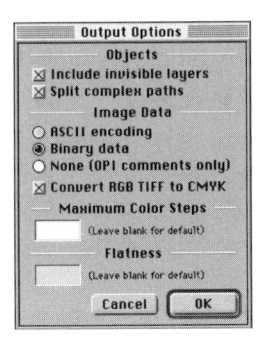

Printing Invisible Layers

If you've turned off the display of layers to speed up your publication's display on screen, you can print them by checking Include Invisible Layers. If you don't want to print invisible layers, leave this option unchecked.

Split Complex Paths

Uncheck the Split Complex Paths checkbox when your publication contains TIFFs you've pasted into complex paths (anything with more curves than a rectangle). Why? Each time FreeHand fails to print a path, it simplifies the path (that is, cuts the path up into smaller, more manageable segments) and sends it to the printer again. If the path contains a TIFF, this means you'll spend extra time waiting for FreeHand to download the TIFF each time it sends the path (or portions of the path). Otherwise, leave this checkbox on.

Tip:
Print Only
What You Need

If you've already printed proofs of an illustration, and only need to alter one part of the illustration and proof that change, consider putting the change on another layer, then printing only that layer. This way, you won't have to wait for the entire publication to print.

Image Data

The options in this section determine how—and if—TIFF images you've placed in your FreeHand publication get sent to your printer, or to an EPS or PostScript file you save to disk.

ASCII Encoding. Choose ASCII Encoding when you're creating a file you intend to transfer to a computer other than a Macintosh, or when you're connected to your printer through a serial cable.

Binary Data. Choose Binary Data to send images in a more compact form than ASCII Encoding (note that this also means a smaller file size, if you're saving the file).

OPI Comments Only. Choose "None (OPI Comments Only)" when you'll be linking to a high-resolution version of the image using an OPI system, such as Kodak's Prophecy. When you turn this option on, FreeHand includes cropping and scaling information for any TIFFs you've placed in your publication, but doesn't include the TIFFs themselves.

PageMaker 6 has trouble printing TIFFs in FreeHand EPS files when you import. This has to do with the OPI image data in your FreeHand EPS. See "FreeHand, TIFFs, and PageMaker 6" in Chapter 4, "Importing and Exporting."

Convert RGB TIFF to CMYK. Check this option to include a color-separated version of any RGB TIFFs you've placed in your publication. You'll get better separations, however, if you separate the RGB TIFF to CMYK in Photoshop (or elsewhere) before you place it in FreeHand.

Maximum Color Steps. When you're printing to a slide recorder, or when you're creating an EPS you plan to convert using a color prepress system (such as those made by Crosfield or Scitex), enter 256 in this field. If you still have trouble printing or converting the file, enter a lower number. You need to do this because some of these devices can handle only a limited number of colors at a time. Otherwise, leave this field blank.

Flatness   As discussed in Chapter 2, "Drawing," flatness is a property of PostScript paths that specifies how many tiny straight line segments a PostScript RIP has to draw to render a curve. The higher the value you enter for flatness, the fewer line segments your printer's RIP will have to draw—which means faster printing times. Even on a 300-dpi printer, the resolution of most laser printers, you won't see a difference between flatness setting of three and a flatness setting of zero, but the former will print much faster. In fact, some paths won't print at all, on any printer, unless you set their flatness to something greater than zero.

Enter a value in this field to set a flatness value for all the paths in your publication. Any flatness settings you've applied to individual paths using the Object Inspector override any value you enter here.

FreeHand and PPDs

PostScript Printer Description files (PPDs) describe your printer to FreeHand and to your printer driver. PPDs are not, and should not be confused with, printer drivers. Printer drivers are pieces of software that direct information from your system and applications to a hardware port—usually, your Macintosh's printer port. For some applications, the printer driver does the work of translating the application's documents into PostScript; this isn't the case for FreeHand, which generates its own PostScript.

PPDs work in conjunction with printer drivers to give applications information about the printer (what paper sizes are available? what's the resolution of the printer? what do the printer error messages mean?) and to customize the printer's operation for the application (what PostScript routine does the application use to render halftones?).

FreeHand uses the printer driver on your system, and uses PPDs to optimize printing for a specific printer.

PPDs—Who's on First?

Because of a territorial dispute—between your applications (FreeHand in particular) and your printer driver—you can get caught in a loop. You create a file, choose a PPD, and save the file. When you open the file, a different PPD is selected in the Print Options dialog box. In fact, every time you open the file, the same—incorrect—PPD appears, no matter what PPD you chose before you saved the file.

This isn't a feature.

What's going on here? Both FreeHand and your printer driver want to be the entity responsible for your PPD choices. If you've chosen a PPD using the driver options available in the Chooser, this choice appears in all your FreeHand documents. Follow these steps to make the PPD choices you make in FreeHand's Print Options dialog box stick.

Note: This will only work with Apple's LaserWriter 8 driver or Adobe's PSPrinter 8 driver (or newer versions of these drivers). The Apple LaserWriter 7.1.2 driver (the previous version) doesn't let you set a PPD for the printer.

1. Select Chooser from the Apple Menu.

2. Click the LaserWriter 8 driver icon. Make sure that the correct printer shows up in the printer list to the right. If not, select it by clicking on the name.

3. Click the Setup button that appears below the list of available printers. The Chooser displays the Current Printer Description File dialog box.

4. Click the Select PPD button. The Select PostScript Printer Description File dialog box appears.

5. Click the Use Generic button.

6. Press Return (or click the OK button) to close the dialog box and apply your change.

If, on the other hand, you'd prefer to let your printer driver choose the PPD, select the PPD you want, or click Auto Configure, in the Select PostScript Printer Description File dialog box and leave it at that.

Rewriting PPDs

You can edit your PPDs to add custom page sizes, to add new sets of screen angles, to download PostScript routines automatically, and to do a variety of other things.

What's in a PPD?

Table 7-3 (on the following pages) is a listing of some of the keywords you'll see when you open a PPD file. I haven't tried to cover every keyword and entry you'll find in a PPD, mainly because FreeHand doesn't use all of them. I've included keywords you might want to change, as well as keywords you shouldn't change.

FreeHand 5 and 5.5 use PPDs conforming to version 4.0 of the Adobe PPD specification for PPDs. If you can't see your PPD in the list of available PPDs, you've probably got an old PPD. You can probably find an new one online (for the locations of Adobe and Macromedia-related sites, see Appendix C, "Resources").

Adding Custom Paper Sizes to PPDs

The main reason to edit PPDs is to add custom paper sizes. If you find yourself entering the same numbers in the Page Size dialog box over and over again, it's a job for custom page sizes. Once you've added a custom page size to a PPD file, the size appears on the Paper size popup menu when the PPD file is selected.

If you're creating your publications on page sizes other than the paper size of the printed piece, stop (unless you're creating signatures, or have some other good excuse). Remember that paper size equals printer RAM. Your jobs will print faster if you use a paper size that's no larger than your publication's page size plus crop marks (which adds about 60 points in each dimension).

You can add custom paper sizes to PPDs for any printer that can accept variable page sizes. Usually, imagesetters can accept variable page sizes and laser printers can't.

To add a custom paper size to a PPD file, follow these steps.

1. Back up the PPD file you intend to edit. Remember that if you make a backup copy of the file you'll be able to return to where you started if you make a mistake. Without the backup, you'll have to go beg a copy of the PPD from your friends, who'll laugh at you.

TABLE 7-3 Keywords in PPDs

Keyword	Example	What is it?
*PSVersion	*PSVersion: "(52.3) 320"	Version of PostScript in the printer's ROMs. Change this value if your printer has a different PostScript version than that listed in the PPD.
*Include:	*Include "MyPageSizes.txt"	Includes a file at this point in the PPD. You can have any number of "*Include" keywords in a PPD.
*DefaultResolution	*DefaultResolution: 2400x2400dpi	Default resolution of the printer. If you usually run your printer in a different resolution than the one you see here, change the resolution here.
*Resolution	*Resolution 1200x1200dpi: " 1200 statusdict /setresolution get exec "	Sets the resolution of the printer, for those printers capable of switching resolutions via software commands (imagesetters, mostly). If you don't know the routine to change the setting on an imagesetter (they're all different), leave this value alone and change the resolution from the image-setter's control panel.
*ColorDevice	*ColorDevice: False	Tells FreeHand whether the selected printer is a PostScript color printer or not.
*FreeVM	*FreeVM: "992346"	Amount of the printer's virtual memory (VM) FreeHand can work with before having to flush fonts, etc. If you know your printer has more—or less—memory available, increase or decrease this value. Usually, a printer's startup page shows you how much VM the printer has available. If yours doesn't—or if you've turned off the

PRINTING   561

TABLE 7-3   Keywords in PPDs (continued)

Keyword	Example	What is it?

*FreeVM (continued)		printer's startup page and don't feel like turning it on again—download the following code (your printer will print a page with the memory amount on it):
		`%%show FreeVM`
		`/Helvetica findfont`
		`12 scalefont setfont`
		`72 72 moveto`
		`/memString 256 string def`
		`vmstatus exch sub memString`
		`cvs show`
		`showpage`

*Password	*Password: "0"	Provides a password for the printer. Do not change this, or if you do, make sure you remember the password. If you don't know the password, you might have to replace chips on your motherboard to be able to use your printer again. I can't think why Adobe put this keyword into their interpreter. In fact, I'm vaguely upset by the notion you'd want to prohibit someone on your network from printing on your printer (why not simply *ask* them?). **Note:** The editor and copy editor for this book have both supplied arguments for keeping people off some printers. Luckily, it's my book, and I see no reason to repeat their fascist ravings here.
*FileSystem	*FileSystem True	Lets FreeHand know if the selected printer has a hard disk attached to it. If this value is "True", FreeHand checks the printer's hard disk for downloadable fonts before looking

TABLE 7-3 Keywords in PPDs (continued)

Keyword	Example	What is it?
*FileSystem (continued)		for them on the current system. If you have a hard disk attached to your printer, set this keyword to "True"; otherwise, leave it at "False". If you have a printer that can be attached to a hard disk, FreeHand queries the printer to see if it has a hard disk attached. If you change this setting to "True", FreeHand doesn't have to ask.
*DeviceAdjustMatrix	*DeviceAdjustMatrix: "[1 0 0 1 0 0]"	Don't change this unless your printer chronically distorts the pages you're printing. If your printer does distort images, you'll have to calculate the percentage of distortion vertically and horizontally and enter it in the matrix. If you found that your printer was always stretching an image by five percent vertically, you'd change the matrix to [.95 0 0 1 0 0]. If your imagesetter is doing this, you probably ought to call a service technician. Don't even think about changing for 300-dpi printers—they're not accurate enough for it to make a difference. See the PostScript Language Reference Manual for more (lots more) information on adjusting matrices. El Greco was just Rembrandt with a matrix adjustment.
*ScreenAngle	*ScreenAngle: "45"	Sets the screen angle the printer uses to print halftones. Change this value if you want a different default screen angle for your printer. Any setting you make in the Halftone screen dialog box overrides this value.

TABLE 7-3 Keywords in PPDs (continued)

Keyword	Example	What is it?
*DefaultScreenProc	*DefaultScreenProc: Dot	Sets the default halftone screen drawing procedure for the printer. This procedure is defined in the "*ScreenProc" keyword listing.
*ScreenProc	*ScreenProc Dot: "{abs exch abs 2 copy add 1 gt {1 sub dup mul exch 1 sub dup mul add 1 sub }{dup mul exch dup mul add 1 exch sub }ifelse }" *End	Halftone screen drawing procedures for the printer. You could enter "*ScreenProc Line: "{ pop }"" or "*ScreenProc Ellipse: "{ dup 5 mul 8 div mul exch dup mul exch add sqrt 1 exch sub }"" instead, but you've got to remember to call them from the "*DefaultScreen-Proc" keyword to get them to work.
*ScreenFreq	*ScreenFreq: "120"	Sets the screen frequency the printer uses to print halftones. If you don't like it, change it. Any setting you make in the Halftone Screen dialog box overrides this value.
*DefaultTransfer	*DefaultTransfer Normalized	Sets the default transfer function for the printer.
*DefaultPageSize	*DefaultPageSize: Letter	Sets the default paper size for your printer. The keyword for the paper size corresponds to the name of a defined paper size existing either in the printer's ROMs or in the PPD file. For more on creating custom paper sizes, see the section "Adding Custom Page Sizes to PPDs," earlier in this chapter.
*PageSize	*PageSize Letter: "letter"	Sets up a paper size. If your printer has variable page sizes (imagesetters usually do; laser printers usually don't), this entry could be: "*PageSize Letter.Extra: "statusdict begin 684 864 0 1 setpageparams end""

TABLE 7-3   Keywords in PPDs (continued)

Keyword	Example	What is it?
*DefaultPaperTray	*DefaultPaperTray: None	If you have a printer with more than one paper tray, change this to the tray you want as your default. The tray selection for your printer is defined in the "*PaperTray" section of the PPD.
*PaperTray	*PaperTray Letter: "statusdict begin lettertray end"	Defines available paper trays for your printer.
*DefaultImageableArea	*DefaultImageableArea: Letter	Sets the default imageable area (the area inside a paper size that the printer can actually make marks on) for the printer. The available imageable areas for your printer are set up using the "ImageableArea" keyword.
*ImageableArea	*ImageableArea Letter.Extra: "0 1 684 864"	Sets up the imageable area for a defined page size (in the example, a page size named "Letter.Extra").
*DefaultPaperDimension	*DefaultPaperDimension: Letter	Sets the default paper dimension for the printer. You set up paper dimensions using the "*PaperDimension" keyword.
*PaperDimension	*PaperDimension Letter.Extra: "684 864"	Sets up the paper dimension for a specific page size (in the example, a page size named "Letter.Extra"). Enter the width and height of the paper, in points. For a wide orientation page, the entry would read "*PaperDimension Letter.Extra.Wide: "864 684"".
*VariablePaperSize	*VariablePaperSize: True	Tells FreeHand whether your printer can accept variable paper sizes. Most imagesetters can; most laser printers can't. If your printer can accept variable paper sizes, the Paper popup menu in

(continued on next page)

PRINTING   565

TABLE 7-3   Keywords in PPDs (continued)

Keyword	Example	What is it?
*VariablePaperSize (continued)		FreeHand's Print Options dialog box will include Other. If you choose Other, you'll be able to enter a custom paper size in the Page Size dialog box and print to whatever size of paper you want (within the imagesetter's capabilities). You can also add your own custom page sizes to PPDs of printers capable of accepting variable page sizes. Changing this value from "False" to "True" does not give your printer the ability to accept variable page sizes.
*DefaultInputSlot	*DefaultInputSlot: Lower	Sets the default paper feed for your printer, if your printer has more than one input slot (an NEC LC 890 Silentwriter is an example of a printer with two input slots). The available input slots are set up by the entries in the "*InputSlot" keyword.
*InputSlot	*InputSlot Lower: "statusdict begin 1 setpapertray end"	Defines the available input slots for your printer.
*DefaultManualFeed	*DefaultManualFeed: False	Makes manual feed the printer's default paper feed. Don't change this unless you habitually use your printer's manual feed.
*ManualFeed	*ManualFeed True: "statusdict begin /manualfeed true store end"	Sets up the printer's manual feed mechanism, if it has one.
*Font	*Font Times-Bold: Standard "(001.002)"	Lets FreeHand know that a font is resident in the printer. Add fonts to this list if you're sure they're going to be on your printer's hard disk or memory. FreeHand will ask your printer if it has a certain downloadable font installed, unless it finds the font in this list. If you *(continued on next page)*

TABLE 7-3 Keywords in PPDs (continued)

Keyword	Example	What is it?
*Font (continued)		enter the font in this list, FreeHand doesn't have to ask and prints faster. To add a font, type: `*Font: PostScriptFontName: Standard "(001.001)"` The PostScript name of the font can be a bit tricky to figure out. The best way to do it is to create a text block containing the font in FreeHand and print the file to disk as PostScript or create an EPS. Then open the file with a text editor and look at the way FreeHand names the fonts near the start of the file. The numbers following the font name are the font type and the font version. Most fonts, these days, are Type 1 (or "001"). Unless you know the font version, just enter "001" for the version.
*DefaultFont	*DefaultFont: Courier	Defines the default font for your printer. This is the default font that gets used if FreeHand can't find the font used for text in your publication. If you're tired of Courier, you can change it to any other printer-resident font you want.

2. Open the copy of the PPD with your word processor.

3. Anywhere after the "*Include" line, enter three lines defining your new page size. The lines are shown below. Variables you enter are shown in italics.

```
*PageSize PageSizeName: "statusdict begin x y offset
orientation end"
*ImageableArea PageSizeName: "0 0 x y"
*PaperDimension PageSizeName: "x y"
```

PageSizeName is the name you want to use for your custom page size. This name should not have spaces in it.

x is the width of the custom page size, in points (if you're an inch monger, just multiply the inch measurement by 72 to get the distance in points).

y is the height of the custom page size, in points.

Offset is a value used to offset the paper size from the edge of the imagesetter's paper (or film) roll. This value should almost always be "0".

Orientation is either "1" or "0". "0" means normal orientation (with the height of the paper being measured along the length of the imagesetter's paper roll, and type in normal orientation printing across the roll); "1" means transverse (where the width of the paper is measured along the length of the imagesetter's paper roll). Here's a custom page size for a 576-by-1,152-point (eight-by-16-inch) paper size with a normal orientation.

```
*PageSize PageSizeName: "statusdict begin 576 1152 0 0 end"
*ImageableArea PageSizeName: "0 0 576 1152"
*PaperDimension PageSizeName: "576 1152"
```

4. Save your edited PPD file to the Printer Descriptions folder in the Extensions folder (in your system folder) as text only. Give it a different name than the original PPD.

5. Open FreeHand.

6. Press Command-P to display the Print dialog box. Press the Change button to display the Print options dialog box. If you edited the PPD file you currently have selected, you'll have to select another PPD, and then select the edited PPD to read the new page size information into FreeHand. Once you've selected the edited PPD file, your new page sizes should appear in the Page size popup menu.

If the new page sizes didn't appear in the Page size popup menu, or if the PPD can't be opened, you probably forgot to save the file as text only. Return to your word processor and try that.

Preparing a FreeHand File for Imagesetting

I've listened long and carefully to the grievances of imagesetting service bureau customers and operators. I've heard about how this designer is suing that service bureau for messing up a job, and I've heard imagesetter operators talking about how stupid their clients are and how they have to make changes to the files of most of the jobs that come in. I've listened long enough, and I have one thing to say.

Cut it out! All of you! There's no reason that this relationship has to be an adversarial one. Before you throw this book across the room, let me explain. I don't mean to sound harsh. I just think that we can all cooperate, to everyone's benefit.

Designers and illustrators, you have to learn the technical chops if you want to play. That's just the way it is. The technical challenges are no greater than those you mastered when you learned how to use an airbrush, X-Acto, or a rapidograph. Your responsibility to your imagesetting service bureau is to set your file up so that it has a reasonable chance of printing (the guidelines in this book should help) and to communicate to your service bureau exactly how it is you want your publication printed (or, if you're creating a PostScript file, to make sure that the settings in the publication are correct).

Service bureau folks, you've got to spell out the limits of your responsibility. If you don't think you should be fixing people's files, don't do it. If you do think it's your responsibility, tell your customer up front you'll fix the files, and charge them for the time. And if you get a customer who knows what they're doing, give them a discount. This will encourage everyone else.

Okay, back to the book.

Printing PostScript to Disk

If you know what you're doing, the best way to prepare your publication for printing at an imagesetting service bureau is to print a PostScript file to disk. If you've set up your printing options correctly, the file will include everything that is needed to print the publication. This way, all your service bureau has to do is download the file, instead of having to open the file, set the printing options, link to any images included in the file, and print. The only things that can go wrong are related to film handling and processing—the wrong film's used, the film's scratched, or the film's been processed incorrectly.

This means, however, that you have to be dead certain of the printing options you want before you print to disk, because it's difficult or impossible to change things after that.

What are the most critical things you have to look out for?

Links to images. Make sure any images you want to print (any that aren't on the background layer) are linked.

Tiling. If you're not tiling, make sure tiling (manual or automatic) is off. If you are, make sure you're tiling the way you want to. If you're tiling manually, you'll have to print a separate PostScript file to disk for each tile you want to print.

Scaling. It's easy to forget that you've scaled things for printing on your proof printer. Make sure that this is set to the scaling you want (generally 100 percent).

Separations/Composite. If you want to get separations from your service bureau, make sure you choose Separations in the Print dialog box. An obvious point, but I've forgotten it at least once.

Printer Type. If you don't choose the right printer type, your publication may not print, and may even crash the service bureau's imagesetter. They hate this, so pick the type of imagesetter they use from the popup menu. You might check with the service bureau to see if they have a custom PPD they'd like you to use.

Page Size. Pick a page size at least large enough to contain your page. If you're printing separations, pick a page size that's at least 60 points wider and taller than your page size so that printer marks (crop marks and registration marks) can be printed. Also make sure that you understand the page orientation you're working with—wide or tall; normal or transverse.

Screen Ruling. If you haven't set a screen frequency for each item in your publication using the Halftone palette, enter the screen ruling you want here. Any screen frequency you entered in the Halftone palette overrides any entry you make here.

Printer Marks. If you're printing separations, you can live without separation names and the file's name and date, but you've got to have the crop marks and registration marks if you want your printer to speak to you again. I turn them all on most of the time.

Negative/Positive Emulsion Up/Down. Are you printing negatives or positives? Emulsion up or down? Set it here.

Inks. What inks do you want to print? If you don't set them to print here, don't look askance at your service bureau when you don't get an overlay/separation for the ink. If you don't want an ink to print, make sure you turn it off or expect to pay for an additional piece of film.

Tip:
Don't Forget Your Custom PostScript Files

If you're using a custom UserPrep file, or if you're using FreeHand extension (AGX1) files (for more on creating and using both types of files, see Chapter 8, "PostScript"), and you're giving your service bureau your FreeHand file (rather than a PostScript file), make sure you include these files with your file. Without the files, any special effects you've used won't print. If you do send these files to your service bureau, let them know that they need to put them in the same folder as their copy of FreeHand before they print.

If you print to disk, FreeHand includes the relevant information from these files in your PostScript file, so you won't need to provide them to your service bureau.

Tip:
Learning About FreeHand's PostScript

The best way to learn about how FreeHand makes images using PostScript is to create simple files, print them to disk as PostScript, and then look at the PostScript file with a word processor. How does FreeHand draw a line? A box? Text? It's all easy to see in the PostScript FreeHand prints to disk. Having good PostScript books around is good, but FreeHand has its own dialect, and the best way to learn that dialect is to look at lots of examples of FreeHand's own PostScript.

How is a printed-to-disk PostScript file different from an EPS file? The former contains all the instructions needed by a PostScript printer to render the page, including all of FreeHand's crop marks, page size information, and, specifically, the PostScript page-printing operator *showpage*.

The EPS file, on the other hand, counts on the application it's placed into for things like crop marks and page-positioning information. An EPS file doesn't include any of the options you've chosen in FreeHand's Print and Print Options dialog boxes, while the printed-to-disk PostScript file includes all those options. In addition, the EPS file usually includes an attached PICT resource (Macintosh EPS) or TIFF (MS-DOS) for screen preview, while the printed-to-disk PostScript file doesn't.

Taking a FreeHand Publication to a Service Bureau

If you don't print your publication to disk as PostScript before taking it to your imagesetting service bureau (that is, you've chosen to ignore my earlier advice out of sloth, gluttony, or because your service bureau has told you they'd rather have the publication file), you have to worry about the same things as I mentioned earlier in "Printing PostScript to Disk." You have a powerful ally, however, in FreeHand 5's new "Report" feature (see Figure 7-9).

1. Choose "Report" from the File menu. FreeHand displays the Document Report dialog box.

2. Choose the reporting options you want. Click one of the buttons in the Category section of the Document Report dialog box to display the options for that category. If you're preparing a report for an imagesetting service bureau, you'll want to turn on the External Files option in the Document Info category, and the Fonts Used option in the Text Info category.

3. When you've set the reporting options you want, press Return (or click the Report button). FreeHand displays the Document Report Viewer dialog box.

4. At this point, you can read the report, or save the report to a text file (click the Save button), or click the Print button to print the report. If you're taking your FreeHand publication to an imagesetting service bureau, print the report and send it with your file.

In addition to the report, and all the files you've placed in a FreeHand publication, your imagesetting service bureau will also want a printed example of the publication.

FIGURE 7-9
Preparing a report for an imagesetting service bureau

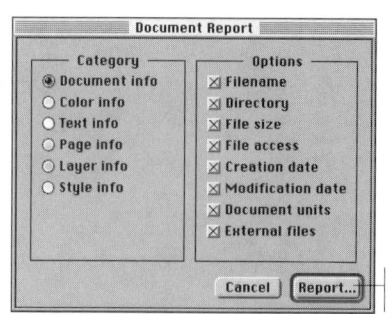

Choose Report from the File menu, and FreeHand displays the Document Report dialog box. The most important reporting categories (from your service bureau's point of view) are those concerning fonts, separations, and external files.

Click the Report button to generate your report.

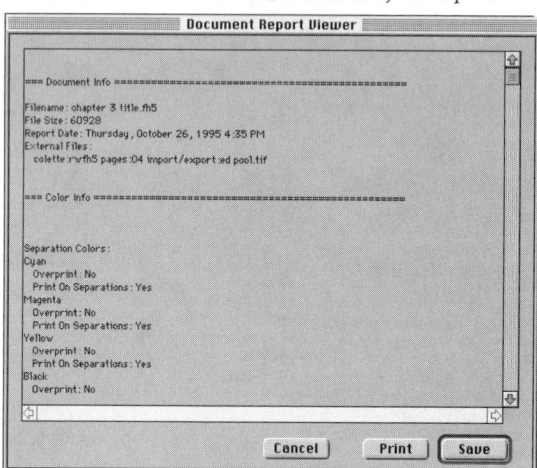

FreeHand creates and displays a report on the vital statistics of the current publication. You can print or save the report.

The Golden Rules

These rules are mentioned elsewhere in this book, but all the service bureau operators I know think I should repeat them again here. The times I mention here are averages, based on a series of benchmarks.

Use blends, not graduated fills. Blends that are created to match your printer's resolution and the line screen you intend to use print more than two times faster than graduated fills covering the same area. This assumes that you're not pasting the blend inside another object, which takes longer. For more on creating blends instead of graduated and radial fills, see Chapter 2, "Drawing."

Use filled objects, not clipping paths. Illustrator users are used to making fountains (what FreeHand calls "graduated fills") using a blend, then placing the blended objects inside a clipping path. In

FreeHand, you should avoid doing this whenever possible, because it takes over five times as long to print as a simple graduated fill of the same path (depending, of course, on the complexity of the clipping path).

Use duplicated objects, not tiled fills. Tiled fills are a wonderful thing—as long as you're basing them on objects with basic lines and fills. As soon as you create a tiled fill containing a graduated or radial fill, watch out! Our benchmarks show that tiled fills containing complex objects take more than twice as long to print as an identical series of duplicated objects.

Remember that page size equals printer RAM. The size of your page corresponds directly to the amount of printer RAM consumed when you try to print the publication. A four-by-four-inch card centered on a letter-size page takes almost twice as much time to print as the same card laid out on a four-by-four-inch page. For more on page setup and page size, see "Printing and Page Setup," earlier in this chapter.

Increase flatness whenever possible. When you're printing to high-resolution imagesetters, the difference between a flatness setting of three and a flatness setting of zero isn't noticeable, but the path with a flatness of three prints almost four times as quickly. For more on flatness, see "Flatness" in Chapter 2, "Drawing."

Don't draw what you can't see. Your printer or imagesetter has to process everything on your publication's page, so why make it do extra work rendering objects that'll never be seen on the printed publication's page?

Simplify your paths. If you're working with complex paths created by autotracing images, try reducing the number of points in each path using Simplify from the Path Operations submenu of the Arrange menu (see "Simplify," in Chapter 2, "Drawing").

Avoid overscanning. When you're scanning images, it's natural to assume that you should scan them at the highest resolution available from your scanner to create the sharpest possible scans. In fact, image data scanned at a resolution greater than two times the screen frequency you intend using to print your publication does not add to the sharpness of the images—which means that the file takes up more space on disk than necessary, and takes longer to send to your printer. See "TIFFS, Line Screens, and Resolution" in Chapter 4, "Importing and Exporting."

Don't import things when you don't have to. Whenever possible, always Copy and Paste from one FreeHand publication to another, rather than exporting and importing EPS graphics. If you have a FreeHand EPS, go to the original file and copy the elements you want out of it. If you're working with an Illustrator EPS, open the file (if possible), rather than placing it. In my tests, placed EPSes took up to 16 times as long to print as the same images pasted from another FreeHand file or converted from an Illustrator EPS.

Printing Troubleshooting

It's going to happen to you. Files are going to take hours to print, and some aren't going to print at all. Or they're going to print in some way you hadn't expected. While this book can be viewed as an extended treatise on printing troubleshooting, this section deals with a few of the most common printing problems and how to fix them.

First of all, what makes a file hard to print? TIFFs, PostScript fills and lines, custom fills and lines, graduated fills, radial fills, and paths with lots of points and curves all do their part to increase the amount of time your publication spends churning around in a printer's RIP. When I say paths with lots of points, I mean paths with more than 100 points—the kind you get when you autotrace the scanned picture of Aunt Martha. Don't forget composite paths, either. At some point, one of these is going to trip you up. When that happens, you'll see a PostScript error message.

PostScript error messages can be cryptic in the extreme, and, best of all, seldom say what they really mean. Almost all of the PostScript errors that have the word "VMError" in them mean that your printer's run out of memory while processing the document. If you see error messages with the word "limitcheck" in them, something in your document is pushing your printer (or

PostScript) past an internal limit. If you see these errors, you're going to have to apply some or all of the golden rules to your publication. In particular, try splitting some of the more complex paths in your publication and increasing the flatness of some or all of the paths in your publication.

There are two errors that have to do with downloadable fonts that are easily fixed.

- PostScript error: "limitcheck" Offending command: "framedevice"

- PostScript error: "VMError" Offending command: "array"

If you get these error messages, go to the Page Setup dialog box and click the Unlimited Downloadable Fonts checkbox. This should fix the problem.

If you see an error containing the word "syntaxerror," you've probably made a mistake in one of the custom PostScript fills or lines you're using. Generally, these are misplaced brackets or parentheses. Look through your code and see what you've missed.

Tip:
When TIFF Images Look Terrible

If your job prints, but your bilevel TIFF and paint-type images look terrible (that is, they look like they have moiré patterns in them), you probably need to magic-stretch them to match them to the printer's resolution. See "Resizing Images to Your Printer's Resolution" in Chapter 4, "Importing and Exporting," for more on magic-stretching.

Tip:
When TIFF Images Don't Print

If your job prints, but lacks a TIFF image or paint-type graphic, you probably lost your link to the image. This often happens when you take the FreeHand file to an imagesetting service bureau for printing (rather than giving them a PostScript file). Remember to take any linked TIFF or paint-type files along when you go to your service bureau, or print your file to disk as PostScript while the files are still linked; they'll be included in the PostScript file.

If you're having this problem with FreeHand EPS files you've placed in a PageMaker 6 publication, see "FreeHand, TIFFs, and PageMaker 6" in Chapter 4, "Importing and Exporting."

Tip:
Image Polarity and Calibration

Lots of people (including me) have said that the polarity of your image (whether it's positive or negative) should be controlled at the imagesetter. We said this because we'd had problems with old versions of PostScript ROMs not inverting images. At this point, PostScript ROMs and software developers' image polarity controls are in sync, and calibration routines for several color separation programs require that you use the application's image polarity controls. Use the image controls in your printing application, instead of setting the polarity at your imagesetter, unless you're working with PostScript ROMs 47.1 or earlier.

Fortune Cookie

I love fortune cookies. "Look afar, and see the end from the beginning," one fortune told me. It could've been talking about printing with FreeHand. From the time you press Command-N to create a new file, you really should be thinking, "How am I going to print this thing?"

Whenever possible, examine the processes you use to create publications in the light of the "golden rules" presented earlier in this chapter. You can almost always make something simpler from your printer's point of view without compromising the appearance of your publication.

Finally, as I always say, if something doesn't work, poke at it.

CHAPTER

PostScript

8

RUDDIGORE

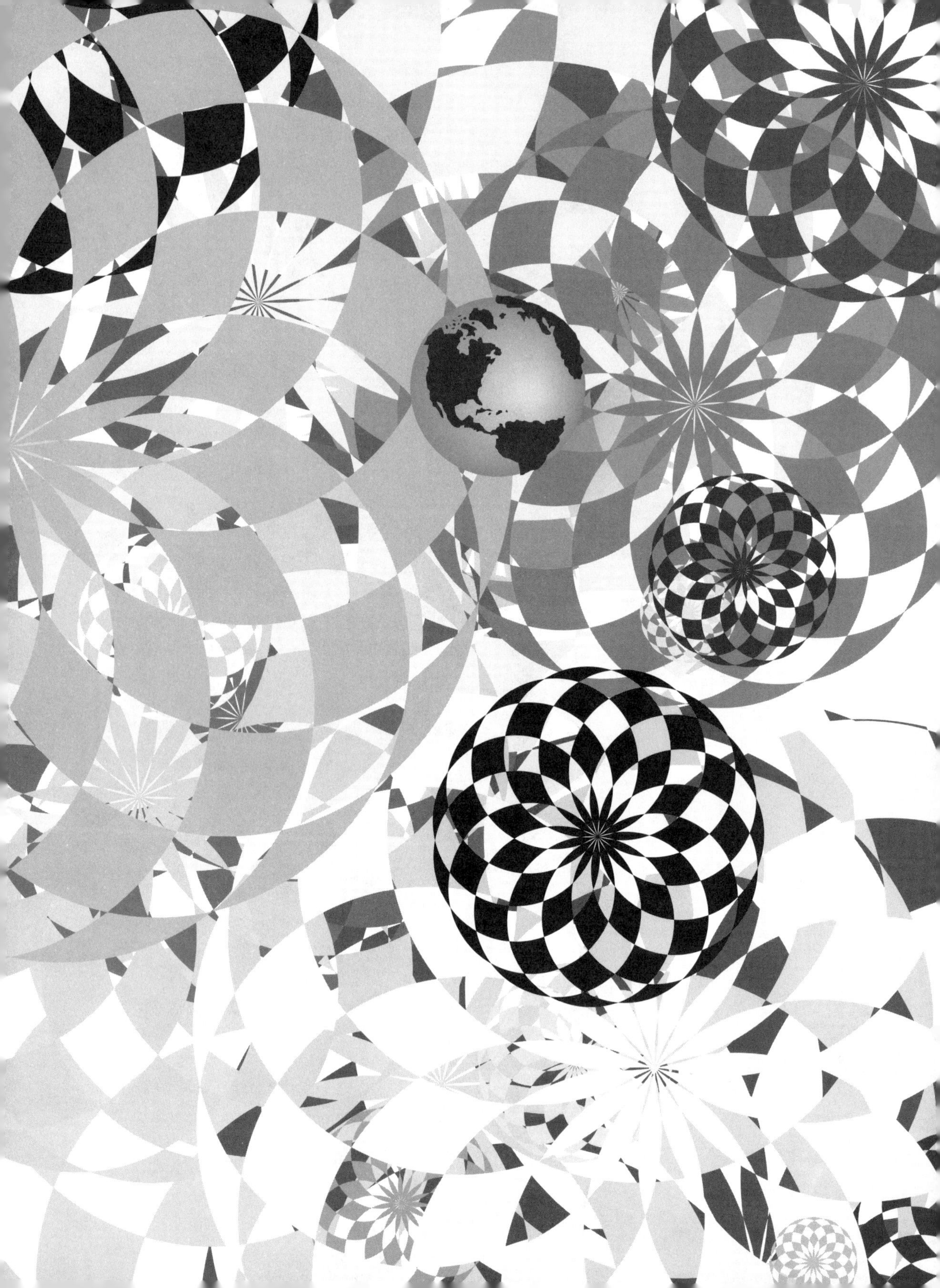

CHAPTER EIGHT ❧ POSTSCRIPT

PostScript

is the engine that makes desktop publishing go. If you already know all there is to know about PostScript and how your printer uses it and/or just want to know how to use it in your FreeHand publications, skip the next section. I'm about to explain PostScript, laser printing, imagesetting, and the meaning of life as I understand them, in as few words as possible. Everyone else, take a deep breath.

What Is PostScript?

PostScript is a page-description language—a programming language for describing graphic objects. It's been said that page-description languages tell your printer how to make marks on paper. This isn't quite true—your printer already knows how to make marks. Page-description languages tell your printer *what marks to make.*

PostScript has emerged as the best of the commercially available page-description languages (other page-description languages being Hewlett-Packard's PCL5, Xerox's Interpress, and Imagen's Impress—these last two being "ancient history" by the standards of the computer world). This doesn't mean it's perfect, just that it's the highest standard we've got.

579

Inside your PostScript printer, there's a computer dedicated to controlling the printer. This computer interprets the PostScript sent to it by your Macintosh and turns it into a bitmap the size of the printer's page. The combination of printer hardware (processor and memory) and software (the version of the PostScript language in the printer's ROMs) is often called a raster image processor (RIP) because it turns a set of drawing commands into a raster image (or bitmap). You'll often hear someone talk about "ripping" a page; they mean they're running it through the RIP.

After the printer receives and processes the information for a page, the RIP transfers the bitmap from its memory to a photosensitive drum using a laser beam. The laser doesn't actually move—its beam bounces off a rotating mirror on its way to the drum. The areas where the drum is charged attract the powdered toner in the printer. When it's time to print the page, paper is pulled into the printer so that the sticky bits of toner are transferred from the drum to the paper. In an imagesetter, the laser beam directly exposes lithographic (black and white) film or paper.

What's PostScript Got to Do with FreeHand?

You can almost think of FreeHand as PostScript wearing a user interface. This isn't to say that FreeHand's internal database is PostScript (it's not), but that FreeHand approaches drawing objects the same way that PostScript does. And then there's printing. Try printing a FreeHand publication on something other than a PostScript printer, and you're in for a disappointment.

How can you use PostScript to extend FreeHand? There are three basic approaches.*

- ◆ You can write your own EPS files.
- ◆ You can examine and modify FreeHand's PostScript.
- ◆ You can create your own PostScript and add it to FreeHand.

---

* You can get all of the PostScript code, PostScript special effects (including more than 100 new PostScript fills), and ResEdit tools discussed in this chapter on the companion disk for this book—along with lots of other FreeHand extensions and tools. I'm distributing the disk myself, for $20. To get a copy of the disk, just drop me a line (see my contact information in Appendix C, "Resources").

Writing Your Own EPS Files

If you want to write your own PostScript files and place them in FreeHand, you'll have to convert them from "raw" PostScript to EPS. Mostly, this means you need to add the following few lines to the beginning of your file.

```
%!PS-Adobe-2.0 EPSF-1.2
%%BoundingBox: lowerLeftX lowerLeftY upperRightX upperRightY
%%EndComments
```

The variables following "%%BoundingBox" are the measurements of the image your PostScript code creates, in points. Usually, "lowerLeftX" and "lowerLeftY" are both zero. If you're not sure what the size of your image is, print the file and measure it.

The PostScript code you use inside an EPS should not include the following PostScript operators.

banddevice	exitserver	initclip
letter	nulldevice	setsccbatch
legal	renderbands	setmatrix
stop	erasepage	grestoreall
initmatrix	copypage	note
framedevice	setpageparams	initgraphics
quit		

Figure 8-1 shows an example EPS file—and what it looks like when you print it.

When you place an EPS you've created this way in FreeHand, you'll see a box, just as if you were looking at the graphic in Keyline view. This is because the PostScript file doesn't look like anything until it's been run through a PostScript interpreter, and your Macintosh, unfortunately, doesn't have one.

Software PostScript (and PostScript clone) interpreters do exist, however. The one I'm the most familiar with is Transverter Pro, from TechPool, which does a good job of adding preview images to EPS graphics (see Appendix C, "Resources," for an address, and Appendix A, "System," for a description). In addition, you can view raw PostScript files using Adobe Systems's Acrobat, provided you

FIGURE 8-1
EPS file

```
%!PS-Adobe-2.0 EPSF-1.2
%%BoundingBox: 0 0 612 792
%%Creator:(Greg Stumph)
%%Title:(Fractal Tree)
%%CreationDate:(9-25-90)
%%EndComments
%% set up variables
/bdf
   {bind def} bind def
/depth 0 def
%% maxdepth controls how many branchings occur
%% exceeding 15 will be VERY time consuming
/maxdepth 10 def
%% after branching "cutoff" times, the branch angles increase
%% set cutoff higher than maxdepth to supress this
/cutoff 4 def
/length
   {rand 72 mod 108 add} bdf
/ang
   {rand 10 mod 10 add} bdf
/sway
   {rand 60 mod 30 sub} bdf
/NewLine
   {sway length 3 div sway length 3 div
   0 length rcurveto currentpoint
   depth 1 sub maxdepth div setgray
   stroke translate 0 0 moveto} bdf
/down
   {/depth depth 1 add def
   depth cutoff gt
     {/ang
        {rand 30 mod 20 add} bdf
     } if
   } bdf
/up
   {/depth depth 1 sub def
   depth cutoff le
     {/ang
        {rand 10 mod 10 add} bdf
     } if
   } bdf
%% FractBranch is the loop that does all the work,
%% by calling itself recursively
/FractBranch
   {.8 .8 scale
   down NewLine
   depth maxdepth lt
     {ang rotate gsave FractBranch grestore
     ang 2 mul neg rotate gsave FractBranch grestore} if
   up
   } def
gsave
```

FIGURE 8-1
EPS file
(continued)

```
306 72 translate 0 0 moveto
10 setlinewidth
1 setlinecap
currentscreen 3 -1 roll
pop 65 3 1 roll setscreen
FractBranch
grestore
%%End of file
```

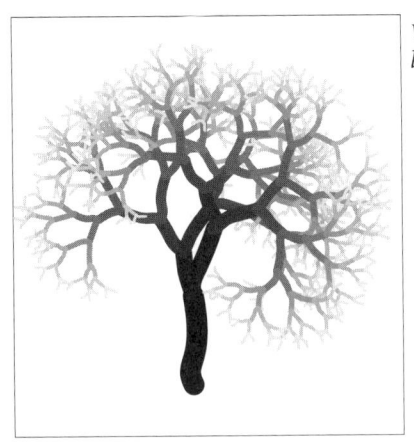

What this EPS file looks like when you print it.

have the Acrobat Distiller application (it is, after all, most of a PostScript interpreter).

Looking at FreeHand's PostScript

If you're curious, or if you're creating your own UserPrep file or external resource file, you should also take a look at FreeHand's PostScript to see if there's something there you can use. Knowing FreeHand's PostScript can keep you from "reinventing the wheel" when you write your own code.

One of the most beautiful things about PostScript is that it's just text—which means you can open it in any word processor.

While you can create PostScript files by turning on File in the LaserWriter driver, I use FreeHand's Export command, and choose Generic EPS. Files created this way are a little bit smaller and are guaranteed to contain only FreeHand code.

The first time you open a FreeHand PostScript or EPS file, what you see can be rather intimidating. What is all this stuff?

The most important code can be found between the lines

`%%BeginResource: procset Altsys_header 4 0`

and

`%%EndProlog`

Everything between these two lines is one or another of FreeHand's PostScript dictionaries (see Figure 8-2). Specifically, you should look at the PostScript definitions following "/supdict 65 dict def" and "/ropedict 85 dict def." These are the support routines for FreeHand's custom PostScript fills and strokes. If you can't see these dictionaries, make sure the file you've printed to disk contains at least one custom stroke or fill.

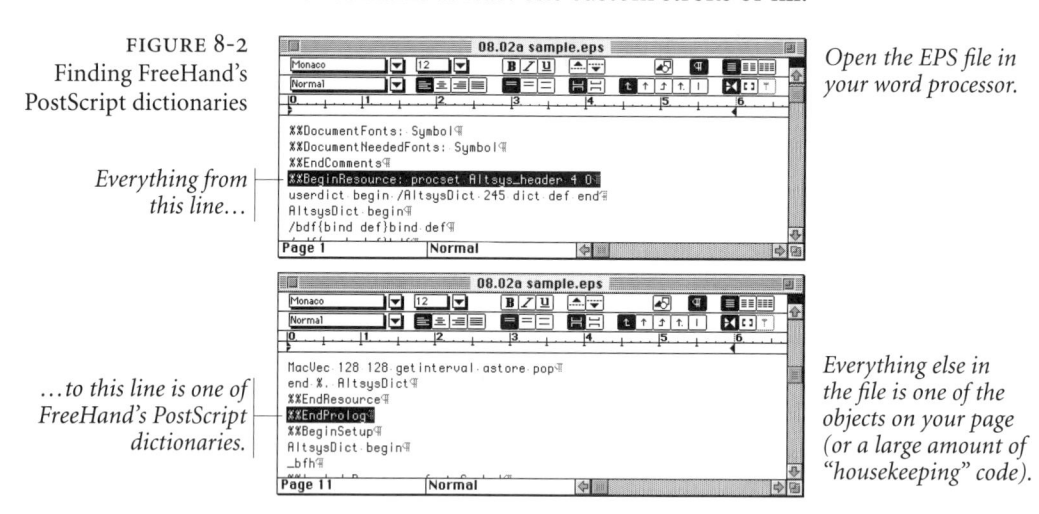

FIGURE 8-2
Finding FreeHand's
PostScript dictionaries

Everything from this line...

...to this line is one of FreeHand's PostScript dictionaries.

Open the EPS file in your word processor.

Everything else in the file is one of the objects on your page (or a large amount of "housekeeping" code).

If you're looking for the objects you've drawn, scroll to the end of the file, then scroll up a couple of screens. When you see the line "%%BeginPageSetup," you've reached the start of a FreeHand page (while your publication might contain more than one page, I advise examining FreeHand's PostScript one page at a time—it's less confusing). Scroll down until you see a line ending with "m"—it's the start of the first path you've drawn (see Figure 8-3).

Don't be scared—you don't have to know this stuff to enter most of the new PostScript strokes and fills in this chapter. The code is pretty well annotated with comments (by software engineering standards) and you should be able to understand some of it just by looking at it. PostScript comments are preceded by a "%" and are ignored by PostScript interpreters.

FIGURE 8-3
Finding what
you've drawn

Here's the start of a path drawn in FreeHand.

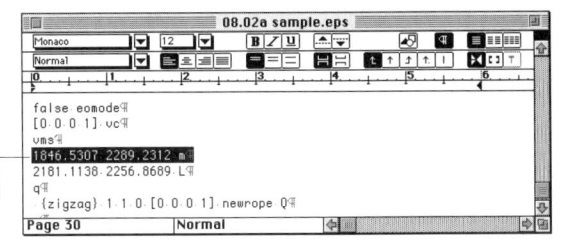

What't the rest of the code you can see in the example screen mean?

```
false eomode
[0 0 0 1] vc
vms
1846.5307 2289.2312 m
2181.1138 2256.8689 L


q
   {zigzag} 1 1 0 [0 0 0 1] newrope Q
```

Turns off overprinting.
Sets the color to black.
Manages printer memory.
Moves to the coordinates shown.
Draws a path to these coordinates, from the coordinates in the previous line.
Manages printer memory ("gsave")
Applies the custom line style Zigzag.

If you're having trouble making sense of the PostScript file, remember that procedures begin with a "/" and end with a "}def" or "}bdef". Here's an example of a procedure.

```
%%procedure for picking a random integer
/randint {rand exch mod } def
```

Looking at FreeHand's PostScript Resources

The Post resources inside FreeHand contain all of FreeHand's PostScript code. If you're creating your own PostScript code, or if you're creating external resource files, you'll probably find it helpful to take a look at these resources.

To open FreeHand's Post resources using ResEdit (a free programmer's tool from Apple available from user groups and Apple's Internet site, ftp.apple.com), follow the steps below (see Figure 8-4). If you haven't created a template for the Post resource class, you might want to skip ahead to "Creating External Resource Files" to find out how. It's much easier to look at and edit these resources if you use a template (ResEdit's existing POST template won't work).

1. Launch ResEdit.

FIGURE 8-4
Viewing FreeHand's
PostScript resources

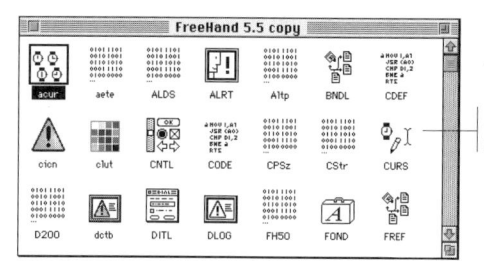

Open a copy of FreeHand with ResEdit.

ResEdit displays the resources inside FreeHand.

Double-click the Post resource class.

ResEdit displays a listing of the Post resources in FreeHand.

Double-click one of the Post resources...

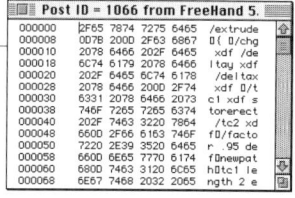

...and ResEdit displays the contents of the resource.

If you haven't created a template for Post resources, you'll see something like this.

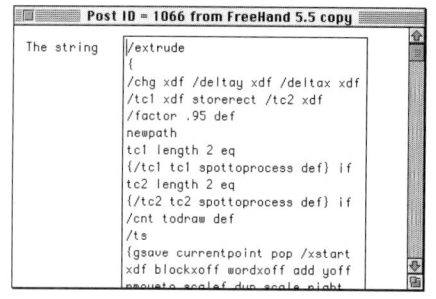

If you've skipped ahead and created a resource template for the Post resource class, you'll see something like this.

2. Locate and open your FreeHand application. Always work on a copy of FreeHand so that you don't inadvertently damage the application.

3. Type "post" to scroll down to the Post resource class and press Return to open the class (or double-click the icon).

4. ResEdit displays a list of the Post resources in FreeHand.

5. Double-click any one of the resources to see its contents.

6. When you're finished looking at the resources, close the file or quit ResEdit.

The resources are labelled by number, and it can take a while to locate the code you want. Since I've already gone through the resources, I can tell you where things are (see Table 8-1). When you see "\n" inside these resources, read it as a carriage return.

TABLE 8-1
Selected FreeHand Post resources

Resource ID:	What's in it:
1066	Zoom text effect (known internally as "extrude")
1067	Inline text effect
1085	AltsysDict, FreeHand's main PostScript dictionary
1086	PostScript error handler, the code that prints PostScript error messages on your pages when something goes wrong
1127	Code for drawing crop marks
1128	Code for drawing registration marks
1147	supdict, which contains procedures used by the custom fill and custom stroke effects
1148	ropedict, the PostScript dictionary containing support routines for custom PostScript strokes
1149	texturedict, the PostScript dictionary containing code for rendering FreeHand's textured fills (Coquille, Sand, Denim, etc.)
1150	Bricks fill effect
1151	Tiger Teeth fill effect
1152	Circles fill effect
1153	Squares fill effect
1154	Hatch fill effect
1155	Random Leaves fill effect
1156	Random Grass fill effect
1157	Noise fill effect
1158	Black-and-White Noise fill effect
1160	Neon stroke effect
1161	Burlap textured fill

TABLE 8-1
Selected FreeHand Post resources (continued)

Resource ID:	What's in it:
1162	Denim textured fill
1163	Sand textured fill
1164	Coarse Gravel textured fill
1165	Fine Gravel textured fill
1166	Light Mezzo and Heavy Mezzo textured fills
1167	Medium Mezzo textured fill
1168	Coquille textured fill
1169	Arrow stroke effect
1170	Braid stroke effect
1171	Crepe stroke effect
1172	Snowflake stroke effect
1173	Teeth stroke effect
1174	Two Waves stroke effect
1175	Three Waves stroke effect
1176	Wedge stroke effect
1177	Star stroke effect
1178	Cartographer stroke effect
1179	Checker stroke effect
1180	Dot stroke effect
1181	Diamond stroke effect
1182	Right Diagonal stroke effect
1183	Left Diagonal stroke effect
1184	Rectangle stroke effect
1185	Ball stroke effect
1186	Squiggle stroke effect
1187	Swirl stroke effect
1188	Zigzag stroke effect
1189	Roman stroke effect
1190	Heart stroke effect

What's the point of all this? If you know where something is, you can change it, which is what most of the rest of this chapter is about. If you're happy with everything about the way FreeHand prints, or don't feel the urge to create your own PostScript effects, or aren't curious, you can skip the rest of the chapter. If you want to change the way FreeHand prints crop marks, or add new PostScript line and fill effects, or really know what's going on under the hood, read on.

Variables in FreeHand's PostScript

Did you ever wonder how FreeHand tells your printer to change to a new font, scale the font, and draw a string of text? If you used ResEdit to open Post resource ID 1228 and 1054 inside FreeHand, you'd see the resources shown in Figure 8-5.

FIGURE 8-5
Filling out the form

When you print (or export a file as an EPS), FreeHand takes the information (in this example, some text set in Sabon) in your publication and merges it with PostScript from its Post resources.

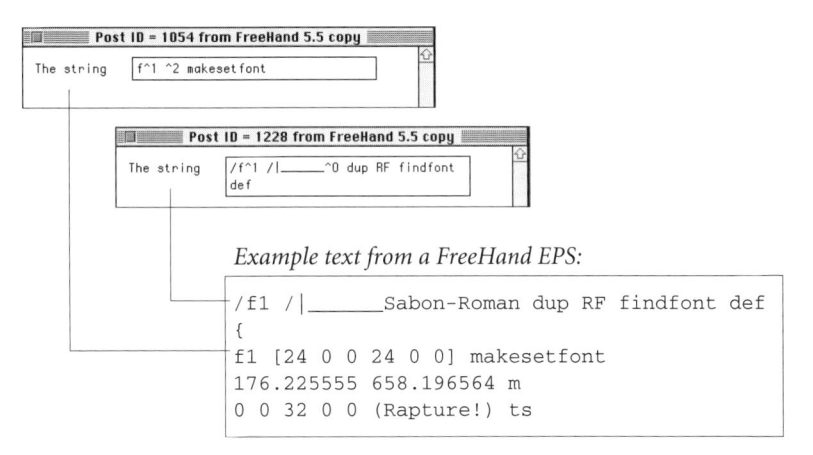

```
Post ID = 1054 from FreeHand 5.5 copy
The string    f^1 ^2 makesetfont
```

```
Post ID = 1228 from FreeHand 5.5 copy
The string    /f^1 /|_____^0 dup RF findfont
              def
```

Example text from a FreeHand EPS:

```
/f1 /|_____Sabon-Roman dup RF findfont def
{
f1 [24 0 0 24 0 0] makesetfont
176.225555  658.196564 m
0 0 32 0 0 (Rapture!) ts
```

Compare the example with the Post resources. Do they look similar? You bet—the Post resource is a blank form for the code FreeHand sends (to your printer or to disk) when it specifies a font. The characters preceded by a caret (^) are FreeHand's internal representations of the data it'll use to fill out the form. Some of the tags are pretty easy to figure out—in this example, "^1" in Post ID 1228 equals "1" and "^0" equals "Sabon-Roman."

"^2" in Post ID 1054 is a little more complicated—it's an array containing the font's scaling. The example text is 24 points and hasn't been scaled horizontally (if it had been, you'd see a different number in the first position in the array).

Changing FreeHand's PostScript

There's more to opening FreeHand's PostScript resources with ResEdit than merely snooping around, of course. Once you have an idea of where things are, you can change them.

If you do change FreeHand's resources, however, bear in mind that you do so entirely at your own risk. These techniques are not supported by Macromedia or Peachpit Press—though I'll take a shot at helping you if you get stuck (see Appendix C, "Resources," for contact information).

Making Textured Fills Transparent

If you want FreeHand's textured fills (Burlap, Denim, Coquille, etc.) to print with a transparent background, you can edit the Post resource that controls the way they print. This is one of the simplest, easiest, and most useful changes you can make to FreeHand's Post resources.

First, if you haven't already skipped ahead to build yourself a Post resource template, do so now. The example screens I'll show use the template, not the hexadecimal display.

To make FreeHand's textured fills transparent, follow these steps (see Figure 8-6).

1. Start ResEdit. Locate and open a copy of FreeHand.

2. Locate and select the Post resource class, and open it by pressing Return (or by double-clicking on the icon). ResEdit opens FreeHand's Post resource class and displays a list of all the Post resources inside FreeHand.

3. Select and open Post resource ID 1149.

4. Scroll through the resource until you see the following lines.
   ```
   gsave
   [0 0 0 0] vc
   filler
   grestore
   ```

5. Type "%%" in front of each of these lines.
   ```
   %%gsave
   %%[0 0 0 0] vc
   %%filler
   %%grestore
   ```

FIGURE 8-6
Making textured fills transparent

Default (textured fill prints with an opaque background).

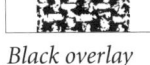

Edited version (textured fill prints with a transparent background).

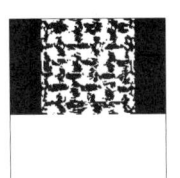

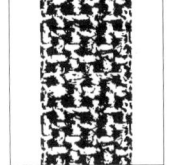

Color 1 overlay   Black overlay   Color 1 overlay   Black overlay

Use ResEdit to open a copy of FreeHand. Locate and open Post resource ID 1147.

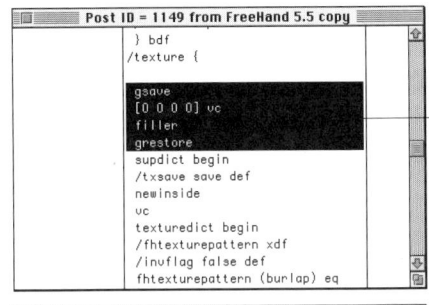

Scroll through the resource until you locate these four lines of text.

Type "%%" before each of the four lines and save this copy of FreeHand.

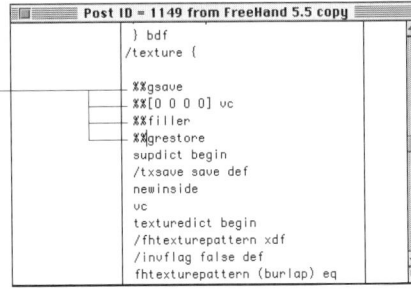

When you use this copy of FreeHand, textured fills will print with transparent backgrounds.

6. Press Command-S to save the edited copy of FreeHand. Quit ResEdit.

When you print textured fills from this copy of FreeHand, they'll print with transparent backgrounds (though they'll still be opaque on screen). What, exactly, this means depends on whether you've set the color you've applied to the textured fill to overprint or not, and whether the color is defined as a spot or process color.

If you're working with a spot color, and overprint the spot ink, the textured fill simply overprints any objects behind the textured fill—no part of the fill is knocked out of those objects. If, on the other hand, you've set the ink to knock out, FreeHand knocks out the solid areas of the textured fill from any objects behind the filled object. (Note that this is bound to produce trapping problems, as you can't trap the pattern inside the textured fill.) If you're working with a process color, the solid areas in the textured fill are knocked out of any objects behind the fill regardless of the overprinting settings of the process inks.

If you're using this technique, and want an opaque background behind one of your textured fills, you'll have to draw an opaque shape behind the object containing the fill. It's a small price to pay.

Overprinting TIFFs

If you read Chapter 4, "Importing and Exporting," you'll remember that I complained about FreeHand's lack of a separate control for overprinting grayscale TIFFs. This is no problem when you're overprinting the ink you've used to color the TIFF, but what if you can't do that?

To find out what was going on, I printed a file to disk (with Separations turned on in the Print dialog box), then opened the file with Microsoft Word and looked through the file for anything that seemed suspicious. Immediately after the TIFF image in the PostScript file, I saw the following line.

```
[0 0 0 0] vc 0 0 21.6001 22.3201 rectfill
```

There it was: the grail. And all you have to do is comment out that line (which sets the color of the box drawn behind the TIFF), and the TIFF will overprint. Make the change in the resource, and all grayscale TIFFs will overprint (see Figure 8-7).

The following steps show you how. We won't alter FreeHand itself—instead, we'll create an external resource file. This way, you can turn your new "feature" on and off without editing FreeHand.

1. Launch ResEdit.

2. Locate and open a copy of FreeHand.

3. Open the Post resource class. ResEdit displays all the Post resources in FreeHand.

4. Select Post resource ID 1211 and press Command-C. Close the copy of FreeHand (if you're asked if you want to save changes, click No).

POSTSCRIPT 593

FIGURE 8-7
Overprinting
grayscale TIFFs

Select Post resource ID 1209, and copy it to the Clipboard.

Press Command-N to create a new resource file. Give the file a name and save it.

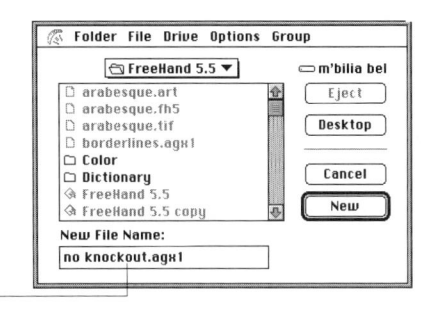

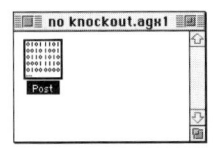

Paste the Post resource from the Clipboard into the new file.

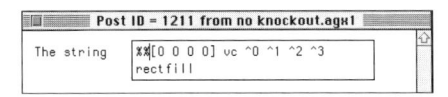

Open the Post resource class, then double-click the Post resource (there should be only one) to open it. Type "%%" before the first line of the resource and close the resource.

Choose Get Info from the File menu for the file you just created. ResEdit displays the Info dialog box.

Type "AGX1" in the Type field.

Type "FH50" in the Creator field.

Save and close the file.

5. Press Command-N to create a new resource. Name it "no knockout.agx1" (or something like that) and save it in the same folder as your copy of FreeHand. ResEdit creates your new, empty resource file.

6. Press Command-V to paste the Post resource you copied out of FreeHand into your new resource file.

7. Open the Post resource class and open the single Post resource inside. Scroll to the end of the resource and type "%%" at the start of the text.

        %%[0 0 0 0] vc 0 0 21.6001 22.3201 rectfill

8. Choose Get Info for the file from the File menu. In the Type field, type "AGX1". Type "FH50" in the Creator field. Save your file and quit ResEdit.

The next time you start FreeHand, you'll see a dialog box asking if you want to load the resource or not (see Figure 8-8). You do, so press Return (or click the OK button). To get rid of this annoying message, you'll have to add an Xvrs resource to your external resource file (see "Creating External Resource Files," later in this chapter).

FIGURE 8-8
An overly grim dialog box

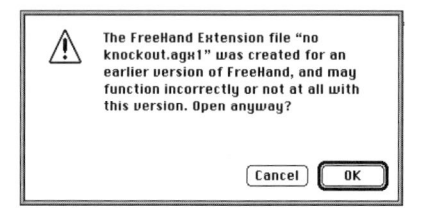

> The FreeHand Extension file "no knockout.agx1" was created for an earlier version of FreeHand, and may function incorrectly or not at all with this version. Open anyway?
>
> Cancel   OK

When you print, your grayscale TIFFs won't knock out of objects behind them. When you want your grayscale TIFFs to knock out again, just move the file out of the FreeHand folder and restart FreeHand, or, better, draw a box behind them.

Creating Your Own PostScript Effects

There are several different ways to enter your own PostScript code.

- You can attach your own PostScript code to FreeHand objects by choosing PostScript in the Fill Inspector or the Stroke Inspector and entering up to 255 characters of code.

- You can create your own PostScript effects, defining them as procedures, and save them in a special file named "UserPrep". Then you can activate those procedures by typing the procedure names (and appropriate parameters) in the PostScript sections of FreeHand's Stroke and Fill Inspectors. This gets you around the 255-character limit.

♦ You can create your own PostScript effects and turn them into FreeHand external resource files. Once you do this, they'll appear when you choose Custom from the Fill Type or Stroke Type popup menus in the Fill or Stroke Inspector.

Typing PostScript in the Fill and Stroke Inspectors

When you choose PostScript from either the Fill Type or Stroke Type popup menus in the Fill Inspector or Stroke Inspector, a large field appears at the bottom of the Inspector. You can type up to 255 characters of PostScript code in this field (or you can paste in text you've entered elsewhere). Press Return, and FreeHand applies the code you enter here to the selected object as a PostScript fill or stroke effect.

In some ways, this is the easiest way to get PostScript you've written into FreeHand, provided the code fits in the field. The trouble is, 255 characters isn't a lot of code. You can cut down the number of characters used by making your variable and procedure names shorter ("ls" instead of "lineStart," for example), but this only works up to a certain point.

In fact, it sometimes looks like FreeHand accepts more than 255 characters in this text edit field—the field accepts the characters without complaint. But when you press Return, FreeHand will truncate the contents of the field, leaving only 255 characters.

There are three ways around this limitation. You can rely on procedures that you know are already defined in FreeHand and use them in your PostScript code, you can rely on procedures you've created in your own UserPrep file, or you can create your own external resource files. These three techniques are covered later in this chapter.

The following steps show you how to apply a simple PostScript stroke effect (see "PostScript Strokes" in Chapter 2, "Drawing").

1. Draw a path.

2. Press Command-Option-L to display the Stroke Inspector.

3. Choose PostScript from the Stroke Type popup menu. The PostScript Code field appears in the Stroke Inspector.

4. Type PostScript code in the field (you can delete the default code "stroke").

5. Press Return to apply your PostScript stroke.

The selected path won't look any different on screen, but when you print to a PostScript printer, the effect you've typed is applied to the path.

Figure 8-9 shows a few stroke effects you can enter. As you enter this code, you'll see procedures that don't look like "normal" PostScript. That is, instead of typing "exch def" you'll type "xdf". I can do this because I know FreeHand's already defined "xdf" as "exch def"—it's a kind of shorthand. For a list of PostScript shortcuts defined by FreeHand, see Table 8-2.

FIGURE 8-9
PostScript strokes

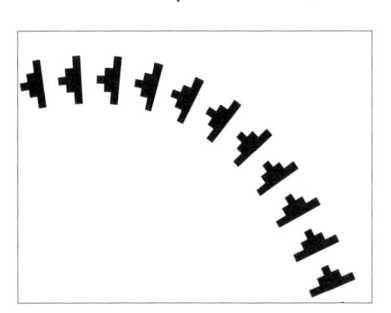

Example PostScript stroke code
```
currentlinewidth /lw exch cvi
def gsave [lw lw 4 mul] 0
setdash lw 6 mul setlinewidth
stroke grestore gsave [lw lw 4
mul] lw setdash lw 3 mul
setlinewidth stroke grestore
gsave [lw lw 4 mul] lw 2 mul
setdash lw setlinewidth stroke
grestore
```

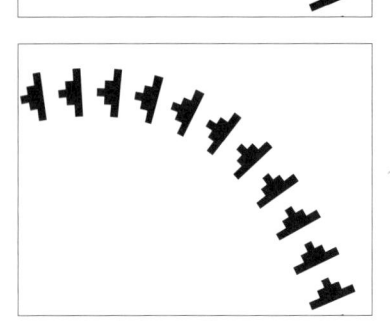

Shorthand version of above
```
currentlinewidth /lw exch cvi
def q [lw lw 4 mul] 0 d lw 6
mul w S Q q [lw lw 4 mul] lw d
lw 3 mul w S Q q [lw lw 4 mul]
lw 2 mul d lw w S Q
```

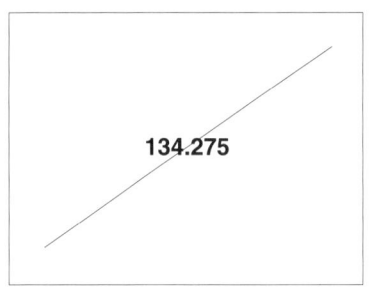

Dimension line code
```
pathbbox /t xdf /r xdf /b xdf
/l xdf /dx r l sub def /dy t b
sub def S /ts 20 string def /
Helvetica-Bold findfont 9
scalefont setfont l b trans-
late dx 2 div dy 2 div 3 sub m
dx 2 exp dy 2 exp add sqrt ts
cvs stringwidth pop 2 div neg
0 rmoveto ts show S
```

FIGURE 8-9
PostScript strokes
(continued)

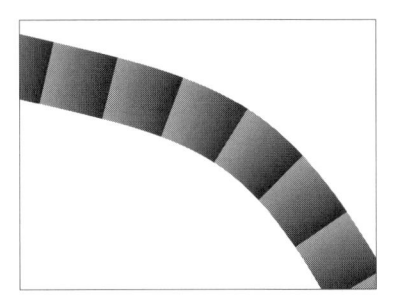

Graduated line code
```
cvc /CC xdf /ks 25 def /kp 1 1
ks div sub def 0 1 ks { /c xdf
[1 ks 1 sub] c 2 add d cvc
length 4 eq {cvc {kp mul}
forall 4 array astore /cvc
xdf}{cvc 0 get kp mul /nt xdf
cvc 0 nt put} ifelse cvc vc q
S Q } for CC vc
```

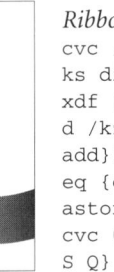

Ribbon line code
```
cvc /CC xdf /ks 25 def /kp .5
ks div def 0 1 ks 2 mul {/c
xdf [1 ks 2 mul 1 sub] c 2 add
d /kz c ks le {{kp sub}}{{kp
add}} ifelse def cvc length 4
eq {cvc {kz} forall 4 array
astore}{cvc 0 get kz /nt xdf
cvc 0 nt put cvc} ifelse vc q
S Q} for CC vc
```

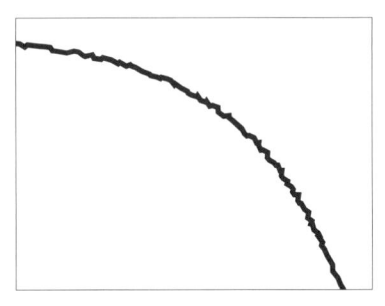

Shaky line code
```
23 srand 0 setflat /ri {cvi
rand exch mod} def flattenpath
{newpath m} {2 {1 dup 2 mul ri
sub add exch} repeat L} {} {}
pathforall S
```

PostScript fill effects work just like PostScript stroke effects. You can type up to 255 characters in the PostScript Code field (see "PostScript Strokes" in Chapter 2, "Drawing").

1. Draw a rectangle.

2. Press Command-Option-F to display the Fill Inspector.

3. Choose PostScript from the Fill Type popup menu. The PostScript Code field appears at the bottom of the Fill Inspector.

4. Enter PostScript code in the field.

5. When you're through entering code, press Return to apply your PostScript fill. The rectangle fills with "PS".

Figure 8-10 shows a few more PostScript fill effects.

TABLE 8-2
FreeHand's shorthand for commonly used procedures

Name:	What it does:
F	Fills the current path with the current color
f	Closes the current path, then fills it with the current color
S	Strokes the current path with the current line weight, color, and dash pattern
s	Closes the current path, then strokes it
q	Saves the current graphic state (more or less the same as PostScript's "gsave" operator)
Q	Restores the previously saved graphic state (like PostScript's "grestore" operator)
w	Sets the stroke width. Same as the PostScript operator "setlinewidth"
n	Same as the PostScript operator "newpath"
d	Sets the dash pattern of a path. Same as the PostScript operator "setdash"
xdf	Defines the current variable name with whatever's on top of the operand stack. Same as "exch def"
vc	Sets the current color
cvc	Current color array (every time you use "vc", "cvc" updates)

Creating and Using a UserPrep File

If you've created some PostScript stroke or fill effects or have borrowed them from some other source (such as this book, other PostScript books, or the text files you found on someone's CorelDraw disks) and want to use them in FreeHand, the simplest thing to do is to create a PostScript dictionary of your own (see Figure 8-11).

1. Using a word processor or a PostScript programming tool such as LaserTalk from Adobe Systems, create a series of procedures you want to use.

2. Save the procedures as a text-only file named UserPrep, and place the file inside the folder containing your copy of FreeHand.

FIGURE 8-10
PostScript fills

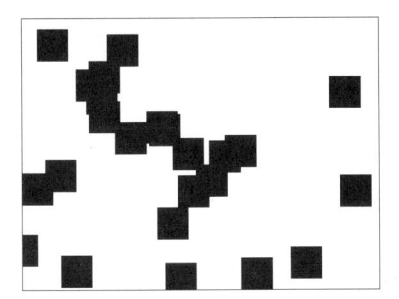

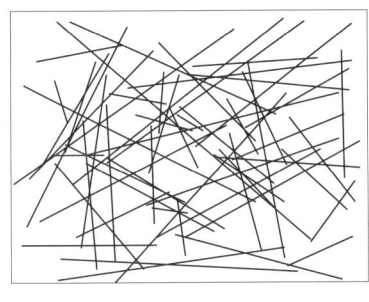

Random Squares code
```
23 srand pathbbox clipper /kt
xdf /kr xdf /kb xdf /kl xdf n
/dx kr kl sub def /dy kt kb
sub def /ri {cvi rand exch
mod} def /sz 12 def kl sz sub
kb sz sub translate 0 0 m /rl
{rlineto} def 24 {dx ri dy ri
m sz 0 rl 0 sz rl sz neg 0 rl
f} repeat
```

Random Triangles code
```
23 srand pathbbox clipper /kt
xdf /kr xdf /kb xdf /kl xdf n
/dx kr kl sub def /dy kt kb
sub def /ri {cvi rand exch
mod} def /sz 12 def kl sz sub
kb sz sub translate 0 0 m /rl
{rlineto} def 24 {dx ri dy ri
m sz 0 rl sz 2 div neg sz rl
f} repeat
```

Scribble code
```
23 srand pathbbox clipper /kt
xdf /kr xdf /kb xdf /kl xdf n
/dx kr kl sub def /dy kt kb
sub def /ri {cvi rand exch
mod} def /xy {dx ri dy ri} def
kl kb translate 0 0 m 60 {q xy
m xy xy xy C .5 w S Q} repeat
```

Straight Scribble code
```
23 srand pathbbox clipper /kt
xdf /kr xdf /kb xdf /kl xdf n
/dx kr kl sub def /dy kt kb
sub def /ri {cvi rand exch
mod} def /xy {dx ri dy ri} def
kl kb translate 0 0 m 60 {q xy
m xy L .5 w S Q} repeat
```

3. In FreeHand, select a path to which you want to apply one of your new PostScript effects.

4. Display the Fill or Stroke Inspector.

5. Choose PostScript from the Fill Type or Stroke Type popup menu.

6. Type the name of your procedure in the PostScript code field, preceding it with any variables it requires.

7. Press Return to apply your effect to the selected path.

8. Print your publication. If you get a PostScript error or if nothing prints, you've made a mistake in either your UserPrep or the way you entered the procedure. Find it and fix it. Errors containing the words "nostringval",

FIGURE 8-11
Using UserPrep

A sample UserPrep file. This file defines one PostScript fill effect, Scribble.

```
%%UserPrep
/scribble
%%on stack: random number seed, line weight, number of lines
{/ns xdf
/lineWeight xdf
/seed xdf
seed srand lineWeight w
flattenpath pathbbox clip
/top xdf
/right xdf
/bottom xdf
/left xdf
cvc /CVC xdf
cvc length 4 eq
  {/colorChange{cvc {newTint} forall 4 array astore vc} def}
  {/colorChange{cvc 0 get {newTint} mul /tint xdf cvc 0 tint put vc} def
} ifelse
/randint {rand exch mod} def
/newTint {/random {100 randint .01 mul} def random mul} def
/xy
  {rand right left sub cvi mod left add rand
  top bottom sub cvi mod bottom add
} bdf
ns {n xy m xy xy xy C colorChange S CVC vc} repeat
} def
%%End UserPrep
```

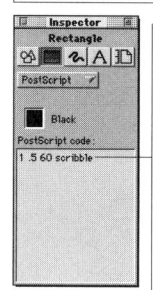

Type the parameters your new fill effect expects in the Fill Inspector, followed by the name of the procedure. In this example, you'd type a seed for the random number generator, the line width, and the number of lines you want, followed by "scribble" (the name of the fill).

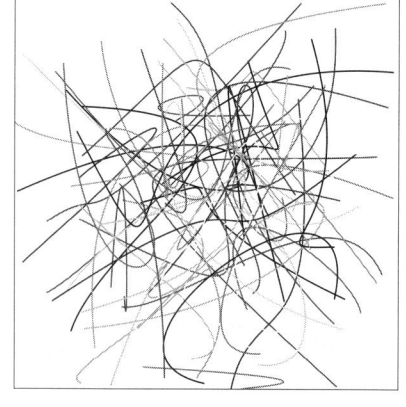

Scribble PostScript fill effect

"nocurrentpoint", and "stack underflow" are usually caused by entering a variable improperly before the procedure name in the PostScript Code field (in either the Fill or Stroke Inspector).

Creating External Resource Files

One of FreeHand's most significant features is that you can extend the program using external resource files. How does this work? FreeHand, on startup, loads files of type AGX1 it finds in its folder. FreeHand loads the resources found in these files as if they were resources found inside your copy of FreeHand. If the resource IDs in your AGX1 files match the IDs of resources that FreeHand's already loaded, the resources in the external files override the internal resources.

Almost any preexisting resource in FreeHand can be replaced by an external resource file, and whole new resources can be added. External resource files, such as the ones we'll create in this chapter, aren't the same as FreeHand's Xtras—you won't be able to add charting modules to FreeHand using external resource files.

If you're interested in learning how to write FreeHand Xtras (something that's way beyond the scope of this book), call Macromedia customer service and ask for a FreeHand Xtras Software Development Kit (see Appendix C, "Resources," for contact information). It's free.

Don't take these limitations too hard. The number of things you can do with external resource files is mind-boggling. The FreeHand extensions that I find most exciting are the ones that change the way FreeHand prints objects and the ones that add new PostScript strokes and fills. I've placed most of this book's discussion of external resource files in this chapter because these exciting modifications and additions have to do with PostScript.

Why use external resource files to add PostScript effects instead of creating a UserPrep file? Because it's too easy to make mistakes entering variables for an external UserPrep. External resources make it easy to remember what variables a procedure needs, because you can add your own buttons, fields, and popup menus in the Fill and Stroke Inspectors. Creating external resource files is much more difficult than creating a UserPrep file, but it's worth it.

Creating resource templates. Before you can create any external resources for FreeHand, you've got to create four resource templates in ResEdit. Don't let that deter you, though. This part is easy. You don't have to know the theory of how this stuff works—I don't. I just know what to do to get the results I want, and I'm happy to share the results of my trial-and-error experimentation with you.

We'll be creating templates named GnEf, Post (PostScript; this resource type differs from ResEdit's built-in "Post" and "POST" resource templates, so don't think you can skip creating this one), UIrz, and Xvrs. We'll add the templates to a copy of ResEdit, which we'll then use to create external resource files. If you developed any FreeHand 3 external resource files, you should note that the LnEf, FlEf, and Scrn resources are not used by FreeHand 4 and 5, and that the Post resource has a new format. "Great," I said when I first opened FreeHand 4 with ResEdit. "Everything I know is wrong."

I used ResEdit 2.1.3 to create my templates, and I strongly suggest you use this version or later. Versions 2.1 and after are light-years ahead of earlier versions in terms of their stability, capability, and ease of use. If it gets much better, they'll have to start charging money for it.

I cannot thank Apple Computer enough for this tool, which makes it (relatively) easy for Macintosh users to augment and customize their system software and applications. Nothing like ResEdit exists on any other platform. The one problem is distribution: although it's "free," Apple charges a small fee for distribution. Consequently, you won't find it on commercial online services or in shareware collections. It is on Apple's Internet site (ftp.apple.com), and many user groups have paid the small fee to distribute it.

We'll create the Post resource template first, following the steps below (see Figure 8-12).

1. Make a copy of ResEdit and open the copy with ResEdit.

2. Locate and select the TMPL resource (you can just type "T" to move to the resource). Double-click to open it. A listing of available templates appears.

3. Press Command-K to create a new template. We're going to use Command-K again several different times in this procedure, to do several different things. What

FIGURE 8-12
Creating ResEdit templates

Open a copy of ResEdit.

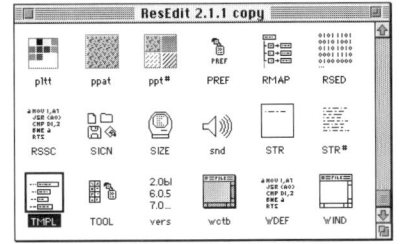

Double-click the TMPL resource class.

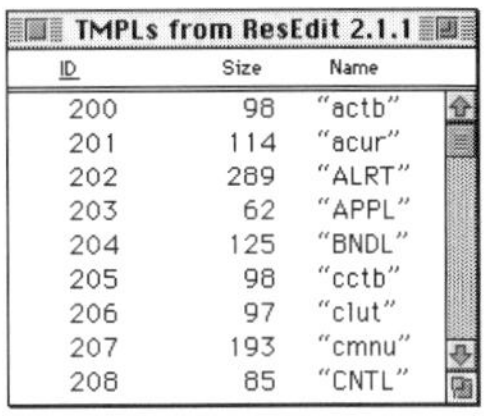

ResEdit displays a list of resource templates.

Press Command-K to create a new template. ResEdit displays a window where you can edit the definition of the template.

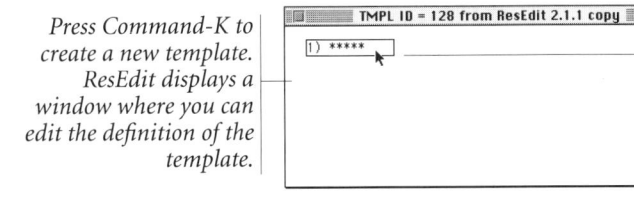

Select the first field tag in the template and press Command-K.

ResEdit creates two new fields.

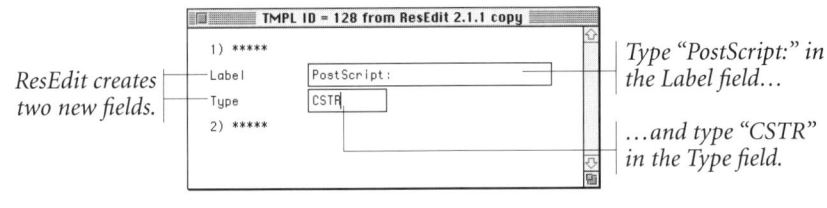

Type "PostScript:" in the Label field…

…and type "CSTR" in the Type field.

Press Command-I. ResEdit displays the Info window for your new resource.

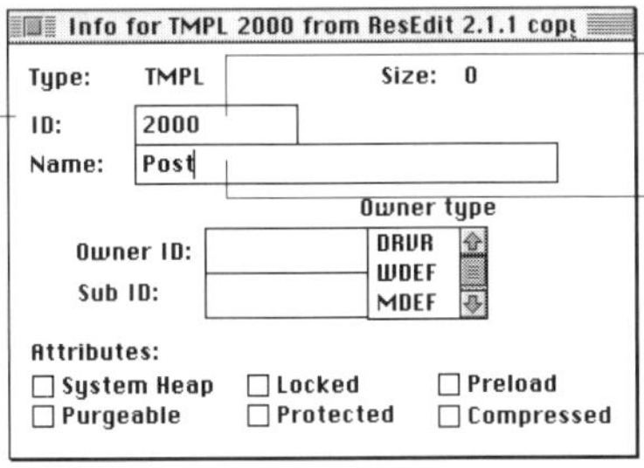

Type an ID number for the resource here.

Enter a name (in this case, "Post") for the template here.

Press Command-W twice to close the Info window and the TMPL window, and save the copy of ResEdit.

Command-K does varies depending on the context you're in (usually changing based on what you've got selected). Command-K generally means "create another one," with the object being created determined by what window you're in or what you've got selected. In this case, a new, empty template appears.

4. Select the field tag "1)*****" in the template window and press Command-K to create a new field. Two new fields, Label and Type appear, along with the field tag "2)*****".

5. Type "PostScript:" in the Label field, then type "CSTR" in the Type field.

6. Press Command-I to display the Info window for the template. Type a fairly high number (I use 2000) in the ID field. You do this to keep the new resource ID from conflicting with the preexisting templates. Press Tab to move to the Name field. Type "Post" in the Name field and press Command-W twice to close both the Info window and the TMPL window.

Your new resource template appears in the listing of templates.

Follow the same procedure to create three more resource templates, entering the values shown in Table 8-3 in each field as you create it. The labels aren't technically necessary—they just make the resources a little easier to decipher. Some data types (such as AWRDs and ALNGs) don't need labels—they're just byte padding in the resource and aren't displayed when you open the resource with the template.

We've just built four new ResEdit tools for creating and editing FreeHand's external resource files. Save your changes and quit this copy of ResEdit. We'll be using the copy of ResEdit we've modified, so you can throw away the original copy of ResEdit (just kidding—back it up so that you'll always be able to retrace your steps if something doesn't work).

To make sure that you've correctly created the templates, follow these steps (see Figure 8-13).

1. Open the modified copy of ResEdit.

2. Press Command-N to create a new file. Type a name for the file and press Return. A new file window opens.

3. Press Command-K to create a new resource. ResEdit displays the Select New Type dialog box.

4. Scroll through the list of templates until you find one of the templates you added to this copy of ResEdit. Select one and press Return to close the dialog box.

If you've built the new templates correctly, ResEdit creates a new resource and opens a view of the resource that's formatted

TABLE 8-3
Template parameters

Name:	Field:	Label:	Type:
Xvrs	1	Just enter 0	CSTR
GnEf	1	Version:	DWRD
	2	Type:	DWRD
	3	Number of parameters:	DWRD
	4	Name:	CSTR
	5		AWRD
	6	User name:	CSTR
	7		AWRD
	8	PostScript resources needed:	OCNT
	9	*****	LSTC
	10	ID# (-1000)	DWRD
	11	*****	LSTE
	12	PostScript to invoke effect:	CSTR
	13		ALNG
	14	UIrz ID:	DLNG
	15	*****	LSTB
	16	Type:	DLNG
	17	Minimum:	DLNG
	18	Maximum:	DLNG
	19	Default:	DLNG
	20	*****	LSTE
UIrz	1	Number of items:	DWRD
	2	*****	LSTB
	3	Type:	CSTR
	4		AWRD
	5	Frame:	RECT
	6	Resource ID:	DWRD
	7	Flags:	H004
	8	Title:	CSTR
	9		AWRD
	10	Tag:	DLNG
	11	*****	LSTE

FIGURE 8-13
Testing the resource templates

Create a new resource file.

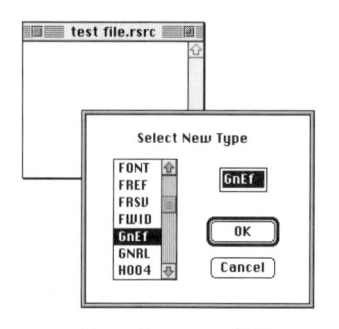

Press Command-K to add a new resource.

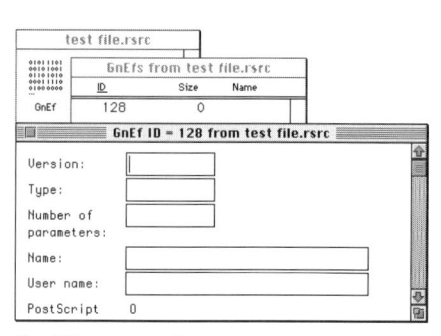

ResEdit creates the resource and displays the resource template.

according to the template's instructions. If this doesn't happen, go back to the steps above and try to figure out what went wrong. Are you sure you're using the copy of ResEdit you modified?

Test all four of the templates. When you're through, you can throw this dummy resource file away.

What do these resources do? When you choose a custom fill or stroke from the Inspector's popup menu, FreeHand looks for a GnEf matching the menu item. The GnEf then tells FreeHand where to look for the UIrz resource, which contains the text edit fields, buttons, and color wells that appear in the Inspector. Values in the GnEf then set the defaults for the Inspector items. The GnEf also tells FreeHand the IDs of the Post resources the effect needs to print and how to invoke the effect when it's applied to a path.

GnEfs are the key to FreeHand's custom stroke and fill resources (see Figure 8-14).

Creating new PostScript lines and fills. Even if you don't know PostScript, this section shows you how to add a variety of new PostScript strokes and fills to FreeHand. If you do know PostScript, the examples in this section will show you how to fit your code into FreeHand's scheme of things. There are really three ways to add PostScript strokes and fills to FreeHand.

◆ Add new lines and fills based on support routines already inside FreeHand.

◆ Add new lines and fills based on support routines outside of FreeHand (in an external resource file).

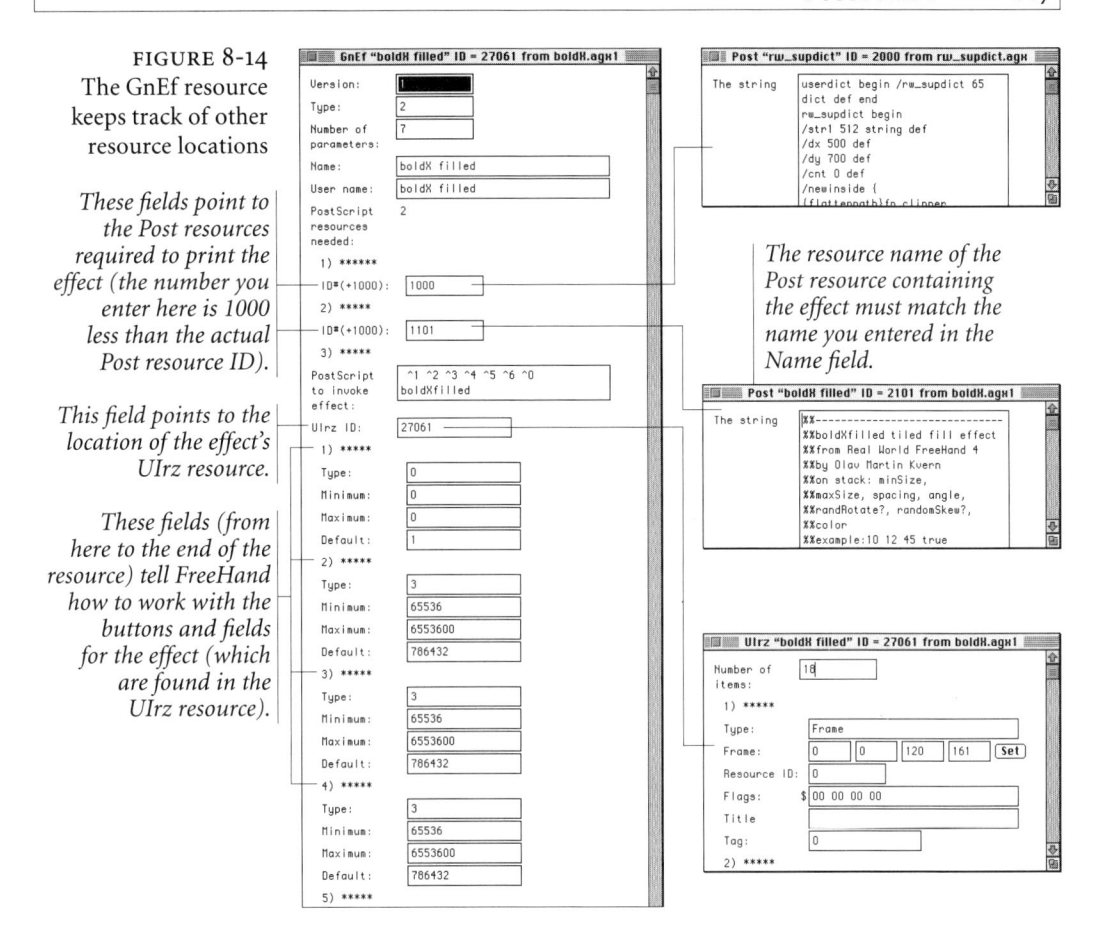

FIGURE 8-14
The GnEf resource keeps track of other resource locations

These fields point to the Post resources required to print the effect (the number you enter here is 1000 less than the actual Post resource ID).

This field points to the location of the effect's UIrz resource.

These fields (from here to the end of the resource) tell FreeHand how to work with the buttons and fields for the effect (which are found in the UIrz resource).

The resource name of the Post resource containing the effect must match the name you entered in the Name field.

- Mixing and matching the two above methods.

What's the big deal about support routines? While you can create a simple PostScript line by typing PostScript code in the PostScript dialog box, remember that you're limited to 255 characters. If you want an effect that repeats some shape along a path or changes shape randomly, you'll probably need more room. Most PostScript is based on pieces of code that are used over and over again to do some particular function (picking a random integer, for example). These pieces of code are called support routines. They can't create the effect you want by themselves, but they keep you from having to reinvent the wheel (that is, retype the same routines) every time you want to create a new PostScript effect.

Why would you want to use FreeHand's existing routines? FreeHand's PostScript user dictionary contains routines for repeating an object along a path (stroke effects), for filling a path with a repeated shape (fill effects), and for filling a path with a randomly rotated and scaled shape (more fill effects). I don't know about you, but it would take me literally years to write PostScript code that'd do these things. And there's more good stuff inside FreeHand for you to take advantage of. The drawback to using the internal support routines? You have to know what they are and how to use them.

Why would you want to use your own routines? Because you know them better. If you're a PostScript hack like David Blatner of PSpatterns fame, you've already written totally different routines for doing the same things (and different things, too) and have a certain number of PostScript effects you created for FreeHand 3 you want to convert to FreeHand 5 external resources.

Clearly, mixing and matching has the potential to give you the best of both worlds. Whenever possible, you can use the code that Altsys spent blood, sweat, and person-years creating. And then, when necessary, you can create your own support dictionary to do things beyond the scope of the built-in code.

Creating Custom PostScript Strokes

You can use FreeHand's built-in custom stroke drawing routines to create virtually any line pattern you can imagine. Here's how it works. FreeHand's custom PostScript stroke routines (found in the "newrope" procedure) take instructions for one object and repeat that object along a path. The procedures scale, space, and color the objects on the path according to the values you enter in the Stroke Inspector (see Figure 8-15).

Creating a GnEf resource. First, we need to fill in a GnEf resource for our custom stroke (see Table 8-4).

1. Start ResEdit and create a new resource file.

2. Press Command-K and create a new GnEf resource. Fill in the fields in the GnEf resource as shown in Table 8-4.

3. Press Command-I and give the GnEf resource an ID that's higher than that of any GnEf ID in FreeHand (above 23000

FIGURE 8-15
How FreeHand draws custom PostScript lines

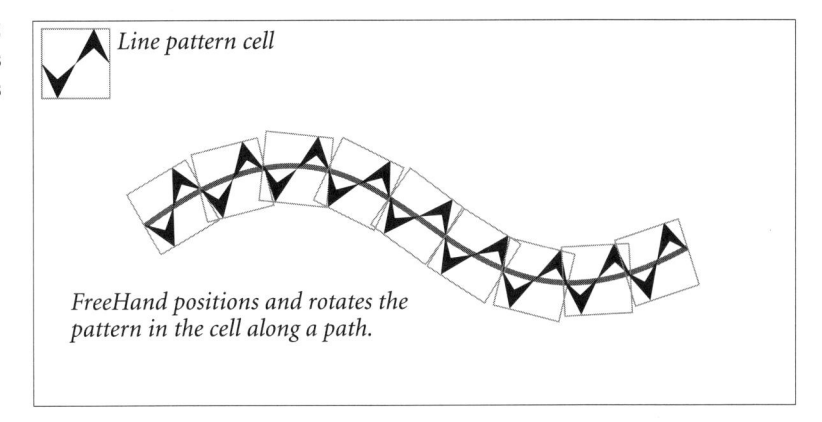

Line pattern cell

FreeHand positions and rotates the pattern in the cell along a path.

is safe, but keep the ID number under 28000—I've gotten weird "out of memory" errors for higher IDs). Enter the same name for the effect as you entered in the User name field of the GnEf.

4. Save your work.

Tip:
On Beyond Z

When you're creating new custom PostScript stroke effects, you've got to make sure that they appear on the Stroke Inspector's popup menu following the built-in effects. To do this, type characters in front of the names of your effect so they'll get sorted to the end of the list. I use "~" ("~Hexagon", for example).

Getting the PostScript code you need. Next, we'll create the PostScript for your new custom stroke effect. The heart of a FreeHand

TABLE 8-4
Creating a GnEf resource for a custom stroke effect

Field:	Example:	What it means:
Version	1	Version number
Type	3	Type (2 = custom fill, 3 = custom line)
Number of parameters	4	Number of PostScript parameters—all custom fill effects have four: color, width, length, and spacing

TABLE 8-4
Creating a GnEf resource for a custom stroke effect (continued)

Field:	Example:	What it means:
Name	~Hexagon	The internal name for your custom stroke effect. This name must match the name of the last Post resource you refer to. Use a tilde (~) or other character to put your new effect at the end of the popup menu (see "On Beyond Z," later in this chapter, for the reason we need to do this).
User name	~Hexagon	Name of the custom stroke effect as you want it to appear on the popup menu in the Stroke Inspector. Again, see "On Beyond Z," later in this chapter, for the reason for the tilde (~).
Post resource #1	145	Location of supdict (this resource ID is 1000 less than the actual Post ID—the actual Post containing the support dictionary is 1145).
Post resource #2	146	Location of ropedict (again, this ID is 1000 less—the actual Post ID is 1146).

TABLE 8-4
Creating a GnEf resource for a custom stroke effect (continued)

Field:	Example:	What it means:
Post resource #3	1200	This is the location of the PostScript you need to draw the object you're repeating along the path (again, this number is 1,000 less than the actual ID of the Post resource you're referring to).
PostScript to invoke effect	{~Hexagon} ^1 ^2 ^3 ^0 newrope	PostScript needed to draw the effect. The variables ^1, ^2, ^3, and ^0 refer to the Width field, the Length field, the Spacing field, and the color in the color well, respectively.
UIrz ID	0	All custom PostScript stroke effects use the same UIrz.

Control:	Field:	Value:
Control 1	Type	0 0 = color well, 2, 3 = text edit field, in points, 4 = text edit field, in degrees, 6 = text edit field, integer, 7 = boolean (a checkbox), 8 = text edit field, percentage
	Minimum	0
	Maximum	0
	Default	0

TABLE 8-4
Creating a GnEf resource for a custom stroke effect (continued)

Control:	Field:	Value:
Control 2	Type	3
	Minimum	0*
	Maximum	19660500*
	Default	1572840*
Control 3	Type	2
	Minimum	0*
	Maximum	19660500*
	Default	1572840*
Control 4	Type	3
	Minimum	0
	Maximum	19660500*
	Default	1572840*

* Multiply the measurement you want by 65,535 to come up with the value you enter here.

custom stroke effect is a kind of cell—like a tiny FreeHand page that's one unit square. The size of the unit itself doesn't matter because the scale of the cell gets determined later by the values you enter in the Width and Length text edit fields in the Stroke Inspector. The zero point of this line-drawing cell is at its center, and all of FreeHand's drawing commands (which you use to construct the line pattern) get their coordinates relative to this zero point.

You can create an enlarged version of this cell to use in plotting the placement of line segments and paths inside the cell, as shown in Figure 8-16.

1. Open FreeHand and press Command-N to create a new file.

2. In the Document Inspector, select Custom from the popup menu. Enter "0p100" for both the width and height of the page, and enter a bleed amount of "0p50".

3. In the Setup Inspector, enter "0p10" in the Grid Size field and press Return.

FIGURE 8-16
Coordinate matrix for creating custom lines

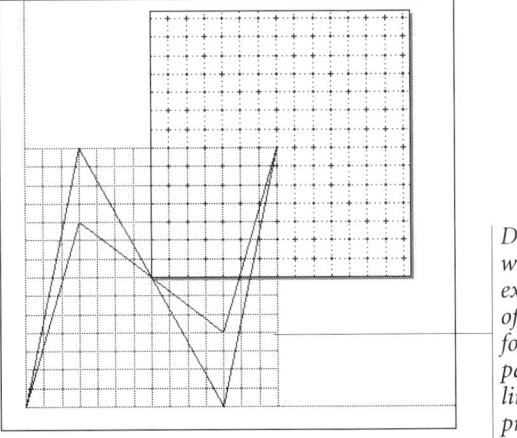

Draw whatever you want in this area, then export the graphic in one of the Adobe Illustrator formats and extract the pattern for your custom line using your word processor.

4. Create a grid that's 100 points square, drawing grid lines every ten points.

5. Select the grid, press Command-G to group it, and press Command-Option-B to display the Object Inspector (if the Inspector's not visible, display it first by pressing Command-I).

6. Type "-50" in both the X and Y fields and press Return. FreeHand moves your grid so that its center point is precisely above the bottom-left corner of your publication's page.

7. Send the grid to the background layer.

Now that you can use the grid as a guide for creating your new line style, draw anything you want inside the grid. When you've got something you think would make a good line pattern (start with a simple shape), export the file as an Adobe Illustrator file (any format), and then use a word processor to extract the line pattern from the EPS graphic.

Why not export the graphic as a Generic EPS file? Because the coordinate system used in FreeHand's EPS is based on the lower-left corner of the pasteboard—not on the lower-left corner of the page (see Figure 8-17). This makes absolutely no difference to applications importing or printing the EPS, but makes it more difficult to use this technique. Illustrator format keeps things simple, which is just what we want, in this case.

1. Open the file with your word processor.
2. Delete everything preceding the first line ending with an "m" ("moveto") instruction.
3. Delete everything from the end of the last line ending with an "L" or a "C" to the end of the file.
4. Delete any occurrence of "vmrs", "vmr", "vms", "u", or "U" remaining in the file.

At this point, the file contains only the commands for drawing the shape (or shapes) you drew.

FIGURE 8-17
Which would you rather work with?

FreeHand version
```
1735.3014 1559 m
1692 1533.9998 L
1648.6986 1558.9998 L
1648.6986 1609 L
1692 1634.0002 L
1735.3014 1609.0002 L
1735.3014 1559 L
```

Illustrator version
```
43.3014 -25 m
0 -50.0002 L
-43.3014 -25.0002 L
-43.3014 25 L
0 50.0002 L
43.3014 25.0002 L
43.3014 -25 L
```

Once you've got the line pattern, you can plug it into a couple of PostScript routines. Type the code shown below, replacing the variables shown in italics with the names you want your routines to use and with the line pattern you extracted from the EPS graphic in the previous procedure.

```
%%call FreeHand's set of stroke effect procedures
ropedict begin
%%Enter the name for your custom line here
/linePatternName
{
blocksetup
%%paste your drawing commands here
drawingCommands
%%enter "s" instead of "f" to stroke the path
f
Q} def
end
```

Here's an example line pattern.

```
ropedict begin
/~Hexagon
{
blocksetup
```

POSTSCRIPT 615

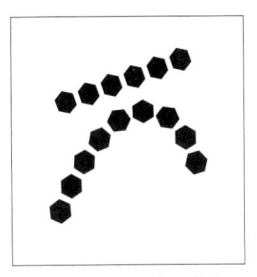

Printed example of the Hexagon custom stroke

```
.01 .01 scale
43.3014 -25 m
0 -50.0002 L
-43.3014 -25.0002 L
-43.3014 25 L
0 50.0002 L
43.3014 25.0002 L
43.3014 -25 L
f Q} def
end %%Make sure you add a space or a return here!
```

Creating a Post resource. Now that we've gotten the code we need, it's time to create a Post resource (see Figure 8-18).

1. If you're not still in ResEdit, start ResEdit and open the external resource file you've been working on.

2. Press Command-K and add a new Post resource.

3. Open the Post resource you created and paste the code from your word processor into the resource.

4. Set the Post resource ID to the last ID you entered in the GnEF (in our earlier example, you'd use ID 2200). Give the Post resource the same name as you've entered in the User name field of the GnEf (in our example, "~Hexagon").

5. Save the resource file.

Adding an Xvrs Resource. The last thing you need to do, before you launch FreeHand and test your new custom stroke effect, is to add an Xvrs resource to your external resource file. If your external resource file contains an Xvrs resource, FreeHand won't complain about the file during startup (see Figure 8-19).

1. Open the resource file you added the GnEf and Post resources to.

2. Create a new resource of type Xvrs.

3. Enter "0" (or anything, for that matter) in the Xvrs resource.

4. Give the Xvrs resource an ID of 9999.

5. Save your file.

FIGURE 8-18
Creating a Post resource

Press Command-K to create a new resource. ResEdit displays the Select New Type dialog box.

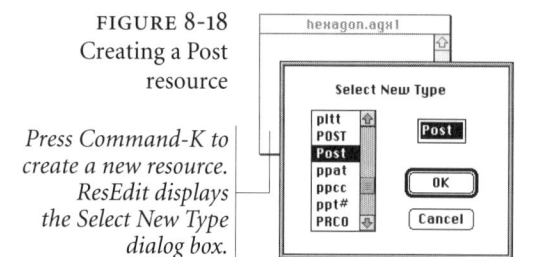

Choose Post from the list of resource types, or type "Post" in the field.

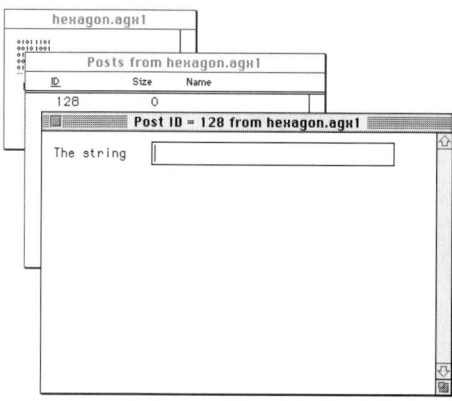

ResEdit displays a new Post template.

Copy text out of your word processor and paste it into the Post resource.

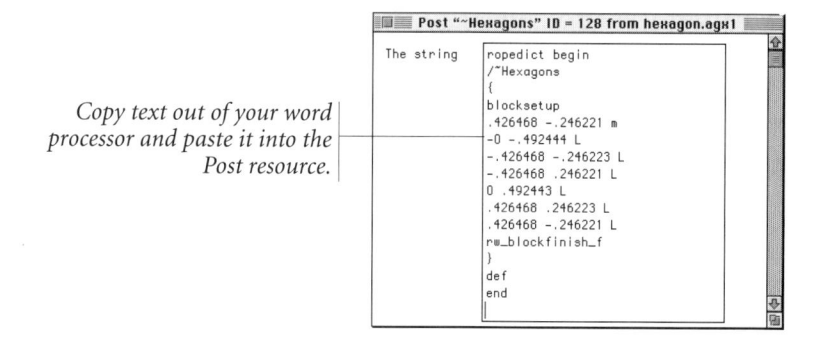

FIGURE 8-19
Creating an Xvrs resource

Press Command-K to create a new resource. ResEdit displays the Select New Type dialog box.

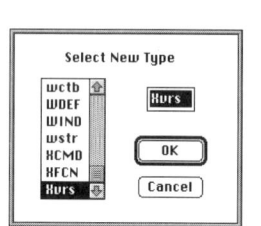

Choose Xvrs from the list of resource templates, or type "Xvrs" in the field.

ResEdit creates a new Xvrs resource.

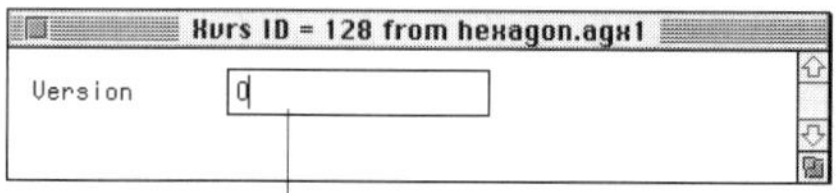

Type anything in this field.

Press Command-I to display the Info window for the Xvrs Resource.

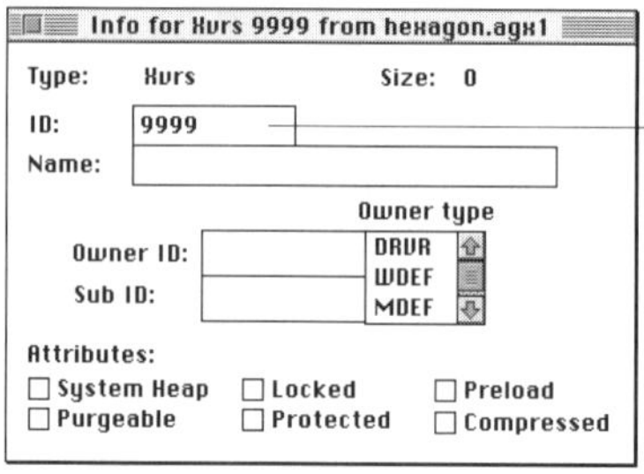

Type 9999 in this field.

Tip:	In some cases, you might want to omit Xvrs resources from your external resource files because you might want to choose which external resource files FreeHand loads. To keep the resource from loading, click the Cancel button when FreeHand displays the "earlier version" message. If you do this, you won't have to move files around in the Finder to keep FreeHand from loading them.
Omitting Xvrs Resources on Purpose	

Setting the resource file's type and creator. If an external resource file doesn't have the correct file type and creator, FreeHand ignores it. Here's how to add those key bits of information (see Figure 8-20).

1. Choose Get Info for *filename* (where *filename* is the name you gave the file when you created it) from the File menu. ResEdit displays the Info dialog box for the file.

2. Type "AGX1" in the Type field and type "FH50" in the Creator field.

3. Press Command-W to close the dialog box. ResEdit asks if you want to save your changes. You do, so click Yes.

4. Quit ResEdit.

Testing your new external resource file. Test your new external resource file by opening FreeHand, drawing a path, and pressing Command-Option-L to display the Stroke Inspector. Choose Custom from the Stroke Type popup menu. Can you see your example stroke effect on the Effect popup menu? If so, select it. If not, run

FIGURE 8-20
Setting the file type and creator

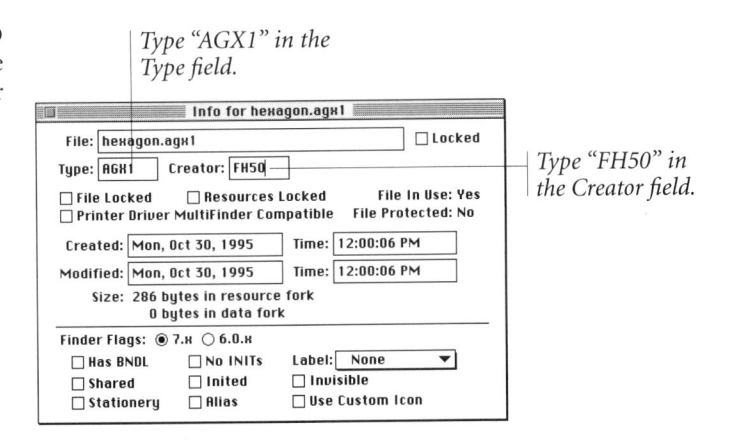

through the procedures above and try to see where you made an error (I got tired of getting errors because of mismatches between the PostScript procedure name, the "User name," and the "Internal name," so I started using the same name for all three purposes).

Apply the stroke effect to a path and try printing the file. If it prints, congratulations! You've just added a stroke effect to your copy of FreeHand. If it doesn't print, it's most likely you've either typed something wrong or have made an incorrect entry in the Post resource containing the drawing commands (suspect this first if you get an "undefined" PostScript error).

This is where LaserTalk comes in handy; you can troubleshoot your PostScript by stepping through it, line by line, while in direct communication with your printer.

Adding a preview of your stroke effect. As far as I know, you won't be able to add a preview image of your custom stroke effect, as FreeHand does for its built-in effects. At this point, I can get *something* to appear in the preview window, but it's never what I want. If you figure it out, please give me a call!

Tip:
Space Out

Make sure that you add a space or a carriage return following the last character of your PostScript code. If you don't, characters FreeHand sends following your effect might get appended to one of your procedure names, resulting in PostScript files that won't print. This is especially true for the PostScript you enter in the GnEf—FreeHand's going to put a "Q" right at the end of it. If there's no space, you're going to be in trouble.

Creating Custom Fill Effects

Because you can create tiled fills inside FreeHand, there's not much need to create fill effects that simply repeat one pattern over and over again. If you want a fill effect that randomly resizes, scales, or skews a pattern inside a filled object or if you want to create a tiled effect where each tile rotates around its center point, however, custom fills are just the ticket.

Creating a UIrz resource for a custom fill. The contents of the UIrz resources are the buttons, fields, and static text you see in the

Fill Inspector. Your custom fill effect can use as many controls as you can shoehorn into the Inspector (not many!).

Creating UIrz resources is a complex process, and the only way I can think of to make it easier is to show you how to create an example custom PostScript fill. I'll try to explain what we're doing as we work through the process.

Start ResEdit and create a new resource file in your FreeHand folder. Set the file's type to AGX1 and its creator to FH50 (if you've forgotten how to do this, refer back to the procedure for creating external resource files, earlier in this chapter). Create a new UIrz resource and fill it in as shown in Table 8-5.

The Flags field in the UIrz resource tells FreeHand how to format and how to interpret the control. Table 8-6 shows what the different flags mean.

Different flags can be added together. To produce a color well you can drag color swatches out of (00020000) or drop color swatches into (00010000), which also displays the name of the color to the right of the color well (00080000), and displays that name in nine-point Geneva (00000002), you'd enter 000B0002 ("B" because 8 + 2 + 1 = B in the hexadecimal universe—where you count 0, 1, 2, 3, 4, 5, 6, 7, 8, 9, A, B, C, D, E, F).

TABLE 8-5
Example UIrz Resource

Item:	Field:	Enter:	What it does:
Number of items		18	Sets the number of user interface items displayed by this fill effect.
1	Type	Frame	"Frame" is the area of the Inspector that the effect's controls take up. Every UIrz resource starts with a frame.
	Frame	0 0 121 161*	This rectangle takes up (more or less) all of the available space in the Inspector (that is, everything but the Inspector buttons and the Fill Type popup menu).

* FreeHand's rectangles—whether they're for a Frame, a TextView, a BtnView, or a ColorWell, are measured, PostScript-style, from their lower-left corners. The lower-left corner of the Inspector, therefore, is 0,0. The measurements are in pixels.

TABLE 8-5
Example
UIrz Resource
(continued)

Item:	Field:	Enter:	What it does:
1 (continued)	ID	0	Leave this at zero for the UIrz resources you create.
	Flags	00000000	See Table 8-6 for a description.
	Title		If the control has a title, enter it here. Otherwise, leave this field blank.
	Tag	0	Leave this set to zero for the UIrz resources you create.
2	Type	ColorWell	Creates a FreeHand color well.
	Frame	7 140 115 160	Defines a frame for the color well. Note that this frame is wide enough to display the name of any color you drop into it.
	ID		0
	Flags	000B0002	
	Title		
	Tag	0	
3	Type	TextView	Creates both static text (labels) and text edit fields.
	Frame	76 106 108 122	
	ID	0	
	Flags	00030002	
	Title		
	Tag	0	
4	Type	TextView	
	Frame	42 106 74 122	
	ID	0	
	Flags	00030002	
	Title		
	Tag	0	

TABLE 8-5
Example
UIrz Resource
(continued)

Item:	Field:	Enter:	What it does:
5	Type	TextView	
	Frame	76 87 108 103	
	ID	0	
	Flags	00030002	
	Title		
	Tag	0	
6	Type	TextView	
	Frame	76 68 108 84	
	ID	0	
	Flags	00030002	
	Title		
	Tag	0	
7	Type	BtnView	Creates buttons—checkboxes, radio buttons, and icon buttons.
	Frame	6 49 116 63	
	ID	0	
	Flags	00050002	
	Title	Random rotation	
	Tag	0	
8	Type	BtnView	
	Frame	6 36 116 48	
	ID	0	
	Flags	00050002	
	Title	Random skewing	
	Tag	0	
9	Type	TextView	
	Frame	1 106 40 122	
	ID	0	
	Flags	00800002	
	Title	Size:	
	Tag	0	

TABLE 8-5
Example
UIrz Resource
(continued)

Item:	Field:	Enter:	What it does:
10	Type	TextView	
	Frame	1 87 74 103	
	ID	0	
	Flags	00800002	
	Title	Spacing:	
	Tag	0	
11	Type	TextView	
	Frame	1 68 74 84	
	ID	0	
	Flags	00800002	
	Title	Angle:	
	Tag	0	
12	Type	TextView	
	Frame	108 68 120 84	
	ID	0	
	Flags	00000002	
	Title	°	
	Tag	0	
13	Type	MUView	Draws a dotted line across the Inspector, separating different sections.
	Frame	0 136 121 137	
	ID	0	
	Flags	00002002	
	Title		
	Tag	0	
14	Type	MUView	
	Frame	0 65 121 66	
	ID	0	
	Flags	00002002	
	Title		
	Tag	0	

TABLE 8-5
Example
UIrz Resource
(continued)

Item:	Field:	Enter:	What it does:
15	Type	MUView	
	Frame	0 32 121 33	
	ID	0	
	Flags	00002002	
	Title		
	Tag	0	
16	Type	TextView	
	Frame	1 3 121 15	
	ID	0	
	Flags	00040002	
	Title	Real World FreeHand 5.5	Your message here
	Tag	0	
17	Type	TextView	
	Frame	40 125 76 138	
	ID	0	
	Flags	00040002	
	Title	min:	
	Tag	0	
18	Type	TextView	
	Frame	74 125 110 138	
	ID	0	
	Flags	00040002	
	Title	max:	
	Tag	0	

Creating a GnEf resource for a custom fill. You create GnEf resources for custom fills exactly as you would for a custom stroke effect (see "Creating a GnEf Resource," earlier in this chapter). For our example custom fill, enter the values shown in Table 8-7.

Creating a Post resource for a custom fill. I drew the "X" shape using the FreeHand grid file we created (see "Getting the PostScript Code You Need," earlier in this chapter), exported it as an

TABLE 8-6
Selected UIrz flags
and what they mean

Item:	Flag:	What it means:
Any	00000002	Display text in nine-point Geneva
MUView	00002000	Draw a gray line on either side of the text
ColorWell	00010000	Color swatches can be dropped in
	00020000	Color swatches can be dragged out
	00080000	Display the color name to the right of the color well
TextView	00008000	Left-align text
	00040000	Center text
	00800000	Right-align text
	00010000	Draw a border around the text
	00020000	Editable field
	00400000	Italicize text
	00080000	Make text bold
BtnView	00010000	Button toggles when clicked (like a checkbox)
	00040000	Button is a checkbox
	00080000	Button is a radio button
	00100000	Button is an icon button

Illustrator 1.1 file, and extracted the drawing commands from the Illustrator file using Word. I then pasted the drawing commands into a fill procedure (which I derived from FreeHand's own Squares custom fill). Figure 8-21 shows examples of this fill effect.

Enter the text shown below in your word processor.

```
%%boldXfilled tiled fill effect
%%from Real World FreeHand 5
%%by Olav Martin Kvern
%%on stack: minSize,
%%maxSize, spacing, angle,
%%randRotate?, randomSkew?,
%%color
```

TABLE 8-7
Example GnEf

Field:	What you enter:
Version	1
Type	2
Number of parameters	7
Name	boldXfilled
User name	boldXfilled
PostScript resource 1	145
PostScript resource 2	1101
PostScript to invoke effect	^1 ^2 ^3 ^4 ^5 ^6 ^0 boldXfilled
UIrz ID	27061

Field:	Label:	What you enter:
UIrz item 1*	Type	0
	Minimum	0
	Maximum	0
	Default	1
UIrz item 2	Type	3
	Minimum	65535
	Maximum	6553500
	Default	786432
UIrz item 3	Type	3
	Minimum	65535
	Maximum	6553500
	Default	786432

* The GnEf resource refers to the UIrz controls in order and starts counting following the Frame item in the UIrz. In this case, the color well is UIrz item #1, UIrz items 2 and 3 set the minimum and maximum size of the "X," and UIrz items 5 and 6 are the checkboxes controlling random rotation and random skewing, respectively. When FreeHand uses the values from these items in the PostScript it sends to the printer (as directed by the GnEf), everything shifts down by one—the value in UIrz item 1 is plugged in for variable "^0", the value for UIrz item 2 is entered for "^1", and so on.

TABLE 8-7
Example GnEf
(continued)

Field:	Label:	What you enter:
UIrz item 4	Type	4
	Minimum	-23592960
	Maximum	23592960
	Default	1966080
UIrz item 5	Type	7
	Minimum	0
	Maximum	1
	Default	0
UIrz Item 6	Type	7
	Minimum	0
	Maximum	1
	Default	0

```
%%example:10 12 45 true
%%[0 0 0 1] boldXfilled
supdict begin
/boldXfilledLoop
{ystart spacing ystart abs
{/ycur xdf
xstart spacing xstart abs
{q ycur m
currentpoint translate
%%random rotation?
randomRotate true eq
{360 randint rotate} if
%%random skewing?
randomSkew true eq
{
/xSkew 360 randint def
/ySkew 360 randint def
[1 xSkew sin ySkew sin neg 1 0 0] concat} if
%random scaling?
randomScale true eq
{maxSize minSize sub randint minSize add /size xdf} if
%%scale the tile
size 100 div dup scale
q
%%start drawing commands
-25 -50 m
-50 -25 L
-25 0 L
-50 25 L
```

```
-25 50 L
0 25 L
25 50 L
50 25 L
25 0 L
50 -25 L
25 -50 L
0 -25 L
-25 -50 L
%%end drawing commands
f
Q
Q
} for
} for
}
def
end
/boldXfilled
{
supdict begin
q newinside
/color xdf
colorchoice
/randomSkew xdf
/randomRotate xdf
/angle xdf
/spacing xdf
/maxSize xdf
/minSize xdf
minSize maxSize eq
{/randomScale false def minSize /size xdf} {/randomScale
true def} ifelse
/xstart x1 x2 add 2 div neg spacing sub def
/ystart y1 y2 add 2 div neg spacing sub def
dx 2 div dy 2 div translate
angle rotate boldXfilledLoop
Q end
} def
```

Now that we've got the code we need, it's time to create a new Post resource.

1. Start ResEdit (if it's not already running) and open the external resource file you've been working on (if it's not already open).

2. Add a new Post resource.

3. Paste the code from your word processor into the Post resource.

FIGURE 8-21
Your new custom fill effect

4. Press Command-I to display the Info dialog box for the resource. Set the resource's ID to 2101 (remember, it's 1000 higher than the number you entered in the GnEf). Name the Post resource "boldXfilled".

5. Save the resource file.

Add an Xvrs resource to the file (see "Adding an Xvrs Resource," earlier in this chapter) and save the file. The next time you start FreeHand, you should see a new menu item "boldXfilled" on FreeHand's list of custom fills in the Fill Inspector. When you choose this item from the popup menu, FreeHand should display the controls for your new effect in the Inspector.

PostScript Postscript

Though this has been the hardest chapter in the book to write, I feel I've only scratched the surface of what you can do with FreeHand and PostScript. Once I figure out how to do text effects, I may even have to create an addendum to this book. Or, this being a book by Peachpit Press, maybe we can do *The Little FreeHand PostScript Fills Book*. Now there's an idea!

Appendices
Index

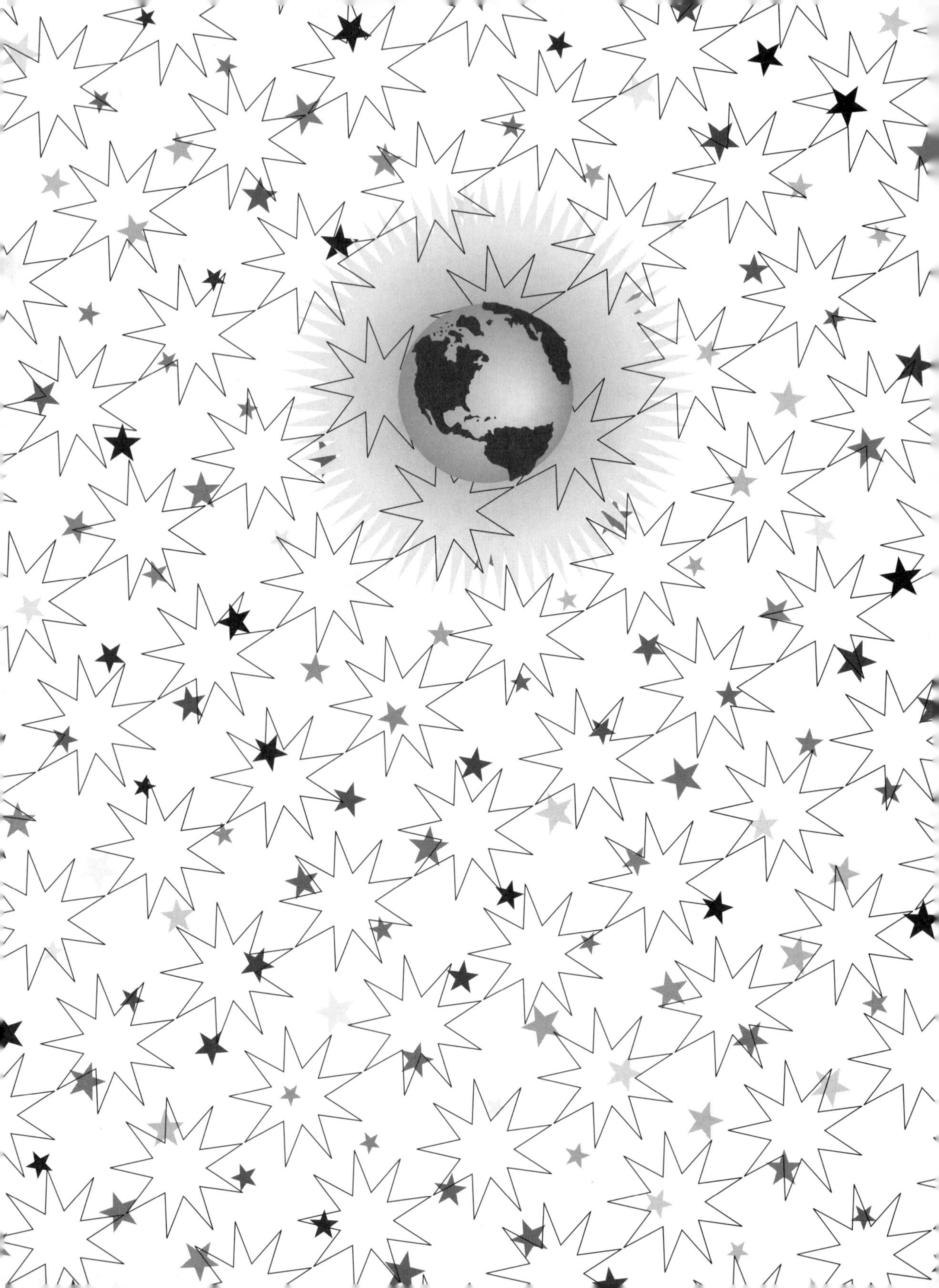

APPENDIX A 🎣 SYSTEM

Like any other desktop publishing tool, FreeHand does not exist in a vacuum. Sure, you can create great-looking publications without using a single other program—but the usefulness and power of FreeHand can be multiplied many times by having an array of utilities and System resources available.

Sometimes these additional tools perform just one, limited function; sometimes they're entire applications in their own right. In either case, having them around either improves your FreeHand productivity or (essentially) adds capabilities to FreeHand.

The first thing you need is a system configuration that is both reliable and that fits you like a glove. Your Macintosh should respond to your directions exactly the way you want it to, without crashing in mid-operation or doing anything you didn't expect.

In this chapter (indeed, in the rest of the book), I'm assuming that you're using System 7.0 or higher, and all the illustrations and explanations are based on that assumption.

System

Your Macintosh system is made up of the System file itself and your extensions, control panel devices (which I'll refer to as "cdevs"), Apple Menu items, and fonts. Extensions contain supplements and changes to the system software that get loaded when you start your Macintosh. Control panel devices are utilities that let you change characteristics of your system or extensions (like the background screen pattern, or what network type you're using). Cdevs sometimes contain extension-like material as well that gets loaded at startup. Part of an extension (or cdev with code) is in RAM all the time, waiting for you to do whatever it is that activates it.

Apple Menu items are small utility programs that get put in the Apple Menu Items folder in the System Folder. (Actually, anything you put in this folder automatically shows up on the Apple menu; it's just that Apple Menu items are put here by default.)

Fonts are resources which, when dragged onto the System Folder icon, are placed in the System file (in System 7.0.x) or Fonts folder (in System 7.1). Or, you can use a font-management utility like MasterJuggler or Suitcase to tell the system where the fonts are. Once fonts are installed on your system, applications (such as FreeHand) can call on and use them.

The following are a few more of my "golden rules."

- ◆ Have only one System file per Macintosh.

    You can use a utility to "bless" one of several Systems on a Macintosh, but I've never seen it work well. The only reason to try this is if you're working with a KanjiTalk or Chinese System and need to switch back and forth between localized Systems. Otherwise, don't. If you need to store unused fonts somewhere, store them in suitcase files, not in an unused System file.

- ◆ Don't switch to the most current System version until it's been around for a couple of months.

    Some System versions are buggy—some are even withdrawn by Apple after they've been in circulation for awhile. What you really need is an idiot friend who always installs the newest System version as soon as it's available—even before they're released (I'm this way, actually). Let them lose work because of incompatibilities and bugs. Then ask them about the new System software. Once their level of bitching and whining declines, you know it's safe to upgrade (by this time they're on to a new version, anyway).

◆ When you update your System, check all of your extensions and control panels for compatibility.

Check your applications, too, but you'll generally have more problems with the items that live inside the System folder. Most of the problems I had when I updated from System 6 to System 7 revolved around the extensions and cdevs I use (although the worst problems actually had to do with the ROMs in my video board).

If you suspect your extensions and cdevs are causing your problems, turn them off. To do this, restart your Macintosh and hold down Shift after you see the "happy Mac" icon (see "Extension Managers," later in this Chapter).

◆ Don't work on a live System file with ResEdit.

I lose work all the time doing this. It's a stupid thing to do.

◆ When you update your System, make sure that you use the Installer application—don't drag items over.

Apple's Installer application (used by most developers and Apple itself to install new software) sometimes needs to install low-level system resources which can't be simply dragged over. Many of the system updaters have these resources. Note that for applications that don't use the Apple Installer—such as FreeHand—many items that you need aren't automatically copied and aren't available by clicking the Customize button. In this case, you need to look at the disks, find the items you need, and copy them over manually. Do this as a last resort, however.

◆ Less is not more, but can be less trouble.

Every extension and cdev you use takes up RAM, and the more extensions and cdevs you have, the more likely it is that they'll conflict with each other or with your applications. Do you really need to have a rainbow-colored cursor? Or a rotating globe instead of a watch? Like the tree in the garden of Eden, the Macintosh gives us the ability to make our systems as weird and stupid as we want. Rule of thumb: If you're running more than 10 extensions/cdevs on a Macintosh with eight megabytes of RAM, it's time to exercise some restraint. Tell the snake you're not interested.

◆ Before you blame the application, check your System.
    As far as I can tell, 50 percent of the technical support calls to Macintosh application developers are about funky Systems, multiple Systems, corrupted font files, etc.

◆ Your system is more than your System.
    As wonderful as the Macintosh system is, a real desktop-publishing system includes other applications: word processors, other page-layout tools, font-editing software, utilities, and image-editing programs. The whole of the software on your Macintosh should be greater than the sum of its parts.

Extensions and Control Panels

As I mentioned earlier, extensions and (some) cdevs are little applications that are loaded when your system starts up. Part of an extension or cdev is always active in your Macintosh's memory, waiting for you to do something it needs to respond to.

ATM and TrueType. In the early days of Macintosh, you had to have a screen font for every size of type you used—unless you didn't mind your type looking jagged on screen. These days, Adobe Type Manager (ATM) produces smooth-looking characters on your screen (as smooth as they can be at your screen's resolution) from your Type 1 PostScript printer fonts. If you don't have the printer fonts, ATM won't produce better-looking type. Apple's TrueType fonts, which are included with System 7, also produce smooth type on screen.

Should you buy lots of TrueType fonts? Or should you get ATM and use PostScript Type 1 fonts? Which font format is better from FreeHand's point of view? While FreeHand supports TrueType, ATM and PostScript Type 1 fonts are your best bet. For me, the deciding factor is that PostScript Type 1 fonts print well on PostScript imagesetters. And—there's no nice way to say it: TrueType fonts don't.

MasterJuggler and Suitcase. These two extensions make everything about working with fonts easier and quicker, because you can add fonts to your system without opening the Font/DA Mover (pre-System 7), dragging them onto your System icon (System 7.0.x), or dragging them into the Fonts folder in your System folder (System 7.1 or newer). With either MasterJuggler or Suitcase, you can load and unload fonts in seconds, without having to claw your way through folders in the Finder. System 7 was supposed to make these extensions obsolete. It didn't.

That said, these two extensions do about the same things. I like MasterJuggler better, because it's got a better user interface and a great application launcher (again, so I don't have to dig through folders to find an application to launch—or clutter my desktop with aliases), but Suitcase is marketed by a larger company and gets updated (to keep up with system changes) more often.

Tip:
Where You Should Put Your Fonts

If you're using a font-management utilty (such as MasterJuggler or Suitcase), keep your outline (or printer) fonts in the same folder as the suitcase containing the bitmap (or screen) fonts. This folder can be anywhere.

If you're not using a font-management utility, store your bitmap fonts in the System file itself; or, in systems newer than System 7.1, in the Fonts folder.

Tip:
When FreeHand Can't Find Your Fonts

If you're using MasterJuggler or Suitcase and FreeHand is having trouble finding your outline fonts, put them into the correct location in the System folder: the Extensions folder in System 7.0.x, or the Fonts folder in System 7.1. Then restart your Macintosh.

Can FreeHand find the fonts now? If not, you're probably using an outdated version of your font management program (at the time of this writing, the current version of MasterJuggler is 1.9, and the current version of Suitcase is 2.1.4)—or an old version of ATM (the current version is 3.8).

Until you can update these utilities, you'll need to keep your fonts in your Fonts folder (under System 7.1; if you're using System 7.0.x, put the bitmaps in the System file and put the outlines in the Extensions folder). This is an inconvenience for people who like to keep their fonts in other folders, in other places. But this is the real world, and reality encompasses certain unpleasant facts. What's more important—keeping the fonts in another folder, or being able to use them? You choose.

ATR. Adobe Type Reunion (ATR) combines your font families into groups on your font menus (see Figure A-1). Instead of having separate menu choices for Minion and Minion Black, ATR shows you a menu item for "Minion," and lists "Regular" and "Black" on a submenu attached to the font family's name.

Previous versions of ATR didn't work very well with FreeHand (FreeHand would lose track of its filters while ATR was running), but the most current version (1.1) works just fine.

FIGURE A-1
Adobe Type Reunion

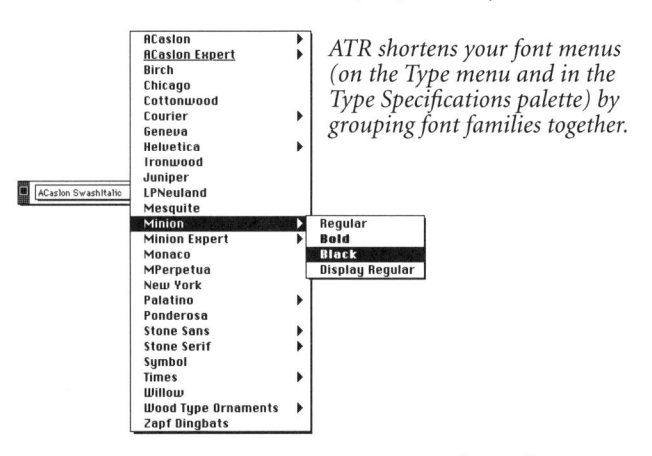

ATR shortens your font menus (on the Type menu and in the Type Specifications palette) by grouping font families together.

Super Boomerang. Super Boomerang, from the Now Utilities package, is a cdev that is active only when you're in a "standard file" dialog box (these are the dialog boxes where you see a listing of files you can open, save, or place). When Super Boomerang's running, a menu appears across the top of those dialog boxes (you can see it in many of the screen shots in this book). The File and Folder menus show you files and folders you've been working with recently. You can use this menu to switch from file to file, folder to folder, and volume to volume quickly, or you can use Boomerang's keyboard shortcuts to move even more quickly (see Figure A-2). You can also permanently add files and folders to these menus.

Do you frequently go to an Open or a Place dialog box and forget what file name you wanted—or where you left the file? If

FIGURE A-2
Super Boomerang

Super Boomerang displays a menu across the top of standard Open, Save, and Place dialog boxes.

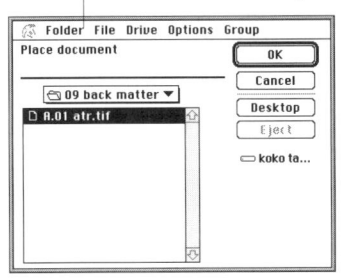

Super Boomerang's File and Folder menus display files and folders you've used recently. You can attach specific files and folders to the menus and assign keyboard shortcuts to them (Command-F, for example, takes me to my "fonts and DAs folder").

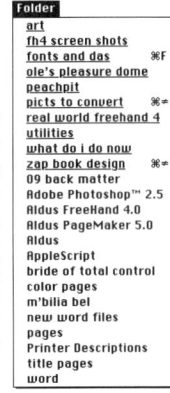

Choose Find from the Super Boomerang Options menu, and you can direct Super Boomerang to search your system for a files (or even for text inside files).

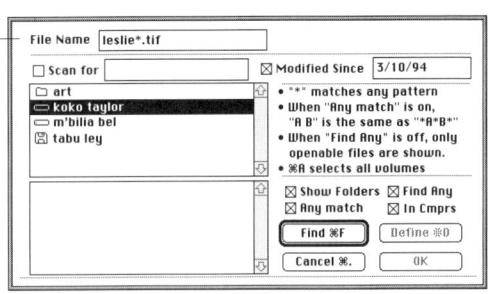

you do, you'll love Super Boomerang's Where Is feature. Choose Where Is from Super Boomerang's Options menu (or press Command-?), and Super Boomerang displays a nifty little dialog box that'll help you find your file. Whatever you named it. Wherever it is (see Figure A-3). Super Boomerang can even search the contents of files for text—and it does so with frightening speed.

QuicKeys. QuicKeys (version 2.1 or higher), from CE Software, is an extension that you use to create keyboard shortcuts and macros (a macro is a series of tasks performed in a sequence). If you find yourself wishing for more keyboard shortcuts in FreeHand (like a shortcut for the Move palette, to name only the most needed), get yourself a copy of QuicKeys and add them.

Tip:
Apply and close

As much as I love FreeHand's palettes, I find it's too easy to forget to close them when I don't need them—especially the Transform palette and the Align palette. The result? Sometimes, I lose sight of my publication. Figure A-3 shows how to create a QuicKey that applies the changes you've made in a palette, then closes the palette.

638   REAL WORLD FREEHAND 5.0|5.5

FIGURE A-3
Apply and close QuicKey

Display the QuicKeys control panel (unless you've changed the default, you can press Command-Option-Return).

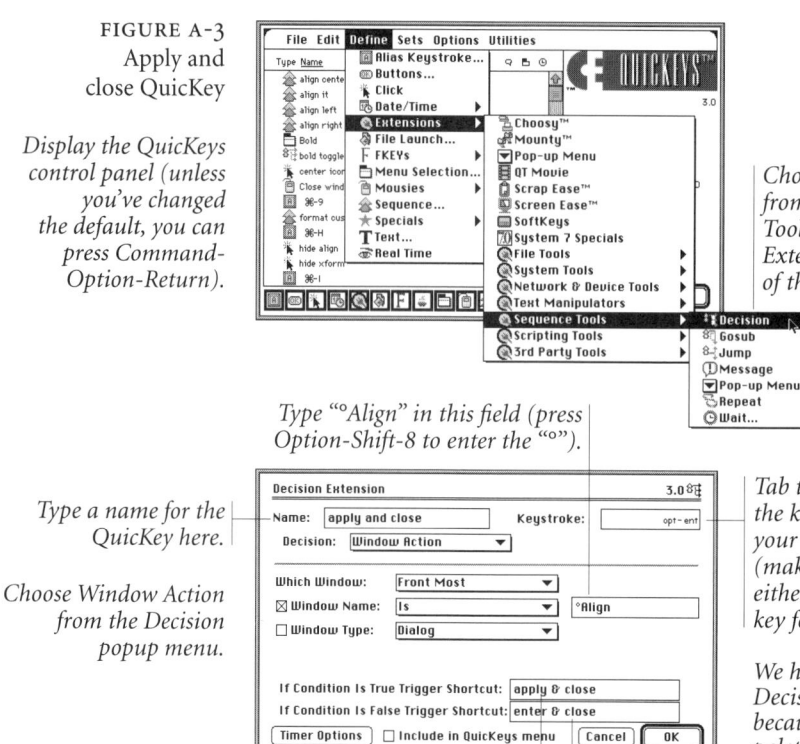

Choose Decision from the Sequence Tools submenu of the Extensions submenu of the Define menu.

Type "°Align" in this field (press Option-Shift-8 to enter the "°").

Type a name for the QuicKey here.

Choose Window Action from the Decision popup menu.

Tab to this field and press the keys you want to use for your keyboard shortcut (make sure you include either the Return or Enter key for this QuicKey).

We have to use a Decision QuicKey, because the Align palette (alone of all the palettes) doesn't apply its changes when you press Return (or Enter).

Enter these names—we'll create the QuicKeys that match them later.

Choose Sequence from the Define menu to create a new Sequence QuicKey.

QuicKeys displays the Sequence dialog box.

Type the same name for this QuicKey as you entered in the If Condition is True Trigger Shortcut field in the Decision Extension dialog box.

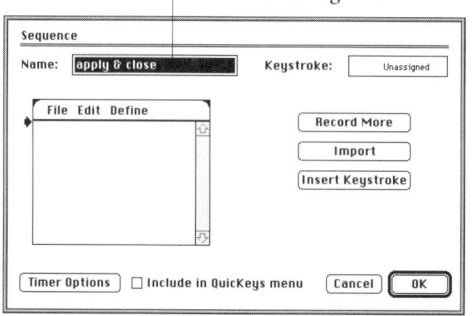

Choose Buttons from the Define menu to create a new Button QuicKey.

APPENDIX A: SYSTEM 639

FIGURE A-3
Apply and
close QuicKey
(continued)

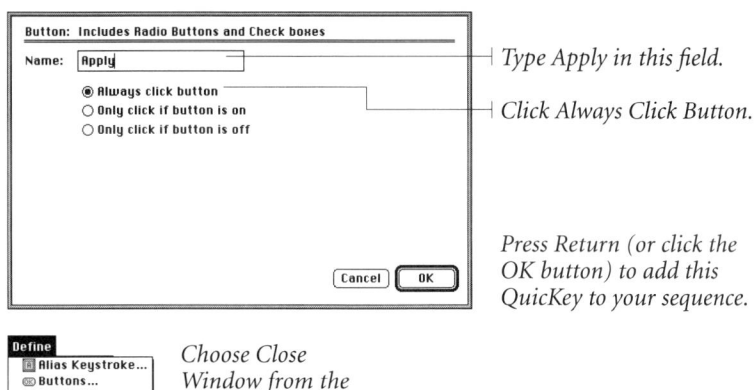

→ Type Apply in this field.

→ Click Always Click Button.

Press Return (or click the
OK button) to add this
QuicKey to your sequence.

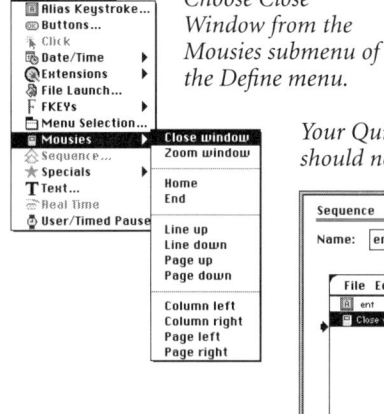

Choose Close
Window from the
Mousies submenu of
the Define menu.

Your QuicKey sequence
should now look like this.

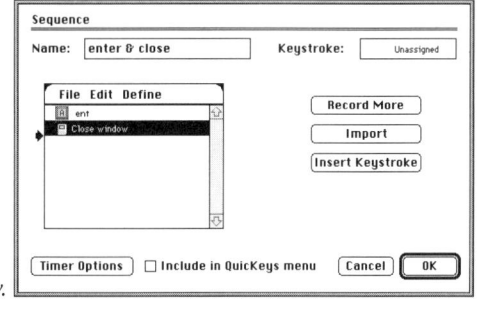

Save this Sequence QuicKey.

Using the techniques shown earlier in this
figure, create another Sequence QuicKey.

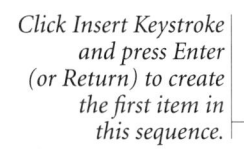

Click Insert Keystroke
and press Enter
(or Return) to create
the first item in
this sequence.

Choose Close Window
from the Mousies
submenu of the Define
menu to create this
sequence item.

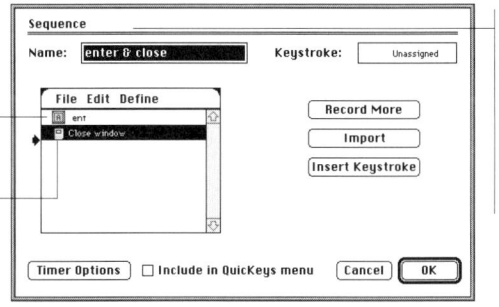

Type a name for the second
Sequence QuicKey here.
This name should match
the name you entered in
the If Condition is False
Trigger Shortcut field in
the Decision Extension
dialog box.

Close QuicKeys. Next, test the QuicKey. Select some objects and press
Command-Shift-A to display the Align palette. Choose an alignment
and press Option-Enter (or whatever keystroke you've assigned to
the QuicKey). If everything's working, FreeHand will apply the
alignment and close the Align palette. This QuicKey works well
with every palette but the Type Specifications palette.

Extension managers. If you use extensions and cdevs to add features to your Macintosh system, you need an extension manager, such as Startup Manager from the Now Utilities package, or the System 7.5 Extension Manager (where do they get these crazy product names?). Usually, extension managers are cdevs that set themselves up to load before any other cdevs or extensions, and control which other extensions and cdevs load, and (in some cases) in what order they load (see Figure A-4).

FIGURE A-4
Extensions Manager

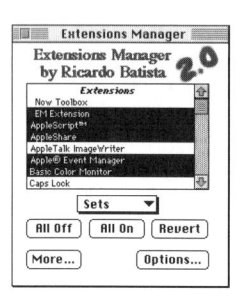

What's the use of this? I have a pressure-sensitve drawing tablet. The tablet is controlled by a cdev. I don't like having the tablet on all the time—mostly because the cdev conflicts with the cdev that makes my modem work. So, using Extension Manager, I keep two "sets" (or lists of which extensions and cdevs to load)—one for when I want to use the tablet; one for when I want to use the modem.

Extension managers also come in very handy when you're trying to track down extension/cdev incompatibilities—you can turn startup files on and off, one (or more) at a time, to find out which one's giving you trouble.

Utilities

While I might caution you against large numbers of extensions and cdevs, utilities are another thing. You can never have too many utilities.

ResEdit. Simply put, you cannot do without this utility if you want to customize your programs to better fit the ways that you work.

And if you want to create external resources for FreeHand it's essential (technically, you could use the Think C utility SARez, or similar resource compilers for other programming environments).

In the old days, ResEdit was a terrifying and unstable product—more prone to demolish any file it touched than make it more useful. These days, ResEdit is still a little rough around the edges, but it's safe enough for your kids to play with.

FreeHand's resources are set up beautifully from ResEdit's point of view—usually each resource does only one thing. Heck, some of them are even labelled. Get yourself a copy of ResEdit and start investigating a copy of FreeHand.

File-compression utilities Like work expanding to fill the time available for it, your files expand to fill the amount of space you have on your hard drive. StuffIt, DiskDoubler, and (my favorite) Compact Pro compress files so that they take up less space on your disk (now if I could only find a work compression utility!).

All these programs compress FreeHand PostScript files to less than a third of their original size (the degree of compression varies depending on the file's contents), which is a great thing to do when you're taking your file to an imagesetting service bureau or sending files to someone using a modem. Your service bureau may even prefer getting compressed files—ask them.

Torquemada the Inquisitor. So you want to search through a text file for every occurrence of "<B>" and change it to "\b"? That's pretty easy—just about any word processor can do that. But what if you want to find "<B>", followed by an indeterminate amount of text ending with "<P>" and change it to "\b", followed by the same, unspecified text and replace the "<P>" with "\plain"? This is hard for most word processors, but it's easy for Torquemada the Inquisitor, an incredible search and replace (or, as the youngsters say, "find and change"—never having seen WordStar) utility. Torquemada can only search text-only files—but that covers both text-only and RTF, the two text formats FreeHand can import. Think about it—you've got to be able to do search and replace to clean up text files, and Torquemada's free (see Figure A-5).

FIGURE A-5
Torquemada
the Inquisitor

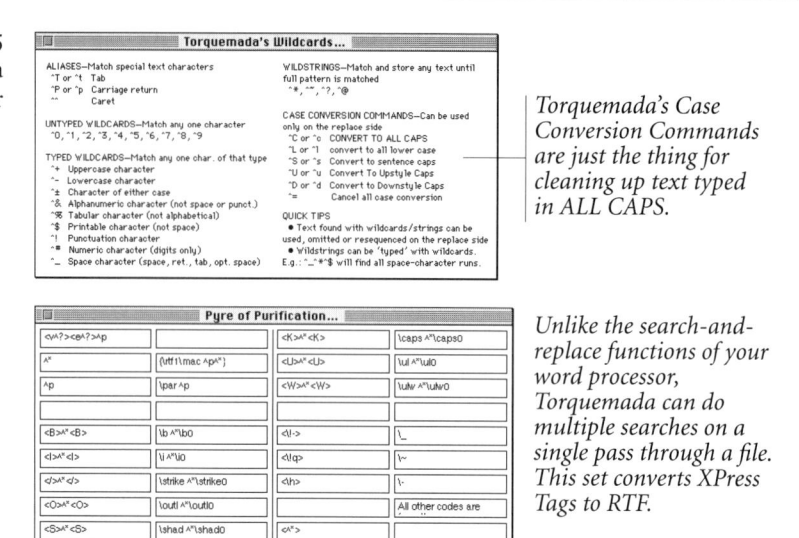

Torquemada's Case Conversion Commands are just the thing for cleaning up text typed in ALL CAPS.

Unlike the search-and-replace functions of your word processor, Torquemada can do multiple searches on a single pass through a file. This set converts XPress Tags to RTF.

3-D Rendering Applications

I love taking paths I've drawn in FreeHand to 3-D applications, such as Adobe Dimensions, Ray Dream's addDepth and Ray Dream Designer (version 3.0—I expect 4.0 works well, too, but I don't have it yet). Once I've imported the paths, I can extrude them, rotate them in 3-D space, or apply textures to their surfaces. It's hours of fun—and, once you get into rendering the objects, I do mean *hours*!

Adobe Dimensions. At around $100, Dimensions is a good way to get into 3-D—and it's sometimes bundled with other Adobe products by mail-order outfits (which means it's free, if you're already planning to buy the Adobe product). Dimensions has an edge over addDepth in one area—wrapping paths around a curved surface (though it can't wrap a TIFF or other bitmap image around a surface generated from a FreeHand path).

To get FreeHand paths into Adobe Dimensions, you'll have to export the paths in the Aldus FreeHand 3 or Illustrator (any version) file format—Dimensions can't open FreeHand files.

APPENDIX A: SYSTEM 643

Dimensions can export files as FreeHand 3 files, so you can bring the results of your 3-D experiments back into FreeHand and add them to your layouts

See Figure A-6 for an example of a FreeHand path extruded and altered in Dimensions.

FIGURE A-6
FreeHand paths and Adobe Dimensions

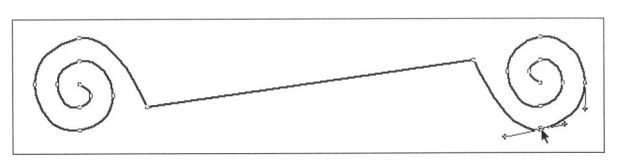

Create a path in FreeHand and save it as a FreeHand 3 file.

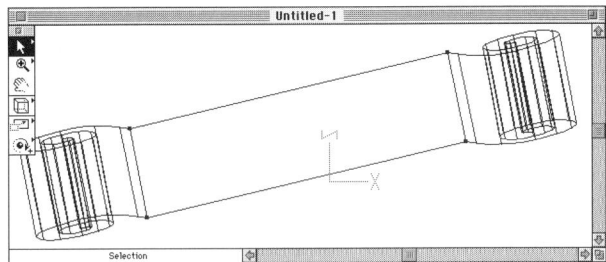

Import the path into Dimensions and use the Extrude command to add depth to the path.

Create some text in FreeHand. Convert the text to paths and export it as a FreeHand 3 file.

In Dimensions, select the extruded path and choose Artwork Mapping from the Appearance menu. Click the Import button and import the text you exported from FreeHand.

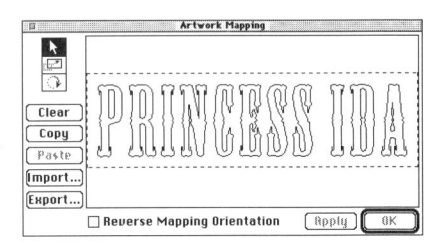

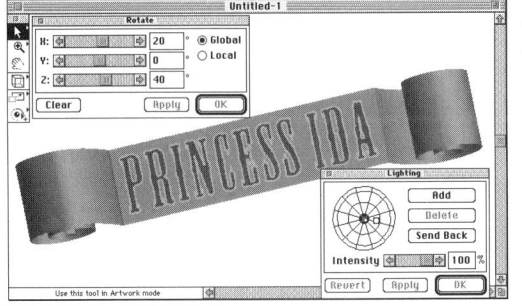

Render the artwork in Dimensions, and export it as a FreeHand 3 file. You can then open and edit the FreeHand 3 file in FreeHand.

Ray Dream addDepth. AddDepth can't, at the time of this writing, open FreeHand files from version 4, 5, or 5.5, or FreeHand EPSes. This doesn't mean you're out of luck, however—addDepth can read and write FreeHand 3 files. This makes it, of the three programs mentioned here, the most convenient to use. Export your files as FreeHand 3, open and edit them in addDepth, and then save them as FreeHand 3 files (which you can open in FreeHand). addDepth doesn't support everything you can create in FreeHand, as noted below.

- Graduated and radial fills you've created in your FreeHand publication don't transfer to addDepth (paths with these fill types applied show up in addDepth without their fills). Blends, however, are supported by addDepth. If you want a graduated fill, use addDepth's Gradation fill.
- Patterned fills, textured fills, PostScript fills, and custom fills are not supported by addDepth.

FIGURE A-7
FreeHand paths and Ray Dream addDepth

Create some text in FreeHand. Convert the text to paths and export it as a FreeHand 3 file.

Import the FreeHand file into addDepth. Rotate and extrude the paths, then click on a shader you want to use in the Shaders window or create your own (in this example, I've chosen the Metallic Shader). Save the file in the FreeHand 3 format, and you can open and edit it in FreeHand.

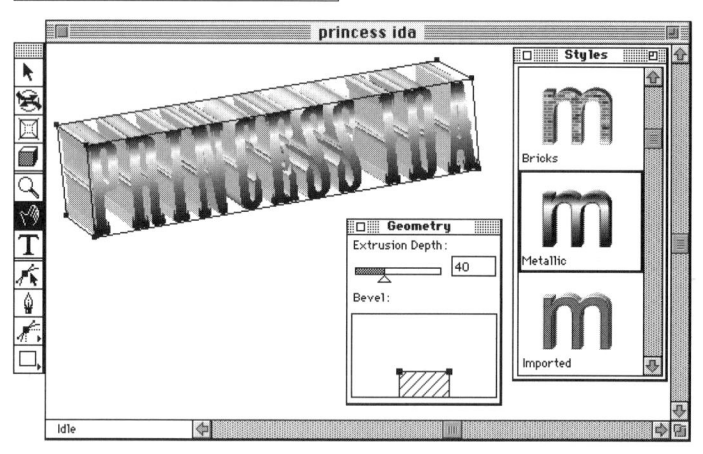

Printed example.

- adDepth supports only solid basic strokes—no dashed strokes, patterned strokes, custom strokes, or PostScript strokes.

- Any imported artwork in the FreeHand 3 file is not included when you open the file in addDepth.

- addDepth can't handle text that's been bound to a path. Convert the text to paths, however, and you'll have no problem.

- addDepth doesn't support FreeHand's text effects (Zoom, Inline, and Shadow).

For an example of the 3-D effects you can achieve with addDepth, see Figure A-7.

Ray Dream Designer. I have to admit it—I like this program (even though the documentation is skimpy in the extreme). Designer is a very capable 3-D drawing and rendering program—and it costs a third of what similar programs (such as the excellent Alias Sketch) cost. As far as I can tell, this is because Designer (as of version 3.02, anyway) doesn't contain any animation features.

While Designer can open FreeHand 3 files, getting FreeHand paths into Designer isn't as easy as getting them into addDepth or Dimensions. At the time of this writing, Designer couldn't import FreeHand 4 files. Designer can, however, export rendered scenes as TIFF (or—ugh!—bitmap PICT) files you can place in FreeHand.

Getting a FreeHand path into Designer for the first time isn't at all easy, so I'll show you how in the following steps (see Figure A-8).

1. In FreeHand, export the objects you want to import into designer as a FreeHand 3 document.

2. Switch to Designer and choose FreeForm from the Objects menu. Designer's Perspective window changes to show you a cross-section (cross-sections are the basic building blocks of 3-D scenes in Designer).

3. Choose Import Artwork from the Sections menu (at the top of the Perspective window, not on the main menu bar).

FIGURE A-8
FreeHand paths and Ray Dream Designer

Draw some objects in FreeHand and export them as a FreeHand 3 file.

In Ray Dream Designer, display the FreeForm window and Choose Import Artwork from the Sections menu. Apply Shaders and textures to the imported paths...

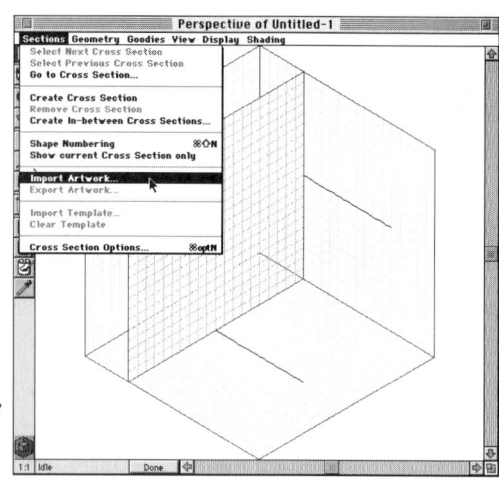

...and render them (rendering at high resolution takes time, so you might want to schedule all your rendering for times you're not planning to use your Macintosh—like when you're sleeping).

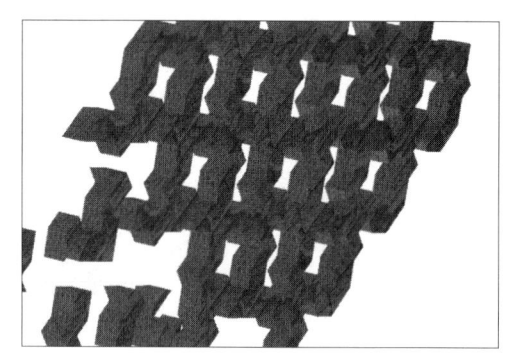

Paths rendered with Ray Dream Designer's Stone Wall Shader.

Designer displays the Import Artwork dialog box. Pick a file name and press Return (or click OK).

4. Designer imports the artwork and places it on the selected cross section. Designer converts any text in the FreeHand publication to paths. At this point, you can work with the paths in the converted FreeHand file as you would any other object in Designer.

Image Tools

Desktop design, illustration, and page layout rely on three things: type, line drawing, and images. FreeHand covers the first two items well. Photoshop handles the last item better than anything else (I have heard good things about Fractal Design's Painter, Sketcher, and Dabbler, too).

Adobe Photoshop. If you can buy only one other application (in addition to FreeHand), it should be Photoshop. When you want to work with bitmaps—be they scanned photographs or freeform paintings, Photoshop is the place to do it.

There's no way I can cover an application the size of Photoshop in this appendix, but I can throw in a favorite tip.

Tip:
Smoother
graduated fills
with Photoshop

When you create a graduated fill that goes a long distance—say, 25 inches or so—the bands between the gray steps in the graduated fill become very obvious. Even if you're working with 256 shades of gray, there just aren't enough different gray shades available to make a smooth graduation. What can you do?

To create a smooth blend using Photoshop, follow these steps (see Figure A-9).

1. Create a blend in FreeHand.

2. Export the blend in the Adobe Illustrator 3.0 format.

3. Open the Illustrator file with Photoshop. As Photoshop opens the file, it displays the EPS Options dialog box. Enter the resolution and size you want and press Return. Photoshop opens the file, converting the blend to a bitmap as it does so.

4. Choose Add Noise from the Noise submenu of the Filters menu. Photoshop displays the Add Noise dialog box.

5. Type a number in the Amount field. You'll have to experiment to see what works best for you—I like to enter "3", "5", or "7". Press Return, and Photoshop adds a little bit of noise to the image. When you print, this noise smooths the optical transitions between gray bands.

6. Place the TIFF in FreeHand, replacing the original blend in your publication.

FIGURE A-9
Smoother blends
with Photoshop

FreeHand blend from 40 to 60 percent gray. Some banding should be visible.

Open the blend in Photoshop and add some noise to smooth the transitions between gray bands (in this case, I entered "3" in the Amount field in Photoshop's Add Noise dialog box).

DeBabelizer. DeBabelizer is a file conversion utility for images. If you want to change an image from one image format to another—especially if you've got lots of files to convert or are working with an exotic file type (such as an Apple II color image), DeBabelizer is for you (see Figure A-10).

When you've got hundreds of PICT screen shots you want to convert to TIFFs—a situation I've faced several times as I produce books for other people—DeBabelizer can save the day. Instead of opening each PICT file (cursing the person who created it) in Photoshop and then saving the file as a TIFF (cursing some more as I do so), I can give DeBabelizer a list of files to convert and go home for the evening. While I'm away, DeBabelizer converts the PICTs to TIFFs, and has them waiting for me in the morning. Thanks to DeBabelizer, I am a better, more tolerant person.

FIGURE A-10
DeBabelizer

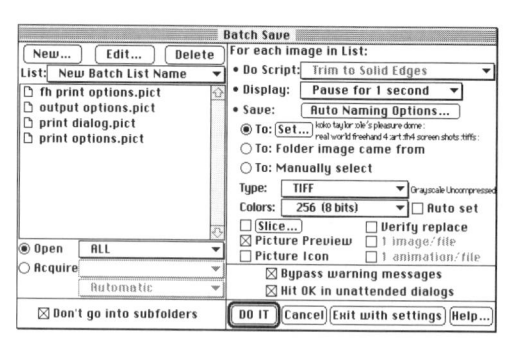

Adobe Acrobat

I admit that I've been confused about Adobe Acrobat. At first glance, Acrobat seems like the perfect software for large organizations and their large computer networks. With Acrobat, those corporations can make the move to the "paperless office," with their employees distributing memos, sales reports, and training manuals—all without having to push paper through a printer. This is great—for those corporations. But what does that have to do with you and me?

I've been using it for two things: document interchange, and as a software PostScript RIP. Before I talk about that, however, I'd better talk a little about Acrobat.

Which Acrobat?

The pieces that make up Acrobat come in several different packages.

The simplest is the Acrobat Reader. It can display the contents of PDF files, navigate through them, and print them. It's also the cheapest piece—it's free. You can download it from most of Adobe's online sites (see Appendix C, "Resources").

The best deal, in my opinion, and provided you have a CD-ROM drive, is to get the Acrobat reader on CD. When you do this, you also get a ton of great stuff in PDF format: the complete works of Shakespeare, for example, and historical documents of the United States (I'm always looking things up in the Constitution).

The Adobe Acrobat 2.1 package contains the Acrobat Search and Acrobat Exchange applications, and the PDF Writer. Acrobat Search gives you a way of searching the text of multiple PDF files. Acrobat Exchange does everything the Acrobat Reader does, and can also create and edit PDF files.

The PDFWriter is a piece of system software that works just like a printer driver. Select the PDFWriter in the Chooser and then print to it from your application. As you print, the PDFWriter takes the instructions your application would have sent to the printer, and writes them to disk as a PDF.

When you buy the Acrobat Pro package, you get all of the software mentioned above, plus the Acrobat Distiller. The Distiller can take PostScript code from virtually any source and turn them into PDFs—it's a software PostScript RIP (a somewhat limited one). Why would you use the Distiller instead of the PDFWriter? Use the Distiller if the publications you're working with contain TIFF images or EPS graphics—or if you're having trouble using the PDFWriter ("trouble" means that objects are dropping out of the PDF files you create).

Getting There from Here

To me, the most exciting aspect of Acrobat is the prospect of interchanging documents between applications. For years now, desktop publishing has lacked a standard file format for moving publications from one application to another. As it turns out, PDF makes a pretty good standard—better than Illustrator 1.1, in any case (PDF can include images).

What if you want to use a laid-out PageMaker page in FreeHand? Copying PageMaker elements out of PageMaker and pasting them into FreeHand works pretty well (provided you follow the directions in "Clipboard Control," in Appendix B, "Your FreeHand Installation"), but can be cumbersome—especially for multipage publications. Instead, try the following steps.

1. Print your PageMaker file to disk as PostScript (if you're using PageMaker 6, you can choose Create Adobe PDF from the File menu and skip to Step 3).

2. Open the PostScript file with the Acrobat Distiller. This creates a PDF file on your disk.

3. Open the PDF file with FreeHand. Once you've opened the page in FreeHand, you can use any of FreeHand's tools or commands to edit it—everything's been converted into FreeHand objects.

Software PostScript RIP

As someone who loves working with PostScript, I've lamented the lack of a real PostScript programming environment—complete with PostScript interpreter—on the Macintosh. Sure, I can always connect with the PostScript interpreter in my printer, but it's slow. Instead, I do my PostScript programming on my NeXT machine, which uses PostScript to control its display—but it's not always practical to do so. Now, at last, the Acrobat Distiller gives me the ability to see the result of my PostScript code on-screen.

You can't just open PostScript code, however, using the Acrobat Distiller—so how can you get your code into a PDF file? Follow these steps.

1. Create an EPS containing your PostScript code.

2. Place the EPS in FreeHand.

FIGURE A-11
Seeing What You'll Get

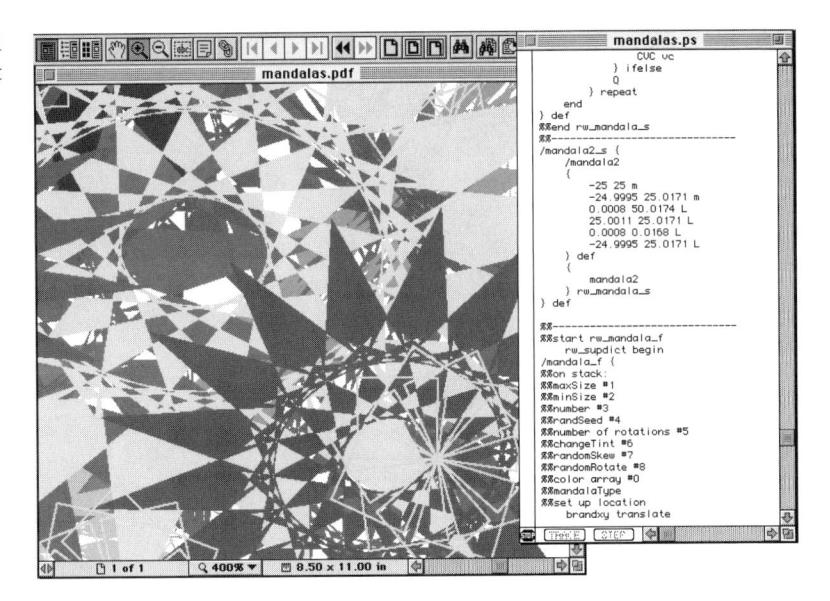

3. Print your publication to disk as PostScript.

4. Open the PostScript file you just created with the Acrobat Distiller. The Distiller creates a PDF file from the arbitrary PostScript code in your file.

5. Now you can view the result of your PostScript code using the Acrobat Viewer, or open the PDF using FreeHand 5.5.

PostScript Tools

If you're creating your own PostScript dictionaries or external resource files for stroke and fill effects, or if you're just trying to find out why your last publication didn't print, you need some tools for working with PostScript. Here are a few of my favorites.

LaserTalk. LaserTalk is the essential PostScript utility. With LaserTalk, you can communicate directly with the PostScript interpreter in your printer, and, better yet, *you can see what's going on* (see Figure A-11). If you're serious about creating PostScript effects for FreeHand, you've got to get LaserTalk.

FIGURE A-12
LaserTalk

LaserTalk puts you in direct contact with the PostScript interpreter in your printer.

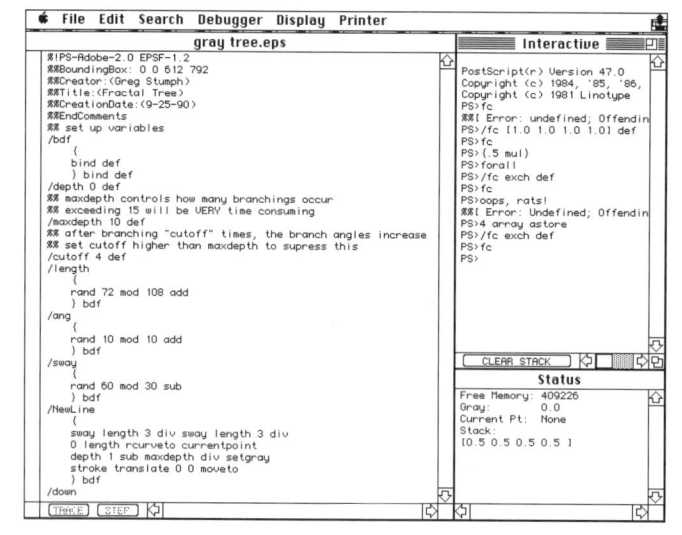

NeXT machine. Stop laughing, I'm serious. The black boxes made by NeXT, Inc., before they got out of the hardware business to go head-to-head with Microsoft in the operating system business (it's okay to laugh again, at this point) are worth having even if all you do with them is develop PostScript code. It's because they use PostScript to control their screen display—you can actually see your PostScript effects on screen (see Figure A-13). Because the NeXT is perceived as an dead platform (heck, it *is* a dead platform), you can pick them up fairly cheaply.

FIGURE A-13
The Nextstep operating system uses PostScript to drive its screen display

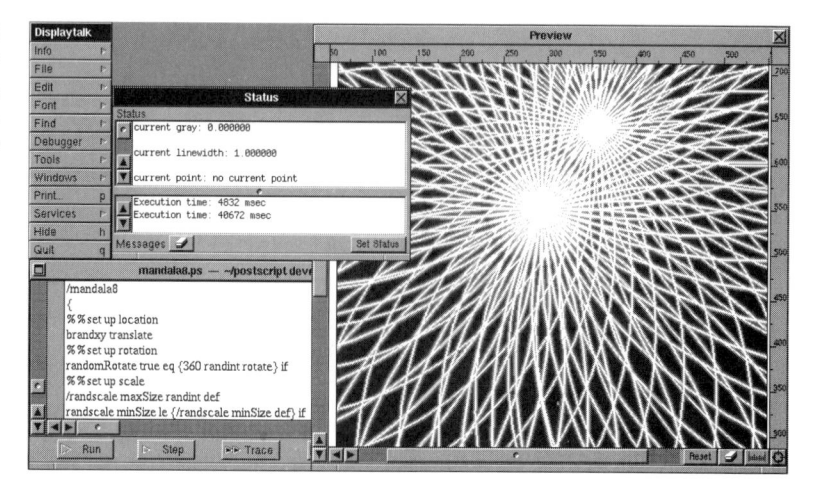

APPENDIX B 🙦 YOUR FREEHAND INSTALLATION

FreeHand comes with many megabytes of subsidiary files, most of which end up on your hard drive when you install FreeHand. What is all of this stuff? Where does it all go? Table B–1 shows you what's where, and why, for a standard FreeHand installation. If you change folder names, or drag files around after you've installed them, things will look different.

| Tip: Use the Default Installation | Why ask for trouble? Leave your FreeHand files where FreeHand's installer thinks they should go. Ideally, of course, FreeHand could find the files wherever you put them, with whatever names you cared to give them—ideally. We don't live in an ideal world, however. And neither does FreeHand. FreeHand looks for specific files in specific folders. If it can't find them, it can't use them.

Always install your copy of FreeHand from copies of the original product disks, rather than by dragging the files off another drive or fileserver. It's too easy to miss all of the subsidiary files that aren't inside the application folder.

In spite of this admonition, it's okay to change the name of your FreeHand folder and put it anywhere you want.

| FreeHand Preferences | FreeHand stores the current settings of the Preferences dialog boxes, the location and state of all the palettes, and a variety of other, esoteric information in the FreeHand Preferences file, which you'll find in your Preferences folder in your System Folder.

653

TABLE B-1   What's installed when you install FreeHand

Folder*:	File:	What it is:
System:Extensions: Printer Descriptions	Various PPDs	PostScript Printer Description files, which customize printing for a specific printer model. These are the printer models that appear in the Open PPD dialog box when you click Select PPD in the Print Options dialog box. If you don't have, and don't intend to use printers for which you have PPDs (including imagesetters at your service bureau), you can throw away those PPD files.
System:Preferences	FreeHand Preferences	A text file containing your FreeHand preference settings (see "FreeHand Preferences," in this appendix for a description of the file's contents).
	FreeHand Help.note	Notes you've taken while using FreeHand's online help. If you don't use online help, you can throw this file away.
System:Preferences: Macromedia	FreeHand Xtra Info Cache	This file helps FreeHand keep track of your Xtras. If you throw it away, it'll take longer to launch FreeHand, and FreeHand will just make another one.
FreeHand**	FreeHand	You know, FreeHand.
	ReadMe	A text file containing late-breaking information about FreeHand. Do read this file—there's often good stuff in it. I printed the file and threw it away; what you do with it is up to you (provided you read it, first).
	FreeHand Defaults	FreeHand defaults template file. You can open this file and change FreeHand's defaults, or add your own default colors, layers, and styles.
	What's New in FreeHand 5.5	An Acrobat PDF file containing information on FreeHand 5.5's new features. You'll only see this (obviously) if you've upgraded to FreeHand 5.5. This is the only documentation for FreeHand 5.5.
FreeHand:Colors	Various color libraries (files labeled with the file extension .BCF or .ACF)	FreeHand's color libraries. Don't delete these unless you really have no intention of using a color from a specific color library. You can, however, shorten the Color List's popup menu by moving some of these files to another folder. You can import colors from color libraries in any folder.

*In this table, I'll use the Macintosh's own shorthand for referring to folder locations. Instead of saying "In the Proximity folder in the Dictionary folder in the FreeHand folder," I'll say "FreeHand:Dictionary:Proximity."

**In this table, I'll generally use "FreeHand," rather than "FreeHand 5" and "FreeHand 5.5." Most of the filenames cite one version or the other, but I'm sure you'll figure it out.

TABLE B-1 (continued) What's installed when you install FreeHand

Folder:	File:	What it is:
FreeHand:Dictionary	prxlngst.rsl	A file that keeps track of installed dictionaries. Do not delete or move this file.
FreeHand:Dictionary: Proximity	prxlngst.lng	Another file that keeps track of installed dictionaries. Do not delete or move this file.
FreeHand:Dictionary: Proximity:US English	USFHN.bpx, USFHN.msp, USFHN.nfo, USFHN.udc, and USFHN00.vpx	FreeHand's hyphenation and spelling dictionaries. Don't throw these away. If you have dictionaries for other languages installed, you'll see them in the FreeHand: Dictionary:Proximity folder, as well.
FreeHand:Help	EHelpEngine™ 4.0	The viewer application for FreeHand's online help files. Don't throw this away unless you never use (or plan on using) FreeHand's help system.
	FreeHand Help Doc, FreeHand Help Media	FreeHand's online help. FreeHand has a very good context-sensitive online help system, so you might want to keep these files around. If you never use online help, you can throw these files away.
FreeHand:Fonts	Type 1 PostScript fonts	You can use these fonts in any application—though you'll have to install them, first.
	UnStuffit	FreeHand's Type 1 PostScript font files are saved in compressed Stuffit archives. To decompress them, you need this application. If you already have Stuffit, you can delete this file.
FreeHand: Sample Illustrations	Various FreeHand publications	Sample FreeHand publication files. Install these files if you want to take a look at the way they're built—but you should be aware that they don't always demonstrate the best way to do things in FreeHand. These files take up quite a bit of disk space, so you might want to delete them once you've finished examining them (or just not install them in the first place).
FreeHand:Snap Sounds	FH Snap Sound 1- FH Snap Sound 9	Sounds FreeHand plays when you have the Snap Sounds turned on in the Sounds Preferences dialog box (see "Sounds" in Chapter 1, "FreeHand Basics," for more on snap sounds).

TABLE B-1 (continued) What's installed when you install FreeHand

Folder:	File:	What it is:
FreeHand:UserPrep Files	UserPrep ReadMe	A file explaining the contents of the various UserPrep files in this folder.
FreeHand:UserPrep Files	Various UserPrep files	To use any of the UserPrep files in this folder, put the file in your FreeHand folder and enter the name of the file in the Name of UserPrep File field in the Expert Import/Output Preferences dialog box.
FreeHand:UserPrep Files	Hyphen.prp	Use this UserPrep file if you're printing to a RIP made by Hyphen (a manufacturer of PostScript clone interpreters).
FreeHand:UserPrep Files	MoreBanding.prp	If you're having trouble printing to a PostScript Level 2 color printer (that is, you're getting lots of "limitcheck" errors), use this UserPrep file. Your printed pages won't look as good, but at least they'll print.
FreeHand:UserPrep Files	Scitex.prp	Use this UserPrep file if you're printing to Scitex RIPs that support the ScitexVignette operator (not all of them do).
FreeHand:UserPrep Files	SeikoOverprint.prp	If you're printing to a Seiko ColorPoint2 printer with 4-color media loaded, use this UserPrep file. You'll be able to see the effect of FreeHand's overprinting and trapping on your color proofs.
FreeHand:UserPrep Files	Slides.prp	This UserPrep file improves printing of graduated and radial fills to film recorders equipped with the VBS Professional Output Manager.
FreeHand:UserPrep Files	SmoothRadsGrads.prp	Use this UserPrep file when you're printing to 300-600 dpi monochrome printers and want to see less banding in your radial and graduated fills. This UserPrep slows down printing.
FreeHand:UserPrep Files	Tiles.prp	If you're having trouble printing tiled fills on Level 2 PostScript RIPs attached to imagesetters, use this UserPrep file. Don't use this file unless you're having trouble, however, as it slows down the printing of *all* tiled fills.
FreeHand:Xtras	Various Xtras	FreeHand Xtras, such as Smudge (the Smudge tool), Spiral (the Spiral tool), and Trap (the Trap Xtra).

You can edit this file to change your preferences, but you've got to remember it's a "live" file—FreeHand writes changes to the file every time you quit the program (if not more frequently).

All of the coordinates in the FreeHand Preferences file are in pixels, and are measured from the lower-left corner of your screen (PostScript-style).

Your FreeHand Preferences file might look a little different (that is, some keywords might appear in different places in your file). Don't worry about this—sometimes FreeHand writes things in a different order than the one shown here.

Xtras from Elsewhere

FreeHand 5 can run almost any plug-in designed to work with Illustrator 5.5, and FreeHand 5.5 adds the ability to use plug-ins created for Photoshop. In addition, FreeHand's Software Developers' Kit (or SDK) offers software developers the ability to create Xtras that go beyond those created for Illustrator or FreeHand. I've been working on plug-ins for PageMaker and Xtensions for XPress, and I think that, from the developer's point of view, FreeHand is the most advanced thing in shrink-wrap.

Illustrator Plug-Ins

Funny thing—some of the most useful Xtras you'll ever put on your Xtras menu are the ones that come with Adobe Illustrator. If you've got both Illustrator and FreeHand, all you have to do is put an alias to your Illustrator Plug-Ins folder in your FreeHand Xtras folder (some FreeHand partisans also suggest another method, which also saves considerable disk space). The next time you start FreeHand, you'll see the Illustrator plug-ins on various submenus of your Xtras menu. The following are a few of my favorite of Illustrator's plug-ins (see Figure B-1).

- Add Anchor Points. Every time you run this plug-in, FreeHand adds a point halfway between each point on any paths you've selected. While this doesn't sound like a big deal, it can come in handy—especially when you're transforming paths as shown on page 445.

FIGURE B-1
Useful Adobe Illustrator plug-ins

Illustrator's Export plug-in can export selected text in more formats than FreeHand's Export command.

When you import text typed in ALL CAPS, you can turn to Illustrator's Change Case plug-in.

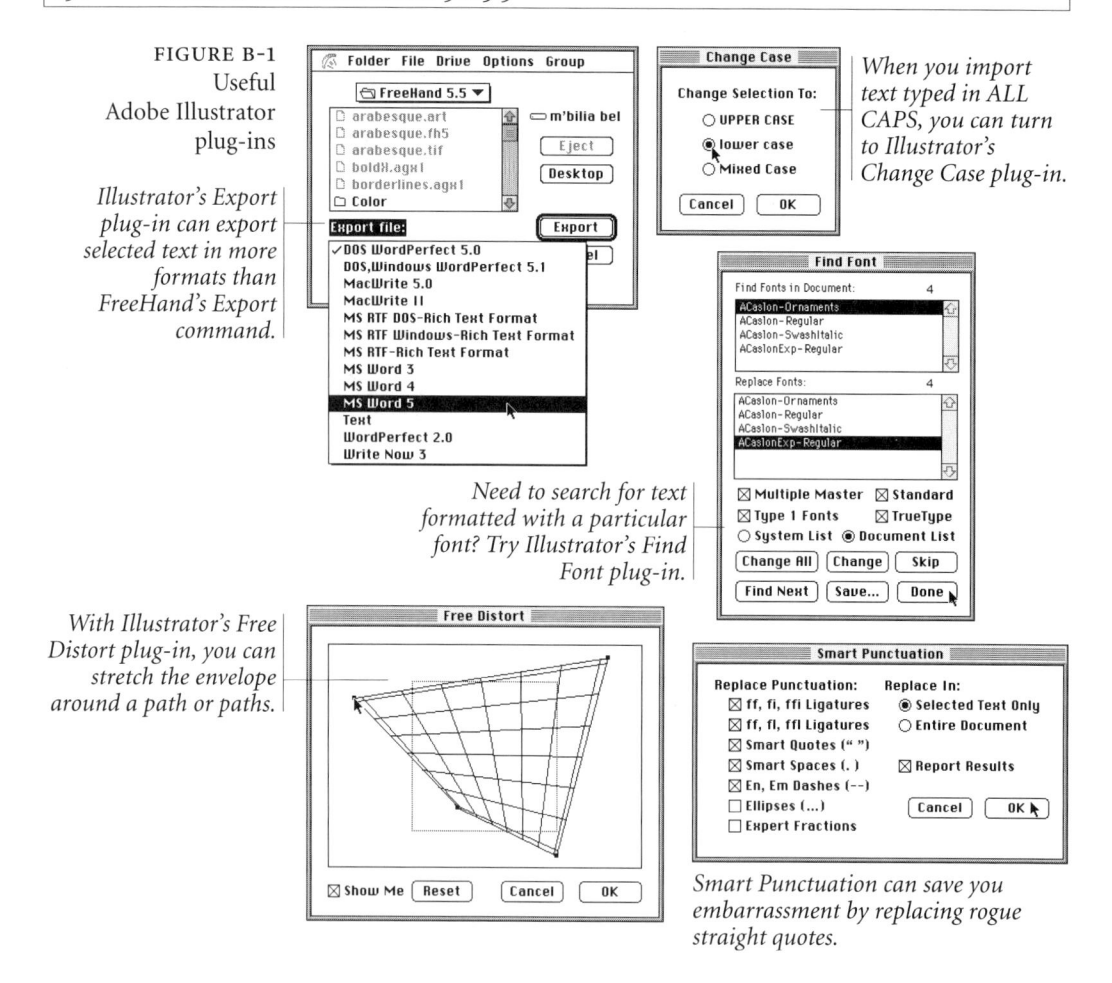

Need to search for text formatted with a particular font? Try Illustrator's Find Font plug-in.

With Illustrator's Free Distort plug-in, you can stretch the envelope around a path or paths.

Smart Punctuation can save you embarrassment by replacing rogue straight quotes.

- Find Font. FreeHand's Find command won't help you if you're looking for type that's been formatted with a specific font—which is all this plug-in does.

- Change Case. Don't you hate it when you import text that's typed in ALL CAPS? This Illustrator plug-in can go some distance toward fixing your problem. It's very simple-minded and won't help you with sentence caps, or title caps, but it might keep you from assaulting a co-worker.

- Export. Want to export something *less* than all of the text in your publication? This Illustrator plug-in exports only the text you've selected, and it exports it in more file formats than you can from "stock" FreeHand.

◆ Smart Punctuation. This plug-in searches through text (either the selected text or all of the text in the publication), finding certain characters and combinations of characters, and replacing them with characters the plug-in and I think are appropriate (though we don't always agree). It's a great last-minute check for typographic gaffes.

KPT Vector Effects

One of the best "idea generators" in Photoshop is the collection of filters titled "Kai's Power Tools" (or KPT—"Kai" is Kai Krause, a Photoshop power user and plug-in developer). Now, MetaTools (formerly HSC), the distributor of KPT, has come out with a collection of filters for Illustrator, which they're calling "KPT Vector Effects" (or VEX). These plug-ins were originally written by Shree Krotay, and have been acquired for distribution by KPT.

As part of the distribution agreement, the filters' user interface has been made to look like—and act like—the other KPT products. This may or may not be a good thing, depending on your point of view. I'm of two minds about Kai's interfaces, myself. When I'm fishing for ideas (what my office mates call "screwing around"), the non-standard controls don't bother me at all. When I'm actually trying to get something done, on the other hand, they can drive me nuts.

Are these as much fun as KPT for Photoshop? That depends on whether you'd rather blast bits or bend beziers. I like 'em, though I sometimes curse parts of the user interface. They're not quite as mind expanding as their Photoshop cousins, but I suspect they're more useful.

KPT VEX includes a variety of effects (there are a dozen in the pre-release package I received), and I don't have the space to cover them all here (this isn't, after all, a product review). Here are a few of my favorites, in no particular order (see Figure B-2).

◆ KPT 3D Transform. FreeHand's 3D Rotation tool is great, but it doesn't add sides to make paths you're rotating look more like solid, three-dimensional objects. The KPT 3D Transform Xtra does this, and does it almost as well as a dedicated 3D rendering application (such as Adobe Dimensions) would.

FIGURE B-2
KPT Vector Effects

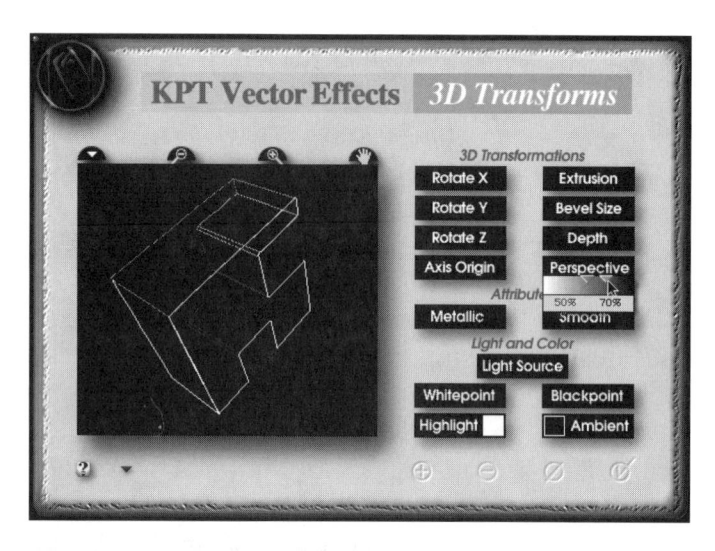

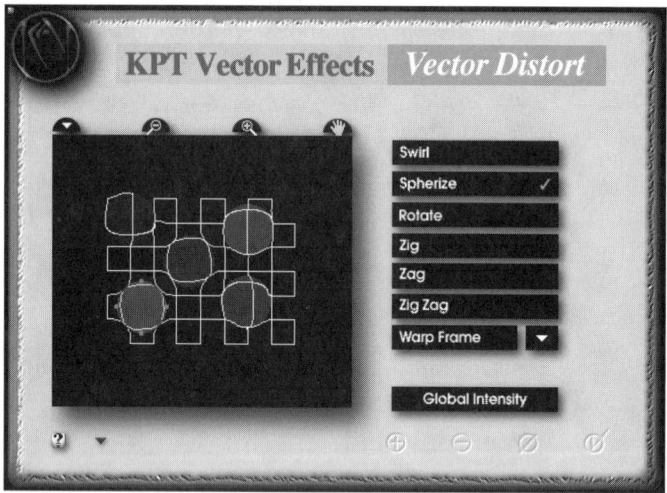

- KPT Emboss. This Xtra does something very simple—producing the illusion of a raised, "embossed" surface—but it does it very well. You can create embossing effects using FreeHand's native tools, but KPT Emboss makes it easier.

- KPT Sketch Roughen. I'm generally against the practice of stacking objects on top of each other (why print what you can't see?), but I'll make an exception in the case of the KPT Sketch Roughen plug-in. KPT Sketch Roughen makes your

FreeHand artwork look a little messier. It does this by stacking mutated copies of your artwork on top of each other, producing the same effect as we do when sketching objects by hand.

- ◆ KPT Vector Distort. This Xtra gives you a way of stretching or distorting the envelope of a path—it's a lot like Illustrator's Free Distort plug-in. But it does it very differently. When you first display KPT Vector Effects, you'll see a rectangle surrounding an area of your artwork in the preview window. In VEX terms, this is an "influence."

    You can adjust this area in the preview window, making it cover more or less of the artwork, or you can change its behavior—influences can apply different types of distortions, from "Swirl" (something like Illustrator's Twirl plug-in) to Spherize (which makes it look as if you're holding a wide-angle lens in front of the artwork). Are you getting this? You can apply different types of distortions to different parts of your path, all at once.

    Once you have an influence in place, you can create another by choosing "New Influence" or "Duplicate Influence" from the plug-in's pop-up menu. To delete an influence, select it and press Delete.

Extensis DrawTools

First, I have to state that I have a connection to Extensis Corporation—I developed (with Debra Kosky) six plug-ins that'll be part of Extensis' PageTools 2.0 for PageMaker. I do not, however, make any money from the sale of DrawTools.

DrawTools is a set of Xtras for FreeHand (and plug-ins for Illustrator). The main part of DrawTools is DrawTools Shape, which adds a floating palette to FreeHand (see Figure B-3). The DrawTools Shape palette controls seven different effects. You can map paths onto a sphere, cylinder, cone, or diamond. You can also distort paths by projecting them onto "waves," or by stretching and squashing them with the Free Distort option. It's almost as many effects as KPT VEX, all hiding in one palette.

Draw Tools also includes a series of Xtras for working with color. The Multitone Xtra changes the colors of objects to a specified set of colors; the Grayscale Xtra changes color objects into their grayscale equivalents; the Color Mixer gives you a way of replacing colors in your publication, and you can use the Edit Curves Xtra to adjust the saturation of colors in your publication. The Random Replace Colors Xtra randomly changes the colors used in your publication or in the selected objects.

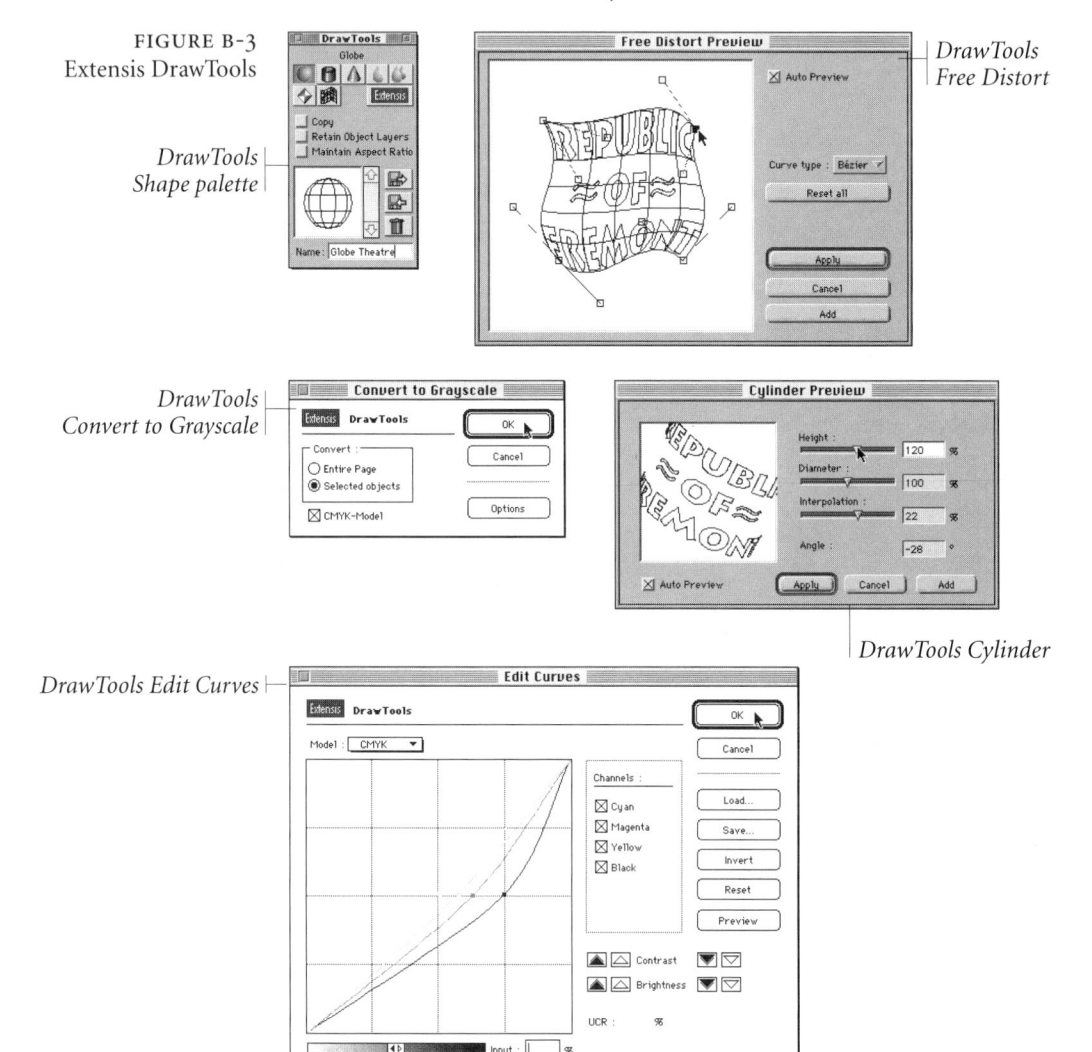

FIGURE B-3
Extensis DrawTools

DrawTools Shape palette

DrawTools Free Distort

DrawTools Convert to Grayscale

DrawTools Cylinder

DrawTools Edit Curves

FreeHand Easter Eggs

Many programs have hidden jokes and silly things in them. FreeHand is no exception. Some people hate the idea that software engineers ever have any fun, and fume about having anything silly in their software. If you are one of those people, please skip the rest of this appendix.

Confetti or Worms

When you hold down Option and click the picture in the About FreeHand dialog box, FreeHand displays an animated squiggle that runs around inside the confines of the dialog box. I've been told these squiggles are supposed to look like confetti, but they look more like hyperactive worms to me. Exhaustive research shows that you can have up to 20 worms active at time (see Figure B-4).

FIGURE B-4
Confetti (Worms)

FernHead

Try this: hold down Command and Caps Lock as you choose About FreeHand from the Apple menu. FreeHand displays a very silly dialog box (see Figure B-5). That's Samantha Seals Mason, Goddess of FreeHand, dressed up as "Pat" (the androgynous figure in the official About box).

Turn off Caps Lock and type "beavis" (if you're running a 68040-based Macintosh—PowerMac users have to type "ppcbeats" and some other five-letter word I've promised not to pass on for fear of enraging a major integrated circuit manufacturer), and FreeHand displays the dialog box shown in Figure B-6 (or my name's not Rival Monk Tavern).

FIGURE B-5
Samantha as Pat

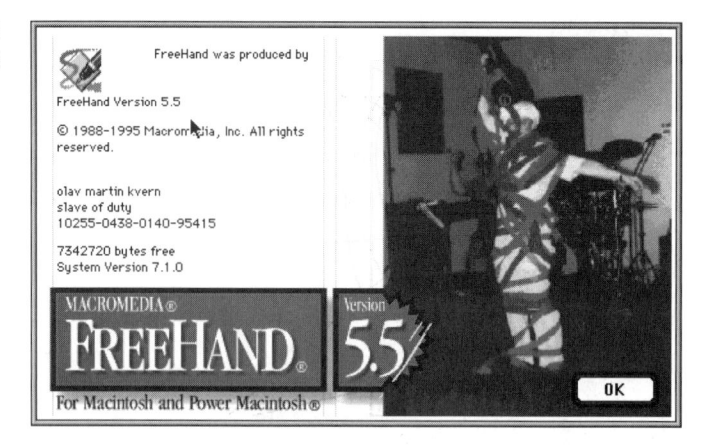

FIGURE B-6
Anagram screen

Here's a complete (as far as I know) list of the anagrams (for "Macromedia FreeHand," of course) that appear.

I Am Comrade FernHead	Monarch Dead; I Am Free!	America Hand Freedom
Deafen Homeric Drama	A Charred Amino Fed Me	Afraid Men Do Reach Me
Romance Her Deaf Maid	Hand-Carried Ammo Fee	A Comedian Framed Her
Academia Herd For Men	Harm Of American Deed	A Confirmed Head Mare
I'm A Charred Famed One	Madame Dacron Heifer	Adore Fancied Hammer
Defame Richmond Area	Fire Ahead, Commander	Redefined Roach Mama
Ah, Deformed American	Head Comedian Farmer	Chairmen Adored Fame
Harm A Redefined Coma	Fear Mr. Comedian Head	Her Admired Acne Foam
More Dharma Defiance	Command Diarrhea Fee	Manic Forehead Dream
Menaced Idaho Farmer	I Faced Her Memoranda	Harem Of Admired Acne
I Recommend Far Ahead	Her Odd American Fame	Can Mom Feed Diarrhea?
In A Crammed Forehead	Adhered In Foam Cream	Frame A Mediocre Hand
Each Admired For Name	A Former Dead Machine	

APPENDIX C RESOURCES

This appendix tells you where to get the things mentioned in this book. First of all, you can write to me or send me a message on Compuserve. I'd love to know what you thought of the book (even if you didn't like it—I took my best shot, but I can't correct my aim unless I know I've missed). I'd also love to hear about any fabulous FreeHand tips and tricks you've come up with (so I can steal them for the next editon).

Olav Martin Kvern
1619 Eighth Avenue North
Seattle, Washington 98109-3007
(206) 285-0308 (fax)
CompuServe: 76636,2535
America Online: Olav Kvern

Adobe Systems, Incorporated
Adobe Illustrator, Adobe Dimensions, Adobe Photoshop,
Adobe Type Manager, Adobe Type Reunion,
Adobe PostScript, LaserTalk, Adobe PageMaker, Adobe Persuasion,
Adobe TrapWise
1585 Charleston Road
Mountain View, California 94039
(415) 961-4400
World Wide Web: http://www.adobe.com
CompuServe: Go ADOBE

Aladdin Systems, Incorporated
StuffIt Deluxe
Deer Park Center, Suite 23A-171
Aptos, California 95003
(408) 685-9175

AlSoft
MasterJuggler
P.O. Box 927
Spring, Texas 77383
(800) 257-6381
(713) 353-9868 (fax)

ANPA
Newspaper Association of America
11600 Sunrise Valley Drive
Reston, Virginia 22091
(703) 648-1367

Apple Computer
MacDraw, ResEdit
20525 Mariani Avenue
Cupertino, California 95014
(408) 996-1010

CE Software
QuicKeys
1801 Industrial Circle
West Des Moines, Iowa 50265
(515) 224-1995

Extensis
DrawTools
55 SW Yamhill, 4th Floor
Portland, Oregon 97204
(503) 274-2020
(503) 274-0530 (fax)

Focoltone
Springwater House
 Taffs Well, Cardiff   CF4 7QR
United Kingdom
(44) 222-810-962

Macromedia Corporation
FreeHand
600 Townsend,
San Francisco, California 94103
(415) 252-2000
World Wide Web: http://www.macromedia.com
CompuServe: Go MACROMEDIA
America Online: Macromedia

MetaTools (formerly HSC Software)
KPT Vector Effects
6303 Carpinteria Avenue
Carpinteria, California 93013
805-566-6200

Microsoft Corporation
Microsoft Word, Microsoft Excel, RTF Specification
One Microsoft Way
Redmond, Washington 98052
(206) 882-8080

Now Software
Now Utilities (including *Super Boomerang*)
520 S.W. Harrison Street, Suite 435
Portland, Oregon 97201
(503) 274-2800
(503) 274-0670 (fax)

Pantone
55 Knickerbock Road.
Moonachie, New Jersey 07074
(201) 935-5500

Seattle Gilbert & Sullivan Society
Thespis, Trial by Jury, The Sorcerer, H.M.S. Pinafore, The Pirates of Penzance, Patience, Iolanthe, Princess Ida, The Mikado, Ruddigore, The Yeomen of the Guard, The Gondoliers, Utopia Limited, The Grand Duke, and, yes, even Sullivan & Burnand's *Cox and Box*
P.O. Box 15314
Seattle, Washington 98115

Greg Swan
Torquemada the Inquisitor
P.O. Box 1724
Andover, MA 01810

Symantec
Suitcase
175 West Broadway
Eugene, Oregon 97401
(800) 441-7234

Toyo Ink Manufacturing Company Ltd.
3-13, 2-chome Kyobashi
Chuo-ku, Tokyo 10
Japan
(4 81) 3-2722-5721

TruMatch
25 West 43rd St., Suite 802
New York, New York 10036
(212) 302-9100

/ (Slash character) 585
^ (Caret character) 589
{ } (Curly brackets) 385
% (Percent character) 180, 584
+ (Plus sign) 204, 310
" (Quotation marks) 296-297
\n symbol in Post resources 587
{ } (Curly brackets) 385
1-bit TIFFs 346. *See also* TIFFs
2-D effects 458-459
3-D display, turning off 87-88
3-D effects 447, 458-459
3-D rendering applications 642-646, 659-660
3-D Rotation tool 465-466
3-D Transform plug-in 659-660
4-bit TIFFs 359. *See also* TIFFs
8-bit (256-color) display 74, 476
8-bit TIFFs. *See also* TIFFs
    bit depth 354
    gray level settings 359
    importing 346
12%-800% page views 33-34
16-bit color display 476
24-bit color display 476
24-bit TIFFs 346. *See also* TIFFs
30 or 45 degree oblique projection grid 222
256K view 34

A

About message in Library dialog box 488
Above field in Paragraph Inspector 304, 306
Absurd numbers in Rotate palette 442
Abutting pages 26
Accuracy 56-57
    EPS preview images or bounding boxes 86, 401-402
    fixed leading method 270
    flatness 115-116
    guide positioning 12-14
    in transformations
        reflecting on specific axes 448-449
        rotation angles 442
        scaling by specific percentage 437-438
        skewing precisely 452
    locations of objects 34-36
    most accurate views 34-36
    moving objects precisely 61-62, 433-434
    PICT preview images 347
    pixels and grid increment mismatches 30-31
    scaling objects 48
    text block size or position 253
.ACF file extension 486
Acquiring images 370-371
Acrobat

Acrobat Pro 649
converting FreeHand files to PDF 420-421
displaying PostScript 581, 583, 650-651
Distiller 649
    creating PDF files 421
    displaying PostScript 581, 583, 650-651
document interchange 648-651
Exchange 649
opening PDF files in FreeHand 344
PDFWriter 649
PostScript RIP 648-651
Reader 649
Search 649
Viewer 651
Acronyms, skipping hyphenation in 295
Active pages 97, 543
Active windows 7
Add Anchor Points plug-in 657
Add Arrow on Color List 480-481, 508
Add Guides dialog box 13-14
Add-ons. *See* Xtras
Add Pages command and dialog box 25-26
Add Words to Dictionary option 95
addDepth 644-645
Additions. *See* Xtras
Adjust Display Color option 74-76
Adjusting matrices in PPDs 562
Adobe Acrobat. *See* Acrobat
Adobe Dimensions 642-643
Adobe Fetch 86
Adobe Illustrator. *See* Illustrator
Adobe PageMaker. *See* PageMaker
Adobe Photoshop. *See* Photoshop
Adobe PostScript. *See* PostScript
Adobe PPD specifications 559
Adobe PrePrint Pro 528
Adobe PSPrinter 8 driver 558
Adobe Streamline 346
Adobe Table Editor 349
Adobe TrapWise 470, 512
Adobe Type Manager 268-269, 634
Adobe Type Reunion 265, 636
Agfa Cristal Raster 473, 533
AGX1 files 593-594, 619
    converting clipboard contents 100
    external resource file type 617
    including custom PostScript files for service bureaus 570
Aldus FreeHand. *See* FreeHand
Aldus PageMaker. *See* PageMaker
Aldus Persuasion. *See* Persuasion
Aldus Table Editor 349
Align feature 461
Align palette 18-19, 20, 462-464

Alignment
    aligning objects 461-464
    auto-expanding text blocks 233-234
    baseline alignment in text joined to paths 326-327
    locking objects 462, 463
    tab alignment 298-299, 300, 302
    text alignment
        codes in RTF files 386
        converting to Illustrator 1.1 410
        converting XPress Tags to RTF 389-390
        distributing characters converted to paths 334-335
        hanging punctuation 296-297
        paragraph formatting 289
        setting best-looking text 291
        setting QuicKeys for 290-291
        text joined to paths 325, 326
Alignment guides. *See* Ruler guides
Alignment Inspector palette 21, 289. *See also* Align palette
All But Standard 13 font option 542
All caps text 388, 658
All Foreground Layers print option 69
All On and All Off commands 66
All Visible Foreground Layers print option 69
Alphabetizing color names 505
Alternate fonts. *See* Font substitution
AltsysDict dictionary 587
Always Binary Image Data option 100
Always Review Unsaved Documents upon Quit option 97
Always Use Text Editor option 82, 236
Anagrams 664
Anchoring graphics in text 337-340
Angles
    axonometric projection 223-224
    characters in text joined to paths 327-329
    Constrain field 51
    control handles on points 122-123, 124, 125
    graduated fills 186-187
    oblique projection 220-222
    of constraint for drawing tools 31
    of reflection 448
    of rotation 5, 440, 441
    of skewing 452
    pie chart wedges 213-216
    screen angles in Print Options dialog box 554
    star points 42-43
    tiled fills 190
Annotations in PDF files 421

669

Antialiasing option 413
Apple color model 502-503. *See also* HSB color model
Apple Color Picker dialog box 74-75, 76
Apple File Exchange 382
Apple Menu items 632
Application-level defaults 23-24
Apply button 20, 358, 360
Applying styles 311, 314-316
 dragging and dropping 84-85, 315-316
 preferences 98-99
 text style masks 318-321
Applying Text Editor changes 236
Arc dialog box 126-127
Arc tool 126-127
Arcs 52
 adding to paths 111-112
 adjusting curve 130-131
 automatic curvature 132, 133
 converting CAD drawings to FreeHand 352-353
 creating 126-127
 drawing with Pen tool 120-121
 Option-dragging shortcut 131
 simplifying 137-138
Area charts 211-213
Aromatic Puce 318
Arranging pages 26-27
"array" error messages 575
Arrays in FreeHand's PostScript 589
Arrow custom stroke 179, 588
Arrow keys, nudging with 79, 429, 435
Arrowhead Editor dialog box 176-177
Arrowheads and tailfeathers on lines 176-177
Ascent option in text joined to paths 327
ASCII Encoding option
 exporting 394
 printing 541, 556
ASCII files
 exporting text-only files 392
 importing 344, 349, 382
 opening 349
Assault prevention techniques 658
ATM (Adobe Type Manager) 268-269, 634
ATR (Adobe Type Reunion) 265, 636
Attaching graphics to text 337-340
Attributes
 defining styles by attributes 198-199, 313-314
 formatting attributes of multiple paths 197
 inheritance in styles 200-203, 204-205
 like attributes in blending 151
 text style masks 318-321
Auto-Apply Style to Selected Objects option 98-99, 311
Auto-expanding text blocks 84, 230, 232-235
Auto-Rename Changed Colors option 73
Auto Tile print option 542
Automatic curvature 132, 133
Automatic embedding 378-379
Automatic hyphenation 294-295
Automatic tiling 542
Automatic tracing 172-173
Automatic trapping 470

Automatic updating of edition files 416
Autoskewing text 328
Autotracing 172-173
Axes
 axonometric projection grids 223-224
 charts
  bar and column charts 208-209
  line and area charts 211-213
  setting zero point for 207
  stacked bar and column charts 210-211
 control handles 122-123, 124, 125
 object transformations 48
 of movement constraint 433
 of reflection 447-450
 of transformations 427
Axonometric projection techniques 223-224, 453-454

B

Background colors of text blocks 72-73
Background image EPS files 376
Background layers 63
 switching to foreground 68
 tracing objects on 48-49, 170-172
Bacteria, drawing at actual size 6
Bad habits of those who should know better
 page size 27
 paths with billions and billions of points 150
 pounding on imagesetters with wastebaskets xxiii
 unjustified justification 290
Balance Columns field 261-262
Ball custom stroke 179, 588
Banding
 avoiding 551, 647-648
 moiré patterns in images 360-361
 printed blends 153
Bar charts 208-211
Base fonts 265
Baseline shift 272-273
 codes in RTF files 385, 387
 converting XPress Tags to RTF 389
Baselines of text
 inline graphics 339-340
 leading methods 270-273
 options for text joined to paths 326-327
Basic fills 182-184, 275. *See also* Fills
Basic shapes 54-55, 56, 107-109
Basic shapes tools 38-39, 106
Basic strokes 173-177, 275, 279. *See also* Strokes
Basing styles on attributes 198-199, 313-314
Basing styles on examples 196-198, 311-313
Basing styles on other styles 84, 200-203, 204
Basing styles on selected objects 98-99
.BCF file extension 486
Begging behavior of cartographers 236
Behavior of inline graphics 338
Below field in Paragraph Inspector 305, 306
Benchmarks for printing times 573
Bend-O-Matic 131
Better (but Slower) Display option 89
Beveled joining on strokes 175
Bezier control points. *See* Control handles

Bezigon tool. *See* Point tool (please!)
Bilevel bitmaps. *See* Bitmaps
Bilevel TIFFs. *See also* TIFFs
 applying colors to 498
 converting grayscale TIFFs to bilevel 356-357
 importing 346
 missing or poor quality printing 575
 Object Inspector controls 356-357
 scaling to target printer's resolution 360-362, 437
 scanning line art 355-356
 TIFF controls 356-357
 transparent backgrounds 356-357
Binary Data option 394, 541, 556
Binary image data 100
Bind to Path command 324
Bit depth 354, 506
Bitmap-only PICT files 86, 347
 embedding as TIFF 379
 exporting from FreeHand 392
 rastering objects into bitmaps 412-414
Bitmap PICT Previews option 86, 347
Bitmap textured fills 193, 590-592
Bitmapped strokes 178
Bitmaps
 applying colors to 498
 converting bitmaps in PICT files to TIFFs 347
 dithering 413
 importing 54-56
 missing or poor quality printing 575
 Object Inspector controls 356-357
 PNTG file types 346
 rastering objects into bitmaps 412-414
 scaling to target printer's resolution 32, 360-362, 437
 TIFF controls 356-357
 TIFF file type 346
Black and white graphics 412
Black and White Interface option 87-88
Black and white noise custom fill 185, 587
Black color or ink
 desaturating colors 503
 in color printing process 472
 knocking out or overprinting 520
 saturating colors 505
 values in color definitions 489
Black dots in Text Editor 338
Blank fields in palettes 266, 274
Blank text styles 318-321
Bleed area 8, 26
 allowing for on press sheets 547
 in publication window 4
 relationship to page size and paper size 8, 550
 setting in Document Inspector 29
Blend command 148, 155-156, 160, 170
Blending 151-164
 adding percentages to colors 501-502
 blends in converted Illustrator EPS files 375
 calculating steps 32, 152-154
 choosing colors 474
 compared to graduated fills 572
 creating new colors based on blend steps 157-158

INDEX

editing blends 156-157
equations 153, 154
in perspective drawings 219, 220
multi-color blends 162-164
naming colors 504
positioning colors 162-164
printing on prepress or film
    recorders 395
problems creating blends 156
process color tint builds 508-509
reference points 151-152
trapping graduated fills 520-522
Blob tool. *See* Variable Stroke tool
Blue color values 489-490
Bold italic text style 265, 269
Bold text style 269
    converting XPress Tags to RTF 389
    in RTF codes 386
    problems printing correct font 265
Bond paper sizes 549
Bookmarks in PDF files 421
Borders
    on edition files 416, 418
    on text blocks 258-261
Bottom handles of text blocks 252
Bounding boxes
    adding to PostScript files 581
    aligning objects 461, 462
    displaying objects while dragging 92-93
    dragging objects quickly 432-433
    exporting zoom text effects 285
    problems with exported EPS
        files 401-402
    X marks in 373
Boxes. *See* Bounding boxes; Link boxes;
    Rectangles and squares
Braid custom stroke 179, 588
Breaking
    links to edition files 416
    links to imported files 419, 420
    links to text blocks 255
    paragraphs between columns 307
Bricks custom fill 185, 587
Brightness controls in Image dialog box 358
Budgetary constraints
    color separations 536
    printing 474
Buffered Drawing option 89-90, 253-254,
    261, 369
Build Paragraph Styles Based On Shared
    Attributes option 84, 313, 318
Bureaucrats in early days 539
Burlap textured fill 193, 587
Butt caps on strokes 174
Buttons
    creating in Inspector user interface 601,
        618, 621
    Flags field values in UIrz resource 625

C

C patterns in fills 186
Cabinet projections 221
CAD programs, importing from 352-353
Calibrating imagesetters 534
Calibrating monitors 74-76, 476
Calligraphic Pen tool 43, 45-46, 120
Calling PostScript routines in UserPrep

files 180-181, 598-601
Cancel Publisher button 418
Cancel Subscriber button 416
Canceling
    object selection 57
    publishing or subscribing 414, 418
    text block selection 254
Canines on graphic designers 466
Capitalization errors, finding 94, 242
Capitalized words 242, 295
Caps on lines 174, 408
Caret character (^) 245, 589
Carriage returns
    compared to end-of-line characters 239
    converting XPress Tags to RTF 390
    ending every line in text-only files 382
    ending paragraphs 288
    in PostScript code 180, 587, 618
    in RTF codes 386
    in text joined to paths 325
    not using unless necessary 250
    searching for in text 245
    using instead of tabs 298
Cartographer custom stroke 179, 588
Cartographers, begging behavior of 236
Case of text
    changing 658
    in RTF files 388
    in spelling dictionary 95
    search patterns 244
Cavalier projections 221
Cavern, Olive 243
cdevs 631-640
CE Software QuicKeys. *See* QuicKeys
Cells (PostScript stroke grid cell) 612-613
Cells (text blocks) 229-230, 256
Center of rotation 47, 441
Center points
    of objects
        drawing from center out 107
        resetting coordinates to center 438
        rotating or reflecting around 47-48
        scaling from 436, 437, 438, 439
        scaling objects around 48, 109
        skewing around with 48, 451
    of paths 657
    of radial fills 188-189
Centered paragraph rules 308
Centered tabs 298, 386
Centered text 289
    centering text vertically in objects 462
    converting XPress Tags to RTF 390
    in RTF codes 386
    text joined to paths 325, 326
Central projection 216-220
ch symbol in Info bar 5
Chainsaw tool (Knife tool) 46-47
Change Case plug-in 658
Changing Objects Changes Defaults
    option 80-81
Changing the View Sets the Active Page
    option 97
Channels, splitting in CMYK TIFFs 530-532
Character formatting 262-264
    automatic copyfitting 321-323
    baseline shift 272-273

blank fields in Type Specifications
    palette 266
color 275-280
compared to paragraph
    formatting 262-263
fonts 264-269
kerning 286-288
leading 270-274
stretching characters 280
text effects 280-286
type size 269
type styles 269
Character Inspector palette 21, 22
    baseline shift 272-273
    kerning 287
    leading methods 270-274
    leading problems 274
    stretching characters 280
    text effects 280-286
Character pairs, kerning 287
Characters
    baseline shift 272-273
    character formatting 262-264
    converting to paths 146, 332-337
    greeking text 91-92
    moving cursor character by
        character 237
    special characters
        codes in RTF files 387
        hanging punctuation 296-297
        inserting 238-240
        searching for 243, 245
    stretching 280
    tab characters. *See* Tabs
    text joined to paths 326-329
    type size and leading methods 270
    weird characters in text files 382
    wildcard characters 245
Charting techniques 206-224
Charts
    creating 206-216
    importing from Excel or
        Persuasion 350-352
Check marks on Layers palette 63, 66
Checkboxes, creating in Inspector
    interface 621
Checker custom stroke 179, 588
Checking spelling 94-95, 240-243
Checkmarks on Layers palette 63, 66
Child styles 200-203, 204
Chokes (trapping technique) 514
    example 515-516
    reversing chokes and spreads 527-528
    trapping color TIFFs 526
    trapping lines 518-519
    trapping process colors 524
    trapping text 519-520
Chooser settings for PPDs 558
Circles. *See* Ellipses and circles
Circles custom fill 185, 587
Classical method of drawing 134
Clay tablets 539
Cleaning up text 243
Clearing. *See* Deleting
Clipboard
    converting contents on exit 100
    copying with 70

672 REAL WORLD FREEHAND 5.0|5.5

Clipped EPS images 401-402
Clipping paths. *See also* Cropping
   color changes on object
      boundaries 457-458
   disappearing objects 140
   dragging selected points of clipping
      path 430-431
   in PDF files 421
   moving paths without moving
      contents 363-364
   on imported images 456
   outline and vignette masks for
      TIFFs 364-367
   print times 572-573
   techniques 454-460
   transparent and translucent
      effects 458-460
   trapping images with 526
   using Paste Inside multiple
      times 455-456
Clone command 70-71
Cloning 82. *See also* Duplicating
   before path operations 169
   color changes on object
      boundaries 457-458
   flipping and flopping techniques 139
   repeating transformation on cloned
      objects 429
   shortcuts 429
   transparent and translucent
      effects 458-460
   trapping across color boundaries 516, 517
   trapping lines 518-519
Close box in publication window 4
Close Cut Paths option 46-47
Closed paths 139-141
   changing to open paths 140
   converting CAD drawings to
      FreeHand 352-353
   converting to Illustrator 1.1 409
   determining if closed or open 144
   expanding stroke into two new paths 167
   filling 182-194
   flowing text inside paths 329-330
   insetting new path inside object 168-169
   punching or uniting 166-167
Closing
   Text Editor box 237
   Toolbox and palettes 86-87
CMYK color model
   choosing in Color Mixer palette 481-482
   color names 72
   considerations for use 477-478
   creating FreeHand bitmap images 412
   creating new colors 485-486
   darkening colors 502-503
   determining colors in images 506
   in color libraries 489
   lightening colors 503
   naming colors 504
   renaming changed colors
      automatically 73
   text colors in RTF files 385
CMYK TIFFs
   bit depth 354
   converting RGB to CMYK 556

stochastic screening 530
Coarse gravel textured fill 193, 588
Code
   PostScript
      accessing in UserPrep files 598-601
      adding space or return after last
         character 618
      end of file code in Illustrator 411
      examining in EPS files 583-585
      FreeHand shorthand 598
      in GnEf resources 611
      operators that shouldn't be in EPS
         files 581
      pasting into Inspector 180
      techniques for entering 594-595
      using support routines
         effectively 606-608
   PPD keywords 559-567
   RTF files 386-387
Color. *See* Colors
Color Control Xtra 501-502
Color field boundaries 457-458
Color folder 484
Color libraries 486-493
   adding colors from 482-485
   example of text file 491
   importing 484
   supported libraries 478-479
Color List Names option 72-73
Color List palette 18-19, 20, 479-481
   adding color names 504
   adding new colors 485-486
      Color-Xtra-created colors 501
      from blends 158-159
      from color libraries 482-485
   alphabetizing color names 505
   applying colors 173-174, 275-276, 496-497
   deleting unused colors 505
   displaying 481
   dragging colors 182-183
   replacing one color with
      another 495-496
Color List Shows Container Color
   option 275
Color List Shows Text Color option 275, 276
Color Mixer palette 18-19, 20, 74
   applying colors 173-174
   creating new colors 485-486
   displaying 481
   dragging colors 182-183
   editing colors 493-496
Color Mixer Uses Split Color Well option 74
Color Mixer Xtra 662
Color models 477-478
   choosing for new colors 485-486
   in color libraries 489
   in Color Mixer palette 481-482
Color overlays. *See* Color separations
Color photographs. *See* Color TIFFs
Color Preferences dialog box 72-76
Color prepress systems 395, 529, 556-557
Color proofs 102, 476
Color sample books. *See* Color libraries
Color separations 353, 528-535
   avoiding rosettes 472-473

checking settings before
      imagesetting 569
   converting RGB TIFFs to CMYK 394, 556
   FM screening 533-535
   matching color names 484-485
   matching color specifications 486
   preseparating color TIFFs 353, 367-368
   print settings 544-545
   printing names on 484
Color swatches 478-479
   applying colors 496-497
   color wells 74
   creating new colors 486
   creating tints 480
   dropping on Add arrow 481
   rows and columns in color
      libraries 487-488
Color tables in RTF files 385
Color TIFFs. *See also* TIFFs
   applying colors to grayscale TIFFs 353
   choosing inks 474
   importing 54-56, 346
   magic stretch 361-362
   preseparating 367-368
   scanning at optimal resolution 573-574
   separating 528-535
   trapping 526
Color wells 74. *See also* Drag-and-drop
   techniques
   applying colors 173-174, 182-183, 356
   creating custom wells in Inspector user
      interface 620
   double-clicking to display Color List 481
   dragging color swatches into 162, 182-183, 496
   UIrz resource values 619, 624
Color wheel dialog box 74-75, 76
Colors. *See also* Color List palette; Color
   Mixer palette; Process colors; Spot colors;
   Tints palette
   adding percentages to colors 501-502
   alphabetizing names 505
   applying
      drag-and-drop techniques 78-79, 479
      to groups 497-498
      to objects 496-500
      to text 275-280
      to TIFFs 356
   blending 153-154, 157-158, 159-164
   changing to specified set 662
   choosing colors and inks 474-478
   choosing for trapping 528
   color libraries 482-485, 486-493
   color models 477-478
   converted Illustrator EPS files 375
   copying from another FreeHand
      file 500-501
   creating FreeHand bitmap images 412
   creating new colors 157-158, 485-486, 505-507
   darkening 502-503
   deleting 500, 505
   desaturation 503
   displaying
      adjusting color display 74-76
      comparing to printed samples 75-76,

INDEX 673

475-476
display preferences 72-76
simulating spot colors with
    process 509-510
    viewing colors on screen 476-477
dithering onscreen 74
editing 74, 181-182, 493-496
exporting to color libraries 486-490
Extensis DrawTools Xtras 662
Eyedropper tool 505-507
fill colors
    basic fills 182-184
    converting to Illustrator 1.1 409
    graduated fills 186-187
    radial fills 188-189
FreeHand 5 color enhancements 469-470
grid color 76
guide color 12
guides 76
halftones 353
highlighted rules 282
importing
    from Illustrator 492
    from other applications 492-493
    from PageMaker 490-492
lightening 503
matching
    color names in imported
        images 484-485
    Eyedropper tool 506
    in scanned images 505-507
names 72-73, 174, 484-485, 488, 504, 505
object defaults 80-81
path color in text joined to paths 328
printing
    color PostScript printers 475
    color printing process 470-473
    color proofs 476
    comparing to printed samples 75-76, 475
problems
    converting process colors to
        spot 403-404, 481
    rasterizing images 414
process colors
    converting process colors to
        spot 403-404, 481
    converting spot colors to process 481, 493-495
    simulating spot color display 509-510
    tint builds 508-509
randomizing 504-505, 662
renaming automatically 73
replacing
    one color with another 495-496
    randomly replacing 662
    with grayscale equivalents 662
    with specified set 662
RTF color tables 385
saturation 505, 535, 662
separating and preseparating 528-535
shifting color definitions 403-404
shortcuts for editing colors 482
spot colors
    blending two spot-colored
        objects 154-155
    converting process colors to

spot 403-404, 481
    converting spot colors to process 481, 493-495
    graduated fills 186
    importing into QuarkXPress 403-404
    simulating display with process
        colors 509-510
    tint builds 507-510
stroke colors
    basic strokes 173-174
    converting to Illustrator 1.1 410
    editing strokes 181-182
    on paragraph rules 309
    patterned strokes 178
text colors 275-280
    avoiding fuzzy type 280
    converting XPress Tags to RTF 389
    in RTF files 385, 386
    in text styles 314
    zoom text effect 284-285
tints 507-510
trapping 510-528
Xtras 470, 501-507, 662
Colors dialog box. *See* Color List palette; Color Mixer palette; Tints palette
Column charts 208-211
Column Inspector palette 21, 22, 256-258
Columns
    in color libraries 487-488
    in text blocks 229-230, 255-258
        adding borders to 259-261
        balancing text in 261-262
        column breaks in RTF files 385
        end of column characters 239, 240
        problems displaying rules 261
        rules 259-261
        setting best-looking text 291
        text flow within 257-258
        wrapping tabs 299-300
Commands, adding to popup menus 601
Comments in PostScript code 584
Commercial printers. *See also* Printing
    color printing process 470-473
    dot sizes in screening 533
    FM-screened images 535
    gentle advice about using 102
    hi-fi color 473
    labeling overlays for 552
    negative, positive, and emulsion settings
        for film 553
    preferring named colors from color
        libraries 483
    press sheet sizes 547-549
    seeking advice from 536
    trap widths 515
    trapping process 510, 512
Compact Pro 641
Companion columns in text 300, 304
Complexity of publications 454, 573
Composite paths 145-148
    characters converted to paths 146, 332-335
    correcting direction 149
    editing subpaths 147-148
    filling 182-194
    filling transparent area 146
    in converted Illustrator EPS files 375

    joining additional paths to 147
    losing information in exported files 400
    punching holes with Punch
        command 166
    simplifying self-crossing paths 150
    splitting into individual paths 146
Composite proofs 544-545, 569
Compound paths. *See* Composite paths
Compuserve GIF images 349
Concave lens effect 464-465
Concentric fills. *See* Radial fills
Condensed type 280
Cone shapes, mapping paths onto 661
Confetti easter egg 663
Configuration of installed files 653-657
Configuration of System resources 631-640
Connector points 52, 53
    creating while drawing 134
    creating with Point tool 47, 125
    curve control handles 114-115
Connector tool. *See* Point tool
Consecutive hyphens in text blocks 295
Constitution of the United States 649
Constrain field in Setup Inspector 31, 51, 108
Constraining
    direction of objects being dragged 433
    drawing with Line tool 43
    Freehand tool 118
    lines while drawing 108-109
    object movements 61
    rectangles and ellipses 107
    resizing around shape's center 109
    setting up oblique projection grids 222
    skewing effects 451
Container Color option 73
Containers for text. *See* Text blocks
Contents of paths
    moving 430-432
    reflecting 449
    rotating 441, 444
    scaling 435, 436
    skewing 452, 453
Continuous-tone film recorders 395
Contrast controls in Image dialog
    box 358-359
Control handles 51, 52-53, 130-133
    adjusting with multiple points
        selected 132
    connector points 52, 125
    controlling line segment curve 115
    converting to Illustrator 1.1 409
    corner points 52, 122-123
    curve points 124
    dragging out of points 52, 122-123
    in converted Illustrator EPS files 375
    moving points 138
    no control handles on selected
        points 130-131
    placing points with Pen tool 120-121
    retracting 131, 132, 133
    turning off automatic curvature for
        points 132, 133
Control panel devices 631-640
Controls, creating in Inspector user
    interface 611-612, 619-623

Convert Editable EPS When Placed
    option 343, 372, 373, 378
Convert PICT Patterns to Grays
    option 85-86, 350
Convert RGB TIFF to CMYK option 394,
    556
Convert to Paths command 332, 459-460
Convert to Process command 492
Converting
    CAD drawings to FreeHand
        elements 352-353
    clipboard contents on exit 100
    curve points to corner points 121-122,
        124
    custom guides to paths 16
    EPS files
        FreeHand files to Illustrator
            1.1 404-411
        Illustrator EPS files to
            FreeHand 374-375, 492
        placed EPS files 372
        PostScript files to EPS graphics 581
        previous FreeHand version EPS
            files 348
        to FreeHand elements 85, 348,
            373-374
    files to another format
        importing and exporting 421-422
        using Acrobat 420, 649-650
    FreeHand elements into
        bitmaps 412-414
    imported object-PICTs 206-207
    non-FreeHand files by opening 343
    paths to guides 11, 12
    PICT elements to FreeHand
        elements 348, 349-353
    PICT patterns to grays 350
    process colors to spot 481
    spot colors to process 403-404, 481, 492,
        493-495
    text to paths 332-337
        centering text vertically in objects 462
        paragraph rules 259
        problems 333
        what happens to rules 308
    TIFFs
        grayscale TIFFs to bilevel 356-357
        RGB TIFFs to CMYK 556
    XPress Tags text to RTF 388-391
Convex lens effect 464-465
Cookie cutter effects. See Punch command
Coordinate systems
    in EPS files 398
    in Illustrator and FreeHand 614
    matrices for PostScript effects 612-613
Coordinates
    axis of rotation 442
    basic shapes on page 55
    centers of objects 438, 442
    comparing Illustrator and FreeHand EPS
        descriptions 406
    corners of objects 438
    cursors 5
    in Object Inspector 429, 434
Copies, number to print 540
Copy command
    compared to importing 574

exporting FreeHand elements 400-401
Copyfit Inspector palette 21, 22
    automatic copyfitting 321-323
    balancing text in columns 261-262
    first line leading methods 273-274
Copying
    arrowheads into Stroke Inspector 177
    CAD drawings into FreeHand 352-353
    charts or graphs from other
        applications 206-207, 350-352
    color names 495-496
    colors from another file 500-501
    compared to importing 574
    elements from other applications 349
    exporting objects by copying 400-401
    formatting by creating styles 196-198,
        311-314
    formatting during search and
        replace 247
    object PICTs out of FreeHand 391
    objects 70-71, 190
    Post resources from FreeHand 592
    repeating last transformations 71
    setting Option-drag defaults 82
    styles 202-204, 205
    tab settings 304, 306
    text 248-249, 382-383
    tiled fills 190, 191
Coquille textured fill 193, 588
Corner handles
    resizing objects 439
    resizing paths with text flowed inside 330
    resizing text blocks 250-251
Corner points 52, 53
    as easiest to use 54
    converting curve points to 121-122, 124
    converting FreeHand files to Illustrator
        1.1 409
    placing
        while drawing 135-136
        with Pen tool 120-122
        with Point tool 47, 122-123
Corner radius 107
    adding arcs to paths 111-112
    changing 110
    choosing 42
    specifying for rectangles 55
Corner tool. See Point tool
Corners on rectangles. See Corner radius
Correct Direction command 148, 149, 170
"Could not complete the 'Set page info'
    command..." 28
Count option (numerical guides) 13-14
Courier font 542
Cover weight paper sizes 549
Cracked mirror effect 660
Crashing problems with Photoshop plug-
    ins 370
Create File dialog box 541
Create PICT Image Xtra 412-414
Create Publisher command 417
Creators
    evil space gods 224
    external resource files 593-594, 617, 619
    graphic files 346
Crepe custom stroke 179, 588
Cristal Raster 473, 533

Cromalin color proofs 102, 476
Crop command 167-168, 170
Crop marks
    checking settings before
        imagesetting 570
    considering in paper size 545, 549-550
    in FreeHand's Post resources 587
    settings 552
Cropped-off printouts 550
Cropping
    clipping paths 454-456
    contents inside a path 430-431
    Crop command 167-168
    images 370-371
Crosfield color prepress system 529
Cuneiform in early bureaucracy 539
Curly brackets ({ }) 385
Current percentage field in Copyfit
    Inspector 323
Current Printer Description File dialog
    box 558
Cursor Key Distance option 79
Cursors
    dragging to scroll page 36-37
    for tools 39-40
    moving text cursor 237
    playing sounds when over snap points 94
    position in Info Bar 5
    shadow cursors in rulers 9
Curve control handles. See Control handles
Curve levers. See Control handles
Curve points
    control handles 114-115
    converting to corner points 121-122, 124
    converting to Illustrator 1.1 409
    placing
        while drawing 134
        with Pen tool 120-122
        with Point tool 47, 124-125
Curve tool. See Point tool
Curved corners on rectangles. See Corner
    radius; Rounded corners
Curved line segments. See Arcs
Custom arrowheads 177
Custom dash patterns 176
Custom fills 184-186
    editing 186
    losing information in exported files 399
    printing problems 574
Custom guides 11-17, 80
    converting to paths 16
    guide color 76
    Guides layer 63
    playing sounds for guide events 93
Custom paper sizes, problems 550
Custom strokes 177-180
    losing information in exported files 399
    printing problems 574
Custom tints. See Tints
Cut command 455
Cut Contents command 366, 456
Cut-off EPS images 401-402
Cutting
    holes in paths. See Punch command
    objects with layer information 80
    paths with Knife tool 46-47
    text 382-383

INDEX   675

cv symbol in Info bar 5
cvc string in PostScript code 598
Cyan color or ink 472, 489, 503, 505
Cylinder shapes, mapping paths onto 661
Cylinders in color printing process 471

D

d character in PostScript code 598
Dainippon Ink and Chemicals,
    Incorporated 478
Darken Colors Xtra 502-503
Darkening colors 501
Dash characters 239-240
Dash Editor dialog box 175-176
Dashed lines 175-176, 407
Dashed patterns 282
Data, plotting for charts 207, 208-209
Dates, printing on overlays 552
DCS and DCS2 files 54, 348, 367, 528
DeBabelizer 346, 349, 648
Decimal points in text, aligning 298-299
Decimal tabs 298-299, 387
Decreasing color saturation 503
def statement in PostScript code 584
Default Line Weights option 97-98
Default Template for New Documents
    option 95-97
Defaults
    line weights 97-98
    multiple default files 96-97
    setting FreeHand defaults 23-24
    setting object defaults 80-81
    styles in defaults file 206
    tab settings 298
    templates 95-97
    text auto-expansion 234
    text block size 84, 228
    UserPrep files 99
    zero point location 10
Define Style Based on Selected Object
    option 98-99
Defining colors in color libraries 489-490
Defining styles
    fills, lines, and strokes 196-199, 200-204
    preferences 98-99
    text style masks 318-321
    text styles 311-314
Degrees
    angles in oblique projection 220-222
    in pie charts 213-215
Delete Empty Text Blocks Xtra 232
Delete Unused Named Colors Xtra 505
Deleting
    ATM font database file 269
    carriage returns in text-only files 382
    colors 500
    default code in PostScript field 181
    empty text blocks 232
    fills 194
    guides 14-16, 80
    inline graphics 338
    layers 65-66, 80
    linked text blocks 255
    local formatting 204-205
    objects pasted inside paths 456
    pages 27
    paths after Intersect command 165

paths after operations 169
paths after Punch command 166
paths outside cropping area 167-168
screen preview images 376-377
strokes 182
tab markers 300, 302
text flowed inside paths 330
unused colors 505
Delivering files to service bureaus 571-572
Democratic mating cycles 466
Denim textured fill 193
Dental offices 113
Depth. *See* Bit depth; Perspective
Desaturate Colors Xtra 503
Descent option in text joined to paths 326
Deselecting
    objects 57
    text blocks 254
Designer 3-D application 645-646
Desktop Color Separation files. *See* DCS files
Desperation
    converting XPress Tags to RTF 388-391
    vignette masks 365
Dialog boxes of the future 71
Diamond custom stroke 179, 588
Diamond shapes, mapping paths onto 661
DIC color library 478
Dictionaries
    AltsysDict 587
    hyphenation dictionaries 294
    in UserPrep files 598-601
    PostScript fill and stroke dictionaries 584
    spelling dictionary 95, 242
    support routines in 606-608
Diffusion dithers in stochastic
    screening 530-532
Dimension lines, creating with
    PostScript 596
Dimensions 3-D application 642-643
Dimetric projection 223-224
Direction of paths. *See* Winding
Director 412-414
Disabled plug-ins 370
Disappearing rules or borders 259, 261, 308
Discretionary hyphens (dishys) 240, 245,
    294, 387, 390
DiskDoubler 641
DiskTop 344
Display. *See* Displaying; Screen display
Display Border option 259, 261, 309
Display Color Setup dialog box 74-75, 510
Display Overprinting Objects option 91
Display Preferences dialog box 253, 280
Display Text Effects option 89, 281
Displaying. *See also* Screen display; Views
    Align palette 462
    Color List palette 481
    Color Mixer palette 481
    Copyfit Inspector 261
    Fill Inspector 182
    fills 89
    grid 29
    hidden tools 39
    Info Bar 5
    layers 66-67
    Layers palette 64
    linked and embedded graphics 378

multiple windows 7
objects while dragging 92-93
overprinting objects 91
palettes 19-20, 22-23, 86-88
path operations palette 170
PostScript strokes 180-181
problems with EPS preview images 373
simulated spot colors 509-510
Stroke Inspector palette 173
Styles palette 196
swatches of colors before editing 74
text block borders 258-259, 261
Text Editor box 236-237
text effects 89, 280-281
text joined to paths 328
TIFFs at high resolution 90
transparent text blocks 253
type reduction percentage 323
Type Specifications palette 264
Xtra Tools palette 506
Distiller (Acrobat) 420-421, 583, 649,
    650-651
Distorted objects or text
    3-D Rotation tool 465-466
    DrawTools Shape palette 661-662
    Fisheye Lens tool 464-465
    fixing printer's distorted images 562
    Free Distort plug-in 658
    inline graphics 338
    KPT Vector effects 659-661
    moiré patterns in images 360-362
    skewing in perspective drawings 453-454
    skewing objects 450-454
    text joined to paths 327-329
Distribute Widths command 334-335
Distributing
    characters converted to paths 334-335
    objects at even intervals 461-464
    text evenly in columns 261-262
Dither 8-Bit Colors option 74
Dithering
    bitmap images 413
    colors 74
    in stochastic screening 530
Divider line in Layers palette 63
Document Inspector palette 21
    active pages 97
    moving between pages 38
    overriding printing options 32
    page orientation 545
    page size 545
    pasteboard changes 76-77
    playing with pages 24-32
    scrolling 25-26
    shortcuts 22
    zooming in 24-25
Document interchange 420, 649-650
Document-level preferences 76-77
Document Preferences dialog box 76-77,
    95-97
Document Report dialog box 571-572
Document Report Viewer dialog
    box 571-572
Document Setup button 29
Documents
    changing defaults 23-24, 80-81
    copying styles to 205

creating single-page file from a multi-
    page document 396
document-level preferences 76-77
moving around in 33-38
multiple open publications 7
page setup 24-33
simplifying 101
Dodecagons. *See* Polygons
Dot custom stroke 179, 588
Dot size in screening 533
Dots in Text Editor 338
Dots per inch (dpi)
  blend steps for printer
      resolution 153-154
  equations for printing gray levels 551
  stochastic screening 532
  TIFF resolution and screen
      frequency 354-356
Dotted display of drawn paths 44, 117
Dotted lines in tabs 302
Downloadable fonts
  converting to paths 333-334
  copying FreeHand elements for
      export 401
  in EPS images 402-403
  in pasted FreeHand elements 401
  locating on printer's hard disk 561-562
  printing problems 32-33, 333-334, 575
Downloading EPS files 375
dpi (dots per inch). *See* Dots per inch (dpi)
Drafting techniques 216-224
Drag and Drop a Paragraph Style
    options 84-85, 316
Drag-and-drop techniques. *See also* Color
    swatches; Color wells
  applying styles 84-85, 315-316
  color techniques 479
      adding colors to Color List 159
      applying colors 496-497
      blending 161
      fill colors 184
      removing colors 182, 194
      stroke colors 173-174, 182
      text fill colors 276-277
      text stroke colors 279
      TIFF colors 356
  compared to using styles 194
  graduated fills 186-187
  linking and unlinking text
      blocks 254-255
  pick distance 78-79
  radial fills 188-189
  rearranging layers 68
  tab settings 300-301
  UIrz resource values for color wells 619,
      624
Dragging
  constraining drag direction 433
  copying paths 82
  creating text blocks 228-229
  drag magnification technique 35-36
  drag-placing 345
  generic instructions for transforming
      objects 426, 427
  guides to delete 14-15
  guides to scroll windows 80
  Knife tool across objects 46-47

line segments into curves 131
objects 92-93, 429, 432-433
page icons on pasteboard 26-27
reflecting objects 447-448
resizing text blocks 232-233
rotating objects 441
ruler guides 11-17
scaling objects 439
zero point 10-11
Dragging a Guide Scrolls the Window
    option 15, 80
Draw Dotted Line option 44, 117
Drawing
  basic shapes 107-109
  charts or graphs 206-224
  constraining tool movements or
      shapes 49-51
  drawing tools 38-39, 105-106
  Ellipse tool 43
  Freehand tool 118
  Line tool 108-109
  objects from center out 107
  path-drawing techniques 133-138
  path winding 113-114, 149
  Pen tool 120-122
  Point tool 122-125
  pressure sensitivity 44-45, 119, 120
  Rectangle tool 40-42
  Sketch Roughen plug-in 661
  undoing path segments 117-118
Drawing tablets 44-45, 119, 120
Drawing tools 38-39, 105-106
DrawTools Shape palette 661-662
Drivers. *See* Printer drivers
Drop shadows on text 283
Duotones, creating 498-500
Duplicate command (Document
    Inspector) 27
Duplicate command (Edit menu) 70-71
Duplicate command (Layers palette) 69
Duplicate command (Styles palette) 202
Duplicate words, finding 94, 242
Duplicating. *See also* Cloning; Copying
  styles 202-204
  transformation commands 426, 428-429
Dynamic Scrollbar option 79-80

E

Easter eggs 663-664
Edges of EPS images 401-402
Edit Color dialog box (PageMaker) 489
Edit Curves Xtra 662
Edit Guides command and dialog box 13,
    15, 16
Edit Image button 357
Edit Original command 418
Edit Style dialog box 314, 317
Edit Tab dialog box 302-305
Editable EPS files 343, 372, 373-374
Editable EPS When Placed option 85
Editable objects in PDF files 420
Editing
  arrowheads 177
  blends 156-157
  color libraries 487-490
  colors 493-496
      adding percentages to colors 501-502

changing spot colors to
    process 509-510
Color Control Xtra 501-502
randomizing 504-505
renaming automatically 73
splitting color well 74
contents of non-FreeHand files 343
dashed line patterns 176
edition files 418
EPS files 85, 372, 373-374
fills 186, 190-192, 193-194
guides 16-17
objects pasted inside a path 456
paths. *See also* Paths
  characters converted to paths 332
  dragging points of clipping
      path 430-431
  in blends 157-158
  objects pasted inside a path 456
  subpaths 147-148
PICT resources in ResEdit 376-377
resources in resource files 592-594
strokes 178-180, 181-182
styles 201, 310, 316-317
  changing parent and child styles 203
  dragging and dropping 84-85
  fill- and stroke-only styles 196-198
  formatting by editing styles 195, 200
  redefining 200, 201
subselecting shapes in groups 59-60
tabs 304
text 40, 228-240
  directly on page 82
  options and defaults 82-85
Text tool 40
Editing Preferences dialog box
  expert preferences 97-99
  general editing preferences 78-80
  object editing preferences 80-82
  text editing preferences 82-85
Edition files 415-418
Elements. *See* Objects
Ellipse tool 39, 41, 43
  constraining 50
  drawing with 54
Ellipses and circles
  basic shape properties 54-55
  constraining to circles 31, 50
  converting CAD drawings 352-353
  converting to paths 110-111
  creating arc segments of specific
      radius 111-112
  drawing 31, 43, 107-108
  resizing 109-110
  winding in 114
Em dash characters 240
Em measurement in kerning 287
Em space characters 239, 240, 245
Embed TIFF/EPS upon Import Rather than
    Link option 100, 372, 378
Embedding
  applying Photoshop filters to
      graphics 370
  edition files 416
  embedded graphics in RTF files 388
  extracting embedded graphics 380-381

INDEX

FreeHand files in exported EPS
    graphics 395-396
  graphics in FreeHand files 378-380
  inserting graphics in text 337-340
  placed EPS files 372
Empty square handles 230
Empty text blocks, finding 232
Emulsion settings 553, 570
En dash characters 240
En space characters 240, 245
Encapsulated PostScript files. *See* EPS files
End-of-column characters 239, 240, 245, 288
End-of-file codes in Illustrator 411
End-of-line characters 239, 240
  converting XPress Tags to RTF 390
  in RTF codes 387
  searching for in text 245
  unnecessary 250
End-of-story symbol in link boxes 232
End points of paths 144
Engineers, option name long-windedness and 316
Enhancing images in duotones 499
Enlarging objects. *See* Resizing; Scaling
Enlarging views. *See* Views
Entering text. *See* Typing
EPS files
  bitmapped images in 347
  bounding boxes 401-402, 461
  comparing PostScript in files 570-571
  converting
    EPS to FreeHand objects 85
    FreeHand EPS files into Illustrator 1.1 404-411
    previous FreeHand version EPS files 348
    RGB TIFFs to CMYK 556
    to PDF 649
  creating 392-397
    for OPI 529
    invisible EPS files 376-377
    nonprinting graphics 377-378
    your own EPS files 375-376
  double-clicking in PageMaker 418
  downloadable fonts 402-403
  embedded in RTF files 388
  .EPS extension 397
  exporting 344, 392-397
    compared to printing to disk 541
    converting text to paths 334
    downloadable fonts in files 401
    embedding files in exported EPS graphics 395-396
    for OPI systems 394
    FreeHand's exporting capabilities 391-392
    Generic EPS files 396-397
    matching color names 484-485
    matching color specifications 486
    PICT preview images 86
    text with zoom text effect 285
    writing PostScript files as EPS 581-583
  extracting 381
  importing 54-56, 346-349
    applying colors to imported files 498

colors from Illustrator graphics 492
  colors from PageMaker 490-492
  compared to copying 574
  compared to opening 372-378
  FreeHand EPS files 373-374
  locked colors 493
  managing linked files 419-420
linking or embedding 100, 372, 378
magic stretch 361-362
opening
  compared to importing 372-378
  formats FreeHand can open 344, 348-349
PageMaker problems with EPS TIFFs 397-399
PostScript
  editing headers 406-407
  examining PostScript in EPS files 583-585
  example of PostScript code 582-583
  preseparating images 367-368, 528, 529
  publishing edition files as 417
  salvaging older EPS files 404-411
EPS Import Filter dialog box (PageMaker) 398-399
EPS Rasterizer dialog box (Photoshop) 414
Equations
  blend steps for printer resolution 153-154
  converting XPress Tags measurements to twips 390, 391
  degrees in pie charts 214
  gray levels 551
  resolution in resized TIFF images 355
  screen frequency and printer resolution 354-356
  simulating spot color with process 509-510
  sizes of objects in blends 154
  sizes of scanned TIFF files 354
Equilateral polygons. *See* Polygons
Error handlers in Post resources 587
Error messages
  "array" 575
  "Could not complete the 'Set page info' command..." 28
  custom UserPrep files 600-601
  "framedevice" 575
  "limitcheck" 550
  "nocurrentpoint" 601
  "nostringval" 600
  printing 574-575
  "stack underflow" 601
Errors in spelling or capitalization 240-243
Even columns 261-262
Even/Odd Fill option 146
Evenly spacing objects across page. *See* Distributing
Evil space gods 224
Excel 206, 349, 350-352
Excess text in text joined to paths 325
Exchange (Acrobat) 649
Exiting FreeHand 100
Expand Stroke command and dialog box 12-13, 148, 167-168, 170
Expanded type 280
Expanding text blocks automatically 84,

230, 232-235
Expert Document Preferences dialog box 95-97
Expert Editing Preferences dialog box 97-99
Expert Import/Export Preferences dialog box 99-100
Export command 392
Export Document dialog box 392
Export plug-in 658
Exporting 344
  bitmap PICT files 392
  bitmaps for Photoshop filters 412-414
  choosing output options 392-397
  color libraries 486-490
  colors 479
  copying 400-401
  data with Publish and Subscribe 415-418
  embedded graphics 380-381
  EPS files
    embedding FreeHand files in EPS 395-396
    EPS bounding box problems 401-402
    examining PostScript 583-585
    Generic EPS files 396-397
    imported TIFF images 394
    Macintosh EPS 397
    MS-DOS EPS 397
    nonprinting EPS files 377-378
    PageMaker problems with EPS TIFFs 397-399
  FreeHand 5 files in FreeHand 4 76-77
  FreeHand's exporting capabilities 391-393
  generic instructions 392-393
  grave warnings 392
  Illustrator formats 399-400
  import/export preferences 85-86
  one page from multi-page document 396
  PostScript code in Illustrator format 613, 623-624
  selected text 658
  text with inline graphics 340
  text with zoom text effect 285
Exporting Preferences dialog box 86
Extended characters 238-240
Extending FreeHand's capabilities. *See* Xtras
Extension Manager 640
Extensions, system 631-640
External files
  externally stored files 379
  listing in reports 571
External resource files
  compared to UserPrep files 601
  creating 592-594, 601-608
  custom fills and strokes 595, 608-628
  loading 594
  overprinting grayscale TIFFs 592-594
  sending to service bureaus 570
  testing custom strokes 617-618
Extra leading method 270-271
Extracting embedded graphics 380-381
Extracting inline graphics 338
Extraterrestrial plots 224
Eyedropper tool 505-507
Eyestrain, alleviating 236

F

F or f characters in PostScript code 598
Fake duotones, creating 498-500
Family publications and color matching 505
Fascism and type 29
Faster screen redraw. *See* Screen display
Fear of styles 195
Felt-tip marker effects 281-282
FernHead 663-664
Fetch preview images 86
FH50 file creator 593-594, 617, 619
Fields
    creating in Inspector user interface 601, 618
    in GnEf resources 609-612
    in resource templates 603-604, 605
    in UIrz resources 618-624
    typing code in Inspector 595-599
File-compression utilities 641
File creators 593-594, 617, 619 344
File extensions
    .BCF and .ACF 486
    .EPS 397
File formats
    choosing for export 392-393
    conversion utilities 349
    EPS file types 347
    graphic files 346-349
    importing files 346-349
    interchange formats 420
    PDF files 420-421, 649, 650-651
    PICT and EPS 346-349
    printing to disk as PostScript 541-542
    problems opening or importing formats 349
File interchange formats 420
File names
    exported color libraries 487
    MS-DOS EPS exported files 397
    opening multiple files 7
    printing names on overlays 552
File print option 541
File size 86, 100, 354, 378
File types. *See* Creators; File formats
Filenames. *See* File names
Files
    color libraries 486-487
    creating reports before printing 571-572
    DCS separations 529
    default template files 95-97
    delivering to service bureaus 571-572
    document preferences 76-77
    embedding in exported EPS graphics 395-396
    external resource files 592-594, 601-608
    FreeHand Defaults file 23-24
    FreeHand Preferences file 653
    including in PPDs 560
    installed file configuration 653-657
    linked files 419-420
    listing external files in reports 571
    opening compared to importing or placing 343-344
    PPD files 559
    preparing for service bureaus 568-572

reducing number you need to keep 395-396
subscribing to editions 415-416
UserPrep files 99, 598-601
Fill button on Color List 479-480, 496
Fill Inspector palette 21, 22
    accessing code in UserPrep files 599-600
    applying colors with 275, 496
    attributes in styles 196
    code for PostScript fills 188, 594, 595-599
    controlling overprinting 512-513
    deleting or editing fills 193-194
    displaying 182
    dropping colors into color well 182-183
    filling text blocks 259
    tiled fills 190
Fills 182-194
    adding percentages to colors 501-502
    applying
        color fills 479-480, 496-498
        to characters converted to paths 332
        to text 275-277, 497
    basic fills 182-184
    blends
        blending paths 151
        calculating steps for printer resolution 32
        creating graduated or radial fills 159-160
    converting to Illustrator 1.1 409
    custom fills 184-186
    defaults for objects 80-81
    disappearing 140
    display options 89
    dithered colors in 74
    dragging and dropping 184, 186-187, 188-189
    editing 193-194
    fill-only styles 196-198, 199
    following shape of object 160
    graduated fills 186-187, 520-522, 525-526
    in groups
        coloring fills in groups 497-498
        transforming group's fills 81, 426, 428
    in text blocks 259
    joining paths with different fills 148
    patterned 188
    PostScript
        examples 599
        external resource files 618-628
        fill dictionary 584
        fills 188
        typing code for custom fills 595-599
    radial fills 188-189, 522-523, 525-526
    simplifying 101
    text-block color fills 72-73
    textured fills 193, 590-592
    tiled fills 189-192
    transforming with paths
        reflecting 449
        rotating 441, 444
        scaling 435, 436
        skewing 452, 453
    transparent and translucent effects 458-459

trapping
    controlling overprinting 512-513
    graduated and radial fills 520-522, 525-526
    knocking out 183-184
    overprinting 183-184
    overprinting black inks 520
    overprinting graduated fills 186
    Trap Xtra 526-528
Fills checkbox 192, 430-432
Film output 470-473, 535, 553
Filters, Photoshop 368-371, 379, 412-414. *See also* Xtras
Final output devices. *See also* Printers
    blend steps for printer resolution 153-154
    page orientation 28-29
    paper and page sizes 27-28
    problems printing correct font 265
    resizing images to printer's resolution 360-362, 437
    setting printer resolution 32, 361-362
Find Capitalization Errors option 94
Find Duplicate Words option 94
Find Font plug-in 658
Find palette 243
Finding
    all instances of fonts 658
    empty text blocks 232
    incorrect punctuation 658-659
    linked files 419-420
    text 243-248
Fine gravel textured fill 193, 588
First Blend field 152-153, 156-157
First line indents 295-297, 298, 386. *See also* Indents
First line leading 273-274
First page of files 26
Fisheye Lens tool 464-465
Fit On Paper printing option 544
Fit Page view 33-34
Fixed leading method 270-271
Fixed space characters 239, 240
Fixed Width option in Calligraphic Pen tool 45
Flags field in UIrz resources 619, 624
Flatness 115-116
    converting to Illustrator 1.1 408
    exporting EPS files 395
    print settings 557
    printing times 573
FlEf resources 602
Flipping. *See also* Reflecting
    flipping and flopping technique 139
    inline graphics 338
    objects 48, 447-450
Floating graphics 337-340
Floating palettes. *See* Palettes
Flow Inside Path command 329
Flowing text in linked text blocks 254-255, 257-258
Fluorescent inks 528
Fluorescent lighting 476
Flush Zone text setting 290, 294
FM screening 533-535
Focoltone color library 478
Font numbers 386, 410

Font size. *See* Type size
Font substitution 265, 266-269
   blank fields in Type Specifications palette 266
   in PDF files 421
   in RTF files 387
   printing to disk 542
   problems printing correct font 265
   SuperATM 268-269
Font tables 385
Fontographer Type 3 fonts 332
Fonts 264-269. *See also* Text; Type
   ATM 634
   configuring systems 632
   converting
      characters to paths 332, 333-334
      information to Illustrator 1.1 410
      XPress Tags to RTF 389
   downloadable fonts
      converting text to paths 333
      copied FreeHand elements 401
      in EPS images 402-403
      LaserWriter options 32-33
      problems printing 574-575
   exporting FreeHand elements 401
   finding all instances of fonts 658
   font substitution 266-269
   handling in PostScript 589
   ideal spacing 292
   in converted Illustrator EPS files 375
   in EPS images 402-403
   in PDF files 421
   including when printing to disk 542
   listing resident fonts in PPDs 565-566
   PostScript Type 1 and 3 fonts 332, 634
   problems with 32-33, 574-575, 635-636
   RTF font tables 385
   screen fonts, printer fonts, and type styles 265, 634-636
   setting best-looking text 291
   setting up QuicKeys 266-267
   TrueType 332, 634
   Type Specifications palette 263, 264
   utilities and configuration 634-636
Fonts folder 268
Footers in RTF files 388
For Position Only images 530
Forced justification 289-290, 325, 326
Foreground layers 49, 63, 68
Formatting. *See also* Fills; Strokes; Styles
   attributes of multiple paths 197
   character formatting 262-264
   defining styles by attributes 198-199, 313-314
   guides 12-13
   local formatting compared to styles 194-195, 310
   overriding 204-205
   text
      during search and replace 247
      formatting stripped from text-only files 382
      importing formatted text 384-388
      in text blocks 232
      in Text Editor 236
      paragraph formatting 288-309
      text style masks 318-321

      text styles 309-321
Fortune cookies 576
Fountains. *See* Graduated fills
Fractal tree code 582-583
Fractilize Xtra 130
Fragmenting objects 660
Frame in Inspector user interface 619
"framedevice" error messages 575
FrameMaker 396-397
Frames (planes of projection) 217
Free Distort plug-in 658
Freeform paths. *See* Paths
FreeHand
   Aldus FreeHand 2.0 - 4.0 348
   application and document defaults 23-24
   as out-of-control video game 94
   changing FreeHand's PostScript 590-594
   color enhancements in version 5 469-470
   configuration of installed files 653-657
   coordinate system compared to Illustrator 614
   creating PDF files 344
   direct links to PageMaker 418
   easter eggs 663-664
   embedding files in exported EPS graphics 395-396
   examining PostScript in EPS files 583-585
   extending with PostScript 580
   extensions. *See* Xtra Tools palette
   loading external resource files 594
   new features xxix-xlii
   opening previous versions of files 348
   PostScript code shorthand 598
   resources 585-589
   salvaging older EPS files 404-411
   Software Developer's Kit 657
   Tao of 101-102
   Xtras. *See* Xtras
FreeHand 4 Compatible Page Placement option 76-77
FreeHand Defaults file 23-24, 95, 206
Freehand dialog box 117
Freehand Knife tool option 46
FreeHand Preferences file 653, 657
Freehand tool 39, 41, 43-46, 50, 116-120
Freehand Tool dialog box 43-45, 119-120
Full Height rule option 259-260
Full-scale oblique projection 221
Full spectrum lighting 476
Full Width rule option 260
Fun house mirror effect 660

G

Gaping holes in blends 154
General Editing Preferences dialog box 78-80
Generic EPS files, exporting 396-397, 583
GIF files 349
Global changes to formatting. *See* Styles
Glowing type tricks 336-337
Gluttonous files 571
GnEf resources
   creating for custom fills 623, 625
   creating for custom strokes 608-612
   example 607
   functions of 606

   template 602, 605
Goddess of FreeHand 663-664
Golden rules of service bureaus 572-574
Golden rules of system configuration 632-634
Goofy lines 229, 254-255
Grabber Hand, scrolling with 36-37
Graduated fills 186-187. *See also* Blending
   adding percentages to colors 501-502
   advantages of blends 159-160, 572
   applying colors to 497-498
   banding problems 647-648
   calculating steps using printer resolution 32
   changing fills to 186
   characters converted to paths 332
   display options 89
   dithered colors in 74
   exporting for prepress or film recorders 395
   overprinting 186
   printing problems 572, 574
   rendering in Illustrator format 400
   splitting complex paths to simplify files 394
   trapping 520-522, 525-526
Grape color matching 505
Graphic file formats. *See* File formats
Graphic styles 195, 196. *See also* Styles
Graphics. *See* Imported graphics; Objects; *names of specific file formats*
Graphing techniques 206-224
Grave warnings
   changing FreeHand's PostScript 590
   converting PICT patterns to grays 86
   exporting PICTs from FreeHand 392
   large cropped TIFFs 363
   passwording printers 561
   patterned fills 188
   patterned strokes 178-180
   rapidographs and extraterrestrials 224
   renaming colors 484
   stochastic screening 530
   zoom text effect 285
Gray level controls in Image dialog box 359-360
Gray shades
   blend steps for printer resolution 153-154
   converting grayscale graphics to bitmaps 412
   converting PICT patterns to grays 85-86, 350
   halftones 353
   pixels in bilevel TIFFs and bitmaps 360-362
   replacing colors with gray shades 662
   resolution and screen frequency 354-355, 551
   tint density settings 551-552
Grayed names in Type Style popup 269
Grayed TIFF images 170-171
Grayscale TIFFs. *See also* TIFFs
   applying colors to 353, 498
   converting to bilevel 356-357
   dithered bitmaps in stochastic screening 472, 530-533

duotones 499
importing 346
magic stretch 361-362
Object Inspector controls 356-357
overprinting 592-594
scanning at optimal resolution 573-574
splitting channels of CMYK TIFFs 531
Grayscale to Bitmap dialog box (Photoshop) 532
Grayscale Xtra 662
El Greco's matrix adjustments 562
Greek Type Below *N* Pixels option 91-92
Greeked text 91-92, 269-270
Green color or ink 473, 490
Grid Color dialog box 76
Grid Color option 76
Grid command 29
Grids. *See also* Snap to Grid command
 axonometric projection 223-224
 grid color 76
 grid distance settings 29-31
 line-drawing cell for PostScript strokes or fills 612-613, 623-624
 multiview perspective 219-220
 oblique projection 221-222
 playing sounds for grid events 93
 problems placing objects exactly on grid 30-31
 single-view perspective 218-219
Gripper edge on print jobs 547
Grouping
 applying colors to groups 497-498
 characters converted to paths 332
 converting to Illustrator 1.1 410
 displaying bounding boxes 461
 displaying grouped paths in Object Inspector 434
 groups as objects 56
 keeping layer information 80
 multiple inline graphics 338
 resizing proportionally 109-110
 selecting groups as a whole 60
 setting text wrap 331
 subselecting items in groups 59-60
 transforming groups 81, 426, 428
Groups Transform as Unit by Default option 81
Grow box (Zoom box) 4
Guide Color dialog box 76
Guide Color option 76
Guide Position dialog box 17
Guides 11-18. *See also* Custom guides; Ruler guides
 adding precisely 12-14
 color 76
 dragging to scroll window 80
 Guides layer 63
 playing sounds for guide events 93
 positioning 16-17
 tracking tabs 82-83
 wide guides 12-13
Guides dialog box 12-14, 16-17
Guides layer 12, 63, 68, 69

H

H field (Object Inspector) 234-235, 440
H field (Skew palette) 452

h symbol in Info bar 5
Hairlines 174, 280
Half-scale oblique projection 221
Halftone palette 18-19, 20, 197
Halftones 353
 avoiding when tiling print jobs 543
 compared to stochastic screening 472
 dot sizes in screening 533
 equations for printing 551
 FM-screened images 535
 halftone-only styles 198
 including screens in preseparated TIFFs 368
 overriding screen angles 554
 patterned strokes 180
 printer's screen angles 562
 problems in transverse paper orientation 550-551
 screen drawing procedures in PPDs 563
Hand-sketched effect 661
Handles. *See* Control handles; Selection handles
Hanging indents 303
Hanging punctuation 296-297
Hanging text out of text blocks 303
Hard disks attached to printers 561-562
Hard-to-see text, working with 236
Hatch custom fill 185, 587
Header files for DCS images 529
Headers in files 388, 406-407
Headings
 side heads 300, 304
 spreading across columns 289-290
Heart custom stroke 179, 588
Heavy mezzo textured fill 193, 588
Height
 auto-expanding text blocks 232-235
 objects 57, 440
 page size 28
 paper size 545-546, 567
 resizing imported TIFFs 356
 rows in text blocks 256-257
Hell color prepress system 529
Helvetica font 542
Hexadecimal addition 619
Hexadecimal codes for special characters 387
Hexagons. *See* Polygons
Hi-fi color 473
Hideous text styles 318
Hiding
 hidden layers 66-67
 hidden text in RTF files 388
 hidden tools 39
 Info Bar 5
 palettes 19-20, 22-23, 64, 196, 486
 text ruler 230-231
 Toolbox and palettes 23, 86-87
Hiding Palettes Hides the Toolbox option 23, 86-87
High-fidelity color 473
High-resolution images 398-399
High-Resolution TIFF Display option 90, 170, 378, 506
Highlight dialog box 282
Highlight text effect 281-282, 309
Highlights in duotone images 499

HLS color model 477, 481-482, 502-503
Holes in blends 154
Holes in composite paths. *See* Punch command
Holes in text styles 318-321
Hollow square handles 230
Horizon in perspective rendering 217, 218
Horizontal auto-expansion 233, 234-235
Horizontal axes of charts 207
 line and area charts 211-213
 plotting 207-213
 stacked bar and column charts 210-211
Horizontal axes of objects 48
Horizontal object scaling 436, 437
Horizontal reflecting of objects 448
Horizontal ruler. *See* Rulers
Horizontal rules in text blocks 260-261
Horizontal Scale field 280
Horizontal skewing 327-329, 450, 451
Horizontal text scaling 385, 410
Horizontal TIFF scaling 356
Horse color matching 505
Howling, making more time for 466
HSB color model
 adjusting monitor colors 75
 choosing in Color Mixer palette 481-482
 considerations for use 477
 creating new colors 486
 darkening colors 502-503
 lightening colors 503
Hue, lightness, and saturation. *See* HLS color model
Hue, saturation, and brightness. *See* HSB color model
Hydrophobic and hydrophilic printing plate surfaces 471
Hyperactive worm easter egg 663
Hyphens and hyphenation
 as paragraph formatting 288
 controls 294-295
 discretionary hyphens 240, 387
 em dashes 240
 en dashes 240
 number of consecutive hyphens 295
 searching for hyphens in text 245
 setting best-looking text 291
Hypnosis, spirals and 127

I

ICEfields 473, 534-535
Icon buttons in Inspector user interface 621
Icons, page 26-27, 38
ID numbers 604, 609
Idiot friends and their uses 632
Ignore Columns Less Than *N* % field 322
Ignoring words in spellcheck 242
Illustrator 207
 converting FreeHand data to Illustrator 1.1 407-410
 coordinate system compared to FreeHand 614
 creating charts in 207
 exporting files in Illustrator formats 391, 393, 399-400
 exporting PostScript code as 613, 623-624
 importing

INDEX

colors from 492
compared to opening files 348
file formats 346
Illustrator EPS files 374-375
method of drawing 135
opening files in FreeHand 344, 348, 374-375
using plug-ins in FreeHand 657-659
Image database preview images 86
Image dialog box 357-360
Image PICT files. *See* Bitmap-only PICT files
Imageable area of printers 564
Imagesetters
  custom paper sizes 559, 566-567
  delivering files to service bureaus 571-572
  figuring paper, film and page sizes 27-28
  FM screening 533
  gentle advice about using 101
  paper and page orientation 545-546
  paper size 8, 27-28, 545, 559, 566-567
  positive or negative images 576
  pounding on with wastebaskets xxiii
  preparing files for 568-572
  problems printing correct fonts 265
  screen angles 554
  signatures 547-549
  understanding PostScript 580
Import/Export Preferences dialog box 99-100
Import placing 343
Imported graphics 54-56
  applying colors to 498
  as objects 56
  extracting embedded graphics 380-381
  importing EPS files 372-378
  in RTF files 388
  inline graphics 337-340
  linking and embedding 378-380
  links to imported graphics 357
  resizing TIFFs 356
  rotating 465
  trapping 526
  working with OPI 529-530
Importing
  charts or graphs 206-207
  color libraries 484
  colors 481
    from other applications 492-493
    to or from PageMaker 490-492
  compared to copying and pasting 574
  cropping images while importing 370-371
  drag-placing 345
  EPS files 372-378
    compared to opening 348
    created from PostScript 581
    FreeHand EPS files 373-374
    Illustrator EPS files 374-375
    into page-layout programs 398, 401-404
    solving bounding box problems 401-402
  files compared to opening 343-344, 348
  generic instructions 344-345
  import placing 343
  linking and embedding 378-380

embedding rather than linking 100
links to imported graphics 357
managing linked files 419-420
object PICTs 349-353
PICTs 348, 349-353
problems importing files 349
problems importing into PageMaker 398
problems with bounding boxes 401-402
text files 382-391
with Publish and Subscribe 415-418
Importing/Exporting Preferences dialog box 85-86, 350
Incandescent lighting 476
Inches 30
Include Fetch Preview option 86
Include FreeHand Document in EPS option 391-392, 393, 395-396
Include Invisible Layers export option 394
Increasing color saturation 505
Increasing percentages of colors 501-502
Incrementally spacing guides 13-14
Indents 295-297
  as paragraph formatting 288
  hanging indent settings 303
  in RTF codes 386
  on tab ruler 298
  using tabs with 298
Index entries in RTF files 388
Influences in distortion effects 661
Info Bar 5
Info dialog box (ResEdit) 376, 594
Inherited attributes in styles 200-203, 204
Ink-level overprinting 513
Ink List in Print Options dialog box 553-554
Inks
  checking settings before imagesetting 570
  choosing colors 474-478
  controlling overprinting 513
  defining colors 474
  duotones 499
  fluorescent inks 528
  hi-fi color 473
  in color printing process 471, 472
  knocking out black inks 520
  listing 553-554
  metallic inks 528
  printing names on overlays 552
  reversing chokes and spreads 528
  spot or process 472, 474-475, 553
  trapping special inks 528
  varnishes 528
Inline Effect dialog box 282
Inline graphics 337-340
Inline text effect 282, 587
Input slots in printers 565
Inserting text into text blocks 382-383
Insertion points 237
Inset Path command and dialog box 148, 168-169
Inset Path operations 170
Inset rule option 259-260
Inside colors of radial fills 188
Inspector palette 18-19, 21-22. *See also* names of specific Inspector palettes
Installed configuration 653-657

Installer application 633
Inter-paragraph spacing. *See* Letterspacing; Wordspacing
Interchange formats 420, 649-650
Internally stored files 379
Intersect command 148, 164-166, 170
Invisibility. *See also* Hiding; Transparency
  hidden text in RTF files 388
  hidden tools 39
  invisible EPS files 376-377
  invisible layers 66-67, 394, 555
  invisible objects 573
  invisible text blocks 232
Isis Imaging ICEfields 473, 534-535
Isometric projections 223, 445-447
Italic text 265, 269, 386, 389

J

Join Elements command 81
Join Non-Touching Paths option 81
Join Objects command 145
Joining
  additional paths to composite paths 147
  composite paths 145-148
  lines 175
  paths 144, 148
  text to paths 324-329
Justified text 289-290
  converting XPress Tags to RTF 390
  Flush Zone setting for last line 294
  in RTF codes 386
  justifying characters converted to paths 334-335
  text joined to paths 326
  word- and letterspacing suggestions 292-293

K

Kai's Power Tools 368, 659-661
Keep *N* Lines Together field 261-262, 307
Kent, Clark 466
Kerning 286-288
  around inline graphics 338
  changing in text blocks 250, 252
  converting to Illustrator 1.1 410
  converting XPress Tags to RTF 391
  flowing text inside paths 330
  in converted Illustrator EPS files 375
  range kerning in RTF codes 387
  tracking compared to range kerning 287-288
Key commands or shortcuts. *See* Shortcuts
Keyline view
  controlling with Layers palette 63
  problems viewing text effects 281
  switching to 5-6, 66-67
  viewing text on paths 324
Keys, nudging with 429, 435
Keywords
  in color library files 488-490
  in PPDs 559-567
Knife tool 39
  constraining 50
  drawing 136-137
  options 46-47
  shortcuts 41
  splitting paths 142-143

Knife Tool dialog box 46-47, 137
Knocking out
    basic fills 183-184
    basic strokes 174
    black inks 520
    color fields 516-518
    graduated fills 186
    in chokes 515-516
    in spreads 515
    ink settings 553-554
    lines 518-519
    objects or inks 513
    patterned strokes 178
    text 519-520
    textured fill problems 591-592
Kodak's Prophecy system 394, 556
KPT 3D Transform plug-in 659-660
KPT Sketch Roughen plug-in 661
KPT Vector Distort plug-in 660-661
KPT Vector Effects 659-661
Krause, Kai 659
Krotay, Shree 659
Kurta tablets 44-45, 119
Kvern misspellings of interest 243
Kvern never in dictionaries 95

L

Labels
    creating in Inspector user interface 620
    in resource templates 603-604, 605
Landscape (wide) page orientation 28, 545-546
Languages for hyphenation dictionaries 294
LaserTalk 375, 618, 651-652
LaserWriter 8.0 and 8.1.1 drivers 540, 558
LaserWriter Options dialog box 32
LaserWriter Print Options dialog box 540
LaserWriters 403
Last Blend field 152-153, 156-157
Launching. *See* Opening
Lawnmower color matching 505
Layers 62-70
    changing order 67-68
    changing viewing mode 6, 66-67
    copying layer and objects 69
    creating new layers 64-65
    default layers 62-63
    deleting 65-66
    displaying or hiding 66-67
    gentle advice about using 101
    invisible layers 394, 555
    keeping layer information for objects 80
    locking and unlocking 69-70, 462
    losing information in exported files 392, 400
    moving objects to another layer 64
    naming or renaming 70
    printing and nonprinting 68-69, 555
    switching between foreground or background 68
    tracing objects on 49
Layers palette 18-19, 20
    changing order of layers 67-68
    changing viewing modes 6
    checkmarks and icons 63
    copying layer and objects 69
    displaying and hiding 64

divider line 63
organizing and controlling elements 62-70
Remember Layer Info option 80
switching layers between foreground and background 68
Layout guides. *See* Custom guides; Guides; Ruler guides
Leaders on tabs 302-303
Leading 270-274
    automatic copyfitting 321-323
    changing in text blocks 250, 252
    converting to Illustrator 1.1 410
    first line leading 273-274
    flowing text inside paths 330
    inline graphics 338, 340
    problems with multiple leading in lines 272, 274
    RTF codes 386
Left-aligned tabs 298, 386
Left-aligned text
    converting XPress Tags to RTF 389
    RTF codes 386
    setting alignment 289
    text joined to paths 325, 326
    word- and letterspacing suggestions 292-293
Left Diagonal custom stroke 179, 588
Left-justified text 290
Left text indent 295-296, 298, 386
Length of custom strokes 179
Lens distortion 464-465
Letterspacing
    in automatic copyfitting 321-323
    setting best-looking text 291
    setting in Spacing Inspector palette 292
Level 1 and 2 output devices. *See* PostScript printers
Levers. *See* Control handles
Libraries, color. *See* Color libraries
Library dialog box 483-484, 487
Light mezzo textured fill 193, 588
Lighten Colors Xtra 503
Lightening colors 501, 503
Lighting, office 476-477
Lightness controls in Image dialog box 358
Like attributes 151
"limitcheck" error messages 550, 574-575
Limiting. *See* Constraining
Line art, scanning 355-356
Line breaks in PostScript code 180
Line breaks in text 298
Line charts 211-213
Line ends. *See* Arrowheads and tailfeathers on lines; Caps on lines; Miter limits
Line joins 175, 352, 408
Line screens. *See* Screen frequency
Line segments. *See also* Lines
    as objects 56
    connector points 125
    converting CAD drawings to FreeHand 352-353
    corner points 122-124
    curvature 114-115, 130-131
    curve points 121-122, 124
    curving while drawing 120-121
    flatness settings 557

join options 175
    Option-dragging 131
Line spacing in text. *See* Leading
Line tool 39, 41, 43
    constraining 50
    drawing straight lines 54
Line weights. *See also* Strokes
    converting to Illustrator 1.1 408
    creating spreads 515
    defaults 97-98
    predefined 173
    setting to none in imported PICTs 352
    transforming group line weights 81
Linear graduated fills 186
Lines. *See also* Line segments; Link lines; Paths; Rules; Strokes
    arrowheads and tailfeathers 176-177
    as objects 56
    caps 174, 408
    constraining 50
    converting to Illustrator 1.1 408
    creating separating line in Inspector palette 622
    curved line segments 52
    default weights 97-98
    drawing 43, 54, 108-109, 118
    extra lines in imported PICTs 350
    in paths 51-54, 112-116
    join options 175
    line ends (caps) 174, 408
    miter limits 175
    predefined line weights 173
    straight line segments 52
    trapping 518-519
Lines of sight in perspective rendering 217
Lines of text
    first line leading 273-274
    last line of justified text 294
    leading 270-274
    line breaks in text 298
    problems with multiple leading in lines 272
Lines per inch (lpi)
    blend steps for printer resolution 153-154
    equations for printing gray levels 551
    OPI separations 529
    resolution and screen frequency for TIFFs 354-356
    stochastic screening 532
Link boxes 229-230, 231-232, 254-255
Link lines 229, 254-255
Linking
    data with Publish and Subscribe 415-418
    direct links between FreeHand and PageMaker 418
    OPI links 530
    text blocks 54, 254-255
        breaking links 255
        link boxes 231-232
        text joined to paths doesn't display 326
    to external files
        applying Photoshop filters to linked files 370
        before imagesetting 569
        graphics 378-380

INDEX 683

listing external files in reports 571
managing linked files 419-420
placed EPS files 372
relinking to files 420
updating imported graphics 357
to high-resolution images in
   PageMaker 398-399
turning off linking 100
Links button 357, 379
Links dialog box 379
Listing external files 571
Listing guides 15
LnEf resources 602
Loading colors into Eyedropper tool 506
Loading external resource files 594
Local formatting
   compared to styles 194-195, 310
   compared to text style masks 318
   deleting 204-205
   information in RTF files 385
   overriding 204-205
Locate Center control in Fill Inspector 188
Locate File dialog box 419-420
Lock command 461
Lock Guides command 14
Lock symbols 63, 69-70, 461
Locking
   layers 63, 69-70, 462
   objects 461, 462, 463
Logarithmic graduated fills 186
Logos 24
Long-windedness of FreeHand
   engineers 316
Losing links 420
Low-resolution screen display
   linked graphics 378
   TIFF display 90
Lowercase letters 94, 95
lpi (lines per inch). *See* Lines per inch (lpi)

M

MacDraw 349
Macintosh EPS export option 397
Macromedia Director 412-414
Macromedia FreeHand. *See* FreeHand
Macron character ( ) 285
Magenta color or ink 472, 489, 503, 505
Magic stretch 32, 361-362
Magnetic pull. *See* Snap to *commands*
Magnification
   changing views 6, 33-36
   FreeHand's grid 29
   in Document Inspector 24-25
Magnification field 36
Magnification popup menu 4, 6
Magnifying Glass tool 33-34, 39, 41, 49
Make Compound command
   (Illustrator) 375
Make Process command 494
Manual feed printing 565
Manual tiling 542-544
Manually downloading fonts 403
Manually tracing objects 170-172
Manually updating edition files 416
Margins
   page margins in RTF files 388
   tiles in tiled fills 191

Masks, outline and vignette 364-367
Masks, text styles 318-321
Mason, Samantha Seals 663-664
MasterJuggler 268, 635
Match Case option 244
Matching colors in objects 505-507
MatchPrints 102
Mating cycles in political parties 466
Matrices, adjusting in PPDs 562
Max field in Copyfit Inspector 321-323
Maximum Color Steps option 395, 556-557
Maximum magnification 6, 36
McSink 382
Measurement systems. *See* Units of measure
Medium mezzo textured fill 193, 588
Memory consumption
   applying Photoshop filters 369
   autotracing 172
   copying objects 70
   creating FreeHand bitmap images 412, 414
   downloadable fonts in EPS
      images 402-403
   dynamic scrollbars 79
   extensions and control panels 633-634
   flatness and printing 116
   listing printer memory 560-561
   missing screen previews for EPS files 373
   number of open publications 7
   number of Undo's available 78
   off-screen drawings 89
   printing large paper sizes 559
   printing smaller pages 573
   ungrouping characters converted to
      paths 332-333
Menu items, adding to popup menus 601
Merging styles 206, 318-321
Mesopotamians as bureaucrats 539
Messy artwork effect 661
Metallic inks 528
MetaTools 659-661
Microsoft Excel 206, 349, 350-352
Microsoft RTF specification 391
Microsoft Windows 397
Microsoft Word 349, 385
Millimeters 30
Min field in Copyfit Inspector 321-323
Minimize/maximize box (Zoom box) 4
Minimum zoom amount 36
Mirror images of objects. *See* Reflecting
Missing Fonts dialog box 267, 268
Missing images in print jobs 575
Misspelled words 240-243
Miter joining on strokes 175
Miter limits 175, 408
Mixed colors in color libraries 489
Models, color. *See* Color models
Modifying Leading option 322, 323
Moiré patterns 360-362, 472
Money, tight
   color separations 536
   printing budgets 474
Monitors. *See* Screen display
Mounted beggars 422
Move icon 61
Move palette
   contents of cropped TIFFs 363-364

displaying 433
moving objects 61-62, 429, 433-434
tiled fills 192
moveto PostScript operator 408
Moving
   around in documents 33-38
   centers of radial fills 188-189
   constraining tool movements 50
   contents and fills of paths 430-432
   contents of cropped TIFFs 363-364
   cursor through text 237
   cycling through open palettes 20
   guides 11-17
   Info Bar 5
   linked files 419, 420
   objects 60-62, 429-435
      by dragging 432-433
      to another layer 64
      with Move palette 61-62, 429, 433-434
      with nudge keys 435
   pages on pasteboard 26-27
   points 122, 138-139
   scrolling pages 36-38
   styles to another publication 205
   tab markers 300-301
   text blocks by resizing 250, 253
   through Inspector fields 20
   tiled fills 190-191, 192
   zero point in rulers 10-11
MS-DOS EPS export option 397
Multi-Color Fill dialog box 162
Multi-Color Fill Xtra 162-164
Multicolumn and multirow text
   blocks 255-258
   balancing text in columns 261-262
   column and row rules 259-260
   flowing text inside paths 330
   text flow within 257-258
Multiple default templates 96-97
Multiple guides, deleting 16
Multiple layers
   deleting 65-66
   hiding 66
Multiple open publications 7
Multiple paragraphs, creating styles
   from 311-313
Multiple paths, formatting 197
Multiple windows 7
Multitone Xtra 662
Multiview perspective 219-220

N

n character in PostScript code 598
Name All Colors Xtra 504
Name of UserPrep File option 99
Names
   color libraries 487, 488
   colors 481
      adding named colors 483
      deleting unused names 505
      "home team wins" rule 500
      in color libraries 488
      in converted Illustrator EPS files 375
      in Stroke Inspector 174
      matching names 484-485
      naming colors 504

new colors 486, 508
    preferences 72-73
    renaming automatically 73
custom paper sizes in PPD files 567
custom strokes 609, 610
edition files 417
exported files 393
layers 65-66, 70
linked files 419
matching resource names 607
option name long-windedness 316
Post resources 615
PostScript names of fonts 566
print files 541
styles 196-197, 199, 202, 205-206, 312
Negative film, printing 553, 570, 576
Negative gray level setting 359-360
Negative numbers 156, 433, 442
Neon custom stroke 179, 587
Nested groups 60
Network printing 556
New command (Color List palette) 157-158, 159
New command (Layers palette) 65-66
New command (Styles palette) 196
New Default-Sized Text Containers Auto-Expand option 84, 228, 234
New features in FreeHand xxix-xlii
New Window command 7
"newrope" procedure 608
NeXT machines 652
Next page, moving to 5
Next style settings 314
"nocurrentpoint" error message 601
Noise custom fill 185, 587
Nonbreaking space characters 239, 240, 245, 387
None (OPI Comments Only) option 394, 556
None option
    removing fills 194
    removing strokes 182
    text joined to paths 325
Nonprinting EPS files 377-378
Nonprinting grid. See Grids
Nonprinting guidelines. See Ruler guides
Nonprinting layers 63, 68-69
Normal gray level setting 359-360
Normalize option in transfer function 552
"nostringval" error message 600
Now Utilities
    Startup Manager 640
    Super Boomerang 636-637
Nudging objects 79, 429, 435
Number of Steps field 152, 156-157
Number of Undo's option 78
Numbers
    aligning with decimal tabs 298-299
    in Move palette fields 433
    in Rotate palette fields 442
    negative in First and Last Blend fields 156
    page numbering on pasteboard 26
Numerical scaling 48
Numerically-positioned guides 12-14

O

O symbol in Ink List 554
Object-by-object drawing 89
Object Inspector palette 21, 22, 56-57
    automatic curvature 132, 133
    blending 152-153, 156-157
    closing paths 140
    converting curve points to corner points 124
    corner radius of rectangles 42, 110
    filling transparent areas in composite paths 146
    flatness 116, 557
    linking controls 379
    moving objects 434
    properties for basic shapes 55
    retracting control handles 132, 133
    scaling objects 440
    text auto-expansion 234
    text block size or position 253
    text joined to paths 326-327
    TIFF controls 356-357
    Transforms As Unit option 426, 428
Object-level overprinting 512-513
Object-oriented graphics 346-347. See also EPS files; PICT files
Object-PICT files 347-348, 349-353
    containing bitmapped images 348
    exporting 344
    importing 206-207
    magic stretch 361-362
    preview images 86
Objects 56-57. See also Paths
    aligning 461-464
    applying styles 199-200
    blending 151-164
    centers shown in Info Bar 5
    closed or open paths 144
    color changes on object boundaries 457-458
    constraining movement 61
    coordinates on palettes 438
    copying styles with 205
    defaults for 80-81
    dragging 92-93, 432-433
    dragging to scroll page 36-38
    drawing basic shapes 54-55, 107-109
    duplicating entire pages 27
    in FreeHand Defaults file 24
    in imported PICTs 350, 352
    inline graphics 337-340
    locking 461
    moving 60-62, 429-435
    nudging 79
    on layers
        hiding 66-67
        moving to another layer 64
        on deleted layers 65
    orthographic views 445
    overprinting 512-513
    pasting inside clipping paths 454-460
    perspective rendering 216, 217
    reflecting 48, 447-450
    rotating 47, 440-447
    scaling 435-440
    selecting
        position relative to rulers 9
    setting Pick Distance 78-79
    techniques 57-60
    through stacks of objects 59
    sharing common boundary 139
    skewing 450-454
    snapping to grid or guides 79
    tracing 48-49, 170-173
    transforming 426, 427
    wrapping text around 330-331
Oblique angles. See Oblique projection techniques; Skewing
Oblique projection techniques 220-222, 453-454
Observers in perspective rendering 216, 217
Offscreen drawing 89
Offset cylinders 471
Offsetting
    copies of objects 70-71
    custom paper sizes in PPD files 567
    tiled fills 190-191, 190-192
Old and tired designers 280
Opaque text blocks 253
Open paths 139-141, 144
Open Prepress Interface (OPI) 394, 529-530, 556
Opening
    EPS files to convert 85
    FreeHand
        loading external resources 594, 601
        restoring last view 76
        restoring zipped palettes 87
    FreeHand 5 files in FreeHand 4 76-77
    FreeHand resources in ResEdit 585
    multiple publications 7
    multiple windows 7
    other file formats
        compared to importing 343-344, 348
        Illustrator EPS files 374-375
        PICT files 348
        problems 349
    PageMaker pages in FreeHand 650
    PPD files 559, 566-567
Operations palette 18-19, 170
OPI-compliant prepress systems
    linking to images in PageMaker 398-399
    overriding options for printing 100
OPI (Open Prepress Interface) 394, 529-530, 556
OPI reader (PageMaker) 398
Optimizing. See Printing speed; Screen display
Option-copying objects. See Copying
Option-Drag Copies Paths option 82
Option name long-windedness 316
Orange ink 473
Order
    of colors in Color List 481
    of layers 67-68
    of path creation. See Winding
Orientation
    characters in text joined to paths 327-329
    paper and pages 545-546
        custom paper sizes in PPD files 567
        line screen problems in transverse paper orientation 550-551
Original paths, deleting or cloning after

INDEX 685

operations 81-82, 169
Orphans 305-307
Orthographic views of objects 445, 453
Outline fonts 332, 333, 635
Outline masks 364-365
Outline viewing mode. *See* Keyline view
Outlined text 387, 389
Outlines of objects. *See* Borders; Chokes (trapping technique); Spreads (trapping technique); Strokes
Outlining
   characters in text 282
   expanding path's stroke into two new paths 167-168
   insetting new path inside object 168-169
   objects. *See* Tracing
Output Options command and dialog box 394-397, 541, 555-557
Outside colors of radial fills 188
Overlap *N* Points field 542
Overlapping adjacent colors. *See* Trapping
Overlapping bleed areas 26
Overlapping paths
   creating new paths from intersections 164-166
   punching holes with 166
   selecting through subpaths 148
   simplifying self-crossing paths 150
   uniting into single path 166-167
Overlapping points 144
Overlapping print margins 542
Overprint checkbox 183
Overprinting
   at color field boundaries 516-518
   basic fills 183-184
   basic strokes 174
   black inks 520
   displaying overprinting objects 91
   duotones 499
   graduated fills 186, 520-522
   grayscale TIFFs 592-594
   highlighted rules 282
   in chokes 515-516
   in spreads 515
   lines 518-519
   object-level and ink-level overprinting 174, 512-513
   paragraph rules and text effects 309
   process-color fills 525-526
   settings in Print Options dialog box 553-554
   spot-color radial fills 522-523
   spot-color tint builds 507
   text 275, 279, 519-520
   text effects and rules 309
   textured fill problems 591-592
Override Output Options when Printing option 100
Overriding
   black ink overprinting 520
   copying styles to another publication 205
   FreeHand's internal resources 601
   ink-level overprinting 174, 513
   ink settings 553, 554
   printing options 32-33
   screen angles 554

styles and local formatting 204-205, 310
units of measure 29-30
Overset text 232, 255, 326

P

P symbol in Ink List 553
Padlock icons 63, 69-70, 461
Page Curl plug-in 368
Page-description languages 579-580
Page-layout programs 344, 401-404
Page numbers on pasteboard 26
Page Setup command and dialog box 32-33
Page size 27-28
   bleed area and paper size relationship 8, 27-28
   checking settings before imagesetting 569
   custom page size problems 28
   in PPDs 563, 564-565
   in press sheets 547-549
   PostScript printer page sizes 545
   printing smaller pages 573
   setting up 25-26, 27-28
Page Size dialog box 29
PageMaker
   converting files to XPress 420
   converting pages to FreeHand 650
   converting RGB TIFFs to CMYK 394
   direct links to FreeHand 418
   EPS Import Filter dialog box 398
   exporting and importing colors 486, 490-492
   importing FreeHand files into 401-404
   linking to high-resolution images 398-399
   opening PDFs in FreeHand 344
   OPI reader 398
   printing downloadable fonts 403
   problems with EPS bounding boxes 401-402
   problems with EPS TIFFs 397-399
Pages
   adding 25-26
   arranging 24-33
   bleed area 8
   changing active page 97
   changing page views 5, 33-38
   deleting 27
   deleting all guides 16
   disappearing in FreeHand 4 76-77
   displaying in multiple windows 7
   duplicating 27
   exporting more than one page 393
   finding in PostScript code 584
   grid 29-30
   in PDF files 421
   in publication window 4
   margins in RTF files 388
   objects on 51-56
   orientation 28-29, 545-546
   page icons 4, 5, 26-27, 38
   page numbers 26, 541
   pasteboard 8, 26, 76-77
   positioning in signatures 547-549
   printing page spreads 543-544
   printing ranges of pages 541

problems adding pages or changing size 28
rearranging on pasteboard 26-27
scrolling 36-38
setting guides on multiple pages 13
setting up pages 24-33, 545-549
size 27-28, 29
   bleed area and paper size relationship 8, 27-28
   checking settings before imagesetting 569
   custom page size problems 28
   in PPDs 564-565
   in press sheets 547-549
   PostScript printer page sizes 545
   printing smaller pages 573
   setting up 25-26, 27-28
   tiled printing options 542-544
   turning 38
Paint-type graphics. *See* Bitmaps
Pale-colored text, working with 236
Palettes 18-23. *See also names of specific palettes*
   applying changes and closing QuicKey 637-639
   applying changes with 20
   cycling through open palettes 20
   display options 86-88
   DrawTools Shape palette 661-662
   hiding or zipping 22-23, 87
   shortcuts 20
   shrinking to title bar 22-23
   tabbing through fields 20
Palettes Preferences dialog box 86-88
Panic engendered by styles 195
Pantone color libraries 475, 478, 494
Paper, choosing 475
Paper feeds in printers 565
Paper orientation 545-546, 550-551, 567
Paper size
   adding custom paper sizes to PPDs 559, 566-567
   bleed area and page size relationship 8, 27
   choosing 549-551
   designing for press sheets 547-548
   imagesetting custom paper sizes 550
   memory requirements of large paper sizes 559
   press sheet sizes 547-549
   scaling print jobs to 544
   setting in PPDs 563, 564-565
Paper Size dialog box 550
Paper source, choosing 541
Paper tray settings 564
Paragraph formatting 288-309
   alignment 289-291
   automatic copyfitting 321-323
   compared to character formatting 262-263
   Flush Zone text setting 294
   hanging punctuation 296-297
   hyphenation 294-295
   in RTF codes 385, 390
   indents 295-297
   leading 270-274
   paragraph rules 307-309

paragraph spacing 304-306, 307
spacing 291-294
tabs 297-306
widows 305-307
Paragraph Inspector palette 21, 22
hanging punctuation 296-297
keeping lines together 261-262, 307
paragraph rules 307-309
text indents 296
Paragraph Rule Width dialog box 308
Paragraph rules 281, 307-309
Paragraph styles 84-85, 309-321
Paragraphs
formatting 288-309
joining more than two to a path 325
keeping lines together 305-307, 307
new paragraph markers in RTF codes 387
Ragged Width option 293
selecting 238, 288-289
space above and below in RTF codes 387
styles 84-85, 309-321
Parent styles 200-203, 204, 314
Partial text styles 318-321
Passwords for printers 561
Paste command 574
Paste In button 190
Paste Inside command 455. *See also* Clipping paths; Contents of paths
avoiding Split Complex Paths option 394
color changes on object boundaries 457-458
creating clipping paths 454-460
cropping TIFFs 362-364
moving contents of paths 430-432
outline and vignette masks for TIFFs 364-367
simplifying objects 101
transparent and translucent effects 458-460
trapping across color boundaries 516, 518
using multiple times 455-456
Pasteboard
differences in size in FreeHand 5 76-77
displaying in Document Inspector 24, 25
in coordinate system 398
in publication window 4
making more room 28
pages and stored elements on 8
problems adding pages or changing size 28
rearranging pages 26-27
Pasting. *See also* Paste Inside command
CAD drawings into FreeHand 352-353
charts or graphs from other applications 206-207, 350-352
code into PostScript stroke box 180
color names 496
compared to importing 574
custom arrowheads into Stroke Inspector 177
elements from other applications 349
graphics into text 337-340
keeping object layer information 80
Post resources into resource files 593
styles into another publication 205

text into text blocks 248-249, 382-383
TIFFs inside a path 353
Pat of the About box 663-664
Path-drawing tools 38-39, 106, 116-125
Path operations 148-168
Path Operations Consume Original Paths option 81-82, 169
Paths 51-54, 112-116
adding midpoints automatically 657
applying styles 194-195
as objects 56
blending 151-164
bounding boxes 461
characters converted to paths 259, 332-337
clipping paths 454-460
closing after cutting 46-47
composite paths 145-148
compound paths 137
converting
CAD drawings to FreeHand 352-353
EPS paths to Illustrator 1.1 407-410
Illustrator EPS files to FreeHand 374-375
paths to guides 11, 12, 16
rectangles and ellipses to paths 110-111
copying 82
creating
differences between tools 39
drawing techniques 133-138
Freehand tool variations 43-46, 116-117
new paths from intersecting paths 164-166
with basic shape tools 106-107
with Freehand tool 43-46, 116-120
with Knife tool 137
with Pen tool 46
cropping 167-168
deleting or cloning after operations 169
direction
after reflection 449-450
after rotating 444, 445
correcting path direction 149
reversing direction 114
winding 113-114
editing
expanding stroke into two new paths 167-168
insetting new path inside object 168-169
paths in blends 157-158
strokes 181-182
extra paths in imported PICTs 350
filling 182-194
flatness 115-116, 557
flowing text inside paths 329-330
formatting attributes of multiple paths 197
gentle advice about using 101
grouped and ungrouped 434
joining 81, 144, 147
moving 60-62, 429-435
contents and fills 430-432
paths without moving contents 363-364

paths without moving fills 192
open and closed 79, 139-141
Operations palette 170
overprinting 513
pasting TIFFs inside 137, 353
path operations preferences 81-82, 169-170
PostScript code
comparing Illustrator and FreeHand 404-406
finding path beginning in code 584, 585
preserving original paths 81-82
punching holes with Punch command 166
rotating selected points 444, 445
rounded corners with specific radius 111-112
scaling 435, 436
selecting 58-59
simplifying 137-138, 150
splitting 142-143
complex paths 394
composite paths into individual paths 146
Split Complex Paths print option 555-556
with Knife tool 46-47
text joined to paths 324-329
transformation Xtras 464-466
undoing path segments 117-118
uniting overlapping paths 166-167
Patterned fills 188, 498
Patterned strokes 178-180
Patterns
consisting of FreeHand objects. *See* Tiled fills
converting PICT patterns to grays 86, 350
moiré patterns in images 360-362
of custom strokes 179
textured fill trapping problems 591-592
PDF files 420-421, 649, 650-651
PDFWriter 649
Pen tool 39, 41, 46
constraining 50
drawing with 120-122
Illustrator method of drawing 135
Pentagons. *See* Polygons
Percent character (%) 180, 584
Percentage leading method 270-271
Percentages
in object scaling 437-438
in pie charts 213-216
in Spacing Inspector 292-293
of colors
adding percentages to colors 501-502
adding percentages to multiple colors 501-502
desaturating 503
lightening 503
saturating 505
Performance hits. *See* Memory consumption; Screen display
Personal names in dictionaries 243
Perspective projection 216-220. *See also* Skewing

INDEX

using blends 219, 220
using rotation techniques 445-447
using skewing techniques 453-454
Persuasion 206, 349, 350-352
Photographs. *See* TIFFs
Photoshop 647-648
   applying filters to graphics 379
   as swiss army knife 349
   creating FreeHand bitmaps for
      Photoshop 412-414
   duotones 499
   exporting FreeHand files for 397
   preseparated images 367, 528
   running plug-ins in FreeHand 349,
      368-371
   stochastic screening 530-533
   vignette masks 365
Picas 29-30, 30
Pick Distance option 78-79
PICT files 346-349. *See also* Bitmap-only
   PICT files
   bitmap-only PICT files and object-PICT
      files 347-348
   converting PICT patterns to grays 86,
      350
   copying FreeHand elements 391,
      400-401
   embedded in RTF files 388
   exporting from FreeHand 391-392
   importing 54-56
      compared to opening 348
      extra elements in imported files 350
      from CAD programs 352-353
      object-PICTs 206-207
      PICT graphics 349-353
   patterned stroke compatibility 180
   PICT resources in ResEdit 376-377
   preview images 86, 347
   publishing edition files as 417
PICT2 files 391-392
Pie charts 213-216
Pixels 346, 360-362
Place command 85, 345
Place Document dialog box 345
Place gun cursor 345
Placeholders for linked files 419
Placing. *See* Importing
Plain text style 269, 389
Plan (orthographic) views of objects 445,
   453
Planes of perspective 223-224. *See also*
   Skewing
Planes of projection 216-224
Platforms, exporting for 396-397
Play Sounds When Mouse is Up option 94
Plotting data for charts 207-216
Plug-ins. *See* Xtras
Plus sign (+) in Styles palette 204, 310
PMS colors. *See* Pantone color libraries
PNTG file types 346
Point handles. *See* Control handles
Point size of type. *See* Type size
Point tool 39, 41, 47
   as Ole's favorite 54
   classical method of drawing 134
   constraining 50
   drawing point-by-point 122-125

Pointer shapes. *See* Cursors
Pointer tool 39, 40, 41
   constraining 50
   dragging with 429
   scaling with 110, 439
   selecting with 57
Points (in paths) 51-54, 113. *See also*
   Connector points; Corner points; Curve
   points; Snap to Point command
   adding midpoints automatically 657
   as objects 56
   center points of objects 48
   connector points 52
   control handles 51, 114-115
   corner points 52, 53, 121-122, 123
   creating
      drawing point-by-point 122-125
      Tight Fit option 44, 45, 117
      when splitting paths 142-143
      with Freehand tool 116
      with Pen tool 120-122
      with Point tool 47, 122-123
   curve points 52, 53, 121-122, 123
   dragging selected points of clipping
      path 430-431
   in converted Illustrator EPS files 374-375
   moving 60-62, 122, 138-139
   on stars 42-43
   order of placing. *See* Winding
   playing sounds for FreeHand events 93
   problems printing paths with lots of
      points 574
   reference points in blending 151-152
   rotating
      around specific points 442-443
      selected points 444, 445
   scaling around specific points 438
   selecting 58, 132, 138-139
   snapping together 79
   splitting 46-47, 142-143
   turning off automatic curvature 132, 133
   which type to use 52-54
Points (units of measure) 29-30
Polarity of images, settings 576
Polygon tool 39, 41, 42-43
   constraining 50
   drawing with 54
   setting type of polygon 107
Polygon Tool dialog box 42-43
Polygons
   drawing 42-43, 107-108
   rotating while drawing 107-108
   winding 114
Popup stroke menu 609-610
Portable Document Format files 420-421,
   649, 650-651
Portrait (tall) page orientation 28, 545-546
Positioning
   guides 12-14
   highlighted rules 282
   objects precisely 56-57
   tabs 302-305
   text 254-255, 257-258
   TIFFs 356
   zipped palettes 87
Positive film, printing 553, 570, 576
Positive numbers 433, 442

Post resource template 602-606
Post resources
   creating for custom fills 623-628
   creating for custom strokes 615, 616
   editing textured fill background 590-592
   examining in FreeHand 585-589
   FreeHand resource IDs 587-588
   functions of 606
   referring to in GnEf resources 607, 611
   variables in PostScript 589
POST template in ResEdit 585
Posterization
   avoiding in print jobs 551
   gray level setting 359-360
   Posterize option in transfer function 552
PostScript 579-580
   comments 584
   converting PostScript files to
      EPS 581-583
   converting to PDF 649
   custom strokes as PostScript 178
   dictionaries 584, 587
   displaying with Acrobat Distiller 650-651
   entering code
      adding space or return after 618
      for custom fills and strokes 180-181,
         595-599, 609, 612-615
      FreeHand code shorthand 598
      techniques 594-595
   examples
      custom fills 624-627
      custom strokes 596-597, 615
      EPS files 582-583
      UserPrep files 600
   extending FreeHand with 580
   external resource files
      creating 601-608
      creating resource templates 602-606
      for custom PostScript fills 618-628
      for custom PostScript strokes 608-618
      including files for service bureaus 570
      support routines 606-608
      testing 617-618
      turning effects off and on 592-594
   FreeHand PostScript output
      examining exported EPS files 583-585
      examining files printed to
         disk 570-571
      in EPS files 347
      operators that shouldn't be in EPS
         files 581
      procedures in 585
   FreeHand resources
      changing FreeHand 590-594
      editing textured fill
         background 590-592
      examining resources in
         FreeHand 585-589
      support routines 606-608
      variables in resources 589
   interpreters 581
   printing
      limits on gray shades 354-356
      print error messages 574-575
   UserPrep files
      creating 598-601
      including for service bureaus 570

utilities 651-652
version in printer's ROMS 560
Postscript custom fills 184-186
PostScript errors, avoiding 101
PostScript files (printing to disk) 541-542
PostScript fills 188
  applying colors to 498
  characters converted to paths 332
  custom fills 184-186
  losing information in exported files 399
  syntax errors in 575
PostScript Job printing option 541
PostScript Printer Description files. See PPDs
PostScript printers
  available page sizes 545
  color PostScript printers 475
  Level 1 or Level 2 RIPs 542
PostScript strokes 180-181, 399
PostScript Type 1 and 3 fonts 332, 634
PPDs
  adding custom paper sizes 559, 566-567
  Adobe PPD specifications 559
  compared to printer drivers 557
  editing 559-567
  keywords 559-567
  problems finding PPDs in list 559
  problems keeping PPD selected 558
  tint density information 552
Practical jokes with colors 504-505
PrairieSoft DiskTop 346
Precision. See Accuracy
Preferences command and dialog box 71-100
  color preferences 72-76
  document preferences 76-77, 95-97
  editing preferences 78-80, 97-99
  expert preferences 95-100
  import/export preferences 85-86, 99-100
  object editing preferences 80-82
  palette options 86-88
  screen redraw preferences 88-93
  sound preferences 93-94
  spelling preferences 94-95
  text editing preferences 82-85
Prefix text in color libraries 489
PrePrint Pro 528
Preseparating color images 353, 367-368, 529
Preserving original paths after operations 81-82
Press Match color proofs 476
Press sheets, printing 547-549
Pressure-sensitive drawing tablets 44-45, 119, 120
Pressure-sensitive Knife tool 46
Preview command 5
Preview Drag option 92-93, 432-433
Preview images 347
  adding for custom stroke effects 618
  Adobe Fetch 86
  breaking link and reattaching 375-376
  creating with PostScript interpreters 581
  deleting 376-377
  exporting FreeHand elements 401
  for EPS files 347, 396
  linked graphics 378

missing 373
PICTs 86
Preview mode 5-6, 63, 66-67
Previewing
  changes to TIFF images 358, 360
  edition files 416
  sounds 93
  Text Editor changes 236
Previous page, moving to 5
Primary colors 503, 505
Print dialog box 32, 540-545
Print Options dialog box 540
  displaying edited PPDs and page sizes 567
  nonprinting layers 68-69
  overprinting controls 513
  overriding screen angles 554
  overriding settings 174
  paper orientation 545-546
  problems keeping PPD selected 558
  settings 553-554
Printer Descriptions folder 567
Printer drivers
  LaserWriter 8 and 8.1.1 540
  PDXWriter 649
  PPDs and drivers 557
Printer fonts 265, 332, 333, 402-403, 635
Printer marks 545, 549-550, 552, 570
Printers. See also Commercial printers; Final output devices; Imagesetters; PPDs; Printing; Service bureaus
  checking settings before imagesetting 569
  choosing PPDs 549
  color capacity 560
  color PostScript printers 475
  flatness 115-116
  gray levels 551
  hard disks attached to 561-562
  listing resident fonts 565-566
  memory and downloadable fonts 403
  page sizes 563, 564-565
  paper sizes 545, 549-551, 563, 564-565
  passwording 561
  positive or negative images 576
  PPDs and printer drivers 557
  printing on other platforms 556
  resolution
    determining blend steps 153-154
    gray levels 551
    listing in PPDs 560
    screen frequency and printer resolution 354-356
    setting target printer resolution 27-28, 361-362
  screen angles 554
  slide recorders 556
  troubleshooting printing 574-576
  understanding PostScript 580
  virtual memory 560-561
Printing. See also Commercial printers; Final output devices; Imagesetters; PPDs; Printers; Printing speed; Service bureaus
  advantages of blends 159
  amount of printer's memory 561
  bleeds 8
  building files that will print 572-574

color printing process 470-473
color separations 536
creating reports before printing 571-572
delivering files to service bureaus 571-572
displaying overprinting objects 91
downloadable fonts 401
duotones 499
flatness settings 557
FM-screened images 535
halftones 353
ink lists 553-554
layers 63, 68-69, 555, 556
linked and embedded graphics 378
movable type and romance novels 539
output options 394-397
  emulsion 553
  file names, dates, or inks on overlays 552
  negatives or positives 553
  overriding options 100
  page and paper orientation 545-546
  page and paper size 27-28, 545, 549-551
  page ranges and number of copies 540-541
  page setup options 545-549
  page spreads 543-544
  printer marks 552
  scaling print jobs 544
  screen angles 554
  settings in Print dialog box 540-545
overriding options 100
paper source 541, 565
PICT patterns 86
PostScript to disk 541-542, 568-570
PPDs
  adding custom paper sizes 559, 566-567
  keywords 559-567
  printer types and PPDs 549
problems
  custom paper sizes 550
  downloadable fonts 32-33
  keeping PPD selected 558
  missing images 575
  PageMaker problems with EPS TIFFs 397-399
  troubleshooting printing 574-576
resolution and gray levels 32, 551
separations 353, 528-535, 544-545
signatures 547-549
simplifying publications 101, 150
specifying UserPrep files 99
TIFFs 353, 556-557
tiling
  large layouts 27-28
  options 542-544
  to slide recorders 556
  trapping 510, 512
  understanding PostScript 580
Printing cylinders 471
Printing head 471
Printing plates 471
Printing speed
  blends and blend steps 153-154
  building files for faster printing 572-574

INDEX   689

characters converted to paths 334
flatness settings 116, 557
grayscale or bilevel TIFFs 357
imported FreeHand EPS files 373-374
patterned strokes 178
resident fonts 565-566
stochastic screening 530
vignette masks 365
Printing tower 471
Problems. *See* Troubleshooting
Procedures, PostScript 599-600
Process colors
    avoiding fuzzy type 280
    color libraries 478-479, 489
    color model considerations 477-478
    color names 72
    comparing printed samples 475
    considerations for use 474-475
    converting spot colors to 474, 493-495
    creating new colors 485-486
    duotones 498
    Flamenco screening 472
    importing
        from PageMaker 490-492
        from QuarkXPress 491-492
        into QuarkXPress 403-404
        matching in EPS and publication 486
    in blends 153-154, 154-155
    in converted Illustrator files 375
    inks 472, 553
    patterned strokes 178
    proofing on color PostScript printers 475
    simulating spot colors with 509-510
    text color in RTF files 385
    tint builds 508-509
    tints 478
    trapping 514, 523-526
    Xtras 501-507
    zoom text effect 285
Projection
    axonometric projection 223-224, 453-454
    cabinet projection 221
    cavalier projection 221
    central projection 216-220
    dimetric projection 223-224
    full-scale and half-scale oblique projection 221
    isometric projection 223, 445-447
    oblique projection 220-222, 453-454
    perspective projection 216-220, 445-447, 453-454
    planes of projection 217
    trimetric projection 223
Prominent canines on graphic designers 466
Prophecy system 394, 556
Proportional resizing
    of objects 48, 436, 437, 439
    scaling graphics while placing 345
    text blocks or text 250
    transforming group's strokes and fills 426, 428
PS symbol in fills 188, 597
PSPrinter 8 driver 540, 558
Publication window 4-18
Publications. *See* Documents; Files
Publish and Subscribe 415-418

Publisher applications 415
Publisher dialog box 417
Publisher Options command and dialog box 418
Punch command 148, 166, 170
Punctuation
    hanging 296-297
    searching and replacing 658-659

Q

Q or q characters in PostScript code 598
QuarkXPress
    converting files to PageMaker 420
    converting RGB TIFFs to CMYK for 394
    converting XPress Tags to RTF 388-391
    EPS bounding box problems 401-402
    importing FreeHand files 401-404
    importing named colors 486
    importing spot and process colors 403-404
    opening PDF files in FreeHand 344
    printing downloadable fonts 403
QuickDraw 347
QuickEdit Acquire plug-in 370-371, 379
QuicKeys 637-639
    alignment QuicKeys 290-291
    applying changes and closing palettes 637-639
    changing fonts 266-267
    resetting color display 511
    simulating spot color with process 510
Quickly moving objects 432-433
Quitting FreeHand
    converting clipboard 100
    reviewing unsaved documents 97
Quotation marks (") 296-297

R

Radial fills 188-189
    advantages of blends 159-160
    applying colors to 498
    calculating steps using target printer resolution 7
    characters converted to paths 332
    display options 89
    dithered colors 74
    exporting for color prepress or film recorders 395
    printing problems 574
    rendering in Illustrator format 400
    splitting complex paths to simplify files 394
    trapping 522-523, 525-526
Radio buttons, creating in Inspector user interface 621
Radius of rectangle corners. *See* Corner radius
Rag left alignment. *See* Right-aligned text
Rag right alignment. *See* Left-aligned text
Ragged Width text setting 291, 293
Rainbows 162
RAM. *See* Memory consumption
Random grass custom fill 185, 587
Random leaves custom fill 185, 587
Random Replace Colors Xtra 662
Randomize Named Colors Xtra 504-505
Range kerning 287-288

converting XPress Tags to RTF 391
    in RTF codes 387
Range Kerning field in Character Inspector 288
Ranges between guides 13-14
Rapidographs and ancient Greeks 224
Raster Image Processor (RIP) 580
Rasterizing elements 412-414
Ray Dream addDepth 644-645
Ray Dream Designer 645-646
Read Embedded OPI Image Links option (PageMaker) 398
Reader (Acrobat) 649
Rearranging pages 26-27
Reblending 157
Rectangle custom stroke 179, 588
Rectangle tool 39, 40-42
    constraining 50
    drawing with 54
    properties of shapes 106-107
    setting corner radius 107
Rectangle Tool dialog box 42
Rectangles and squares
    basic shape properties 54-55
    constraining to squares 50
    converting to paths 110-111
    corner radius 110
    drawing 31, 40-42, 107-108
    resizing 109-110
    winding 114
Red color values 490
Redefine command 200, 201
Redefine Style dialog box 201, 317
Redefining styles 316-317
Redraw Preferences dialog box 88-93
Redraw While Scrolling option 79-80, 90
Reducing Glass tool 33-34, 49, 50
Reducing view magnification 6
Reference points 151-152, 156
Reflect Axis field 449
Reflect palette 448-449
Reflecting
    flipping and flopping technique 139
    flipping objects 48, 447-450
    paths changing direction 114, 449-450
Reflection tool 39, 48, 447-448
Registration marks
    checking settings before imagesetting 570
    considering in paper size 545, 549-550
    in FreeHand's Post resources 587
    settings 552
Releasing custom guides 16
Relinking to files 357, 420
Rembrandt, matrix adjustments and 562
Remember Layer Info option 80
Remember Location of Zipped Palettes option 87
Remember Window Size and Location option 76
Remove command (Color List) 500
Remove command (Document Inspector) 27
Remove command (Layers palette) 65-66
Remove From Path command 324, 330
Remove Overlap command 148, 150, 170
Removing. *See* Deleting

Renaming
    colors 73, 484
    layers 64, 70
    styles 206
Rendering applications 642-646, 659-660
Rendering objects as printed (Preview mode) 5-6
Reordering colors in Color List 481, 505
Repeated words, searching for 242
Repeating patterns of FreeHand objects. *See* Tiled fills
Repeating Photoshop effects 370
Repeating transformation commands 71, 426, 428-429
Repellent text styles 318
Replacing
    colors in publications 662
    embedded graphics with links 380
    incorrect punctuation 658-659
    linked graphics with embedded 380
    one color with another 495-496
    text 245-247
Report command 571-572
Repositioning. *See* Moving
Republican mating cycles 466
Resampling scanned images 355
ResEdit 640-641
    examining Post resources in FreeHand 585-589
    external resource files 618-628
    file types 346
    invisible EPS files 376-377
    nonprinting EPS files 377-378
    reattaching preview images 375-376
    resource templates 602-606
    stupid things to do 633
    textured fill background edits 590-592
Resetting
    color display with QuicKeys 510, 511
    coordinates to object centers or corners 438
    original TIFF settings 358, 360
    zero point to default position 10
Resize box in publication window 4
Resizing
    inline graphics 338
    objects or paths. *See* Scaling
    palettes to title bars 22-23
    text blocks or text 84, 232-235, 250-253
Resolution
    blend steps for printer resolution 153-154
    default and set resolution for printers in PPDs 560
    displaying TIFFs at high resolution 90
    equations for printing gray levels 551
    flatness and 115-116
    FM screening 534
    OPI separations 529-530
    resized TIFF images 355
    resizing images to printer's resolution 360-362, 437
    scanned resolution of TIFF images 354
    scanning line art 355-356
    screen frequency and printer resolution 354-356
    setting printer resolution 32, 361-362

tint densities 551-552
Resource IDs 603
Resource templates 602-606
Resources
    creating new resource files 592-594
    examining in FreeHand 585-589
    external resource files 592-594, 601-608
    for custom strokes 608-612
    functions of 606
    GnEf resources 607, 623, 625
    Post resources 623-628
    resource templates 602-606
    Xvrs resources 615-617, 628
Restore Last View When Opening Document option 76
Restoring
    document views 76
    objects pasted inside paths 456
    original document defaults 24
    original TIFF settings 358, 360
    overridden styles 204-205
    window size and location 76
    zero point to default position 10
    zipped palettes onscreen 87
Retaining original paths after operations 81-82
Retract buttons 132, 133
Retracting control handles 131, 132, 133
Return key 180. *See also* Carriage returns
Reverse Direction command 114, 148, 149, 170
Reverse Traps option 527-528
Reversed type, working with 236
Reverting
    to original document defaults 24
    to original style 204-205
    to original TIFF settings 358, 360
Reviewing unsaved documents 97
Rewriting PPDs 559-567
RGB color model
    adjusting monitor colors 75
    choosing in Color Mixer palette 481-482
    color names 72
    considerations for use 477-478
    converting RGB TIFFs to CMYK 556
    creating bitmap images 412
    creating new colors 485-486
    darkening colors 502-503
    defining colors 490
    in color libraries 489
    lightening colors 503
    naming colors 504
    text colors in RTF files 385
RGB TIFFs 354, 506, 528, 556
Rich Text Format files. *See* RTF (Rich Text Format) files
Right-aligned tabs 298, 386
Right-aligned text
    converting XPress Tags to RTF 389
    in RTF codes 386
    setting alignment 289
    text joined to paths 325, 326
    word- and letterspacing suggestions 292-293
Right Diagonal custom stroke 179, 588
Right-justified text 290
Right text indent 295-296, 298, 386

RIP-based FM screening systems 533
RIPs (Raster Image Processors) 580, 650-651
Roman custom stroke 179, 588
Roman versions of fonts 265
Romance novels in history of type 539
ROMs 580
ropedict PostScript dictionary 587, 610
Rosettes in color printing 472-473
Rotate Around Path text orientation option 327
Rotate palette 214, 441-443
Rotating
    3-D Rotation tool 465-466
    building pie charts 214
    contents and fills 444
    direction of paths after rotating 444, 445
    inline graphics 338
    multiple objects 443
    objects 47, 440-447
    polygons while drawing 107-108
    storing angles of rotation 440
    using in perspective drawings 445-447
Rotation Angle field 442
Rotation tool 39, 47, 440-441, 465-466
Rough sketch effects 661
Round caps on strokes 174
Round joining on strokes 175
Rounded corners
    adding to paths 111-112
    corner radius 42, 110
Rounding measurements in RTF files 385
Rows
    in color libraries 487-488
    in text blocks 229-230, 255-258
        adding borders to 259-261
        problems displaying rules 261
        text flow within 257-258
RTF (Rich Text Format) files
    converting XPress Tags to RTF 388-391
    exporting from FreeHand 392
    formatting not imported in RTF files 385, 388
    importing 343-344, 349, 384-391
    Microsoft specification 391
    obtaining latest specification 391
    opening 349
    RTF codes 386-387
Ruler guides 80. *See also* Custom guides; Snap to Guides command
    axonometric projection 223-224
    color 76
    Guides layer 63
    moving layer up or down 67-68
    multiview perspective 219-220
    oblique projection 221-222
    playing sounds for guide events 93
    positioning 11-17
    single-view perspective grid 218-219
    Snap to Guides command 17-18
Rulers 4, 9
    tab rulers on text blocks 230-231
    tracking tabs 82-83
    zero point 10-11
Rules
    around rows or columns 259-261
    behind text 281-282

INDEX

problems displaying 261
text effects and 281, 307-309
through text 283
underlining text 284
Running heads or footers 388
Running Photoshop plug-ins 368-371

S

S or s characters in PostScript code 598
Sand textured fill 193, 588
Saturate Colors Xtra 505
Saturation
   adjusting 662
   Desaturate Colors Xtra 503
   FM-screened images 535
   Saturate Colors Xtra 505
Saving document reports 571-572
Saving files
   FreeHand 5 files in FreeHand 4 76-77
   reviewing before quitting 97
Scale Factor % field 437-438
Scale options in printing 544
Scale palette 435, 436, 437-438
Scales in oblique projection 220
Scales of charts 207-216
Scaling
   checking print scale settings before
      imagesetting 569
   displaying scaling percentage 356
   horizontal text scaling 280, 385
   images
      bitmaps to original size 437
      TIFFs 356
      to target printer resolution 32,
         360-362, 437
   inline graphics 338
   objects 435-440
      around specific points 438
      proportionally 48, 109-110
      rectangles and ellipses 109-110
      to target printer's resolution 32,
         360-362, 437
      with Object Inspector 56-57, 440
      with Pointer tool 439
      with Scale palette 437-438
      with Scaling tool 48, 435-437
   paths
      compared to Inset Path
         command 168
      with text flowed inside 330
   techniques in perspective
      drawings 445-447
   tiled fills 190
Scaling tool 39, 48, 435-437
Scanning. See also TIFFs
   line art 355-356
   optimizing resolution 573
   plug-ins 370-371
   size and resolution of images 354-356
Scitex color prepress system 529
Screen angles 554, 562
Screen display
   black and white interface 87-88
   blend display 159-160
   colors
      8-bit (256-color) display 74
      adjusting display 74-76

calibration 74-76, 476
   choosing colors from printed
      samples 475
   color preferences 72-76
   HSB color model 75
   controlling with Layers palette 63
display speed
   drawing with dotted lines 117
   Keyline or Preview modes 6
   off-screen and object-by-object
      drawing 89
   redrawing while scrolling 79-80, 90
   slow scrolling 90
Draw Dotted Line option 44, 117
fill display 89
greeking text 91-92
images
   high-resolution TIFF display 90
   large cropped TIFFs 363
   object PICT previews 86
   monitor settings 506
   objects being dragged 92-93, 433
   screen redraw preferences 88-93
   text effects display 89
Screen fonts 265, 635
Screen frequency
   checking settings before
      imagesetting 569
   duotones 499
   equations 354-356, 551
   halftone-only styles 198
   in PPDs 563
   lines per inch 153-154
   scanned resolution of TIFF images 354
   scanning at optimal resolution 573
   transverse printing and rotated
      publications 550-551
Screen preview images. See Preview images
Screen redraw. See Screen display
Screen ruling. See Screen frequency
Screens. See also Halftones
   Flamenco screening 472
   FM screening 533-535
   hi-fi color 473
   in color printing process 472-473
   stochastic screening 472-473, 530-535
Scrn resources 602
Scrollbars 4, 5, 79-80
Scrolling 36-38
   dragging guides to scroll 80
   in Document Inspector 25-26
   redrawing while scrolling 90
SDK (Software Developer's Kit) 657
Search (Acrobat) 649
Searching for text
   FreeHand files 243-248
   PDF files 649
Seattle Mariners 422
Select All command 57
Select PostScript Printer Description File
   dialog box 558
Selecting
   groups 59-60
   guides 14
   more than one color to add 483-484
   objects
      centering selected object in

window 34
   in Keyline or Preview modes 6
   position relative to rulers 9
   rotating multiple selected objects 443
   techniques 57-60
   through stacks of objects 59
   with Pointer tool 40
paths 58-59
   after splitting 142
   subpaths of composite paths 147
   with joined text 324
points 58, 138-139
   multiple points 132, 138
   reference points in blends 156
   rotating selected points 444, 445
text 238
   joined to paths 324
   paragraph rules 308
   paragraphs 288-289
   to apply styles 314
   with multiple formatting
      attributes 266
Selection handles 57
   defining bounding boxes 461, 462
   displaying 57
   resizing objects 439
   text auto-expansion shortcuts 235
   text blocks 83-84, 230-231, 250-253
Selection rectangle (marquee) 57-58, 132,
   138, 143
Sensitivity of Pick Distance option 78-79
Separating color images. See Color
   separations
Separating line in Inspector user
   interface 622
Separation Names option 484
Separations print option 544-545
Serial cables, printing over 556
Service bureaus
   creating file reports before
      printing 571-572
   delivering files 571-572
   gentle advice about using 102
   golden rules 572-574
   preparing files 568-572
Set Links dialog box 379
Set Parent command and dialog
   box 202-203
Setting up pages 24-33
Setup Inspector palette 21
   constraining angle 118
   measurement units 9
   printer resolution 361-362
   setting up pages 29-32
   tool constraint values 31
Shadow cursors in rulers 9
Shadow text style 387, 389
Shadows
   drop shadows on text 283
   in duotone images 499
Shakespeare 649
Shape-drawing tools 38-39
Shared attributes in styles 84
   basing styles on examples 311-313
   text style masks 318-321
Sharpening images 535
Shatter plug-in 660

Shift-selecting techniques 57-58
Shifting baselines. *See* Baseline shift;
    Baselines of text
Shoe color matching 505
Shortcuts
    changing page views 33-34
    Clone and Duplicate commands 70-71
    Create PICT Image dialog box 413
    displaying palettes 20, 22-23
    displaying rulers 9
    dragging line segments into curves 131
    editing colors 482
    hiding and zipping palettes 22-23
    kerning 287
    locking objects 461
    moving text cursor 237
    nudging with arrow keys 429, 435
    opening Text Editor box 236-237
    path operations palette 170
    PostScript code shorthand 598
    QuicKeys for changing fonts 266-267
    reducing or enlarging type size 269
    screen display of objects being
        dragged 433
    selecting or deselecting
        objects 58
        paragraphs 289
        text 238
        text blocks 254
        tools 41
    special characters 240
    switching between tools and Magnifying
        Glass 34
    text auto-expansion 233, 235
    transforming objects 426, 428-429
    viewing modes for layers 67
Show Path option 328
Show Selection option 241, 244
Show Text Handles When Text Ruler Is Off
    option 83-84, 230
Showing. *See* Displaying
Shrinking palettes to titlebars 22-23
Side handles of text blocks 252
Side heads in text columns 300, 304
Sides on polygons 42-43
Signatures 547-549
Silly things in FreeHand 663-664
Simplify command 134, 137-138, 148, 150,
    170
Single paths, formatting attributes 197
Single-view perspective 218-219
Single widowed lines or words of
    paragraphs 305, 307
Size of files 86, 100, 354, 378
Size of pages. *See* Page size
Sizing. *See* Resizing; Scaling
Sketch Roughen plug-in 661
Skew Horizontal or Vertical text orientation
    options 327
Skew palette 452
Skewing
    3-D Rotation tool 465-466
    inline graphics 338
    objects 450-454
    text joined to paths 327-329
    using in perspective drawings 453-454
Skewing tool 39, 48, 450-452

Skip Capitalized hyphenation option 295
Skipping words in spellcheck 242
Slanting objects. *See* Skewing
Slash character (/) in PostScript code 585
Slide recorders, printing to 556
Slothful files 571
Slow screen redraw. *See* Screen display
Slowly dragging objects 432-433
Small caps text formatting 388
Small text sizes, working with 236
Smart Punctuation plug-in 658-659
Smooth points. *See* Curve points
Smoothing path edges 413
Smoothness of curves. *See* Flatness
Smudge dialog box 162
Smudge tool 161-162
Snakes, what to tell 634
Snap Distance option 17, 79
Snap Sounds Enabled option 93
Snap to Grid command 31, 79, 93
Snap to Guides command 17-18, 79, 93
Snap to H-Guide or V-Guide options 93
Snap to Point command 79, 93, 144,
    221-222
Snowflake custom stroke 179, 588
Soap operas xxii, 397
Soft returns. *See* End-of-line characters
Software Developer's Kit 657
Software engineers' problems 274
Software soap operas xxii, 397
Solarize gray level setting 359-360
Son of More Preferences dialog box 71
Sort Color List by Name Xtra 505
Sounds, playing 93-94
Sounds Preferences dialog box 93-94
Space characters
    adding after PostScript code 618
    em spaces 239, 240
    en spaces 240
    entering code for PostScript strokes 180
    nonbreaking spaces 239, 240
    searching for in text 245
    text effects 286
    thin spaces 240
    using tabs instead 298
Spacing
    as paragraph formatting 288
    automatic copyfitting 321-323
    before and after paragraphs 304-306,
        307, 387
    changing in text blocks 250, 252
    distributing characters converted to
        paths 334-335
    in custom strokes 179
    in substituted fonts 268
    kerning 286-288
    last line of justified text 294
    objects evenly across page. *See*
        Distributing
    paragraph formatting 291-294
    setting in Spacing Inspector 292
    three entirely objective things 291
Spacing Inspector palette 21, 22, 292-294,
    295
Special characters
    hanging punctuation 296-297
    macrons ( ) 285

RTF codes 387
    searching for 243, 245
    typing 238-240
Specifying attributes in styles 198-199,
    313-314
Speed. *See* Printing speed; Screen Display
Spelling 94-95, 240-243
Spelling palette 241
Spelling Preferences dialog box 94-95, 242
Spherize distortion effect 661
Spiral dialog box 128-129
Spiral tool 127-129
Spirals 127-129
Split Complex Paths option 394, 555-556
Split Element command 332
Split Object command 142, 143, 146
Splitting
    color wells 74
    complex paths 394
    paths or points 46-47, 142-143
    text flowed inside paths 330
    text from paths 324
Spot colors
    avoiding fuzzy type 280
    color libraries 478-479, 489
    color model considerations 477
    comparing printed samples 475
    considerations for use 474-475
    converting to process 474, 481, 493-495
    creating new colors 485-486
    graduated fills 186, 520-522
    importing
        from other applications 492-493
        from PageMaker 490-492
        into QuarkXPress 403-404
        matching in EPS and
            publication 484-485
    in blends 153-155
    inks 472, 528, 553
    overprinting and textured fills 591-592
    radial fills 522-523
    renaming colors 484
    simulating display with process
        colors 509-510
    tint builds 507-510
    tints 478
    trapping 514-518, 520, 528
    Xtras 501
    zoom text effect 285
Spread Size field in Print Options dialog
    box 470
Spreads (page spreads) 543-544
Spreads (trapping technique) 514
    example 515
    process color trapping 523-524
    reversing chokes and spreads 527-528
    Trap Xtra 526-528
    trapping lines 518
    trapping text 519-520
Square caps on strokes 174
Squares. *See* Rectangles and squares
Squares custom fill 185, 587
Squiggle custom stroke 179, 588
"stack underflow" error message 601
Stacked bar and column charts 210-211
Stacked screens. *See* Tint builds
Stacking order of layers, changing 67-68

INDEX 693

Standard file formats 650
Star custom stroke 179, 588
Stars, drawing 42-43
Starting points of tiled fills 190-191
Startup Manager 640
Static text in Inspector user interface 620
Status bar (Info Bar) 5
Steps in blending 152-154, 156-157
Stochastic screening 472-473, 530-535
Stories
    applying styles 314-316
    checking spelling 240-243
    copyfitting 321-323
    flowing inside paths 329-330
    in deleted linked text blocks 255
    linking together 230-231, 254-255
    searching and replacing text 243-248
    selecting all paragraphs in 289
    selecting text in 238
    symbols in link boxes 231-232
    text flow within columns and rows 257-258
Storing elements on pasteboard 8
Storing imported graphics 378-380
Straight Knife tool option 46
Streamline 346
Streets paved with gold 422
Strikethrough dialog box 283
Strikethrough text effect 283, 309
Strikethrough type style 388
String variables in FreeHand's PostScript 589
Stroke button on Color List 479-480, 496
Stroke Inspector palette 21, 22
    accessing code in UserPrep files 599-600
    applying colors or strokes 173, 496
    code for PostScript strokes 180-181, 594, 595-599
    custom strokes 177-180
    dropping colors into 173-174
    editing strokes 181
    overprinting 513
    paragraph rule strokes 309
    removing strokes 182
    text or text block strokes 259, 277-279
    using attributes in styles 197
    values for PostScript strokes 608
stroke PostScript operator 409
Stroke Widths submenu 173, 181
Stroked text effect 387
Strokes 173-182
    applying
        color strokes 479-480, 496-498
        to text 277-279, 497
    arrowheads and tailfeathers 176-177
    Basic stroke type 173-177
    blending paths 151
    caps 174
    characters converted to paths 332
    converting to Illustrator 1.1 410
    custom strokes 177-180, 179
    dashed 175-176
    default weights 97-98
    defaults for objects 80-81
    editing 181-182
    glowing type trick 336-337
    join options 175

joining paths with different fills 148
miter limits 175
overprinting 174, 513-514
patterned strokes 178-180
PostScript strokes 180-181
    code for custom strokes 595-599, 609, 612-615
    examples 596-597, 615
    external resource files 608-618
    stroke dictionary 584
predefined line weights 173
removing from paths 182
scaling with paths 435, 436
stroke-only styles 196-198, 199
text
    on paragraph rules 309
    on text block backgrounds 72-73
    on text block borders 259
    on text joined to paths 328
transforming group's strokes 426, 428
trapping 518-519, 526-528
width 174
StuffIt 641
Stupid things to do with ResEdit 633
Style numbers in RTF codes 386
Styles 194-206
    + (plus sign) by names 310
    adding to defaults file 206
    applying 182, 199-200, 279-280, 314-316
    basing one style on another 200-203
    compared to local formatting 194-195, 310
    copying to another publication 205
    creating 196-199, 200-204
    defining by attributes 198-199, 313-314
    duplicating 202-204
    editing 201, 316-317
        changing parent and child styles 203
        merging two into one 206
    fill- and stroke-only styles 196-198, 199
    gentle advice about using 101
    graphic and text styles 195, 196
    halftone-only styles 198
    losing information in exported files 392, 399
    overriding 204-205
    renaming 196-197, 199
    setting preferences 98-99
    style sheets in RTF files 385
    text style defaults 84-85
    text style masks 318-321
    text styles 309-321
Styles palette 18-19, 20
    + (plus sign) 310
    applying strokes 173
    applying styles 199-200
    displaying 196
Subpaths of composite paths 147-148
Subscribe To command and dialog box 415-416
Subscriber applications 415
Subscriber dialog box 415-416
Subscriber Options dialog box 416, 418
Subscribing 415-416, 418
Subscripted text (baseline shift) 272-273, 387, 389
Subselecting in groups 59-60

Substituting fonts. *See* Font substitution
Suffix text in color libraries 489
Suggested spellings for words 241, 242
Suitcase 268, 635
Sumerians (Mesopotamians) in early bureaucracy 539
supdict PostScript dictionary 587, 610
Super Boomerang 636-637
SuperATM 268-269
Superimposed text 459-460
Superman 466
Superscripted text (baseline shift) 272-273, 387, 389
Support routines 584, 606-608
Surprises in FreeHand 663-664
Swatches. *See* Color swatches
Swirl custom stroke 179, 588
Swirl distortion effect 661
Switching
    between Freehand tool variations 43-44, 116
    between linked and embedded graphics 380
    between multiple publications 7
    between page views 33-36
    between tools and Magnifying Glass 34, 41, 49
    cycling through open palettes 20
    default templates 96-97
    layers between foreground and background 68
    to new System version 632
    to Pointer tool temporarily 40, 41
Symbol font 542
Symbols
    in link boxes 231-232
    inserting special characters 238-240
    on tools 39
"syntaxerror" messages 575
System configuration 631-640
System file 267, 631-634

T

Tab characters or tab stops. *See* Tabs
Tab key 254
Tab ruler 230-231, 298
Table Editor 349
Table-like columns and rows. *See* Multicolumn and multirow text blocks
Table-making applications 349
Table of contents markers in RTF files 388
Tabs 297-306
    alignment 300, 302
    as paragraph formatting 288
    codes in RTF files 386-387
    converting XPress Tags to RTF 390-391
    copying settings 304, 306
    deleting 300, 302
    Edit Tab dialog box 302-305
    hanging indents 303
    leaders 302
    searching for in text 245
    setting 299-301
    style settings 314
    tracking on ruler and page 82-83
    unnecessarily ending lines with 250
    using with indents 298

wrapping tabs 300, 304, 385
Tagged Image Format files. *See* TIFFs
Tagging text with styles 310, 311
Tailfeathers 176-177
Tall page orientation 28, 545-546
Tall paper sizes 545-546
Tall tales about Polygon tool 106
Tao and FreeHand 101-102
Target printer resolution option 32
Target printers. *See* Final output devices; Imagesetters; Printers
Tavern, Rival Monk 663
Technology Without An Interesting Name standard 370
TechPool Transverter Pro 581
Teeth custom stroke 179, 588
Templates
   FreeHand defaults template 23-24, 95-97, 206
   resource templates 602-606
Temporary preview drag 93
Testing
   external resource files 617-618
   resource templates 604-606
Text 227. *See also* Stories; Text blocks; Type
   alignment 233-234, 289-291, 325, 326
   auto-expanding text blocks 232-235
   automatic copyfitting 321-323
   baselines 272-273, 326-327
   blank fields in palettes 266
   case of text 388
   centering vertically in objects 462
   changing case 658
   checking spelling 94-95, 240-243
   cleaning up 243
   colors
      applying colors to 275-280, 497
      color changes on object boundaries 457-458
      displaying applied color 72-73
      in RTF files 385, 386, 389
   converting
      characters to paths 259, 332-337
      EPS text to Illustrator 1.1 407, 410-411
      text file conversion utilities 382
      text in converted Illustrator EPS files 375
   copying 248-249
   editing 82, 236-237
   effects 89, 280-286
   entering and editing 40, 228-240
   exporting 340, 344, 392, 658
   eyestrain and small text 236
   fills 275-277
   finding and replacing 243-248
   first line leading 273-274
   Flags field values 625
   flowing
      inside paths 329-330
      within columns and rows 257-258
   fonts 264-269
   formatting
      by replacing 247
      character formatting 262-264
      entire text in text blocks 232
      hyphenation 294-295

indents 295-297
kerning 286-288
leading 270-274
not supported in RTF files 385, 388
paragraph formatting 288-309
space before and after paragraphs 304-306, 307
spacing 291-294
styles 279-280
type size 269
type styles 269
glowing type tricks 336-337
greeked text 91-92, 269-270
handles 83-84
highlighting 281-282
horizontal scaling 280, 385
importing text files 382-391
   in PDF files 421
inline graphics 337-340
insertion points 237
joining to paths 324-329
kerning 286-288
label text in Inspector palette 618
leading 270-274
linking stories 230-231, 254-255, 326
multicolumn and multirow text blocks 255-258, 261-262
options and defaults 82-85
paragraph rules 307-309
problems
   avoiding fuzzy type 280
   fonts 32-33, 574-575, 635-636
   text joined to path doesn't display 326
   weird characters in text 382
resizing text and text blocks 84, 230, 250-253
RTF codes 386-387
rulers 230-231, 298
selecting 238
special characters 238-240
spiraling 127-128
striking through 283
tabs 82-83, 297-306
text blocks 54, 56, 248-262, 255-258. *See also* Text blocks
text styles 309-321, 314-316
transparent text 459-460
trapping 519-520
underlining 284
widows 305, 307
wrapping around objects 330-331
Text blocks 54, 56, 248-262. *See also* Text
   accurate size or position 253
   alignment in text joined to paths 325, 326
   as objects 56
   auto-expanding text blocks 84, 230, 232-235
   borders and fills in 258-261
   breaking into single-line text blocks 400
   coloring background 497
   colors 275-280
   controls 229-232
   converting characters to paths 332
   copying text 248-249
   creating blocks
      before inserting text 382-383

by clicking or dragging 228-229
square blocks 345
with Text tool 40
deleting empty text blocks 232
deselecting 254
displaying borders 261
displaying text effects 89
fill and stroke color names 72-73
finding empty blocks 232
flowing text inside paths 329-330
handles 83-84
hanging text outside 296-297
in PDF files 421
insertion points 237
link boxes 231-232
linking 230-231, 254-255, 326
losing information in exported files 399, 400
multicolumn and multirow 229-230, 255-258
   balancing text 261-262
   borders on rows and columns 259-261
   text flow 257-258
   wrapping tabs 299-300
opaque or transparent during editing 253
options and defaults 82-85
resizing blocks and text 84, 230, 250-253
rules
   problems displaying rules 261
   strokes on paragraph rules 309
selecting all paragraphs in 289
selection handles 230-231
styles 279-280
tab rulers 230-231, 298
text wrap 330-331
unlinking 255
Text Color option 73
Text containers. *See* Text blocks
Text Editing Preferences dialog box 82-85
Text Editor box 236-237, 338
Text effects 309, 388
Text Inspector palette 21. *See also* Alignment Inspector; Character Inspector; Paragraph Inspector; Spacing Inspector
Text on a path 286
Text-only files
   exporting from FreeHand 392
   opening or importing into FreeHand 344, 349, 382
Text ruler 230-231, 298
Text styles 195, 196, 309-321
   applying 314-316
   creating 311-314
   default style names 312
   editing 316-317
   next style 314
   text style defaults 84-85
   text style masks 318-321
Text tool 39, 40, 41, 228
Text weight paper sizes 549
Text wrap 330-331, 338-340, 418
Text Wrap command and dialog box 330-331
Textured fills 193, 590-592
texturedict PostScript dictionary 587

INDEX   695

Thicker command 181
Thin space characters 240, 245
Thinner command 181
Three-dimensional effects 447, 458-459, 659-660
Three-dimensional rendering applications 642-646, 659-660
Three-Dimensional Rotation tool 465-466
Three Waves custom stroke 179, 588
Thumbnail Fetch images 86
Thumbnail views 24-25, 28
Thumbnails in PDF files 421
TIFFs 346, 353-371
   1-bit, 8-bit, and 24-bit 346
   applying Photoshop filters 368-371
   avoiding Split Complex Paths print option 394, 555-556
   bilevel TIFFs 346, 355, 356-357
   bit depth 354
   bounding boxes 461
   brightness and contrast 358-359
   color 346
      applying colors to 498
      converting to CMYK in exported files 394
      matching colors in 505-507
      preseparating 367-368
      RGB and CMYK TIFF bit depth 354
      separating 528
      trapping 526
   converting bitmap-only PICT files to 347
   converting to PDF 649
   cropping with Paste Inside command 362-364
   duotones 498-500
   embedding 100, 378
      bitmap PICTs as TIFFs 379
      TIFFs embedded in RTF files 388
   FM screening 534
   grayscale 346
      converting to bilevel 356-357
      gray level controls 359-360
      overprinting 592-594
   halftone-only styles 198
   halftones 353
   importing 54-56, 348
   line art 355
   links to imported TIFFs 357
   losing in exported files 399
   managing linked files 419-420
   Object Inspector controls 356-357
   outline and vignette masks 364-367
   PageMaker problems with EPS TIFFs 397-399
   pasting inside paths 137, 353, 362-364, 394
   printing
      missing or poor quality image 575
      options and settings 556-557
      PageMaker problems with EPS TIFFs 397-399
      problems 574
   resizing imported TIFFs 356
   resolution
      high-resolution display 90
      resized TIFF images 355

      resizing to printer's resolution 360-362, 437
      scanning resolution 354
      screen frequency 354-356
   size of files 354-356
   stochastic screening 530-535
   tracing 170-173
   transparent backgrounds 356-357
Tiger teeth custom fill 185, 587
Tight Fit option 117
   Calligraphic Pen tool 45
   Freehand tool 44
   Knife tool 47
Tight tracing option 49
Tiled fills 189-192
   applying colors to 498
   characters converted to paths 332
   compared to duplicating objects 573
   moving paths with 430-432
   rotating 444
   splitting complex paths 394
Tiling printed pages 27-28, 542-544, 569
Times font 542
Tint builds 474, 507-510
Tint reduction option 528
Tints
   avoiding fuzzy type 280
   considerations for use 478
   custom tints 482
   darkening and lightening 501, 503
   defining colors 474
   graduated fills 186
   in halftones 353
   tint densities 551-552
   trapping graduated fills 520-522
Tints palette 18-19, 20, 182
Tips you bought this book for
   accurate tracing 171-172
   avoiding fuzzy type 280
   avoiding tiling 27-28
   breaking text into single-line text blocks 400
   calculating steps in diagonal blends 154
   changing formatting with styles 202
   closing paths with irregular line 140-141
   converting from process to spot colors 403-404
   converting grayscale TIFFs to bilevel 356-357
   default template problems 96
   deleting multiple layers 65-66
   flipping and flopping 139
   getting more pages on pasteboard 28
   greeking all text on a page 92
   knocking out or overprinting black 520
   printing more than 999 copies 540
   replacing one color with another 495-496
   resizing objects proportionally 109-110
   scanning line art 355-356
   setting grid for easy object placement 30-31
   solving EPS bounding box problems 401-402
   stacking zipped palettes 87
Tao of FreeHand 101-102
temporary preview drag 93

text style masks 318-321
transparency and the Intersect command 165-166
zooming to precise areas of page 34
Title bars 22-23
Titular long-windedness of engineers 316
TMPL resource class 602-603
Toggling palettes 19-20
Toolbox palette 4, 18-19
   displaying 20
   hiding when palettes are hidden 86-87
   setting display preferences 23
   symbols on tools 39
   tool descriptions 38-51
Tools 38-51. *See also names of specific tools*
   constraining tool movements or shapes 49-51
   constraint values 31
   path-drawing tools 116-125
   shortcuts for selecting 41
   which to use 105-106
   Xtra Tools palette 18-19, 126-130, 464, 506
Top handles of text blocks 252
Top noise custom fill 185
Torquemada the Inquisitioner 389, 641-642
Toyo color library 479
Trace Background option 49
Trace Edges command (Inline text effect) 282, 587
Trace Foreground option 49
Tracing
   object edges 167-168
   objects 48-49, 170-173
Tracing tool 39, 48-49, 170-173
Tracing Tool dialog box 172
Track Tab Movement with Vertical Line option 82-83
Tracking 287-288
Transfer Function print option 551-552
Transfer functions 563
Transform it again shortcut 426, 428-429
Transform palette 18-19, 20, 48. *See also Move palette; Reflect palette; Rotate palette; Scale palette; Skew palette*
   generic transforming instructions 426, 427
   subpanels 426
Transformation tools 39
Transforming 425
   3D Transform plug-in 659-660
   generic instructions 426, 427
   grouped objects 426, 428
   inline graphics 338
   line weights and fills 81
   locking objects against 461
   preserving original paths 81-82
   shortcuts 426, 428-429
   transformation Xtras 464-466
Transforms As Unit option 426, 428
Translucency 458-460
Transparency
   bilevel TIFFs 356-357
   characters converted to paths 333
   creating transparent and translucent effects 458-459
   deleting preview images 376-377

superimposed text 459-460
textured fills 193, 590-592
TIFFs in stochastic screening 532
transparency operations 170
transparent areas within shapes 145, 146.
    See also Composite paths
    using with Intersect command 165-166
    viewing text blocks during editing 253
Transparency dialog box 165-166
Transparency operations 170
Transporting files to another machine 420
Transverse orientation 545-546, 550-551, 567
Transverter Pro 581
Trap Color Method option 528
Trap dialog box 527
Trap Width option 527
Trap Xtra 526-528
Trapping 510-528
    chokes and spreads 514
    choosing colors for trapping 528
    color boundaries 516-518
    gentle advice about using 101
    graduated fills 186, 520-522, 525-526
    imported images 526
    line widths in spreads 515
    lines 518-519
    manual trapping 513-514
    object-level and ink-level overprinting 512-513
    overlapping differently colored objects 517-518
    process colors 514, 523-526
    radial fills 522-523, 525-526
    reversing chokes and spreads 527-528
    spot colors 514-518, 522
    Spread Size field 470
    text 519-520
    textured fill problems 591-592
    Trap Xtra 470, 526-528
    TrapWise 470, 512
TrapWise 470, 512
Triangles, building pie charts with 214-216
Tricks that no longer work 432
Trim margins on print jobs 547
Trimetric projection 223
Trimmed-off page edges. *See* Bleed area
Troubleshooting
    adding pages or changing size 28
    converting process colors 403-404, 481
    creating blends 156
    custom paper sizes 28, 550
    default templates 96
    external resource files 618
    fills
        banding in fills 647-648
        textured fills 591-592
    graphics
        cut-off EPS images 401-402
        EPS preview images 373
        PageMaker problems with EPS TIFFs 397-399
        rasterizing images 414
    objects dropping out of PDF files 649
    opening or importing formats 349
    Photoshop plug-ins 370
    poking at things 576

positioning objects on grid 30-31
PPDs not in list 559
printing 550-551, 574-576
rules displaying incorrectly 261
text
    bound to paths 333
    font problems 32-33, 265, 333-334, 575, 635-636
    fuzzy type 280
    leading problems 272, 274
    small or pale text 236
    text effect display 281
    weird characters in text 382
True confessions
    adjusting monitor color display 75
    calibration and lighting 477
    connector points 52, 125
    crayons and color 469
    fixed leading 270-271
    foolishness and the Enter key 237
    knowing exactly how much to reflect 448
    Ole's love of woodcuts 136
    Ole's method of drawing 135-136
    pounding on imagesetters with wastebaskets xxiii
    scaling objects 439
    senility of graphic designers 97
    Spiral dialog box controls 128
    Type Specifications palette 263-264
    US Constitution 649
    Zapf Chancery 268
    zip code problems 240
TrueType fonts 332, 634
TruMatch color library 479
Turning pages 38
TWAIN Acquire plug-in 370
Twips 385, 390, 391
Two-dimensional objects 458-459
Two Waves custom stroke 179, 588
Type 227. *See also* Fonts; Text; Text blocks
    automatic copyfitting 321-323
    avoiding fuzzy type 280
    baseline shift 272-273
    basis for design 29
    character formatting 262-264
    colors 275-280
    converting characters to paths 332-337
    defaults for 80-81
    fills 275-277
    font substitution 266-269
    fonts 264-269
    glowing type tricks 336-337
    kerning 286-288
    leading 270-274
    stretching characters 280
    text effects 280-286
    trapping 519-520
    type size 269
    type styles 269
    whirlwind history 539
    widows 305, 307
Type 1 and Type 3 fonts 332
Type Reunion 636
Type size 269
    automatic copyfitting 321-323
    avoiding fuzzy type 280
    converting to Illustrator 1.1 410

converting XPress Tags to RTF 387
    in leading methods 270
    in RTF codes 386
    kerning compared to tracking 287-288
    kerning measurements 286
    rounding in RTF files 385
    Type Specifications palette 263
Type Specifications palette 18-19, 20
    blank fields in 266
    formatting 263-264
    text with multiple formatting attributes 266
    type size 269
    type styles 269
Type styles 269
    compared to using screen fonts 265
    in Type Specifications palette 263
    indicating in RTF files 385
    not supported in FreeHand 388
Typefaces. *See* Fonts
Typing
    auto-expanding text blocks 84, 230, 232-235
    PostScript code into Inspector 595-599
    text 228-238, 330
    Text Editor 236-237

U

UIrz resource template 602, 605
UIrz resources
    creating for custom fills 618-624
    Flags field values 619, 624
    functions of 606
    referring to in GnEf resources 607, 611
Unavailable type styles 269
Underline text effect 284, 309
Underline type style 388
Undo command 78
Undoing
    changes to original TIFF settings 358, 360
    inline graphics 338
    number of Undo's 78
    Paste Inside command 456
    path segments 117-118
Ungroup command 333
Ungrouping
    keeping object layer information 80
    rectangles and ellipses 111
    transformed objects 426
    ungrouped path display in Object Inspector 434
Uniform scaling option 437
Union command 148, 166-167, 170
United States Constitution 649
Units of measure
    choosing for charts 207-216
    in rulers 9
    kerning 286-287
    leading methods 270-274
    RTF files 385
    setting measurement systems 29-30
    twips 385
Unjoining text from paths 324
Unlimited Downloadable Fonts option 32, 575
Unlinking text blocks 255

INDEX   697

Unlocking
    layers 69-70, 462
    objects 461, 462
Unnamed colors 504
Unplaced text
    in linked text blocks 255
    in text joined to paths 326
    symbol in link boxes 232
Unsaved documents, reviewing 97
Unsharp Mask filter 368
Unused colors 505
Unzipping palettes 22-23
Updating
    graphics with Publish and
        Subscribe 415-418
    imported TIFFs or graphics 357
    links 379
    styles 316-317
Uppercase letters 94, 95
Use CMYK Names option 504
Use Maximum Value option 528
Use RGB Names option 504
Use Tint Reduction option 528
User dictionaries 242
User interface in Inspector palette 618-619
UserPrep files 99
    compared to external resource files 601
    creating 594, 598-601
    including for service bureaus 570
Utilities 640-642

V

V field in Skew palette 452
v symbol in Info bar 5
Vanishing points 216, 217
    in zoom text effect 285
    multiview perspective 219-220
    single-view perspective grid 218-219
Variable Blob tool (Variable Stroke
    tool) 44-45, 116, 118-119
Variable paper sizes in PPDs 563, 564-565
Variable Stroke tool 44-45, 116, 118-119
Variable Width option in Calligraphic Pen
    tool 45
Varnishes 528
vc string in PostScript code 598
Vector Distort plug-in 660-661
Version numbers of color libraries 488
Versions of FreeHand 76-77, 404
Vertical axes of charts 207-213
Vertical axes of objects 48
Vertical object reflecting 448
Vertical object scaling 356, 436, 437
Vertical object skewing 450, 451
Vertical ruler. *See* Rulers
Vertical rules in text blocks 259-260
Vertical tab-tracking lines 82-83
Vertical text alignment 289, 462
Vertical text auto-expansion 233, 234-235
Vertical text skewing 327-329
Vertical text spacing 304-306
VEX (KPT Vector Effects) 659-661
Video games, setting up FreeHand as 94
View menu commands 33
View mode popup menu 4, 5-6
Viewer (Acrobat) 651
Viewing
    colors 476-477
    document reports 571-572
Views
    changing active page 97
    changing in Layers palette 66-67
    changing page views 33-38, 49
    choosing magnification 6
    controlling with Layers palette 63
    most accurate views in FreeHand 34-36
    Preview and Keyline mode 5-6
    restoring on opening 76
    setting with Layers palette 6
    zooming in Document Inspector 24-25
Vignette masks 365-367
Violet ink 473
Virtual memory in printers 560-561
Visual problems with small text 236
Vividness of colors, changing 503, 505
"VMError" messages 574-575
Vortex of Ed 381

W

w character in PostScript code 598
W field (Object Inspector) 234-235, 440
Wacom tablets 44-45, 119
Wastebaskets, using to pound on
    imagesetters xxiii
Wave distortions 661
Wedge custom stroke 179, 588
Weights of lines. *See* Line weights
Werewolves 466
When Creating a New Graphic Style
    options 98-99
When Exiting, Convert to Clipboard
    option 100
White space in tiled fills 191
White text, working with 236
Whole Word option 244
Wide angle lens effect 464-465
Wide page orientation 28, 545-546, 550
Wide paper sizes 545-546
Widows, controlling 305-307, 307
Width
    auto-expanding text blocks 232-235
    columns in text blocks 257-258
    custom paper sizes in PPD files 567
    highlighted rules 282
    line weights for spreads 515
    objects 57, 440
    pages 28-29
    paper 545-546
    paragraph rules 308
    paths 408
    resizing imported TIFFs 356
    strokes 119, 174, 179
    trapping width 527
Width Knife tool option 46
Wildcards 245
Winding 113-114
    after reflection 449-450
    after rotating 444, 445
    reversing path direction 114, 149
Windows
    changing page view 33-38
    opening multiple windows 7
    publication window and elements 4-18
    scrolling by dragging guides 80
Windows (Microsoft) 397
Winged pigs 422
Word (Microsoft) 349, 385
Word processors
    comparing PostScript in files 570-571
    creating
        EPS files 375
        UserPrep files 598-601
    editing
        color libraries 487-490
        EPS files 373
        PPD files 559, 566-567
    examining PostScript in EPS
        files 583-585
    importing files 344
Word wrap 330-331
Words
    adding to dictionaries 95, 242-243
    checking spelling 240-243
    searching for entire words 244
Wordspacing
    automatic copyfitting 321-323
    changing 250, 252
    flowing text inside paths 330
    setting best-looking text 291
    Spacing Inspector palette 292
World Series 422
Worms easter egg 663
Worms of text 326-327
Wrapping tabs 299-300
    in RTF files 385
    marker on tab ruler 298-300
    setting side heads 300, 304
Wrapping text 330-331, 338-340, 418

X

X and Y fields
    Document Inspector 28
    Fill Inspector 190-191
    Object Inspector 434
    Rotate palette 442
    Scale palette 438
    TIFF controls 356
X marks in EPS bounding boxes 373, 396
xdf string in PostScript code 598
XPress. *See* QuarkXPress
XPress Tags text 388-391
Xtra Tools palette 18-19, 126-130, 464, 506.
    See also names of specific tools or Xtras
Xtras
    Extensis DrawTools 661-662
        Color Mixer Xtra 662
        DrawTools Shape palette 661-662
        Edit Curves Xtra 662
        Grayscale Xtra 662
        Multitone Xtra 662
        Random Replace Colors Xtra 662
    FreeHand's Xtra tools 464, 506
        3-D Rotation tool 465-466
        Eyedropper tool 505-507
        Fisheye Lens tool 464-465
        Spiral tool 127-128
    FreeHand's Xtras
        Color Control Xtra 501-502
        color Xtras 470, 501-507
        Create PICT Image Xtra 412-414
        Darken Colors Xtra 502-503

The Mac is not a typewriter
Robin Williams

This best-selling, elegant guide to typesetting on the Mac has received rave reviews for its clearly presented information, friendly tone, and easy access. Twenty quick and easy chapters cover what you need to know to make your documents look clean and professional. $9.95 *(72 pages)*

The Official Photo CD Handbook: A Verbum Interactive Guide
Michael Gosney, et al.

With Photo CD, Kodak's breakthrough technology, you don't have to wait for tomorrow's electronic cameras to join the digital photography revolution. Learn how to use and store digital images and media files without spending a fortune. Two CDs include mutimedia presentations, valuable Photo CD utilities, and 68 MB of usable images, backgrounds and sounds. $39.95 *(384 pages, w/2 CD-ROMs)*

Photoshop 3 for Macintosh: Visual QuickStart Guide
Elaine Weinmann and Peter Lourekas

Completely revised for Photoshop 3, this indispensable guide is for Mac users who want to get started in Adobe Photoshop but don't like to read long explanations. QuickStart books focus on illustrated, step-by-step examples that cover how to use masks, filters, colors, and more. $19.95 *(295 pages)*

The Photoshop 3 Wow! Book (Mac Edition)
Linnea Dayton and Jack Davis

This book is really two books in one: an easy-to-follow, step-by-step tutorial of Photoshop fundamentals and over 150 pages of tips and techniques for getting the most out of Photoshop version 3. Full color throughout, *The Photoshop Wow! Book* shows how professional artists make the best use of Photoshop. Includes a CD-ROM containing Photoshop filters and utilities. $39.95 *(286 pages, w/CD-ROM)*

Photoshop in 4 Colors
Mattias Nyman

Find step-by-step procedures and detailed explanations on how to reproduce and manipulate color images using Photoshop and QuarkXPress. A terrific, invaluable resource for those who need high-quality color output. $22.95 *(80 pages)*

Photoshop in Black and White, 2nd Edition
Jim Rich and Sandy Bozek

Updated to cover versions 2.5 and 3.0, this book explains how to adjust black-and-white images of any type for reproduction. Topics inlude image characteristics; adjusting highlights, shadows, and midtones; sharpening images; and converting from color to greyscale. Appendices cover scanning, resampling and calibration. $18 *(44 pages)*

QuarkXPress Tips & Tricks, 2nd Edition
David Blatner, Phil Gaskill, and Eric Taub

The smartest, most useful shortcuts from *The QuarkXPress Book*—plus many more—are packed into this book. You'll find answers to common questions as well as insights on techniques that will show you how to become a QuarkXPress power user. Includes a CD-ROM with useful XTensions and demos. $34.95 *(448 pages, w/CD-ROM)*

Real World Scanning and Halftones
David Blatner and Steve Roth

Master the digital halftone process—from scanning images to tweaking them on your computer to imagesetting them. Learn about optical character recognition, gamma control, sharpening, PostScript halftones, Photo CD and image-manipulating applications like Photoshop and PhotoStyler. $24.95 *(296 pages)*

For more titles, check us out on the World Wide Web:
http://www.peachpit.com
or call 510-548-4393 for a catalog.

Order Form

USA 800-283-9444 • 510-548-4393 • FAX 510-548-5991
CANADA 800-387-8028 • 416-447-1779 • FAX 800-456-0536 OR 416-443-0948

Qty	Title	Price	Total
		SUBTOTAL	
		ADD APPLICABLE SALES TAX*	
		SHIPPING	
		TOTAL	

Shipping is by UPS ground: $4 for first item, $1 each add'l.

*We are required to pay sales tax in all states with the exceptions of AK, DE, HI, MT, NH, NV, OK, OR, SC and WY. Please include appropriate sales tax if you live in any state not mentioned above.

Customer Information

NAME

COMPANY

STREET ADDRESS

CITY   STATE   ZIP

PHONE (   )   FAX (   )
[REQUIRED FOR CREDIT CARD ORDERS]

Payment Method

❏ CHECK ENCLOSED   ❏ VISA   ❏ MASTERCARD   ❏ AMEX

CREDIT CARD #   EXP. DATE

COMPANY PURCHASE ORDER #

Tell Us What You Think

PLEASE TELL US WHAT YOU THOUGHT OF THIS BOOK: TITLE:

WHAT OTHER BOOKS WOULD YOU LIKE US TO PUBLISH?

MAC   PEACHPIT PRESS • 2414 Sixth Street • Berkeley, CA 94710